Advancing the Human Right to Health

Advancing the Human Right to Health

Edited by

José M. Zuniga

Stephen P. Marks

Lawrence O. Gostin

OXFORD
UNIVERSITY PRESS

OXFORD
UNIVERSITY PRESS

Great Clarendon Street, Oxford, OX2 6DP,
United Kingdom

Oxford University Press is a department of the University of Oxford.
It furthers the University's objective of excellence in research, scholarship,
and education by publishing worldwide. Oxford is a registered trade mark of
Oxford University Press in the UK and in certain other countries

First Edition published in 2013

Published in the United States of America by Oxford University Press
198 Madison Avenue, New York, NY 10016, United States of America

British Library Cataloguing in Publication Data
Data available

Library of Congress Control Number: 2013940000

ISBN 978–0–19–966161–9

Foreword

Paul Hunt

Adopted in 1946, the Constitution of the World Health Organization (WHO) states that the 'enjoyment of the highest attainable standard of health is one of the fundamental rights of every human being without distinction of race, religion, political belief, economic or social condition' (WHO, 1946). Two years later, Article 25 of the Universal Declaration of Human Rights (UDHR) extended the foundations for the international legal framework for the right of everyone to the enjoyment of the highest attainable standard of physical and mental health, commonly known as the right to the highest attainable standard of health, or the right to health. Since then, the right to health has been codified in numerous legally binding international and regional human rights treaties, as well as constitutions and other national laws, generating a burgeoning jurisprudence and literature.

Commemorating the 65th anniversary of the UDHR, this important volume provides a rich and timely contribution to the deepening literature on the right to the highest attainable standard of health. Some of the essays in *Advancing the Human Right to Health* set out the big picture, such as the relationship between public health and the right to health; while others are issue specific, such as access to medical products, vaccines, and technologies. Some contributors look at the right to health in particular countries, ranging from low- to high-income States; while others reflect on the future challenges and opportunities. All deserve our careful attention.

As United Nations (UN) Special Rapporteur on the right to the highest attainable standard of health from 2002 to 2008, I wrote some 30 reports, including annual reports on my communications to governments—'communications' being diplomatic code for letters of complaint for alleged violations of the right to health. Some of my reports look at thematic issues, such as sexual and reproductive rights, access to medicines, mental disability, water and sanitation, maternal mortality, the skills drain, the health-related UN Millennium Development Goals, and indicators and benchmarks.

One report to the UN General Assembly sets out *Human Rights Guidelines for Pharmaceutical Companies in Relation to Access to Medicines*. Another group of my reports considers the enjoyment of the right to health in particular countries, such as Mozambique, Peru, Romania, Uganda, Lebanon/Israel (following the war of mid-2006), Sweden, and India—two countries of which (Peru and India) form a part of the country case study section of this volume. One of my additional country reports looks at donors' human rights responsibilities of international assistance and cooperation in health by exploring Sweden's role in relation to, first, Uganda's health sector and, second, the health-related activities of the World Bank and International Monetary Fund. Under the rubric of country reports, I also reported on the World Trade Organization, Guantánamo Bay, and the pharmaceutical company GlaxoSmithKline. Two of these reports (Guantánamo Bay and Lebanon/Israel) were co-authored with other UN 'special procedures'. All of these country reports were preceded by visits to the place or institution in question, except Guantánamo Bay, where the United States denied me entry. Three of the 'special procedures' working with me on this report were invited to visit Guántanamo Bay, but US authorities imposed unacceptable conditions on their invitation (i.e. no private interviews with detainees) and so our report was prepared without the benefit of a visit from any of us.

Perhaps it is because of these endeavours that I am especially appreciative of the fine collection of essays contained in *Advancing the Human Right to Health*, including national studies on the right to health. It is not easy to move from the general to specific, abstract to operational, international to national, yet this is what we have to do. It is only by striving to apply the right to health to specific issues, and national (and subnational) polices, programmes, projects, and practices, that we will grasp the potential of this fundamental—but complex and extensive—human right. By learning from national studies, such as those in this collection, we can find ways to give proper attention to the best available technical evidence and also respect the values embodied in legally binding human rights.

In recent years, the health and human rights community has developed a way of 'unpacking' or analysing the right to health with a view to making it easier to understand and apply. Promulgated by the Committee on Economic, Social and Cultural Rights (CESCR) in 2000, General Comment 14 represents a crucial stage in the development of this right to health framework. Looking back, General Comment 14 was one of the CESCR's most influential achievements during the years I served as an CESCR member. In recent years, numerous individuals and organisations have applied and refined this right to health framework, making it more accessible, specific, and operational. The framework has a number of elements, including freedoms and entitlements, obligations of immediate effect, the rebuttable presumption of non-retrogression, the duty to address disadvantage, active and informed participation, international assistance and cooperation, monitoring and accountability, and so on. The framework is becoming a common language for talking about the right to health, and it is used, to one degree or another, in a number of the contributions to this volume.

Nobody suggests that the right to health framework provides answers to some of the complex issues raised by health, such as how to deal with competing health priorities within a finite budget. The framework addresses a prior, and more elementary, problem: how to move beyond the one-line right to health formulations found in legal texts and towards a more detailed understanding of the key components of the right to the highest attainable standard of health. Of course, in a sense, the framework is not new: for the most part, health policymakers and practitioners have known its key components for many years. But the record shows that, when the chips are down, some of these components are overlooked. Fees are introduced without properly reflecting on access for the impoverished. Programmes are implemented without appropriate outreach to rural communities. Projects are formulated without active and informed participation. Policies are adopted without effective monitoring and accountability arrangements. The early and routine consideration of the right to health framework will reduce the frequency of such oversights and help to ensure that health-related interventions are responsive, equitable, and of good quality. Moreover, when the right to health 'lens' is applied to countries it helps to identify some of the pressing health issues needing attention. The application of the framework led to my examination of undocumented people in Sweden, for example, as well as neglected diseases in Uganda. As history demonstrates, without the right to health framework or 'lens,' undocumented people and neglected diseases are routinely overlooked.

For my part, not only did I apply—in practice—the right to health framework to specific issues and countries, I also sought to extend and refine it. General Comment 14 is a powerful instrument but it is not perfect. With the benefit of hindsight, it is strangely silent on some issues without which it is impossible to operationalize the right to health, such as the critical importance of effective, responsive, integrated health systems that are accessible to all. Advised by health experts, I endeavoured to address this, and some other, General Comment 14 lacunae.

The essays in this volume confirm that the right to the highest attainable standard of health is a site of struggle and should be seen as one important element in a strategy for progressive social change. The operational impact of the right to health depends upon multiple variables. Progressive governments must be persuaded to integrate the right across their policymaking processes, in accordance with their legal obligations. Health workers must grasp the potential of the right to help them achieve their professional objectives and understand that monitoring is not accountability, but one step towards accountability. Human rights mechanisms must take this fundamental human right seriously and its meaning must be further clarified. Activist judges and lawyers have to be willing to learn from health workers and find innovative ways to vindicate the right. Civil society organizations have to campaign around health and human rights. More right to health tools must be fashioned. Disadvantaged individuals, communities, and populations must apprehend that the right empowers them by granting entitlements, placing legal and moral obligations on others. This in turn calls for greater imagination in fashioning accountability mechanisms that are accessible and responsive to all. The WHO and other international organizations must be prevailed upon to champion the right to the highest attainable standard of health. Importantly, health and human rights needs political leadership at the highest levels, exemplified by former Mexican Minister of Health, Julio Frenk, whose contribution to this volume is a reflection upon Mexico's ongoing efforts to achieving the right to health for its citizens.

Today, there are numerous health movements and approaches, including health equity, primary healthcare, health promotion, social determinants, health security, continuum of care, biomedical, macroeconomics, and so on. All are very important. It is misconceived, however, to regard human rights as yet another approach with the same status as the others. Like ethics, the right to the highest attainable standard of health is not optional—and, like ethics, it recurs throughout all other approaches. However, the right provides the only perspective that is both underpinned by universally recognized moral values and reinforced by legal obligations. Of course, it does not provide neat answers to numerous complex health issues, any more than does any other single approach. Nonetheless, as *Advancing the Human Right to Health* confirms, the right to the highest attainable standard of health has a profound contribution to make towards building healthy societies and equitable health systems.

Over the last 65 years, the right to the highest attainable standard of health has come a long way. The challenges remain enormous and diverse. Our commanding challenge is to take the right to health out of the law books—and beyond easy exhortation and rhetorical remonstration—and apply it operationally in health policies and practices in communities and elsewhere. This means we have to engage in respectful, open-minded collaboration across disciplines. In its turn, multidisciplinary collaboration demands we gather evidence of impact of the right to the highest attainable standard of health.

These are among the challenges confronting us. Thankfully, this indispensable volume will help us navigate the way ahead.

Notes

This chapter was written in the author's personal capacity. The United Nations (UN) reports referenced in this Foreword are available online at <http://www.essex.ac.uk/hrc/research/projects/rth/default.aspx>.

Reference

WHO. (1946). *Constitution of the World Health Organization*. World Health Organization (WHO): New York, NY.

Preface

José M. Zuniga, Lawrence O. Gostin, and Stephen P. Marks

Along a continuum from the right to health in perspective to the right to health in action—and punctuated by challenges and opportunities on the road to its realization—*Advancing the Human Right to Health* offers a systematic analysis of the international right to health, one of the most fundamental human rights in the International Bill of Human Rights.

The right to health in perspective

The book's first section, *The right to health in perspective*, contains chapters that take the 'long view'—providing a thoughtful account of the key parameters of the right, together with key strategies to achieve it, and why the right is so essential.

The section begins with Chapter 1 written by Co-Editor, Stephen P. Marks, which provides an insightful historical and contemporary examination of the emergence and scope of the universal human right to health. He explains how the right emerged among States and stakeholders, as well as what its scope can, and should, be—now and in the future. Professor Marks introduces key concepts surrounding the right to health (and socioeconomic rights more generally) such as progressive realization. He uses his language carefully, particularly the notion of a 'universal' right to make the essential point that the right to health applies to everyone and in all regions. There can be no exceptions.

Chapter 2 turns to one of the key strategies for implementing and enforcing the right to health: litigation. Litigation on the right to health has taken place with respect to some of the great health issues of our time, such as tobacco control, AIDS, and access to medicines. Oscar A. Cabrera and Ana S. Ayala examine legal cases at both the international level and in domestic courts to demonstrate the vast potential of using judicial bodies to achieve the international right to health. Professor Cabrera leads the Bloomberg/Tobacco Free Kids initiative at the O'Neill Institute for National and Global Health Law at Georgetown University Law Center. And, accordingly, he has a breadth of experience in devising and implementing litigation strategies.

Exploring how we move the right to health from concept to practice, Chapter 3 provides insights from Helena Nygren-Krug, former head of the World Health Organization (WHO) portfolio on health and human rights. She describes progress made in advancing the right to health, including challenges and opportunities, and concludes with practical ways on how to take the agenda forward. The right to health is only meaningful to the extent we ensure that States are implementing this right, and the only way to know whether there is effective implementation is through careful monitoring and evaluation. The use of clear indicators towards progress is essential if we are to significantly advance human health.

Ariel Pablos-Mendéz and Lesley Stone, both from the US Agency for International Development (USAID), next discuss economic development for health as a key driver of stronger, more productive States. There are many States that lack the capacity to fully ensure the conditions in which everyone can be healthy. To guarantee the right to health, therefore, it is not only necessary to hold States accountable, but also to provide them with the capacity to meet the needs of their populations. This requires both bilateral and multilateral assistance. It also requires changing the traditional paradigm of 'donors' and 'recipients', moving towards a paradigm shift of mutual responsibilities. Higher-income States, and the international community as a whole, should partner with lower-income States to ensure a fair allocation of scarce resources. This requires not just adequate funding, but also ensuring that States regain full 'ownership' of their national strategies, activities, and programmes.

The section ends with a chapter in which Eric A. Friedman and Co-Editor Lawrence O. Gostin examine the 'pillars' of the right to health. What does the right to health entail in its deepest and richest sense? It certainly has a legal and normative dimension, enshrining a key entitlement for individuals and populations. But it is also a tool of litigation, advocacy, and social mobilization. We are engaged in an international campaign for a Framework Convention on Global Health, which is based on the human right to health. This chapter shows how the right to health can be deployed to make a fundamental difference in the lives of all individuals—particularly the most disadvantaged.

The right to health in action

The chapters in Section 1 offering 'long-view' perspectives lead naturally into the right to health in action. Indeed, the framework outlined in the book's first five chapters remains theoretical unless and until it finds application in actual country settings. Case studies provide context for analysing the right to health and assessing whether and to what extent this right has influenced critical decision-making at the local and national levels regarding allocation of resources, definition of policies, and creation of institutional structures that make a difference in people's lives.

The 12 case studies in Section 2, *The right to health in action*, reflect a wide range of approaches to progressive realization of the right to health, reflecting different demographics, resource constraints, legal systems, political and social structures, as well as economic incentives. Central to this inquiry is whether and to what extent the national constitution or some other legal text has formally enshrined the right to health and whether the State has ratified the International Covenant on Economic, Social and Cultural Rights (ICESCR), creating thereby a legal obligation to take measures with a view to the full realization of the right to health.

In order to establish a basis for comparison across countries, the authors drew from a basic template for the country studies, although considerable latitude was left to each author to adapt the structure of the chapter to particular features of each country. Nevertheless, they all begin with a reference to the country's history and an overview of the state of the nation's health, often including a review of data related to endemic diseases, food security, morbidity/mortality, maternal-child health, and similar statistical informational essential to the background within which the right to health has been advanced or not.

The second common feature of each country case study is an assessment of the country's human rights laws and accountability frameworks, whether political, judicial, or social. Next, the chapters examine the achievement and obstacles to ensuring availability, accessibility, acceptability, and quality of care or health services. Where appropriate, each case study also examines the limitations on human rights under domestic laws to protect public health. Many chapters include a history of human rights violations or coercive measures affecting health policies and health systems. Since each country presents specific constraints, the case studies examine the evolving responses and future national directions towards realizing the right to health, as well as whatever unique issues might be exemplified by the country.

Indeed, each country case study included in this section offers unique insights into the challenges and opportunities for the progressive realization of the right to health. The first nine case studies concern countries where the right to health has been, at least to some extent, interpreted as being provided for by the constitution or some other foundational legal text.

In Chapter 6, Donna J. Barry, Kate Greene, Wesler Lambert, Fernet Léandre, and Loune Viaud consider the role of the right to health in the face of extreme poverty following decades of political and economic oppression in Haiti, highlighting the importance of rights-based approaches to international aid. In Chapter 7, Raymond A. Atuguba explores the health financing issues that ultimately led to the development of Ghana's National Health Insurance Scheme, a key development in its progressive realization of the right to health. In Chapter 8, Ravi Duggal details how the rights to health and development have interacted throughout the progression of India's Five-Year Plans. In Chapter 9, Charles Ngwena, Rebecca Cook, and Ebenezer Durojaye assess the role of constitutional protections for the right to healthcare and their judicial interpretation in post-apartheid South Africa. In Chapter 10, Raul C. Pangalangan reviews the Philippine experience with translating a constitutionally protected right to health into health programmes, regulation, and legislation aimed at protecting vulnerable populations and improving the health of all. In Chapter 11, Philip D. Chen and Di Wu recount how health and food safety reform have played a central role in progressively realizing the right to health of the Chinese, many of whom face unique challenges accessing care due to geographic or occupational status. In Chapter 12, Armando De Negri Filho documents recent legal and political developments regarding the constitutional right to health in Brazil, where a broad social acceptance of this right continues to propel movement towards an equitable universal health system. In Chapter 13, Ariel Frisancho describes how citizen participation in social change has had a formative impact in progressive realization of the right to health in Peru, an upper-middle income country characterized by high levels of inequality. And, in Chapter 14, Julio Frenk and Octavio Gómez-Dantés explain how Mexico's System of Social Protection in Health has successfully translated a 'democratization of health' into a social rights-based approach to health characterized by priority setting in the definition of comprehensive benefits and financial protection against catastrophic health expenditures.

The last three case studies focus on countries with a high level of per capita income but which do not expressly recognize a constitutional right to health. In Chapter 15, Matthew Weait evaluates the role of the UK's National Health Service in promoting fair and equitable access to healthcare in the absence of a legally enforceable right to health. In Chapter 16, Hiroaki Matsuura and Eriko Sase explore the role of human security in fulfilling health rights in Japan, where an ageing society is learning how to recover from a highly disruptive natural disaster. Finally, in Chapter 17, Alicia Ely Yamin and Jean Connolly Carmalt review both the progress and shortcomings of the world's wealthiest nation—the United States—in addressing health disparities, including through recent reform efforts.

These selected case studies provide only a small window into the world of strategies for domestic implementation of the right to health. Many more countries have valuable experiences to share, and our understanding of the relationships between health and human rights continues to be advanced by further documentation and evaluation of the trajectories of right to health frameworks and rights-based approaches in other settings. As the right to health continues to be defined—as well as adapted alongside developments in public health and medical research—policy makers and activists have a tremendous opportunity to learn from these shared experiences. With health system reform increasingly being set as a top priority in nations of all income levels, attempts to move towards more equitable systems should be usefully informed by evidence-based approaches to the progressive realization of the right to health as described in many of this section's country case study chapters.

The right to health: challenges and opportunities

The myriad human rights enshrined in the Universal Declaration of Human Rights (UDHR) and various conventions and covenants are considered universal, indivisible, interconnected, and interdependent human rights. Yet, as elucidated in the case study chapters, some of these rights are denied or made difficult to implement and enforce due to numerous obstacles, and their realization is dependent on multiple stakeholders and the cultural, economic, political, social, and other realities that give context to our daily lives. Additionally, in various instances, rights themselves appear to be in conflict with one another, introducing, and in some instances, exacerbating existing tensions around implementing and enforcing one right over another for different individuals (or subsets of individuals).

The 11 chapters in Section 3 of the book draw upon the its first section and place into greater context, on an issue-by-issue basis, the challenges that States face in translating the right to health into action, as written about in the book's second section. And, while there are acknowledged shortcomings in the range and scope of issue-specific chapters included in the closing section (e.g. disability, non-communicable diseases, sexual orientation, and gender identity), many of these issues are referenced in various chapters throughout the book. Yet, the issues specifically addressed in the book's third section focus our individual and collective efforts to break down barriers that prevent us from, or at least slow our progress towards, achieving the human right to health for all.

The section begins with Chapter 18 and offers a global perspective from colleagues at the WHO and Joint United Nations Programme on HIV/AIDS (UNAIDS), who chronicle how the HIV/AIDS movement helped to catalyse the right to health agenda in the mid-1980s. They further posit that a human rights-based approach can facilitate progress in addressing the social, economic, and other inequalities exacerbated by the global HIV pandemic, as well as endemic malaria and tuberculosis (TB) epidemics that cause unnecessary suffering and hastened deaths for millions of people.

We next transition to the use of tobacco, which is one of the major risk factors for non-communicable diseases, and has a profound impact on low- and middle-income countries where its use is high and where socioeconomic as well as health inequalities are rampant. In Chapter 19, Professor Cabrera and Professor Gostin offer perspectives on the recent alignment of tobacco control and human rights-based advocacy, litigation, and other agendas. They also offer details about a specific effort to build alliances between tobacco control and human rights practitioners.

Providing insight into ongoing struggles to engender social transformation in relation to women's health, Dr Yamin chronicles the progressive clarification of norms and the integration of human rights discourse within the women's health movement in Chapter 20. In addition, she describes efforts—some successful, others less so—to operationalize rights-based approaches to women's health within the context of the United Nations (UN) Millennium Development Goals (MDGs).

Given documented human rights violations in correctional facilities worldwide, Joanne Mariner and Rebecca Schleifer next note in their chapter how the enjoyment of the right to health in prisons is conspicuous by its absence, and they delve into the international standards that should guarantee prisoners' right to health. Our colleagues from Amnesty International and Human Rights Watch, respectively, also review strategies for ensuring these standards are met somewhere at the nexus of 'positive' and 'negative' rights.

In Chapter 22, Professor Marks and Adriana L. Benedict examine the issue of access to medical products, vaccines, and medical technologies from the perspective of a human right predicated upon two other rights: the *right to health* and the *right to benefit from scientific progress*. In addition to discussing evolving international human rights standards, the authors address domestic implementation and litigation barriers related to the international trade regime, and strategies for incentivizing research and development of health goods to address diseases that have a disproportionate burden in developing countries.

Millions of children under the age of five are underweight worldwide, and childhood malnutrition is a cause of death for millions of children every year. Yet, as the World Food Programme's Martin W. Bloem and Saskia de Pee discuss in their chapter, meeting people's nutritional needs is not considered a human right, even though reducing overall undernourishment and the percentage of underweight children under the age of five are among the indicators assigned to the hunger element of MDG 1—'Eradicate extreme poverty and hunger.' The authors thus argue for enshrining a right to the prevention of chronic undernutrition.

The health workforce, too, has an important role in advocating, facilitating, and protecting the right to health. In Chapter 24, Co-Editor José M. Zuniga and Imane Sidibé review the human resources for health crises plaguing numerous countries around the globe and their effects on advancing the right to health. They also address the need to protect and empower health workers in various settings, while holding them accountable when they engage in human rights abuses and violations, including torture.

In a segue from one aspect of the previous chapter, Amnesty International's Michael Bochenek describes the various ways in which torture and other ill-treatment are prohibited by the UDHR, an international covenant and a convention, as well as regional treaties. He also cites how those legal instruments are violated during policing practices and in the name of countering terrorism, including via State complicity.

Victoria Sutton next details in Chapter 26 human rights issues in relation to emergencies and disasters, including the magnitude 7.0 earthquake that struck Haiti in 2010, which challenge public health aid. She does so while exploring the influence of Article 25 of the UDHR on the response to public health emergencies, including bioterrorism, international environmental disasters, and international conflicts.

Despite the seemingly glacial pace of progress being made in the science of genomics a decade after the initial sequencing of the human genome, Lisa Eckstein proposes in her chapter the need to think optimistically and thus to map a path leading to judicial, ethical, and contextual implementation of genomic sciences. Her chapter includes two insightful case studies—one reviewing the use of genomics as a tool to improve HIV treatment, the other looking at ongoing efforts to apply pharmacogenomics to the global cardiovascular disease epidemic.

Because so much in life is prioritized on the basis of funding, the section ends with Chapter 28, in which Joia S. Mukherjee reviews how governments, while having the major responsibility for fulfilling the right to health, have traditionally been constrained by limited resources to finance the realization of the right to health. She argues, though, that this responsibility must not rest solely with the governments of the world's poorest countries. It is only with large-scale and ongoing international solidarity, as well with civil society fully engaged as both partner and watchdog, that these governments can address the right to health in a sustainable way.

Finally, serving as logical book-ends around this volume of work are a Foreword and a Conclusion penned by the former as well as the current UN Special Rapporteur on the right to the highest attainable standard of health, respectively. They remind us of the urgency to build upon the somewhat limited albeit commendable progress made in securing the right to health for all, offering a timely reminder that all stakeholders must redouble their efforts to achieve the human right to health.

In developing this book, we have done so from the standpoint that health is foundational, as a person cannot engage in all of the activities and human interactions that bring meaning to life without health. Health is also vital to communities because a healthy population enables countries to be productive, with rich cultures and societal well-being. And, although no right can guarantee that all individuals or populations will be fully healthy, what the right to health can accomplish is to ensure the conditions in which people can be healthy and safe.

We have thus aimed to ensure that in its structure *Advancing the Human Right to Health* approaches the right to health from the broadest view possible. We are hopeful that through its rich content—offering the collective wisdom of authors from around the world—the book also meaningfully contributes to efforts to advance the human right to health in every locale and community on the globe.

Acknowledgements and Dedication

José M. Zuniga

Each year on 10 December, the world celebrates Human Rights Day, commemorating the adoption of the Universal Declaration of Human Rights (UDHR) on that day in 1948. The year 2013 marks the 65th anniversary of that inaugural moment in contemporary human rights, and represents an opportunity for individual and collective reflection on progress and shortcomings in the realization of the full range of rights to which human beings are entitled, without distinction, including the right to health.

The 2013 publication of *Advancing the Human Right to Health* is more than a retrospective on the past 65 years; it seeks to provide a perspective on the global response to one of the great moral and legal challenges to the 21st century, namely, living up to the promise of the human right to health, as enshrined not only in Article 25 of the UDHR ('Everyone has the right to a standard of living adequate for the health and well-being of himself and of his family, including food, clothing, housing, and medical care and necessary social services'), but also in multiple international human rights treaties.

I am deeply grateful to my Co-Editors, Lawrence O. Gostin and Stephen P. Marks, for committing their time and expertise to provide the editorial leadership without which such a book project would perish. We were honoured to work with thought-leaders from around the world who, through their contributions to this book, provide context while analysing the complex economic, ethical, legal, medical, political, and sociocultural obstacles to achieving the right to health. Complacency in front of these challenges condemns millions to unnecessary suffering and premature death. My Co-Editors and I thus wish to acknowledge the robust analyses and insightful conclusions of the 49 authors who, despite their hectic schedules, contributed the thematic chapters and country case studies.

The Co-Editors are particularly grateful to Vincent Congiu, without whose dedication and efforts this work would not have been completed. During the course of its development and production, we counted on Adriana Benedict, who demonstrated the highest standards of competence and resourcefulness in both editing and researching support for the book. We acknowledge Eric A. Friedman, who provided invaluable assistance in identifying some of the case study authors. We also express our gratitude to Imane Sidibé for her editing support during the page proof process. Additionally, valuable research and organization assistance was provided by Sara Green, Amy Levin, Jennifer Manne, Ramya Naraharisetti, Sarah Raifman, Neha Sangwan, Aastha Sharma, Vera Sistenich, and Alexandra Zimbelman. Finally, we thank Oxford University Press for commissioning this book, and acknowledge Nicola Wilson, our Commissioning Editor, and Caroline Smith, our Assistant Commissioning Editor.

In closing, just as I opened by referencing an important date in the right to health movement, I end here with another, albeit one marked with great lingering sadness for many of us—both personally and professionally. On 2 September 2013 we will mark the 15-year anniversary of the untimely loss of Jonathan Mann, a key figure in the early fight against HIV/AIDS and a pioneer in advocating the human right to health, who perished along with 228 other victims of the Swissair Flight 111 tragedy. He inspired us all in advocating the inextricable link between health and human rights:

> [M]odern human rights, precisely because they were initially developed entirely outside of the health domain and seek to articulate the societal preconditions for human well-being, seem a far more useful

> framework, vocabulary, and form of guidance for public health efforts to analyze and respond directly to the societal determinants of health than any imperative from the biomedical or public health traditions. (Mann, 1997)

Advancing the Human Right to Health builds on that visionary perspective of the right to health, which I am convinced will continue to challenge and inspire professionals and practitioners alike. It is to Dr Mann and to all who continue this noble work the world over that this book is dedicated.

Reference

Mann, J.M. (1997). Medicine and public health, ethics, and human rights. *The Hastings Center Report*, 27(3), 6–13.

Contents

List of Abbreviations

AIDS	acquired immune deficiency syndrome
ART	antiretroviral therapy
ARV	antiretroviral
AU	African Union
CAT	Convention against Torture and Other Cruel, Inhuman or Degrading Treatment or Punishment
CEDAW	Convention on the Elimination of All Forms of Discrimination against Women
CERD	Convention on the Elimination of All Forms of Racial Discrimination
CESCR	Committee on Economic, Social and Cultural Rights
CHW	community health worker
CIDA	Canadian International Development Agency
CIPIH	Commission on Intellectual Property Rights, Innovation and Public Health
CMH	Commission on Macroeconomics and Health
CRH	Convention on the Rights of the Child
CRPD	Convention on the Rights of Persons with Disabilities
CVD	cardiovascular disease
ECHR	European Convention on Human Rights
ECS	European Committee of Social Rights
ECtHR	European Court of Human Rights
FAO	Food and Agriculture Organization
FCGH	Framework Convention on Global Health
FCTC	Framework Convention on Tobacco Control
FDA	Food and Drug Administration
GDP	gross domestic product
GIVS	Global Immunization Vision and Strategy
HDI	Human Development Index
HIV	human immunodeficiency virus
ICCPR	International Covenant on Civil and Political Rights
ICERD	International Convention on the Elimination of All Forms of Racial Discrimination
ICESCR	International Covenant on Economic, Social and Cultural Rights
ICPD	International Conference on Population and Development
ICTY	International Criminal Tribunal for the former Yugoslavia
IDB	Inter-American Development Bank
ILO	International Labour Organization
IMF	International Monetary Fund
JALI	Joint Action and Learning Initiative
JLI	Joint Learning Initiative
LGBT	lesbian, gay, bisexual, and transgender
MDG	Millennium Development Goal
MOH	Ministry of Health
MSF	Médecins Sans Frontières
MSM	men who have sex with men
NATO	North Atlantic Treaty Organization
NCD	non-communicable disease
NGO	non-governmental organization
OAS	Organization of American States
ODA	Official Development Assistance
OECD	Organization for Economic Cooperation and Development
OHCHR	Office of the High Commissioner for Human Rights
OPEC	Organization of the Petroleum Exporting Countries
PAHO	Pan-American Health Organization
PEPFAR	President's Emergency Plan for AIDS Relief
PHR	Physicians for Human Rights
PIH	Partners in Health
R&D	research and development
SAP	structural adjustment programme
SARS	severe acute respiratory syndrome

STI	sexually transmitted infection
TAC	Treatment Action Campaign
TB	tuberculosis
TRIPS	Trade-Related Aspects of Intellectual Property
UDHR	Universal Declaration of Human Rights
UN	United Nations
UNAIDS	Joint United Nations Programme on HIV/AIDS
UNCAT	United Nations Committee Against Torture
UNESCO	United Nations Educational, Scientific, and Cultural Organization
UNFPA	United Nations Population Fund
UNHCR	United Nations High Commissioner for Refugees
UNHRC	United Nations Human Rights Council
UNICEF	United Nations Children's Fund
UNODC	United Nations Office on Drugs and Crime
USAID	US Agency for International Development
WFP	World Food Programme
WHO	World Health Organization
WMA	World Medical Association
WTO	World Trade Organization

List of Contributors

Raymond A. Atuguba
Senior Lecturer in Law
University of Ghana, Legon
Accra, GHANA

Ana S. Ayala
Associate
O'Neill Institute for National and Global Health Law
Georgetown University Law Center
Washington, DC, USA

Britta Baer
Technical Officer
Gender, Equity, and Human Rights Team
World Health Organization
Geneva, SWITZERLAND

Andrew Ball
Senior Strategy and Operations Adviser
Department of HIV/AIDS
World Health Organization
Geneva, SWITZERLAND

Donna J. Barry
Policy and Advocacy Director
Partners in Health
Boston, MA, USA

Adriana L. Benedict
Juris Doctor Candidate
Harvard Law School
Cambridge, MA, USA

Martin W. Bloem
Chief Nutrition and HIV/AIDS Policy
World Food Programme
Rome, ITALY

Michael Bochenek
Director of Law and Policy
Amnesty International
London, UK

Oscar A. Cabrera
Executive Director
O'Neill Institute for National and Global Health Law
Georgetown University Law Center
Washington, DC, USA

Philip D. Chen
Project Director
China Health Law Initiative
Georgetown University Law Center
Washington, DC, USA

Brian Citro
Senior Research Officer
UN Special Rapporteur on the right to health
Lawyers Collective
New Delhi, INDIA

Jean Connolly Carmalt
Assistant Professor of Law, Politics, and Society
Drake University
Des Moines, IA, USA

Rebecca Cook
Faculty Chair
University of Toronto
Toronto, ON, CANADA

Ravi Duggal
Programme Officer
International Budget Partnership
Mumbai, INDIA

Ebenezer Durojaye
Senior Researcher
University of the Western Cape
Cape Town, SOUTH AFRICA

Lisa Eckstein
Doctor of Juridical Science Candidate
Georgetown University Law Center
Washington, DC, USA

Julio Frenk
Dean of the Faculty
Harvard School of Public Health
Boston, MA, USA

Eric A. Friedman
Project Leader
Joint Action and Learning Initiative
O'Neill Institute for National
and Global Health Law
Georgetown University Law Center
Washington, DC, USA

Ariel Frisancho
National Manager
CARE Peru
Lima, PERU

Octavio Gómez-Dantés
Director for Analysis and Evaluation
Carso Health Institute
Mexico City, MEXICO

Lawrence O. Gostin
Professor of Law/Faculty Director
Georgetown University Law Center
Washington, DC, USA

Kate Greene
Associate Director
Advocacy & Policy
Partners in Health
Washington, DC, USA

Anand Grover
UN Special Rapporteur on the
right to health
United Nations Human Right Council
New Delhi, INDIA

Paul Hunt
Professor of Law
University of Essex School of Law
Colchester, Essex, UK

Wesler Lambert
Deputy Executive Director
Zanmi Lasante
Port-au-Prince, HAITI

Fernet Léandre
Co-Executive Director
Zanmi Lasante
Port-au-Prince, HAITI

Mihir Mankad
Senior Research Officer UN Special
Rapporteur on the right to health
Lawyers Collective
New Delhi, INDIA

Joanne Mariner
Senior Crisis Response Adviser
Amnesty International
London, UK

Stephen P. Marks
François-Xavier Bagnoud Professor
of Health and Human Rights
Harvard School of Public Health
Boston, MA, USA

Hiroaki Matsuura
Departmental Lecturer
School of Interdisciplinary Area Studies
University of Oxford
Oxford, UK

Joia S. Mukherjee
Associate Professor of Medicine
Harvard Medical School
Boston, MA, USA

Armando De Negri Filho
Coordinator
Executive Committee of the World
Social Forum
Porto Alegre, BRAZIL

Charles Ngwena
Professor of Law
University of Pretoria
Pretoria, SOUTH AFRICA

Helena Nygren-Krug
Senior Adviser
Human Rights and Law
Joint United Nations Programme on HIV/AIDS
Geneva, SWITZERLAND

Ariel Pablos-Mendéz
Assistant Administrator for Global Health
US Agency for International Development
Washington, DC, USA

Raul C. Pangalangan
Professor of Law
University of the Philippines
Quezon City, PHILIPPINES

Saskia de Pee
Senior Technical Advisor
Nutrition and HIV/AIDS
World Food Programme
Rome, ITALY

Aafje Rietveld
Medical Officer
Global Malaria Programme
World Health Organization
Geneva, SWITZERLAND

Eriko Sase
Adjunct Professor
Graduate School of Medicine
The University of Tokyo
Tokyo, JAPAN

Rebecca Schleifer
Advocacy Director
Human Rights Watch
New York, NY, USA

Imane Sidibé
Programme/Research Manager
International Association of Providers of AIDS Care
Washington, DC, USA

Lesley Stone
Health Policy and Legislative Analyst
US Agency for International Development
Washington, DC, USA

Victoria Sutton
Associate Professor of Law
Texas Tech University School of Law
Lubbock, TX, USA

Loune Viaud
Co-Executive Director
Zanmi Lasante
Port-au-Prince, Haiti

Matthew Weait
Professor of Law and Policy
School of Law Birkbeck
University of London
London, UK

Diana Weil
Coordinator, Policy and Strategy
Stop TB Department
World Health Organization
Geneva, SWITZERLAND

Di Wu
Associate
O'Neill Institute for National and Global Health Law
Georgetown University Law Center
Washington, DC, USA

Alicia Ely Yamin
Director
Programme on Health Rights of Women and Children
Francois-Xavier Bagnoud Center for Health and Human Rights
Harvard University
Boston, MA, USA

José M. Zuniga
President/CEO
International Association of Providers of AIDS Care
Washington, DC, USA

Section 1

The right to health in perspective

Chapter 1

The emergence and scope of the human right to health

Stephen P. Marks

Introduction

The right to health occupies a prominent place among the internationally recognized human rights, although its formulation and further elaboration are relatively recent. This chapter examines the emergence and scope of the right to health in the corpus of international human rights norms.

Human rights, including the right to health, constitute a set of norms governing the treatment by States and non-State actors of individuals and groups on the basis of ethical principles incorporated into national and international legal systems. Thus, the source of human rights is to be found in the norm-creating process of national and international legal systems, which provides the formal validation of normative positions. The positions emerge from ethical reasoning in moral philosophy or religious faith—what we might term the deeper origins of human rights—or from political claims, which emerge from social mobilization. In plain language, this means that the right to health has emerged from a process of people successfully advocating and eventually obtaining formal recognition in law and policy that they are entitled to—and the State must ensure that they have—an opportunity to lead a healthy life.

The process of formal recognition of the right is incomplete and involves many institutions and reference documents, which are described in the second part of this chapter on the emergence of the right. What elements of a healthy life are properly included in its normative content is the subject of the third part of this chapter. How the right can be advanced is summarized in the fourth part of this chapter, which focuses on the means and methods employed to translate the normative aspirations of this right into justiciable and enforceable legally binding obligations. Many more specifics on the content of the right and the efforts to advance its realization at the national and international levels are provided throughout this book. The conclusion will relate the definitional issues discussed to the broader range of issues explored in other chapters.

The emergence of health in the corpus of international human rights

Health in the WHO Constitution

The early formulation of norms we characterize today as human rights is inseparable from historical and philosophical manifestations of human striving for justice. The deepest origin of human rights no doubt derives from basic human instincts of survival of the species and manifestations of empathy and altruism that evolutionary biology is only beginning to explain (Harris, 2010;

Wilson, 2012). In legend, literature, religion, and political thought, justice and eventually the concept of human rights became socially constructed over time into complex webs of social interaction striving towards a social order in which human beings are treated fairly as individuals and collectivities. The best-known histories of the human rights movement tend to begin with the ancient religions and societies (Ishay, 2007, 2008; Lauren, 1998; Lauterpacht, 1950/1973).

The current catalogue of human rights—at least those enumerated in the International Bill of Human Rights—consists of some 50 normative propositions, expanded by a score of specialized United Nations (UN) treaties, a half-dozen regional human rights treaties, and hundreds of international norms elaborated in the fields of labour, refugees, armed conflict, and criminal law. This corpus of human rights law, enriched by declarations, programmes of action, and other formulations of human rights in the process of becoming legally binding, is the source of the norms that properly fall within the category of international human rights. This body of internationally recognized norms is one of the responses of the community of nations to the horrors of World War II and the commitment to constructing a world order 'to save succeeding generations from the scourge of war, which twice in our lifetime has brought untold sorrow to mankind' (UN Charter, 1945, Preamble). The setting up of a system of UN agencies, such as the World Health Organization (WHO), was another. The prevailing zeitgeist for these normative and institutional developments explains the way health was defined and recognized as a human right by the WHO.

Health is defined in the Preamble to the 1946 WHO Constitution as 'a state of complete physical, mental and social well-being and not merely the absence of disease or infirmity' (WHO, 1946). The preamble further affirms 'the enjoyment of the highest attainable standard of health is one of the fundamental rights of every human being without distinction of race, religion, political belief, [or] economic or social condition' (WHO, 1946). The WHO definition was broadened by the 1978 Declaration of Alma-Ata on Primary Health Care, which strongly reaffirmed the definition, calling it 'a fundamental human right' and adding 'that the attainment of the highest possible level of health is a most important world-wide social goal whose realization requires the action of many other social and economic sectors in addition to the health sector' (WHO, 1978). The Declaration of Alma-Ata also contains a pledge to progressively develop comprehensive healthcare systems to ensure effective and equitable distribution of resources for maintaining health. It has been regretted that, despite this language in the Constitution, 'WHO intentionally neglected human rights discourse during crucial years in the development and implementation of the right to health, [and] . . . did so to the detriment of public health' (Meier, 2010).

The WHO definition, understandable in the context of the immediate aftermath of World War II, was not considered contentious when proposed to the Preparatory Committee that drafted the Constitution (Tobin, 2012). Apparently the wording reflects the language of Henry Sigerist in his books *Medicine and Human Welfare* (1941) and *Civilization and Disease* (1943), which influenced his friend, the Yugoslav delegate Andrija Štampar, who played a significant role in drafting the definition (Bok, 2008). It has been highly contested over the years, and several alternatives have been proposed since. Sisella Bok, in her perceptive analysis of the philosophical issues surrounding the WHO definition, finds this a 'mystifying definition' and argues that the terms 'complete' and 'social'—and, even 'well-being'—contribute to the confusion, which was only prolonged by the Declaration of Alma-Ata (Bok, 2008). She quite helpfully points out that Article 12 of the International Covenant on Economic, Social and Cultural Rights (ICESCR), discussed in the section entitled 'Health in the UN human rights treaty system', while drawing on the WHO definition, departs from it by avoiding the terms 'complete', 'social', and 'well-being' (Bok, 2008). This is true for most other formulations of the right, with the exceptions of the relevant Inter-American treaty (which reproduces the exact words of the WHO definition), and the African Charter, which adds 'spiritual health', a proposal which failed in the WHO in 1999

(Bok, 2008). However, as argued in the later section on health-related human rights, even the term 'social' can be helpful if dealt with from a human rights perspective (as proposed) rather than in the sense of the social engineering of totalitarian regimes, as Bok correctly warns against (Bok, 2008).

This clarification is important for understanding the meaning of the right to health in two ways. First, the critique of the nebulous character of the WHO definition of health, which is of little operational value, does not apply to the definition and interpretation of the right to health as it has evolved into an operational concept. Second, proposals to narrow the definition of health to a biostatistical conception are not necessarily useful for the right to health. For example, Norman Daniels correctly notes that the WHO definition leads to the misconception that health is 'all there is to well-being or happiness' (Daniels, 2008). However, his insistence on an alternative definition focusing on the normal functioning of our species measured by biomedical statistics is of very limited value to promoting the human right to health, although it may be quite useful for some aspects of public health practice. The intent of the WHO definition was to expand from the negative definition (absence of disease) to positive aspects, consistent with the emerging focus on 'social medicine' in the 1940s (Meier, 2010). The human rights texts use one version or another of 'highest attainable standard of physical and mental health', leaving to subsequent elaboration the specifics of what it takes to reach that standard and what features of health will be considered relevant.

The biostatistical conception has the advantage of using objective biological definitions of a healthy organism, without excluding issues of equity or social determinants, which can be raised in the context of health policy but are not definitional to health. From a human rights perspective, the concept of 'the enjoyment of the highest attainable standard of health' is preferable to the biostatistical conception used by Daniels and colleagues for several reasons. First, the biostatistical conception relates to the measurement of an individual's health but says little about what a human rights-inspired health policy should strive to achieve for the population. The appeal is strong to rely on a biostatistical definition because it can be measured and interventions can be identified. However, it is only partially useful for bodies entrusted with assessing compliance with the right to health. It is certainly helpful for members of the Committee on Economic, Social and Cultural Rights (CESCR), for example, to receive data on infant mortality, maternal mortality, life expectancy, and all the other markers of healthy organisms. However, their determination of adequacy of government efforts to realize the right to health would be hampered considerably if all they were interested in were these biostatistical markers. The CESCR's guidelines focus primarily on measures taken to ensure health outcomes rather than the statistical data relating to those outcomes (UN, 2009). Monitoring bodies also need to look at the health system, inequalities, and the various dimensions of the normative content of the right as discussed in the second part of this chapter.

Similarly, Backman and colleagues demonstrated in their 2008 *Lancet* article the value of an assessment of health systems and the right to health by applying 'a manageable set of indicators' to 194 countries with the purpose, among others, of deepening 'the understanding of the important role of health data and indicators in relation to the progressive realization of the right to health' (Backman et al., 2008). Of the 72 indicators selected, only a half-dozen would be considered as based on a biological definition of a healthy organism (such as infant mortality rate, maternal mortality ratio, and life expectancy). The vast majority of the indicators related to recognition of the right to health, non-discrimination, health information, participation, financing, awareness, and accountability. The aim, it should be stressed, of the CESCR and the *Lancet* study is to assess compliance with the right to health, not the health of a person or population.

Second, reliance on statistical measures of conformity to 'normal' functioning of the organism may in fact lead to positions that are antithetical to human rights. For example, if a statistically significant norm for biological health includes sexual drive directed towards reproduction as 'normal', then individuals whose sexual drive is directed exclusively or mainly towards same-sex relations, would be 'unhealthy' biostatistically and therefore pathological. From a human rights perspective, persons preferring same-sex relations and who are supported by the health system and other elements of society in their sexual orientation would be considered—other conditions being equal—healthy physically, mentally, and socially. Persons with disabilities both physical and mental fall below the biostatistical standard for being 'healthy' but from a human rights perspective can be considered as enjoying the right to physical, mental, and social health if the health system meets their special needs. The deviation from the statistical norm would not be relevant to the realization of the right to health. Of course, Daniels acknowledges that for some people 'the functional deficit does not compromise health at all, even though it clearly involves what medicine considers pathology' (Daniels, 2008). His point, however, is that the definition of health should be expanded from the absences of disease to the absence of pathology, including disability and injury. His view is that 'health is normal functioning of our species' based on 'scientific methods of the biomedical sciences to characterize pathology, as well as on our growing understanding of epidemiology, including social epidemiology, to clarify what we need to function normally' (Daniels, 2008).

In sum, while the WHO definition raises complex philosophical issues, it has been used without the confusing concepts of 'complete' and 'well-being', for further normative and practical elaboration of the right to health. The arguments for a narrow statistical definition of health as absence of pathology do not carry over into the instrumental value of a broader definition of health in the context of the right to health, as the experience with the definition of this right after the WHO Constitution demonstrates.

The right to health in the UDHR

The right to health resurfaced two years after the WHO Constitution as a component of the right to an adequate standard of living in Article 25(1) of the 1948 Universal Declaration of Human Rights (UDHR): 'Everyone has the right to a standard of living adequate for the health of himself and of his family, including food, clothing, housing and medical care and necessary social services, and the right to security in the event of unemployment, sickness, disability, widowhood, old age or other lack of livelihood in circumstances beyond his control' (UN General Assembly, 1948). This wording was proposed by the Latin American delegations to the drafting committee of the Commission on Human Rights with the UN Secretariat playing a major role (Morsink, 1999). According to Johannes Morsink's analysis of the drafting of the UDHR, the Secretariat drew on 'the Latin American socialist tradition' as well as some 13 national constitutions containing this right (Morsink, 1999) and subsequently proposed a separate article on the right to medical care. Citing an Indian proposal for an article reading 'every human being has the right to health', he notes that former colonies were more willing to recognize such a right than North Atlantic countries, whose constitutions tended not to recognize the right to health. Nevertheless, the drafting committee adopted a US proposal, drawing on the WHO constitution, stating, 'Everyone, without distinction of economic and social condition, has the right to the highest attainable standard of health. The responsibility of the State and community for the health and safety of its peoples can be fulfilled only by provision of adequate health and social measures' (Morsink, 1999). However, the final draft—after several intermediate versions—added the three rights to food, clothing, and housing 'seen as means to the end of [healthcare]', and 'necessary social services' (Morsink, 1999).

Health in the UN human rights treaty system

From the initial formulations of the WHO Constitutions and the UDHR, the right to health was included in the major UN human rights treaties adopted since, primarily the ICESCR of 1966. By the time the UN started transforming the UDHR into a treaty, the Cold War altered the political landscape. The broadening of the definition and the illustrative examples of steps States should take to realize the right were the result of the WHO's 'significant role in the initial drafting of Article 12' (Alston, 1979). It was the Director-General of the WHO who submitted in April 1951 a draft text on the right to health to the Commission on Human Rights, including the broad WHO definition of health, as well as measures relating to the social determinants of health and the responsibilities of governments (Meier, 2010). The approach to the drafting of the ICESCR differed from that of the UDHR in treating this right on its own rather than within an enumeration of components of the right to an adequate standard of living. The second salient feature was to go well beyond health-care to cover a 'positive definition of health' (Meier, 2010). The third was to enumerate illustrative steps to be taken to realize this right. Working with the International Labour Organisation (ILO) delegate, the WHO delegate convinced the drafters to include the illustrative steps in paragraph 2 of Article 12 (Alston, 1979). Unlike the ILO, which had experience with drafting and monitoring its own standards and preferred that the Covenant should express each right in a brief clause, the WHO felt the need to push for more detailed provisions regarding the scope and substance of the right to health (Alston, 1979).

After a change in leadership at the WHO in 1953, the organization ceased to play an active role in the drafting of the Covenant article, reflecting, as Meier explains, the shift in the WHO's discourse on health 'from the social medicine focus on human rights and . . . toward curative [healthcare] . . . a biomedical vision of health, emphasizing antibiotics, medical technologies, and private urban hospitals as a means to achieve economic growth' (Meier, 2010). As a result, the WHO declined even to comment on the evolving draft right to health article of the Covenant and by 1957 the 'WHO had lost credibility to effect change within the UN Secretariat and among State delegations' (Meier, 2010). For example, it did not prevent the deletion of the definition of health drawn from the WHO Constitution and of the term 'social', or the weakening of other provisions. Nor did it contribute to the work of the Commission on implementation measures in the 1960s (Alston, 1979). After the adoption of the final text in 1966, Meier explains, the 'WHO claimed no ownership or responsibility over the new Covenant's obligations on health' (Meier, 2010). The final text of Article 12, consisting of 118 words, nevertheless, draws heavily on the initial contribution of the WHO before 1953 and remains the most detailed in the Covenant.

The right to health in Article 12 is in two parts: a general affirmation in paragraph 1, and a partial enumeration of steps in paragraph 2. The general part defines the right as 'the right of everyone to the enjoyment of the highest attainable standard of physical and mental health'. Then comes an illustrative, non-exhaustive list of five 'steps to be taken . . . to achieve the full realization of this right', namely:

- The provision for the reduction of the stillbirth-rate and of infant mortality and for the healthy development of the child;
- The improvement of all aspects of environmental and industrial hygiene;
- The prevention, treatment and control of epidemic, endemic, occupational and other diseases;
- The creation of conditions which would assure access to all medical service and medical attention in the event of sickness.

Table 1.1 Right to health definitions

International Convention on the Elimination of All Forms of Racial Discrimination of 1965 (CERD)	'The right to public health, medical care, social security and social services' (Article 5 (e) (iv))
Convention on the Elimination of All Forms of Discrimination against Women of 1979 (CEDAW)	'The right to protection of health and to safety in working conditions, including the safeguarding of the function of reproduction . . . [and] to eliminate discrimination against women in the field of [healthcare] in order to ensure, on a basis of equality of men and women, access to [healthcare] services, including those related to family planning [and] ensure to women appropriate services in connection with pregnancy, confinement and the post-natal period, granting free services where necessary, as well as adequate nutrition during pregnancy and lactation' (Articles 11.1 (f) and 12)
Convention on the Rights of the Child of 1989 (CRC)	'The right of the child to the enjoyment of the highest attainable standard of health and to facilities for the treatment of illness and rehabilitation of health . . . ', followed by an enumeration of six measures to 'pursue full implementation of this right' (Article 24)
Convention on the Rights of Persons with Disabilities of 2006 (CRPD)	'. . . persons with disabilities have the right to the enjoyment of the highest attainable standard of health without discrimination on the basis of disability', followed by an enumeration of six 'measures to ensure access for persons with disabilities to health services that are gender-sensitive, including health-related rehabilitation' (Article 25)

Variations on this definition are found in the major UN human rights treaties, specifically CERD, CEDAW, CDC, and CRPD (see Table 1.1).

The right to health in the regional treaty system

Regional human rights treaties also define the right to health. Article 11 of the European Social Charter of 1961 (as revised in 1996) stipulates States' obligation to take measures 'to remove as far as possible the causes of ill-health; to provide advisory and educational facilities for the promotion of health and the encouragement of individual responsibility in matters of health; to prevent as far as possible epidemic, endemic and other diseases, as well as accidents'; and the duty 'to ensure that any person who is without adequate resources and who is unable to secure such resources either by his own efforts or from other sources, in particular by benefits under a social security scheme, be granted adequate assistance, and, in case of sickness, the care necessitated by his condition, (European Social Charter, 1996). Article 16 of the African Charter on Human and Peoples' Rights of 1981 affirms 'the right to enjoy the best attainable state of physical and mental health [and the obligation of the State to] take the necessary measures to protect the health of their people and to ensure that they receive medical attention when they are sick' (African Charter on Human and Peoples' Rights, 1981). Article 14 of the African Charter on the Rights and Welfare of the Child of 1990 stipulates that 'Every child shall have the right to enjoy the best attainable state of physical, mental, and spiritual health,' with paragraph 2 listing ten measures towards this end (African Charter on the Rights and Welfare of the Child, 1990). Article 10 of the Additional Protocol to the American Convention on Human Rights in the Area of Economic, Social and Cultural Rights of 1988 states that 'Everyone shall have the right to health, understood to mean the enjoyment of the highest level of physical, mental and social well-being,' and lists six measures in paragraph 2 to ensure this right (American Convention on Human Rights in the Area of Economic, Social & Cultural Rights, 1988). This pattern was followed in Article 39 of the Arab Charter on Human Rights (2004), which entered into force in 2008 and stipulates in paragraph 1: 'The State Parties recognize the right of every member of society to the enjoyment of the highest attainable standard of physical and mental health and the right of the citizen to free basic healthcare services and to have access to medical facilities without discrimination of any kind'; and in paragraph 2 the following measures to be taken by State Parties:

- Development of basic healthcare services and the guaranteeing of free and easy access to the centres that provide these services, regardless of geographical location or economic status;
- Efforts to control disease by means of prevention and cure in order to reduce the morality rate;
- Promotion of health awareness and health education;
- Suppression of traditional practices which are harmful to the health of the individual;
- Provision of the basic nutrition and safe drinking water for all;
- Combating environmental pollution and providing proper sanitation systems; and
- Combating drugs, psychotropic substances, smoking and substances that are damaging to health. (Arab Charter on Human Rights, 2004)

Although case law is not very abundant under these regional treaties, it is expanding through the African Commission on Human and Peoples' Rights (ACHPR) (e.g. ACHPR 2001–2002, ACHPR 2002–2003; see Chirwa, 2008); the Inter-American Commission on Human Rights (IACHR) (e.g. IACHR, 2001; see Melish, 2008); the European Court of Human Rights (ECtHR) (e.g. ECtHR, 1994; ECtHR, 2008; see Clements & Simmons, 2008); and the European Committee of Social Rights (ECSR) (ECSR, 2009; see Khaliq & Churchill, 2008). As noted by Malcolm Langford, 'the number of avenues for social rights litigation [including the right to health] at the regional and international level expanded' with the establishment of these regional bodies (Langford, 2008).

The normative content of the right to health

While one can theorize on what the right to health entails, a consensus has emerged over the past 20 years that the CESCR (created to monitor the ICESCR) by and large captured the essential elements in its General Comment No. 14 on the right to health (CESCR, 2000). The right to health does not mean the right to be healthy, the CESCR explains, because being healthy is determined in part by healthcare but also by genetic predisposition and social factors (CESCR, 2000). Thus, the scope of the right to health covers both specific elements of the health system (obligations) and the realization of other human rights that contribute to health (specific health-related human rights).

Obligations of the health system

Since the essence of the right to health is access to the conditions necessary for the realization of healthy lives, it is the duty of the State to ensure those conditions, whether through a regulated market or through government services. In this regard, the CESCR provided a framework that has been widely accepted to identify what is expected to ensure that health facilities, goods, and services, including the underlying determinants of health, are available, accessible, acceptable, and of good quality (CESCR, 2000). The CESCR explains each term. 'Availability' refers to facilities, goods, and services not only of the health system (such as hospitals, clinics, trained medical and professional personnel, medicines, etc.) but also the underlying determinants of health (such as safe and potable drinking water and adequate sanitation). The 'accessibility' requirement has four overlapping dimensions: accessible without discrimination, physically accessible, economically accessible (i.e. affordable), and accessible health-related information. The 'acceptability' dimension refers to respect for medical ethics and cultural sensitivities. Finally, the 'quality of care' dimension relates to health facilities, goods, and services being scientifically and medically appropriate and of good quality (such as 'skilled medical personnel, scientifically approved and unexpired drugs and hospital equipment, safe and potable water, and adequate sanitation') (CESCR, 2000).

These four dimensions are not very different from—in fact they are surprisingly congruent with—the dimensions of the practice of public health. As Sofia Gruskin and Daniel Tarantola put it, 'the added value of a human rights approach to health is in systematizing attention to these issues, requiring that benchmarks and targets be set to guarantee that any targets set are realized progressively, and ensuring transparency and accountability for what decisions are made and their ultimate outcomes' (Gruskin and Tarantola, 2008).

Expanding on theses dimensions of the right to health, the CESCR enumerates what is expected of governments to comply with their obligations to respect, protect, and fulfil the right to health. These three obligations (with the third sometimes expanded into the obligations to promote and to provide) have become the standard approach of treaty bodies and thematic rapporteurs. They have a distinct value for health practitioners, who quite understandably wonder what the right to health would require them to do differently than they already are doing to promote improvements in health delivery with a sensitivity to issues of equity and social justice, not uncommon among health professionals.

While these obligations are to be met within the context of the progressive realization, the CESCR took the bold step of enumerating a subset of obligations belonging to a 'core minimum', which is not subject to progressive realization:

> (1) to ensure the right of access to health facilities, goods and services on a *non-discriminatory* basis, especially for vulnerable or marginalized groups; (2) to ensure access to the *minimum essential food* which is sufficient, nutritionally adequate and safe, to ensure freedom from hunger to everyone; (3) to ensure access to *basic shelter, housing and sanitation*, and an adequate supply of safe and potable *water*; (4) to *provide essential drugs*, . . . defined by WHO's Action Programme on Essential Drugs; (5) to ensure *equitable distribution* of all health facilities, goods and services; [and] (6) to adopt and implement a *national public health strategy and plan of action*, on the basis of epidemiological evidence, addressing the health concerns of the whole population. (Emphasis added; CESCR, 2000, paragraph 43)

It is worth quoting in full what the CESCR identified as how the national plan of action should be devised and reviewed, namely, 'on the basis of a participatory and transparent process'. Moreover, these plans 'shall include methods, such as right to health indicators and benchmarks, by which progress can be closely monitored'. Finally, the strategy and plan of action 'shall give particular attention to all vulnerable or marginalized groups'.

The CESCR added a set of 'obligations of comparable priority' to:

- ensure reproductive, maternal (pre-natal as well as post-natal) and child healthcare;
- provide immunization against the community's major infectious diseases;
- take measures to prevent, treat and control epidemic and endemic diseases;

- provide education and access to information concerning the main health problems in the community, including methods of preventing and controlling them; [and]
- provide appropriate training for health personnel, including education on health and human rights. (CESCR, 2000, paragraph 44)

From a legal perspective, governments that fail to meet those core and equivalent obligations are not in compliance with the Covenant; from the public health perspective, these core obligations are indicative of priorities for the health system based on the right to health. Beyond these core obligations relating to healthcare and the underlying determinants of health, the normative content of the right to health directly involved with the health system, concern, as the first Special Rapporteur pointed out, freedoms, such as 'the right to control one's health, including the right to be free from non-consensual medical treatment and experimentation' (UN, 2003). Finally, the normative content of the right to health dependent on the health system includes specific entitlements in such areas as maternal, child, and reproductive health; occupational health; and prevention, treatment, and control of diseases, including access to essential medicines (UN, 2003). These features of the normative content are expanded by other health-related human rights.

Health-related human rights

The CESCR listed 14 human rights as 'integral components of the right to health', including 'the rights to food, housing, work, education, human dignity, life, non-discrimination, equality, the prohibition against torture, privacy, access to information, and the freedoms of association, assembly and movement' (CESCR, 2000, paragraph 3). Human rights have been categorized in various ways, the most common being to distinguish economic, social, and cultural from civil and political rights, although the contemporary value of such categorization has been questioned (Marks, 2009). For the purpose of relating the core internationally recognized human rights to the realization of health and well-being, it is proposed here to group human rights into three categories, corresponding to the three domains covered in the WHO definition (physical, mental, and social) translated into concepts that are meaningful in moral philosophy and human rights. Physical health overlaps with rights concerning the physical existence and integrity of humans ('rights of existence'); mental health is broadened here to cover those rights that protect the autonomy of thought and action of individuals ('rights of autonomous action'), it being understood that this category is quite different from prevention and treatment of mental illness; and social well-being, that is, those rights that involve social interactions of individuals and groups from the family to the political, cultural, and international communities ('rights of social interaction'). These are not tight categories fitting into the definition of health, but rather a way of grouping health-related human rights that is intended to be meaningful from the perspective of physical, mental, and social well-being. The purpose of including these three categories in a discussion of the scope of the right to health is to draw attention to the fact that deprivations of physical integrity, restrictions on autonomous action, and reduced opportunities for social interaction all have an impact on the full realization of the right to health while often constituting human rights violations themselves.

Rights of existence

Foremost among the human rights relating to 'physical integrity' is the right to not be arbitrarily deprived of life. As defined internationally, the right to life does not ban death resulting from lawful acts of warfare or capital punishment, although international humanitarian law limits the former and newer protocols and regional conventions, supported by UN resolutions and by social movements, define the death penalty as a violation of human rights (Schabas, 1998). The right to death with dignity is sometimes claimed as the human rights grounding for domestic legislation on the subject (Biggs, 2001). Although there is no explicit international human right to death, some scholars construe this right from various recognized rights, such as the rights to dignity and freedom from cruel inhuman or degrading treatment (Paust, 1995).

Another controversial aspect of the right to life relevant to the right to health is the tension between the claim that it includes the right to life of the foetus from the moment of conception, and the claim that reproductive rights of the pregnant woman include the right to voluntary termination of her pregnancy. The right to an abortion is recognized in various national legal systems but not explicitly in international human rights due in large part to opposition by Catholic and Islamic countries. As Jonathan Wolf summarized the debate, 'many have argued from a religious perspective that contraception, and even more so, abortion, are morally unacceptable, and so not only is it right to restrict access to services and information about them, but it is even wrong to offer them' (Wolf, 2012). This issue is authoritatively discussed in another chapter in this volume (see Yamin, Chapter 20, 'Women's health and human rights: struggles to engender social transformation').

Physical integrity is protected in various ways. Special standards, developed in the context of the UN's work on crime prevention and treatment of offenders, apply to the treatment of detainees, as well as the rights and responsibilities of lawyers, prosecutors, judges, and law enforcement officers. For example, the UN Standard Minimum Rules for the Treatment of Prisoners stipulates that '[a]ll accommodation provided for the use of prisoners . . . shall meet all requirements of health, due regard being paid to climatic conditions and particularly to cubic content of air, minimum floor space, lighting, heating and ventilation' (UN, 1955, rule 10). With regard to medical services, the Standard Minimum Rules require that they 'should be organized in close relationship to the general health administration of the community or nation' (rule 22) and make special provisions for mental health, dental services, obstetric and paediatric care for incarcerated women, prevention of the spread of infectious disease, and the role of the medical officer with regard to food, hygiene, sanitation and similar conditions of incarceration (UN, 1955). This issue is addressed in greater detail in another chapter of this publication (see Mariner & Schleifer, Chapter 21, 'The right to health in prison').

More recent standard-setting activity has focused on impunity, accountability of high government officials, and compensation for victims of human rights violations. Special treaties and procedures exist for torture, disappearance, and summary and extra-judicial execution (see Bochenek, Chapter 25, 'Combating torture and other ill-treatment').

Political violence resulting in massive harm to populations entails a wide range of human rights violations affecting the right to health. Certain acts of grievous harm to physical and mental integrity, when 'part of a widespread or systematic attack directed against any civilian population', may constitute crimes against humanity, punishable under international law. The Rome Statute of the International Criminal Court of 17 July 1998 (which entered into force on 1 July 2002) lists the following acts as falling within this particular violation of human rights:

> (a) Murder; (b) Extermination; (c) Enslavement; (d) Deportation or forcible transfer of population; (e) Imprisonment or other severe deprivation of physical liberty in violation of fundamental rules of international law; (f) Torture; (g) Rape, sexual slavery, enforced prostitution, forced pregnancy, enforced sterilization, or any other form of sexual violence of comparable gravity; (h) Persecution against any identifiable group or collectivity on political, racial, national, ethnic, cultural, religious, gender . . . or other grounds that are universally recognized as impermissible under international law, in connection with any act referred to in this paragraph or any crime within the jurisdiction of the Court; (i) Enforced disappearance of persons; (j) The crime of apartheid; [and] (k) Other inhuman acts of a similar character intentionally causing great suffering, or serious injury to body or to mental or physical health. (UN, 1998)

Special treaties and procedures for prevention and repression of certain human rights violations considered as international crimes—such as genocide, torture, slavery, racial discrimination, and various forms of terrorism—are part of human rights law, as well as of international criminal law and international humanitarian law. International humanitarian law, established to protect victims of armed conflict (injured and shipwrecked combatants, prisoners of war and civilian populations notably under occupation) was codified in the four Geneva Conventions of 12 August 1949 and the Additional Protocols of 1977, and is sometimes referred to as the law of human rights in times of armed conflict (see Sutton, Chapter 26, 'Emergencies, disasters, conflicts, and human rights').

Disability rights were not included in the International Bill of Human Rights, but specific human rights standards have been developed for persons with disabilities and mental illness, in particular, the Convention on the Rights of Persons with Disabilities (CRPD), adopted in 2006, with extensive provisions on health in Article 25.

The right to 'a standard of living adequate for the health and well-being' of oneself and one's family was defined in the UDHR as including 'food, clothing, housing and medical care and necessary social services', as well as 'the right to security in the event of unemployment, sickness, disability, widowhood, old age or other lack of livelihood in circumstances beyond [one's] control' (UN General Assembly, 1948). Subsequently, the rights to health, work, safe and healthy working conditions (occupational health), adequate food and protection from malnutrition and famine, adequate housing, and social security (that is, a regime covering long-term disability, old age, unemployment and other conditions) have been further elaborated. The rights to work and to decent conditions of work have been the responsibility of the ILO since 1919, and specific rules have been developed through some 200 ILO conventions and recommendations, constituting a highly developed subfield of human rights. The other rights relating to an adequate living standard have also been expanded upon by treaties, international conferences and summits, and the work of Special Rapporteurs and treaty bodies. This broad range of human rights norms covers the essential components of the social determinants of health. In this regard, the World Conference on Social Determinants of Health in 2011 discussed 'using the human rights approach and tools to address health inequities and strengthen the implementation of actions in the social determinants framework' (WHO, 2011).

Complementing these rights of physical existence and integrity, human rights protecting autonomy of action also contribute to the right to health.

Rights of autonomous action

Several human rights fall within the category of rights that preserve and protect the human value of each person and his or her autonomy and freedom of action. Dignity tends to be mentioned as both the basis for all human rights and a right per se. If dignity means the worth and honour due to any human being in accordance with the social context, in which failure to respect dignity results in humiliation, then the right implies measures to eliminate both acts and omissions, such as discrimination, mistreatment, or lack of an adequate standard of living. However, some courts have applied an objective concept of dignity according to which certain acts (such as making a spectacle of a disability) violate the right to dignity even if consented to by the alleged victim.

The great civil liberties—freedom of oral and written expression, freedom of conscience, opinion, religion or belief—as well as rights to a fair hearing and an effective remedy for violations of human rights, and protection of privacy in domicile and correspondence, all support the autonomy of individuals to act without interference from the State or others. The implications for mental health of these freedoms are easy to identify. Similarly, freedom from arbitrary detention or arrest, torture, or other forms of cruel, inhuman or degrading punishment or treatment, and humane conditions of detention for those legally deprived of their liberty, have obvious implications for physical and mental health. Human rights standards in UN and regional texts provide the definitions and means of redress for these rights. A separate but related human right is that of informed consent to medical experimentation, which was included in post-1945 enumerations of rights due to the abhorrent abuse of that right during World War II (see Zuniga & Sidibé, Chapter 24, '*Primum non nocere* and the right to health').

Equality and non-discrimination are human rights that are at the same time principles for the application of all other human rights, because they require that all persons be treated equally in the enjoyment of their human rights and that measures be taken to remove discriminatory practices on prohibited grounds. According to the CESCR, the first dimension of accessibility of the right to health is non-discrimination, according to which 'health facilities, goods and services must be accessible to all, especially the most vulnerable or marginalized sections of the population, in law and in fact, without discrimination on any of the prohibited grounds' (CESCR, 2000, paragraph 12). The CESCR further reminds State Parties that the:

> Covenant proscribes any discrimination in access to [healthcare] and underlying determinants of health, as well as to means and entitlements for their procurement, on the grounds of race, colour, sex, language, religion, political or other opinion, national or social origin, property, birth, physical or mental disability, health status (including HIV/AIDS), sexual orientation and civil, political, social or other status, which has the intention or effect of nullifying or impairing the equal enjoyment or exercise of the right to health. (CESCR, 2000, paragraph 18)

It also stresses the protection of the vulnerable members of society 'by the adoption of relatively low-cost targeted programmes' (CESCR, 2000, paragraph 18).

Related to freedom of expression is the right to what is called the 'moral and material interests' in any literary, artistic, or scientific creation. Thus copyrights, patents, and other intellectual property rights fall into this category of human rights to the extent that they relate to an individual's creative energies and products; however, intellectual property rights are less justified as 'human rights' when owned by corporations and utilized to market products for return on investment, as confirmed by the CESCR in its 2005 General Comment 17 (UN, 2005; see also Marks & Benedict, Chapter 22, 'Access to medical products, vaccines, and medical technologies').

Freedom of movement means the right to reside where one pleases to leave any country, including one's own, and to return to one's country. The limitation on this right 'necessary to protect . . . public health' (ICCPR, 1966) is the prime example of human rights accommodating the public health imperative of quarantining in times of epidemic. This limitation has been interpreted as allowing public health to be invoked 'as a ground for limiting certain rights in order to allow a State to take measures dealing with a serious threat to the health of the population or individual members of the population. These measures must be specifically aimed at preventing disease or injury or providing care for the sick and injured' (UN, 1984). Public health may also be a justifiable ground for limiting international travel, for example, in times of pandemic influenza (WHO, 2007b).

The right to seek and enjoy asylum from persecution is also a human right, which has been developed and expanded by international refugee law, the practice of the UN High Commissioner for Refugees (UNHCR), and recent codes relating to internally displaced persons. This right, like many others, is not absolute: limitations may be imposed, for example, in times of epidemic, as long as certain safeguards, defined in human rights law, are observed.

Rights of social interaction

The third set of rights that are also determinants of health relate to the participation of individuals in their society. Social well-being—an element of health—relates to group rights, education, family, access to and participation in culture, political participation, gender and reproductive rights, the environment, and development, all of which are the subject of specific human rights with health implications.

The basic human rights texts affirm a limited number of group rights, notably the rights of 'peoples' to self-determination, that is, to 'determine their political status and freely pursue their economic, social and cultural development' and to permanent sovereignty over natural resources (ICCPR, 1966; ICESCR, 1966). They also enumerate the rights of persons belonging to minorities to practise their religion, enjoy their culture and use their language. (ICCPR, Article 27.) Indigenous peoples have defined rights that take into account their culture and special relation to the land (UN, 2007). Health figures prominently among the concerns of minorities and indigenous peoples. For example, Article 24 of the Declaration on the Rights of Indigenous Peoples contains the following article on the right to health, in addition to several other health-related provisions relating to children, the environment, and the right to development:

- Indigenous peoples have the right to their traditional medicines and to maintain their health practices, including the conservation of their vital medicinal plants, animals and minerals. Indigenous individuals also have the right to access, without any discrimination, to all social and health services.
- Indigenous individuals have an equal right to the enjoyment of the highest attainable standard of physical and mental health. States shall take the necessary steps with a view to achieving progressively the full realization of this right.

The right to education includes compulsory primary education, availability and accessibility of secondary education and equal access to higher education, and the role of parents in choosing their child's education institution. Of course, health education includes any learning experience that helps individuals and communities improve their health, and much of the essential knowledge and attitudes people need for healthy lives are communicated in an educational setting. In addition to the right to education, rights of the child have been codified in several instruments, primarily the 1989 Convention on the Rights of the Child (CRC), which makes 'the best interest of the child' the primary consideration and defines rights relating to the child's identity, health and access to healthcare, expression of opinion, conditions of adoption, and protection from abuse, torture, capital punishment, and traditional practices prejudicial to the child's health (CRC, 1989).

Participation takes at least three forms in international human rights. Political participation includes the right to run for office and to vote in genuine and periodic elections. Cultural participation means primarily the right to participate in the cultural life of the community, whether through access to visual and performance art or through artistic creation and the protection of writers, artists and performers. The third meaning of participation relates to efforts to realize human rights whether through the exercise of freedom of association or protection of human rights defenders in accordance with a 1998 declaration, officially entitled Declaration on the Right and Responsibility of Individuals, Groups and Organs of Society to Promote and Protect Universally Recognized Human Rights and Fundamental Freedoms. All these types of participation contribute to the individual's integration into society and ability to influence his or her condition in society, all of which contribute to a healthy life.

Health issues loom large in human rights standard-setting and policy determination regarding gender, sexual, and reproductive rights, which have profound implications for social interaction. The basic human rights texts have been supplemented by a specialized Convention on the Elimination of All Forms of Discrimination against Women (CEDAW) of 1979. Considerable advances in mainstreaming women's rights as human rights were made at the international conferences in Vienna (human rights focus, 1993), Cairo (population focus, 1994), and Beijing (women focus, 1995). Further developments have been made to deal with violence against women (through a

1993 Declaration and a Special Representative to study the problem) and traditional practices harmful to health, such as female genital cutting or mutilation, which State Parties to the CRC and CEDAW agree to abolish (CEDAW, 1979; CRC, 1989) and about which the WHO, the United Nations Children's Fund (UNICEF), and the United Nations Fund for Population Activities (UNFPA) issued a joint plan of action in 1994. Moreover, the committee monitoring CEDAW issued General Recommendation No. 14 on 'Female Circumcision—FGM—Female Genital Mutilation' in 1990 calling on State Parties to 'take appropriate and effective measures with a view to eradicating the practice of female circumcision' (UN, 1990).

Reproductive rights begin with 'The right of men and women of marriageable age to marry and to found a family' (ICCPR, Article 23(2)) which is closely related to the right of 'men and women . . . to decide freely and responsibly on the number and spacing of their children' (UN, 1990), and 'to be informed and to have access to safe, effective, affordable and acceptable methods of family planning of their choice' (UN, 1994a). Various internationally-approved programs and plans of action have set out in considerable detail the specific ways in which this right can be realized and thus enhance health within the family setting and in the context of reproductive rights (see Yamin, Chapter 20, 'Women's health and human rights: struggles to engender social transformation').

In the same way that the distinction between civil and political, and economic, social, and cultural rights is losing its relevance in the post-Cold War era (Marks, 2009), so too is the third category of solidarity or third-generation rights less helpful as a distinct category than it was 20 years ago (Alston, 2001; Marks, 1981). The 'third generation' referred to a set of rights emerging after first-generation civil and political rights and second-generation economic, social, and cultural rights, which reflect certain global values such as peace, a healthy environment, development, communication, humanitarian intervention or assistance, and the like. Some governments and commentators wanted to raise these broad objectives to the level of human rights, notwithstanding the complex matter of defining the rights- and duty-holders and the precise obligations involved. Nevertheless, the rights to a healthy environment and to development, in particular, continue to have support and have been approved though UN resolutions and regional treaties, with a strong health component.

For example, in 1972 the UN Conference on the Human Environment, which created the United Nations Environment Programme (UNEP), proclaimed in its Declaration of the United Nations Conference on the Human Environment that 'man's environment, the natural and the man-made, are essential to his well-being and to the enjoyment of basic human rights—even the right to life itself' (UN, 1972). The African Charter provides that 'all peoples shall have the right to a general satisfactory environment favourable to their development' (African Charter on Human and Peoples Rights, 1981). Article 22 of the Draft Principles on Human Rights and the Environment, presented by the Special Rapporteur on human rights and the environment, provides that, 'All States shall respect and ensure the right to a secure, healthy and ecologically sound environment' (UN, 1994b). At the conclusion of the June 2012 UN Conference on Sustainable Development (Rio+20), the Heads of State and Government affirmed numerous times the importance of human rights and recognized 'that health is a precondition for and an outcome and indicator of . . . sustainable development', calling 'for the full realization of the right to the enjoyment of the highest attainable standard of physical and mental health', and recognizing the importance of 'universal health coverage to enhancing health, social cohesion and sustainable human and economic development' (UN General Assembly, 2012, paragraph 139). In 2012, the Human Rights Council appointed the first Independent Expert on human rights obligations relating to the enjoyment of a safe, clean, healthy and sustainable environment, whose mandate includes contributing a human rights perspective to follow-up processes to Rio+20.

As far as the right to development is concerned, the 1986 Declaration provides that 'States should undertake, at the national level, all necessary measures for the realization of the right to development and shall ensure, *inter alia*, equality of opportunity for all in their access to . . . health services' (Declaration on the Right to Development, 1986). The high-level task force on the implementation of the right to development, established by the Commission on Human Rights in 2004, completed its work in 2010, including extensive analysis and proposals relating to the health dimensions of the right to development (UN, 2010).

This selection of rights relating to minority and indigenous rights, education, cultural and political participation, family, environment, and development underscores the social dimensions of a healthy life, the realization of which improves many of the social determinants of health. These and all other dimensions of the right to health and health-related human rights remain lofty aspirations unless and until they become subject to obligations of duty-holders and mechanisms of accountability.

Means and methods for implementing the right to health

The typical approach to public health consists of four steps: (1) identify the problem through the systematic collection of data; (2) identify the causes of the problem using research on causes, risk factors, and potential interventions; (3) design, implement, and evaluate interventions; and (4) test, monitor, and evaluate effectiveness of promising interventions in diverse settings, and monitor and adapt them to enhance their impact and cost-effectiveness. This approach, familiar to public health professionals, differs from the typical process through which human rights objectives are met. When a right to health framework is introduced, it can complement the public health approach, but the means and methods are of a different nature.

The effective realization of the right to health, like any human right, depends on a process of norm elaboration and enforcement. In the domestic system, law is binding, and the courts and the police are available to use force to compel compliance. In the international human rights regime, the term 'enforcement' refers to coerced compliance, while the more common term 'implementation' refers to supervision, monitoring, and general effort to hold duty-holders accountable. Implementation is further subdivided into promotion—preventive measures to ensure respect for human rights in the future—and protection—responses to violations that have occurred. The means and methods of implementation may be summarized in three forms of promotion and five forms of protection, all of which are relevant to the realization of the right to health.

Promotion (information and education, institutions, further standard-setting)

Promotion of human rights is achieved through developing awareness, standard-setting and interpretation, and creation of national institutions. Awareness of human rights is a precondition to acting on them and is advanced though dissemination of knowledge (publications, information campaigns) and human rights education at all levels. Standard-setting refers to the drafting of human rights texts at the UN level, principally the Human Rights Council and its predecessor Commission on Human Rights, as well as other bodies, such as the Commission on the Status of Women, and UN specialized agencies, such as the ILO and the WHO, as well as the regional organizations (Council of Europe, Organization of American States (OAS), African Union (AU), Arab League, Association of South East Asian Nations (ASEAN)) discussed earlier. These norms are interpreted by various international courts and treaty-monitoring bodies. The third preventive or promotional means of implementation is national institution-building, which includes improvements in the judiciary and law enforcement institutions and the creation of specialized bodies such as health officers in national commissions for human rights and human rights officers in ministries of health.

Thus, the institutions described earlier have contributed to the standard-setting, monitoring, and interpretation of the right to health. Although, as Meier (2010) stresses, the WHO 'lost its human rights compass' from 1953 to 1973, in recent years it has made modest advances in its promotional role, mainly through the work of the Department of Ethics and Social Determinants (formerly the Department of Ethics, Equity, Trade and Human Rights), such as the publication *25 Questions and Answers on Health and Human Rights* (WHO, 2002) and *The Right to Health Factsheet* (WHO, 2007a). Among the treaty bodies, the CESCR has contributed significantly to the interpretative function of the promotional role through General Comment No. 14, discussed earlier. Another significant promotional function is carried out by the Special Rapporteur on the right of everyone to the enjoyment of the highest attainable standard of physical and mental health, whose mandate covers reporting on thematic topics, in addition to the protection functions discussed later. Other 'thematic' rapporteurs deal with health-related issues, such as food, housing, and toxic waste.

Protection (monitoring and evaluation, complaints and litigation)

The protection of human rights involves a complex web of national and international mechanisms to monitor, judge, denounce, and coerce States, as well as provide relief to victims.

Monitoring compliance with international standards is carried out through the reporting and complaints procedures of the UN treaty bodies and regional human rights commissions and courts. States are required to submit reports, and the monitoring body—often guided by information provided by non-governmental organizations (NGOs)—examines progress and problems with a view to guiding the reporting country to do better. Several optional procedures allow individuals and groups (and sometimes other States) to petition these bodies for a determination of violations, including alleged violations of the ICESCR, once the optional protocol to that effect, which the UN General Assembly adopted and opened for signature in 2008, entered into force in May 2013. The quasi-judicial bodies, such as the Human Rights Committee (which monitors the ICCPR) or the ACHPR (which monitors the African Charter), utilize various forms of fact-finding and investigation and issue their views. Another monitoring mechanism is the Universal Periodic Review (UPR). All countries and all rights come under review of the UPR, including—surprising though this may be—the United States on the right to health, even though it has not ratified the ICESCR. The United States came under review in 2010, including with respect to its record on realizing the right to health, as did other reporting countries (UN, 2011).

Special procedures have been established in the UN through which working groups, independent experts and Special Rapporteurs are mandated to study countries or issues, including taking on cases of alleged violations, and report back on their findings and request redress from governments. Numerous right to health issues are raised by the country reports and urgent actions on individual communications, not only in those of the Special Rapporteur on the right to health but also in those of the procedures dealing with adequate housing; arbitrary detention; the sale of children; child prostitution and child pornography; enjoyment of a safe, clean, healthy, and sustainable environment; extreme poverty; indigenous peoples; environmentally sound management and disposal of hazardous substances and wastes; violence against women; and safe drinking water and sanitation.

The second means of protection is adjudication of cases by fully empowered human rights courts, the main ones being the European Court of Human Rights, the Inter-American Court of

Human Rights, and the African Court of Human and Peoples' Rights. At the national level, the trend of court cases invoking the right to health has been increasing (Byrne, 2009), although this trend has been criticized because 'the successful litigants tend to come from economically and socially more advantaged groups' (Wolf, 2012). Jonathan Wolf conjectures that this trend is 'damaging health equity and cost-effectiveness' (Wolf, 2012). The scale on which adjudication distorts health priorities is probably insignificant, and it is certainly consistent with the judicial function to determine that an individual right to health claim would impinge on the State's capacity to ensure the right to health for the population in general. For example, after deferring to State and medical authorities to reach rational decisions on the allocation of scarce resources (South Africa Constitutional Court, 1998), the South African Constitutional Court decided that the courts can determine whether State authorities have chosen the means that are reasonable to realize the right to health and order them to take additional steps if necessary (South Africa Constitutional Court, 2002). More examples are analysed in another chapter of this publication (see Cabrera & Ayala, Chapter 2, 'Advancing the right to health through litigation').

Political supervision refers to the authority of bodies made up of representatives of States to adopt resolutions judging the policies and practices of States. The Commission on Human Rights and its successor the Human Rights Council, the UN General Assembly, the Committee of Ministers of the Council of Europe, and the Assembly of OAS have all adopted politically significant resolutions denouncing governments for violations of human rights and demanding that they redress the situation. They often also call for compensation to the victims. This form of sanction may appear toothless since it is not backed up with coercive force; in practice, however, many governments—fearing reputational, economic, or trade consequences—take quite seriously such political naming and shaming and go to considerable lengths to avoid it, including by improving their human rights performance with respect to the right to health.

The use of coercion is available only to the Security Council, which can use its powers under Chapter VII of the UN Charter to impose sanctions, cut off communications, create ad hoc criminal tribunals, and authorize the use of force by Member-States or deploy UN troops to put an end to a threat to international peace and security, which it has on occasion interpreted to include human rights violations. Human rights considerations were part of the use of Chapter VII in Bosnia, Haiti, Iraq, Libya, Somalia, and other locations. This forceful means of protecting human rights is complex and dangerous and can have harmful health consequences, as has been the case with sanctions imposed on Haiti and Iraq (Marks, 1999), or the spread of cholera allegedly from infected peacekeepers in Haiti (Piarroux et al., 2011). If used properly, forceful intervention can be a modern and legitimate form of the 19th-century doctrine of humanitarian intervention, according to which States use armed force to halt atrocities committed in another State while respecting the principles of necessity, proportionality, disinterestedness, and collective action. The North Atlantic Treaty Organization (NATO) sought to employ such a doctrine in Kosovo in 1999, but, without the necessary authorization from the Security Council, engaged in a legitimate but illegal use of force. Each case of action (e.g. no-fly zones over Iraq since 1991) or inaction (e.g. Rwanda in 1994) regarding the use of armed force for human rights purposes has ethical and legal difficulties. Nevertheless, the legitimacy and legality of authorized force in response to a human rights crisis is now well established (Marks & Cooper, 2010).

The final means of responding to human rights violations is through *humanitarian relief* or assistance. Provision of food, blankets, tents, medical and sanitary assistance, and other forms of aid saves lives and safeguards the health of persons forcibly displaced often as a result of large-scale human rights violations or natural disasters. Refugees and internationally displaced persons come under the protection of the UNHCR, which deploys massive amounts of aid, along with the

International Committee of the Red Cross, UNICEF, World Food Programme (WFP), United Nations Development Programme (UNDP), the UN Office for the Coordination of Humanitarian Affairs, and other agencies, as well as major NGOs like Oxfam, CARE, and the International Rescue Committee. The complex relations with the host country and among the entities seeking to alleviate suffering in such humanitarian emergencies remain problematic, although there is little doubt that this method of implementing the right to health remains essential (Fidler, 2007; Harvard Humanitarian Initiative, 2011).

Conclusion

Every country in the world has accepted that human rights are universal and is bound by at least one treaty containing a provision on the right to health. All are challenged, in one way or another, to achieve progress with respect to this right. The normative content of the right to health has evolved from a contested definition of health and affirmation of it as a 'fundamental right of all human beings' to treaty norms in the principal UN and regional human rights regimes with an impressive amount of interpretative work by treaty bodies, and regional and national judicial bodies. The content of the right is best understood as covering both the dimensions of the right that are the responsibility of the health system and the health-related human rights that focus on physical integrity, personal autonomy, and social interactions.

The richness of the right to health and health-related human rights is of little value without effective means and methods of promotion and protection at the national and international levels. The 12 country case studies featured in this book illustrate the variety of national experience with both the recognition of the right and the means and methods of promotion and protection. Other chapters provide a rich tapestry of theory and practice of international litigation, health development as nation-strengthening, healthcare financing, health systems, and the health workforce. Still other chapters address right to health approaches to access medical products, vaccines, and technologies; to AIDS, malaria, and tuberculosis (TB); to women's health; to genomics; to conflicts and disasters; to food and nutrition; to torture; and to prisons. It has been almost a half-century since the highest attainable standard of physical and mental health was affirmed as a human right in an international treaty, and this array of thematic issues is illustrative of how far the international community has come in that period.

Three final observations may be made in conclusion. First, there is no doubt—notwithstanding the failure of the United States to ratify the ICESCR although the country is bound by a least one other treaty affirming the right—about the status of the right to health among the internationally recognized human rights. One of the consequences has been the trend of national constitutions to contain a right to health provision following closely the wording of the international standard (Kinney & Clark, 2004). Second, the practice of treaty bodies, special procedures, and judicial bodies has significantly enriched the normative content of this right. Third, the moral and legal force of the human right to health as it has evolved has empowered activists to challenge certain major and politically charged obstacles to global health, whether access to antiretroviral treatment for HIV-affected individuals, effective tobacco control, inadequate access of vulnerable populations to healthcare facilities, conditions of detention in places such as Guantánamo Bay, and numerous other issues. In sum, the human right to health has evolved from a timid and confusing initial formulation in 1946 to a robust norm firmly anchored in national and international law but still in need of considerably more effort to reach the full potential of affecting profoundly the resource allocation and policy determination of health systems globally.

References

African Charter on Human and Peoples' Rights. (1981). *African Charter on Human and Peoples' Rights ('Banjul Charter')*. OAU (now AU) Doc. CAB/LEG/67/3 rev. 5, 21 I.L.M. 58 (1982), entered into force 21 October 1986.

African Charter on the Rights and Welfare of the Child. (1990). *African Charter on the Rights and Welfare of the Child*. Adopted by the Organization of African Unity (now called the African Union), entered into force 1999.

Alston, P. (1979). The United Nations' specialized agencies and implementation of the International Covenant on Economic, Social and Cultural Rights. *Columbia Journal of Transnational Law*, 18, 79–118.

Alston, P. (2001). Peoples' rights: their rise and fall. In P. Alston (Ed.), *Peoples' Rights*, pp. 259–293. Oxford University Press: Oxford.

American Convention on Human Rights in the Area of Economic, Social and Cultural Rights. (1988). *American Convention on Human Rights in the Area of Economic, Social and Cultural Rights ('Protocol of San Salvador')*. Adopted at San Salvador, El Salvador on November 17, 1988, at the eighteenth regular session of the General Assembly.

Arab Charter on Human Rights. (2004). *Arab Charter on Human Rights*. Entered into force 15 March 2008.

Backman, G., Hunt, P., Jaramillo-Strauss, C., *et al.* (2008). Health systems and the right to health: an assessment of 194 countries. *Lancet*, 372, 2047–2085.

Biggs, H. (2001). *Euthanasia, Death with Dignity and the Law*. Hart Publishing: Oxford.

Bok, S. (2008). Rethinking the definition of health. *The International Encyclopedia of Public Health*, 6, 590–597.

Byrne, I. (2009). Enforcing the right to health: Innovative lessons from domestic courts. In A. Clapham and M. Robinson (Eds.), *Realizing the Right to Health*, pp. 525–38. Rüffer & Rub: Zurich.

CEDAW (1979). *Convention on the Elimination of All Forms of Discrimination against Women*. UN General Assembly: New York, NY.

CESCR. (2000). *General Comment 14: The right to the highest attainable standard of health (article 12 of the International Covenant on Economic, Social and Cultural Rights)*. Committee on Economic, Social and Cultural Rights (CESCR): Geneva.

Chirwa, D.M. (2008). African regional human rights system. In A. Langford (Ed.), *Emerging Trends in International and Comparative Law*, pp. 323–338. Cambridge University Press: New York, NY.

Clements, L. and Simmons, A. (2008). European Court of Human Rights. In A. Langford (Ed.), *Emerging Trends in International and Comparative Law*, pp. 409–427. Cambridge University Press: New York, NY.

Convention on the Rights of the Child (CRC). (1989). *UN Convention on the Right of the Child*. United Nations: New York, NY.

Council of Europe. (2009). *Right to Health and the European Social Charter*, Secretariat of the European Social Charter. Available at: <http://www.coe.int/t/dGHl/monitoring/Socialcharter/Theme%20 factsheets/FactsheetHealth_en.pdf> (accessed 12 November 2012).

Daniels, N. (2008). *Just Health. Meeting Health Needs Fairly*. Cambridge University Press: New York, NY.

European Social Charter. (1996). *European Social Charter (revised)*. Council of Europe: Strasbourg.

Fidler, D. (2007). Governing catastrophes: security, health and humanitarian assistance. *International Review of the Red Cross*, 89, 247–270.

Gruskin, S. and Tarantola, D. (2008). Health and human rights: overview. In K. Heggenhougen and S.R. Quah (Eds.), *International Encyclopedia of Public Health*, pp. 137–146. Elsevier: New York, NY.

Harris, S. (2010). *The Moral Landscape: How Science Can Determine Human Values*. Free Press: New York, NY.

Harvard Humanitarian Initiative. (2011). *Disaster Relief 2.0: The Future of Information Sharing in Humanitarian Emergencies*. UN Foundation & Vodafone Foundation. Technology Partnership: Washington, DC.

ICCPR. (1966). *International Covenant on Civil and Political Rights*. UN General Assembly: New York, NY.

ICESCR. (1966). *International Covenant on Economic, Social and Cultural Rights*. Entry into force 3 January 1976. UN General Assembly: New York, NY.

Ishay, M. (2007). *The Human Rights Reader: Major Political Essays, Speeches, and Documents from Ancient Times to the Present* (2nd ed.). Routledge: New York, NY.

Ishay, M. (2008). *The History of Human Rights: From Ancient Times to the Globalization Era, With a New Preface*. Norton and Co.: New York, NY.

Khaliq, U. and Churchill, R. (2008). *The European Committee of Social Rights in Langford*. Cambridge University Press: New York, NY.

Kinney, E.D. and Clark, B.A. (2004). Provisions for health and health care in the constitutions of the countries of the world. *Cornell International Law Journal*, 37, 283–355.

Langford, M. (2008). The justiciability of social rights: From practice to theory. In M. Langford (Ed.), *Social Rights Jurisprudence. Emerging Trends in International and Comparative Law*, pp. 1–45. Cambridge University Press: New York, NY.

Lauren, P.G. (1998). *The Evolution of International Human Rights: Visions Seen*. University of Pennsylvania Press: Philadelphia, PA.

Lauterpacht, H. (1973). *International Law and Human Rights*. Garland: New York, NY. (Original work published 1950.)

Marks, S.P. (1981). Emerging human rights: A new generation for the 1980's? *Rutgers Law Review*, 33, 435–452.

Marks, S.P. (1999). Economic sanctions as human rights violations: Reconciling political and public health imperatives. *American Journal of Public Health*, 89, 1509–1513.

Marks, S.P. (2009). The past and future of the separation of human rights into categories. *Maryland Journal of International Law*, 24, 208–241.

Marks, S.P. and Cooper, N. (2010). The responsibility to protect: watershed, or old wine in a new bottle. *Jindal Global Law Review (India)*, 2, 86–130.

Meier, B.M. (2010). Global health governance and the contentious politics of human rights: Mainstreaming the right to health for public health advancement. *Stanford Journal of International Law*, 46, 1–50.

Melish, T.J. (2008). The Inter-American Commission on Human Rights. In A. Langford (Ed.), *Emerging Trends in International and Comparative Law*, pp. 339–371. Cambridge University Press: New York, NY.

Morsink, J. (1999). *The Universal Declaration of Human Rights: Origins, Drafting and Intent*. University of Pennsylvania Press: Philadelphia, PA.

Paust, J.J. (1995). The human right to die with dignity: A policy-oriented essay. *Human Rights Quarterly*, 17, 463–487.

Piarroux, R., Barrais, R., Faucher, B., *et al.* (2011). *Understanding the cholera epidemic, Haiti. Emerging Infectious Diseases*. Available at: <http://dx.doi.org/10.3201/eid1707.110059> (accessed 20 July 2012).

Schabas, W.A. (1998). International law and abolition of the death penalty. *Washington and Lee Law Review*, 55, 797–846.

South Africa Constitutional Court. (1998). *Soobramoney* v. *Minister for Health*. Constitutional Court of South Africa. 1 SA 765.

South Africa Constitutional Court. (2002). *Minister of Health and Others* v. *Treatment Action Campaign and Others*. (10) BCLR 1033 (CC).

Tobin, J. (2012). *The Right to Health in International Law*. Oxford University Press: New York, NY.

UN. (1945). *Charter of the United Nations*, 26 June 1945, 59 Stat. 1031, T.S. 993, 3 Bevans 1153, entered into force October 24.

UN. (1955). *Standard Minimum Rules for the Treatment of Prisoners*, adopted by the First United Nations Congress on the Prevention of Crime and the Treatment of Offenders, held at Geneva in 1955, and approved by the Economic and Social Council by its resolutions 663 C (XXIV) of 31 July 1957 and 2076 (LXII) of 13 May 1977.

UN. (1972). *UN Conference on the Human Environment.* United Nations (UN): New York, NY.

UN. (1984). *United Nations, Economic and Social Council, U.N. Sub-Commission on Prevention of Discrimination and Protection of Minorities, Siracusa Principles on the Limitation and Derogation of Provisions in the International Covenant on Civil and Political Rights*, UN Doc E/CN.4/1984/4, Annex. United Nations (UN): New York, NY.

UN. (1986). *The Declaration on the Right to Development*, 4 December 1986, UN Doc A/41/RES/128. United Nations (UN): New York, NY.

UN. (1990). *United Nations Committee on the Elimination of Discrimination against Women (CEDAW), CEDAW General Recommendation No. 14: Female Circumcision.* UN Doc A/45/38 and Corrigendum. Available at: <http://www.unhcr.org/refworld/docid/453882a30.html> (accessed 12 November 2012).

UN. (1994a). *United Nations Report of the International Conference on Population and Development.* UN Doc A/CONF.171/13, 18 October. United Nations (UN): New York, NY.

UN. (1994b). *Draft Principles on Human Rights and the Environment.* E/CN.4/Sub.2/1994/9, Annex I. United Nations (UN): New York, NY.

UN. (1998). *United Nations Rome Statute of the International Criminal Court*, circulated as document A/CONF.183/9 of 17 July 1998 and corrected by procès-verbaux of 10 November 1998, 12 July 1999, 30 November 1999, 8 May 2000, 17 January 2001 and 16 January 2002. United Nations (UN): New York, NY.

UN. (2003). *United Nations Commission on Human Rights, 59th session*, Report of the Special Rapporteur, Paul Hunt, submitted in accordance with Commission resolution 2002/31, UN Doc. E/CN.4/2003/58, 13 February. United Nations (UN): New York, NY.

UN. (2005). *General Comment No. 17: The right of everyone to benefit from the protection of the moral and material interests resulting from any scientific, literary or artistic production of which he or she is the author.* UN doc. E/C.12/GC/17, 12 January. United Nations (UN): New York, NY.

UN. (2007). *United Nations. Declaration on the Rights of Indigenous Peoples.* UN Doc. A/61/RES/295, Annex, 13 September. United Nations (UN): New York, NY.

UN. (2009). *Guidelines on treaty-specific documents to be submitted by States parties under articles 16 and 17 of the International Covenant on Economic, Social and Cultural Rights.* United Nations Committee on Economic, Social and Cultural Rights. UN Doc. E/C.12/2008/2, annex. 24 March. United Nations (UN): New York, NY.

UN. (2010). *Report of the High Level Task Force on the Implementation of the Right to Development on its Ninth Session.* United Nations. Human Rights Council. UN Doc. A/HRC/15/WG.2/TF/2, Add. 1 (Consolidation of findings) and Add. 2 (Right to development criteria and operational sub-criteria). United Nations (UN): New York, NY.

UN. (2011). *Report of the Working Group on the Universal Periodic Review. United States of America*, Human Rights Council, Sixteenth session, UN Doc. A/HRC/16/11, 4 January. United Nations (UN): New York, NY.

UN General Assembly. (1948). *Universal Declaration of Human Rights, Doc 217A (III).* UN General Assembly: New York, NY.

UN General Assembly. (2012). *The Future We Want.* UN General Assembly: New York, NY.

Wilson, E.O. (2012). *The Social Conquest of Earth.* W.W. Norton & Co.: New York, NY.

Wolf, J. (2012). *The Human Right to Health.* W.W. Norton & Co.: New York, NY.

WHO. (1946). *Preamble to the Constitution of the World Health Organization.* World Health Organization (WHO): New York, NY.

WHO. (1978). *Declaration of Alma-Ata.* World Health Organization (WHO): Geneva.

WHO. (2002). *25 Questions and Answers on Health and Human Rights.* World Health Organization (WHO): Geneva. Available at: <http://whqlibdoc.who.int/hq/2002/9241545690.pdf> (accessed 12 November 2012).

WHO. (2007a). *The right to health.* Fact sheet N°323. World Health Organization (WHO): Geneva. Available at: <http://www.who.int/mediacentre/factsheets/fs323/en/index.html> (accessed 12 November 2012).

WHO. (2007b). *WHO global influenza preparedness plan. The role of WHO and recommendations for national measures before and during pandemics.* World Health Organization (WHO): Geneva. Available at: <http://www.who.int/csr/resources/publications/influenza/WHO_CDS_CSR_GIP_2005_5/en/index.html> (accessed 1 October 2012).

WHO. (2011). *World conference on social determinants of health: meeting report, Rio de Janeiro, Brazil, 19-21 October 2011.* World Health Organization (WHO): Geneva. Available at: <http://www.who.int/sdhconference/resources/wcsdh_report/en/index.html> (accessed 12 November 2012).

Chapter 2

Advancing the right to health through litigation

Oscar A. Cabrera and Ana S. Ayala

Introduction

Litigation can play an important role in advancing the right to health. It has led courts to order bans on smoking and the provision of medicines, as well as strike down abortion restrictions that have contributed to maternal death. Yet experience with right to health litigation has led to fundamental questions about the ability of the judiciary to advance health, including the appropriateness of courts in adjudicating complex policies with significant budgetary implications and whether litigation promotes health equity.

The main purpose of this chapter is to provide the reader with an insight into some of the aspects and areas of contention around right to health litigation, which can be taken into account as the reader delves into the discussions in the chapters that follow. However, we ultimately conclude that right to health litigation is a response to a government's inability to adequately address the health needs of its people, and whether litigation ultimately promotes health equity and advances the right to health depends not only on the type of litigation, but also the political, economic, and social context present in the country at the time. To set the stage, this chapter begins with a brief overview of the history of right to health litigation, including litigation that protects health through the use of other health-related rights that are socioeconomic, civil, or political in nature, such as the right to life. The chapter next introduces some of the main arguments used to challenge the increasing use of the courts to promote the right to health and the public policymaking that this often entails or engenders. These arguments question whether courts are breaching democratic principles, such as separation of powers, when they order the provision of medicines or treatments, or rule on regulatory aspects of the health system. This chapter then explores whether a codified right to health is necessary to foster right to health litigation, and the effects that individual litigation may have on effectuating broader systemic changes that could benefit population health. We end the chapter with a brief discussion on whether courts are promoting or undermining one of the central tenants of the right to health: health equity.

The history and evolution of right to health litigation

The atrocities of World War II and the resulting international commitment to prevent their reoccurrence paved the way for the Universal Declaration of Human Rights (UDHR, 1948), a recognition by governments of the fundamental rights held by every human being—among them, the right to health (Article 25)—and the international commitment to uphold the rights as 'a common standard of achievement' (Preamble).

The UDHR and other international human rights instruments have contributed to setting an international normative standard for health policy and formed the basis of right to health litigation (Meier & Yamin, 2011). Over the years, these instruments have been used by international bodies and regional bodies, such as the Inter-American Commission on Human Rights, as well as by domestic courts. In fact, Argentina has granted both the UDHR and the International Covenant on Economic, Social and Cultural Rights (ICESCR), among other human rights treaties, the same legal status as its national Constitution. These international instruments that are incorporated through article 75.22 of Argentina's Constitution are meant to complement the rights already enshrined elsewhere in that Constitution. As such and coinciding with Argentina's return to democracy in the late 1990s, this incorporation of international human rights instruments has encouraged litigation for the protection of human rights, including the right to health (Bergallo, 2011).

The global trend of rapidly increasing right to health litigation did not begin until the advent of antiretroviral therapy (ART) in the mid-1990s, which proved successful in reducing AIDS-related morbidity and mortality (Yamin, 2011). Until then, health and human rights had been generally treated as two separate issues (Gruskin et al., 2007). However, discrimination, marginalization, and stigmatization of people living with HIV became an obstacle for prevention and care programmes, clarifying the intimate relationship between health and human rights (Gruskin et al., 2007; Mann et al., 1999).

Health and human rights have been described as having three interconnected relationships, each relationship yielding practical results (Mann et al., 1999). The first relationship understands that health policies, programmes, and practices have an impact on human rights. This understanding is derived from the fact that central functions of public health, which are primarily carried out by the State, can at times come into conflict with human rights and at other times, they may benefit human rights. A recognition of this relationship is essential to both achieving an optimal balance when public health objectives conflict with human rights and when the promotion of public health simultaneously promotes human rights (Mann et al., 1999). Similarly, the second relationship recognizes the impact that human rights violations have on health. This relationship is captured not only in serious human rights violations, such as torture, but also in violations of, if not all, most human rights. Finally, the third relationship recognizes that the promotion and protection of health results in the promotion and protection of human rights, as they both seek to define and further the well-being of the person (Mann et al., 1999).

The advent of ART, and its success in prolonging the lives of people living with HIV/AIDS, drove rights advocates to expand their efforts beyond asserting equality rights to framing access to antiretroviral (ARV) drugs as a human rights issue (Meier & Yamin, 2011). International developments strengthened domestic efforts to ensure access to ARV drugs. For example, United Nations (UN) actors, such as the UN High Commissioner for Human Rights, the Committee on Economic, Social and Cultural Rights (CESCR), and the UN Special Rapporteur on the right to health, played an important role in defining State rights-based obligations to respect, protect, and fulfil an HIV/AIDS policy (Meier & Yamin, 2011). In 1997, then-UN Secretary-General Kofi Annan stressed the central role that human rights plays in UN work (UN, 1997). This recognition has been considered important to bringing health and human rights one step closer to realization (Gruskin et al., 2007).

During the 1980s and 1990s, a number of countries also underwent significant structural reform (Brinks & Gauri, 2008; Yamin, 2011) and adopted new constitutions that vigorously enshrined economic and social rights, including the right to health (Cooper, 2011; Meier & Yamin, 2011). Such was the case in Latin America, where both democratization and neoliberal reforms gave way to the adoption of new constitutions (and modifications of existing ones) that recognized economic and social rights as fundamental in order to lessen the effects of new market-based economies (Brinks & Forbath, 2010–2011). Following military dictatorship, the Brazilian Constitution was redrafted in 1988 to include a number of individual rights, including the right to health. As discussed later, the Brazilian Constitution's provisions aimed at the realization of the right to health are impressively comprehensive, as they set up a universal public health system and outline how the system must be administered and financed. The *movimiento sanitarista*, a social movement created in opposition to the military dictatorship and whose aim was to universalize the country's healthcare system, played a central role in the formulation and inclusion of the right to health in the Constitution (Brinks & Gauri, 2008). Also as later discussed, Brazilian courts have ruled on a striking amount of health-related cases, most of them founded on right to health claims.

In South Africa, which transitioned from an oppressive white minority rule to a constitutional democracy during the 1990s, the Constitutional Court has perceived the socioeconomic conditions present during the adoption of the new Constitution—high level of unemployment, inadequate social security, and lack of access to clean water and adequate health services—to be fundamental to the newly formed government. The Constitutional Court's view on the justiciability of socioeconomic rights, combined with the devastation experienced in the country because of its HIV epidemic, placed the right to health at the centre of promoting social justice and framed litigation as a mode of social transformation in South Africa (Cooper, 2011).

In India, the internal conflict of the 1970s, marked by rampant human rights violations and the rise of the 'public interest litigation movement', brought about a change in the perception of how the judiciary should interpret the Constitution. Unlike civil and political rights, social and economic rights, while recognized as being fundamental, are not directly justiciable under the Indian Constitution. However, in the 1970s, the Indian Supreme Court expanded the justiciable right to life to include socioeconomic rights, such as nutrition, clothing, and shelter (Sellin, 2009). As described later, health-related litigation has been meaningful and significant in India.

The uniqueness of HIV/AIDS as a threat to public health on a global scale, the availability of life-saving and -enhancing ARV drugs, and the adoption of progressive constitutions in various countries at the time created the perfect environment for the rise of right to health litigation. HIV disease was seen as particularly targeting already marginalized populations, and access to ARV drugs clearly justified the justiciability of the right to health. Moreover, the disease presented a well-defined obligation for the State. In addition, advocates were able to bring claims based on rights on which courts had experience adjudicating, such as the right to freedom from discrimination (Yamin, 2011).

Other historical developments also paved the way for increased litigation in the area of health and human rights, such as the economic crises of the 1980s and the responding economic structural adjustment programmes implemented in the affected countries (Yamin, 2011). Nevertheless, for the purposes of this discussion, it is fair to state that HIV/AIDS-related litigation played a key role in shaping right to health litigation at the global scale.

Much can be learned from the history and evolution of right to health litigation over the past few decades. Specific circumstances of a given time and place can significantly influence the results of litigation. While the UDHR, the ICESCR, and other international legal instruments, such as the CESCR's General Comment 14 on the right to health, provide guidance on how countries are to implement human rights, implementation at the country level requires modification, or domestication, to fit the country's specific social context. Otherwise, international human rights norms remain aspirational ideals (O'Connell, 2012). Courts play an important role in the domestication process by interpreting human rights standards found in international law, treating them as part of domestic law, and applying them to the reality of the country.

Additionally, it is worth noting that the rights used to resolve health issues have varied across countries and derive from either the socioeconomic or the civil and political realms. These rights include freedom from discrimination, as well as the rights to due process, water and sanitation, and a clean and healthy environment. Yet, the volume of 'right to health litigation' produced in a country is not necessarily dependent on the type of rights already enforced. This is evident in the discussion of specific countries' experiences. However, prior to delving into these experiences, it is necessary to describe some of the principal arguments on the use of courts to address issues involving policy, which is almost inevitable when addressing right to health matters.

Are courts undermining or reinforcing democratic principles?

Judges have increased their participation in defining public policies, a realm traditionally within the purview of a government's political branches—not the courts'. What has been termed the 'judicialization of politics' refers to the expansion of the judiciary's adjudication methods into areas that are traditionally dealt with by politicians and administrators (Vallinder, 1995), namely, the making of public policies (Tate, 1995). The expansion of judicial power into the political arena has driven some to question the democratic legitimacy of the court in such instances. Specifically, some scholars have argued that judicial intervention in social and economic rights is especially problematic because cases involving these rights often involve questions of resource allocation (Desai, 2009; Landau, 2012–2010; Michelman, 2003). An analysis of two main arguments offered against judicial intervention in public policymaking, particularly regarding economic and social rights adjudication, reveals that these arguments may need further exploration and reflection.

Democratic legitimacy

The standard objection is that the judiciary lacks the legitimate authority to define generally applicable policies, especially where complicated trade-offs are at stake, including resource allocation. In entering the realm of public policymaking, as the non-elected branch of government traditionally in charge of interpreting—and not making—laws, courts violate fundamental democratic principles, such as public participation and separation of powers (Tate, 1995). Some consider the area of social and economic rights particularly problematic, as it usually requires the court to adjudicate over policy and financial matters (Christiansen, 2009).

However, others have argued that courts reinforce the democratic system and rule of law when filling gaps left by the political branches of government in the enforcement of social and economic rights. Experience has shown that courts have endeavoured to protect health when the political branches of government could or would not (Meier & Yamin, 2011). Courts can ensure the accountability of the other branches of government by promoting transparency, compelling public officials to justify their use of power, and regulating the use of power to prevent or remedy violations of rights or democratic processes (Gloppen et al., 2004). Thus, courts can be seen as playing an important role in both protecting the rule of law and guaranteeing the checks and balances integral to a democratic system.

A case adjudicated by the Constitutional Court of Colombia—T-760/08—captures the potential of courts to reinforce democratic accountability by demanding measures from the political branches of government to secure people's rights. The Court grouped 22 *tutelas* (individual appeals for the judicial protection of fundamental rights) (Yamin et al., 2011) together to reflect the various failings of the health system. All the claims concerned the inability of the system to adequately deliver health services as guaranteed by national law. According to the Court, the failure of governmental bodies responsible for regulating the system to make the decisions and thus implement policies necessary for guaranteeing the right to health led many people to other choice than to file a *tutela*. As a result, the Court argued, a large percentage of all the *tutelas* filed with the Court were based on right to health claims that stemmed from the problems inherent in the health system (Sentencia T-760/08, 2008, Part II, Sec. 2). Asserting the right to health as a justiciable and fundamental right, the Court ruled in favour of the claimants and ordered that the responsible authorities undertake the necessary measures to resolve the systemic issues present in the health system. Ultimately, the measures amounted to the extensive restructuring of Colombia's health system so that it adhered to rights principles, such as non-discrimination, participation, and accountability (Yamin et al., 2011). Among the orders issued by the Court was the requirement that the reform adopted be financially sustainable (Sentencia T-760/08, 2008, Part II, Secs. 6.1.1.2.2, 6.1.2.2.2, Order No. 22).

The judgment in case T-760/08 has been considered to be exceptionally far-reaching (Yamin et al., 2011). Some have questioned the Court's constitutional ability to call for structural changes in the health system. Others argue that the Court had only interpreted existing legislation, holding the political branches accountable for failing to adequately regulate what was well within their mandate, and encouraged a much needed debate about the right to healthcare in the country and the need for reform (Yamin et al., 2011). Courts in Colombia have therefore become a legal recourse of last resort for those affected by an unregulated health system unable to deliver basic health services (Yamin et al., 2011). Notably, Colombian courts have a strong tradition of judicial independence and broad jurisdiction that includes addressing structural problems through judicial review of laws approved by the legislature (Cepeda-Espinoza, 2011). It should come as no surprise that the Constitutional Court of Colombia has issued 'sweeping' structural decisions, when compared to other countries (Yamin et al., 2011).

In India, higher courts are said to be vital to the protection of the democratic process (Sudarshan, 2006) and have amply addressed policy issues. In fact, distinguishing among policymaking, policy implementation, and the interpretation of law has become difficult to the extent that the higher judiciary can be said to be co-governing (Sudarshan, 2006). Courts in India have helped filled policy gaps in a variety of areas, such as tobacco control, the environment, labour, nutrition, the regulation of blood banks, drugs, emergency care, mental healthcare, reproductive services, and the issuance of guidelines in the areas of medical negligence and malpractice by public actors (Brinks & Gauri, 2012; Parmar & Wahi, 2011). For example, in *Paschim Banga Khet Mazdoor Samity* v. *State of West Bengal*, the Indian Supreme Court ordered the government to create a blueprint for primary care to handle emergency conditions requiring immediate medical care, such as the serious head injuries sustained by the petitioner. Likewise, in *Rakesh Chandra Narayan* v. *Union of India*, the Court ordered the State to improve the conditions of a mental hospital; said order was based on the Chief Judicial Magistrate's findings during a visit he paid to the mental institution. Among others, he found that the hospital's wards had no doors or windows, some patients were lying on the floor with 'a single blanket [serving] both as mattress and cover', the hospital lacked mosquito nets, patients were either naked from lack of available clothes or were wearing 'torn shirts and pants', there was an 'acute shortage of water', 'there was no account of the stock of medicines', and 'life-saving drugs were not stored properly in the absence of a refrigerator' (*Chandra Narayan*, 1989, p. 3). Based on the Chief Judicial Magistrate's report reflecting the failings of the government to provide adequate living conditions and treatment to patients in the hospital, the Court saw 'no reason why the management of the hospital should be left exclusively to the Health Department of State of Bihar' and found that 'the participating Governments should not be associated in such management' (Chandra Narayan, 1989, p. 10). Rather, the Court found it necessary to intervene in the management of the hospital and created a Committee of Management, chaired by a judge of the city's high court, to monitor progress. Such cases reflect the extent to which the Indian Supreme Court has used its liberal powers of review to fill the gaps left by other branches of government.

Furthermore, the failings of democratic processes on their own terms can justify judicial public policymaking. Where government does not properly represent the majority of voters (which is often the case), the representative branches of government may not adequately allocate resources where they are needed. In such cases, a democratically legitimate judiciary can specify and enforce the obligations of the government by rationally analysing the extent to which the elected branches of government have failed to address the needs of a population lacking voter agency (Desai, 2009–2010). In this instance, the justiciability of economic and social rights can enforce democratic governance by ensuring that due attention is given to interests that might otherwise be ignored (Desai, 2009–2010).

Institutional capacity

A second argument against judicial public policymaking is that courts lack the institutional capacity to evaluate and influence specific policies. In the area of social rights, critics argue that the judiciary lacks competency to adequately address resource allocation and running programmes because they are unable to properly measure the 'vague' content of such rights (Landau, 2012). In this view, democratically elected branches are better positioned to gauge complex trade-offs involved in decisions about resource allocation (Desai, 2009–2010). When courts intervene to assist the parties before them, they may unwittingly be drawing scarce public resources away from other areas, which can be detrimental to health equity, a matter that will be elaborated further later. According to this view, the legislature is the appropriate body to identify the 'basic' needs of the population and measures needed to address them, as well as to appropriately set government priorities (Klein, 2007–2008). As discussed in more depth later, in countries such as Brazil, where courts have adopted an expansive view of the right to health, where the impact of judgments issued is limited to the claimant(s) involved, and where at least some evidence suggests that claims are brought largely by individuals belonging to higher socioeconomic classes, there is concern that resources are being siphoned from health programmes to the fulfilment of individual orders.

However, others have argued that courts and the legislature actually employ similar approaches to resource allocation in their decision-making. Based on studies conducted across a number of countries, some experts have concluded that courts and legislatures take similar factors into account, including popular demands, infrastructure issues, government priorities, and resource allocation (Gauri & Brinks, 2008). Moreover, right to health litigation does not always have costly implications for the public purse. For example, tobacco control litigation, unlike typical social rights litigation, does not require public resources to ensure greater protection of the right in question, such as the right to health and freedom of access to information. Unlike the development of a plan for access to housing, the promotion of smoke-free environments protects health with a minimal use of resources.

Concerns over the lack of democratic legitimacy of the judiciary may be overshadowed by the health needs of the population, as courts can indeed fill gaps in the fulfilment of the right to health left by the political branches of government. In the T-760/08 case, the Constitutional Court of Colombia considered the systemic problems in the health system to constitute violations of the Constitution and what led petitioners to seek recourse in the constitutional justice system (Sentencia T-760/08, 2008, Part II, Sec. 2). The Court's order to substantially restructure the health system was a response to the State's failings in meeting the minimum requirements for the fulfilment of the right to health.

Having considered some of the principal concerns raised about the democratic legitimacy of the judiciary, particularly for the purposes of evaluating the role of courts in defining the right to health, we now turn to a related debate: the impact of courts on health outcomes and the promotion of health equity.

Does a codified right to health lead to greater litigation on the right to health?

Deferring to in-depth analyses already developed by experts in the field, this section briefly discusses the effects of a codified right to health on the amount of litigation generated in a country. In a 2008 analysis of 186 constitutions, 135 (73%) of them contained health-related provisions (Perehudoff, 2008). Some have argued that an explicit right to health within a country's constitution invites right to health litigation and is important for the promotion and implementation of the international human right to health (Gauri & Brinks, 2008; Kinney & Clark, 2004). The inclusion of a right to health in the constitution expresses a national commitment to the right, and sets a policy imperative for the country (Kinney & Clark, 2004). Others argue that this holds only when the right, as written in the constitution, is not limited by a clause stipulating progressive realization within available resources (Gloppen, 2011).

Right to health litigation is possible even in some countries where the judiciary has created a right to health or interpreted it within other rights, such as the rights to life, dignity, and non-discrimination (Gloppen, 2011). Interestingly, these countries sometimes experience higher rates of right to health litigation than countries with an explicit right to health in their constitutions. For example, the Mexican Constitution contains a rather robust right to health provision, which not only guarantees every person a right to healthcare (tit. I, ch. I, art. 4), but also places special focus on the need to protect the health of children (tit. I, ch. I, art. 4) and indigenous women (tit. I, ch. I, art. 2(B)(V) and (VIII)). Nevertheless, in countries such as India that do not have an enshrined right to health, courts have adjudicated a greater number of right to health cases. This may be in part related to stricter standing and procedural rules in constitutional litigation that limit the role of courts in adjudicating public policies (Cabrera & Madrazo, 2010; Cabrera and Carballo, forthcoming), and in part due to Mexico's efforts in fostering greater health equity through legislative reform, discouraging the need for litigation. For instance, the 2003 healthcare reforms included the financially sustainable expansion of healthcare coverage to 50 million Mexicans who had been previously excluded; the use of cost-effectiveness analyses to maximize benefits from the use of available resources; the improvement of facilities, equipment, drug supply availability and distribution; as well as the quality of services (Frenk & Gómez-Dantés, 2009).

In India, without an express constitutional right to health, the courts have read in a right to health as an integral part of the right to life, enshrined in Article 19 of the Indian Constitution. In *Paschim Banga Khet Mazdoor Samity*, where the petitioner had fallen off a train, sustained injuries, and was denied emergency care in seven different hospitals, the Indian Supreme Court declared medical assistance as essential for the protection of the right to life (*Paschim Banga Khet Mazdoor Samity*, 1996). Likewise, the Court proclaimed a fundamental right to health in *Consumer Education and Research Centre* v. *Union of India*, mandating that workers receive compulsory health insurance as an integral part of the right (*Consumer Education and Research Centre*, 1995). The Court even referred to international legal provisions, including Article 25 of the UDHR, to establish health as a fundamental human right in *C.E.S.C. Ltd. Etc* v. *Subhash Chandra Bose and Ors.* (*C.E.S.C. Ltd. Etc.*, 1992). In *State of Punjab & Ors.* v. *Mohinder Singh Chawla Etc.*, the Court confirmed that '[i]t is now settled law that right to health is an integral to right to life' (*Singh Chawla*, 1997).

More recently, in the maternal health case *Laxmi Mandal* v. *Deen Dayal Harinagar Hospital & Ors.*, the High Court of Delhi underscored the interrelatedness of the right to health not only with the right to life, but also with the right to food. Moreover, according to the Court, the right to health should be interpreted as including 'the right to access government (public) health facilities and receive a minimum standard of treatment and care', as well as 'the enforcement of the reproductive rights of the mother and the right to nutrition and medical care of the newly born child and continuously thereafter till the age of about six years' (*Laxmi Mandal*, 2010).

While the inclusion of an explicit right to health in a country's constitution does not necessarily lead to a high volume of right to health litigation in a country, the specificity of the provision enshrining a right to health as to State obligations can have a significant effect on the volume of right to health litigation produced in a country: Brazil offers a case in point. Brazilian courts hear approximately 125 cases per one million of population (compared to three cases per ten million in South Africa) (Brinks & Gauri, 2008). In the southern state of Rio Grande Sul alone, between 2002 and 2009, health-related cases jumped from 1126 to 17,025 annually—which amounts to a 1412% increase (Biehl et al., 2012). The 1988 Brazilian Constitution not only establishes health as a fundamental right (Article 5), but also calls for a unified public health system (*SUS—Sistema Único de Saúde*) with universal access to health, regardless of income or whether the person is privately insured (da Silva & Vargas Terrazas, 2011). Under the Constitution, the State must guarantee through 'social and economic policies' (Article 196), both health actions and health services (Article 197). Further, the Constitution details what these actions and services should look like, how the health system should be funded and administrated (Article 198), and its duties and objectives (Article 200). In fact, the Constitution's guarantee is so material that, for example, 88% of health-related litigation in the Brazilian state of Rio Grande Sul cited the constitutional right to health (Biehl et al., 2012). The Constitution's effects on the amount of litigation were augmented by legislation that guaranteed universal access to ART, as well as by the existence of an individual claims mechanism through which individuals could ensure access to health services and treatment.

Civil law countries with accessible judicial processes for individual rights-claims that provide individuals with judicial protection of their fundamental rights, such as *tutela* or *amparo* (defined as a remedy for the protection of constitutional rights), often have higher rates of right to health litigation for claims will only provide remedies for the claimants involved. By contrast, in countries where collective action is more prominent, such as South Africa, there tends to be less jurisprudence, as these actions aim at having a broader impact.

In the case of Colombia, the Constitution contains an explicit right to health with a concrete set of obligations (Article 49). But the Constitutional Court has had a shifting interpretation on the nature of the right to health's justiciability. The right to health is not included in the Constitution's chapter that enumerates justiciable fundamental rights (tit. II, ch. 1). Rather, the right to health is included in the chapter listing social, economic, and cultural rights (tit. II, ch. 2). Nevertheless, the legal nature of the right to health has undergone significant changes. It was not until the Constitutional Court developed the theory of connectivity (or *conexidad*) through case law that the right became justiciable (Sentencia T-491/92, 1992, Fundamentos Jurídicos, §2; Sentencia T-328/93, 1993: Fundamentos Jurídicos, §9; see also Sentencia T-406/92, 1992, Part II, Sec. C(1)(c)). According to this theory, the right to health acquired justiciability as long as it was linked to a fundamental right, such as the right to life (Sentencia T-491/92, 1992, Fundamentos Jurídicos, §2). Most recently, the Court abandoned the connectivity approach and determined that the right to health is justiciable independently from its connection to other rights (T-760/08, 2008: Part II, Sec. 3).

Despite this shifting interpretation, Colombia has produced a significant amount of right to health jurisprudence. Between 1999 and 2005, 328,191 individual *tutelas* related to the right to health were filed with the Constitutional Court, 80% of which were granted. In 2008 alone, 90,000 *tutelas* were filed. In Costa Rica, whose Constitution also does not contain an explicit right to health, the number of *amparo* cases related to health grew from 1000 to 11,000 during the first ten years of Sala IV, Costa Rica's constitutional tribunal (Yamin & Parra-Vera, 2009).

Therefore, as observed in the Brazilian case, the distinct specificity of constitutional right to health guarantees, the courts' expansive interpretation of the right to health (Motta Ferraz, 2011), the individuals' entitlement to sue the government at any level (Motta Ferraz, 2011), and the existence of an individual claims mechanism are all factors that can contribute to high volumes of right to health litigation. In countries such as Colombia and Costa Rica, the *tutela* and *amparo* mechanisms play an important role in generating considerably more right to health litigation. Whether increased litigation leads to better health outcomes is a separate question that is addressed in the next section.

Are courts advancing social justice and ensuring health equity?

The conversation emanating from scholarship on right to health litigation has increasingly focused on whether such litigation leads to what many believe should be its ultimate goal: health equity. Questions raised in this debate include whether courts are disproportionally serving the interests of only the political and economic elites and middle classes by providing them with greater access to the health system, and whether it is enough to look at claimants to measure the level of impact courts have on health equity (Gauri & Brinks, 2008). In this endeavour, experts have tried to identify the factors that determine the level of impact on health equity.

Measuring the impact of litigation on health outcomes

Evidence on the question of whether the litigation of health rights has indeed improved health outcomes and has led to the adequate distribution and allocation of resources is limited. However, there have been several rigorous efforts to analyse the impact of health rights litigation, though with conflicting results. What is clear is that much research is still needed in this area.

The formula developed by Gauri and Brinks assessed the impact of litigation in a country by measuring: (1) the extent of implementation of relevant cases, (2) the direct effects on the parties involved in the cases, and (3) the indirect effect on policy (Gauri & Brinks, 2008). Moreover, the type of case will determine the case's redistributive impact (Brinks & Gauri, 2012). 'Provision' cases (where a duty is imposed on the government to cover or directly provide a service) in India, Brazil, and South Africa do have an impact, as they are intended to benefit a significantly larger set of individuals (Brinks & Gauri, 2008). Brazil exemplifies this trend. 'Regulation' cases (where the courts impose or remove governmental duties that affect regulation) have wider impact, as the rulings extend beyond the immediate litigants and to users of the system. Yet the effectiveness of the ruling is more likely to be undermined by problems in its enforcement and implementation (Brinks & Gauri, 2008). For example, in general, the impact regulation cases in South African regulation has been blunted by a lack of implementation of court rulings on the part of the government (Brinks & Gauri, 2008).

In terms of whether litigation promotes health equity, Brinks and Gauri observe that having an individual claims mechanism, such as Brazil's, could lead to greater health inequity given that litigation appears to be more prevalent in the urban sector and more accessible to wealthier individuals (Brinks & Gauri, 2008, 2012). This issue is explored further later. Likewise, unlike collective claims, privately funded individual litigation can result in greater inequality (Brinks & Gauri, 2008).

Mæstad and colleagues suggest another way of measuring impact of litigation on health outcomes at different levels: the direct impact on the litigants, the impact on health policy, and the impact on the population as a whole. With respect to the direct impact on litigants, they carefully frame their analysis around three questions (Mæstad et al., 2011):

- Which additional health services were ordered by the court?
- What are the health benefits that can be provided through these services?
- How has the particular litigation affected the financial and nonfinancial costs of access to health services?

Based on their empirical studies of India, South Africa, and four Latin American countries (Argentina, Brazil, Colombia, and Costa Rica), the authors conclude that individual litigation involving medical treatment, which is more prominent in the four Latin American countries than in India and South Africa, is most likely to have the strongest direct impact on the litigant. Conversely, while collective or structural cases can lead to direct policy change in India and South Africa, courts are less receptive to claims and less effective in enforcement (Mæstad et al., 2011). Implementation then depends on external contributing factors, such as pressure from civil society (Mæstad et al., 2011).

Moreover, as pointed out by Brinks and Gauri, the judicial processes of individual claims for the protection of fundamental rights that are present in countries such as Brazil, Colombia, and Costa Rica have raised concerns over their ability to promote good health outcomes. Individual claims have led to saturation of the courts and are said to have little impact on health outcomes in the country (Motta Ferraz, 2009). Although these processes were traditionally intended as special 'emergency' tools for the protection of fundamental rights, they have become a health rationing system of their own, in which courts assume an administrative role and determine on a case-by-case basis whether an individual should receive a particular treatment. Courts in India are overwhelmed with reviewing rulings issued by lower courts on writ petitions (Sudarshan, 2006). Likewise, courts in Brazil and Colombia are saturated with claims. In fact, there is concern that the large number of health-related individual claims filed and granted in Brazilian courts is causing a shift in resources and undermining the public health system (Motta Ferraz, 2009). Yet, some experts argue that the restricted direct impact of individual litigation can be counterbalanced with the systemic enforcement of cases, which is essential to effecting policy change (Gloppen & Roseman, 2011). For example, in Brazil and Costa Rica, a specific number of successful individual claims on a particular drug or treatment lead health officials to include it in the public health plan. This practice has resulted in the integration of a number of medicines in the Brazilian public health plan (Mæstad et al., 2011).

Additionally, some have claimed that the beneficiaries of social rights litigation are not the poorest, but rather, the middle or lower-middle classes (Gloppen & Roseman, 2011). For example, in India, there are few courts relative to the size of the population. Lower courts are significantly backlogged. The Supreme Court and High Courts, which have been commended for the progressive jurisprudence they have issued, are more accessible to elites (Sudarshan, 2006). Moreover, a recent study on whether litigation of the right to health leads to health equity in Brazil concluded that courts do not necessarily bring health equity and that a number of conditions that are external to litigation need to be present to advance social justice (da Silva & Vargas Terrazas, 2011). These external conditions include the limited access of those who are poor to both financial resources and information (da Silva & Vargas Terrazas, 2011). The study particularly underscored that the granting of individual claims in Brazil and in other Latin American countries does not necessarily make courts the ideal instrument for promoting equity (da Silva & Vargas Terrazas, 2011).

By contrast, a more recent study argues that right to health litigation is in fact accessible to Brazil's low-income population. Indeed, according to the study, poor patients are taking advantage of the public legal assistance available to them and the receptivity of the Brazilian courts to access medicines (Biehl et al., 2012). Nevertheless, the study also recognized and underscored the need for courts to promote health as a collective right and ensure universal access to medicines rather than 'merely responding to individual cases' (Biehl et al., 2012). Moreover, despite their observations on individual litigation, Brinks and Gauri more recently concluded that evidence does not indicate that litigation only benefits the better-off (Brinks & Gauri, 2012).

Given the conflicting views of experts on the subject, at this time it is difficult to definitively determine whether litigation leads to health equity. As discussed, some evidence suggests that, in at least some cases, right to health litigation may benefit low-income individuals and have a positive impact on health equity. What is clear is that more research is needed to identify: (1) what factors lead to successful policy changes in some cases, but not in others; (2) what factors facilitate poorer populations' access to courts to protect their health; and (3) what political and legislative agenda is needed to institute and utilize these factors. In this manner, it may be possible to efficiently use right to health litigation to consistently promote health equity.

Conclusion

Underlying the discussion in this chapter is the fact that political, economic, and social contexts play an important role in whether a country can advance the right to health through litigation. The discussion may leave more questions unanswered than it has answered. However, we hope to have presented sufficient information about some of the issues that have been debated on right to health litigation and the adequacy of using courts for the promotion of health, providing the reader with context for the chapters that follow.

If in the eyes of some, the judiciary oversteps its boundaries by issuing decisions that affect policy change, courts do so in response to the other branches' inability or unwillingness to adequately meet the needs of the population. Until the health system can adequately address the needs of the population, people will continue to resort to courts to protect their health. A number of factors, beyond the mere inclusion of a right to health in a country's constitution, interact to encourage or inhibit right to health litigation—and the potential for courts to compensate for failings of the other branches of government. And while, according to some studies, abundant right to health litigation may not necessarily guarantee good health outcomes, it has the potential to lead to significant policy changes and relief for individual litigants. Yet such extensive use of courts to secure the right to health is also a marker of the failings of the health system, which can best be resolved through meaningful reform rather than through individual litigation.

References

Bergallo, P. (2011). Courts and the right to health: achieving fairness despite 'routinization' in individual coverage cases? In A. Yamin and S. Gloppen (Eds.), *Litigating Health Rights: Can Courts Bring More Justice to Health?*, pp. 43–75. Harvard University Press: Cambridge, MA.

Biehl, J., Amon, J., Socal, M., *et al.* (2012). Between the court and the clinic: lawsuits for medicines and the right to health in Brazil. *Health and Human Rights*, 14(1), E36–E52.

Brinks, D. and Forbath, W. (2010–2011). Social and economic rights in Latin America: Constitutional Courts and the prospects for pro-poor interventions. *Texas Law Review*, 89, 1943–1955.

Brinks, D. and Gauri, V. (2008). A new policy landscape: legalizing social and economic rights in the developing world. In V. Gauri and D. Brinks (Eds.), *Courting Social Justice: Judicial Enforcement of Social and Economic Rights in the Developing World*, pp. 303–352. Cambridge University Press: New York, NY.

Brinks, D. and Gauri, V. (2012). *The Law's Majestic Equality? The Distributive Impact of Litigating Social and Economic Rights*. World Bank Policy Research Working Paper. No. 5999. World Bank: Washington, DC.

Cabrera, O. and Carballo, J. (forthcoming). Tobacco control litigation: broader impacts on health rights adjudication. *The Journal of Law, Medicine & Ethics*.

Cabrera, O. and Madrazo, A. (2010). Human rights as a tool for tobacco control in Latin America. *Salud Pública de Mexico*, 52, S288–S297.

Cepeda-Espinoza, M.J. (2011). Transcript: social and economic rights and the Colombian Constitutional Court. *Texas Law Review*, 89, 1699–1705.

C.E.S.C. Ltd. Etc v. *Subhash Chandra Bose And Ors* (1992). AIR 573 (India).

Christiansen, E. (2009). Using constitutional adjudication to remedy socio-economic injustice: comparative lesson from South Africa. *UCLA Journal of International Law and Foreign Affairs*, 13, 369–405.

Consumer Education and Research Centre v. *Union of India* (1995). AIR 922, 1995 SCC (3) 42 (India).

Cooper, C. (2011). South Africa: health rights litigation: cautious constitutionalism. In A. Yamin and S. Gloppen (Eds.), *Litigating Health Rights: Can Courts Bring More Justice to Health?*, pp. 190–229. Harvard University Press: Cambridge, MA.

da Silva, V.A. and Terrazas, F.V. (2011). Claiming the right to health in Brazilian courts: the exclusion of the already excluded? *Law & Social Inquiry*, 36, 825–853.

Desai, D. (2009–2010). Courting legitimacy: democratic agency and the justiciability of economic and social rights. *Interdisciplinary Journal of Human Rights Law*, 4, 25–42.

Frenk, J. and Gómez-Dantés, O. (2009). The democratization of health in Mexico: extending the right to health care. In A. Clapman and M. Robinson (Eds.), *Swiss Human Rights Book Volume 3: Realizing the Right to Health*, pp. 463–471. Rüffer & Rub: Zurich.

Gauri V. and Brinks, D. (2008). Introduction: the elements of legalization and the triangular shape of social and economic rights. In V. Gauri and D. Brinks (Eds.), *Courting Social Justice: Judicial Enforcement of Social and Economic Rights in the Developing World*, pp. 1–37. Cambridge University Press: New York, NY.

Gloppen, S. (2011). Litigating health rights: framing the analysis. In A.Yamin and S. Gloppen (Eds.), *Litigating Health Rights: Can Courts Bring More Justice to Health?*, pp. 17–39. Harvard University Press: Cambridge, MA.

Gloppen, S. and Roseman, M.J. (2011). Introduction: can litigation bring justice to health? In A. Yamin and S. Gloppen (Eds.), *Litigating Health Rights: Can Courts Bring More Justice to Health?*, 1–16. Harvard University Press: Cambridge, MA.

Gloppen, S., Gargarella, R., and Skaar, E. (2004). Introduction: the accountability function of the courts in new democracies. In S. Gloppen, R. Gargarella, and E. Skaar (Eds.), *Democratization and the Judiciary: The Accountability Function of Courts in New Democracies*, pp. 1–4. Frank Cass Publishers: London.

Gruskin, S., Mills, E., and Tarantola, D. (2007). History, principles, and practice of health and human rights. *Lancet*, 370, 449–455.

Kinney, E. and Clark, B. (2004). Provisions for health and health care in the constitutions of the world. *Cornell International Law Journal*, 37, 285–355.

Klein, A. (2007–2008). Judging as nudging: new governance approaches for the enforcement of constitutional social and economic rights. *Columbia Human Rights Review*, 39, 351–422.

Landau, D. (2012). The reality of social rights enforcement. *Harvard International Law Journal*, 53, 190–247.

Laxmi Mandal v. *Deen Dayal Harinagar Hospital & Ors.* (2010). W.P.(C) 8853/2008 (India).

Mæstad, O., Rakner, L., and Motta Ferraz, O. (2011). Assessing the impact of health rights litigation: a comparative analysis of Argentina, Brazil, Colombia, Costa Rica, India, and South Africa. In A. Yamin and S. Gloppen (Eds.), *Litigating Health Rights: Can Courts Bring More Justice to Health?*, pp. 273–303. Harvard University Press: Cambridge, MA.

Mann, J., Gostin, L., Gruskin, S., *et al.* (1999). Health and human rights. In J. Mann, M.A. Grodin, S. Gruskin, *et al.* (Eds.), *Health and Human Rights: A Reader*, pp. 7–20. Routledge: New York, NY.

Meier, B. and Yamin, A. (2011). Right to health litigation and HIV/AIDS policy. *Journal of Law, Medicine and Ethics*, Spring, 81–84.

Motta Ferraz, O. (2009). The right to health in the courts of Brazil: worsening health inequities. *Health and Human Rights Journal*, 11, 33–45.

Motta Ferraz, O. (2011). Brazil: health inequalities, rights, and courts: the social impact of the judicialization of health. In A. Yamin and S. Gloppen (Eds.), *Litigating Health Rights: Can Courts Bring More Justice to Health?*, pp. 76–102. Harvard University Press: Cambridge, MA.

Müller, F. and Wehbe, L. (2008). Smoking and smoking cessation in Latin America: a review of the current situation and available treatments. *International Journal of Chronic Obstructive Pulmonary Disease*, 3, 285–293.

O'Connell, P. (2012). International standards on socio-economic rights. In *Vindicating Socio-Economic Rights: International Standards and Comparative Experiences*, pp. 22–47. Routledge: London.

Parmar, S. and Wahi, N. (2011). India: citizens, courts, and the right to health between promise and progress? In A. Yamin and S. Gloppen (Eds.), *Litigating Health Rights: Can Courts Bring More Justice to Health?*, pp. 155–189. Harvard University Press: Cambridge, MA.

Paschim Banga Khet Mazdoor Samity & Ors. v. *State of West Bengal & Anor.* (1996). AIR SC 2426, 4 SCC 37 (India).

Perehudoff, S.K. (2008). *Health, Essential Medicines, Human Rights & National Constitutions.* Vrije Universiteit Amsterdam: Amsterdam.

Rakesh Chandra Narayan v. *Union of India.* (1989). AIR 348, 1988 SCR Supl. (3) 306 (India).

Sellin, J. (2009). Justiciability of the right to health – access to medicines: the South African and Indian experience. *Erasmus Law Review*, 2, 445–464.

Sentencia C-830/10. (2010). Corte Constitucional [C.C.][Constitutional Court], Sala Plena, M.P.: Luis Ernesto Vargas Silva, (Colom.).

Sentencia T-328/93. (1993). Corte Constitucional [C.C.] [Constitutional Court], Sala Segunda, M.P.: Eduardo Cifuentes Muñoz (Colom.).

Sentencia T-406/92. (1992). Corte Constitucional [C.C.] [Constitutional Court], Sala Segunda, M.P.: Ciro Angarita Barón (Colom.).

Sentencia T-491/92. (1992). Corte Constitucional [C.C.] [Constitutional Court], Sala Segunda, M.P.: Eduardo Cifuentes Muñoz (Colom.).

Sentencia T-760/08 (2008). Corte Constitucional [C.C.] [Constitutional Court], Sala Segunda, M.P.: Manuel José Cepeda Espinoza (Colom.).

State of Punjab & Ors. v. *Mohinder Singh Chawla Etc.* (1997). 2 SCC 83 (India).

Sudarshan, R. (2006). Courts and social transformation in India. In R. Gargarella, P. Domingo, and T. Roux (Eds.), *Courts and Social Transformation in New Democracies: An Institutional Voice for the Poor?*, pp. 153–168. Ashgate Publishing Limited: Hampshire.

Tate, C.N. (1995). Why the expansion of judicial power. In C.N. Tateand T. Vallinder (Eds.), *The Global Expansion of Judicial Power*, pp. 27–38. New York University Press: New York, NY.

UN. (1997). *Renewing the United Nations: A Programme For Reform, Report of the Secretary-General.* U.N. GAOR, 51st Session, Agenda Item 168, U.N. Doc. A/51/950.

UN General Assembly. (1948). *Universal Declaration of Human Rights. Resolution 217 A (III).* UN General Assembly: Paris. Available at: <http://www.unhcr.org/refworld/docid/3ae6b3712c.html> (accessed 22 March 2012).

Vallinder, T. (1995). When the courts go marching in. In Tate, C.N. and Vallinder, T. (Eds.), *The Global Expansion of Judicial Power*. New York University Press: New York, NY.

Yamin, A. (2011). Power, suffering, and courts: reflections on promoting health rights through judicialization. In A. Yamin and S. Gloppen (Eds.), *Litigating Health Rights: Can Courts Bring More Justice to Health?*, pp. 333–372. Harvard University Press: Cambridge, MA.

Yamin, A., and Parra-Vera, O. (2009). How do courts set health policy? The case of the Colombian Constitutional Court. *PLoS Medicine*, 6, 147–150.

Yamin, A., Parra-Vera, O., and Gianella, C. (2011). Colombia: judicial protection of the right to health. In A. Yamin and S. Gloppen (Eds.), *Litigating Health Rights: Can Courts Bring More Justice to Health?*, pp. 103–131. Harvard University Press: Cambridge, MA.

Chapter 3

The right to health: from concept to practice

Helena Nygren-Krug

Introduction

Today, more than ever, the question of how to address the right to health in a way that is pragmatic, feasible, and legitimate is both acute and necessary. Governments are struggling to find ways to reduce social spending in the context of the global financial crisis. Meanwhile, people across the world are becoming increasingly aware that their governments have human rights obligations. Taking to the streets, people are demanding that economic and social rights be respected, protected, and fulfilled. How can we reconcile this legitimate demand with increasingly scarce resources? Sixty-five years after the adoption of the Universal Declaration of Human Rights (UDHR), human rights remain at the periphery of national and global health governance. Much more work is needed to ensure that mechanisms are in place both nationally and internationally to allow for transparent and participatory decision-making about how to set priorities and allocate resources in ways which ensure the progressive realization of the right to health.

In recent years, there has been a wealth of actions and initiatives to advance the right to health across regions and countries. It would be timely to harvest these with a view to distilling good practices which could be shared and replicated. Finally, there is a pressing need to strengthen the normative framework of the right to health in order to generate greater consensus on its scope and content, including core obligations.

Where have we been? Key milestones, challenges, and opportunities

The World Health Organization (WHO) Constitution (1946) was visionary in its understanding of both health, and of health as a human right (WHO, 1946). It recognized health as a complete state of physical, mental, and social well-being and not merely the absence of disease or infirmity (WHO, 1946). Moreover, it was the first international legal instrument to recognize 'the enjoyment of the highest attainable standard of health' as 'one of the fundamental rights of every human being without distinction of race, religion, and political belief, economic, or social condition' (WHO, 1946). The WHO was established shortly after the United Nations (UN) was created, to serve as its specialized agency for health. In the aftermath of the holocaust and atrocities of World War II, human rights were high on the international agenda. The need to establish a set of universal norms to govern the relationship between governments and their peoples was an urgent priority. The UDHR was adopted in 1948. During the drafting process, the WHO worked closely to ensure the incorporation of Article 25, which recognizes the right to an adequate standard of living, including social security and medical care (Meier, 2009). With the advent of the Cold War, human rights became polarized into two separate categories. The West argued that civil and political rights had priority and that economic and social rights were mere aspirations. The Eastern bloc argued the contrary; that rights to food, health, and education were paramount and civil and political rights secondary. Hence two separate treaties were created in 1966—the International Covenant on Economic, Social and Cultural Rights (ICESCR) and the International Covenant on Civil and Political Rights (ICCPR).

Article 12 of the ICESCR constitutes the most authoritative reference for the right to health at the international level. It sets out that State Parties recognize the right of everyone to the enjoyment of the highest attainable standard of physical and mental health (ICESCR, 1966), and includes a non-exhaustive catalogue of actions to be taken. While the ICESCR mandates State Parties 'to take steps, individually and through international assistance and cooperation, especially economic and technical, to the maximum of available resources, with a view to achieving progressively the full realization' of the right to health, it does not prescribe what those steps should be (ICESCR, 1966).

The WHO's engagement with the right to health ended soon after the organization's establishment; the global environment characterized by the Cold War likely being the main reason for this engagement. Major scientific breakthroughs, such as antibiotics derived from penicillin, further oriented the WHO's agenda towards diseases and away from health (Burci & Vignes, 2004). Nevertheless, a major milestone was the adoption of the Declaration of Alma-Ata in 1978, which upheld the right to health as a social goal (Declaration of Alma-Ata, 1978). Meanwhile, on the ground in many low-income countries, structural adjustment programmes (SAPs) were generating 'free market' programmes and policies requiring privatization and deregulation as well as the removal of trade barriers.

An international human rights movement emerged in the West, centring its work on civil and political rights, such as the right to a fair trial, the right to vote, freedom of expression, and freedom from torture. Effective strategies of naming, shaming, documenting, and reporting drew attention to abuses of these types of rights. As a result, the public at large became sensitized to civil and political rights. Still today, people, particularly the more senior generation (which tends to constitute the current decision-makers) understand the term 'human rights' to encompass mainly such rights.

It was the HIV/AIDS movement which brought human rights back onto the public health agenda. Initially, the focus was on stigma and discrimination. With the Cold War ending, and the advent of antiretroviral therapy (ART), the right to health also came to the forefront. At the national level, constitutional provisions on the right to health began to generate significant litigation in countries demanding access to HIV medicines (Biehl et al., 2009). This mirrored a trend of resolutions adopted by the UN Commission on Human Rights (UNCHR), recognizing access to medications as a fundamental element of the right to health (Hogerzeil & Mirza, 2011).

The end of the Cold War thus marks the most significant paradigm shift in the history of the right to health. The international community unanimously endorsed the interdependence of *all* human rights—civil, cultural, economic, political, and social—and pledged to treat them on an equal footing. The respect, protect, and fulfil framework applicable to all human rights helped to further break down the dichotomy (CESCR, 2000). Human rights and development were no longer 'ships crossing in the night' (Alston, 2005). The UN reform programme initiated in 1997, made human rights a cross-cutting priority and urged human rights mainstreaming in the work of all UN agencies (Annan, 1997).

State sovereignty, a traditional principle often used as a shield behind which authoritarian regimes could hide, slowly began to be redefined. Human rights were unanimously endorsed by UN Member-States 'as the first responsibility of governments' (World Conference on Human

Rights, 1993). Health, when addressed as a human right, would no longer be considered a domestic issue, hidden behind Article 2(7) of the UN Charter (UN Charter, 2012). Instead, it should be integral to Article 1(3); 'a legitimate concern of the international community' (World Conference on Human Rights, 1993).

Addressing health as a human right subjects the State to a range of monitoring and accountability mechanisms at the international, national, and regional levels. These include courts and treaty-bodies as well as intergovernmental mechanisms such as the Universal Periodic Review (UPR) and special rapporteurs, which have been established to engage in dialogue with States, making them answerable for their actions. The WHO increased its engagement in human rights, both internally, initiating a high-level process to develop a strategy for human rights mainstreaming, as well as externally, actively advocating for heightening attention to health on the UN human rights agenda, both in the charter and treaty-based bodies of the UN human rights system (Brundtland, 2003).

In relation to collaboration with the UN human rights treaty bodies, the bedrock of international human rights law, an important milestone was achieved in 2000, when the WHO worked closely with the Committee on Economic, Social and Cultural Rights (CESCR) to flesh out the right to health through the adoption of General Comment 14. Decades of neglect of economic and social rights had resulted in these rights, in particular the right to health, remaining 'immature'. An additional obstacle, although not insurmountable, was the complexity of the right to health. In essence, the right to health is a claim to a set of arrangements (laws, institutions, policies, and practices) which generate an *enabling environment* that can best secure good health. While non-binding, General Comment 14 provides greater specificity on the broad, yet binding, provisions of Article 12 of the ICESCR. Although already out of date in some respects, General Comment 14 is increasingly used by courts, both nationally and internationally, to interpret provisions relating to the right to health.

General Comment 14 set out the framework of AAAQ—availability, accessibility, acceptability, and quality (CESCR, 2000). Among these, accessibility is arguably acquiring the status of customary international law as well as being enshrined in treaty law. The Convention on the Elimination of All Forms of Discrimination against Women (CEDAW), for example, addresses economic accessibility by explicitly requiring pre and post-natal services to be 'free services where necessary' (CEDAW, 1967). The Free Healthcare Initiative launched in 2010 in Sierra Leone demonstrates how accessibility in the context of poverty may require nothing less than free services (Oxfam, 2012; Save the Children and Health for All Coalition, 2012). A more recent treaty, the Convention on the Rights of Persons with Disabilities (CRPD), in turn, provides an extensive list of facilities and services, including health facilities, for which obstacles and barriers to accessibility must be identified and eliminated.

Also in the year 2000, the Millennium Declaration was adopted and the UN Millennium Development Goals (MDGs) became the mantra for most UN agencies. Even though the Millennium Declaration was anchored in human rights, the blunt but more tangible and, and above all, measurable MDGs quickly took over the agenda. Results-based management was introduced, helping channel efforts towards demonstrating progress to reach the MDGs by 2015. Meanwhile, in low-income countries, SAPs became transformed into Poverty Reduction Strategy Papers (PRSPs), which in turn attempted to further align themselves with the MDGs. 'The Voices of the Poor' study demonstrated that people living in poverty understood why they were ill and why they were poor, and often have ideas about what can be done to remedy their situation, yet they were ignored by those with power, including health service authorities (Dodd & Munch, 2002).

With the terrorist attack of 9/11 on US soil, a radically different political environment overshadowed geopolitics, with antiterrorism and security concerns crowding out efforts to advance the unchartered landscape of economic and social rights. The international human rights agenda reverted back to safeguarding civil and political rights such as freedom from torture and the right to due process. Severe acute respiratory syndrome (SARS) and the fear of pandemics helped catapult the broader security agenda into the public health arena where HIV had already paved the way as a 'security issue' (UN Security Council, 2000, 2011). The WHO focused on preparing for pandemics and adopted the International Health Regulations in 2005 (WHO, 2008). Discussions on the right to health gravitated towards the UNCHR, which had a culture and tradition of voting when not able to reach consensus. In 2002, the UNCHR adopted a resolution which appointed a UN Special Rapporteur on the right to health (hereinafter referred to as 'the Special Rapporteur') (UNCHR, 2002).

In some ways the relationship between the WHO and this mechanism was and is complementary. The work of the Special Rapporteur has helped highlight a range of health challenges in reports to the UN Human Rights Council (UNHRC) (and its predecessor the UNCHR) as well as to the UN General Assembly. Despite occasional overlaps, the mandate of the rapporteur, as an independent voice, has filled an important void raising visibility and awareness on the right to health. On the other hand, the mandate has in some ways diverted attention away from the potential leadership role that the WHO could play and where the technical expertise lies. In this context, the absence of a special procedure on the right to work is noteworthy. The International Labour Organization (ILO), another UN specialized agency, has taken a lead in defining labour rights through a number of treaties underpinned by monitoring mechanisms along with recommendations and technical assistance. While the constitutions of the WHO and the ILO are similar in terms of the powers they invoke, the unique tripartite structure of the ILO gives an equal voice to workers, employers, and governments, facilitating the development of labour standards. While egregious violations of labour standards persist, at least there is easy access to the standards that should apply (ILO, 2012).

Other UN specialized agencies have also played a normative role, shaping and operationalizing rights falling within their mandates. In 2004, after two years of intense negotiations, the Food and Agricultural Organization (FAO) Council unanimously adopted the Voluntary Guidelines on the Progressive Realization of the Right to Adequate Food (FAO, 2005). The FAO Right to Food Unit has since been active in strengthening in-country capacity to implement this right, *inter alia,* by issuing a methodological toolbox which gives guidance on topics such as assessment, legislation, education, budgeting, and monitoring (FAO, 2009).

The UNHRC now adopts resolutions on the right to health with consensus, and health topics are proliferating both in the UNHRC and its subsidiary bodies, from maternal mortality and nutrition to neglected tropical diseases such as leprosy and noma. Conversely, with a slower but also steady pace, health challenges are being framed as human rights issues in the deliberations at the World Health Assembly (WHA) (WHO, 2011b). This trend is also noticeable in how development issues are being reshaped. Most recently, the World Summit on Social Development ('Rio+20') called for the full realization of the right to health along with a range of other economic and social rights (UN Conference on Sustainable Development, 2012). Framing development challenges as rights marks an interesting shift as we transition from the MDGs in 2015.

Human rights are now also explicit in many bilateral donor policies (BMZ, 2012; DANIDA, 2012; Norwegian Ministry of Foreign Affairs, 2012; SIDA, 2012; Swiss Federal Department of Foreign Affairs, 2012). This has reportedly shifted the perception of the accountability relationship, away from donor/recipient to one of peoples/government as well as elevated attention to *process*, addressing questions such as meaningful participation, attention to marginalized groups, and the rule of law. Guided by the Paris Declaration on Aid Effectiveness (2005), the new aid architecture is arguably creating more fertile ground for the right to health to flourish, recognizing the importance of national ownership and policy coherence (OECD, 2012). Grounded in national constitutions as well as treaty obligations, the right to health remains intact even when governments change, providing solid directives to guide the formulation of the health sector strategic plans and other important roadmap documents (WHO et al., 2011). As such, the right to health can help ministries of health and governments, more broadly, stay on track when pushed around by donors and investors. But it can also help donors and investors as it requires checks and balances, monitoring, and accountability. This latter dimension has supported the flourishing of a 'human rights-based approach' within the UN system and beyond (Human Rights-Based Approach Portal, 2012).

Most importantly, there have been myriad actions at the national level to advance the right to health as part of a wider awakening to human rights. An important trend is that of enshrining the right to health in new constitutions. A recent example is Kenya, in which its 2010 Constitution promulgates a strong and comprehensive commitment to the right to health in line with its obligations as State Party to the ICESCR (Kenyan Constitution, 2010). There is also a trend of increased civil society engagement in the right to health, which is encouraging as other economic and social rights clearly have benefitted from such support. With the adoption of the new Kenyan Constitution, for instance, there was an effort led by the People's Health Movement campaign for the right to healthcare to engage and mobilize a wide range of stakeholders to generate bottom-up demand for the implementation of the constitutional provisions (Owuor, 2012).

Several non-governmental organizations (NGOs) with long-standing experience in human rights lobbying and advocacy have moved into the health arena, in recent years, such as Amnesty International with its campaign on maternal mortality (Amnesty International, 2012). Also there are examples of NGOs, with extensive experience in HIV and human rights, broadening their agenda, such as Section 27 (Section 27, 2012). Finally, there is a growing human rights movement dedicated to economic and social rights, more broadly, playing a strong role in strategic advocacy as well as in developing innovative tools such as for budget and expenditure analysis, assessing how governments are allocating resources in ways conducive to the progressive realization of economic and social rights.

Around the world, people, more than ever, are aware that they are 'rights-holders'; neither objects of charity, nor obedient, powerless, and voiceless masses. They are putting pressure on governments honour their human rights obligations, raising expectations of good governance, including transparency and participation. In response, there is new and innovative legislation as well as mechanisms set up in countries. For example, India's Right to Information Act (2005) requires public authorities to proactively publish information as well as allows citizens to request information (Indian Parliament, 2005). The National Health Assembly in Thailand, established under the National Health Act (2007), is, in turn, an example of how community and intersectoral participation, to inform the development of health policies, can be institutionalized (Health Assembly, 2012; National Health Commission Office of Thailand, 2012). The Patient Protection and Affordable Care Act (Affordable Care Act) of 2010, as part of recent US healthcare reform, is another example of legislation which moves the right to health agenda forward. In a societal context characterized by powerful private sector interests and a culture of individualism, as well as a lack of constitutional recognition of the right to health, the Affordable Care Act constitutes an important milestone in substantially decreasing the number of uninsured Americans and safeguarding key human rights principles such as freedom from discrimination on the basis of health status by requiring insurance companies to cover all applicants and offer the same rates regardless of pre-existing conditions (US Congress, 2010).

Approximately 150 million people worldwide are facing catastrophic healthcare costs and 100 million are being pushed into poverty because of direct health payments each year (WHO, 2011a). The global financial crisis, at the top of the agenda of national governments today, begs the question of how to safeguard the right to health in the face of austerity measures. The CESCR has clarified that the principle of maximum available resources requires governments to fully explore both spending and the generation of fresh resources through tax reform and other revenue-generating avenues. Measures likely to lead to retrogression in the enjoyment of rights, such as cuts to social protection, can only be enacted 'after the most careful consideration of all alternatives' (CESCR, 2000). Further, recovery policies must be temporary, covering only the period of the crisis, and both necessary and proportionate, as well as non-discriminatory in character (CESCR, 2012). Finally, the CESCR affirms that in order to comply with human rights standards, crisis response measures must safeguard basic minimum levels of economic, social, and cultural rights. What is meant by the basic minimum level and how to ensure that this will be safeguarded will be discussed in the next section.

To conclude this section, despite some key milestones in the development of the right to health, particularly during the window of opportunity presented at the start of the new millennium, progress has been slow. While the right to health now figures more prominently than ever—across different fora, initiatives, agencies, legal frameworks, speeches, and resolutions—its normative framework remains weak. Moreover, practical guidance on how to safeguard the right to health in today's complex environment, characterized by political and financial instability, is scarce.

Ongoing efforts to enhance accountability

Despite its fragile normative framework, there has been a keen effort, in recent years, to subject the right to health to accountability, a hallmark principle of human rights (Newell & Wheeler, 2006). Indeed, addressing health as a human right shifts the paradigm, from responding to *needs* to the fulfilment of *rights*, and from the optional realm of *charity* to the mandatory realm of *law*. Framing health as a human right generates different forms of accountability—from soft to hard. Within the first category is the initiative of the UN human rights treaty bodies to identify indicators and benchmarks to monitor State Party performance (International Human Rights Instruments, 2006a, 2006b). A harder form of accountability is litigation. Both take us to fundamental conceptual questions about the right to health, including the principle of progressive realization and the minimum core content, along with raising a range of practical challenges.

For the purpose of monitoring human rights in the context of State Party reporting, the UN human rights treaty bodies have adopted a conceptual framework encompassing three types of indicators:

- *Structural indicators*, which aim to link States' commitment to and acceptance of obligations under international human rights standards;
- *Process indicators*, which assess efforts undertaken to meet those obligations through implementation of policy measures and programmes; and
- *Outcome indicators* which measure the results of those efforts as regards the concerned populations' enjoyment of human rights.

For each human right, a number of 'attributes' were then identified. For the right to health, these attributes conform with the catalogue of actions set out in Article 12 of the ICESCR (ICESCR, 1966). Indicators were selected and matched to these attributes (International Human Rights Instruments, 2006a).

While there is a wealth of statistics and data available and applicable to economic and social rights, compared to civil and political rights, nevertheless, who and what gets counted still remains an issue. The WHO estimates that 40 million, or approximately one-third of births are not registered each year (WHO, 2012a). Improving the monitoring of vital events—births, deaths, and causes of death—in countries is a major prerequisite to being able to effectively monitor and implement the right to health. Another challenge is how to select appropriate indicators, recognizing that despite availability of statistics on disease monitoring and health systems performance, the level of disaggregation required for an adequate human rights analysis is often not available. By definition, people who are marginalized live on the edges of society and are sometimes invisible to policymakers. Women are still disproportionately represented to the number of men among the poor, particularly in developing countries as well as economies in transitions (UN Department of Economic and Social Affairs, 2010). Fortunately, there is a strong push for more sex disaggregated data across the UN system and beyond thanks to a commitment to gender mainstreaming (UN General Assembly, 2010). This still leaves huge gaps in information. The principle of equality requires attention to *all* population groups which are consistently excluded. While context specific, these often include children; adolescents; the elderly; people living with HIV; ethnic, religious, and linguistic minorities; lesbian, gay, bisexual, transgender, and intersex (LGBTI) people; people with mental or physical disabilities; migrants (including undocumented and migrant workers); internally displaced people; refugees; slum-dwellers; prisoners; homeless persons; and indigenous peoples (WHO, 2006).

While the question of distinguishing the *inability* from the *unwillingness* of a State to comply with its right to health obligations comes to the forefront explicitly when confronted with individual cases, and not the State Party reporting process, the question of how to measure a State's commitment to the right to health is, nevertheless, central to the selection of 'structural indicators'. Reviewing a country's constitution could be one way. Another is assessing the real growth rate in health spending (Save the Children, 2012). Overall, there is a major gap in so-called 'structural indicators' as most health indicators, including the health-related MGDs cover process and outcome indicators. For example, the MDGs on maternal mortality include indicators on maternal mortality ratio (outcome) and skilled birth attendants (process) but are silent on the question of the commitment of the State to addressing maternal mortality (WHO, 2012b). While health outcomes may be improving in a country, this may be due to the work of NGOs without the government's involvement. The right to health requires the State to play the role as active steward, even if it does not need to be directly involved in service delivery. Moreover, the right to health is an obligation of the State *as a whole*, requiring the State to assess the potential impact on the right to health of actions by different sectors (e.g. ministries of trade, finance, and planning). The obligation to *protect* the right to health further requires the State to regulate non-State actors, (i.e. third parties), to ensure that they act in conformity with the right to health. These include those which have an obvious impact upon the enjoyment of the right to health, such as health insurance companies, which need to be regulated to ensure coverage of poor populations. Yet it also includes the whole range of actors in the business sector whose effects on health may be more or less obvious, such as the car manufacturing, tobacco, alcohol, and food industries.

By allowing States to set their own benchmarks and providing illustrative indicators rather than mandatory ones, the question of minimum core obligations for the right to health has been avoided in the context of identifying indicators for the State Party reporting process. However, it is central to litigation at the national level and will, undoubtedly, also be so in the context of allegations under the optional protocols of the UN human rights treaty bodies (UN General Assembly, 1999, 2008). While guidance on the right to health is scarce, particularly in relation to fundamental questions such as priority-setting, people are increasingly demanding its implementation. As a result, judges are 'hammering out' the right to health on an ad hoc basis as they are faced with adjudicating court decisions, using different entry points and approaches. In Colombia, for example, where the Constitutional Court ordered a dramatic restructuring of the country's health system in 2008, as a result of intense litigation, the Court distinguished an essential minimum core of the right to health, which is immediately enforceable, as opposed to other elements subject to progressive realization taking into account resource constraints (Yamin & Vera, 2009). This approach contrasts with the South African Constitutional Court, which has rejected the notion of a minimum core that can be enforced without regard to resources, and has instead focused on 'reasonableness' (*Mazibuko* v. *City of Johannesburg*, 2009).

The concept of a minimum core content of the right to health, as articulated in General Comment 14, places an obligation on State Parties to ensure 'the satisfaction of, at the very least, minimum essential levels of each of the rights enunciated in the Covenant' (CESCR, 2000). It was planted in General Comment 14 in the form of a laundry list of core obligations reminiscent of the Alma-Ata Declaration (WHO, 1978). Critics say that the list of so-called core obligations is too prescriptive. Others say that it is not prescriptive enough. Essential medicines have been claimed successfully under the right to health in courts, precisely because it is clear what is meant by essential medicines and so what is needed, they contend, is a model list of essential health services (WHO, 2012C). At the national level, there are plenty of examples which could inform such a debate. In the area of healthcare delivery, for example, Chile has focused on defining standards in its Regime on Health Guarantees (World Bank, 2012).

A review of the case law reveals that the 'curative side' of the right to health appears to have been claimed in the courts more frequently and, in this context, applicants claiming life-saving treatment appear to have been most successful. How will issues that predominantly concern populations living in poverty be upheld as integral to the right to health if this right is being shaped through litigation in courts to which they often have limited access? Realizing the right to health is as much about ensuring nutritious food, safe and potable water, and healthy environmental and occupational working conditions as it is about ensuring access to medicines and health services (CESCR, 2000). In fact, realizing the underlying determinants may yield more health in a population than curative health services (Commission on the Social Determinants of Health, 2008).

While there seems to be consensus nowadays among WHO Member-States that everyone should have access, i.e., that access should be universal, there seems to be less clarity about access to what, and who should be responsible for ensuring this access (WHO, 2012d). Whereas primary healthcare was to be made accessible at 'a cost that the community and country can afford' (WHO, 1978), in contrast, General Comment 14 states that 'it is particularly incumbent on State Parties and other actors in a position to assist, to provide international assistance and cooperation, especially economic and technical' which enable developing countries to fulfil their core and other obligations (CESCR, 2000; ICESCR, 1966).

There are recent initiatives to clarify and elaborate extraterritorial obligations in the field of economic, social, and cultural rights (Maastricht Principles on Extraterritorial Obligations, 2011). In this context, as a bare minimum, there is growing recognition and consensus that States should 'do no harm', i.e. *respect* the right to health of people in other countries. At present, the Ministry of Development of Country X may be providing generous aid to the health sector of Country Y, while the Ministry of Trade of Country X is stifling the ability of Country Y to access generic medicines (Grover, 2009). How to ensure that the actions of one State do not impede the ability of another to meet its right to health obligations is a pressing priority if we are going to advance the right to health in today's globalized world.

Another example of how the human rights paradigm is expanding in order to be relevant and effective in the face of today's challenges, is the effort to articulate the human rights responsibilities of the private sector. More work is needed to clarify and to monitor the responsibilities of the private sector in relation to health as well as address conflicts of interest. This is a tremendous challenge given the vast influence of the corporate sector, already deeply entrenched in the field of global health as major donor (McCoy et al., 2009), participant in health negotiations (UN General Assembly, 2012; WHO Russia, 2011), and as partner in global health initiatives (public–private partnerships) (Richter, 2004).

Meanwhile, away from the processes and debates aimed at redefining applicable legal frameworks, concrete ideas are being floated, particularly among civil society and academics, about how to ensure a minimum core content of the right to health, from the creation of a world health insurance (Ooms et al., 2006) to adopting a global convention which sets out the roles and responsibilities of different actors (JALI, 2012), and raising revenue through a G-20-wide financial transaction tax (International Network for Economic, Social and Cultural Rights, 2012).

Any exploration of the core content should be reviewed and redefined so that it looks both ways. Not just at what the rights holder should be entitled to, which may take the discussion in the direction of essential health services. It should also generate a more progressive understanding of the right to health in our complex and interdependent world where a range of core competencies of a government are needed for it to play the role of steward and effective duty-bearer. When the ICESCR was adopted in 1966, it was premised on the notion that State Parties had sufficient political and economic space to develop the best combination of policies adapted to their domestic context towards the realization of the right to health. Nowadays, a multitude of 'push and pull factors', in the shape or form of trade agreements (multilateral and bilateral), investment treaties, austerity measures, and foreign debt, influence the ability of the government to comply with its right to health obligations. Addressing 'more upstream' issues such as capacity for research and development, and policy coherence across government sectors is crucial if we are to go beyond monitoring government performance to building capacity to enable the State to live up to its right to health obligations.

Ways forward

For the right to health to flourish it needs to be brought 'back home' to the public health community. While the public health community—populated by medical doctors, epidemiologists, economists, and others—has embraced a range of slogans and paradigms over the years (from primary healthcare to social determinants and universal coverage, all of which have 'the imprint' of human rights), the language of human rights still remains foreign. For public health professionals, the comfort zone tends to be ethics. Where economists prevail, in turn, the discourse is often about 'clients' and 'commodities' (United Nations Foundation, 2012).

In many countries, the medical profession, from which a large part of the public health community derives, is a powerful actor that tends more towards self-protection than self-policing (Brinkerhoff, 2004). In this context, human rights principles, and the movement behind them, may appear threatening, undermining existing power structures, and questioning authority. Some public health officials, moreover, view human rights work to be adversarial and activist, whereas their work is considered science-based and cooperative. The answer is that the right to health needs everyone and all types of strategies. It needs the activists but it also needs the scientists, the health professionals, and the government bureaucrats. It needs shaming and blaming, documenting and reporting, and finger-pointing and demonstrating. Yet it also needs research, analysis, guidelines, tools, and training—all the familiar areas of work of today's mainstream public health professional.

Shielded from high-level politics, an inventory needs to be developed, detailing actions to advance the right to health. This exercise would need to be interdisciplinary, involving economists, epidemiologists, lawyers and health professionals, academics, parliamentarians, national human rights institutions, civil society movements, and rights-holders themselves. Numerous questions need to be answered: How can a constitutional provision on the right to health best be formulated? What type of institutional mechanisms (e.g. to ensure participatory processes) need to be put in place to ensure that health policies are informed by the right to health? How can priority setting be informed by human rights? How can we 'unpack' the principle of progressive realization? How can the private sector be regulated to safeguard the right to health? Which types of international and bilateral agreements are most likely to impact upon the ability of a government to safeguard the right to health? What types of competencies and skills does the government need to play its stewardship role?

An evidence-informed 'tool box' containing practical guidance and good practice examples would be useful and timely. The work involved in developing this tool box, could, in turn, inform a debate among Member-States about how to strengthen the normative content of the right to health and what is required to ensure its implementation. While it is high time to open the floor, and to open it wide and deep, launching an urgent and necessary debate about how to close the gap between the right to health in theory and the right to health in practice, the groundwork needs to be done first in order to avoid excessively political and sometimes circular debates such as those faced in the context of the right to development (Office of the High Commissioner for Human Rights, 2012).

Hearings could be launched at local, national, regional, and global levels about what works and needs to be done. These may, in turn, stimulate other initiatives. Perhaps a global advocacy campaign on the right to health could be launched, involving a cross section of relevant stakeholders? Or what if some bold and enlightened WHO Member-States came together and decided to start sharing their performance, candidly and boldly, in meeting their right to health obligations, and constructively commenting on each other's performance in a quest for mutual learning? What if this then went one step further, generating the establishment of a peer-review mechanism? A UPR focused on the realization of the right to health? An annual award for the State which has made most progress over the past year, against a set of agreed indicators, or for simply having demonstrated initiative, innovation, and commitment, for example, by establishing a sustainable financing mechanism or passing a piece of progressive legislation? Just as the list of research ideas is endless so, too, is this list of creative ways to stimulate action to move forward.

An underlying challenge is that global decision-making processes are often inaccessible to those most concerned. This holds particularly true for health issues which are often treated as technical and scientific, requiring elite expertise and knowledge. However, there is increased pressure to allow for greater transparency and participation. In the context of the UNHRC, for example, this has resulted in the webcasting of live proceedings, including the UPR, enhancing the ability for those at home to know what their government is saying about its human rights record and that of others. At the end of the day, real change will only happen when people most affected by the lack of the realization of the right to health can engage themselves in claiming their rights. How to build the capacity to demand the realization of rights of people themselves, particularly those most vulnerable or marginalized, as well as ensure that there is safe and meaningful 'space' at local, national, and international levels for these voices to be heard and to have an influence in policymaking are priority challenges.

Conclusion

Sixty-five years after the adoption of the UDHR, gaps are widening both within and between countries (World Bank, 2005). There is also another encouraging trend—the awakening of people, all around the world, to human rights, including the right to health. For those of us working in public health, we can choose to observe how people are demanding the right to health as part of a bigger process of societal transformation. From time to time, we can even be part of the process, as we produce a guideline, which is used by slum-dwellers to argue for a right to safe drinking water, or a statistic which demonstrates that the right to life may be at stake when a government uses meagre resources to purchase fighter jets while maternal health services are in disrepair.

Yet we can also choose to join the groundswell, even charting its course. This means engaging in a common agenda—the realization of the right to health—while we all can and should, undoubtedly, play different roles, building on our comparative advantages, whether we are part of civil society, government, or international agencies. Engaging in the agenda to advance health as a human right means that a range of existing legal frameworks, monitoring mechanisms, tools, processes, and actors at all levels—local, national, international—come into play. We need to strengthen these as well as fill gaps where needed. Areas ripe for priority attention—one substantive and the other process-oriented—and which are both mutually reinforcing are the strengthening of the normative framework of the right to health itself, as well as creating space for dialogue and engagement. Ultimately, 'the realization of economic and social rights is inherently a political undertaking, involving negotiation, disagreement, trade-offs, and compromise' (Arbour, 2005).

The WHO is in the midst of a reform process in order to ensure that it is 'equipped to address the increasingly complex challenges of the health of populations in the 21st century' (WHO, 2012e). The process of reform is Member-State-driven and inclusive (WHO, 2012e). Hopefully, the WHO's unique constitutional mandate on the right to health, its global coordinating function, and its power to generate norms and standards will be strengthened in this context. As Margaret Chan, the WHO Director-General, heeded when opening the Special Executive Board meeting on WHO reform: 'The world needs a global health guardian, a custodian of values, a protector, and defender of health, including the Right to Health' (Chan, 2011).

Note and acknowledgements

The author is a former staff member of the World Health Organization (WHO). The author alone is responsible for the views expressed in this publication and they do not necessarily represent the decisions, policy, or views of the WHO. The author would like to thank Britta Baer, also staff member at the WHO, and Josefin Mattsson, intern at the WHO, for their help in referencing this chapter.

References

Alston, P. (2005). Ships passing in the night: the current state of the human rights and development debate seen through the lens of the Millennium Development Goals. *Human Rights Quarterly*, 27, 755–829.

Amnesty International. (2012). *Explore: A Woman Every 90 Seconds, Why is Maternal Mortality a Human Rights Crisis?* Amnesty International: London. Available at: <http://www.amnesty.org/en/campaigns/demand-dignity/issues/maternal-mortality/rights-journey/evidence/maternal-mortality> (accessed 12 August 2012).

Annan, K.A. (1997). *Renewing the United Nations: A Program for Reform*. Report by the UN Secretary-General: New York, NY. Available at: <http://www.undp.se/assets/Ovriga-publikationer/Renewing-the-United-Nations.pdf> (accessed 15 August 2012).

Arbour, L. (2005). *Freedom From Want—From Charity to Entitlement*. UN High Commissioner for Human Rights: Geneva. Available at: <http://www.ohchr.org/EN/NewsEvents/Pages/DisplayNews.aspx?NewsID=3004&LangID=E> (accessed 21 August 2012).

Biehl, J., Petryna, A., Gertner, A., *et al.* (2009). Judicialisation of the right to health in Brazil. *Lancet*, 373, 2182–2184.

BMZ. (2012). *The Importance of Human Rights in German Development Policy*. Federal Ministry for Economic Cooperation and Development. Available at: <http://www.bmz.de/en/what_we_do/issues/HumanRights/allgemeine_menschenrechte/deutsche_entwicklungspolitik/index.html> (accessed 8 February 2013).

Brinkerhoff, D.W. (2004). Accountability and health systems: towards conceptual clarity and policy relevance. *Health Policy and Planning*, 19, 371–379.

Brundtland, G. (2003). *Statement to the 59th Commission on Human Rights*. World Health Organization: Geneva. Available at: <http://www.who.int/dg/brundtland/speeches/2003/commissionhumanrights/en/index.html> (accessed 15 August 2012).

Burci, G.L. and Vignes, C.-H. (2004). *World Health Organization*. Kluwer Law International: The Hague.

CEDAW. (1967). *Convention on the Elimination of All Forms of Discrimination against Women*. UN General Assembly: New York, NY.

CESCR. (2000). *General Comment 14: The right to the highest attainable standard of health (article 12 of the International Covenant on Economic, Social and Cultural Rights)*. Committee on Economic, Social and Cultural Rights (CESCR): Geneva.

CESCR. (2012). *Letter from CESCR Chairperson to States Parties in the context of the economic and financial crisis*. Committee on Economic, Social and Cultural Rights (CESCR): Geneva.

Chan, M. (2011). *Opening Address at the Executive Board Special Session on WHO Reform of the WHO Director General*. World Health Organization: Geneva. Available at: <http://www.who.int/dg/speeches/2011/who_reform_01_11/en/index.html> (accessed 9 November 2012).

Commission on the Social Determinants of Health. (2008). *Closing the Gap in a Generation: Health Equity Through Action on the Social Determinants of Health*. World Health Organization: Geneva.

DANIDA. (2012). *Human Rights and Democracy*. Ministry of Foreign Affairs: Denmark. Available at: <http://um.dk/en/danida-en/activities/strategic/human-right-demo/> (accessed 31 August 2012).

Dodd, R. and Munch, L. (2002). *Dying for Change. Poor People's Experiences of Health and Ill-Health*. World Health Organization and the World Bank: Geneva and Washington, DC. Available at: <http://www.who.int/hdp/publications/dying_change.pdf> (accessed 30 August 2012).

FAO. (2005). *Voluntary Guidelines to Support the Progressive Realization of the Right to Adequate Food in the Context of National Food Security*. Food and Agriculture Organization (FAO): Rome. Available at: <http://www.fao.org/docrep/meeting/009/y9825e/y9825e00.htm> (accessed 10 August 2012).

FAO. (2009). *Methodological Toolbox on the Right to Food*. Food and Agriculture Organization (FAO): Rome. Available at: <http://www.fao.org/righttofood/publi_02_en.htm> (accessed 16 August 2012).

Grover, A. (2009). *Report of the UN Special Rapporteur on the Right of Everyone to the Enjoyment of the Highest Attainable Standard of Physical and Mental Health. Right to Health in the Context of Access to Medicines and Intellectual Property Rights*. A/HRC/11/12. UN Human Rights Council: Geneva.

Health Assembly. (2012). *Health Assembly*. National Health Commission Office of Thailand, Nonthaburi. Available at: <http://www.samatcha.org> (accessed 30 August 2012).

Hogerzeil, H.V. and Mirza, Z. (2011). *The World Medicines Situation 2011: Access to Essential Medicines As Part of the Right to Health*. World Health Organization: Geneva.

Human Rights Based Approach Portal. (2012). *The Human Rights Based Approach to Development Cooperation: Towards a Common Understanding Among UN Agencies*. United Nations Human Rights Based Approach Portal: New York, NY. Available at: <http://hrbaportal.org/the-human-rights-based-approach-to-development-cooperation-towards-a-common-understanding-among-un-agencies> (accessed 3 October 2012).

ICESCR. (1966). *International Covenant on Economic, Social, and Cultural Rights.* Adopted by the UN General Assembly, 993 UNTS 3UN Art. 12.1. United Nations High Commissioner for Human Rights: Geneva.

ILO. (2012). *Promoting Jobs, Protecting People.* International Labor Organization (ILO): Geneva. Available at: <http://www.ilo.org/global/lang--en/index.htm> (accessed 21 August 2012).

Indian Parliament. (2005). *Right to Information Act No. 22 of 2005.* Indian Parliament: New Delhi.

International Human Rights Instruments. (2006a). *Report on Indicators for Monitoring Compliance with International Human Rights Instruments.* Human Rights Instruments: Geneva. Available at: <http://daccess-dds-ny.un.org/doc/UNDOC/GEN/G06/419/60/PDF/G0641960.pdf?OpenElement> (accessed 28 August 2012).

International Human Rights Instruments. (2006b). *Report on Indicators for Promoting and Monitoring the Implementation of Human Rights.* Human Rights Instruments: Geneva. Available at: <http://daccess-dds-ny.un.org/doc/UNDOC/GEN/G08/423/62/PDF/G0842362.pdf?OpenElement> (accessed 28 August 2012).

International Network for Economic, Social and Cultural Rights. (2012). *Joint Open Letter on the Human Rights Imperative of a Financial Transaction Tax (FTT).* Available at: <http://www.escr-net.org/node/364881.html> (accessed 29 June 2012).

JALI. (2012). *Joint Action and Learning Initiative on National and Global Responsibilities for Health.* Joint Action and Learning Initiative (JALI): Washington, DC. Available at: <http://www.jalihealth.org/about/about-us.html> (accessed 21 August 2012).

Kenyan Constitution. (2010). *The Constitution of Kenya, 2010* (promulgated on 28 August 2010). Adopted by Referendum on 4 August 2010. National Council for Law Reporting with the Authority of the Attorney General: Kenya. Available at: <http://www.kenyalaw.org/klr/fileadmin/pdfdownloads/Constitution_of_Kenya__2010.pdf> (accessed 1 October 2012).

Maastricht Principles on Extraterritorial Obligations of States in the area of Economic, Social and Cultural Rights. (2011). Available at: <http://www.maastrichtuniversity.nl/web/file?uuid=0fc38bc3-63f8-4c99-8b4f-d0d27fb607ef&owner=bdfe7683-80b5-4222-9540-09e8ce89e8cf> (accessed on 8 February 2013).

Mazibuko v. *City of Johannesburg.* (2009). *CCT 39/09.* South Africa Constitutional Court.

McCoy, D., Chand, S., and Sridhar, D. (2009). Global health funding: how much, where it comes from and where it goes. *Health Policy and Planning,* 24(6), 407–417.

Meier, B.M. (2009). *The Highest Attainable Standard: The World Health Organization, Global Health Governance, and the Contentious Politics of Human Rights.* Dissertation Submitted, Columbia University, New York, NY. Available at: <http://www.unc.edu/~meierb/Meier%20-%20Dissertation%20-%20Final.pdf> (accessed 20 August 2012).

National Health Commission Office of Thailand. (2012). *National Health Commission Office of Thailand: Synergy to Wellbeing.* National Health Commission: Nonthaburi. Available at: <http://www.nationalhealth.or.th/> (accessed 30 August 2012).

Newell, P. and Wheeler, J. (2006). *Making Accountability Count.* Institute of Development Studies: Brighton.

Norwegian Ministry of Foreign Affairs. (2012). *Norway's Human Rights Dialogue.* Ministry of Foreign Affairs: Oslo. Available at: <http://www.regjeringen.no/en/dep/ud/selected-topics/human-rights/norways-human-rights-dialogues.html?id=506849> (accessed 31 August 2012).

OECD. (2012). *Paris Declaration on Aid Effectiveness (2005).* Organization for Economic Cooperation and Development (OECD): Paris. Available at: <http://www.oecd.org%2Fdataoecd%2F11%2F41%2F34428351.pdf&ei=lopyUJG4LsTitQao14CwAQ&usg=AFQjCNHP0sRtXXj87zK2zbeKN5QhzJ4FZA> (accessed 8 October 2012).

Office of the High Commissioner for Human Rights. (2012). *Development is a Human Right for All.* High Commissioner for Human Rights: Geneva. Available at: <http://www.ohchr.org/EN/Issues/Development/Pages/DevelopmentIndex.aspx> (accessed 10 August 2012).

Ooms, G., Derderian, K., and Melody, D. (2006). Do we need a world health insurance to realize the right to health? *PLoS Medicine,* 3, 2171–2176.

Owuor, E.O. (2012). *People's Health Movement Kenya (2010)—Report on the right to health care campaign: Assessment phase.* Peoples Health Movement: Kenya. Available at: <http://www.phmovement.org/sites/www.phmovement.org/files/RapportKenya.pdf> (accessed 31 August 2012).

Oxfam. (2012). *Making a Difference to Maternal Health: The Evidence from Sierra Leone.* Oxfam: London. Available at: <http://www.oxfam.org.uk/education/resources/mothers_day_2011/files/Case%20study%20Sierra%20Leone.pdf> (accessed 10 August 2012).

Richter, J. (2004). Public-private partnerships for health: a trend with no alternatives? *Society for International Development*, 47, 43–48.

Save the Children. (2012). *Health Sector Budget Advocacy—A Guide for Civil Society Organizations.* Save the Children: London.

Save the Children and Health For All Coalition. (2012). *Free Health Care in Sierra Leone—One Year On. National Public and Stakeholder's Perceptions of the Free Health Care Initiative.* Save the Children, Health For All Coalition: Westport, CT. Available at: <http://healthforallcoalition.org/publications/one-year-on-final-report/> (accessed 15 August 2012).

Section 27. (2012). *Catalyst for Social Justice.* Section 27: Braamfontein. Available at: <http://www.section27.org.za/> (accessed 21 August 2012).

SIDA. (2012). *Democracy, Human Rights and equality used to combat poverty.* Swedish International Development Cooperation Agency (SIDA): Stockholm. Available at: <http://www.sweden.gov.se/sb/d/14232> (accessed 31 August 2012).

Swiss Federal Department of Foreign Affairs. (2012). *Human Rights.* Federal Department of Foreign Affairs: Berne. Available at: <http://www.eda.admin.ch/eda/en/home/topics/human/humri.html> (accessed 31 August 2012).

UN Charter. (2012). *Charter of the United Nations.* United Nations: New York, NY.

UNCHR. (2002). *The Right of Everyone to the enjoyment of the highest attainable standard of physical and mental health.* UN Commission on Human Rights: Geneva.

UN Conference on Sustainable Development. (2012). *The Future We Want: Outcome document of the United Nations Conference on Sustainable Development.* United Nations Conference on Sustainable Development: Rio de Janeiro.

UN Department of Economic and Social Affairs. (2010). *The World's Women 2010. Trends and Statistics.* United Nations: New York, NY. Available at: <http://unstats.un.org/unsd/demographic/products/Worldswomen/WW_full%20report_color.pdf> (accessed 1 October 2012).

UN General Assembly. (1999). *Optional Protocol to the Convention on the Elimination of All Forms of Discrimination Against Women.* United Nations General Assembly: New York, NY.

UN General Assembly. (2008). *Optional Protocol to the International Covenant on Economic, Social and Cultural Rights.* United Nations General Assembly: New York, NY.

UN General Assembly. (2010). *Mainstreaming a gender perspective into all policies and programmes in the United Nations system.* United Nations General Assembly: New York, NY.

UN General Assembly. (2012). *Resolution A/66/L.1: Political Declaration on the Prevention and Control of Non-communicable Diseases.* United Nations General Assembly: New York, NY.

United Nations Foundation. (2012). *UN Commission on Life-Saving Commodities.* United Nations Foundation: Washington DC. Available at: <http://www.everywomaneverychild.org/resources/un-commission-on-life-saving-commodities> (accessed 1 October 2012).

UN Security Council. (2000). *Responsibility of the Security Council in the maintenance of international peace and security: HIV/AIDS and international peacekeeping operations: Resolution 1308.* United Nations Security Council: New York, NY.

US Congress. (2010). *Patient Protection and Affordable Care Act (PPACA).* United States Congress: Washington, DC.

WHO. (1946). *Constitution of the World Health Organization as adopted by the International Health Conference, New York, 19–22 June, 1946; signed on 22 July 1946.* World Health Organization (WHO): New York, NY.

WHO. (1978). *Declaration of Alma-Ata*. World Health Organization (WHO): Geneva. Available at: <http://www.who.int/publications/almaata_declaration_en.pdf> (accessed 20 August 2012).

WHO. (2006). *Human Rights, Health and Poverty Reduction Strategies*. World Health Organization (WHO): Geneva.

WHO. (2008). *International Health Regulations (2005)*. World Health Organization (WHO): Geneva.

WHO. (2011a). *Health Systems Financing: The Path to Universal Coverage*. World Health Organization (WHO): Geneva.

WHO. (2011b). *Health and Human Rights Newsletter No. 3*. World Health Organization (WHO): Geneva. Available at: <http://www.who.int/hhr/news/newsletter_2011.pdf> (accessed 8 February 2013).

WHO. (2012a). *Health Metrics Network and World Health Organization welcome birth registration resolution*. Word Health Organization (WHO): Geneva.

WHO. (2012b). *Millennium Development Goal 5*. World Health Organization (WHO): Geneva. Available at: <http://www.who.int/maternal_child_adolescent/topics/maternal/mdg/en/index.html> (accessed 20 August 2012).

WHO. (2012c). *WHO Model List for Essential Medicines*. World Health Organization (WHO): Geneva.

WHO. (2012d). *Sixty-fifth World Health Assembly: Daily Notes on Proceedings*. World Health Organization (WHO): Geneva. Available at: <http://www.who.int/mediacentre/events/2012/wha65/journal/en/index5.html> (accessed 12 August 2012).

WHO. (2012e). *WHO Reform*. World Health Organization (WHO): Geneva. Available at: <http://www.who.int/about/who_reform/en/index.html> (accessed 10 August 2012).

WHO Russia. (2011). *First Global Ministerial Conference on Healthy Lifestyles and Noncommunicable Disease Control, Moscow*. World Health Organization and Ministry of Public Health and Social Development of the Russian Federation: Moscow.

WHO, SIDA, and OHCHR. (2011). *Human Rights and Gender Equality in Health Sector Strategies: How to Assess Policy Coherence*. World Health Organization: Geneva.

World Bank. (2005). *Equity and Development: World Development Report 2006*. World Bank: Washington, DC.

World Bank. (2012). *Chile: Regime of Explicit Health Guarantees (Plan AUGE)*. World Bank: Washington DC. Available at: <http://siteresources.worldbank.org/EXTSOCIALDEV/Resources/3177394-1168615404141/3328201-1192042053459/Chile.pdf?resourceurlname=Chile.pdf> (accessed 18 August 2012).

World Conference on Human Rights. (1993). *Vienna Declaration and Programme of Action*. Adopted at the World Conference on Human Rights: Vienna.

Yamin, A.E. and Vera, O.P. (2009). The role of courts in defining health policy: the case of the Colombian Constitutional Court. *PLOS Medicine*, 6, 0147–0150.

Chapter 4

Health development as nation strengthening

Ariel Pablos-Mendéz and Lesley Stone

Introduction

The founder of Brazil's National Health Insurance, Sérgio Arouca, noted that health reform is a process of building citizenship and developing civilization (Campos, 2012). The text of the Universal Declaration of Human Rights (UDHR) acknowledges the rich and deep interconnection between health and development (UN General Assembly, 1948). The right to health will be fully realized when all of the UDHR's words ring true—everyone has a standard of living adequate for his or her health and well-being, including food, clothing, housing, medical care, and necessary social services. Indeed, health and development are locked in a virtuous circle where improvements in health are reflected in growing social and economic capital, and strengthened economies offer greater opportunities to improve health. The current political and economic landscape presents a pivotal moment—though the recent economic downturn calls into question future levels of donor funding, a vision of equitable health systems that protect the rich and poor alike is once again gaining momentum. Continuing commitments to the right to health will strengthen both people and nations.

Health and equity—moral imperatives

As civil rights activist, the Rev. Martin Luther King, Jr., said, 'Of all the forms of inequality, injustice in [healthcare] is the most shocking and inhumane' (King, 1966). Illness strikes without regard to merit. Thus, everyone should be able to access healthcare and public health programmes, which improve the ability to contribute to society, without sinking into poverty. The potential to practise family planning, treat your children with antibiotics when needed, survive childbirth, recover from diarrhoea, and access other basic health interventions is fundamental to human life and should not depend on where a person is born. This core belief, internationally agreed upon in the UDHR, has been buoyed by the success the world has had in preventing death and illness and by the effect that good population health has on development.

The link between health and other facets of human need was recognized at the time the UDHR was drafted. Its articulation of the right to health demonstrates the understanding that health is intimately connected with income status and other indicia of development (UN General Assembly, 1948, Article 25):

- Everyone has the right to a standard of living adequate for the health and well-being of himself and of his family, including food, clothing, housing, and medical care and necessary social services, and the right to security in the event of unemployment, sickness, disability, widowhood, old age or other lack of livelihood in circumstances beyond his control.

- Motherhood and childhood are entitled to special care and assistance. All children, whether born in or out of wedlock, shall enjoy the same social protection.

The aspirations of the drafters were rooted in a belief in equality and the possibility of achieving the vision of a world where basic human needs would be met. The conception of health as intertwined with an adequate standard of living has guided development investments in the ensuing years and been the subject of study.

Donors have understood the importance of health to building strong and stable nations. From 1995 to 2010, international aid for health more than tripled, from US$7.9 billion to US$26.9 billion (Sachs, 2012). Contributions of donor government agencies in health, at all levels, to developing countries and to multilateral institutions (or Official Development Assistance, ODA, for health), grew as a share of overall ODA as well during that time, from about 14% to 17% (Kates et al., 2010). This growth was due in part to political will ignited by moral consciousness and fuelled by real, measureable gains made in global health.

Investment in health development is, in large part, a success story. Smallpox was completely eradicated in the 1970s, and polio cases have dropped by 99% since 1988 (WHO, 2012a). Gains in technology and political commitment have created widespread immunization, water and sanitation, and antimalaria bed net campaigns. Behaviour change communication programmes to increase breastfeeding and use of oral rehydration solutions have reduced child deaths from diarrhoea by more than 80% since the 1980s (WHO & UNICEF, 2009). More than 4 million fewer children are dying each year (UNICEF, 2010), and nearly half as many women die in labour than before the boom in spending (WHO, 2012b). And these gains have been more dramatic in low- and middle-income countries, which suffer the greatest burden (UNICEF, 2011; WHO, 2012b). Growing economies and improvements in other sectors, such as education, agriculture, democracy, and livelihoods, help these children survive to lead full lives and help improve their communities and economies.

This chapter will describe some of the myriad ways in which health development strengthens nations. Health drives economic growth and in turn, improvements in economic standing can be funnelled back into health. This chapter will then describe the way forward—celebrating success, tackling new challenges, and moving towards expanded access to health. For John F. Kennedy, the United States' 35th President, the 'ultimate day' was the day 'when all nations can be self-reliant and when foreign aid will no longer be needed' (Kennedy, 1961), is within the reach of our children or grandchildren. We continue this peaceful revolution of human progress, with partners in the developed and developing world, towards the day when the right to health is realized for all.

The connection between better health and stronger nations

Health development builds stronger nations through a number of different avenues, and the relationship between health and other social determinants makes it a key indicator of development. Improved health is linked to stronger economies through direct impacts, demographic changes, greater human capital, and increased investment. In turn, as the second half of the virtuous circle, strengthened economies can lead to improved health. Health programmes can also lead to better governance and stronger institutions that are more accountable to their people. Finally, good health improves social stability and security. The result of health development is more resilient nations.

Economic growth and human capital

Health is linked to economic growth, one of the keys to stronger nations. In a seminal discussion of the links between health and economic development, the Commission on Macroeconomics and

Health (CMH) found that avoidable disease costs the poorest countries hundreds of billions of US dollars (WHO, 2001). These costs are disproportionately borne by lower-income groups, which generally have access to lower quality water, housing, medical care, and information. Thus, countries with poor health outcomes have a difficult time achieving sustained growth, and health status seems to explain an important part of the difference in economic growth rates between countries, even when controlling for other variables (WHO, 2001).

One way health affects economies is the 'demographic dividend'. As countries gain their economic footing, there is a trend towards demographic changes that lead to further economic growth. A reduction in fertility rate, which may be reinforced by greater child survival, results in the working-age population growing at a faster pace than the dependent population. Gains in women's rights and fewer children to care for also allow for a further expanded workforce, as more women become formally employed. Families are able to invest more in each child because there are fewer children sharing resources for food, health, and education.

The result is rapid economic expansion due to a boom in workers as compared to dependents and increased rates of savings. These changes are thought to account for a substantial portion (one-third to one-half) of the rapid economic growth in East Asia (Bloom & Williamson, 1998). One recent analysis suggests that if the desire that African women have to plan their families is met, it could lead to a 33% higher gross domestic product (GDP) per person by 2040 (Futures Group, 2011).

But the extent of the economic benefits of changing demographics are not a given. Social, economic, and political institutions must be structured to encourage and support economic growth. Investments in education, policies that support fair employment, tax and savings incentives, and the empowerment of women are among the policies that help determine whether a nation seizes this window of opportunity. While the extent of the demographic dividend's economic benefit may be variable, the change in demographics and ensuing growth is due in large part to the better health of children and adults.

Population health is also linked to the ability of children to learn, labour productivity, and increased investment, each of which is important for a strong nation. Children who have proper nourishment and are not burdened by disease are able to learn more quickly, resulting in lifelong benefits. Illness causes frequent absences from school, and malnourishment or anaemia makes children more susceptible to illness and dampens their cognitive abilities. The positive effects of health on education and later, income, are well established. In one study in Kenya, de-worming primary school students reduced absenteeism by 25%, and even had an effect in nearby schools in which de-worming had not yet taken place because of reduced transmission (Cohen & Bloom, 2005).

But boosting the ability of children to learn paves the way for an educated society and all of its benefits. The effect of health on education has special implications for girls. Girls are more likely to suspend schooling if a family member falls ill and needs care. Thus protecting health can reduce educational disparities between the genders, inching closer to the vision of equality outlined in the UDHR.

Developing good health leads to stronger, more productive bodies as well as minds. Many diseases strike people in the prime of life, causing breaks in their most productive years. Studies have investigated the serious economic implications for individuals and families. In Indonesia, anaemic men were found to be 20% less productive than their non-anaemic counterparts (WHO, 2001). Workers who tend to get sick are more likely to have lower wage rates (World Bank, 1993). Poor health also leads to more missed work. In a study of tuberculosis (TB) in India, the average daily wage earner with TB lost more than 80 days' wages due to the effects of a bout with TB

(Muniyandi et al., 2006). But the scope of the problem is not defined simply by lost wages. Eleven per cent of children in the study dropped out of school, and 20% of the children studied had to take up work in order to make up the income lost to ill parents (Muniyandi et al., 2006). The result is a strain on the younger generation's ability to reach its full potential.

Conversely, good health translates into greater income. Basic health interventions, such as nutrition, sanitation, and malaria control, have been linked to economic benefits. Male Guatemalans who had access to a protein-packed supplement when they were young were able to earn an average of 46% higher wages than their counterparts who did not have access to the improved nutrition, potentially through increased cognitive abilities. Progress in water and sanitation reduces infectious diarrhoea, bringing benefits that range from US$3 to US$34 per dollar invested (Hutton & Haller, 2004). High prevalence of malaria has been linked to a reduction in economic growth across an economy, likely due to lost time at school and work and higher levels of anaemia in the population (Gallup & Sachs, 2001). Health is critical to the development of the human capital needed to contribute to the economy and civil society (Box 4.1).

Box 4.1. Health development and human capital: Botswana

Botswana's first HIV case was diagnosed in 1985 (Kates & Leggoe, 2005). By 2002, almost 40% of the adult population of that sub-Saharan African country was HIV infected (McGregor, 2002). Botswana is a country rich in natural resources and generally considered to be well-governed. The government called for a war on AIDS, with strong leadership from then-President Festus Mogae and then-Minister of Health Joy Phumaphi, who proclaimed that the country was 'engaged in a fight to the death' (McGregor, 2002). With an average life expectancy declining to under 40 years of age, Botswana became the first African country to offer antiretroviral drugs for free to all who needed them.

The problem was urgent and complex, affecting individuals, families, and society as a whole. While there are greater demands on the health system, many of the nurses, physicians, and public health professionals needed to fight the disease are themselves ill. The number of orphans needing care skyrocketed from 65,000 in 2002 (McGregor, 2002) to 120,000 by 2005 (Kates & Leggoe, 2005). In 2003, only 7.3% of adults with advanced HIV infection were receiving antiretroviral therapy (ART) and infants of infected mothers had a one in five chance of being born infected (Government of Botswana, 2012).

To fight the growing epidemic, the Government of Botswana created a National AIDS Coordinating Agency (NACA) in 1999, as well as a national strategic plan for HIV/AIDS. They also called on the international community to help. The United States, United Kingdom, Germany, European Union, Japan, Norway, and Sweden, as well as the Bill and Melinda Gates Foundation, the Global Fund to Fight AIDS, Malaria, and Tuberculosis (Global Fund), and pharmaceutical companies worked with the government to protect the nation's most precious natural resource—the people.

Political will, along with health development, has meant a rapid scale-up of interventions for people living with HIV/AIDS. In 2002, only a few thousand received the needed ART for which they were clinically eligible (UNAIDS, 2003). By 2005, 56% of those in need were on ART (Kates & Leggoe, 2005), and by 2010, ART coverage reached 93% (USAID-Botswana, 2011). A similarly optimistic trend occurred with testing of pregnant women—by 2010, more than 95% of pregnant women with HIV received ART for prevention of mother-to-child transmission

(USAID-Botswana, 2011). As a result, prevalence rates have been declining; 350,000 were thought to be infected in 2005 (Kates & Leggoe, 2005) while 320,000 were estimated to be infected in 2010 (USAID-Botswana, 2011). Offering more hope, the rate of infected infants born to HIV-positive mothers has dropped from 21% in 2003 to 4% in 2010 (USAID-Botswana, 2011).

The US government, through the US President's Emergency Plan for AIDS Relief (PEPFAR), has supported the AIDS response by filling gaps in service delivery and providing technical support to scale up and roll out services. As a result of the strong national commitment and growing GDP, the latest Partnership Framework agreement between the Governments of Botswana and the United States frames a path towards health aid that focuses on greater technical assistance and the waning provision of services (PEPFAR, 2010). The trajectory towards programmes that are completely sustained by national resources acknowledges the promise of a future of a healthy population and economy, strong enough to support its own needs.

Botswana is an example of the power of strong political will within a country to provide for the health of its people combined with international health development assistance. In 2008, funds for HIV/AIDS programmes consisted of about two-thirds from national public sources and one-third from international partners (PEPFAR, 2010). Data suggest that the number of new HIV infections is up to 50% lower than it would be without universal access to ART (PEPFAR, 2010). The result is a population that is increasingly healthier and better able to contribute to stronger families, communities, and the economy.

Better health can also shift investment patterns. A longer life means decades more of earning potential. When people have the expectation that they will live into old age, they tend to save more for retirement, often in the form of investment into the economy (Bloom & Canning, 2008). The effect of these changes can be seen in whole societies, and are described as a second demographic dividend.

Reducing the burden of disease can broaden opportunities for investment, further strengthening an economy. High rates of disease dampen local and foreign investments in mining, agriculture, tourism, and other industries. When the workforce and clientele are at risk, projects can fail. This was the case in the classic example of the Panama Canal (WHO, 2001). An earlier attempt to build a canal in the late 1800s was thwarted by deaths from yellow fever and malaria. An estimated 10,000 to 20,000 people died of these diseases between 1882 and 1888 (WHO, 2001). The canal was only possible in the early 1900s through intensive vector control measures, such as draining standing water, fumigating to kill mosquitoes, isolating the sick, and developing improved water systems that replaced rain collection barrels (which often served as breeding grounds for disease-carrying mosquitoes). When these measures brought down rates of illness, the canal project was finished, resulting in improved trade flows and economic growth. Similarly, in Sri Lanka, reducing the risk of malaria from 1947 to 1977 resulted in an estimated 9% higher national income in 1977 because areas previously too risky to live in became attractive to settlement, expanding access to land resources (World Bank, 1993).

While improved health is related to economic growth, the fact that a growing economy leads to better health forms a virtuous circle where gains in either economic growth or health lead to optimism for improvements in both areas and stronger nations. A key finding of the 1993 World Development Report by the World Bank, developed in partnership with the World Health Organization (WHO), is that governments need to foster economic environments that enable households to improve their own health. Higher levels of wealth in a country were linked to better health outcomes. In the 1980s, death rates of children under age five fell across the board, but fell twice as much in countries in which average incomes rose by more than 1% than in countries where average income fell (World Bank, 1993).

Higher levels of wealth make room for increased expenditure in healthcare, but also other determinants of health, including improved nutrition, water, and safe housing. Increased economic development can bring greater levels of sanitation, lowering the incidence of common illnesses such as diarrhoea. Improved roads and transportation can reduce accidents, make it possible for more people to get medical care when it is needed, and increase efficiencies in supply chains for medical commodities. Better infrastructure improves health, whether it is a result of health development spending or a benefit of a growing economy.

Economic growth also increases the funding available for education which, in the case of women and girls, is tied to improved family health. Educated people have greater access to health information and are better able to apply it in their lives. In fact, researchers have estimated that about half of the reduction in child deaths from 1970 to 2009 could be attributed to an increase in the educational status of women (Gakidou et al., 2010).

Better governance, accountability, and human rights

Improving community health strengthens more than economies. Supporting robust, democratic, transparent governments can strengthen health delivery and nations simultaneously. The growth in development assistance in health and fear of corruption has led donors to focus on improving governance in general, with potential benefits outside of the health sector. Donors may require transparency and other financial safeguards before transferring funds. Such systems can be used as good practices for other sectors as well.

Even more potently, a virtuous circle can also be seen in the link between health and human rights. Some of the tools (such as training civil society leaders and encouraging transparency in government decision-making) used to strengthen health governance build the social capacity needed for claiming other human rights. Healthy people can better exercise civil and political rights using these and other tools. Completing the circle, discrete health issues have galvanized communities to use civil and political means to demand health.

Programmes that strengthen health institutions and the participation of people in their governance improve health through direct contributions but also by building social capacity. For example, clinics that rely on community boards to set priorities or ensure accountability empower citizens and make the concept of decentralizing power concrete. Strengthening non-governmental organizations (NGOs) and building the skills of citizens to make legitimate demands on their governments are assets that can be used to make claims on other types of rights. Better health can, in general, improve the likelihood that people are able to exercise their civil and political rights—speaking and organizing on behalf of their interests. Governments and institutions are strengthened and legitimized by civic participation.

Stronger civil society can in turn lead to greater demands for the right to health. The application of a rights framework to health has crystallized movements that use civil and political rights to argue for increased access to health in ways that foster sound protection and equity. This can be seen in the evolution of population programmes from the 1960s, where governments were more likely to impose birth control measures without adhering to principles of informed consent and self-determination (Goldberg, 2009). The 1990s brought an internationally agreed upon framing of reproductive health within the human rights rubric, paving the way for individual demands on the State for increased access to medical services and safeguards to protect voluntarism.

A similar situation occurred in relation to the HIV pandemic. Advocates for people living with HIV/AIDS (sometimes more likely to be from populations that societies had marginalized) developed effective political movements that pushed governments to expand access to treatment and improve the protection of equal rights. ACT UP, or the AIDS Coalition to Unleash Power, took to the streets in the United States to advocate policies that supported the health of people living with HIV/AIDS, shining a light on the US HIV epidemic (Morgan, 1988). The Treatment Action Campaign (TAC) of South Africa is another well-known advocacy group. Rallying around access to ART, the group successfully used South Africa's Constitution multiple times in litigation meant to force that country's government to expand access to ART (Heywood, 2009). These movements strengthened the voice of the people and required governments to be more responsive and respectful of the right to health. Thai health leaders speak of 'the triangle that moves the mountain' (Wasi, 2000). Knowledge is one edge of the triangle necessary for improving health. But social movements and political involvement are also required for solving society's most difficult challenges.

Social stability and security

Health development can also improve social stability and security globally. It is apparent that emerging and re-emerging diseases may cross borders and affect everyone—in this regard, strengthening health systems, and expanding access to quality prevention and treatment services is not merely altruistic on the part of donor nations. From a security perspective, high death rates in segments of the population can themselves be destabilizing (Lewis, 2003). Similarly, the CMH noted that a high infant mortality rate is one of the key predictors of State collapse (WHO, 2001). The possibility of an epidemic striking the ranks of the most productive in society and the forewarning signal of high death rates remains. In addition to being morally imperative, health development is important to global peace and security.

Improving health can also provide a common goal with profound effect on the political space within a country. Governments able to provide services the population requires gain legitimacy, increasing stability and making insurgencies less likely. When a population can turn to its government for the basic provision of social services, it is less likely to build parallel, competing structures outside of the political system. Thus, health development is recognized as promoting a nation's stability (Box 4.2).

Box 4.2. Health development and conflict: Timor-Leste

The importance of health development in helping to establish stability can be seen in the case of Timor-Leste. Ruled by Portugal for 500 years, and then occupied by Indonesia for another quarter century, Timor-Leste was officially recognized as independent in 2002. Post-independence hopes gave way to youth unemployment and stifled development until, in 2006, widespread violence resulted in the demise of the first elected government (Perlez, 2006).

In 2007, a new government was sworn in that had to contend with a large internally displaced population and some of the worst health indicators in the region. The battle to improve health was uphill—when Indonesia withdrew in 1999, pro-Indonesia militia groups destroyed the majority of the health infrastructure and only about 25 physicians remained in the country (Tulloch et al., 2003). The new government saw health as a way to increase public trust and ultimately, political stability. Instead of relying on the degraded infrastructure, the Ministry of Health, led by Nelson Martins, created a service model that used mobile health outreach to

Box 4.2: Health development and conflict: Timor-Leste *(continued)*

respond to the citizen's health needs at the community level. The *Servisu Integrado de Saude Comunitaria* (*SISCa*) model brought basic health promotion and treatment directly to villages. Community leaders, councils, and volunteers were engaged to reinforce health promotion messages, encourage participation to register citizens, and ensure appropriate and acceptable care (Wellsbrown & Hafiz, 2012). The World Bank assisted with the financing of the *SISCa* and NGOs provided support as well.

The results included better health indicators between Demographic and Health Surveys conducted in 2003 and 2009, including steady declines in under-five mortality rates, increased immunization coverage, and a doubling of the contraceptive prevalence rate (Ministry of Finance, 2011). Just as important, the programme helped to establish the government's legitimacy and its level of responsiveness to its people. The programme is attributed with bridging political divides and helping to rebuild the nation, not just the health system.

In a similar vein, a call for health has been able to halt wars, if even for a short time. During the 1980s, the United Nations Children's Fund (UNICEF) worked with the Catholic Church in El Salvador to facilitate a break in fighting long enough to allow children to be immunized against polio, measles, diphtheria, tetanus, and whooping cough (Gautum, 2009). The health imperative—that governments and factions understand health as fundamental to society—can be an overarching goal that brings people with different viewpoints to the table.

The past 50 years have demonstrated the ability of health development to contribute to economies and social institutions in important ways. The growing health and economic status of the world, due in part to health development, has ushered in a new era. The future of health development points to new opportunities for health to serve as a pathway to stronger nations.

Seizing the moment—the way forward

The current landscape continues to reflect the interrelationship between the strength of a nation and the health of its people. Where economies are growing, governments have choices to make about the extent of their commitment to the right to health and their human capital. The progress made in health should be celebrated, and is due in part to strengthened civil society, as well as national and international institutions. The way forward must take into account the emerging political and economic landscapes and the shifting of relationships between donors and recipients. There is, in the near future, hope that nations can use their development (including increased economic growth) to amplify gains in health until it is possible for the right to health to be realized for all, by all.

Success and room for progress

Coming together, the world has been able to make significant improvements in life expectancy, brightening the future for millions. A vaccination programme that required global coordination eliminated smallpox. Maternal deaths are down by almost half in the past 20 years (WHO, 2012b). The annual number of new HIV infections has steadily declined since 1997 (UNAIDS, 2011). Vitamin A supplementation and oral rehydration solutions for diarrhoea have saved millions since they were introduced (UNICEF, 2001). These success stories, among many others, compel the realization that great strides are possible in global health.

The statistics also demonstrate a level of current illness that keeps families and nations from reaching their full potential. In 2010, more than 7.5 million children died (UNICEF, 2011), and the growth of one in every three children in the developing world was stunted by malnutrition (de Onis et al., 2011). Today, women in Africa are 100 times more likely to die from pregnancy-related complications than those in the developed world (WHO, 2012b), and AIDS-related complications are still a major killer in Africa (UNAIDS, 2012). Neglected tropical diseases, including trachoma and schistosomiasis, affect over 1 billion people in the world (WHO, 2012c), causing blindness, pain, and death. Clearly, the struggle of the world's poorest people is still vastly harder than that of those at the higher end of the economic spectrum.

New challenges emerge

Trends indicate that the world faces other growing health concerns as well. Pathogens are expected to emerge fivefold faster between 2000 and 2030 (Carroll, 2011). Non-communicable diseases, including cardiovascular diseases, diabetes, cancers, and chronic respiratory diseases are now responsible for more deaths worldwide than all other causes combined (WHO, 2011). The risk factors for these diseases include tobacco use, an unhealthy diet, lack of physical activity, and excessive alcohol use. The impact of these new epidemics could be significantly reduced through proven measures that already exist.

Non-communicable diseases can be influenced by governmental policies, where there is a social compact that allows for a government strong enough and trusted enough to intervene. For example, taxes on tobacco have been proven to reduce usage in some contexts, and restrictions on the availability of potentially dangerous products (such as age requirements for purchasing alcohol) can also help (Leverett et al., 2002). Zoning laws can create communities with adequate space for exercise, and road design and regulation can calm traffic, preventing accidents and injuries. These interventions require a nation that is up to the task of collecting and analysing information, setting rules that are followed by a majority of the community, and fairly enforcing the regulations. As much as health can strengthen nations, strong nations will be able to continue to make advancements in health.

New solutions will also have to be found to tackle mental illness as a development priority. There is growing recognition that the majority of people who suffer from mental disorders are not able to access treatment. This takes its toll in terms of suffering, human capital, and even economic growth (Lund et al., 2011). The World Health Assembly (WHA) has recently urged Member-States to make this area of health a priority (WHA, 2012), and concerted effort could bring gains similar to those seen in physical health.

While the disease profile is changing, so, too are the political and economic landscapes. New players have emerged in the global health arena, including large private donors such as the Bill and Melinda Gates Foundation, and international institutions outside of the United Nations (UN) framework (e.g. the Global Fund, the Global AIDS Vaccine Initiative (GAVI)). In the new landscape, countries that are strong enough to assert their own priorities are able to integrate aid into their own national plans, while others may be less successful at driving the agenda.

Growing economies and spreading access to health

Perhaps the most exciting opportunity is created by unprecedented economic growth across the globe, which fuels an 'economic transition in health'. With the right policies in place, this transition can lead to a reinterpretation of the social pact, where governments organize health spending to gain efficiencies in the health system as a whole, thereby extending care to more people. This, in turn, can help countries avoid erosion of the gains made against poverty.

Driven by better governance, increased trade, new technology, and the demographic dividend, world per capita GDP has rocketed from around US$1000 in 1900 to more than US$7500 in 2008 (Maddson, 2010). This growth affects both the relationship of donors to developing countries and the level of health that is within our sights. Because of this leap, ODA from governments and multilateral organizations is no longer a primary driver in the economy. Such assistance represented as much as 70% of the capital flows entering developing countries in the 1960s (Clinton, 2011). Today, it is only 13%, even though development budgets have continued to increase (Clinton, 2011). Countries that were once aid recipients (e.g. Brazil, Chile, South Korea, and Turkey) are now donors. Such economic independence should be celebrated; for better or worse, it also implies a shortening window of time within which donor assistance has influence on the internal health policies of developing nations.

Many advances in health are gained from new technologies and better sanitation, which are afforded by a higher standard of living. Thus, the jump in GDP expands the possibility that every person could have access to both healthcare and the other determinants of health necessary to reach their full potential. But this is an opportunity, and not a foregone conclusion. The growth in wealth is not equally distributed across societies. The trend is also for a disproportionate amount of growth in spending in the healthcare sector to be in out-of-pocket, private expenditures from individuals at the point of service for healthcare, leading to inefficiencies and inequitable burdens.

For US$40 to US$50 per person, the developing world would be able to reach the health-related UN Millennium Development Goals and ensure access to critical health interventions (Cavanaugh et al., forthcoming). On an average basis, this is affordable given that it is just a fraction of the average world GDP per capita. Even now, it is achievable within many developing countries, and with economies in Asia and Africa growing at 5% or more each year (World Bank, 2011), it will soon be realistic for many countries to afford a basic package of care for all citizens if funding is spent efficiently.

Unrestrained by an organization of the health system that pools risks, the default in increased health spending is in out-of-pocket payments by sick people in need of care. Out-of-pocket payments can account for 50% to 80% of health expenditures in parts of Africa and Asia (Cavanaugh et al., forthcoming). The result is that an illness can force a whole family into poverty. In fact, the 2010 World Health Report estimated that, as a result of health expenses, 'globally, about 150 million people suffer financial catastrophe annually while 100 million are pushed below the poverty line' (WHO, 2010).

This outcome is antithetical to the right to health and the hope that rising economic opportunities present. While the first era of health development served to strengthen countries in large part by empowering human capital, the future will require that strengthened governments organize the system to improve health. In pooling funding for healthcare (such as is done in insurance schemes in a variety countries, including Ghana, Thailand, and the United States), the rich subsidize the poor and the healthy subsidize the sick. If the system is well organized, this has the effect of improving not only equity, but efficiency as well (Box 4.3).

A health system that pools funding can improve quality and efficiency as well as protect people from catastrophic expenditures. By only paying for services from accredited institutions, systems where a substantial proportion of health spending is through insurance can ensure that clinics and hospitals meet a minimum level of quality. Paying for evidence-based interventions may likewise reduce the likelihood that the sick seek treatment from unqualified practitioners. Large health insurance systems have an incentive to ensure quality of medicines as well. Finally, pooled payment

Box 4.3. Ghana's national health insurance

In 2000, the New Patriotic Party (NPP) came into power in Ghana. A key policy platform during the election was to introduce a new system of national health insurance (JLN, 2008). The status quo since 1985, the unpopular 'cash and carry' system, required out-of-pocket payments for medical appointments and medicines, leading to inequality in access to services, as well as delays in seeking medical care and incomplete purchase of medicines. The NPP announced a goal of 50% to 60% of the population being covered by health insurance within ten years of the new scheme's implementation, with a future expansion to universal health insurance coverage (JLN, 2008).

In 2004, Ghana introduced the National Health Insurance Scheme (NHIS), which had, by 2008, provided insurance for 61% of the population (JLN, 2008). The programme relies on both government entities and the private sector to deliver healthcare. A system of accreditation for both public and private care providers helps the government ensure standard levels of care. The benefits package is robust, and covers most routine care. However, it does not cover expensive, highly specialized treatments such as dialysis and organ transplants. In addition, the payment system for providers is not perfect; it can take months for them to be reimbursed for claims.

The system is funded through a 2.5% health insurance levy added to the value added tax (VAT), which tends to grow with the economy, requiring fewer tax hikes (and therefore less political wrangling) in the future. In addition to the VAT, funding comes from payroll contributions and the collection of premiums. The system initially had a surplus, as taxes were collected before benefits were in place, but will require an infusion of cash in the near term.

The NHIS has made great strides towards affordable, accessible care for all in Ghana. In the 2012 election, the NPP was not the only party offering support for the system of extensive health insurance coverage, demonstrating both the citizens' backing of the NHIS and the likelihood of a cash infusion after the election. While the government is still improving various aspects of the programme, the plan is lowering out-of-pocket costs, and allowing more people to access the care they need.

systems can take better advantage of public health interventions that promote consumer demand and healthy behaviours. Individually, out-of-pocket payers may not realize the importance of seat belts, the danger tobacco poses, or the benefits of exercise. When the risks are pooled, the financial benefit of public health interventions is seen by the insurer, who then has a direct economic incentive to design strategies to disseminate information or change policies in order to promote better health outcomes.

When it comes to building a health system that pools financial risk, the experience of countries such as Chile, Ghana, and Thailand prove that expanding coverage and financial protection is possible even while economies are still developing. In fact, the fundamental change in the social compact that must take place to allow for pooled funding may be easier to accomplish while per capita health spending is relatively low. At some point in the expansion of health expenditure, the interests of healthcare providers, clinics, and hospitals, among other special interests, may become entrenched and it may be more difficult to reach an arrangement that is acceptable to all stakeholders.

Building on a record of success, it is possible to envision a future when even the poorest and most remote communities have access to adequate health resources, as well as the social determinants of health. We have joined together, through local, national, and international structures, to eliminate some diseases and fight a good fight against many others. The changing landscape, including the spread of non-communicable disease, demonstrates that fulfilling the right to health remains a complex and moving target. However, recent economic gains (some of which are themselves due to healthier populations) provide hope that many countries will soon be able to afford basic care for their populations. The next frontier in health development is to ensure that systems evolve, through strong governments and with the input of civil society to provide equitable services and public health programmes at an affordable price to all who need them.

Conclusion

By the time of the UDHR's ratification, nations had accepted the moral imperative of health and were conscious of the links between health and development. In the intervening years, experience continues to demonstrate the virtuous cycle between health and development, both through economic growth and the strengthening of institutions and civil society. No country had achieved universal healthcare in 1948 when the UDHR was enacted (Germany was on its way, and the United Kingdom's National Health Service was about to be born). The economic transition of health is allowing a growing number of countries (over 50 now!) to reorganize their health systems with this explicit purpose, which fosters not only better health, but also financial protection and social stability (Huang, 2012). The next frontier is building systems in every country that can tackle health challenges in ways that protect the poor and improve equity.

References

Bloom, D.E. and Canning, D. (2008). *Population Health and Economic Growth, Commission on Growth and Development.* Working Paper No. 24. World Bank: Washington, DC.

Bloom, D.E. and Williamson, J.G. (1998). Demographic transitions and economic miracles in emerging Asia. *World Bank Economic Review*, 12(3), 419–455.

Campos, F. (2012). *The Brazilian Experience: Health Reform, Primary Health, and Innovations in Human Resources for Health*, presented at Harmonization for Health in Africa Ministerial Conference on Health Financing: Tunis.

Carroll, D. (2011). *The Rising Threat of Zoonotic Disease.* Available at: <http://www.isprs.org/proceedings/XXXVII/8-C23/pdf/Carroll.pdf> (accessed 24 October 2012).

Cavanaugh, K., Stewart, S., Levitt-Dayal, M., *et al.* (2012). *The Economic Transition of Health*: Implications for USAID's Approach to Global Health 2011–2020. Unpublished.

Clinton, H. R. (2011). *Keynote at the Opening Session of the Fourth High-Level Forum on Aid Effectiveness.* Available at: <http://www.state.gov/secretary/rm/2011/11/177892.htm> (accessed 24 October 2012).

Cohen, J. and Bloom, D.E. (2005). Cultivating minds, finance and development. *Finance and Development*, 22(2), 8–14.

de Onis, M., Blossner, M., and Borghi, E. (2011). Prevalence and trends of stunting among pre-school children, 1990–2020. *Public Health Nutrition*, 14, 1–7.

Futures Group. (2011). *Sub-Saharan RAPID: The Change We Seek.* Futures Group: Washington, DC.

Gakidou, E., Cowling, K., Lozano, R., *et al.* (2010). Increased educational attainment and its effect on child mortality in 175 countries between 1970 and 2009: a systematic analysis, *Lancet*, 376, 959–974.

Gallup, J.L. and Sachs, J. (2001). *The Economic Burden of Malaria, Commission on Macroeconomics and Health Working Paper Series.* Paper No. WG1:10. World Health Organization (WHO): Geneva.

Gautum, K. (2009). *Harnessing Religions to Advance Well-Being of Children.* Available at: <http://www.gnrc.net/news/2008/03/05/0001> (accessed 24 October 2012).

Goldberg, M. (2009). *The Means of Reproduction: Sex, Power, and the Future of the World.* Penguin Press: New York, NY.

Government of Botswana. (2012). *Summary Table of Indicator Information Across Years*. Available at: <http://www.gov.bw/en/Ministries--Authorities/Ministries/State-President/National-AIDS-Coordinating-Agency-NACA1/Research--Statistics> (accessed 24 October 2012).

Heywood, M. (2009). South Africa's treatment action campaign: combining law and social mobilization to realize the right to health. *Journal of Human Rights Practice*, 1, 14–36.

Huang, Y. (2012). *World Momentum Builds for Universal Health Coverage in the New Global Health Agenda (Council on Foreign Relations)*. Available at: <http://yaleglobal.yale.edu/content/world-momentum-builds-universal-health-coverage> (accessed 24 October 2012).

Hutton, G. and Haller, L. (2004). *Evaluation of the Costs and Benefits of Water and Sanitation Improvements at the Global Level*. World Health Organization: Geneva.

JLN. (2008). *Ghana Country Profile*. Joint Learning Network for Universal Health Coverage. Available at: <http://jointlearningnetwork.org/content/Ghana> (accessed 24 October 2012).

Kates, J. and Leggoe, A.W. (2005). *The HIV/AIDS Epidemic in Botswana; HIV/AIDS Policy Fact Sheet*. Kaiser Family Foundation: Washington, DC.

Kates, J., Wexler, A., Lief, E., *et al.* (2010). *Donor funding for health in low- and middle-income countries, 2001–2008*. Menlo Park, CA: The Henry Kaiser Family Foundation.

Kennedy, J.F. (1961). Special message to Congress on foreign aid. In *Public Papers of the Presidents of the United States: John F. Kennedy, 1 January to 31 December 1961*, pp. 203–206. US Government Printing Office: Washington, DC.

King, Jr., M.L. (1966). Presentation at the *Second Annual Conference of the Medical Committee for Human Rights*, Chicago, 25 March.

Leverett, M., Ashe, M., Gerard, S., *et al.* (2002). Tobacco use: the impact of prices. *Journal of Law, Medicine, and Ethics*, 30, 88–95.

Lewis, S. (2003). *Notes from UN Press Briefing*. Available at: <http://data.unaids.org/Media/Speeches01/sp_lewis_december-2002-trip_08jan03_en.pdf> (accessed 24 October 2012).

Lund, C., De Silva, M., Plagerson, S., *et al.* (2011). Poverty and mental disorders: breaking the cycle in low-income and middle-income countries. *Lancet*, 378, 1502–1514.

Maddson, A. (2010). *Historical Statistics of the World Economy: 1–2008 A*. Available at: <http://www.ggdc.net/maddison/oriindex.htm> (accessed 24 October 2012).

McGregor, L. (2002). *Botswana Battles against Extinction*. Available at: <http://www.guardian.co.uk/world/2002/jul/08/aids/print> (accessed 24 October 2012).

Ministry of Finance. (2011). *National Statistics Directorate: Demographic and Health Survey Final Report: 2009-10* and accompanying *Fact Sheet*. Available at: <http://www.measuredhs.com/Publications/Publication-Search.cfm?ctry_id=117&c=Timor-Leste&Country=Timor-Leste&cn=Timor-Leste> (accessed 24 October 2012).

Morgan, T. (1988). Mainstream strategy for AIDS group. *New York Times*, B-9, 31.

Muniyandi, M., Ramahandran, R., Balasubramanian, R., *et al.*(2006). Socio-economic dimensions of uberculosis control: Review of studies over two decades from tuberculosis research center. *Journal of Communicable Diseases*, 38(3), 204–215.

PEPFAR. (2010). *Botswana Partnership Agreement for HIV/AIDS*. Available at: <http://www.pepfar.gov/documents/organization/153132.pdf> (accessed 24 October 2012).

Perlez, J. (2006, 27 June). East Timor resignation raises hopes for end to violence. *New York Times*.

Sachs, J. (2012). *Aid Works*. Available at: <http://www.project-syndicate.org/print/aid-works> (accessed 30 March 2012).

Tulloch, J., Saadah, F., Maria de Araujo, R., *et al.* (2003). *Initial Steps in Rebuilding the Health Sector in East Timor*. National Academies Press: Washington, DC.

UNAIDS. (2003). *Progress Report on the Global Response to the HIV/AIDS Epidemic, 2003*. Joint United Nations Programme on HIV/AIDS (UNAIDS): Geneva.

UNAIDS. (2011). *UNAIDS World AIDS Day Report 2011: How to Get to Zero: Faster, Smarter, Better.* Joint United Nations Programme on HIV/AIDS (UNAIDS): Geneva.

UNAIDS. (2012). *Together We Will End AIDS.* Joint United Nations Programme on HIV/AIDS (UNAIDS): Geneva.

UN General Assembly. (1948). *Universal Declaration of Human Rights.* UN General Assembly: Paris.

UNICEF. (2001). *A Million Children Saved through Vitamin A Supplementation.* United Nations Children's Fund (UNICEF): Geneva. Available at: <http://www.unicef.org/newsline/01pr13.htm> (accessed 24 October 2012).

UNICEF. (2010). *Level and Trends in Child Mortality.* United Nations Children's Fund (UNICEF): New York, NY.

UNICEF. (2011). *Levels and Trends in Child Mortality.* United Nations Children's Fund (UNICEF): New York, NY.

USAID-Botswana. (2011). *HIV/AIDS Health Profile.* Available at: <http://transition.usaid.gov/our_work/global_health/aids/Countries/africa/botswana_profile.pdf> (accessed 24 October 2012).

Wasi, P. (2000). *'Triangle that Moves the Mountain' and Health System Reform Movement in Thailand.* World Health Organization: Geneva.

Wellsbrown, T. and Hafiz, A. (2012). *Health Systems in Fragile States Case Study: Timor-Leste. Paper submitted to Medicus Mundi International Network Expert Meeting.* USAIDS: Amsterdam.

WHA. (2012). *The Global Burden of Mental Disorders and the Need for a Comprehensive, Coordinated Response from Health and Social Sectors at the Country Level.* World Health Assembly (WHA): Geneva.

WHO. (2001). *Commission on Macroeconomics and Health.* World Health Organization (WHO): Geneva.

WHO. (2010). *The World Health Report: Health Systems Financing: The Path to Universal Coverage.* World Health Organization (WHO): Geneva.

WHO. (2011). *Global Status Report on Noncommunicable Diseases.* World Health Organization (WHO): Geneva.

WHO. (2012a). *Poliomyelitis Fact Sheet No. 114.* Available at: <http://www.who.int.mediacentre/factsheets/fs114/en/> (accessed 24 October 2012).

WHO. (2012b). *Trends in Maternal Mortality: 1990 to 2010.* World Health Organization (WHO): Geneva.

WHO. (2012c). *Why are Some Tropical Diseases Called Neglected?* Available at: <http://www.who.int/features/qa/58/en/index.html> (accessed 24 October 2012).

WHO & UNICEF. (2009). *Diarrhoea: Why Children Are Still Dying and What Can be Done.* World Health Organization (WHO) and United Nations Children's Fund (UNICEF): Geneva.

World Bank. (1993). *World Development Report.* World Bank: Washington, DC.

World Bank. (2011). *GDP Growth (annual %).* Available at: <http://data.worldbank.org/indicator/NY.GDP.MKTP.KD.ZG/countries/CF-ZG-ZQ-8S-4E?display=graph> (accessed 24 October 2012).

Chapter 5

Pillars for progress on the right to health

Eric A. Friedman and Lawrence O. Gostin

Introduction

Each year, nearly 20 million people die—one in three global deaths—as a result of inequities between richer countries and the rest of the world, and within low- and middle-income countries (Garay, 2012). A child entering the world today in sub-Saharan Africa has a life expectancy more than a quarter century shorter than a child born in a wealthy country (UNDP, 2011). Women in the poorest quintile in Southern Asia are five times less likely to be attended by a skilled birth attendant than those in the wealthiest quintile (UNICEF, 2008a). The comparable disparity between wealthier and poorer women in West and Central Africa is three-and-a-half times (UNICEF, 2008b).

These persisting inequities live alongside a far more promising reality for global health. The past several decades have demonstrated that great progress is possible. Child mortality has fallen from 16 million in 1970 to 7.6 million in 2010 (Rajaratnam et al., 2010; UNICEF et al., 2011). Maternal mortality has fallen from more than 500,000 maternal deaths every year to approximately 358,000 in 2008 (WHO et al., 2010). The number of people with HIV/AIDS in sub-Saharan Africa on antiretroviral therapy increased from about 50,000 in 2000 to 5.06 million by the end of 2010 (WHO et al., 2011). In Brazil, the inequality between rich and poor women in their access to skilled birth attendants that are a reality in so much of the world has been close to eliminated, with near universal coverage of skilled birth attendants (Bhutta et al., 2010).

How can the international community bring the first tragic reality in line with the second, far more hopeful reality? The right to the highest attainable standard of physical and mental health can be a force to enable even the world's poorest people to benefit from the immense health improvements that are possible—interventions that are proven and affordable (ICESCR, 1966). Increasingly, civil society and communities, courts, and constitutional assemblies are turning to the right to health as tool for developing a more just society. The six new national constitutions adopted in 2010 all codified the right to health (Kinney & Clark, 2004; Reuters Africa, 2010). Court decisions based on the right to health are burgeoning. Social movements are turning to the right to health in their advocacy. The United Nations (UN) General Assembly has recognized the right to clean drinking water and sanitation—two of the underlying determinants of health (UN, 2010). The days when a government could argue that the right to health was simply aspirational and unenforceable seem distant.

Yet none of this progress has fundamentally changed the gaping inequalities between rich and poor and other marginalized and disadvantaged populations. How, then, is it possible to accelerate and consolidate the progress already made in improving health and closing health inequities?

This chapter outlines a proposed four-part approach to accelerating progress towards fulfilling the right to health and reducing both global and domestic health inequities:

- Incorporating right to health obligations and principles into national laws and policies;
- Using creative strategies to increase the impact of national right to health litigation;
- Empowering communities to claim their right to health and building civil society's health and human rights advocacy capacity; and
- Bringing the right to health to the centre of global governance for health.

These facets will be mutually reinforcing. Empowered communities are more likely to take advantage of the potential for litigation to enforce national policies, while global governance structures could bolster support for public right to health education and establish policy standards.

A global health agreement—a Framework Convention on Global Health (FCGH)—could help construct these pillars (Gostin, 2008). A civil society-led international coalition—the Joint Action and Learning Initiative on National and Global Responsibilities for Health (JALI)—is steering a process to develop just such a treaty (Gostin et al., 2011). The FCGH would aim to dramatically reduce health inequities and establish a post-UN Millennium Development Goals (MDGs) global health agenda rooted in the right to health, placing such right to health principles as equality, accountability, and empowerment—as well as clearly defined responsibilities—at the centre of this agenda in ways that the MDGs did not. The treaty would further elaborate on the right to health, from clarifying and codifying the interpretation of this right by the Committee on Economic, Social, and Cultural Rights (CESCR) to setting clearer standards for progressive realization and maximum of available resource obligations in the International Covenant on Economic, Social, and Cultural Rights (ICESCR, 1966). The FCGH would also establish norms, targets, mechanisms, processes, and specific obligations that would give further life to central principles, such as accountability, participation, non-discrimination, and equality, while incorporating approaches to ensure proper prioritization of health, and of the right to health, in other sectors, such as trade, investment, and the environment.

In the spirit of the principles that comprise the right to health itself, JALI intends the FCGH to be developed through an inclusive and consultative process that amplifies the voices of the people who suffer most from national and global health inequities. To help inform this dialogue, what follows is an exploration of this four-pronged framework to better realize the right to health, and some ideas on how an FCGH could advance each pillar.

Incorporating the right to health into national law and policy

National legal and policy reform should begin at the top, incorporating the right to health into a nation's constitution. A constitutional right to health does not guarantee that the government will respect the right or that health outcomes will improve. However, it does provide a foundation for action, whether catalysing legal and policy reforms or unlocking the potential for litigation to enforce this right where other routes (e.g. constitutional right to life, judicially enforceable international treaties, and legislation) are unavailable or insufficient.

Incorporating the right to health does not require wholesale constitutional reform, but rather can be incorporated as a separate constitutional amendment. Civil society campaigns could valuably direct national attention to this and other socioeconomic rights. Right to health provisions in other constitutions and information on their implementation should be readily available to assist advocates in determining the specific amendment language that they seek, and to build public and political understanding of what such a right would entail and its possible benefits. This is not presently the case.

The World Health Organization (WHO), civil society, and academics could establish an online, dynamic, regularly updated list of all right to health constitutional provisions, and analysis of how these provisions have been interpreted and implemented. This could help expand the scope of the possible, as advocates see how constitutions like Kenya's incorporate rights to such fundamental human needs as sufficient food, water, sanitation, and adequate housing; how Brazil's Constitution demands universal and equal access to healthcare and requires legislation to establish a formula for minimum government health spending on public health activities and services; and how Bolivia's Constitution guarantees citizens' participation in the decision-making processes of the public health system (Constitution of Kenya, 2010; Constitution of the Federative Republic of Brazil, 1988; Constitution of the Republic of Bolivia, 2009).

An FCGH could aid in these efforts, requiring that States make the right to health justiciable. In countries that already have the right to health in their constitutions, or in which the FCGH (or other treaties with the right to health to which they are party) is self-executing, the right to health would already be justiciable. Elsewhere, States might meet this obligation by passing legislation to domesticate the FCGH—or by enacting a constitutional amendment. This requirement would be comparable to provisions in the International Covenant on Civil and Political Rights (ICCPR) obliging parties to develop the possibility of a judicial remedy, and to enforce that remedy, for violations of treaty rights.

Laws, regulations, and policies should incorporate principles of equity, participation, and accountability. Comprehensive approaches to health equity will include non-discrimination legislation with effective sanctions; disaggregating health data and equity targets for poor and marginalized populations with accompanying strategies and time-bound benchmarks; and equitably distributing funding, health workers, and facilities. Legislation should require that all processes involving health-related decision-making engage civil society and community members with standards to ensure that members of marginalized groups are able to fully participate.

Countries could commit through an FCGH to disaggregate health data by sex, rural or urban residence, and other dimensions, and through periodic surveys or other means assess health disparities that may be harming other populations. Health information systems could also be strengthened to capture how health funds are disbursed, both to monitor funding across regions (e.g. whether indigenous areas are receiving disproportionately few funds) and to compare actual disbursements with committed funds, which could reveal corruption or other malfeasance. Perhaps within prescribed minimum benchmarks, equity-related targets could be among the targets in an FCGH, or those that the FCGH commits countries to set for themselves. The treaty could commit countries to a multi-faceted approach—addressing a patient bill of rights, pre- and in-service health worker training, structural measures (e.g. infection control and prevention), and effective complaint mechanisms—to reduce health sector stigma and discrimination. It could also establish guidelines for inclusive health decision-making at sub-national, national, and international levels.

The FCGH could encourage wealthier countries to fund these measures. It might even establish a right to health capacity-building fund to which FCGH parties would contribute, possibly under an agreed formula to ensure that the fund contains at least minimum necessary resources for the full gamut of right to health-related capacity-building activities under the FCGH. This could represent a distinct channel of funding within a larger global health funding mechanism.

Accountability requires that people have the opportunity to understand and question government policies and actions, get answers, challenge responses, and obtain redress for rights violations. Transparency is critical for accountability: India's Right to Information Act of 2005 has proven one of civil society's most important recent new tools to advance human rights (India Together, 2011). Transparency will also help tackle corruption and protect rights, as will powerful, independent anti-corruption bodies.

Improving domestic accountability would be one of the chief goals of an FCGH. It could require countries to develop, implement, monitor and evaluate, and report back on a strategy to improve health accountability at the community level, such as through functioning village health committees, community scorecards, or community monitoring. The treaty could require and support capacity-building for maternal, newborn, and child mortality audits (South Africa Every Death Counts Writing Group, 2008). It could ensure and provide standards for implementing the right to information, akin to India's law, at the least for health and related sectors. The treaty could also prescribe a multitude of measures to improve transparency in health and related sectors, such as publishing (including on the Internet) all health plans and strategies, including in minority languages; discouraging corruption by requiring health ministry officials to publish their private assets online; in general, using open, transparent, competitive bidding processes for ministry of health contracts (and related ministries, such as water); and informing communities of health funds that they are supposed to receive for local health services.

A right to health approach requires adequate funding. Laws could establish minimum funding levels for health, as in Brazil. Governments should use all policy levers to increase funding for health and its determinants. One analysis identified five such levers:

- the proportion of government expenditure that is health-related;
- overall government revenue;
- official development assistance;
- borrowing (deficit financing); and
- monetary policy and financial regulation (Balakrishnan et al., 2010).

To these five levers, a sixth is equally important: ensuring the efficient use of resources.

The WHO conservatively estimates that fully 20% to 40% of the world's health 'spending is consumed in ways that do little to improve people's health' (WHO, 2010). Changed incentive structures for health providers, strategic health sector purchasing, reduced fragmentation of health financing, and greater focus on health equity are just some of the ways to improve efficiency and meaningfully channel available resources to health (WHO, 2010).

Countries should explore innovative approaches to raising revenue, such as taxing unhealthy foods and imposing special levies on large, profitable companies (WHO, 2010). An FCGH might commit countries to implement a minimum number of such approaches, which the treaty could delineate. Beyond establishing domestic and international assistance funding benchmarks, the treaty could state circumstances under which countries are obliged to seek international assistance, owing to domestic resources that are inadequate to meeting their populations' right to health.

The rights approach to health also demands respect for the central, but often violated, public health principles of developing policies based on evidence and adopting an all-of-government approach in advancing the public's health. Countries could develop institutions specifically charged with advocating for and coordinating government efforts to incorporate health and human rights into all policies. For instance, Uganda established a right to health desk in the health ministry, charged with building capacity among health professionals on the right to health, mainstreaming the right to health in the health sector, and advocating the incorporation of right to health-based policies in other sectors (Maiso & PHR, 2009). Parliamentary committees responsible for health or human rights oversight should hold hearings on health *and* human rights. An FCGH could commit governments to establishing a right to health office to coordinate health and right to health approaches in all policies, as well as to educate the public on their right to health, promote health worker education on human rights, motivate support for the right to health within the government, and provide or ensure legal assistance for people when their right to health has been violated (Businge, 2008). The treaty could require a comprehensive public health strategy encompassing social determinants of health, and its funding benchmarks could extend beyond healthcare to address underlying determinants of health.

Codifying the right to health and developing accountability mechanisms will transform sound health policy into enforceable legal requirements. Policies on particular health issues must also integrate human rights standards, such as funding clean needle exchange to reduce HIV transmission among intravenous drug users, domesticating the Convention on the Rights of People with Disabilities (CRPD), and conducting right to health assessments.

Health and right to health assessments are seeing growing use across a great variety of contexts, from assessing health and health-related policies—such as a gender action plan in Pakistan and maternal health policy in Bangladesh—to projects that might at first glance seem to have little relation to health, such as replacing a bridge (Bhat & Clapp, 2011; Naripokkho, 2006; Zahid, 2007). They can lead to critical recommendations. The maternal health policy assessment in Bangladesh, using the Health Rights of Women Impact Assessment Instrument, led to recommendations to strengthen sub-district health advisory committees and have health facilities accommodate social and religious practices. The health impact assessment of replacing the bridge included recommendations to minimize risk of injury to pedestrians and bicyclists and to reduce air pollution and other negative health effects of construction.

An FCGH could set minimum standards on when countries should conduct right to health assessments of policies outside the health sector that could impact health, and require a right to health assessment of the health system itself as a foundation for revising a national health strategy, as well as to assess the impact of health policy changes on the right to health. The treaty could require that countries follow the policy that would most positively affect health or the right to health or, if they do not, to publicly justify the chosen approach and establish processes for affected populations or civil society organizations to challenge the decisions. Beyond right to health assessments, an FCGH might even direct countries to implement specific policies, such as permitting syringe exchange.

Beyond the FCGH itself, how do we give life to this ambitious agenda? As a foundation, government officials need to understand the right to health. Civil society, academicians, and international civil servants all have a role in educating government officials, including parliamentarians, on health and human rights. To enable health in all policies, this education should cover all officials, not only those with an explicit health mandate.

A right to health capacity-building fund in an FCGH could support these efforts. The WHO could train and designate a human rights point person in each of its country offices. Such point people will need to closely collaborate with partners to ensure that their impact extends beyond the health ministry.

Policymakers will need to be convinced of the link between the right to health and improved health outcomes. For example, they need to be convinced that public participation in health decision-making and community-based accountability structures indeed impacts health services and health outcomes. More research is needed, but evidence is emerging (Björkman & Svensson, 2009; Potts, 2008). Organizations supporting these types of mechanisms should carefully monitor and evaluate their impact, and explore possibilities for linking with researchers to develop rigorous evidence of success. Foundations should fund this research and the community monitoring efforts

Table 5.1 Health and human rights tools

Tool	Description	FCGH implementation
Health, human rights, and impact assessments		
Human Rights Impact Assessment for the Formation and Evaluation of Public Health Policies (Gostin & Mann, 1994) (<http://www.hhrjournal.org/archives-pdf/4065262.pdf.bannered.pdf>)	Provides questions to guide public health policies that may burden human rights	These tools will help implement an FCGH mandate on health and human rights assessments, including to incorporate the right to health in health strategies and interventions, and to ensure that policies and projects beyond the health sector that impact health are consistent with the right to health. Some of these tools focus on specific areas that health strategies should address, including the health workforce and reducing health sector discrimination. Many can be used proactively to design health strategies and polices and activities in other sectors that protect and promote the right to health. Civil society can use them to evaluate government implementation of the right to health. The first tool is slightly different, aimed at minimizing the possible burden of public health strategies on other human rights.
Health Rights of Women Assessment Instrument (Bakker et al., 2010) (<http://www.humanrightsimpact.org/fileadmin/hria_resources/HeRWAI_Training/HeRWAI_engels_2010.pdf>)	Instrument to assess impact of policies on women's health rights and develop action plans to better realize women's health rights	
The Assessment of the Right to Health and Health Care at the Country Level: A People's Health Movement Guide (People's Health Movement, 2006) (<http://www.phmovement.org/sites/www.phmovement.org/files/RTH_assmt_tool_0.pdf>)	Guide to assess government implementation of right to health obligations and develop recommendations to address violations	
Health Impact Assessment (HIA): HIA Related Sites (WHO, 2012) (<http://www.who.int/hia/network/related/en/index.html>)	Tools and guidance documents to determine how policies in different sectors will affect the public's health and the health of vulnerable groups	
Human Rights Impact Assessment Tools and Instruments (Human Rights Impact Resource Center, 2012) (<http://www.humanrightsimpact.org/resource-database/toolsets/>)	Various tools to assess the impact of policies on human rights, including rights to health, food, and housing	
Incorporating the Right to Health into Health Workforce Plans: Key Considerations (Health Workforce Advocacy Initiative, 2009) (<https://s3.amazonaws.com/PHR_other/incorporating-right-to-health.pdf>)	Questions to guide policymakers and civil society on incorporating the right to health into health workforce plans and policies	
Ensuring Equality: A Guide to Addressing and Eliminating Stigma and Discrimination in the Health Sector (Peugh & Friedman, 2011) (<http://physiciansforhumanrights.org/library/other/stigma-reduction-guide.html>)	Guide to a comprehensive approach to reduce stigma and discrimination in the health sector	

Enforcing the right to health		
Global Health and Human Rights Database (O'Neill Institute for National, Global Health Law at Georgetown University Law Center, & Lawyers Collective, 2013) (<http://www.globalhealthrights.org>)	Database of more than 350 health and human rights cases from around the world and international instruments and national constitutions from around the world that enshrine health-related rights	An FCGH could encourage or require countries to contribute to this or a similar database, which could assist civil society and legal professionals in using litigation to enforce the right to health, and aid the judiciary in using effective approaches to adjudicate health rights claims, including by prescribing innovative remedies.
Monitoring the right to health		
'Health systems and the right to health: an assessment of 194 countries' (Backman et al., 2008) (<http://www.essex.ac.uk/human_rights_centre/research/rth/docs/lancet.pdf>)	Preliminary set of 72 health and human rights indicators	These indicators, including as they may be further refined, could inform countries in developing right to health-based health strategies, as an FCGH would require; contribute to monitoring implementation of the right to health; and assist in monitoring FCGH compliance.
Maternal Death Audit as a Tool Reducing Maternal Mortality (Mills, 2011) (<http://siteresources.worldbank.org/INTPRH/Resources/376374-1278599377733/MaternalDeathAuditMarch22011.pdf>)	Provides guidance on and a sample form for maternal death audits	This tool could assist countries in implementing a possible FCGH mandate to conduct maternal death audits.

themselves. The health impacts of these empowering community mechanisms can be every bit as great as many of the most powerful biological medicines.

Whether established through an FCGH or an independent effort, a global database collecting information on these initiatives could both help countries and communities design the most effective mechanisms and convince policymakers of their importance. If linked to FCGH, the treaty could encourage States to submit examples of such approaches to the FCGH Secretariat to feed into the database. This should increase uptake of these practices, strengthening accountability to the right to health and thus improving compliance with the FCGH. As part of an FCGH monitoring and evaluation process, States might even be required to report on measures that they are taking—including by making use of the best available evidence, including through the database—to adopt measures that will enhance accountability to the right to health from the community to national levels.

Leadership is essential. Right to health proponents can identify and nurture respected officials in government to chart the way. And they can advocate for government positions mandated to pursue the right to health, like Uganda's right to health desk, and for dynamic individuals to fill such positions.

Motivated policymakers will need the means to effectively implement the right to health. A growing set of health and human rights tools can support this capacity (see Table 5.1), and assure policymakers that FCGH mandates, such as right to health assessments, are feasible. The human rights community can create more advanced tools, such as further practical guidance to policymakers for specific health areas and right to health issues.

Using creative strategies to enhance national right to health litigation

From increasing access to food and medicine to supporting tobacco prevention and control, constitutional provisions and court cases are contributing to healthier populations. AIDS advocates from India and South Africa to Latin America took to the courts to argue that human rights obligate government to provide access to antiretroviral medications—and they won (*Minister of Health & Others* v. *Treatment Action Campaign & Others*, 2002; *Cruz del Valle Bermúdez & Others* v. *Ministerio de Sanidad y Asistencia Social*, 1999; *Asociación Benghalensis* v. *Ministerio de Salud y Accion Social-Estado Nacional*, 2000; Conroy, 2011). In India, the right to food has resulted in cooked meals for millions of school children. A regional human rights commission catalysed the transformation of Paraguay's mental health system from institutionalization to community care (Hillman, 2005). In Colombia, where unsafe abortions are a leading cause of maternal death, the highest court demanded abortion legalization to protect women's health (*Roa Lopez* v. *Colombia*, 2006). And an Indian court prohibited smoking in public places to safeguard the right to life (*K. Ramakrishnan & Another* v. *State of Kerala & Others*, 1999).

Yet even constitutional rights and successful litigation do not always lead to better health. Enforcing an individual's right to health without regard to the cumulative impact of individual cases risks unintended negative effects on equity. Courts may feel institutionally constrained from issuing bold orders, and without a watchful eye upon them, States may fail to implement court directives.

Three steps could take right to health litigation to the next level. First, courts could adapt and build upon the most progressive approaches. Where constitutions do not expressly guarantee the underlying determinants of health, courts can read them into the right to health or life. Courts could be open to claims of immediate enforceability of minimum core obligations.

Courts should constantly interrogate the policy and equity implications of their judgments and of government policies. As South Africa's Constitutional Court insisted in the landmark right to housing case *Government of the Republic of South Africa* v. *Grootboom*, to meet the constitutional standard of reasonableness, the government's housing plan would have to 'provide relief for people who have no access to land, no roof over their heads, and who are living in intolerable conditions or crisis situations' (*Government of the Republic of South Africa* v. *Grootboom*, 2000). Courts could institute a comparable test in all areas connected to health and its underlying determinants.

Pushing the boundaries of the right to health requires engaging some of the most doctrinally difficult challenges: What precisely are the minimum core obligations? What are the proper benchmarks for maximum available resources? What pace of progress does progressive realization require? With respect to the minimum core obligations requirement to ensure 'essential primary care', courts could require a government strategy to achieve universal primary care (CESCR, 2000). Courts could assess whether the strategy is fully funded and adequately prioritizes reaching poor and other marginalized groups. Going a step further, courts could directly require countries to establish and define a benefit package to which everyone would be entitled.

Courts' role in establishing and passing judgment on minimum core obligations has been challenged from several directions. In *Grootboom*, the court doubted its own competence to establish such obligations. The South African Court has also sought a level of deference to the elected branches of government in evaluating the government's implementation of socioeconomic rights. Meanwhile, experience elsewhere suggests that case-by-case challenges of often expensive health services not included in national health benefit packages risk diverting funds from other services that could better meet the needs of the whole population, including its poorer members. This is particularly true when limited access to courts means that the poorest members of the population are unlikely to be the litigants (Ferraz, 2009).

Courts might take a lesson from the Constitutional Court of Colombia in combining the clarity, accountability, and equity of a defined set of minimum health services for all with the inclusive, participatory processes that ensure democratic legitimacy, competence, and equity. In 2008, the Colombian Court required the government to unify two health insurance schemes and to achieve the government's stated goal of universal insurance coverage by 2010. The unification process had 'to be participatory, transparent, and evidence-based, and to include relevant indicators and benchmarks' (Yamin & Parra-Vera, 2010). Rather than determining the benefits of the unified scheme itself, the Court ordered the relevant health authority 'to immediately and on an annual basis comprehensively update the benefits included . . . through a process that included "direct and effective participation of the medical community and the users of the health system," in particular those who would be most affected by policy changes' (Yamin & Parra-Vera, 2010). Such benefits would be immediately enforceable, as would other health services needed to address threats to a person's minimum level of subsistence that the person could not afford (Judgment T-760, 2008; Yamin & Parra-Vera, 2010). The Court recognized resource limitations: the benefits 'need not be infinite but can be circumscribed to cover the health needs and priorities determined by the competent authorities in light of the efficient use of scarce resources' (Judgment T-760, 2008). The benefits plan had to be 'designed to protect the right to health according to the needs of the population', with limitations being 'reasonable and proportionate' (Judgment T-760, 2008).

Universal health coverage could extend to underlying determinants of health. Courts could be deferential if these guaranteed minimums have been developed through an inclusive, participatory process; adhere to requirements of equity; are consistent with maximum resource availability requirements; are regularly reviewed and updated; and are well implemented.

Courts could demand specific, time-bound action, with experts and community members themselves developing the remedy, much as the Colombian Court sought to put the nature of universal coverage in the democratic domain. The approach adopted by the Inter-American Court of Human Rights in *Xákmok Kásek Indigenous Community* could similarly serve as a model. The Court held that the Paraguayan government had a duty to guarantee the right to life to community members, who lacked basic services as they sought to reclaim traditional lands. The Court required Paraguay to prepare a study, involving specialists and community perspectives, on obstacles to healthcare and other basic needs, including food, water, and sanitation. Paraguay was then obliged to adapt its services to the study's conclusions (*Xakmok Kasek Indigenous Community* v. *Paraguay*, 2010). A participatory approach could be linked to substantive parameters encompassing areas including equity and resources to ensure a robust outcome.

Courts are most likely to adopt these approaches if judges and lawyers are well-versed in the right to health. Therefore, a second step to better realize the right to health through litigation is training for legal professionals on health and human rights, courts' approaches in other jurisdictions, and the real-world impact of their decisions (including on equity and implementation). A new global health and human rights database—such as the one being launched collaboratively by the O'Neill Institute for National and Global Health Law at Georgetown University, and the Lawyers Collective in India—opens up new possibilities for cross-border learning. Judges and lawyers could be exposed to innovative applications of socioeconomic rights, such as the South Africa Constitutional Court finding that these rights required an independent anti-corruption body (*Hugh Glenister* v. *President of the Republic of South Africa & Others*, 2011).

The FCGH might require countries to periodically submit relevant cases to the treaty Secretariat to ensure that the database is comprehensive and current, maximizing its potential to aid litigants in protecting their rights and courts in adjudicating and offering the most effective remedies for violations. There is precedent for such a data-sharing requirement. The WHO Global Code of Practice on the International Recruitment of Health Personnel, for example, encourages countries to establish and maintain a database of laws and regulations relevant to health worker migration and recruitment, as well as their implementation. Countries are supposed to provide this information to the WHO every three years (World Health Assembly, 2010).

An FCGH could establish one or several lead agencies, such as the WHO or the UN Office of the High Commissioner for Human Rights (OHCHR), or another process (involving such partners as the International Commission of Jurists) to establish a plan for this training. If such direct support for legal capacity-building within the judicial system stands out among human rights treaties, it builds upon other legal capacity-building stipulations in international law. The other health framework convention, the Framework Convention on Tobacco Control, stands as an important precedent, with its support for technical assistance to develop 'a strong legislative foundation' for tobacco control measures (WHO Framework Convention on Tobacco Control, 2003). Further afield, with the centrality of law enforcement to the treaty—though looking towards prosecutions by the State, rather than potentially against the State—the Convention against Corruption requires that countries, 'to the extent necessary, initiate, develop or improve specific training programmes for its personnel responsible for preventing and combating corruption' (United Nations Convention against Corruption, 2003). This is much as an FCGH might require training for personnel responsible for enforcing the right to health. The Convention against Corruption encourages international technical assistance for this capacity-building, including training through international institutions (United Nations Convention against Corruption, 2003). In the realm of human rights itself, a resolution of the Pan-American Health Organization (PAHO) calls for educating legislative and judicial personnel on human rights standards (PAHO, 2010).

Third, lawyers and civil society organizations need to view court victories as only part of a continuum of change. Compliance is a pervasive problem. In *Grootboom*, seen as a landmark victory for socioeconomic rights, the seemingly victorious plaintiff, Irene Grootboom, died eight years after the judgment, 'still homeless and penniless' (Joubert, 2008). Advocates for victorious parties in right to health cases must follow through to see that policies—and lives—really change.

Change is most likely if advocates combine litigation with a broader strategy. For example, in 2011 Ugandan health and human rights advocates initiated a case against the government to force action to reduce maternal mortality, asserting violations of the rights to life and health, and the rights of women. Civil society organizations have coordinated the litigation with a comprehensive advocacy strategy including petitions, civil society and public mobilization, and media pressure. Since the Centre for Health, Human Rights and Development initiated the case, more than 35 civil society organizations in Uganda have come together to form a coalition advocating for maternal health (Mulumba et al., 2011).

Empowering civil society and communities to claim their right to health

Pressure from civil society and the broader public can generate the political imperative to secure the right to health. Empowering communities to understand and claim their rights represents the third pillar of a health and human rights strategy. This pillar is constructed of public understanding, participation, accountability, and advocacy. It recognizes that more than a set of legal doctrines, human rights demand a fundamental redistribution of power from States to individuals, especially those who have traditionally held the least power.

Incorporating the right to health into laws, regulations, policies, and practices begins with establishing participatory and inclusive policy development processes that provide a privileged place for poor and marginalized communities. Public input and civil society organizations should inform health-related policies and identify areas where policy reform is required. Community involvement in implementing, monitoring, and evaluating policies must follow, so that reforms are carried out effectively, respond to local priorities and realities, and reach those in greatest need. Mechanisms range from the national (e.g. national health assemblies and multi-sector health committees) to the local (e.g. village health committees), and from open processes that engage many people (e.g. regulatory notice comments procedures) to those engaging selected community and civil society representatives (e.g. community health boards).

In addressing community level accountability and offering health decision-making guidelines, an FCGH should insist that countries incorporate ways to ensure meaningful participation of marginalized and vulnerable populations and to emphasize their needs. A central aspect of an FCGH would be to establish standards of universal health coverage, for both healthcare and the underlying determinants of health. Countries could be required to follow inclusive, participatory approaches to translating these global guidelines into specific national standards and policies, and not rely solely on a technocratic approach (e.g. by setting the standards simply by determining most cost-effective interventions that would comply with the global guidelines; such evidence should have a role, but not an exclusive one).

People will be best equipped to pursue the right to health if they understand their rights. Civil society and the media can educate the populace. Journalists will themselves often need to be educated on, and sensitized to, health and human rights. Government institutions have an educational role. The Uganda Human Rights Commission's health rights unit seeks to help 'people realise what they are entitled to in the health units and empower them to demand . . . the services', and offers legal aid to people whose health rights are violated (Businge, 2008). Health workers can be a powerful force for the right to health, respecting it in their own practices, educating patients, and advocating locally and nationally. Their educational curricula should incorporate human rights, including the right to health. An FCGH could commit countries to incorporating human rights into training for all health workers and to establishing an agency—perhaps a governmental entity within the health ministry, or perhaps an empowered independent institution, such as a strong a human rights commission—charged with facilitating implementing the right to health. This should encompass assisting people in claiming this right, including through education on the right to health, and ensuring that people can access legal recourse to remedy violations. Such a requirement would be similar to, if more specific than, the duty in the CRPD to 'maintain, strengthen, designate or establish . . . a framework, including one or more independent mechanisms . . . to promote, protect and monitor implementation of the present Convention' (International Convention on the Protection and Promotion of the Rights and Dignity of Persons with Disabilities, 2006).

Knowledge of the right to health alone is not enough, even when combined with access to the legal system. Civil society capacity-building is needed, including core and programmatic funding; fundraising, budgeting, management, and information technology skills; strategic planning; and training in advocacy strategies and tactics (e.g. budget monitoring and community scorecards). Capacity-building should be supplemented by capacity sharing, that is, facilitating connections among civil society organizations: developing health and human rights networks within countries and regions to share skills, experiences, and lessons, and to join forces in advocacy campaigns. The PAHO human rights resolution incorporates some of these capacity-building measures, namely human rights training for health workers and promoting dissemination of human rights information among civil society organizations (PAHO, 2010).

It is critical that an FCGH support often beleaguered civil society organizations that seek to advance health and other human rights, but find their time consumed by fundraising as much as change-making. This support could be part of the proffered right to health capacity-building fund, or a distinct mechanism, and should encompass less formally organized community groups and networks, whether geographically centred or sharing other common characteristics (e.g. disease status, gender, or disability). Such a fund could overcome the potential ineffectiveness of good intentions not backed by resources, such as the pledge in the Rio Political Declaration on Social Determinants of Health to 'empower the role of communities and strengthen civil society contribution to policy-making and implementation by adopting measures to enable their effective participation for the public interest in decision-making' (World Conference on Social Determinants of Health, 2011).

With increased funding and support should also come measures to augment the accountability of civil society organizations, particularly to the people on whose behalf they work. This accountability could come through their constituents' direct involvement and decision-making authority within the organizations, non-governmental organizations (NGOs) effectively and transparently evaluating their own activities, and regular channels of communication, input, and feedback. Meanwhile, when one or several civil society organizations represent broader civil society, those organizations need to accurately portray the positions and ideas of broader coalitions, report back on results, and gather feedback to contribute to a cycle of meaningful representation.

Health and human rights advocacy cannot be viewed apart from the broader human rights environment that will impact this advocacy, such as freedom of expression and assembly, the right to information, and the free operation of civil society organizations. Feeling their power and control over society threatened, a growing number of regimes have restricted NGOs' ability to register and raise money, especially from foreign sources, and have limited the activities of internationally supported NGOs, including human rights advocacy (International Center for Not-For-Profit Law, 2006; 2009).

The FCGH might require countries to review, rescind, and avoid future laws that could obstruct civil society right to health advocacy through these types of laws. An internationally financed civil society fund might help give some solace to—or more likely, remove a propaganda point from—governments that are skittish about the foreign influence of NGOs. It will provide funds that are clearly not linked to an agenda of any particular country—only to advancing the human rights and well-being of their people.

Bringing the right to health to the centre of global governance for health

Much of this chapter is devoted to showing how an FCGH could help bring the right to health to the centre of global governance for health. This section expands upon this concept to show how the international community could support effective health and human rights policies, progressive litigation, and empowered civil society and communities. These international efforts comprise the fourth pillar and build on ideas enunciated earlier, such as increasing funding for health and human rights organizations; providing technical support to build their capacity; and sharing lessons, facilitating international connections, and developing health and human rights tools and indicators that can be adapted locally.

Beyond this, countries must meet their own right to health obligations in the global arena. These include sustained, sufficient, and predictable development assistance, and protecting and advancing health and human rights in trade, investment, environmental, and other spheres of international law.

An FCGH could codify and expand upon the foregoing responsibilities. It could establish an international financing framework that delineates funding obligations for each country, addressing both domestic and international responsibilities. It could establish new financing mechanisms, and unambiguously specify the priority to be given to health and human rights in other international legal regimes. An FCGH could go further by delineating what such priority would entail in these other areas, from affirmative requirements to address the health impact of climate change when developing adaptation measures to protecting bilateral and regional trade agreements from provisions that could reduce access to medicine. It could require countries to assess the impact of macroeconomic policies on the right to health and avoid any that could undermine the right. The treaty could codify public health and human rights approaches to illicit drug use, which recognize addiction as a health condition requiring treatment and demand respect for the human rights of drug users. A treaty might also establish formal mechanisms of coordination among the WHO, the OHCHR, and key actors in other regimes, such as the World Trade Organization (WTO), World Bank, International Monetary Fund (IMF), International Labour Organization (ILO), UN Office on Drugs and Crime (UNODC), and UN Environment Programme. Civil society and communities, as well as governments, would need to be assured of formative roles in any such mechanism. The WHO and the OHCHR, with their health and human rights mandates, would be well placed to lead such an entity.

The WHO should strengthen its own human rights capacity in line with its constitutional mandate, which recognizes 'the enjoyment of the highest attainable standard of health', as 'one of the fundamental rights of every human being without distinction of race, religion, political belief, economic or social condition' (WHO, 1946). The WHO should assume this leadership role, mainstreaming human rights throughout its programming, increasing its own human rights capacity in terms of staffing, funding, and organizational knowledge, and elevating the priority it gives human rights. It should lead and help coordinate international support for local health and human rights activities and advocate for other international legal regimes to incorporate health and human rights concerns.

Academia and think tanks can make human rights law itself more effective. By analysing the fast-growing body of right to health law, examining how the right is being implemented, and offering new ideas, they can contribute to greater clarity of health and human rights law and to its progressive development. And they can increase understanding on the real-life impact of this law, factors that facilitate and impede its impact, and mechanisms to improve enforcement.

An FCGH and the four pillars of health and human rights

These four pillars—incorporating the right to health into national laws, using creative strategies to increase the impact of national right to health litigation, empowering communities to claim their rights, and bringing the right to health to the centre of global governance for health—are integrally intertwined. Social movements spur legal and policy reform. Legal and policy change creates new opportunities for litigation. Elevating human rights in and integrating it throughout global governance for health will facilitate national progress, even as national processes, priorities, and experiences should inform global action.

An FCGH could help to simultaneously erect all four pillars. A successful FCGH will need to incorporate strong compliance mechanisms. These would begin with regular, public country reports on how they are implementing the treaty. Whether by requiring an inclusive process in developing these State reports, explicitly considering parallel civil society reports in evaluating State compliance, or both, the treaty should ensure that evaluation of compliance is not based simply on States' unsupported statements or approval. Reporting cannot be the end of compliance strategies, however. While countries have considerable self-interest in improving the health of their own and the world's population, the treaty should also include creative incentives for compliance and sanctions for non-compliance. For example, certain forms of international funding might be available or ensured only for countries that are meeting their own funding obligations. Non-compliance might open up the possibility of suspension from the possibility of serving on the WHO Executive Board or UN Human Rights Council. Given the lives on the line, targeted sanctions of the sort usually reserved for traditional national security concerns, such as freezing assets and travel bans on individuals, could be options in severe cases. Any sanctions must themselves adhere to the highest human rights standards and not degrade the health and undermine the rights of the very people they are meant to help.

Critical to a successful FCGH will be a social movement that supports the treaty and the right to health more broadly. A powerful social movement, one that includes labour, environmental, and other broader concerns, can ensure that pressure for compliance comes from domestic as well as international sources. Indeed, a widely supported FCGH with clear standards could be a powerful tool for civil society advocacy in both the global South and North, even in countries that have not themselves ratified the FCGH.

A comprehensive approach to advancing the right to health, backed by a global treaty, could prove a commanding counterweight to competing interests and political forces, advance effective policies and mechanisms for implementing the right to health, further clarify human rights law and attendant obligations, and enhance accountability and enforcement through community, national, and international actions.

Due regard to each pillar, drawing on and adding to innovative right to health approaches and capturing the synergies among the pillars, holds much promise for global health. With bold, systematic, and innovative actions, human rights stand to have a transformative impact in making global health better tomorrow than it is today.

An FCGH could powerfully advance the right to health and close national and global health inequities. The JALI envisions a treaty developed through a broadly inclusive 'bottom-up' process. Ultimately, the most important input into an FCGH will come from the people whose health realities are worlds away from our own. The treaty must speak to the realities of slum-dwellers who live near centres of power yet lack the most basic services, to farmers who find themselves and their children without proper nourishment, and to the orphans and widows, indigenous populations, sexual minorities, women, people with disabilities, and others who often suffer the ugliest discrimination and most extreme poverty. It is their voices that JALI most hopes to hear and incorporate in guiding a process to develop an FCGH.

Acknowledgment

This chapter, adapted for publication in this book, was previously published as Friedman, E.A. and Goston, L.O. (2012). 'Pillars for progress on the right to health: harnessing the potential of human rights through a Framework Convention on Global Health'. *Health and Human Rights: An International Journal*, 14(1):4–19. [Online], Volume 14, Number 1 (12 June 2012)

References

Asociación Benghalensis v. *Ministerio de Salud y Accion Social-Estado Nacional.* (2000). *National Supreme Court of Justice of Argentina, A. 186, XXXIV*. Available at: <http://www.law.georgetown.edu/oneillinstitute/global-health-law/who-hhr/caselaw-detail.cfm?id=1464&b=1> (accessed 7 November 2012).

Backman, G., Hunt, P., Khosla, R., *et al.* (2008). Health systems and the right to health: an assessment of 194 countries. *Lancet*, 372, 2047–2085.

Bakker, S., Plagman, H., and Nederveen, M. (2010). *Health Rights of Women Assessment Instrument*. Available at: <http://www.humanrightsimpact.org/fileadmin/hria_resources/HeRWAI_Training/HeRWAI_engels_2010.pdf> (accessed 7 November 2012).

Balakrishnan, R., Elson, D., Heintz, J., *et al.* (2010). *Maximum Available Resources and Human Rights: Analytical Report*. Available at: <http://www.cwgl.rutgers.edu/globalcenter/publications/marreport.pdf> (accessed 7 November 2012).

Bhat, M. and Clapp, E. (2011). *The Sellwood Bridge Project: A Health Impact Assessment*. Available at: <http://www.apho.org.uk/resource/item.aspx?RID=115411> (accessed 7 November 2012).

Bhutta, Z.A., Chopra, M., Axelson, H., *et al.* (2010). Countdown to 2015 decade report (2000-10): taking stock of maternal, newborn, and child survival. *Lancet*, 375, 2032–2044.

Björkman, M. and Svensson, J. (2009). Power to the people: evidence from a randomized field experiment on community-based monitoring in Uganda. *Quarterly Journal of Economics*, 124, 735–769.

Businge, C. (2008). *Health Rights Unit Launched*. Available at: <http://www.newvision.co.ug/PA/8/13/652335> (accessed 7 November 2012).

CESCR. (2000). *General Comment No. 14: The Right to the Highest Attainable Standard of Health (article 12 of the International Covenant on Economic, Social and Cultural Rights). Committee on Economic, Social, and Cultural Rights (CESCR): Geneva*. Available at: <http://www1.umn.edu/humanrts/gencomm/escgencom14.htm> (accessed 7 November 2012).

Conroy, O. (2011). *Free Second-Line Medication for HIV/AIDS to be Available in Non-Metro Indian Cities from March.* Available at: <http://topnews.us/content/232332-free-second-line-medication-hivaids-be-available-non-metro-indian-cities-march> (accessed 7 November 2012).

Constitution of the Federative Republic of Brazil. (1988). *Arts. 196198.* Available at: <http://www.v-brazil.com/government/laws/constitution.html> (accessed 7 November 2012).

Constitution of Kenya. (2010). *Art. 43.* Available at: <http://www.kenyaembassy.com/pdfs/The%20Constitution%20of%20Kenya.pdf> (accessed 7 November 2012).

Constitution of the Republic of Bolivia. (2009). Art. 40.

Cruz del Valle Bermúdez & Others. v. *Ministerio de Sanidad y Asistencia Social.* (1999). *Supreme Court of Justice of Venezuela, Case No. 15.789, Decision No. 916.* Available at: <http://www.law.georgetown.edu/oneillinstitute/global-health-law/who-hhr/caselaw-detail.cfm?id=1292&b=1> (accessed 7 November 2012).

Ferraz, O.L.M. (2009). The right to health in the courts of Brazil: worsening health inequities? *Health and Human Rights: An International Journal,* 11, 40.

Garay, J. (2012). *Global Health (GH)=GH Equity=GH Justice=Global Social Justice: The Opportunities of Joining EU and US Forces Together.* Available at: <http://eucenter.berkeley.edu/newsletter/winter12/garay.html> (accessed 7 November 2012).

Gostin, L.O. (2008). Meeting basic survival needs of the world's least healthy people: Toward a framework convention on global health. *Georgetown Law Journal,* 96, 331–392.

Gostin, L.O., Friedman, E.A., Ooms, G., *et al.* (2011). *The Joint Action and Learning Initiative: Towards a Global Agreement on National and Global Responsibilities for Health.* Available at: <http://www.plosmedicine.org/article/info%3Adoi%2F10.1371%2Fjournal.pmed.1001031> (accessed 7 November 2012).

Gostin L. and Mann, J.M. (1994). *Human Rights Impact Assessment for the Formation and Evaluation of Public Health Policies.* Available at: <http://www.hhrjournal.org/archives-pdf/4065262.pdf.bannered.pdf> (accessed 7 November 2012).

Government of the Republic of South Africa v. *Grootboom.* (2000). South Africa Constitutional Court: CCT 11/00, Para. 99. Available at: <http://www.saflii.org/za/cases/ZACC/2000/19.html> (accessed 7 November 2012).

Health Workforce Advocacy Initiative. (2009). *Incorporating the Right to Health into Health Workforce Plans: Key Considerations.* Available at: <https://s3.amazonaws.com/PHR_other/incorporating-right-to-health.pdf> (accessed 7 November 2012).

Hillman, A. (2005). Protecting mental disability rights: a success story in the inter-American human rights system. *Human Rights Briefs,* 12, 25–28.

Hugh Glenister v. *President of the Republic of South Africa & Others.* (2011). South Africa Constitutional Court, March 17, CCT 48/10. Available at: <http://www.saflii.org/za/cases/ZACC/2011/6.html> (accessed 7 November 2012).

Human Rights Impact Resource Center. (2012). *Human Rights Impact Assessment (HRIA) Tools and Instruments.* Available at <http://www.humanrightsimpact.org/resource-database/toolsets/> (accessed 7 November 2012).

ICESCR. (1966). *International Covenant on Economic, Social, and Cultural Rights.* G.A. Res. 2200A (XXI), Art. 12. Office of the High Commissioner for Human Rights (OHCHR): Geneva. Available at: <http://www2.ohchr.org/english/law/cescr.htm> (accessed 7 November 2012).

India Together. (2011). *Right to Information in India.* Available at: <http://indiatogether.org/rti/> (accessed 9 August 2011).

International Center for Not-for-Profit Law. (2006). Recent laws and legislative proposals to restrict civil society and civil society organizations. *International Journal of Not-for-Profit Law,* 8, 76–85.

International Center for Not-for-Profit Law. (2009). Barred from the debate: restrictions on NGO public policy activities—letter from the editor. *Global Trends in NGO Law,* 1, 1–12.

International Convention on the Protection and Promotion of the Rights and Dignity of Persons with Disabilities. (2006). G.A. Res. 61/106, Art. 33(2). Available at: <http://www1.umn.edu/humanrts/instree/disability-convention2006.html> (accessed 7 November 2012).

Joubert, P. (2008). *Grootboom Dies Homeless and Penniless.* Available at: <http://mg.co.za/article/2008-08-08-grootboom-dies-homeless-and-penniless> (accessed 7 November 2012).

Judgment T-760. (2008). *Constitutional Court of Colombia, July 31, at Para. 4.4.3.* Available at: <http://www.escr-net.org/usr_doc/English_summary_T-760.pdf> (accessed 7 November 2012).

K. Ramakrishnan & Another v. *State of Kerala & Others.* (1999). *Kerala High Court, India: AIR 1999 Ker 385.* Available at: <http://indiankanoon.org/doc/1480636/> (accessed 7 November 2012).

Kinney, E.D. and Clark, B.A. (2004). Provisions for health and health care in the constitutions of the countries of the world. *Cornell International Law Journal*, 37, 285–355.

Maiso, F. and PHR. (2009). Private communication between Physicians for Human Rights and Dr. Faustine Maiso, Right to Health Officer within the Ugandan Ministry of Health and the World Health Organization (28 July 2009).

Mills, S. (2011). *Maternal Death Audit as a Tool Reducing Maternal Mortality.* Available at: <http://siteresources.worldbank.org/INTPRH/Resources/376374-1278599377733/MaternalDeathAudit March22011.pdf> (accessed 7 November 2012).

Minister of Health & Others v. *Treatment Action Campaign & Others.* (2002). South Africa: Constitution court, CCT 8/02. Available at: <http://www.saflii.org/za/cases/ZACC/2002/15.html> (accessed 7 November 2012).

Mulumba, M., Kabanda, D., and Hafsa, N. (2011). *Holding the Ugandan Government to Account for Maternal Mortality.* Available at: <http://www.equinetafrica.org/newsletter/index.php?issue=130> (accessed 7 November 2012).

Naripokkho. (2006). *HERWAI Study of the Bangladesh National Strategy for Maternal Health.* Naripokkho Organization. Available at: <http://www.humanrightsimpact.org/resource-database/reports/resources/view/6/user_hria_reports/> (accessed 7 November 2012).

O'Neill Institute for National and Global Health Law, WHO, and Lawyers Collective. (2012). *Global Health and Human Rights Database.* Available at: <http://www.ghhrdb.org> (accessed 7 November 2012).

PAHO. (2010). *Resolution CD50.R8: Health and Human Rights.* Pan-American Health Organization (PAHO): Washington, DC. Available at <http://new.paho.org/hq/dmdocuments/2010/CD50.R8-e.pdf> (accessed 7 November 2012).

People's Health Movement (2006). *The Assessment of the Right to Health and Health Care at the Country Level: A People's Health Movement Guide.* Available at: <http://www.phmovement.org/sites/www.phmovement.org/files/RTH_assmt_tool_0.pdf> (accessed 7 November 2012).

Peugh, L. and Friedman, E.A. (2011). *Ensuring Equality: A Guide to Addressing and Eliminating Stigma and Discrimination in the Health Sector.* Available at: <http://physiciansforhumanrights.org/library/other/stigma-reduction-guide.html> (accessed 7 November 2012).

Potts, H. (2008). *Accountability and the Right to the Highest Attainable Standard of Health.* Available at: <http://www.essex.ac.uk/human_rights_centre/research/rth/docs/HRC_Accountability_Mar08.pdf> (accessed 7 November 2012).

Rajaratnam, J.K., Marcus, J.R., Flaxman, A., *et al.* (2010). Neonatal, postneonatal, childhood, and under-5 mortality for 187 countries, 1970–2010: a systematic analysis of progress towards Millennium Development Goal 4. *Lancet*, 375, 1988–2004.

Reuters Africa. (2010). *Madagascar's Gov't Hopes for Recognition After Poll.* Available at: <http://af.reuters.com/article/topNews/idAFJOE6B50AG20101206> (accessed 7 November 2012).

Rio Political Declaration on Social Determinants of Health. (2011). *World Conference on Social Determinants of Health, Para. 12(2)(ii).* Available at: <http://www.who.int/sdhconference/declaration/Rio_political_declaration.pdf> (accessed 7 November 2012).

Roa López v. *Colombia*. (2006). Constitutional Court of Colombia, C-355/06. Available at: <http://www.law.georgetown.edu/oneillinstitute/global-health-law/who-hhr/caselaw-detail.cfm?id=1591&b=1> (accessed 7 November 2012).

South Africa Every Death Counts Writing Group. (2008). Every death counts: use of mortality audit data for decision making to save the lives of mothers, babies, and children in South Africa. *Lancet*, 371, 1294–1304.

UNDP. (2011). *Human Development Report 2011, Sustainability and Equity: A Better Future For All*. United Nations Development Programme (UNDP): New York, NY. Available at: <http://hdr.undp.org/en/media/HDR_2011_EN_Complete.pdf> (accessed 7 November 2012).

UNICEF. (2008a). *State Of The World's Children 2009*. United Nations Children's Fund (UNICEF): Geneva. Available at: <http://www.unicef.org/sowc09/docs/SOWC09-FullReport-EN.pdf> (accessed 7 November 2012).

UNICEF. (2008b). *Progress for Children: A Report Card On Maternal Mortality, Number 7*. United Nations Children's Fund (UNICEF): Geneva. Available at: <http://www.unicef.org/childsurvival/files/Progress_for_Children-No._7_Lo-Res_082008.pdf> (accessed 7 November 2012).

UNICEF, WHO, World Bank, *et al*. (2011). *Levels and Trends in Child Mortality: Report 2011, Estimates Developed by the UN Inter-Agency Group for Child Mortality Estimation*. United Nations Children's Fund (UNICEF): Geneva, Switzerland. Available at: <http://www.unicef.org/media/files/Child_Mortality_Report_2011_Final.pdf> (accessed 7 November 2012).

UN. (2010). *The Human Right To Water And Sanitation*. G.A. res. 64/292. United Nations (UN): New York, NY. Available at: <http://www.un.org/ga/search/view_doc.asp?symbol=A/RES/64/292> (accessed 7 November 2012).

UN Convention against Corruption. (2003). G.A. Res. 58/4, Art. 60. United Nations (UN): New York, NY. Available at: <http://www.unodc.org/documents/treaties/UNCAC/Publications/Convention/08-50026_E.pdf> (accessed 7 November 2012).

World Health Assembly. (2010). *WHO Global Code of Practice on the International Recruitment of Health Personnel: 63.16 May 2021*. World Health Organization (WHO): Geneva. Available at: <http://www.who.int/hrh/migration/code/WHO_global_code_of_practice_EN.pdf> (accessed 7 November 2012).

WHO. (1946). *Preamble to the Constitution of the World Health Organization as adopted by the International Health Conference, New York, 19–22 June, 1946; signed on 22 July 1946*. World Health Organization: New York, NY.

WHO. (2010). *The World Health Report—Health Systems Financing: The Path To Universal Coverage*. World Health Organization (WHO): Geneva. Available at: <http://www.who.int/whr/2010/en/index.html> (accessed 7 November 2012).

WHO. (2012). *Health Impact Assessment (HIA): HIA Related Sites*. World Health Organization (WHO): Geneva. Available at: <http://www.who.int/hia/network/related/en/index.html> (accessed 7 November 2012).

WHO Framework Convention on Tobacco Control. (2003). *World Health Assembly Res. 56.1, Art. 22(1)(b)(i)*. World Health Organization (WHO): Geneva. Available at: <http://whqlibdoc.who.int/publications/2003/9241591013.pdf> (accessed 7 November 2012).

WHO, UNAIDS, and UNICEF. (2011). *Global HIV/AIDS Response: Epidemic Update and Health Sector Progress Towards Universal Access, Progress Report 2011*. World Health Organization (WHO): Geneva. Available at: <http://whqlibdoc.who.int/publications/2011/9789241502986_eng.pdf> (accessed 7 November 2012).

WHO, UNICEF, UNFPA, *et al*. (2010). *Trends in Maternal Mortality: 1990 to 2008*. World Health Organization (WHO): Geneva. Available at: <http://whqlibdoc.who.int/publications/2010/9789241500265_eng.pdf> (accessed 7 November 2012).

Xákmok Kásek Indigenous Community v. *Paraguay*. (2010). Inter-American Court of Human Rights, Series C, No. 214 August 2024, Paras. 300-306. Available at: <http://www.worldcourts.com/iacthr/eng/decisions/2010.08.24_Xakmok_Kasek_v_Paraguay.pdf> (accessed 7 November 2012).

Yamin, A.E. and Parra-Vera, O. (2010). Judicial protection of the right to health in Colombia: from social demands to individual claims to public debates. *Hastings International and Comparative Law Review*, 33, 101–129.

Zahid, R. (2007). *Gender Reform Action Plan—A Breakthrough for Pakistani Women? A Policy Research Using Health Rights of Women Assessment Instrument (Herwai)*. Available at: <http://www.humanrightsimpact.org/resource-database/reports/resources/view/42/user_hria_reports/> (accessed 7 November 2012).

Section 2

The right to health in action

Chapter 6

Haiti: an overview of its right to health history and future directions

Donna J. Barry, Kate Greene, Wesler Lambert, Fernet Léandre, and Loune Viaud

Introduction

The nation of Haiti occupies one-third of the island of Hispaniola with a population of 9.8 million and a nearly even split between urban and rural populations (UNICEF, 2012). Haiti's history has been one of invasion, occupation, slavery, political instability, dictatorship, and, most recently, democracy. However, Haiti's turbulent history, including centuries of explicit and implicit interference by France and the United States, has had a severe impact on its development. It is thus no surprise that Haiti is currently the poorest country in and accounts for the worst health indicators among the countries in the Western Hemisphere (World Bank, 2012a).

After centuries of colonization, during which the indigenous population was killed off and the remaining population consisted of slaves brought from Africa (Jenson, 2005), a 12-year slave revolt ended in 1804 with Haiti becoming the first independent black republic, subsequently inspiring other former slave colonies to rise up and gain independence (James, 1938/2001). The victory was short-lived, with immediate isolation by the United States for fear of reprisals against slavery within its own borders, and commercial embargoes by France and the United States (Dubois, 2005). In addition, in 1827 France demanded payment for lost property by threatening to reinvade the country. Haiti was thus saddled with its first debt, which took 95 years to pay off and augured the country's economic decline (Schuller, 2006). Since the revolution of 1791–1804, Haiti has had 54 presidents (Buss & Gardner, 2008), and the first democratically elected president, Jean-Bertrand Aristide, was deposed twice with US assistance after two separate, fair elections. The past two presidential elections have had relatively peaceful transitions of power (Freedom House, 2012).

While the vast majority of the population has historically lived under the poverty line and continues to do so, from 2005 to 2009 Haiti enjoyed relatively stable economic growth until the devastating magnitude 7.0 earthquake in January 2010 provided yet another hurdle for the impoverished nation to overcome. Just ten months after the earthquake, Haiti experienced an epidemic of cholera, a disease which had not been previously documented in Haiti. As of May 2012, cholera has killed more than 7000 Haitians (MSPP, 2012). Introduced by foreign sources, the cholera epidemic is emblematic of how high levels of poverty and poor access to healthcare, clean water, and sanitation can explode into a crisis situation and lead to deadly consequences for the entire population.

National health overview

Haiti's health indicators compare unfavourably with every other country in the Latin America and the Caribbean (LAC) region. Many discrepancies in common health indicator data exist and, where necessary, ranges are presented. Data have been sourced from Haiti's Ministère de la Santé Publique et de la Population (MSPP), United Nations Children's Fund (UNICEF), and the World Health Organization (WHO). Life expectancy is currently 54 (MSPP, 2011) to 62 years (WHO, 2011), as compared to 73 years for the neighbouring Dominican Republic (PAHO, 2011). Infant mortality stands at 57 (PAHO, 2007) to 64 (WHO, 2011) per 1000 live births and maternal mortality at 630 deaths per 100,000 births or 300 deaths with adjusted rates which were revised by the WHO in 2008 (PAHO, 2007; WHO, 2011). The total fertility rate in Haiti is 3.34, tying with Bolivia for the highest rate in the LAC region (World Bank, 2012b). Contraceptive prevalence is only at 32%, and only 26% of births are attended by professionally trained personnel (WHO, 2011).

Haiti has the highest rates of tuberculosis (TB) (306/100,000) and HIV (2.2%) in the Western Hemisphere (MSPP, 2010), and malaria continues to be a constant danger to unprotected populations. Even before the cholera outbreak, diarrheal disease caused 22% of childhood mortality (WHO, 2011). Immunization coverage for common vaccines such as diphtheria and polio stands at only 59% (UNICEF, 2010).

Malnutrition rates are exceedingly high: 25% of infants are born with low birth weight; 18% of children under five years old are moderately to severely underweight; and 10% of children under five years old suffer from moderate to severe wasting (UNICEF, 2010). Access to clean water in 2008, measured in percentage of population with access to improved water sources, was only 63% nationally, with great disparities between urban and rural populations, the rates for which were 71% and 55%, respectively (UNICEF, 2010). However, since the cholera outbreak, these rates have likely drastically declined. Rates of access to basic sanitation are some of the worst globally. Only 17% of the total population reports having access to improved sanitation facilities, once again masking gross disparities between rural and urban populations, where the rates are 10% and 24%, respectively (UNICEF, 2010).

Access to healthcare is severely restricted by a lack of government resources, poverty levels which curtail private expenditures, a dearth of well-functioning facilities, and very low numbers of professional healthcare workers. External funding for healthcare in Haiti has had a dramatic impact on which sector (public or private) is able to provide services. As of 2009, annual per capita spending on health in Haiti was US$40 (WHO, 2011). This disguises the fact that only US$15 per capita spending is from government revenue; the rest, or 66%, is from external sources (WHO, 2011). Government expenditure as a percentage of total health expenditure is only 22%, and thus private (per person) expenditure as a percentage of total expenditure on health is over 77% (WHO, 2011). Given that 54% of the population lives below the international poverty line of US$1.25 income per day (PAHO, 2007), it is no wonder that 47% of Haitians lack access to healthcare (MSPP, 2010).

Haiti has some of the world's worst healthcare worker per population ratios. There are only 2.5 physicians and 1.1 nurses per 10,000 people and the vast majority of them are located in the capital city, Port-au-Prince, and other large urban centres (Library of Congress, 2006). Officially, Haiti's MSPP has broad coverage with health posts and centres, as well as hospitals, distributed across the country. However, in reality many of these public health services are poorly maintained, equipped, and staffed. A recent study highlighted the irrelevance of this coverage given that 70% of healthcare is provided by non-governmental organizations (NGOs) (Zanotti, 2010).

Haiti's human rights' obligations

The government of Haiti is the primary guarantor of its citizens' human rights and is obligated to respect, protect, and fulfil the right to health. As stated in the preamble of the 1987 Constitution of the Republic of Haiti, the State is required to organize a system of government respecting human rights (Constitution of the Republic of Haiti, 1987). Section A, Article 19 of the Constitution explicitly states, 'The State has the absolute obligation to guarantee the right to life, health, and respect of the human person for all citizens without distinction, in conformity with the Universal Declaration of Human Rights' (Constitution of the Republic of Haiti, 1987). According to Article 23 of the same Section, 'The State has the obligation to ensure for all citizens in all territorial divisions appropriate means to ensure protection, maintenance and restoration of their health by establishing hospitals, health centres, and dispensaries' (Constitution of the Republic of Haiti, 1987).

Haiti is also a signatory and party to multiple international treaties which obligate the government to ensure the right to health. Haiti ratified the International Covenant on Civil and Political Rights (ICCPR) in 1991; the Convention on the Elimination of All Forms of Discrimination against Women (CEDAW) in 1981; the Convention on the Rights of the Child (CRC) in 1995; and the American Convention on Human Rights (Pact of San José) in 1977. In addition, the government signed, and recently ratified the International Covenant on Economic, Social and Cultural Rights (ICESCR) and has signed, but not yet ratified, the Additional Protocol to the American Convention on Human Rights in the Area of Economic, Social and Cultural Rights (Protocol of San Salvador).

Right to health: availability, accessibility, acceptability, and quality

As guaranteed by the constitution, and as a party to and signatory of multiple treaties, the country's government has the obligation to fulfil the right to health for its citizens. However, given centuries of political turmoil, interference of other states, and an inordinately high percentage of foreign assistance and provision of care by international partners, the right to health has been poorly protected and fulfilled. The country's health statistics reflect this inability to assure the availability, accessibility, acceptability, and quality of healthcare.

Availability

While, on paper, it appears that, based on population distribution, healthcare facilities are decentralized and distributed across the country, most public facilities are woefully resourced and thus do not have enough staff or medical supplies, medications, and space to adequately treat the needs of those who present for care. In addition, given that the majority of care is provided through private for-profit and not-for-profit organizations, the government should have the capacity to regulate both what types of care is provided and its quality. However, given that most international funding goes to NGOs rather than to support the government, this regulatory capacity is absent. In addition, given the verticality of foreign assistance, some health issues, such as HIV/AIDS, are well supported, while other important conditions, such as chronic disease, remain under-resourced. Externally funded projects typically only last three to five years and rarely lead to sustainable programmes. Once the foreign assistance has ended or international NGOs lose funding, the programmes are often discontinued. This has been evident in cholera care and treatment programmes, where a withdrawal of foreign assistance and NGOs led to a shortage of prevention and treatment programmes just 18 months into the country's first cholera epidemic (Center for Economic and Policy Research, 2011).

Accessibility

Most of Haiti's specialty care and its best-trained healthcare professionals are located in Port-au-Prince. Basic primary care is available in many parts of the country; however, it is still primarily located in urban areas, even though much of the population lives in remote, rural areas. For those who live in rural areas, transportation costs and distances to clinics and hospitals can be substantial barriers to care.

Not all care through the public sector is free, although the most vulnerable populations do not have to pay fees. These populations include children under five and pregnant women. Most care for HIV/AIDS, TB, and malaria is covered by international assistance and is therefore available free of charge. With the level of poverty in Haiti, any fees for healthcare are cost prohibitive. Given that antenatal care and deliveries are free, one would expect far more facility-based births instead of the mere 26% attended by skilled personnel in facilities in urban areas, and 15% in rural areas (WHO, 2011). In addition, only 54% of pregnant women receive the recommended four antenatal visits (WHO, 2011). These figures highlight the likelihood of hidden fees as well as lack of accessibility to quality facilities to receive antenatal care and give birth.

On a more positive note, Haiti was one of the first low-income countries in the world to start providing treatment for HIV/AIDS. HIV testing and treatment was prioritized early in the country's epidemic, and Haiti was one of the first recipients of a grant from the Global Fund to Fight AIDS, TB and Malaria (Global Fund). The HIV infection rate in the country has declined from 3.8% in 2005 to 1.9% in 2011 (WHO et al., 2011), which highlights how effective and important free care is in the country. And, where HIV/AIDS funding has been spent in public sector facilities, it has led to increased utilization of other services including prenatal care, childhood vaccination, and other primary care (Walton et al., 2004).

Acceptability

Where care is available and provided by well-trained and adequately supported Haitian health professionals, it is culturally appropriate and grounded in medical ethics. Haiti's State medical and nursing schools, as well as a handful of private schools, provide excellent education, and graduates from those programmes are highly sought after in both the public and private sectors. With its proximity to the United States and neighbouring Caribbean islands, as well as decades of political and economic insecurity, the attrition rate for nurses and physicians is particularly high. This 'brain drain' has a substantial effect on the quality and quantity of healthcare provided in Haiti. In some regions, community health workers (CHWs) have helped fill the void in service delivery (Jerome & Ivers, 2010). Because the CHWs are from the communities they serve, care is grounded in community principles and local culture.

Quality

As previously discussed, where healthcare is available in well-equipped health centres with well-supported healthcare professionals, quality care is offered in Haiti. However, health statistics lay bare the fact that much of the care provided in Haiti is of poor quality. Given the paucity of funding with which the MSPP has to ensure the quality of care in Haiti, regulation of the quality of services has not been a high priority. In fact, once again highlighting the influence of foreign assistance on Haiti's health outcomes, it is important to note that quality of care indicators are rarely collected by donors; instead, the number (quantity) of patients in care and treatment has been prioritized. The Global Fund and US President's Emergency Plan for AIDS Relief (PEPFAR), both major funders in Haiti over the past decade, have focused on achieving continual increases of numbers of patients in care and treatment, rather than retention of those patients and the quality of care they receive. However, a number of quality indicators are beginning to be collected and, as a result, quality of care in these programmes may begin to be measured and improved.

Violations of Haitians' right to health

Not only has Haiti's health sector been dependent on foreign assistance and dominated by donor priorities for healthcare, the aid has fluctuated greatly based on the political circumstances. Taking into consideration the large percentage of donor aid spent on healthcare in Haiti, it is critical to examine the consistency of that aid as well as whether its use or conditions have violated or helped fulfil the right to health in Haiti.

US assistance to Haiti has been suspended and reinstated numerous times to achieve political goals. When President Aristide was first elected President in 1990, US foreign assistance rose in support of the democratically elected president and his government after decades of rule by the Duvalier dictators. Seven months after his election, a military coup overthrew President Aristide, and all aid except humanitarian aid was suspended (Hallward, 2007). The Clinton administration helped bring him back to power and restored aid in 1994. Aristide was replaced by René Préval in 1995, but was re-elected in 2000, following elections considered *by some* to be fraudulent. Again, US aid was suspended but was ultimately restored by the Bush administration after a coup forced Aristide out of office in 2004 and a transitional government was established (Hallward, 2007).

The way in which aid to Haiti has been manipulated by more powerful forces is best illustrated by a case study that also relates the obligations, both fulfilled and violated, that donors and non-State actors bear in fulfilling human rights in this impoverished nation. In 1998 the Inter-American Development Bank (IDB) approved a US$54 million dollar loan to the government of Haiti to improve water and sanitation in two communities in Haiti. The projects funded by the loans would decrease the cost of clean water to the poorest residents of these communities—highly important given widespread inaccessibility to clean water and sanitation. Haiti ratified the loans in 2000 and a year later paid its outstanding arrears to the IDB, thus meeting the contractual requirements of the new loans. The loan processing should have begun at that time. However, the United States began expressing concerns about the loans. This concern was politically based and reflected US discomfort with then-President Aristide, rather than being based on the ability of Haiti to comply with or implement the projects funded by the loans. In fact, the United States offered to release a 'hold' on the loans in exchange for political reform in Haiti. The IDB's Articles of Agreement (Inter-American Development Bank, 1996) explicitly prohibit interference in the political affairs of any Member-State. There was a great deal of backroom discussion between the US-based Executive Director to the IDB, the US Department of the Treasury, and the US Embassy in Haiti—all of which was inappropriate based on the IDB's Articles of Agreement.

Because the United States could not formally or publicly prevent the loans from being disbursed, behind the scenes US officials began to delay the loans by requesting a report identifying why the loans had not been released (Center for Human Rights and Global Justice et al., 2008). Other measures were used to postpone the loans, including requesting that the Organization of American States (OAS) comment on the loans over which they had no authority. The delay tactics were successful as Haiti fell into arrears on current and pending loans, including the loans which were being blocked. In late 2001, then Ambassador to Haiti, Dean Curran, inadvertently spoke publicly about

US intentions to block the loans. While public criticism and rallies led to an OAS resolution to normalize relations between Haiti and international financial institutions in the autumn of 2002, Haiti did not have enough foreign currency to begin paying the accrued arrears.

Once again, much negotiating took place behind the scenes in order to block and release the loans, culminating in an agreement in mid-2003, which allowed Haiti to pay its arrears and be eligible for loan disbursement (Center for Human Rights and Global Justice et al., 2008). Yet again, the United States found another tactic to prevent loan disbursal by accusing Haiti of human trafficking, which would have placed it in a category for which sanctions could be applied. Finally, near the end of 2003, the IDB restarted the process to release the loans. But in February 2004, the United States achieved their ultimate goal; President Aristide was removed from office in a *coup d'état* and the loans were once again delayed.

When the *Wòch nan Soley* report was drafted in 2007, the loans had been disbursed and were in the implementation phase. They have now been completed and water and sanitation systems have been improved in Port-au-Paix and Saint Marc. However, beyond publishing and promoting of this report, there is no redress for those whose access to clean water and health was affected by the United States' political interference in the disbursement of the life-saving loans. What the authors of this report ultimately prove is that in countries like Haiti where the State has inadequate resources to fulfil the rights of their own citizens, actors with greater resources and more global influence, like the United States and the IDB, wield significantly more power than the State. These actors have corresponding obligations, at the very least, not to violate human rights:

> Given all these obligations, it is clear that actions taken by the United States in blocking IDB development loans earmarked for water projects in Haiti were a direct violation of the US government's human rights obligations . . . In this case, the United States actively impeded the Haitian State's ability to fulfill the Haitian people's human right to water through its actions, thus breaching its duty to respect human rights. (Center for Human Rights and Global Justice et al., 2008)

Given Haiti's primary reliance on foreign assistance to fulfil its citizens' right to health, there are undoubtedly additional violations of Haitians' right to health which donor entities, bilateral and multilateral, have been either complicit or primary violators, or both.

Evolving responses and obligations: future directions towards the right to health

A shift in the recipients of foreign assistance and the way in which externally funded projects are implemented are critical to improving the right to health in Haiti. New funding and project implementation should be based on a human rights approach to improve the availability, accessibility, acceptability, and quality of health services. However, foreign aid recipients since the 2010 earthquake and subsequent cholera outbreak do not reflect a change despite many promises from donors. Less than 1% of relief or humanitarian funding after the earthquake went to the Haitian government and it has received the least amount of funding as compared to NGOs and other implementers to address the cholera epidemic (Office of the Special Envoy for Haiti, 2012).

If the health of Haitian citizens is to be improved and the right to health for all Haitians fulfilled, an entirely new approach to providing healthcare—which is both domestically and internationally funded—is required. Such an approach must include more input from both the recipients of healthcare and related services, and embrace Haitians coordinating and implementing the health services. The Haitian MSPP and other relevant ministries must be involved in the planning, implementation, regulation, and evaluation of all projects being implemented in their country.

Aid should be based on addressing all health concerns from primary to tertiary care and help strengthen Haitian healthcare institutions, mainly those based in the public sector since they serve the majority of the impoverished population.

More aid should be channelled to and through the MSPP and other relevant ministries including those overseeing food and nutrition, housing, transportation, and water and sanitation. Direct assistance to the government of Haiti in order to provide salary support, operating costs, regulatory oversight, and systems for management and reporting to donors are a priority. Many aid agencies and NGO partners complain that there is no capacity in Haiti's ministries to implement and manage projects. What is rarely, if ever, mentioned by donors and international partners is that these ministries would greatly benefit from the aid in order to increase their capacity as good implementing partners.

Multiple bilateral donors to Haiti, including the United States, have signed on to and are beginning to implement steps to improve aid effectiveness. By pooling external funds for use by recipient governments and engaging more local partners in implementation, pillars of aid effectiveness, the right to health and health indicators are likely to improve in Haiti. In 2011, the US Agency for International Development (USAID) began to reform its procurement process and direct funding to governments and more local, in-country institutions. It remains to be seen if this reform will extend to Haiti.

Haiti's MSPP is reviewing national health financing options. The system now reflects its lack of planning and coordination, and is cobbled together from user fees, additional private out-of-pocket expenditures, and international funding. A new health financing system should also be based on the right to health and improve availability, accessibility, acceptability, and quality. This means the government of Haiti should extend the policy of not requiring user fees for maternal and child health services to include all services in the public sector. The taxation system should be reformed and better staffed so that internal revenue collection can provide a greater share of the resources used for healthcare.

The next few years of aid and health system reform will be critical to improving the health of Haiti's citizens and to building quality, sustainable healthcare to improve the right to health in Haiti. The government of Haiti, along with bilateral and multilateral partners, has the opportunity to rebuild a system based on the right to health and thus meet all Haitians' health needs. Authors contributing to future books such as this one will hopefully find a much improved, rights-based health system in Haiti with its primary outcome being positive health outcomes.

Acknowledgements

The authors acknowledge Meredy Throop and Ashley Ahlholm who conducted background research for the chapter.

References

Buss, T.F. and Gardner, A. (2008). *Haiti in the Balance: Why Foreign Aid Has Failed and What We Can Do About It*. Brookings Institution Press: Washington, DC.

Center for Economic and Policy Research. (2011). *Cholera Cases Down, But Are Past Mistakes Being Repeated?* Available at: <http://www.cepr.net/index.php/blogs/relief-and-reconstruction-watch/cholera-cases-down-but-are-past-mistakes-being-repeated> (accessed 22 August 2012).

Center for Human Rights and Global Justice at New York University School of Law, Partners In Health, Robert F. Kennedy Center for Human Rights, *et al.* (2008). *Wòch nan Soley: The Denial of the Right to Water in Haiti*. The Center for Human Rights and Global Justice: New York, NY.

Constitution of the Republic of Haiti. (1987). National Legislative Bodies: Haiti.

Dubois, L. (2005). *Avengers of the New World: The Story of the Haitian Revolution.* Harvard University Press: Cambridge, MA.

Freedom House (2012). *Countries at the Crossroads 2012 – Haiti.* Freedom House: Washington, DC. Available at: <http://www.unhcr.org/refworld/docid/505c1731c.html> (accessed 9 October 2012).

Hallward, P. (2007). *Damming the Flood: Haiti, Aristide, and the Politics of Containment.* Verso: New York, NY.

Inter-American Development Bank. (1996). *Agreement Establishing the Inter-American Development Bank.* Available at: <http://idbdocs.iadb.org/wsdocs/getdocument.aspx?docnum=781584> (accessed 6 May 2012).

James, C.L.R. (2001). *The Black Jacobins: Toussaint L'Ouverture and the San Domingo Revolution.* Penguin Books: New York, NY. (Original work published 1938.)

Jenson, D. (2005). Nineteenth-century 'postcolonialités' at the bicentennial of the Haitian independence. *Yale French Studies, The Haiti Issue: 1804 and Nineteenth-Century French Studies,* 107, 1–5.2.

Jerome, J.G. and Ivers, L.C. (2010). Community health workers in health systems strengthening: a qualitative evaluation from rural Haiti. *AIDS,* 24(Supp 1), S67–S72.

Library of Congress – Federal Research Division. (2006). *Haiti Country Profile* (May 2006). Available at: <http://lcweb2.loc.gov/frd/cs/profiles/Haiti.pdf> (accessed 22 August 2012).

MSPP. (2010). *Plan Interimaire du Secteur Santé.* Ministère de la Santé Publique et de la Population [Ministry of Public and Population Health, MSPP]: Port-au-Prince. Available at: <http://www.mspp.gouv.ht/site/download/plan_interimaire.pdf> (accessed 20 August 2012).

MSPP. (2011). *Executive Summary – Health.* Ministère de la Santé Publique et de la Population [Ministry of Public and Population Health, MSPP]: Port-au-Prince. Available at: <http://www.mspp.gouv.ht/site/downloads/sante.pdf> (accessed 20 April 2012).

MSPP. (2012). *Ministere de la Santé Publique et de la Population Rapport de Cas.* Ministère de la Santé Publique et de la Population [Ministry of Public and Population Health, MSPP]: Port-au-Prince. Available at: <http://www.mspp.gouv.ht/site/downloads/Rapport%20journalier%20MSPP%20du%2030%20septembre%202012.pdf> (accessed 08 October 2012).

Office of the Special Envoy for Haiti. (2012). *Humanitarian Pledges and Recipients for the Cholera Response from Public Sector Donors [as of March 2012 in USD millions].* Available at: <http://www.haitispecialenvoy.org/download/International_Assistance/4-relief-cholera-status.pdf> (accessed 14 May 2012).

PAHO. (2007). *Health Situation in the Americas: Basic Indicators.* Pan American Health Organization (PAHO): Washington, DC. Available at: <http://www.paho.org/english/dd/ais/BI_2007_ENG.pdf> (accessed 22 August 2012).

PAHO. (2011). *Basic Health Indicators.* Available at: <http://ais.paho.org/phip/viz/basicindicatorbrowaser.asp> (accessed 21 April 2012).

Schuller, M. (2006). *Jubilee USA Network: Break the Chains of Haiti's Debt. 2.* Available at: <http://www.jubileeusa.org/fileadmin/user_upload/Resources/Policy_Archive/haitireport06.pdf> (accessed 22 August 2012).

UNICEF. (2010). *Level and Trends in Child Mortality.* United Nations Children's Fund (UNICEF): New York, NY.

UNICEF. (2012). *At a Glance: Haiti.* Available at: <http://www.unicef.org/infobycountry/haiti_statistics.html> (accessed 8 October 2012).

Walton, D., Farmer, P.E., Lambert, W., *et al.* (2004). Integrated HIV prevention and care strengthens primary health care: lessons from rural Haiti. *Journal of Public Health Policy,* 25(2), 137–158.

WHO. (2011). *World Health Statistics.* World Health Organization (WHO): Geneva. Available at: <http://www.who.int/whosis/whostat/2011/en/index.html> (accessed 3 May 2012).

WHO, UNAIDS, and UNICEF. (2011). *Global HIV/AIDS Response: Epidemic Update and Health Sector Progress Toward Universal Access*. World Health Organization (WHO): Geneva. Available at: <http://www.unaids.org/en/media/unaids/contentassets/documents/unaidspublication/2011/20111130_UA_Report_en.pdf> (accessed 9 October 2012).

World Bank. (2012a). *Haiti Country Bank*. Available at: <http://www.worldbank.org/en/country/haiti/overview> (accessed 8 October 2012).

World Bank. (2012b). *Fertility Rate, Total (Births per Woman)*. Available at: <http://data.worldbank.org/indicator/SP.DYN.TFRT.IN/countries> (accessed 20 August 2012).

Zanotti, L. (2010). Cacophonies of aid, failed state building and NGOs in Haiti: setting the stage for disaster, envisioning the future. *Third World Quarterly*, 31(15), 755–771.

Chapter 7

The right to health in Ghana: healthcare, human rights, and politics

Raymond A. Atuguba

Introduction

Ghana gained independence from the British in 1957, and under the leadership of Kwame Nkrumah, it attained Republican status in 1960. However, after President Nkrumah was overthrown in 1966, Ghana was ruled by military regimes until 1993, except for two brief constitutional democratic interregnums in 1969 and 1979. Ghana also experienced an economic slump in the 1970s and early 1980s, leading to an economic recovery programme, which incorporated the structural adjustment programme of the mid-1980s, led by the World Bank and the International Monetary Fund (IMF). These reforms had many ripple effects, including public and civil service, educational, and ultimately democratic reforms. Today, Ghana is politically stable and has been for over two decades; it has produced crude oil in commercial quantities since 2010; it has stable institutions; and has recently attained the status of a lower middle-income country.

Overview of Ghana's health status

Ghana's population currently numbers 24.9 million (UNDP, 2011) and is expected to double within approximately 28 years (Ghana Statistical Service, 2010). Seventy per cent of men and 58% of women above age 15 are literate (UNDP, 2009). Ghana's gross domestic product (GDP) per capita is estimated to be US$1410 (World Bank, 2011a). In addition, Ghana's Human Development Index (HDI) ranking is 135 out of 187 (UNDP, 2011).

Ghana's health indicators have shown steady improvement over the past few decades. In 1960, Ghanaians could expect to live for just 46 years (UNICEF, 2008). Today, life expectancy is 64.2 years (UNDESA, 2011; World Bank, 2011b). Ghana currently experiences declining mortality in addition to its high fertility rate. The under-five mortality ratio is 69 per 1000 live births (UNICEF, 2011), a substantial decrease from 215 per 1000 in 1960 (UNICEF, 2005).

Although the data indicate progress in the area of health and development, Ghana nevertheless has significant need to improve the health and development outcomes of its population. Between 3.1 and 3.5 million clinical cases of malaria are reported each year; an estimated 14,000 deaths in children under five were attributed to malaria in 2008 (President's Malaria Initiative, 2011). In 2009, United Nations Children's Fund (UNICEF) reported that 260,000 people were living with HIV in Ghana (UNICEF, 2011).

Human rights laws and accountability frameworks

Ghanaians have placed human rights at centre stage during the last two decades of constitutional democratic rule. The Constitution Review Commission was set up in January 2010 to consult with the people of Ghana on necessary revisions to and operation of the 1992 Constitution (Constitution Review Commission, 2011). Chapter 5 of the 1992 Constitution, containing 33 Articles, is dedicated to human rights, while Chapter 6, 'The Directive Principles of State Policy', sets out economic, social, cultural, and developmental rights, including 'the right to good [healthcare]', which has been interpreted by the Constitution Review Commission as a positive recognition of the right to health as a full-fledged right (Constitution Review Commission, 2011).

Right to health in Ghana

While the right to health was incorporated in the language of the 1992 Constitution of Ghana, the courts have not yet issued any decisions interpreting the meaning and scope of the language. Many argue that the Ghanaian State has some affirmative responsibilities towards its citizens in the health domain and that the fundamental right to health is positively enforceable under the Constitution. They argue thus, in light of the omnibus rights provision in Article 33(5), which provides that, '[t]he rights, duties, declarations, and guarantees relating to the fundamental human rights and freedoms specifically mentioned . . . shall not be regarded as excluding others not specifically mentioned which are considered to be inherent in a democracy and intended to secure the freedom and dignity of man' (Constitution of Ghana, 1992).

Healthcare was a key political issue in the 2004 and 2008 presidential campaigns in Ghana (Rajkotia, 2007). The performance of the National Health Insurance Scheme, which was implemented in 2004 as an election promise, remains at the centre stage of national discourse. New opportunities for health policy reform are emerging, which were absent in the days of structural adjustment. Further, new funds for healthcare are available due to increasing willingness of governments and international financial institutions to lend money to Ghana; tax reform; increased economic activity related to new technologies; and new sources of oil and gas production.

This chapter discusses broad issues of human rights, politics, and national and international economic management in light of public concerns about healthcare and the lack of government initiative to take advantage of opportunities to design a health system that meets the needs of its people.

Healthcare in Ghana: access, quality, and financing

Discussions around healthcare policy in Ghana focus on financing, access, and the quality of healthcare services, and often ignore the psychological health dimensions of healthcare.

Access to healthcare services

Serious disparities exist in access to healthcare services in Ghana. In 2003, only 57.7% of the population had access to medical services (Ghana Statistical Service, 2003). Rural populations continue to have less access to care than urban: more than 80% of people in the Greater Accra Region were within 30 minutes of the nearest health facility, compared to 57.7% of the national population in 2003 (Ghana Statistical Service, 2003). Access was lowest (20.9%) in the Upper East Region, one of the poorest regions in the country (Ghana Statistical Service, 2003). Health indicators from the Ghana Living Standards Survey further indicated that about 40% of persons in need of medical services in 2005 to 2006 did not consult medical personnel (Ghana Living Standards Survey, 2005).

Access to care is influenced by demand, as well as the cost of care, and the amount of trained healthcare personnel available. According to the 2007 Human Development Report (HDR), there was one physician to 17,733 persons in 2004 (UNDP, 2007). In northern and western parts of Ghana poor road networks and inadequate infrastructure discourage health personnel from accepting postings in these areas (UNDP, 2007). Medical personnel are overworked, which threatens the quality of medical care. Long waiting times also mean that patients lose precious time attending to their jobs (Wireko, 2008). The high cost of care often results in patient inability to pay for services. Many patients opt for self-medication and present at hospital only when the situation is critical—often too late. Increasing numbers of Ghanaians have returned to alternative medicine in the last two decades, because it is culturally accepted and very accessible. It is not uncommon for someone with a broken bone to visit an herbalist for treatment instead of going to the hospital (Legal Recourses Center, 2008). These factors have led some experts to call for a more vigorous integration of traditional medicine into the healthcare system, much as China and India have done (Akosah-Sarpong, 2008). Recently, the government has established a Traditional Medicine Practice Council and is seeking to incorporate traditional medicine into mainstream medical practice in Ghana.

Quality of care

The quality of the care accessed in Ghanaian public hospitals and healthcare centres is poor and the infrastructure is inadequate. Many patients in critical condition have no beds and diagnostic equipment; where it exists, it is either in disrepair or under-serviced (Dovlo, 2003). As noted earlier, physicians are overworked, which negatively affects the quality of their services. Many patients report they are not treated well at hospitals and health centres. They wait long hours, even when they are in severe pain, and they have to endure chastisement from healthcare workers who are overworked (NHIA, 2012). To the extent that human and physical resources can be bought with cash, financial resources are paramount to realizing the right to health in Ghana.

Financing of health services

The cost of funding healthcare in Ghana has become too high for the government to bear alone (Konrad Adenauer Foundation, 1999). There are five key sources of healthcare financing in Ghana: the government's budget; external donors; healthcare institutions; charitable donations, mainly from religious institutions; and private, out-of-pocket funds, which are equal to the amount spent by the government.

Ghana's health budget has remained stable at around 11% to 12% during the second half of this decade (Azeem & Adamtey, 2006). In 2011, Ghana's public expenditure on health was 4.3% of its GDP (World Bank, 2011a). In a country with significant disease burden, Ghana's health expenditure is relatively small. This has led to a substantial financing gap, which has fallen on the private consumer. A number of policy changes have sought to remedy this consumer burden, yet it has not been an easy task.

The history of financing healthcare in Ghana

By 1985, President Jerry John Rawlings was forced to respond to demands by international financial institutions to make cuts in the country's public expenditures. As a result, his administration passed the Hospital Fees Regulations (Legislative Instrument No. 1313, 1985), which raised fee levels substantially. This instrument mandated fees for consultation, laboratory and other diagnostic procedures, dental and surgical services, medical examinations, and hospital accommodation. Patients were charged full price for their drugs, a process that earned the name 'cash and carry' (NHIS, 2012).

In the 1990s, extensive research was conducted on the negative distributional impact of health policies, including user fees, which had been imposed by international financial institutions on the Ghanaian government during the mid-1980s as part of structural adjustment (Schoepf et al., 2000). Policies that exempt vulnerable populations from fee requirements have failed in practice due to under-enforcement and the inability to take advantage of such benefits. Without the necessary cash, many patients have been detained at health institutions until they can pay their bills. For example, the detention of many mothers after childbirth until their medical bills were settled was, until recently, an everyday phenomenon in Ghana. It is these inhumane features of the cash and carry system of financing healthcare that rekindled national interest in a search for alternatives.

With the adoption of the 1992 Constitution, public discourse began to focus on the human rights dimensions of Ghana's healthcare financing system. Human rights groups argue that it is the duty of the government to develop, deploy, and monitor a system of healthcare financing in accord with basic human rights. The Legal Resources Centre in Ghana secured a ruling on the unconstitutionality of detaining mothers and children for their inability to pay medical bills (*Happy Abaji* v. *Administrator of La Polyclinic*, 2003). In July 2008, the Ghanaian government introduced a policy of free maternal healthcare under the National Health Insurance Scheme (NHIS). The National Health Insurance Council reported that it had already registered a total of 50,924 pregnant women, just 18 days after the inception of the programme (Yeboah & Appiah-Adjei, 2008). Funding for this new policy was provided by the British government and under this policy both the mother and child obtain free healthcare from the first day of pregnancy until a year after delivery. At the beginning of the 21st century, the government began to develop and implement a NHIS as a more sustainable mechanism for financing healthcare.

Ghana's National Health Insurance Scheme

The NHIS was proposed in the 2000 election to abolish the cash and carry system and accelerate improvements in health conditions of the general population, especially the poor. The NHIS recommended a multi-fund health insurance scheme that reflected the demographic configuration of the Ghanaian population. The Bill was passed into law (an Act of Parliament) in 2004 after many drafts and public discussions (NHIA, 2003, 2004).

The NHIS, in sum, sets a low premium; exempts people under age 18 and over 70 years of age and indigents from paying premiums; requires that entire families enrol in health insurance; provides a benefits package that covers 95% of the disease burden in Ghana; has no scheme for co-payments or deductibles; and is funded additionally by sales tax from a small tax net and social security contributions. The Act exempts the following from paying premiums: contributors to the national pension fund, the Social Security and National Insurance Trust (SSNIT); SSNIT pensioners; children under 18 whose parents or guardians are contributors; persons of 70 years and above; and indigents (NHIA, 2003).

The Act provides for the establishment of a National Health Insurance Council (NHIC) to regulate, oversee, and implement the Act to achieve its objectives. It also creates a National Health Insurance Fund (NHIF) composed of revenue from a 2.5% health insurance levy; a percentage (2.5%) of each person's contribution to the Social Security and Pensions Fund; monies allocated to the Fund by Parliament; monies accruing from investments made by the Council; and grants, donations, and voluntary contributions (NHIA, 2003). A benefit package of out-patient services, in-patient services, oral health services, eye care services, maternity care, and emergency care was included in the regulations made under the Act. An annual budgetary allocation has been established for the support of the healthcare needs of the medically indigent. The basic premium is set at about US$5 per year (NHIA, 2003).

The governing body of the NHIS is the NHIC, which is composed of representatives from critical government agencies, such as the Ministries of Health and Finance, and from civil society bodies, such as the Ghana Bar Association (NHIA, 2003). The NHIC registers, licenses, and provides accreditation to residents and providers; supervises and monitors operations; provides various services; issues identity cards and maintains a register; manages the NHIF; and ensures compliance with the Act (NHIA, 2003).

By June 2007, 9.5 million people (47% of the population) had registered with the NHIS, including those in the exempt group and informal sector who had made only partial payments (NHIC, 2007). About 6.5 million people (32% of the population) had been issued identification cards and could access healthcare services from NHIC-accredited providers without paying a fee (NHIC, 2007). Membership registration under the scheme reached an estimated 55% of the population by December 2007; of this, an estimated 48% of the population were card-bearing members who were able to access healthcare services purchased through insurance (NHIS, 2007). Despite these significant gains, problems of access, quality, and financing still exist in Ghana's healthcare system.

Ghana's National Health Insurance Scheme and the right to health

Ghana's NHIS is a typical example of a right to health policy. The right to health provision in Article 12 of the International Convention on Economic, Social and Cultural Rights (ICESCR) recognizes the right of 'everyone to the enjoyment of the highest attainable standard of physical and mental health' (ICESCR, 1976). The obligations of State Parties to the covenant for a full realization of the right include the prevention, treatment, and control of epidemic, endemic, occupational, and other diseases and the creation of conditions that would assure all persons medical services and medical attention in the event of sickness. Ghana ratified the ICESCR in the year 2000.

Assuring access to healthcare, as mandated in the right to health, has had cost implications. The sources of funding for the NHIS must therefore involve the international community, the State, and groups and individuals within the State, public and private alike. While the right to health is not officially considered a fundamental right, which the government is obligated to defend, at the very least, the right to health is part of the calculus that the electorate may use to assess the performance of a government and determine whether to vote them out of power or to allow them to stay in power. In the words of Article 36 of the 1992 Constitution:

> The Directive Principles of State Policy contained in this Chapter shall guide all citizens, Parliament, the President, the Judiciary, the Council of State, the Cabinet, political parties and other bodies and persons in applying or interpreting this Constitution or any other Law and in taking and implementing any policy decisions, for the establishment of a just and free society.
>
> ... The President shall report to Parliament at least once a year all the steps taken to ensure the realization of the policy objectives contained in this Chapter and, in particular, the realization of basic human rights, a healthy economy, the right to work, *the right to good health care* and the right to education. (Emphasis added; Constitution of Ghana, 1992)

A close reading of the NHIA shows that, in addition to replacing the discredited cash and carry system with an alternative scheme of healthcare financing, the Act was seen as necessary for the realization of a human right. The Memorandum to the Bill states that:

> Though the cash and carry system has problems, it cannot be abolished without finding a suitable mechanism for cost recovery in the health sector. There is a need to look for and institute a more humane alternative to the direct out of pocket at point of service user payments involved in the cash and carry system. (Emphasis added; NHIA, 2003)

To what extent does the NHIA respond to the need to institute a healthcare system that accords with the dignity of the human being? This brings us to an examination of the NHIS in practice.

The National Health Insurance Scheme in practice and the limits on securing the right to health

Before the NHIS, the cash and carry system created financial barriers to accessing healthcare, particularly for the poor. After the Health Insurance Act implemented in 2004, Ghanaian residents could access pre-defined healthcare services through District Mutual Health Insurance Schemes (DMHISs) by paying a small contribution, or by being classified under any of the exempt categories in the Act, without the need to pay for such services at the point of delivery. Provision is made under Act 650 for three types of health insurance schemes namely, the DHMISs, the Private Commercial Health Insurance Schemes (PCHISs), and the Private Mutual Health Insurance Schemes (PMHISs). Currently 145 DMHISs and four PMHISs have been granted authority to operate in the country (NHIS, 2012).

However, numerous challenges have constrained the realization of the NHIS. The first major problem is that the NHIS is overly decentralized. The law allows for the establishment of legally autonomous DMHISs in Ghana's 170 administrative districts. This legal and institutional framework has yielded a system which lacks administrative and financial oversight, clear lines of supervision, and due process.

The Act needs to be read alongside the 1992 Constitution of Ghana, especially Articles 23 and 296, which place limits on administrative bodies and administrative officials in terms of their powers. Article 23 requires that administrative bodies and administrative officials act 'reasonably and comply with the requirements imposed on them by law', while Article 296 imposes on administrative bodies and officials limits on how they may exercise discretionary power. The Article requires that the exercise of discretionary power must imply a duty to be fair and candid; a duty not to be arbitrary, capricious, or biased; a duty to act in accordance with the due process of law; and a duty to publish regulations as a guide for exercising such discretionary powers. The Ghanaian courts are increasingly willing to subject the administrative actions of State institutions to scrutiny in order to determine their consistency with the provisions of the Constitution.

In some cases, the District Schemes are unable to provide access to healthcare services for their clients. The contributions they receive are never more than 5% of the total cost of healthcare accessed by their subscribers (Konrad Adenauer Foundation, 1999). To make up the difference, they depend on tax money paid to them through the Authority. When there is a delay in the release of funds from the Authority, the District Schemes are unable to pay their service providers. Many healthcare providers have started denying subscribers treatment because of a huge backlog in outstanding payments to them from District Schemes.

One of the reasons for this backlog is that District Schemes do not have the capacity to efficiently process claims and control fraud, which leads to limited auditing. Other problems confronting the NHIS include poor membership portability due to the fragmented nature of the scheme; poor quality of services by healthcare service providers; non-existent or poor healthcare infrastructure; an ineffective complaints system and limited consumer voice; a medicines list lacking some essential medicines; an ineffective medicines supply chain that translates into higher costs for the scheme; and lack of an effective framework for the review of the medicines list and tariffs. There are also issues related to over-utilization and abuse and high service reimbursement rates.

Another area of concern for the NHIS is the National Health Insurance Fund (the Fund), which aims to subsidize the cost of healthcare services to members of the District Schemes. The management, growth, and disbursement of the Fund are still beset with many challenges and the NHIS must go through a lot of red tape to secure release of monies for the Fund.

Barriers to access remain under the Act. Though stated in the Act that all children are covered by insurance, their coverage is actually dependent on their parent's membership to the District Scheme, which means that in reality, many children are not actually covered. Further, persons suffering from a disability that renders them financially incapacitated are not necessarily covered.

Community participation and local-level decision-making—the strength of community-based health insurance schemes

While the NHIS was the first attempt at nationwide insurance coverage, community-based health insurance schemes at Dodowa (in the Greater Accra Region) and Nkoranza (in the Brong Ahafo Region) had been in operation for many years before the NHIS was instituted, 1992 and 2001, respectively. These schemes have generated significant experiential knowledge on healthcare financing, and specifically, on the strengths and weaknesses of community participation in healthcare (Anie et al., 2001; Atim & Sock, 2000). The ways in which community-based financing mechanisms (including extra-community sources of funding), community mobilization, and community ownership of the insurance schemes have had an impact on those schemes are particularly relevant. An important lesson learnt is that it is imperative that each District Scheme designs a constitution that responds to the local conditions and to which its stakeholders can relate.

New king, new law

Ghana's new government has decided to change the policy and legislative framework of the NHIS. The purpose of the new law is the same as the current law, to ensure that residents of Ghana have access to quality healthcare services; however, the strategy is different.

The new law provides a new framework to address the many challenges that impede the effective implementation of the NHIS. It seeks to abolish the District Schemes and instead set up a unified NHIS to be operated by a National Health Insurance Authority (NHIA), which is answerable to the governing board of the Authority (NHIA, 2003). The two other schemes recognized by the Bill, namely, PCHISs and PMHISs, are to be regulated by the National Insurance Commission (NIC) (NHIA, 2003). The NHIA will have regional and district offices. This assures a decentralized structure for the NHIS. Further, the Bill provides for Regional and District Monitoring and Advisory Committees for the NHIS. These committees are tasked with monitoring the implementation of the scheme in the regions and districts and making recommendations to the Board for improvements.

As an additional measure, the new law uses the mechanism of accreditation of healthcare providers and facilities as a monitoring mechanism for quality control. This includes monitoring for compliance with medicines lists, tariffs, and mechanisms to prevent over- or under-use of healthcare services.

The new law broadens exemption categories under the NHIS to include persons suffering from chronic psychiatric disorders. However, most categories of exempt persons must pass a means test in order to be exempt. The Bill also mandates the Authority to liaise with the Ministry of Social Welfare in order to identify and provide coverage for all the vulnerable.

The new law allows for the centralization of claims processing and payment, which will help avoid denial of services by providers when payments are delayed. The law also allows for greater flexibility in the investment of the Fund and the sources of funding have been expanded. Sin taxes and taxes from recent oil and gas finds in Ghana were initially written into the bill for the benefit of the Fund, but were later removed. Other notable innovations in the new law relate to more precise provisions on data privacy and data security of members of the Scheme. Portions of the Fund are used to finance healthcare infrastructure and improve availability of healthcare personnel.

Future national directions towards the right to health

The Constitution Review Commission of Ghana has made a number of findings, observations, and recommendations for improving healthcare in Ghana. Its report has been accepted by the government for implementation.

The Commission's first observation was to agree with the World Health Organization (WHO) definition of health as 'a state of complete physical, mental and social well-being and not merely the absence of disease or infirmity' (WHO, 1992). By this definition, the Commission acknowledged that mental health is a key element in determining the well-being of a person. The Commission then recommended the immediate passage of a progression Mental Health Law to improve delivery of mental health services in Ghana (CRC Report, 2011). In 2012, a new Mental Health Act was passed in Ghana (Act 846, 2012). The Act provides for the representation of persons with Disability in Councils and Committees that deal with matters affecting mental health; the creation of an authority specifically charged with addressing mental health issues in the country; and the creation of a fund for the Mental Health Authority.

The Commission then called for the passage of the Health Institutions and Facilities Act for better regulation of health facilities. It further called for increased funding to the health sector so that hospitals and healthcare facilities may meet certain minimum standards to be able to continue to operate. In 2011, the Act was passed into law (Act 829, 2011). The Commission also acknowledged subsisting challenges with the NHIS relating to coverage and long-term sustainability as Ghana transforms into a middle-income country and becomes less eligible for international funding in critical areas.

Finally, in his 2011 State of the Nation Address, Ghana's President committed his government to achieving the health-related United Nations (UN) Millennium Development Goals by 2015 by continuing to concentrate on improving health outcomes; and targeting resources towards the health of women and children and the prevention and control of communicable and non-communicable diseases. He also stated that the NHIS will continue to provide financial risk protection against the cost of basic quality healthcare for all citizens in Ghana. He committed to continuing the construction of district hospitals, regional hospitals, staff housing for some regional hospitals, and refurbishment of teaching hospitals. He also promised that following the passage of the Mental Health Act, the government will adopt a community mental healthcare strategy to facilitate the implementation of the Act and pass the necessary legislative instrument to operationalize other aspects of the Act.

In sum, the future projections for the right to health in Ghana include the following:

- The amendment of the 1992 Constitution to provide expressly for the right to the highest attainable standard of health, including access to healthcare services without barriers and a right to a clean and healthy environment;

- The re-enactment of the National Health Insurance Act to provide for robust institutional and funding mechanisms for healthcare for all Ghanaian residents; and
- The implementation of a progressive Mental Health Act to include community-based care.

Conclusion

The Ghanaian Constitution can be interpreted to enforce a right to health, though it is not expressly included. At the very least, the Constitution imposes a duty on the government to take and report on steps for the realization of the right to health of Ghanaians.

In human rights practice, the State has the responsibility to respect the right to health of its people by refraining from discriminatory practices in the provision of health services. Second, the State must protect the right to health of its people by protecting individuals from certain acts of third parties that infringe on their right to health. Finally, the State must provide and ensure access to needed health resources for its population. Guideposts for determining whether the right to health is implemented include availability, accessibility, equality, and quality.

In legal systems where social and economic rights are not well articulated, the right to health can be read through the civil and political right to life. In the African Charter on Human and People's Rights (1979), introduced by the formerly named Organization of African Unity, and other legal frameworks that articulate social and economic rights, the challenge is how those rights should be defined and enforced in a way that requires States to have both the requisite rule of law framework necessary for transparent enforcement and also the programmatic development agenda that ensures the progressive realization of those rights.

In addition, the right to health is clearly interrelated with other rights: poor social conditions, such as poverty; inadequate housing and nutrition; and lack of education can be significant obstacles to the realization of the right to health and the right to life. Realization of the rights to life, to physical integrity, and to privacy is also important for the maintenance of people's health and for the realization of the right to health. The interdependence and indivisibility of economic, social, and cultural rights and civil and political rights becomes visible in this regard and constitutes additional fodder for the struggle for economic and social rights, such as the right to health (Amnesty International, 2005).

As part of its mandate to realize the right to health for all residents of Ghana, the government of Ghana has designed an NHIS as the mechanism for delivering the healthcare needs of the population. The NHIS, however, faces many challenges in fulfilling this purpose. The tried and tested community-based health insurance systems in Ghana were not made the backbone of the NHIS; the DMHISs were autonomous, but not organically grown, and indirectly controlled by the government; and the system, to meet an election promise, was developed for nationwide application at once, and instituted unsustainable coverage and financial rewards to the insured, service providers, and pharmaceutical companies.

To realize the right to health for Ghanaian residents, the current government is reviewing the policy and legislative framework of the NHIS. The review process has been endorsed by the Constitution Review Commission, which has also called for the recognition of the right to health as a full-fledged right as part of Ghana's Constitution.

References

Amnesty International. (2005). *Human Rights for Human Dignity: A Primer on Economic, Social and Cultural Rights*: Amnesty International Publications: New York, NY. Available at: <http://www.amnestyusa.org/Report_Human_rights_for_human_dignity/5_Who_is_responsible/page.do?id=1102192&n1=3&n2=29&n3=231> (accessed 2 November 2012).

Anie, S., Kyeremeh, G., and Anarwat, S.G. (2001). *Mutual Health Organizations: A Quality Information Survey in Ghana*. Working paper. Partners For Health Reform: Bethesda, MD.

Akosah-Sarpong, K. (2008). *Ghana: Striking Health Workers and Traditional Medicine*. Available at: <http://www.africanconservation.org/dcforum/DCForumID27/104.html> (accessed 30 July 2008).

Atim, C. and Sock, M. (2000). *An External Evaluation of the Nkoranza Community Financing Health Insurance Scheme, Ghana, Technical Report No. 50*. Partners for Health Reform: Bethesda, MD.

Azeem, V. and Adamtey, N. (2006). *Budget ceilings and health in Ghana*. A Report Prepared by Centre for Budget Advocacy of ISODEC (Ghana): Accra.

Constitution of Ghana. (1992). *The Constitution of The Republic Of Ghana 1992*. Available at: <http://www.judicial.gov.gh/constitution/second_schedule/home.htm>.

Constitution Review Commission. (2011). *Report of the Constitution Review Commission of Ghana. From a Political to a Developmental Constitution*. Constitution Review Commission: Accra.

Dovlo, D. (2003). *The Brain Drain and Retention of Health Professionals in Africa*. A Case Study Prepared for a Regional Training Conference on 'Improving Tertiary Education in Sub-Saharan Africa: Things that Work!' Accra, 23–25 September. Available at: <http://siteresources.worldbank.org/INTAFRREGTOPTEIA/Resources/dela_dovlo.pdf> (accessed 30 July 2008).

Ghana Living Standards Survey. (2005). *International Household Survey Network*. Available at: <http://surveynetwork.org/home/index.php?q=activities/catalog/surveys/ihsn/288-2005-001> (accessed 2 November 2012).

Ghana Statistical Service. (2003). *Health, Nutrition and Environmental Statistics* Available at: <http://www.statsghana.gov.gh/Health_Nutrition.html> (accessed 2 November 2012).

Ghana Statistical Service. (2010). *Population & Housing Census Summary Report of Final Results*. Available at: <http://www.statsghana.gov.gh/docfiles/2010phc/Census2010_Summary_report_of_final_results.pdf> (accessed 2 November 2012).

Happy Abaji v. *Administrator of La Polyclinic; Minister for Health; and Attorney-General*. (2003). High Court, Accra, Suit No. Misc. 168/2003.

ICESCR. (1976). *International Covenant on Economic, Social and Cultural Rights*. Res 2200A (XXI), 21 U.N. GAOR Supp. (No. 16) at 49. Adopted 16 December 1966, G.A, U.N. Doc. A/6316 993 U.N. T.S. 3, entry into force 3 January 1976.

Konrad Adenauer Foundation. (1999). *Alternative Ways of Funding Health Care: The Role of Stakeholders in Promoting Sustainable Community Health Insurance*. Konrad Adenauer Foundation: Accra.

Legal Resources Centre. (2008). *Report on Healthcare Access in the Bongo and West Mamprusi Districts of Ghana, 18 January 2008*. Legal Resources Centre: Accra.

Legislative Instrument No. 1313. (1985). *Hospital Fee Regulation, 1985*. Republic of Ghana: Accra.

NHIA. (2003). *National Health Insurance Act, 2003 (Act 650)*, entered into force on 12 September 2003. Republic of Ghana: Accra.

NHIA. (2004). *National Health Insurance Regulations (L.I. 1809)*. Republic of Ghana: Accra.

NHIA. (2012). *Final Report on the Policy and Legislative Review of the National Health Insurance Scheme*. Prepared by the Law and Development Associates for the National Health Insurance Authority, January, 2012. (On file with author).

NHIC. (2007). *Quarterly Operational Report Submitted to National Health Insurance Council* (NHIC) by NHIC Secretariat, August 2007 (on file with author).

NHIS. (2007). *Ghana National Health Insurance Scheme: Joint DP Mission Aide Memoire, December 8–13, 2007, p. 1*. Available at: <http://www.moh-ghana.org/UploadFiles/nhis/NHIA%20AIDE%20MEMOIRE%20UPDATED090805115015.pdf> (accessed 2 November 2012).

NHIS. (2012). *The Road to Ghana's Healthcare Financing*. Directorate of Corporate Affairs and Strategic Decisions. Available at: <http://www.nhis.gov.gh/?CategoryID=158&ArticleID=1110> (accessed 2 November 2012).

President's Malaria Initiative. (2011). *Malaria Operational Plan—FY 2011 (Year 4): Ghana*. Available at: <http://www.pmi.gov/countries/mops/fy11/ghana_mop-fy11.pdf> (accessed 2 November 2012).

Rajkotia, Y. (2007). *The Political Development of the Ghanaian National Health Insurance System: Lessons in Health Governance' Health Systems 20/20 Project*. Abt Associates Inc. Bethesda, MD.

Schoepf, B.G., Schoepf, C., and Millen, J.V. (2000). Theoretical therapies, remote remedies: saps and the political ecology of poverty and health in Africa. In J.Y. Kim, J.V. Millen, A. Irwin, *et al.* (Eds.), *Dying for Growth: Global Inequality and the Health of the Poor*, pp. 91–129. Monroe, ME: Common Courage Press.

UNDESA. (2011). Cited in HDR 2011: <http://hdrstats.undp.org/en/countries/profiles/GHA.html> (accessed 2 November 2012).

UNDP. (2007). *Ghana Human Development Report 2007*. United Nations Development Programme (UNDP): Accra. Available at <http://planipolis.iiep.unesco.org/upload/Ghana/Ghana_nhdr_2007.pdf> (accessed 18 August 2012).

UNDP. (2009). *Human Development Report 2009: Overcoming Barriers: Human Mobility and Development*. United Nations Development Programme (UNDP): New York, NY. Available at: <http://hdr.undp.org/en/media/HDR_2009_EN_Complete.pdf> (accessed 18 August 2012).

UNDP. (2011). *Sustainability and Equity: A Better Future for All*. United Nations Development Programme (UNDP): New York, NY.

UNICEF. (2005). *The State of the World's Children*. United Nations Children's Fund (UNICEF): New York, NY.

UNICEF. (2008). *The State of the World's Children 2009*. United Nations Children's Fund (UNICEF): New York, NY.

UNICEF. (2011). *At a Glance: Ghana*. United Nations Children's Fund: New York, NY. <http://www.unicef.org/infobycountry/ghana_statistics.html> (accessed 2 November 2012).

Wireko, V. (2008, 6 August). The National Health Insurance Scheme works. *Daily Graphic*, p. 11.

World Bank. (2011a). *World Development Indicators 2011*. World Bank: Washington, DC. Available at: <http://data.worldbank.org> (accessed 15 May 2011).

World Bank. (2011b). *Human Development Report (HDR) 2011: Sustainability and Equity: A Better Future for All*. Available at: <http://hdr.undp.org/en/reports/global/hdr2011/> (accessed 2 November 2012).

WHO. (1992). *Basic Documents. 39th Edition. CRC Report*. World Health Organization (WHO): Geneva.

Yeboah, L.A. and Appiah-Adjei, G. (2008, 19 July). More pregnant women register under free maternal health care programme. *Daily Graphic*. Available at: <http://www.modernghana.com/news/174979/1/more-pregnant-women-register-under-free-maternal-h.html> (accessed 30 July 2008).

Chapter 8

Health and development in India: moving towards the right to health

Ravi Duggal

Background

India's population is estimated to be close to 1.21 billion, and it is growing at a rate of about 1.64% per year (Census India, 2011). As a capitalist economy, India, with its own multinational corporations, may be competitive with some of the world's developed countries, but an overwhelming majority of people in India come nowhere close to earning the World Bank-defined basis subsistence of US$2 a day. The latest poverty estimate by India's Planning Commission puts the proportion of persons below the poverty line at 27.5%, or more than 315 million people (NSSO, 2007). However this estimate is based on an extremely low level of monthly per capita consumption of Rs. 356.30 (US$9 per month) for rural areas and Rs. 538.60 (US$13 per month) for urban areas. This is far below the globally accepted figure set by United Nations (UN) Millennium Development Goals (MDGs) of US$1 per day for absolute poverty, or Rs. 1200 (US$30) monthly per capita expenditure. With the MDGs estimate for defining poverty, two-thirds to three-quarters of the population are considered to be living in absolute poverty. If all of India's people had an income of US$2 per day needed to transcend poverty the total income would amount to US$800 billion, which translates to a whopping 93% of India's gross domestic product (GDP). India's Human Development Index (HDI) rank is 134 of 187 (UNDP, 2011) and its health indicators place it in the bottom quartile of the world's countries.

The history of India's health policy

As part of the post-World War II reconstruction initiative, the Health Survey and Development Committee, under the chairmanship of Sir Joseph Bhore, was created on 18 October 1943. The formation of this Committee marked the first large-scale undertaking to document the prevailing health conditions in India and recommend a plan for the future. The four-volume Bhore Committee Report was submitted to the Government of India in 1946. It defined eight objectives for its plan for a National Health Service (Bhore, 1946):

- Making adequate provision for the preventive and curative medical care;
- Placing services as close to the community as possible;
- Providing widest possible basis of cooperation between health personnel and the people;
- Enabling involvement of medical and auxiliary professions in health policy formulation; and
- Making available diverse diagnostic, treatment, laboratory, and institutional facilities ('group' practice).

- Making special provisions for vulnerable population groups;
- Providing access to healthcare services irrespective of ability to pay for them; and
- Creating healthy homes, workspaces, and recreational facilities.

The report emphasized a need for a comprehensive and universal healthcare system, and it made recommendations concerning the district health scheme and health organization to provide integrated health services—curative, preventive, and promotive—to the entire population. If implemented, these measures would have been India's first steps on the path to a right to health.

Although the opportunity to build a foundation for the right to health was presented, the development paradigm had no space for such provisions. Indeed, there was no attempt in the post-Colonial period to radically restructure the healthcare system, as per the framework provided by the Bhore Committee. Rather, a series of five-year plans were instituted which seemed to allow the healthcare inequalities to continue to grow. Access opportunities favoured urban populations, physicians were trained for the private sector through State financing, and bulk drugs were supplied at subsidized rates to private formulation units; both measures facilitated the development and strengthening of the private health sector in India.

1950–1975—from managing epidemics to primary healthcare

In the 1950 and 1960s, India's health sector was focused on managing epidemics. Mass campaigns were started to control diseases such as malaria, smallpox, tuberculosis (TB), leprosy, filaria, trachoma, and cholera (Banerji, 1973). During the First (1951–1956) and Second (1956–1961) Five-Year Plans, the basic structural framework of the public healthcare delivery system remained unchanged. Urban areas continued to receive more than three-quarters of the medical care resources while rural areas received 'special attention' under the Community Development Programme (CDP), presenting clear evidence that as early as the beginning of the 1960s the availability of medical care in urban India was already well within the World Health Organization (WHO)'s acceptable standard norm of one hospital bed per 500 persons, whereas rural India was 16 times worse off with regards to these data. The Third Five-Year Plan (1961–1966), discussed the problems affecting the provision of primary healthcare (PHC). It directed attention to the shortage of health personnel, delays in the construction of PHC buildings, and inadequate training facilities for staff required in the rural areas (Planning Commission, 1968). It also pointed to the inadequacy of healthcare institutions, physicians, and other personnel in rural areas, cited as the major shortcomings of the previous Five-Year Plan (Planning Commission, 1968). However, no mention was made of specific steps to reach this goal.

1975–1990—focusing on rural health and formalizing health policy

With the Fifth Five-Year Plan (1974–1979), the government acknowledged that the urban health infrastructure was expanding at the cost of the rural sectors (Planning Commission, 1974). Yet it was only in the Sixth Five-Year Plan (1980–1984), including the announcement of the first National Health Policy (NHP) in 1983, that the transformation of India's rural health infrastructure finally happened.

Until 1983, there was no formal health policy. As a consequence of the global debate on alternative strategies during the 1970s, the signing of the Declaration of Alma-Ata on PHC in 1978, and the recommendations of the Indian Council of Social Science Research (ICSSR), and Indian Council of Medical Research (ICMR) in 1980 (ICSSR-ICMR, 1980), the government decided that 'an integrated, comprehensive approach towards the future development of medical education, research, and health services' was necessary (MOHFW, 1983). During the decade following the 1983 NHP, rural healthcare received special attention. A massive programme of PHC facilities expansion was undertaken in the Sixth (1980–1984) and Seventh (1985–1990) Five-Year Plans to achieve the target of one PHC per 20,000 to 30,000 people and one health sub-centre per 2,500 to 5,000 people.

1990–present—addressing a resurgence of communicable diseases and addressing disease surveillance, health workforce, and other deficiencies

During the Eighth Five-Year Plan (1992–1997), a committee directed to review India's public health status discovered a resurgence of communicable diseases and a need to drastically improve disease surveillance. The Ninth Five-Year Plan (1997–2002), incorporated this Committee's recommendations, and, in addition to improving disease surveillance, for instance, it addressed the healthcare worker shortage through part-time positions and State-specific strategies (Planning Commission, 2003). The Child Survival and Safe Motherhood (CSSM) programme, transformed into the Reproductive and Child Health (RCH) programme on the basis of the ICPD-Cairo agenda, received multi-agency external funding support to provide need-based, demand-driven, high-quality integrated reproductive and child healthcare (Planning Commission, 2003). The Ninth Five-Year Plan also recommended a reformulation of the 1983 NHP, with a focus not only on improving healthcare, but also on measuring and monitoring of the healthcare delivery systems and the health status of the population (Planning Commission, 2003).

The Tenth Five-Year Plan (2002–2007) (Planning Commission, 2002) coincided with the National Health Policy of 2002 (Government of India, 2002), which, for the first time, was drafted with feedback from the public. The 2002 NHP acknowledged that the public healthcare system fell grossly short of defined requirements, the morbidity and mortality due to easily curable diseases were unacceptably high, and resource allocations were generally insufficient. It also found public health infrastructure unsatisfactory; insufficient funding for the outdoor medical facilities; insufficient medical and paramedical personnel; unavailability of consumables; dilapidated, obsolescent, and unusable equipment in many public hospitals; obsolete equipment and minimal availability of essential drugs in the indoor treatment facilities; all of which led to 'overcrowding, and consequentially to a steep deterioration in the quality of the services' (MOHFW, 2001). The 2002 NHP attempted to regulate the private health sector through statutory licensing, and for expressing concerns about establishing a viable referral system, teaching health volunteers simple medical skills, and improving overall health statistics were also admirable. However, ultimately, the 2002 NHP was a collection of unconnected statements, a dilution of the role of public health services, and an unabashed promotion of the private health sector.

The Eleventh Five-Year Plan (2007–2012), like its predecessor, paints a dismal picture of the health services infrastructure in India and stresses the importance of investment in primary health and decentralization. The specific objectives in the health sector are to reduce infant mortality rate to 28, maternal mortality ratio to 1 per 1,000 live births, and total fertility rate to 2.1; to provide clean drinking water for all by 2009; and to halve malnutrition among children under four years and anaemia among women and girls by 2012 (Planning Commission, 2007). The Eleventh Five-Year Plan was guided by the National Rural Health Mission (NRHM), which was launched with the 2005/2006 budget in order 'to provide effective healthcare to the poor, the vulnerable and to marginalized sections of society throughout the country' (MOHFW, 2005). It refers to 18 specific states as an area of focus. This concentrated approach, however, conflicts with the universality of the right to healthcare, thus undermining the very objective of a national health programme. It is evident from the history of programme implementation in India that targeted programmes fail to make an impact as compared to universalized initiatives. A classic example is the Public Distribution System in India which worked well while it was universal but by making it targeted on the poor was significantly weakened. Similarly, the introduction of user fees in public hospitals, with a provision that the poor would get free access, actually destroyed the reputation of the public hospitals because they were now viewed as hospitals for the poor and the middle-class stopped seeking care thus these hospitals lost the constituency that made them credible institutions. While the poor need special support from the public health system, access to services should not be selective because in doing so it distorts the design of universal coverage.

Since universal access to comprehensive primary healthcare and referral services is not stated clearly as a goal, the financing strategy for NRHM consists of 'selective programmes for targeted populations'. Hence separate schemes—e.g. Rs. 10,000 for untied funds for the subcentres, Rs. 100,000 for rural hospital maintenance if Rogi Kalyan Samitis (patient welfare committees that administer use of untied and user fee funds) are formed, Rs. 750,000 per block for training ASHAs (village level health workers referred to as Accredited Social Health Activists)—have been formulated, instead of determining what resources would be required in a proposed package of comprehensive services to implement the strategy effectively.

Thus NRHM so far has been merely tinkering with the system. It has not made any significant structural inroads to making the architectural changes it proudly boasts about in the mission document. This is because while the government on the one hand talks about NRHM, on the other it is letting the corporate sector, including multinational corporations, have an unregulated and open environment to boost the private health sector and profit from it. In fact, NRHM also promotes public-private partnerships and a number of initiatives in this line have been launched, the most talked about being the Chiranjeevi scheme in Gujarat for deliveries in private hospitals but financed by government. Others include Rogi Kalyan Samitis, handing over PHCs/CHCs to private sector/NGOs in Arunachal Pradesh, Gujarat, and Karnataka; and contracting out of specific services in hospitals like laundry, diagnostic, security, and catering services. Further, the use of the insurance route to finance tertiary and secondary care for below poverty line populations through programmes such as the Rashtriya Sawsthya Bima Yojana (National Health Insurance Scheme) and its State-level clones like Arogyashri in Andhra Pradesh, Yeshaswini in Karnataka, and Jeevan Dayi in Maharashtra are draining huge resources from the Ministries of Health. In 2010 to 2011, Rs. 21.98 billion in premiums were re-directed for 189 million insured persons towards such care in the private sector (IRDA, 2012). As a result, an increasing proportion of public resources are being directed for the benefit of the private health sector in addition to various subsidies which already exist. Of note, some of the prominent subsidies to the private health sector include those directed to medical education, with 80% of graduates from public medical schools joining the private sector, tax waivers to Trust/Society-managed hospitals which do not reciprocate the legal responsibilities of treating 10% to 20% of poor patients free of cost, supply of patients whose healthcare is paid by the public sector directly to corporate hospitals, and tax rebates for the importation of medical equipment and supplies.

The government is now reviewing this in its preparation for the Twelfth Five-Year Plan and there has been a substantial debate about pushing hard for universal coverage for healthcare. In this context, the Planning Commission set up an independent High-Level Expert Group (HLEG) to make recommendations for realizing universal coverage. The HLEG has come up with broadly acceptable recommendations after wide-ranging consultations and debates (Planning Commission, 2011). How much of this finds its way into the Twelfth Five-Year Plan can only be known after it is approved.

International human rights commitments

India joined the United Nations on 30 October 1945, and participated in the drafting of the Universal Declaration of Human Rights (UDHR), which influenced the formulation of India's Constitution. As discussed further later, the Constitution made a forceful appeal to the State through the Directive Principles of State Policy to work towards assuring these rights through the process of governance, but it clearly stated that any court could choose not to enforce them.

On 10 April 1979, however, India ratified the International Covenant on Economic, Social and Cultural Rights (ICESCR), which mandates the right to health through Articles 9 and 12. Post-ratification efforts through the Sixth Five-Year Plan and the 1983 NHP were the first steps in honouring this commitment. Indeed, as a result of these measures, the rural public health infrastructure expanded considerably and more resources were allocated to the health sector. Soon thereafter, however, the economic crisis of the 1990s and the unsatisfactory 2002 NHP delivered devastating blows to the health sector.

With the government's commitment to assure the right to the highest attainable standard of health waning, it has become increasingly difficult for India to honour its commitment to the ICESCR. In 2008, the Committee on Economic, Social and Cultural Rights (CESCR) examined the combined second to fifth reports submitted by India under the ICESCR (CESCR, 2008). The CESCR noted, along with the positive aspects relating to the adoption of legislative and judicial measures favouring economic, social, and cultural rights, and was rather forthright in expressing a number of serious problems relating to the right to health (CESCR, 2008). It further noted that certain disadvantaged and marginalized groups suffer from 'widespread and often socially accepted discrimination, harassment, and/or violence'; the ban on sex selection is inadequately enforced; HIV/AIDS infections are rising; trade in human organs is increasing; there is a shortage of access to safe drinking water; serious food insecurity disproportionately affecting disadvantaged and marginalized groups; and the elimination of traditional practices and provisions of personal status laws harmful and discriminatory to women and girls is not advancing (CESCR, 2008). The CESCR also noted with concern that, 'despite the economic growth achieved by the State party, health-care expenditures remain exceptionally low at around 1% of GDP, and that a significant proportion of the population continues to have limited or no access to basic health services, resulting in alarmingly high rates of maternal and infant mortality, as well as high incidences of tuberculosis and other communicable diseases' (CESCR, 2008). Finally it expressed concern that the universal healthcare scheme did not provide for universal coverage, excluding a considerable portion of the population, and 'that the quality and the availability of the health services provided under the scheme have been adversely affected by the large-scale privatization of the health service' (CESCR, 2008). The CESCR also formulated a substantial set of suggestions and recommendations to remedy these deficiencies, including that India 'significantly increase its healthcare expenditure, according the highest priority to reducing maternal and infant mortality rates and to preventing and treating serious communicable diseases, including HIV/AIDS' (CESCR, 2008).

In addition to the ICESCR, India is a party to the WHO Constitution, Convention on the Elimination of All Forms of Discrimination against Women (CEDAW), Convention on the Rights of the Child (CRC) and its additional protocols, Convention on the Elimination of All Forms of Racial Discrimination (CERD), Convention on the Rights of Persons with Disabilities (CRPD), the Alma-Ata Declaration, the Cairo Programme of Action, the Copenhagen Declaration, the Beijing Platform of Action, and the Habitat Agenda.

Since none of the international human rights treaties have been incorporated or transformed into domestic laws in India, they have only an evocative significance and may be used by the Courts or petitioners to derive inspiration (Nariman, 1995). On a number of occasions, therefore, many of these human right treaties that have been ratified by India have been used by the Courts of India in conjunction with the fundamental rights described in the Constitution.

The Constitutional framework

The Constitution did not originally accord health or healthcare the status of a right. There are some instances in case law wherein various directive principles were used to demand access to healthcare, especially in emergency situations. From time to time, Article 21 of the Constitution, 'securing the right to life' has been invoked. These cases are exceptional, however, and even if the Supreme Court or High Courts set a precedent of health as a right, the orders are rarely respected in daily practice. Nevertheless, three articles of the Directive Principles, enshrined in Part IV of the Constitution, provide a basis to for the right to health and healthcare. These articles are:

Article 41. Right to work, to education and to public assistance in certain cases.

Article 42. Provision for just and humane conditions of work and maternity relief.

Article 47. Duty of the State to raise the level of nutrition and the standard of living and to improve public health.

For a small percentage of the working population, the assurance of healthcare exists with social security and social insurance. Because only a select group of people can enjoy this privilege, the nation's healthcare policy is one of discrimination and inequity, thereby violating not only the non-discrimination principle of international law, but also Article 14 of the Constitution (the right to equality), under the chapter on Fundamental Rights.

These constitutional provisions on social security, social insurance, a decent standard of living and adequate public health services, coupled with the collective policy statements and supported by international legal commitments, form the basis of the right to health and healthcare in India. The only legal and constitutional principle missing is the principle of justiciability, or the ability of a text to take effect as a legal rule. The 93rd amendment to the Constitution has provided limited justiciability with regards to education, and it is clear that a similar amendment concerning healthcare should be adopted, especially since inadequate healthcare can put lives at risk.

The current healthcare system

While medical care is largely a State government responsibility, the central government supports preventive healthcare and directs health policy, while retaining some flexibility, which it has often used to expand its sphere of control over the health sector. The central government has pushed various national programmes—including vertical programmes for leprosy, TB, blindness, malaria, smallpox, diarrhoea, filaria, goitres, and now HIV/AIDS—in such a way that States have had little input regarding the design and components of these programmes.

The administrative structure of public healthcare services in India is two-pronged: the Secretariat of the Health Ministry and the Directorate of Health Services. At the central government level there is a Ministry of Health and Family Welfare, the Department of Health, the Department of Family Welfare, the Department of Indian Systems of Medicine and Homoeopathy (ISM&H), and the Directorate General of Health Services. The Departments of Health, Family Welfare, and

ISM&H each have a secretary with a hierarchy of additional, joint, deputy and under-secretaries looking after the various programmes of the three departments. To facilitate interaction between the central government and State governments, there is a Central Council of Health and Family Welfare that is comprised of health ministers and secretaries from each State along with a few nominated members. This Council is also the primary advisory and policymaking body for healthcare in India.

Economic and social inequities

Only a small section of the population, largely called the organized sector, has some form of health insurance coverage. Those working in either the government or private industries can obtain State-mandated social security like the Employee State Insurance Scheme, Central Government Health Scheme, and the Maternity Benefit Scheme. A lucky few may also receive it through employer-provided health services or reimbursements. It is estimated that about 12% of India's population has access to healthcare, as this is the proportion covered by social insurance or some other employer-supported health coverage (Ellis et al., 2000). Such care is sustained at least during the working life of the primary income earning member of the family.

The private health sector constitutes a strong lobby in India so much so that there is virtually no regulation of this sector. The private sector has a virtual monopoly of ambulatory curative services in both rural and urban areas, and more than half of hospital care is run by the private sector (CBHI, 2000). The medical councils only register the qualified physicians and issue them a licence to practice. There is no performance assessment, continuing education, price regulation, or prescription-vetting by either the medical councils or the government. Furthermore, the private healthcare sector is strongly backed by the private pharmaceutical industry (a largely multinational industry) which also constitutes a powerful lobby. It is the strength of the private health sector and the private pharmaceutical industry that has hindered the implementation of progressive policy initiatives, including the recommendations of the Hathi Committee Report, whose recommendations pertained to the removal of irrational drug combinations, generic naming of essential drugs, and the development of a national formulary for prescription practice. Pharmaceutical formulation production in India is presently worth over Rs. 1,000 billion; over 98% of this is in the private sector (Department of Pharmaceuticals & Government of India, 2011).

Thus, India has a large, unregulated, expensive, and dominant private health sector, and an inadequately resourced, selectively focused, and declining quality public health sector; the former has a curative monopoly and the latter carries the burden of preventive and promotive care.

The inequities across classes are most severe between the top 18% and bottom 36% of households. For low-income households, the infant and child mortality rate is two times greater than in high-income households. When further observing low-income households (in comparison to high-income households), the incidence of malaria is three times greater, the incidence of TB is four times greater, malnourishment among women of reproductive age is three times greater, while access to antenatal care is nearly four times less, the number of completed immunization is two times less, and the rate of physician-assisted childbirth is four times less (IIPS, 2000).

Disparities also exist between rural and urban areas. India presently has 17,000 hospitals (34% rural), 25,670 dispensaries (40% rural), and about 1 million beds (23% rural). Note that data on hospitals, dispensaries, and beds pertaining to the private sector are grossly under-reported, and figures for 2001 to 2002 for public facilities also suffer from under-reporting as a number of States do not share data. Thus the actual figures should be much higher, and especially so for the private sector. The rural areas in addition have 24,000 PHCs and 140,000 sub-centres (CBHI, 2011).

However, when these data are represented in proportion to population, it is evident that urban areas have 4.48 hospitals, 6.16 dispensaries, and 308 beds per 100,000 people, in sharp contrast to the rural areas that have 0.77 hospitals, 1.37 dispensaries, 3.2 PHCs, and 44 beds per 100,000 people (CBHI, 2011). The urban hospitals are essentially curative centres, providing outpatient and inpatient services for primary, secondary, and tertiary care. Rural hospitals, conversely, have mostly preventive and promotive services, such as communicable disease control plans, family planning initiatives, and immunization schemes. Curative care programmes are the weakest component of the rural health institutions in spite of a very high demand for such services in those areas. As a result, this demand must be met by either city hospitals or private practitioners.

While there is evidence of substantial improvements of some health outcomes, including infant mortality rate, crude birth rate, crude death rate, and life expectancy, the latest *Human Development Report* shows a downward trend in India's global ranking (UNDP, 2011). This decline, along with slowing growth in India's human development score, may be linked to declining investments and expenditures in the public health sector. In the mid-1980s, public health expenditure peaked because of the large expansion of the rural health infrastructure, but after 1986 there was a decreasing amount of both new investments and expenditures being put into the public health sector (Duggal et al., 1995). This decline is in sharp contrast to the unprecedented increase of out-of-pocket spending, most of which goes to the private health sector.

The right to health

Assessment and recommendations

Availability

Availability of healthcare in India is inadequate because, rather than focusing on increasing the number of rural healthcare centres, training doctors for the public sector, and lowering the cost of prescription drugs, public investment has focused on expanding the curative care options for the urban population, educating a substantial number of physicians for the private sector, and producing bulk drugs at subsidized rates for private buyers.

As noted earlier, disparities exist between rural and urban areas. In addition to disparities related to the numbers of hospitals, dispensaries, and beds per 100,000 people in rural versus urban areas, there is a disparity in the category of services they provide. The urban hospitals are essentially curative centres. Rural hospitals offer primarily preventive and promotive services. The poor, therefore, must often seek medical attention from private providers. However, the lack of guidelines regulating the private sector results in a large proportion of under-qualified private providers who either have training in other systems of medicine (such as the traditional medicine systems *Ayurveda*, *Unani*, and *Siddha*) or lack any training.

A 30% decline in use of the public healthcare facilities in both rural and urban areas over the past decade is partially due to the fivefold increase in cost of seeking treatment in public hospitals (nearly sevenfold in private hospitals), with no parallel increase in the purchasing power of the poorer classes (NSSO, 1998). Decreased use is also attributable to a decline in the investments and expenditures in the public health sector, alongside the privatization of services, deregulation of drug prices, and increased reliance on market mechanisms to address welfare needs (Shukla, 2001).

Moreover, the public hospitals have a shortage of skilled physicians. From 75% to 80% of medical education is provided through State-owned or State-funded institutions at a highly subsidized cost to students (CBHI, 2011). However, 80% of graduates from public medical schools either join the private sector (55%) or migrate abroad (25%), resulting in an inadequate social return (CBHI, 2011). Of note, the Union Ministry of Health is considering compulsory public medical service for a limited number of years for medical graduates from public medical schools as a mechanism to fulfil the needs of the public healthcare system. An option also under consideration is facilitating postgraduate medical education only for those who have completed the minimum public medical service, including in rural areas. Nonetheless, hospitals are currently understaffed by more than 50%, thereby making them ineffective places for care (CBHI, 2011). While urban areas have an adequate number of hospital beds—at a ratio of one bed per 300 persons—rural areas have eight times fewer beds than the required norm of one bed per 500 persons. This urban–rural divide is evidence of gross discrimination based on place of residence, and the rural population is deprived of access to curative care services (CBHI, 2011).

The early public sector participation in drug production was a laudable effort, but over the years it became evident that the focus of the scheme shifted to bulk drug production. Before long, most of the supplies were directed to private formulation units at subsidized rates. Ironically, at present, while 45% of India's drug production is exported, a substantial amount of the necessary drug requirements must be imported (Phadke, 1998).

Accessibility

Accessible care must be non-discriminatory and affordable, allowing all people access to necessary health facilities and relevant information. While India has generally had a serious lack of access to the most basic healthcare services and healthy living conditions, even more alarming is the overwhelming disparity between the health services physically accessible to urban dwellers compared to rural dwellers and wealthy individuals compared to poor individuals. Disparities also exist between different social groups. Two groups in particular suffer from an astonishing disparity in access to healthcare, namely the scheduled castes and tribes, because of their historically disadvantaged status.

Physical and non-discriminatory access to healthcare facilities becomes irrelevant if the provided services are not affordable. All conventions talk about affordability, but they do not discuss services being offered free of charge. Indeed, there is great pressure on the public health system in India to introduce or increase user fees because it might enhance the efficiency of the public health system and force users to be more responsible in seeking healthcare (Peters et al., 2002). Such a policy has been adopted in many states in India, and adverse results can already be seen. For example, there has been a dramatic decline in utilization of public services by the poorest classes, and now their hospitalization rate is six times less than that of the wealthier classes. In fact, the poorer classes have reported such low rates of hospitalization, not because they fall ill less often but because they lack resources to access healthcare, and hence invariably postpone their utilization of hospital services until it is absolutely unavoidable (NSSO, 1998). As a consequence, the wealthy consume approximately three times more of public hospital resources than the poor, even though the poor contribute to public revenues a disproportionately higher amount of their income to access healthcare services due to the government's primary reliance on indirect taxation.

India also fails to provide adequate access to information regarding health issues. While data on public health services are available, data on the private sector are conspicuously absent. The private sector, for instance, does not supply data on communicable diseases, even though releasing this information is mandated by law (the Notifiable Diseases Act). This practice leads to an inaccurate epidemiological database, dangerously affecting the ability to monitor, contain, and prevent certain diseases. Additionally, the local authorities have failed miserably to register and record private health institutions and practitioners, leading to an imprecise estimate of the data quoted regarding the private sector, as studies have occasionally shown. A 1994 survey in Mumbai, for example, showed that the Municipal Corporation only officially accounted for 64% of private hospitals and nursing homes (Nandraj & Duggal, 1996). Similarly, a much larger study in Andhra Pradesh in 1993 revealed missing statistics about the private health sector (Mahapatra, 1993). Although statutory bodies, medical councils have also mismanaged their members' records and have therefore been unable to regulate medical practices. As a result, there are a large number of untrained and unqualified persons practising medicine across India; some estimates quantify this group at more than 50% of all practitioners (Duggal, 2000).

Acceptability and quality

Finally, India falls deplorably short with respect to acceptability and quality of care. As previously explained, there is a clear rural–urban dichotomy in health policy. Urban areas have been provided a somewhat comprehensive healthcare service through the numerous public hospitals and dispensaries while rural areas have been provided with almost exclusively preventive and promotive healthcare services. This phenomenon violates the principle of non-discrimination and equity, an important ethical concern that must be addressed. Furthermore, all too often physicians and hospitals allow themselves to be lured by the pharmaceutical industry to prescribe inappropriate and/or unnecessary drugs (Phadke, 1998), and the medical associations have not yet dealt with this important and worsening trend. In a positive move, however, the government recently mandated the compulsory prescription of generic drugs along with their branded counterparts for physicians (*The Economic Times*, 2011).

Contributing to these problems is the fact that India has no standard protocols for its health services, so monitoring their quality becomes very difficult. While those in the public sector often follow the Bureau of Indian Standard (BIS) guidelines for hospitals, those in the private sector generally do not (BIS, 1989, 1992; Nandraj & Duggal, 1996). Recently, efforts have been initiated in Mumbai to develop an accreditation system. The central government is already considering the possibility of bringing that system to the national level so that it can promote quality of healthcare across all of India (Nandraj & Duggal, 1996).

International cooperation

The larger dependence on external assistance in the health sector began with the India Population Project (IPP) of the World Bank, which were essentially soft loans and not grants as in the past from bilateral and multilateral donors. The first five IPPs focused on development of the health infrastructure, especially in rural areas, dove-tailing with the Minimum Needs Programme. They did make a significant impact in strengthening the infrastructure, but the subsequent IPPs changed the strategy to supporting recurring expenditure. This led to disaster because the dependence on World Bank and various bilateral donors for running various health programmes reduced the government's own funding of these programmes. The big international donors now are the UK Department for International Development (DFID), European Commission, US Agency for International Development (USAID), and the World Bank, which all follow a similar strategy; that is, supporting selective health programmes targeted at specific population groups. This approach is unsustainable and can only distort further the healthcare system of the country and move further away from the rights framework.

In June 2003, the Government of India announced a new policy for bilateral development assistance that called for an end to grant and credit assistance from small bilateral donors to India. Today, small donor agencies are now invited to provide support to the Indian civil society and channel funds through multilateral organizations, who in turn must obtain governmental approval for their work (Saxena, 2005).

International agencies have been exerting influence on Indian policymaking and programme design both within and outside the Five-Year Plans. Whether it was the CDP in the 1950s, intrauterine contraceptive devices and malaria in the 1960s, or RCH and AIDS in the 1990s, most health programmes have been shaped through external collaboration. After the 1980s, the international agencies' influence became stronger with more money flowing in terms of conditional soft loans.

Even more critical than the conditionalities of international aid today is the issue of trade relations, especially between developed and developing countries. There has been a substantial opposition to the proposed free trade agreements between India and the European Union earlier in 2012. These agreements would potentially prevent Indian generic drug companies from manufacturing and exporting cheap and affordable drugs to developing countries worldwide. Known as the pharmacy of the developing world, Indian-produced generic antiretroviral drugs have accounted for more than 80% of the donor-funded developing country market (Waning et al., 2010). These agreements would thus hamper India's ability to procure and distribute essential drugs where they are desperately needed.

Bringing equity in trade will bring about a paradigm shift from international influence to international cooperation. For this to become reality, developed nations will have to accept the principles of the right to development, which will facilitate this shift.

Discussion

After more than half a century of waiting in vain for written policy to assure the people of India a universal and comprehensive healthcare system, the time has come to adopt a human rights approach to the right to health. The right to health is not a societal obligation, but a claim to an entitlement. Health is a positive right that must be fulfilled for everyone, no matter that person's wealth, residence, religion, caste, or gender. A human rights approach would not necessitate that all healthcare resources be distributed according to strict quantitative equality or that society attempt to provide equality in medical outcomes, neither of which would in any case be feasible. Instead the universality of the right to healthcare requires the definition of a specific entitlement be guaranteed to all members of our society without any discrimination.

Core content of a right to health in India

India faces many challenges. It has an overwhelmingly dominant and largely unregulated private health sector, leading to an absence of professional ethics and an absolute disinterest in improving the organization, regulation, and quality of the healthcare system. Its severe lack of regulation results in many unqualified and untrained practitioners attempting to practise medicine. The public health sector, meanwhile, provides selective and limited care. It discriminates on the basis of residence, offering an unacceptably small number of programmes and services to those who live in rural areas. Declining investments in the public sector and wasteful expenditures due to a lack of standard protocols is only aggravating the problem. Perhaps the most difficult obstacle, however, is the poor state of the underlying determinants of health. A substantial portion of the population has unfiltered water, objectionable sanitation, and a shortage of food.

Given the existing challenges, certain initial steps will be necessary to fulfil the right to health for the people of India. First, directive principles must be firmly linked to fundamental rights through a constitutional amendment. Second, a National Health Act (similar to the Canada Health Act) must be implemented to organize the current healthcare system under a common umbrella organization so that both the public and the private sectors are governed by an autonomous national health authority under a single-payer mechanism. Third, a strategy must be developed for pooling resources deployed in the health sector. Fourth, there must be a redistribution of existing health resources, both public and private, according to yet-to-be-specified standard norms to assure physical equity. Fifth, consensus-building must generate a political commitment to securing the right to health.

After these preliminary steps, the State can begin to reform the system using a rights-based approach. First, financial resources should be allocated as block funding on a per capita basis for each population unit of entitlement as per existing norms. This action will redistribute current expenditures and substantially reduce inequities based on residence. Local governments should be given the autonomy to use these resources according to local needs, using a broadly defined policy framework of the public health goals as a guide. Second, local governments should adopt a policy dictating the location of new hospitals as per standard acceptable ratios such as one hospital bed per 500 people and one general practitioner per 1,000 people. Fiscal measures should be instituted to discourage the unnecessary and unhelpful concentration of resources in particular areas. Such location-specific restrictions in setting up practice may be viewed as a violation of the fundamental right to practise one's profession anywhere. It must be remembered that this right is not absolute and restrictions can be placed in concern for the public good. The suggestion here is not to have compulsion but to restrict through fiscal measures. In fact, in the United Kingdom's National Health Service, local health authorities have the right to prevent setting up of clinics if their area is saturated. Third, a strict policy should be implemented requiring public service of medical graduates from public medical schools and specifying the minimum amount of public service necessary for admission to a postgraduate institution. Fourth, the medical councils should be held accountable for assuring that only qualified and licensed doctors with continuing medical education certification are practising. Fifth, essential drugs as per the WHO list should be placed under price control (90% of them are off-patent). Adequate amounts of these drugs must be compulsorily produced or imported so that they are available to and affordable for all people. Sixth, employee-based health schemes should be integrated with the general public health system so that there is no discrimination based on employment. These hospitals and dispensaries are grossly under-utilized and could easily be opened up for public use.

The core content is the minimum level of care, the core entitlement, which should be guaranteed to all members of society, including consideration of components of primary care services such as health education, referral and specialty services, ambulatory access, and pharmaceutical services. It is also essential to specify the minimum standards of the healthcare resources that must be made available to all people regardless of their social, geographical, and financial position. The BIS has supplied its own recommendations regarding the minimum requirements, suggesting a ratio of one physician per 3.3 beds and one nurse per 2.7 beds (BIS, 1989, 1992).

Government officials and policymakers usually question using these described norms because they believe that the numbers are excessive for a poor country such as India and doubt that they have the resources to create that level of healthcare provision. That reaction is incorrect. Consider the morbidity rate in India. The daily rate is 2% to 3% of the population, meaning that approximately 20 million to 30 million patients are handled every day and 7 billion to 10 billion every year (NSSO, 2007). Assuming that all 30 million will seek outpatient care and that each physician can handle about 60 patients per day, a little more than 500,000 physicians would need to be equitably distributed across the country, resulting in a ratio of one physician per about 2,500 people.

Currently, India has more than 1.3 million physicians in all systems combined; if those systems can be integrated through a continuing medical education programme and the physicians redistributed per standard requirements, medical services could be provided in the ratio of one physician per 700 to 1,000 people.

The HLEG report referred to earlier has taken a step in the right direction and its recommendations are in line with the discussion here. It is now a matter of exerting the requisite political will to realize the right to healthcare.

Creating a consensus

The following suggestions lay out some of the events that need to take place if the battle for the right to health is going to be a successful one in India:

- Research and develop a detailed framework for the new healthcare system;
- Hold national and regional conferences on right to health, piquing the interest of a wide array of social action groups;
- Run campaigns on the national and regional level for the right to health;
- File public-interest litigation on the right to health to create a basis for a constitutional amendment;
- Demand justiciability of directive principles from government officials;
- Lobby medical professionals to gain support in the medical community for this improved system;
- Lobby political parties to incorporate the right to health in their manifestos; and
- Pressure international bodies (e.g. the WHO) as well as national bodies (e.g. National Human Rights Commission) to conduct effective monitoring of India's State obligations and demand accountability.

The objective is to have widespread dialogue, secure solid documentation, facilitate legal discourse, and promote an ever-rising awareness of the right to health in India.

References

Banerji, D. (1973). Population planning in India—national and foreign priorities. *International Journal of Health Services*, 3, 773–777.

Bhore, J. (1946). *Report of the Health Survey and Development Committee ('Bhore Committee Report')*. Government of India: Delhi.

BIS. (1989). *Basic Requirements for Hospital Planning CIS:12433 (Part 1)-19883*. Bureau of Indian Standards (BIS): New Delhi.

BIS. (1992). *Basic Requirements for a 100 Bedded Hospital: A Draft Report*. Bureau of Indian Standards (BIS): New Delhi.

CBHI. (2000). *Health Information of India*. Central Bureau of Health Intelligence (CBHI): New Delhi. Available at: <http://www.cbhidghs.nic.in/index.asp> (accessed 7 October 2012).

CBHI. (2011). *National Health Profile of India: 2010*. Central Bureau of Health Intelligence (CBHI): New Delhi. Available at: <http://cbhidghs.nic.in/index2.asp?slid=1125&sublinkid=929> (accessed 24 October 2012).

Census India. (2011). *Size, Growth Rate and Distribution of Population*. Available at: <http://www.censusindia.gov.in/2011-prov-results/data_files/india/Final_PPT_2011_chapter3.pdf> (accessed 7 October 2012).

CESCR. (2008). *40th Session, Periodic Report of the State Party.* Office of the United Nations High Commissioner for Human Rights: India.

Department of Pharmaceuticals and Government of India. (2011). *Annual report 2010–2011.* Available at: <http://pharmaceuticals.gov.in/AnnualReport1011/ch_2.pdf> (accessed 7 October 2012).

Duggal, R. (2000). *Where are we today? Seminar 489.* Available at: <http://www.india-seminar.com/2000/489/489%20duggal.htm> (accessed 24 October 2012).

Duggal, R., Nandraj, S., and Vadair, A. (1995). Health expenditure across states. *Economic and Political Weekly*, 30, 834–844.

The Economic Times. (2011, 17 December). Health ministry prescribes data to boost generic sales. *The Economic Times.* Available at: <http://www.generic-medicine.prabodhan-grahak.org/en/archives/economic_17th.html> (accessed 24 October 2012).

Ellis, R., Alam, M., and Gupta, I. (2000). Health insurance in India—prognosis and prospectus. *Economic and Political Weekly*, 35, 207–217.

Government of India. (2002). *National Health Policy 2002.* Ministry of Health: New Delhi.

ICSSR and ICMR. (1980). *Health for All: An Alternative Strategy. Report of a Study Group.* Indian Council of Social Science Research (ICSSR): New Delhi.

Insurance Regulatory and Development Authority. (2012). *Annual Report 2010–11.* Government of India: New Delhi.

IIPS. (2000). *National Family Health Survey of India, 1998–1999.* International Institute for Population Sciences (IIPS): Mumbai.

Mahapatra, P. (1993). *Social, Economic, and Cultural Aspect of Asthma: an Exploratory Study in Andhra Pradesh, India.* Institute of Health Systems: Hyderabad.

MOHFW. (1983). *National Health Policy 1983.* Ministry of Health and Family Welfare (MOHFW), Government of India: New Delhi.

MOHFW. (2001). *Draft National Health Policy.* Ministry of Health and Family Welfare (MOHFW), Government of India: New Delhi.

MOHFW. (2005). *NRHM Mission Document.* Ministry of Health and Family Welfare (MOHFW), Government of India: New Delhi.

Nandraj, S. and Duggal, R. (1996). Physical standards in the private health sector. *Radical Journal of Health (New Series)*, II-2/3, 141–184.

Nariman, S.F. (1995). Economic, social, and cultural rights and the role of lawyers. *ICJ Review*, 55, 141–152.

NSSO. (1998). *Morbidity and Treatment of Ailments, 52nd Round, Report No.441.* National Sample Survey Organisation (NSSO): New Delhi.

NSSO. (2007). *National Sample Survey 61st Round, Report No.508.* National Sample Survey Organisation (NSSO): New Delhi.

Peters, H., Yazbeck A.S., Sharma, R.R., *et al.* (2002). *A Better Health Systems for India's Poor: Findings, Analysis, and Options.* World Bank: New Delhi.

Phadke, A. (1998). *Drug Supply and Use: Towards a rational policy in India.* Sage Publications: New Delhi.

Planning Commission. (1968). *Third Five-Year Plan.* Government of India: New Delhi.

Planning Commission. (1974). *Fifth Five-Year Plan.* Government of India: New Delhi.

Planning Commission. (2002). *Tenth Five-Year Plan.* Government of India: New Delhi.

Planning Commission. (2003). *Ninth Five-Year Plan.* Government of India: New Delhi.

Planning Commission. (2007). *Eleventh Five-Year Plan.* Government of India: New Delhi.

Planning Commission. (2011). *High Level Expert Group Report on Universal Health Coverage in India.* Available at: <http://planningcommission.nic.in/reports/genrep/rep_uhc0812.pdf> (accessed 24 October 2012).

Saxena, N.C. (2005). External aid to India. *IDS Bulletin*, 36, 56–60.

Shukla, A. (2001). Right to health care. *Health Action*, 14, 6–10.

UNDP. (2011). *Human Development Report*. Available at: <http://hdrstats.undp.org/en/countries/profiles/IND.html> (accessed 7 October 2012).

Waning, B., Diedrichsen, E., and Moon, S. (2010). A lifeline to treatment: the role of Indian generic manufacturers in supplying antiretroviral medicines to developing countries. *Journal of the International AIDS Society*, 13, 35.

Chapter 9

The right to health in post-apartheid era South Africa

Charles Ngwena, Rebecca Cook, and Ebenezer Durojaye

Introduction

South Africa is often referred to as a rainbow nation due to the racial diversity of its 50.5 million people (Statistics South Africa, 2011). South Africa is a middle-income country, and has the largest economy in Africa (Nattrass & Seekings, 2001). While South Africa has a relatively strong economy, millions of its people live in deprivation. Though the economy has been growing, from 1993 to the first quarter of 2012, the growth rate in South Africa's gross domestic product averaged only 3.2% (Trading Economics, 2012). South Africa has one of the highest global income disparities (Nattrass & Seekings, 2001; Terreblanche, 2002), with an overall Gini coefficient of about 0.68 (Bradshaw, 2008). In effect, the country exhibits features of a small first world ensconced within a larger developing world.

Transformation of the political and constitutional landscape of South Africa

On 27 April 1994, a new Constitution with a Bill of Rights was born when the African National Congress (ANC) won South Africa's first ever democratic general election and formed a new government, opening the country to a new era of constitutionalism (Currie & de Waal, 2005). Until then, South Africa had achieved notoriety for institutional apartheid.

The country first adopted, as a temporary measure, the Constitution of the Republic of South Africa Act No. 200 of 1993, which took force on 27 April 1994. In 1996, it adopted the Constitution of the Republic of South Africa No. 108 as a final iteration. The Constitution ended apartheid as a State doctrine. Moreover, its adoption marked the end of the Westminster doctrine of parliamentary sovereignty, supplanting it with supreme law informed by international human rights.

Section 7(2) of the Constitution imposes on the State a duty to respect, protect, promote, and fulfil the Bill of Rights—the cornerstone of democracy in South Africa. Human dignity, equality, and freedom are recognized as foundational values by Section 7(1) of the Constitution. When interpreting the provisions of the Bill of Rights, Sections 39(1)(b) and 233 of the Constitution enjoin courts to consider international law and to achieve, where possible, an interpretation consistent with international law.

The Constitutional Court has underscored the role of equality under the new Constitution (*President of the Republic of South Africa and Another* v. *Hugo*, 1997, (6) BCLR 708, para. 74). In the South African context, substantive equality includes socioeconomic since these may prevent outcome in equality (Albertyn & Goldblatt, 1998). As part of guaranteeing substantive equality, Section 9(2) of the Constitution requires parliament to adopt measures to implement equality and also mandates affirmative action. The commitment to substantive equality is further underscored by the provision of a wide array of health-related socioeconomic rights in the Constitution, including rights of access to:

- an environment that is not harmful to one's health or well-being (Section 24);
- adequate housing (Section 26);
- healthcare services, including reproductive healthcare (Section 27(1) and (2));
- emergency medical treatment (Section 27(3));
- sufficient food (Section 27(1)(b));
- sufficient water (Section 27(1)(b));
- social security (Section 27(1)(c)); and
- [for children] basic nutrition, shelter, healthcare services, and social services (Section 28(1)(c)); and
- [for incarcerated persons] adequate accommodation, nutrition, reading material, and medical treatment (Section 35(2)(e)).

Early in its life, the Constitutional Court confirmed that the socioeconomic rights guaranteed by the Constitution are justiciable in spite of their budgetary implications (*Ex parte Chairperson of the Constitutional Assembly*: In *re Certification of the Constitution of the Republic of South Africa*, 1996, (10) BCLR 1253 (CC), paras. 77–78).

Health of the South African population

The health of the South African population exhibits the dual features of diseases that, on the one hand, resemble countries with large populations which live in conditions of poverty and socioeconomic deprivation, and, on the other hand, typify countries with populations that are not economically deprived and enjoy standards of living that are comparable to those in developed countries. According to Redelinghuys, South Africa's burden of disease can be described as a fourfold burden, namely the burden of: (1) HIV and related diseases; (2) diseases of inequality, poverty, and underdevelopment, notably infectious diseases; (3) chronic diseases of lifestyle; and (4) a high fatality rate related to injury and violence (Redelinghuys, 2012).

South Africa has the highest concentration of people living with HIV. It is estimated that 5.6 million people are living with HIV in the country (UNAIDS, 2010). Among the adult population, the prevalence rate of HIV is estimated at 16.9% (Redelinghuys, 2012). HIV/AIDS accounts for 31% of deaths in the country. South Africa also has a high burden of tuberculosis (TB), which is associated with a high burden of AIDS. Globally, South Africa's TB burden ranks third, accounting for 13% of all deaths in the country (Rispel & Kibua, 2011). Over and above being exacerbated by HIV/AIDS, the TB epidemic has also been exacerbated by poor TB treatment completion rates and multi-drug resistant TB (Redelinghuys, 2012).

South Africa's current infant mortality rate (IMR), mortality rate for under-fives, and maternal mortality rate (MMR) do not bode well and suggest that it will not be able to achieve United Nations (UN) Millennium Development Goal (MDG) targets. Though in recent years antiretroviral therapy (ART) has been effective in reducing mother-to-child transmission of HIV, in 2010, the country's IMR was 46.9 per 1,000, a rate which compares unfavourably with the target of 18 per 1,000 set for 2015 by the MDGs (Day & Gray, 2010; UNDP, 2010). Similarly, while the under-five mortality rate, dropped from 72 per 1,000 in 2005 to 67.3 per 1,000 in 2010, it is also still significantly far from the MDG benchmark of 20 per 1000 (Day & Gray, 2010; UNDP, 2010). South Africa's MMR increased from 369 per 100,000 in 2001 to 400 per 100,000 in 2010. To reduce the MMR by three-quarters, as required by the MDGs, South Africa would need to achieve a target of 38 per 10,000 by 2015 (Day & Gray, 2010; UNDP, 2010).

There are major discrepancies between racial groups with the divide most pronounced between the African and white populations (Redelinghuys, 2012). For example, in 2008, the mortality rate for the African population was 58.5% while that of the white population was 19% (Day & Gray, 2008). At birth, the life expectancy for the African population was 49.2 years, while that of the white population was 63.6 years (Day & Gray, 2008). Such discrepancies are also reflected in the IMR, under-fives mortality rate, and the MMR. The legacy of apartheid has exerted an abiding influence in the creation and sustenance of inequalities in the underlying determinants of health, and the African population accounts for 79% of the population that is poor, with poverty most accentuated among the African rural population (Department of Social Development, 2010).

Historical background to South African healthcare

According to several commentators, historically the South African healthcare system has been afflicted with five primary maladies (African National Congress, 1994; De Beer, 1984; van Rensburg, 2012; van Rensburg & Benatar, 1993; Van Rensburg & Fourie, 1994):

- Dominance of curative-orientated healthcare which has depended on expensive hospital-based care rather than affordable, preventative, community-based care (Health Systems Trust & World Bank, 1995; South African Institute of Race Relations, 1995, 1997).
- Provision of racially segregated health services which was taken to absurd extremes with the creation of separate departments of health by region and race (van Rensburg, 2012).
- Fragmentation of services after the Public Health Act No. 36 of 1919 which created a three-tiered, uncoordinated system of organizing and dispensing healthcare services and was supplanted by the Health Act No. 63 of 1977, that reorganized the health sector but ultimately reinforced the fragmentation of services (van Rensburg, 2012).
- The accentuation of rural–urban discrepancies and inequalities in the provision of services (van Rensburg, 2012).
- The proliferation of the private sector at the expense of the public sector (van Rensburg, 2012).

South Africa's human rights laws

More than any other health-related text in the Constitution, Section 27 is formulated in direct and universal terms, recognizing a right to health for everyone in contrast, for example, to Section 28(1)(c) and Section 35(2)(e) of the Constitution which only confer health rights on children and incarcerated persons, respectively. This section includes the only direct right to health for which the Constitutional Court has provided interpretive guidance. The relevant text of Section 27 is:

> Everyone has the right to have access to healthcare services, including reproductive health care . . . The State must take reasonable and other measures, within its available resources, to achieve a progressive realisation of each of these rights . . . No one may be refused emergency medical treatment. (Constitution, 1996)

The essence of Section 27

In one sense, Section 27 formally confers equality to anyone who wishes to access healthcare services. In this way, Section 27 not only affirms Section 9—the equality clause of the Constitution—but also complements the non-discrimination component of General Comment 14 (CESCR, 2000). In another sense, more pertinent to this analysis, Section 27 addresses availability and accessibility in the broader sense envisaged by General Comment 14 as well as acceptability and quality of care (CESCR, 2000). Specifically, Section 27 is about a positive entitlement (Ngwena, 2000a)—it confers on everyone a right to access health services based on need, simultaneously imposing a positive corresponding duty upon the State to provide health services. Section 27(2), which enjoins the State to take reasonable legislative and other measures, within its available resources, to achieve the progressive realization of each of the rights stated in Section 27(1).

Limiting the right to healthcare services under Section 27

The Constitution limits the right conferred by Section 27 in two main ways, one implicit in Section 27 itself and the other found in Section 36. Section 27(2) which is, similar but not identical to Article 2(1) of the International Covenant on Economic, Social and Cultural Rights (ICESCR), articulates the nature of the positive duty upon the State yet limits the State's duty to using only resources that are *available* to it and meeting health needs on a *progressive* basis. In this way, Section 27(2) implies that: the provision of health services requires resources; resources are finite; and health needs cannot always be met immediately. Furthermore, Section 27 recognizes the constitutional separation of powers between the executive branch and the judiciary branch. Section 27 not only implicitly recognizes the pre-eminent role of the executive branch in health policymaking and resource allocation subject to review for reasonableness, but also subscribes to the notion of progressive realization, as discussed in General Comment 14.

The other limitation is evident in Section 36, the Constitution's general limitation clause. Section 36 allows for limits on the rights outlined in the Bill of Rights to the extent that any limitation is reasonable and justifiable in an open and democratic society based on human dignity, equality, and freedom. Also taken into account are: the nature of the right; the importance of the purpose of the limitation, the nature of the limitation, the relationship between the limitation and its purpose; and the least restrictive means to achieve the purpose. The limitation section allows the courts to interpret claims relating to access to healthcare services purposively and generously but at the same time in a context that recognizes that fundamental rights are relative rather than absolute (Currie & de Waal, 2005). In the context of socioeconomic rights, Section 36 acts as a buffer against the risk of over-individualization of rights (Pieterse, 2006) and the unjustified preference of some rights over others.

Judicial interpretation and application of Section 27

Three cases have been critical in shaping the judicial interpretation and application of Section 27 and are discussed in the following sections.

Soobramoney v. *Minister of Health, KwaZulu-Natal* (1997) (12) BCLR 1696 (CC)

The applicant in *Soobramoney* v. *Minister of Health, KwaZulu-Natal* (hereafter *Soobramoney*) was suffering from chronic renal failure and in a critical condition, and without renal dialysis he faced imminent death. He was refused treatment at a State renal unit because he did not meet the medical criteria for access to this treatment, the provision of which was rationed by the State. The applicant brought an action before the High Court challenging the decision to refuse him dialysis as an infringement of his right to life under Section 11 of the Constitution and his right not to be refused emergency medical treatment under Section 27(3). The High Court found that the guidelines laid down for determining eligibility for dialysis—only patients with acute renal failure or who were candidates for renal transplant were eligible—were based on reasonable grounds which the applicant did not meet. The High Court explained that 'emergency medical treatment' (*Soobramoney* v. *Minister of Health*, 1998) had to be interpreted in the context of finite resources, and it meant treatment that was 'possible and available' (*Soobramoney* v. *Minister of Health*, 1998) ruling that it was not the function of the court to direct the State to make additional funds available, which was a political decision. In any event, the applicant fell outside of the scope of Section 27(3) in that his condition did not constitute an emergency.

The Constitutional Court dismissed the appeal unanimously largely for the same reasons as the High Court, holding that although Section 27(3) was capable of a broader meaning to include ongoing treatment for chronic ailments, it had a narrower constitutional meaning. A broader interpretation was, in any event, untenable as such an interpretation would have the effect of prioritizing the treatment of terminal illness over other forms of care. The Court was also of the view that basing the claim on Section 11—which provides the right to life—was inappropriate, as the Constitution contained specific provisions on access to healthcare, and these sections were contingent upon available resources. The Court was reluctant to interfere with rational decisions taken in good faith by political organs and medical authorities.

Because *Soobramoney* represents the first decision of the Constitutional Court not only on a matter pertaining to the interpretation of a right concerning access to healthcare services but also on the interpretation of a socioeconomic right as a justiciable right, it does not thoroughly illuminate the normative content of Section 27 as a socioeconomic right. Moreover, while General Comment 14 envisages that courts will impugn executive policy decisions that impact on the realization of the right to health, as part of the protective function of the judicial organ of State, *Soobramoney* seemed to give undue deference to the executive organ. There is no promise in *Soobramoney* that the Court is interested in inquiring into whether the State accords due priority to the realization of the right sought by making available resources that *ought* to be available and utilizing such resources effectively, in line with General Comment 14.

The other shortcoming of the *Soobramoney* ruling is the absence of a systematic approach to the determination of a socioeconomic right, thereby offering no clear articulation to derive interpretive assistance from the normative content of the right to healthcare services (Scott & Alston, 2000). The omission of international human rights instruments was significant, not least because Section 39 of the Constitution enjoins the court to consider international law when interpreting provisions of the Bill of Rights. While South Africa had signed but not ratified the ICESCR, the injunction in Section 39 of the Constitution requires neither the international law in question to have been incorporated into domestic law nor the relevant treaty to have been signed or ratified.

Government of the Republic of South Africa and Others v. *Grootboom and Others* (2000) (11) BCLR 1169 (CC)

Government of the Republic of South Africa and Others v. *Grootboom and Others* (hereafter *Grootboom*) revolved around the interpretation and application of the right of access to housing under Section 26 or alternative basic shelter under Section 28 of the Constitution. In *Grootboom*, the respondents were rendered homeless as a result of eviction from informal homes that they had erected on land earmarked for formal low-cost housing. The respondents succeeded on the Section 26 claim in the Constitutional Court. The Court drew particular assistance from the provisions of the ICESCR and their interpretation by the Committee on Economic, Social and Cultural Rights (CESCR). Article 11(1) of the ICESCR provides everyone with the right to an adequate standard of living, including adequate housing. Article 2(1) of the ICESCR is similar to Section 26(2) of the Constitution. The Court looked at the interpretation of the CESCR and made use of General

Comment 3, which explains the obligations imposed by Article 2(1) of the Covenant (CESCR, 1990). Drawing in part from the systematic approach adopted by the CESCR in General Comment 3, the Court was able to unentangle Section 26(2) of the Constitution into three main elements: 'reasonable legislative and other measures'; 'progressive realization of the right'; and 'within its available resources'. (*Government of the Republic of South Africa and Others* v. *Grootboom and Others*, 2000).

The Court noted that resources were a crucial consideration, but reasonableness depended on context. In the *Grootboom* case, the Court concluded that the State was not meeting the obligations imposed by Section 26(2) in that it did not provide relief to the categories of people in desperate need. The Court emphasized that a well-intentioned programme would not pass constitutional muster if it lacked reasonableness. The State had not taken reasonable measures to meet the right in question, notwithstanding that its resources were limited and its housing programme was sincere. At the same time, the Court rejected the CESCR's notion that every substantive socioeconomic right carries a 'minimum core obligation' that is immediately realizable (General Comment 3 at paragraph 10), instead stating that the minimum threshold was dependent on the actual needs and opportunities for the enjoyment of a right. Yet in dismissing the notion of a core minimum, the Court did not rule out the notion of minimum core obligations, saying that, in appropriate cases, evidence can be adduced to show that the State failed to discharge even a 'minimum core service'. In short, the Court favours a flexible, case-by-case approach subject to a 'reasonableness' criterion where there is no prior universal core minimum entitlement as a matter of course.

Minister of Health and Others v. *Treatment Action Campaign and Others* (2002), (10) BCLR 1033 (CC)

Minister of Health and Others v. *Treatment Action Campaign and Others* (hereafter referred to as *Minister of Health and Others*) was an appeal by the government against the decision of the High Court—*Treatment Action Campaign and Others* v. *Minister of Health and Others* (2002), (4) BCLR 356 (T). During the first trial, the applicants challenged the State's decision to confine the dispensation of the antiretroviral drug nevirapine to only 18 pilot sites for the purpose of prevention of mother-to-child transmission of HIV (PMTCT). Before the High Court, the applicants' main argument was that the government's failure to provide universal access to antiretroviral therapy (ART) in the public health sector, specifically for PMTCT of HIV, constituted a series of breaches of constitutional provisions, but mainly Section 27. The government had confined nevirapine to 18 sites because of safety reservations and because it wished to study the social, economic, and public health implications of providing a nationwide programme. The applicants were successful before the High Court, which held that the government's nevirapine programme fell short of a reasonable measure to realize the right of access to healthcare under Section 27. The Court ordered the State to make nevirapine universally available in the public sector and to plan and implement forthwith a comprehensive national programme for PMTCT of HIV. The government appealed this decision to the Constitutional Court.

The Constitutional Court held that while the State was better placed than the courts to formulate and implement policy on HIV, including measures for PMTCT, nonetheless, it had failed to adopt a reasonable measure to achieve the progressive realization of the right of access to healthcare services in accordance with Section 27(2) read with Section 27(1). The policy of confining nevirapine distribution to the 18 pilot sites was unreasonable in that it was too rigid (reaching only 10% of the population of women accessing antenatal care at public facilities). It denied those who were born outside of the pilot sites the opportunity to receive a life-saving drug that could be administered within the available resources of the State. Nevirapine had been recommended for PMTCT without qualification by the World Health Organization (WHO), and the State's own licensing authority—the Medicines Control Council—had registered nevirapine for PMTCT. Applying *Grootboom*, a programme that excludes a significant section of the community cannot pass constitutional muster unless the cost of the programme is beyond the available resources of the State. In this case, the Court found that the cost of each nevirapine treatment—less than US$2—was patently within the means of the State. The Court, in its dicta, also said that it would have reached the same conclusion had the matter been determined according to the State's obligation under Section 28 of the Constitution. The provision of nevirapine to prevent transmission of HIV could be considered 'essential' to the child, whose needs were 'most urgent'.

The Constitutional Court upheld the decision of the High Court but modified the order. It ordered the State to remove restrictions limiting nevirapine to pilot sites; permit, facilitate, and expedite use of nevirapine at public health facilities; and to provide for counselling training outside of the pilot sites. While the Court conceded that the matter of health policy was pre-eminently within the province of the executive branch and that all organs of State should be sensitive to and respect separation of powers, it was concomitantly at pains to emphasize that Section 7(2) the Constitution requires the State to 'respect, protect, promote, and fulfil the rights in the Bill of Rights'. Upon finding an infringement of a fundamental right, courts have competence to grant appropriate relief, including issuing orders that are just and equitable, as mandated by Section 38 and Section 172(1) of the Constitution.

Unlike *Grootboom*, this case was decided without any explicit recourse to international law. In particular, the Court could have built on the Committee on the Elimination of Discrimination against Women (CEDAW) General Recommendation 24: Women and Health, to explain the discriminatory nature of neglecting health care that only women need to ensure that they go safely through pregnancy and childbirth to ensure the birth of a healthy child (CEDAW, 1999). Moreover, as in the *Grootboom* case, the Court deciding the *Minister of Health and Others* case refused to endorse the notion of a minimum core obligation as a 'self-standing independent positive right' (*Government of the Republic of South Africa and Others* v. *Grootboom and Others*, 2000).

Judicial interpretation and application of Section 35 of the Constitution

Section 35 of the Constitution has generated case law pertinent to the notion of a right to health in the context of access to healthcare for those that are in State incarceration. As part of vindicating rights guaranteed by the Constitution, prisoners have brought cases to courts, inter alia, in connection with access to healthcare under Section 35(2)(e), which guarantees an incarcerated person a right to receive 'adequate medical treatment' at the State's expense, and Section 35(f) (iv), which guarantees an incarcerated person a right to be visited and examined by a medical practitioner of his or her choice.

The earliest case to come before the courts was *B and Others* v. *Minister of Correctional Services and Others* (1997), (6) BCLR 789 (C). The issue before the High Court in this case was whether refusal by the Department of Correctional Services to pay for the cost of ART for four prisoners who were HIV-positive was a breach of the right to receive 'adequate medical treatment' under Section 35(2)(e). The Court held that, with respect to prisoners for whom ART had been medically prescribed, there had been a breach. While the Department of Correctional Services had pleaded lack of resources, it failed to submit convincing evidence in support of this claim.

In *N and Others* v. *The Government of South Africa and Others* (2006), 15 prisoners living with HIV claimed that they were entitled to access to treatment in accordance with: Section 27 of the Constitution; Section 35(2)(e) of the Constitution; and the *Operational Plan for Comprehensive HIV/AIDS Care, Management and Treatment of 2003* (*Operational Plan*) (Department of Health, 2003). The High Court ordered the prison authorities to provide treatment and indicate to the prisoners and the Court how access to the treatment would be expedited, noting that the applicants' status as prisoners did not in any way deprive them of their fundamental human rights, including access to life-saving medications. The Court said the State had a duty under Sections 27 and 35 of the Constitution and Section 12 of the Correctional Services Act to provide treatment to the applicants. Applying *Grootboom*, the Court observed that the steps taken by government to assure access to HIV treatment for the prisoners, in accordance with its obligations under Sections 27 and 35(2)(e) of the South African Constitution, were not only slow but inadequate and unreasonable.

Other cases decided under Section 35(2)(e) clearly demonstrate the willingness of South African courts to give life to the constitutional provisions on the right to health, especially with regard to vulnerable groups such as prisoners. In *Stanfield* v. *Minister of Correctional Services* (2004) (4) S.A 43 (C), the Court held that to continue to detain (as opposed to granting parole to) a terminally ill cancer sufferer, despite the fact that the place where he was being detained lacked necessary medical facilities for his treatment, constituted a violation of his right to dignity and to dignified conditions of detention. In *Du Ploy* v. *Minister of Correctional Services*, (2004), 3 All SA 613 (T), Section 35(2)(e) similarly played an indirect role in influencing the overturning of a refusal to grant a medical parole to a prisoner who was in serious need of palliative care that could not be provided by the correctional institution in which the prisoner was detained. In this case, it was held that the refusal of medical parole to the applicant was irrational and unreasonable and thus impugned his rights to: dignity; access to healthcare services; dignified conditions of detention; and to not be subjected to cruel, inhuman, and degrading punishment.

Section 35(f)(iv) has similarly been applied by the courts to ensure that detainees are given conditional parole to secure treatment and care that the State cannot afford to provide for serious ailments. In the case of *S* v. *Mpofana* (1998) (1) SACR 40 (Tk) 45, an applicant for bail alleged, *inter alia*, that he was denied access to a medical practitioner of his choice. On appeal to the High Court, while the decision to refuse bail was upheld, the Court said that an infringement of Section 35(f)(iv) would require the respondent to either provide the applicant access to medical treatment or to restrain the respondent from denying the applicant either access to such treatment or preventing the applicant from challenging the legality of the detention. In *S* v. *Vanqa* (2000) (2) SACR 371 (Tk), an applicant who was awaiting trial suffered from serious asthma attacks while in detention but had not been provided with medical care by prison authorities and was prevented from using medications brought to him in prison by his relatives. It was held by the Court that the inability of the applicant to obtain necessary treatment constituted 'exceptional circumstances' that warranted his release on bail, and the denial of treatment to the applicant amounted to a 'deplorable' violation of Section 35(2)(e) of the Constitution.

While the approach of the South African courts in cases involving incarcerated persons complements the reasoning of the CESCR in paragraph 34 of General Comment 14, courts have missed an opportunity to have recourse to international law as applied to those in State incarceration, such as the WHO's Guidelines on HIV Infection and AIDS in Prisons, and the International Guidelines on HIV/AIDS and Human Rights (WHO, 1993, 1997).

The role of quasi-judicial bodies in implementing the right to health

Under Section 184 of the South African Constitution, the South African Human Rights Commission (SAHRC) is empowered to monitor the implementation of socioeconomic rights. The SAHRC has conducted public hearings to assess the extent to which the South African government is meeting its obligation to realize the right to health (SAHRC, 2007). The SAHRC also has continued to document human rights violations in relation to health and has requested the South African government to take more concrete steps in fulfilling the right to health of its citizens (SAHRC, 2007).

Policy and legislative frameworks on the right to health

The *White Paper for the Transformation of the Health System of South Africa* has been the most important transformative policy instrument for the healthcare sector (Department of Health, 1997). Over and above creating a single national ministry to direct and coordinate health policy in place of the erstwhile racially-fragmented services, two main strategies for reforming the healthcare system and remedying the legacy of gross inequality stand out. One is a paradigm shift toward primary healthcare (PHC). The other is the introduction of the district health system (DHS). Both strategies are intended to render healthcare services accessible in a substantive sense, as envisaged by General Comment 14. The implementation of a PHC system has required a major redistribution of public health resources in favour of equitable geographical allocations. Equally, there is now a de-emphasis on high-technology care in urban and teaching hospitals in favour of providing PHC to historically underserved areas (van Rensburg & Engelbrecht, 2012). Early in its life, the new government embarked on an extensive clinic-building programme in rural areas in an effort to render health services geographically accessible (Benatar, 1997; van Rensburg & Engelbrecht, 2012). The DHS, an instrument for decentralizing and regionalizing healthcare, is now becoming the vehicle for organizing and dispensing healthcare services. If diligently implemented, it should democratize health services and substantially dilute the dominance of the national Department of Health and provincial health authorities in the organization and dispensation of services, thereby overcoming overdependence on hospital-based care and bridging the urban–rural chasm.

The Department of Health has adopted a Patients' Rights Charter (Department of Health, 2000) as a tool for raising awareness about health rights among users and improving the quality of services. The Patients' Rights Charter contains information on rights and responsibilities pertaining to access to healthcare services, and on the complaints mechanism, facilitating the rendition of acceptable and high-quality services as integral components of the right to health.

On the legislative front, one of the earliest measures adopted to ensure access to healthcare was a decree by the State President in 1994 to the effect that all children under the age of six and all pregnant women were entitled to free healthcare services (Government Gazette Notice, 1994; McCoy & Barron, 1996; McCoy & Khosa, 1996). Another early piece of legislation to be passed was the Choice on Termination of Pregnancy Act No. 92 of 1996 (CTOPA). The CTOPA was passed to radically reform abortion law and ensure that women's reproductive health needs are respected, protected, and fulfilled rather than criminalized (Ngwena, 1998), making free abortion services available upon request in the first 12 weeks of pregnancy. Notwithstanding early problems of implementation, vast numbers of women have been able to secure safe and legal abortions (Ngwena, 2000b; Reproductive Rights Alliance, 2000). The validity of the CTOPA has been unsuccessfully challenged in the courts by 'prolife' groups (*Christian Lawyers Association of SA and others* v. *Minister of Health and Others* (1998), (11) BCLR 1434 (T); *Christian Lawyers Association of SA and Others* v. *Minister of Health and Others* (2004), (10) BCLR 1086 (T)).

The new government passed the Medicines and Related Substances Control Act No. 90 of 1997 with a view, inter alia, to render the price of medicines more accessible through a variety of measures, including: parallel importation of medicines; compulsory licensing; institution of price regulation and controls; promotion of generic substitution; and the prohibition of bonuses and rebates (used by drug manufacturers to offer discounts to dispensers of medicines (Gray, 1998).

The drug industry reacted, in part, through court challenges such as the *Pharmaceutical Manufacturers Association of SA and Another* (1999). In this case, the applicants challenged the constitutionality of Section 15 of the Medicines and Related Substances Act, which permits the Minister of Health to prescribe conditions for the supply of more affordable medicines so as to protect public health, notwithstanding patent rights guaranteed under the Patents Act No. 57 of 1978. The applicants withdrew the case following a surge of global public opinion against their action. In *Minister of Health and Another* v. *New Clicks South Africa (Pty) Ltd. and Another* (2005), the applicants challenged the constitutionality of Section 22 of the Medicines and Related Substances Act, which permits the Minister of Health to establish a Price Control Committee to determine prices of drugs in the country and dispensing fees for pharmacists. The Constitutional Court upheld the portion of the Act dealing with price regulation as reasonable to ensure reasonable access to medicines for citizens, as envisaged under Section 22 of the Act. However, the Court struck the provisions dealing with dispensing fees for pharmacists as unconstitutional because it unreasonably destroyed the viability of pharmacists.

As part of rendering medicine accessible, two Pharmacy Amendment Acts have been passed. To promote pharmacy growth in rural areas, the Pharmacy Amendment Act No. 88 of 1997 permits a non-pharmacist to own a pharmacy, provided a pharmacist supervises the dispensation of a prescribed medicine. Pharmacy Amendment Act No. 1 of 2000 requires a pharmacist who applies for registration with the country's pharmacist registration body—the Pharmacy Council—to serve one year of remunerated service in a State health facility as a condition for registration.

Prior to the introduction of the National Health Insurance Scheme, South Africa did not have national insurance provisions for access to healthcare. Only about 20% of the population–mainly those that are in formal employment—are able to access private insurance. The Medical Schemes Act No. 131 of 1998 was passed in an effort to broaden access to medical schemes that finance access to the private health sector. The Act outlawed unfair discrimination based on age, sex, disability, or state of health, in the provision and pricing of healthcare coverage.

The National Health Act No. 61 of 2003 created a national health system and provided for the decentralization of health services to provinces and districts primarily through the establishment of provincial health authorities and district health authorities. Section 4 of the National Health Act put on a statutory footing free healthcare services for pregnant and lactating women, children below the age of six who are not members or beneficiaries of medical schemes, and all persons who are not members of medical schemes. The goal is for the 80% who cannot access the private sector to be guaranteed access to the public health sector. The Act espoused democratic governance of healthcare structures, including and especially the active involvement of the community at a local level.

A bill to amend the National Health Act of 2003, the National Health Amendment Bill of 2012 (Amendment Bill), has been proposed. The proposed amendment is intended to establish monitoring bodies that will ensure quality assurance and provide remedies for patients that experience human rights violations in the healthcare sector. More importantly, Clause 81 of the Amendment Bill seeks to establish an office of ombudsman to receive complaints from patients and ensure that necessary remedies are provided to the complainants in a fair, economical, and expeditious manner. As documented by Human Rights Watch (with respect to maternal deaths in poor provinces), one of the major challenges patients often encounter when seeking healthcare services in public hospitals has been unethical practices by healthcare providers (Human Rights Watch, 2011). Clause 77 of the Amendment Bill establishes the office of the Health Standard Compliance to promote and protect health and users of healthcare services and monitor compliance by health establishments of national norms and standards.

Another important development in the healthcare arena is the recent introduction of the National Health Insurance (NHI) pursuant to Section 3 of the National Health Act. Prior to this, only about

20% of the population—mainly those that are in formal employment—were able to access private insurance (Department of Health, 2011). The NHI aligns itself with General Comment 14 of the CESCR by augmenting the PHC system and seeking to ensure that everyone has access to appropriate, efficient, and quality healthcare services. Social solidarity, effectiveness, equity, and affordability are principles that underpin the NHI, which is being piloted in districts across the country.

Implementing the right to health: lessons from the antiretroviral therapy experience

Timely delivery of high-quality services has been the major challenge for the public health sector. Current healthcare reforms have not succeeded in bridging the chasm between the public sector and the private sector. The widely shared perception that the public health sector provides a third-rate service reflects the reality that the move towards universal PHC has occurred at a faster pace than capacity to deliver requisite services. There are many facilities that are experiencing overcrowding, long waiting periods for patients, shortages of supplies and equipment, poor working conditions, and low staff morale. All of these factors detract from what is envisaged by Section 27 and General Comment 14's requirement of high-quality care.

Moreover, for reasons connected to the government's initial scepticism over the efficacy of ART, literally millions of people living with HIV were at first denied treatment that the State could otherwise afford. It was only in November 2003, when the government adopted the Operational Plan (Department of Health, 2003) that the State unequivocally committed itself to making provisions of ART universally available through a nationwide programme.

The roll-out of this ART programme has had a hesitant start, in part due to delays by the State in committing resources. Essentially, the Operational Plan aimed to provide ART to about 1.5 million people in the country by 2008. At the end of 2010, it was estimated that one million people were receiving ART from private and public health facilities in the country (UNAIDS, 2010). This figure, though significant, represents only about 40% of people in need of HIV treatment, a huge availability shortfall. Also, problems still exist in terms of treatment resistance, dearth of healthcare providers, delay in certification of health facilities to uptake treatment, administrative challenges, and stock-outs in some parts of the country (Navario et al., 2010). Against this backdrop, it cannot, as yet, be said that the ART roll-out meets the tenets of General Comment 14.

For PMTCT, the picture is different. Programme implementation has been better than ART roll-out, primarily because the financial resources and infrastructure required for PMTCT are a tiny fraction of those required for lifelong ART. Even so, it was not until the Constitutional Court ordered the state to provide treatment for PMTCT and thus to act in *Minister of Health and Others* that the it finally did so. In a real sense, *Minister of Health and Others* compelled the government to change its policy and scale up its efforts in developing and implementing a universal nevirapine regimen, one that would be made available and accessible on the basis of need rather than ability to pay, as envisaged by General Comment 14. On account of this increase in services, the number of HIV-positive pregnant women receiving ART for PMTCT increased from about 22% in 2003 to almost 90% at the end of 2009 (UNAIDS, 2010). The challenge now is not so much making PMTCT services available but rather promoting their use among pregnant women. In addition, government will need to address challenges such as shortages of test kits; stigma; insufficient staff assigned to HIV services; late payment of lay counsellors, with consequent absenteeism; and delayed transcription of CD4 count results into patient files, which is required for ART initiation (Sprague et al., 2011).

One of the lessons to draw from the slow uptake of ART use for PMTCT is that achieving availability and accessibility is not enough. The beneficiaries of the services must also be willing to come forward for treatment. Where a particular condition is stigmatized—as is the case with HIV/AIDS—more needs to be done by healthcare providers to promote the acceptability of the treatment offered.

Conclusion

In the post-apartheid era, South Africa has certainly embarked on a major transformative agenda. South Africa's challenge is no longer about creating a Constitution, policy, and legislation that enable the right to health but rather implementation. As discussed in preceding sections, even while accepting that implementation is a progressive process, there is still a long way to go before South Africa can truly claim that healthcare services are available, accessible, acceptable, and of good quality.

References

African National Congress. (1994). *National Health Plan South Africa.* African National Congress: Johannesburg.

Albertyn, C. and Goldblatt, B. (1998). Facing the challenge of transformation: the difficulties in the development of an indigenous jurisprudence of equality. *South African Journal on Human Rights*, 14, 248–276.

Benatar, S.R. (1997). Health care reform in the new South Africa. *New England Journal of Medicine*, 336, 881–895.

Bradshaw, D. (2008). *Determinants of Health and Their Trends: South African Health Review.* Health Systems Trust: Durban.

CEDAW. (1999). *General Recommendation 24: Women and Health*, UN GAOR 1999, UN Doc. A/54/38/Rev.1. Committee on the Elimination of Discrimination against Women (CEDAW): Geneva.

CESCR. (1990). *General Comment 3.* Committee on Economic, Social, and Cultural Rights (CESCR): Geneva.

CESCR. (2000). *General Comment No. 14: The Right to the Highest Attainable Standard of Health (Article 12 of the International Covenant on Economic, Social and Cultural Rights).* Committee on Economic, Social, and Cultural Rights (CESCR): Geneva.

Christian Lawyers Association of SA and Others v. *Minister of Health and Others.* (2004). (10) BCLR 1036 (T).

Constitution of the Republic of South Africa. (1996). No. 108.

Currie, I. and De Waal, J. (2005). *The Bill of Rights Handbook* (5th ed.) Juta: Wetton.

Day, C. and Gray, A. (2008). Health and related indicators. *South African Health Review*, 2008, 239–396.

Day, C. and Gray, A. (2010). Health and related indicators. *South African Health Review*, 2010, 211–353.

De Beer, C. (1984). *The South African Disease: Apartheid Health and Health Services.* South African Research Service: Johannesburg.

Department of Health. (1997). *White Paper for the Transformation of the Health System in South Africa.* Department of Health: Pretoria.

Department of Health. (2000). *Primary Health Care Package for South Africa: A Set of Norms and Standards.* Department of Health: Pretoria.

Department of Health. (2003). *Operational Plan for Comprehensive HIV/AIDS Care, Management and Treatment for South Africa.* Available at: <http://www.info.gov.za/issues/hiv/careplan.htm> (accessed 31 October 2012).

Department of Health. (2011). *National Health Insurance in South Africa: Policy Paper.* Department of Health: Pretoria.

Department of Social Development. (2010). *Progress Review of the Implementation of the White Paper on Population Policy for South Africa (1998) and the ICPD Programme of Action (1994).* Department of Social Development: Pretoria.

Ex parte Chairperson of the Constitutional Assembly. (1996). In *re Certification of the Constitution of the Republic of South Africa*, (10) BCLR 1253 (CC).

Government Gazette Notice. (1994). *Government Notice 657. National Health Act (61/2003): Policy on National Health Insurance*. Department of Health: Pretoria.

Government of the Republic of South Africa and Others v. *Grootboom and Others*. (2000). (11) BCLR 1169 (CC).

Gray, A. (1998). Equity and the provision of pharmaceutical services. *South African Health Review*, 1998, 103–112.

Health Act. (1977). *Health Act No. 63 of 1977*. Government Printers: Pretoria.

Health Systems Trust and World Bank. (1995). *Health Expenditure in South Africa*. Health System Trust: Durban.

Human Rights Watch. (2011). *'Stop Making Excuses': Accountability for Maternal Health Care in South Africa*. Human Rights Watch: New York NY.

McCoy, D. and Baron, P. (1996). *Free Health Care for Pregnant Women and Children under Six in South Africa: An Impact Assessment*. Health Systems Trust: Durban.

McCoy, D. and Khosa, S. (1996). Free health care policies. In D. Harrison, P. Barron, and. J. Edwards (Eds.), *South African Health Review*, pp. 157–164. Health Systems Trust: Durban.

Medical Schemes Act. (1998). *Medical Schemes Act, No. 131 of 1998*. Government Printers: Pretoria.

Minister of Health and Another v. *New Clicks South Africa (Pty) Ltd. and Another*. (2005). (3) SA 231 (CC).

Minister of Health and Others v. *Treatment Action Campaign and Others*. (2002). (10) BCLR 103.

Nattrass, N. and Seekings, J. (2001). Democracy and distribution in highly unequal economies: the case of South Africa. *Journal of Modern African Studies*, 39, 471–498.

Navario, P., Bekker, L., Darkoh, E., *et al.* (2010). Special report on state of HIV/AIDS in South Africa. *Global Health*, 6, 3.

Ngwena, C. (1998). History and transformation of abortion law in South Africa. *Acta Academica*, 30, 32–68.

Ngwena, C. (2000a). Access to health care as a fundamental right: the scope and limits of section 27 of the Constitution. *Journal for Juridical Science*, 25, 1–32.

Ngwena, C. (2000b). Accessing abortion under the choice on termination of pregnancy act: realising substantive equality. *Journal for Juridical Science*, 25, 19–44.

Patents Act. (1978). *Patents Act, No. 57*. Government Printers: Pretoria.

Pharmaceutical Manufacturers Association of SA and Another: In re Ex Parte President of the Republic of South Africa & Others. (1999). (4) SA 788 (T).

Pharmacy Amendment Act. (1997). *Pharmacy Amendment Act, No. 88*. Government Printers: Pretoria.

Pharmacy Amendment Act. (2000). *Pharmacy Amendment Act, No. 1*. Government Printers: Pretoria.

Pieterse, M. (2006). Resuscitating socio-economic rights: constitutional entitlements to health services. *South African Journal on Human Rights*, 22, 473–502.

President of the Republic of South Africa and Another v. *Hugo*. (1997). (6) BCLR 708 (CC).

Redelinghuys, N. (2012). Health and health status of the South African population. In H.C.J. van Rensburg (Ed.), *Health and Health Care in South Africa*, pp. 237–292. Van Schaik: Pretoria.

Reproductive Rights Alliance. (2000). National terminations of pregnancy statistics. *Barometer*, 6, 5–9.

Rispel, L. and Kibua, T. (2011). Wither the MDGs? Stewardship for health in Kenya, Nigeria and South Africa. In K. Kondlo, and C. Ejiogu (Eds.), *Africa in Focus: Governance in the 21st Century*, pp. 240–258. HSRC Press: Cape Town.

Scott, C. and Alston, P. (2000). Adjudicating constitutional priorities in a transnational context: a comment on *Soobramoney's* legacy and *Grootboom's* promise. *South African Journal on Human Rights*, 16, 206–414.

Soobramoney v. *Minister of Health, KwaZulu-Natal*. (1997). (12) BCLR 1696 (CC).

Soobramoney v. *Minister of Health, KwaZulu-Natal*. (1998). (1) SA 430 (D & CLD).

South African Human Rights Commission (SAHRC). (2007). *Public Inquiry: Access to Health Care*. South African Human Rights Commission: Johannesburg.

South African Institute of Race Relations. (1995). *South Africa Survey 1995/1996*. South African Institute of Race Relations: Johannesburg.

South African Institute of Race Relations. (1997). *South Africa Survey 1996/1997*. South African Institute of Race Relations: Johannesburg.

Sprague, C., Chersich, M.F., and Black, V. (2011). Health system weaknesses constrain access to PMTCT and maternal HIV services in South Africa: a qualitative enquiry. *AIDS Research and Therapy*, 8, 1–9.

Statistics South Africa. (2011). *Mid-Year Population Estimates 2011*. Statistics South Africa: Pretoria.

Terreblanche, S. (2002). *A History of Inequality in South Africa 1652-2002*. University of Natal Press: Durban.

Trading Economics. (2012). *South Africa GDP Growth Rate*. Available at: <http://www.Tradingeconomics.com/south-africa/gdp-growth> (accessed 9 August 2012).

UNAIDS. (2010). *Global Epidemic Report*. Joint United Nations Programme on HIV/AIDS (UNAIDS): Geneva.

UNDP. (2010). *South Africa MDG Report 2010*. StatsSA/United Nations Development Programme (UNDP): Pretoria.

WHO. (1993). *Guidelines on HIV Infection and AIDS in Prisons*. WHO Global Programme on AIDS: Geneva.

WHO. (1997). *Prisons and AIDS: UNAIDS Point of View*. Joint United Nations Programme on HIV/AIDS (UNAIDS): Geneva.

van Rensburg, H.C.J. (2012). The history of health care in South Africa. In H.C.J. van Rensburg (Ed.), *Health and Health Care in South Africa*, pp. 61–120. Van Schaik: Pretoria.

van Rensburg, H.C.J. and Benatar, S.R. (1993). The legacy of apartheid in health and health care. *South African Journal of Sociology*, 24, 99–111.

van Rensburg, H.C.J. and Engelbrecht, M.C. (2012). Transformation of the South African healthcare system. In H.C.J. van Rensburg (Ed.), *Health and Health Care in South Africa*, pp. 121–188. Van Schaik: Pretoria.

van Rensburg, H.C.J. and Fourie, A. (1994). Inequalities in South African health care. Part I: the problem—manifestation and origins. *South African Medical Journal*, 84, 95–103.

Chapter 10

The domestic implementation of the international right to health: the Philippine experience

Raul C. Pangalangan

Introduction

This chapter uses the Philippine experience to draw lessons on the human rights approach to health, that is to say, protecting and promoting the health of people through mechanisms that are both legal and international and, more specifically, by converting health needs as a claim of individuals against the State and securing these through international treaties. Located in Southeast Asia, the Philippines is a middle-income archipelago consisting of more than 7,000 islands, ranked 112th in the world by the Human Development Index (HDI) and with a life expectancy at birth at 69 years of age (UNDP, 2012). However, with elevated infant and maternal mortality rates, uncontrolled population growth, and highly unequal access to care, the Philippines faces significant challenges in increasing the overall health of its society. As such, the right to health has remained a focus of definitive importance in Philippine law and politics.

Codifying health rights as international law fundamentally transforms the meaning of rights-based advocacy and, in the Philippines, demonstrates the power and limits of rights claims where law-based State institutions are thinly veneered over the raw power of competing elites. This transformation raises three preliminary issues that form the backdrop of this study on the right to health in the Philippines:

- How accurately can we determine compliance and non-compliance with such treaty obligations? In addition to the old debate about the international enforceability of social and economic rights in general, we thereby challenge the Philippines' own capacity to translate treaty obligations into domestic programmes given constitutional constraints. Until the post-Ferdinand Marcos Constitution of 1987, health claims had not been formally recognized on the constitutional plane, thereby fostering a liberal State initially disabled from ministering to welfare claims. The Philippines frustrates in domestic constitutional law the grand promises it makes in international covenants.
- By internationalizing an erstwhile domestic issue, we disengage the essentially distributional nature of the right to health from the hegemony of national elites. The Philippines' newly restored democracy has merely ratified the rule of the old families, the professional politicians, and the powerful business sector. Stated otherwise, in order for the right to health to trump elite control, it will not suffice merely to globalize what was hitherto a local concern. We must also transform health claims into fixed legal categories (e.g. demandable rights), rather than preserve them as charity extended by benevolent aristocrats (e.g. privilege), or as goods

negotiated in the open market (e.g. commodities). The right to health trumps local resistance by becoming both a legal and an international obligation.

- Since treaties impose obligations on States, we privilege one form of collectivity, the Nation-State, over non-State, family, and village networks of support through which healthcare were hitherto collectivized, thus demoting community-based health reforms. For instance, traditional and alternative medicine has served generations of Filipinos, oblivious to State intervention, but it became visible to treaty-compliance processes only when it was incorporated into statute law. The irony therefore is that health claims must be formalized into rights claims to immunize them from being compromised politically, yet once formalized they become hostage to the flaws and weaknesses of the State.

The right to health under Philippine law: a constitutional framework

Enforceability of treaty obligations in Philippine municipal law

The Philippines has recognized several right to health clauses under the International Covenant on Economic, Social and Cultural Rights (ICESCR), International Convention on the Elimination of All Forms of Racial Discrimination (ICERD), Convention on the Elimination of All Forms of Discrimination against Women (CEDAW), and the Convention on the Rights of the Child (CRC) (UN, 2012). These international obligations form part of domestic law by virtue of the Incorporation Clause of the 1987 Philippine Constitution, which states that the Philippines 'adopts the generally accepted principles of international law as part of the law of the land' (Philippine Constitution, 1987). However, the Supreme Court effectively required that treaty obligations be more specific and detailed before they could be self-executing without the benefit of separate legislation (*Pharmaceutical and Health Association of Philippines* v. *Duque II*, 2007). In *Duque II*, the Court held that international codes on breastfeeding were at best, non-binding 'soft law' that could not have enabled direct enforcement by administrative agencies. However, the Court noted that these treaties described only necessary steps in general terms, and no specific treaty obligations had been 'transformed' into domestic law. Referring to the more specific provisions in the non-binding World Health Organization (WHO) resolutions that categorically barred formula-manufacturers from making nutritional and health claims for breast milk substitutes, the Supreme Court found that these WHO standards did not create binding custom that could thus be 'incorporated' into Philippine law (ICBMS, 1981). Significantly, the Court characterized the WHO resolutions as 'soft law' or 'non-binding norms, principles and practices that influence State behaviour' (*Duque II*, 2007).

Additionally, the Supreme Court has created a hierarchy of rights, giving preference to civil and political rights over social, economic, and social rights—including the right to health (*Mayor Simon* v. *Commission on Human Rights*, 1994). The issue of domestic implementation of international health standards is currently being tested in a case pending before the Supreme Court regarding the implementation of health warnings required by the WHO's Framework Convention on Tobacco Control (FCTC) in the case of *Department of Health* v. *Honorable Tamayo* (*Department of Health* v. *Honorable Tamayo*, 2010).

Constitutional recognition of the right to health

The Philippine Constitution expressly recognizes the right to health. Article II contains the Declaration of Principles and State Policies in which the Constitution sets forth the following directive principle: 'The State shall protect and promote the right to health of the people and instill health consciousness among them' (Philippine Constitution, 1987). That same article provides, in Section 16, that the State shall likewise protect and advance 'the right of the people to a balanced and healthful ecology in accord with the rhythm and harmony of nature' (Philippine Constitution, 1987). The Supreme Court had the occasion to interpret the latter clause in *Oposa* v. *Factoran*, wherein it concluded that a mere directive principle, having used the language of rights, thus created legally enforceable claims that can be invoked directly before courts without waiting for implementing rules by the legislative or executive branches (Bernas, 1988).

The other right to health clauses that have been 'constitutionalized' appear in Article XIII entitled, 'Social Justice and Human Rights', which devotes an entire section to health. Article XIII establishes a particular mode by which the State shall uphold this right through the adoption of an 'integrated and comprehensive approach to health development'. While 'integration' refers to a unified health delivery system that incorporates both public and private sector participation, as well as the utilization of western and indigenous healthcare systems, 'comprehensiveness' refers to the delivery of services and the undertaking of activities relating to health promotion, disease prevention, education, and planning (Bernas, 1988).

Furthermore, Article XIII emphasizes that health services must be made available at affordable costs and free medical care must be given to the poor. It is clear from these clauses that, despite the State's obligation to uphold the right to health for all, a clear bias is established in favour of vulnerable populations—the poor and underprivileged, elderly, disabled, women and children—as cited in *Del Rosario* v. *Bengzon* (CESCR, 2000; *Del Rosario, S.A. & et al.* v. *Secretary of Department of Health,* 1989). Section 14 of the same Article further emphasizes the State's focus on upholding the right to health for working women. A final constitutional clause on the right to health appears in Article XIV entitled 'Education, Science and Technology, Arts, Culture, and Sports'.

International Indicia of Compliance with regard to the right to health

The Committee on Economic, Social, and Cultural Rights (CESCR) considered that the entitlements of the right to health 'include the right to a system of health protection which provides equality of opportunity for people to enjoy the highest attainable level of health' (CESCR, 2000). For instance, the right to health cannot be separated from the right to food, and laws (i.e. an Act for Salt Iodization Nationwide (Republic Act No. 8172, 1995)) and the Philippine Food Fortification Act of 2000 (Republic Act No. 8976, 2000) have been enacted to ensure that children do not suffer from micronutrient deficiencies.

The rights of persons with disabilities are also important health concerns addressed by Philippine law. The Congress has passed a law, the Magna Carta for Disabled Persons, to provide a comprehensive framework intended to assure the rights of persons with disabilities, particularly with regard to access to crucial social services such as healthcare, education, and employment opportunities. This act is in accordance with both the international commitments of the Philippines as well as the explicit mandate of the Philippines Constitution. The Congress has extended the scope of the Magna Carta to ensure that it will be implemented by local government units (Republic Act No. 10070, 2009).

The Traditional and Alternative Medicine Act of 1997 (TAMA) promotes research into and utilization of 'traditional and alternative [healthcare] systems' (Republic Act No. 8423, 1997). Traditional and alternative healthcare and medicine under this law refers to 'knowledge, skills, and practices *on [healthcare]*, other than those embodied in biomedicine [i.e. western medicine]' and 'not necessarily explicable in the context of modern, scientific, philosophical framework' (Emphasis added; Republic Act No. 8423, 1997). To this end, the Philippine Institute of Traditional and Alternative Health Care was created and charged with conducting a study of traditional and alternative medicine, training health workers in the use of such techniques, and formulating rules and guidelines for the regulation of the practice and usage of traditional and alternative medicine (Republic Act No. 8423, 1997). However, implementation has been slow due to the power of an organized physicians' lobby.

Specific aspects of the right to health: domestic programmes and legislation

Maternal, child, and reproductive health

In a country with the highest population growth in Asia, reproductive health is also among the most divisive health rights issues. The Revised Penal Code criminalizes abortion (Republic Act No. 3815, 1930), and punishes both the woman who gets (Article 258) and the physician (Article 259) who performs an abortion. The 1987 Constitution preserves this provision and attempts to insulate it from constitutional challenge by stating that the State 'shall equally protect the life of the mother and the life of the unborn from conception' (Philippine Constitution, 1987). At the same time, the Magna Carta of Women (Republic Act No. 9710, 2009) requires a 'comprehensive, culture-sensitive, and gender-responsive health services and programmes covering all stages of a woman's lifecycle and which addresses the major causes of women's mortality and morbidity', and calls for '[m]aternal care to include pre- and post-natal services to address pregnancy and infant health and nutrition' and '[r]esponsible, ethical, legal, safe, and effective methods of family planning' (Republic Act No. 9710, 2009).

From 1995 to 2010, the infant mortality rate (IMR) in the Philippines declined from 35 per 1,000 live births to 23 per 1,000 live births, although this rate decline lags behind comparable countries such as Thailand and Vietnam (Millennium Development Goals Indicators, 2011). The leading causes of infant deaths are bacterial sepsis, respiratory distress of the newborn, and pneumonia (DOH, 2005). The maternal mortality ratio (MMR) is between 95 to 163 deaths per 100,000 live births (National Statistical Coordination Board, 2012). The 2010 *Philippine Progress Report on the MDGs* states that 'the 2015 target of 52 deaths per 100,000 live births is unlikely to be met. There is also a need to intensify efforts to reduce the HIV and AIDS prevalence' (Millennium Development Goals Indicators, 2011). The 2009 Field Health Service Information System (FHSIS) report reflects the same progress in terms of the number of births that occur in a facility and the number that are attended by a skilled birth attendant. For normal deliveries, 47.08% were home-based; 38.83% were facility-based, with the 8.43% listed as 'others' (FHSIS, 2009). A little more than a third (33.8%) were attended by a physician, 39.1% by midwives, 1.4% by public health nurses, and 19.6% were attended by traditional birth attendants (FHSIS, 2009).

Philippine law requires and provides for free immunization for children under eight years old against various diseases such as tuberculosis (TB), diphtheria, pertussis, tetanus, measles, poliomyelitis, rubella, and hepatitis B (Presidential Decree No. 996, 1976). By 2008, reports indicated that 79.5% of the target population has been fully immunized, with more children vaccinated against hepatitis B (with more than 80% coverage) (National Statistics Office, 2008). Additionally, the Barangay-Level Total Development and Protection of Children Act (Republic Act No. 6972, 1990) provides for the establishment of daycare centres in every *barangay* (community) for children up to six years of age aimed at holistic health monitoring and support services (Republic Act No. 6972, 1990).

The 2009 FSHIS report showed that pre- and post-natal care is still inadequate, with only 59% of pregnant women with four or more prenatal care visits and only 52% of post-partum women initiating breastfeeding (FHSIS, 2009). Under the Rooming-In and Breastfeeding Act of 1992, guidelines were established to encourage and allow public and private hospitals to have the infants 'roomed-in' with the mother within 30 minutes after delivery in the case of normal births or within three to four hours in the case of Caesarean deliveries (FHSIS, 2009). In two qualitative studies assessing women's reproductive health and rights, a reproductive rights group found that nine out of 12 deaths were 'due to scientifically uninformed and erroneous management by traditional birth attendants [leading to] severe and rapid haemorrhage' (Demeterio-Melgar & Pacete, 2007). They further found that the major hurdle to patients was access to public hospitals that typically suffered from patient overload and a lack of basic emergency supplies (Melgar, 2005).

Justiciability concerns

The true picture regarding reproductive rights is best captured in proposed legislation and threatened litigation over these rights. After local groups filed a petition to nullify a de facto ban by the City of Manila against 'artificial' contraception (*Manila Times*, 2007), the city's Mayor, a firm opponent of reproductive rights, issued an order declaring that his city 'promotes responsible parenthood and upholds natural family planning not just as a method but as a way of self-awareness in promoting the culture of life while discouraging the use of artificial methods of contraception like condoms, pills, intrauterine devices, surgical sterilization, and others' (Executive Order No. 003, 2000). The order did not contain an explicit ban on 'artificial' contraception but, given the dynamics of local Manila politics, has resulted in 'as-applied' violations (Demeterio-Melgar & Pacete, 2007).

The Department of Health (DOH) has prohibited an emergency contraceptive drug levonorgestrel as an abortifacient, demonstrating the government's strict interpretation of the constitutional clause in order to prohibit contraceptives that, according to the WHO, 'do not interrupt pregnancy and thus are no form of abortion', but merely suppress ovulation, inhibit fertilization, or prevent implantation (WHO, 1998). Additionally, congressional attempts to advance reproductive rights through domestic legislation have not been met with success due to stiff opposition from the clergy and lay followers of the dominant Roman Catholic Church. There are two bills pending before the current Congress on reproductive rights (House Bill No. 4244, 2011; Senate Bill No. 2865, 2011). The earlier bill, the Reproductive Health Care Act of 2002, was not passed and its opponents, not satisfied with defeating the bill, actively presented their countervailing bill, the proposed Rights of Conscience Act of 2006 (House Bill No. 5028, 2006).

Right to prevention, treatment, and control of diseases

The 2009 FSHIS annual report lists the following as the leading causes of morbidity in the Philippines: acute respiratory infection, acute lower respiratory tract infection and pneumonia, bronchitis/bronchiolitis, hypertension, acute watery diarrhoea, influenza, urinary tract infection, and respiratory TB. With the TB-DOTS programme, there have been significant improvements in implementation and outcomes; 73% of TB cases were detected (DOH, 2010a). Of all detected cases, 89% completed the treatment and 79% were cured (DOH, 2010a). Regarding malaria, the Department of Health reports that among the total endemic population, the proportion of people using/sleeping under insecticide-treated nets has increased from 48% in 2006 to 91.2% in 2009 (National Center for Disease Prevention and Control, 2011). Likewise, the malaria morbidity rate and mortality rate have declined significantly from 50.3 per 100,000 population in 2002 to 13.3 per 100,000 in 2008, and 0.17 per 100,000 population in 2005 to 0.03 per 100,000 in 2009, respectively (National Center for Disease Prevention and Control, 2011).

The Administrative Code of 1987 not only mandated the creation of the DOH, but required it to provide services focused on preventing and controlling specific diseases. Programmes concentrating on the treatment of TB, malaria, schistosomiasis, and other similar diseases have been introduced under the authority of this law (Section 13, Title IX, Chapter 1 (Executive Order No. 292, 1987)). Since then, special laws have been enacted prescribing specific measures for the prevention, control, and treatment of particular ailments judged to be significant threats to the health of the public. For instance, the National Diabetes Act of 1996 mandated the creation of a National Commission on Diabetes and formulation of a National Diabetes Prevention and Control Plan (Republic Act No. 8191, 1996). In 1998, Congress passed the Philippine AIDS Prevention and Control Act (Republic Act No. 8584, 1998), which created the Philippine National AIDS Council (Republic Act No. 8584, 1998) while codifying HIV/AIDS confidentiality and non-discrimination (Republic Act No. 8584, 1998).

Right to health facilities, goods, and services

As early as 1954, Congress enacted Republic Act No. 1082, which strengthened the provision of health and dental care in rural areas by assigning public physicians and dentists to work in each congressional district in the country. A law enacted in 1992 mandated the conversion of municipal health centres in remote areas to five-bed capacity municipal health infirmaries, which would act as public health clinics (Republic Act No. 7609, 1992). In return, basic medical equipment and medicines were assigned by the DOH to the infirmaries (Republic Act No. 7609, 1992). The Barangay Health Workers' Benefits and Incentives Act of 1995 promoted 'participatory strategies such as health education, training of *barangay* health workers, community building and organizing' and provides incentives to communities and local health workers to act as front liners in the Primary Health Care Approach (Republic Act No. 7883, 1995).

The National Health Insurance Act of 1995 (Republic Act No., 7875, 1995), which called for implementing compulsory health insurance, established a national programme for health insurance that seeks to provide each citizen with a mechanism to obtain the financial resources necessary to procure essential health services. Additionally, Republic Act 8344, popularly known as the 'No-Deposit Law', makes it unlawful for hospitals and medical clinics to demand any form of advance payment before they provide healthcare services to a patient with an emergency or serious illnesses (Republic Act No. 8344, 1997). Similarly, legal mechanisms to ensure access to emergency treatment through medical insurance and similar schemes have also been established.

Republic Act No. 6675, commonly known as the Generics Act of 1988, requires the use of generic terminology in the prescription and dispensation of drugs, hopefully encouraging the use of generic drugs that, due to their lower costs, are more accessible to the poor and underprivileged (Republic Act, 6675, 1988). Furthermore, the law requires every drug manufacturer to make their medicines available in generic form (Republic Act, 6675, 1988). The Universally Cheaper Accessible and Quality Medicines Act of 2008 works toward the same end by specifically targeting the prices of medicines through drug ceiling prices (Republic Act, 9502, 2008). It also amended the Intellectual Property Code of the Philippines to entrench a parallel importation mechanism for patented drugs and medicines (Republic Act, 9502, 2008).

Encouragingly, statistics reflect considerable progress in assured medical services. As of May 2012, membership in the Philippine Health Insurance Corporation (PhilHealth) has progressed to 85% of the projected population of 95.98 million (Philippine Health Insurance Corporation, 2012). It is good to note that out of this figure, 39.70 million (41%) belong to the sponsored programme whose premiums are subsidized by national and local government (Philippine Health

Insurance Corporation, 2011). Full subsidy is given to 20.15 million NHTS-sponsored beneficiaries by the national government (Philippine Health Insurance Corporation, 2011). The number of PhilHealth-accredited hospitals has increased to 1687 (Philippine Health Insurance Corporation, 2011). With the release of the DOH's Administrative Order 2011-0029 on the 'streamlining of licensure and accreditation of hospitals', all DOH-licensed facilities are now deemed accredited by PhilHealth (DOH, 2011). This move further enhances both physical and financial access to health services.

A distinct patients' rights approach has emerged in Philippine law. A review conducted by various non-governmental organizations (NGOs) engaged in health advocacy concluded that government hospitals demonstrate a prevalence of discriminatory practices against poor, unmarried women (e.g. being asked to produce marriage certificates to access reproductive health services), youth, prostituted women, ethnic groups, the disabled, and women who had undergone abortions (Melgar, 1999). This discrimination in its mildest form was expressed through rude or disrespectful behaviour, and in its more extreme form resulted in an indifferent and/or irrational use of drugs and medical procedures (Melgar, 1999). Unfortunately, horror stories of government-affiliated physicians verbally and physically abusing patients, particularly women, or denying them treatment are becoming increasingly common (Tadiar, 2002). Despite numerous cases reported and documented, the prosecution of erring physicians, let alone conviction and sanction, remain few and far between, and efforts to enact legislation recognizing and protecting patients' rights have thus far been met with little success (Molino, 2001).

Responsibility for the right to health: domestic and international organizations

Role of the Philippine Department of Health

The Constitutional mandate to 'protect and promote the right to health of the people' is principally carried out through the DOH (Philippine Constitution, 1987). Its responsibilities include defining the national health policy, formulating and implementing a national health plan, providing for health programmes and services, conducting health education and research, and performing health-related regulatory functions (Executive Order No. 292, 1987). It has promulgated executive issuances on the entire range of health concerns: from industrial hygiene with the creation of the Solid Waste Management Task Force (DOH, 1992a), to disease control with the designation of all city health officers as members of the DOH AIDS Prevention and Control Committee (DOH, 1987), to the rights of persons with disabilities with the implementation of community-based rehabilitation programmes (DOH, 1992b). The DOH maintains offices at the regional, provincial, city, and municipal levels to provide efficient health and medical services to people at the grassroots level and to coordinate efforts with agencies set up by local government units (DOH, 1992b).

The Local Government Code of 1991 (Republic Act No. 7610, 1992) required the devolution of several areas of healthcare provision to DOH-supervised LGUs as a key strategy in streamlining the delivery of basic health services. Services and facilities related to general hygiene and sanitation became the responsibility of the lowest local government unit or *barangay*, while the provision of maternal and child care in addition to the containment of communicable and non-communicable diseases have become the responsibility of cities and municipalities, and the provision of hospital and other tertiary care health services have been placed in the care of cities and provinces. Nonetheless, the DOH manages several tertiary and specialty hospitals that are collectively known as

DOH-retained hospitals. Further, the DOH provides resources for the upkeep of certain public projects, including programmes to control TB, malaria, and vaccine-preventable diseases. Importantly, critics of devolution have pointed out that the transfer of power from a central government to a lower, local administration, may lead to a worsening in the delivery of basic services due to the absence of effective controls and the lack of universal standards, as well as deterioration in the quality of services as a result of the lack of local capacity and insufficiency of resources (International Council on Human Rights Policy, 2002).

The DOH has also established the Medium Term Philippine Development Plan for 2004–2010, which states that 'The [healthcare] delivery system, adopting the rights-based and life-cycle approach, shall be responsive to the needs of the population, especially the poor' (Medium Term Philippine Development Plan, 2004). The Plan sets out an ambitious set of priorities in six areas (Medium Term Philippine Development Plan, 2004). Currently, the direction of health reform has shifted toward achieving universal healthcare, as expressed in the 'Aquino Health Agenda: Universal Health Care for All Filipinos' (DOH, 2010b) which was later on adopted by the DOH as the 'Kalusugan Pangkalahatan' [or 'Universal Health Care'] agenda (DOH, 2011).

Role of international aid

The Philippines has enjoyed the benefit of a wide range of bilateral assistance. NGO representatives have expressed concerns about 'tied' aid and conditionalities because they require the engagement of the donor's own nationals and lack stakeholder participation in priority setting, planning, implementation, monitoring, and evaluation. The bilateral and multilateral donors and lenders have invested heavily in the health sector in the Philippines but rarely with any explicit support for the right to health.

United States

In addition to providing assistance in the field of family planning and reproductive health, the US Agency for International Development (USAID) has supported the Philippines in its fight against TB by helping both the public and private sectors institutionalize the DOTS approach. It also sponsors programmes focused on HIV prevention and antibiotic resistance prevention, and in 2006 awarded the Research Triangle Institute a multimillion-dollar contract for the Strengthening Local Governance for Health (HealthGov) Project designed to convince local government units to invest resources in family planning, TB care, and HIV prevention and control. The USAID also funds studies and initiatives to support the health sector reform agenda (USAID, 2012).

Germany

The *Deutsche Gesellschaft für Internationale Zusammenarbeit* (German Agency for Technical Co-operation, or GTZ) is Germany's development agency, and it primarily supports the health sector reform agenda. It has configured its aid as a four-pronged assistance programme focused on helping the national health insurance programme, setting up local health systems, maintaining hospital equipment, and designing a franchising scheme to retail quality low-cost pharmaceuticals. In addition, GTZ's support for PhilHealth has been extensive, including providing human resource consultancies for the ongoing re-engineering work in PhilHealth and funding for an advocacy course.

Japan

The Japanese International Cooperation Agency (JICA) focuses on three health priorities; maternal and child health services (MCH/FP), TB control, and HIV prevention. For all three areas, JICA has placed experts and provided focused grants in both the DOH and project areas. The JICA has also helped the health sector reform agenda by funding health policy training courses for the DOH and PhilHealth staff.

Australia

AusAID has provided assistance to the Integrated Community Health Services Project (ICHSP) and the Women's Health Safe Motherhood project (WHSMP), two major projects implemented by the DOH. The WHSMP's objective is to improve the health, nutrition, and the family status of women along with addressing their health needs at the community level. AusAID also provided support to a landmark malaria control project in Agusan del Sur in Mindanao.

Spain, Italy, and Belgium

The Spanish government has provided aid and soft loans to government hospitals. The Italian government has provided grants to local government units and government hospitals in Metro Manila for the implementation of referral schemes. The Belgian government has offered assistance for health services through its support of agrarian reform beneficiaries all over the country as part of the Belgian Integrated Assistance to Agrarian Reform Project Sites (BIARPS).

The European Union

The European Union assists with the implementation of health projects. It has primarily assisted the WHSMP by supporting community initiatives in the field of HIV prevention. In 2006, the European Commission agreed to provide €33 million to the Philippines' Health Sector Policy Support Programme (HSPSP), and in 2007 the European Commission provided a grant of €12 million to contribute to improving health services in conflict-affected areas of the Southern Philippines, particularly through the 'Mindanao Health Sector Policy Support Programme'.

UN agencies

The United Nations Population Fund (UNFPA) focuses its resources toward population and family planning programmes and has donated contraceptive supplies to the DOH and initiated province-level family planning programmes across the country. The WHO has been supporting the DOH with several grants in health-related areas, including environmental health, drug policies, and health promotion. It has also helped the country in accessing money from the Global Fund to Fight AIDS, Tuberculosis, and Malaria. Among the numerous projects implemented by the United Nations Children's Fund (UNICEF) in the Philippines are the maternal and child health nutrition (MCHN) project and the micronutrient deficiencies control project.

International financial institutions

The Asian Development Bank (ADB) has also provided loans to support the ICHSP, a project that is also supported by AusAID. Outside of the ICHSP, another health-related project is the Early Childhood Development Project (ECDP) run by the Department of Social Welfare and Development. The World Bank provided several major loans to the health sector, including for the WHSMP and the Urban Health National Programme (UHNP). The WHSMP focuses on women's health while the UHNP assists three urban areas (Metro Manila, Cebu, and Cagayan de Oro) provide healthcare services to their residents. The World Bank's most recent project is the 'National Sector Support for Kalusugan Pangkalahatan [Universal Health Care], which has allotted US$300 million for the universal healthcare reforms being pursued in the sector' (World Bank, 2012).

Measuring the implementation of the right to health in the Philippines

Lack of reliable data on health: causes and implications

Although the country's IMR, MMR, crude birth rate, crude death rate, and life expectancy at birth statistics appear impressive, various health professionals and civil society organizations have challenged the reliability of the government's figures. These statistics ignore a significant number of deaths that occur in areas without hospitals or professional healthcare facilities, and as a consequence, remain underreported. It has been estimated that 60% of Filipinos who die have not received medical attention, casting serious doubt on the validity of government statistics (Tadiar, 2002). Furthermore, in the case of maternal and infant deaths that arise out of or relating to abortion, many cases go unreported for fear of legal repercussions due to the illegality of abortion. Inconsistencies within the statistics produced by government agencies, such as those reported by the DOH and the National Statistics Office, cast more doubt on the accuracy of these estimates (Molino, 2001).

Misuse of budgetary allocations as indicia for the 'prioritization' of health

For reasons that will be enumerated in the following sections, figures demonstrating a steady increase in government allocation for health and the corresponding share of health expenditures in GNP should be examined critically.

Artificially magnifying the health budget

The true test of prioritization is per capita spending for health, that is to say, the rise in budgetary allocation must be pegged to the rise in population and discounted by inflation. As of 2007, total health expenditure was P. 234.3 billion comprising 3.2% of the country's GNP. Divided by a population of 95.98 million, per capita spending is at P. 253.49 per person (NSCB, 2007). The figure still fails to meet the WHO's recommended value of 5%. However, the DOH's budget has increased from P. 11.3 billion in 2007 to P. 42.2 billion in 2012 (Republic Act No. 10155, 2012). The new administration has also expressed its commitment to health through the Aquino Health Agenda, so the picture in the next few years may be brighter. Safeguards must be put in place to ensure efficiency in spending as, in the past, healthcare funds have been used for the construction of bus stops, waiting sheds, basketball courts, and infrastructure projects that are susceptible to bloated budgetary estimates and the extraction of 'kickbacks' (Batalla, 2000).

Decentralization of healthcare from national government to local government units

Because of decentralization policies, declining numbers in the health budget do not necessarily translate into a lower governmental priority for health. The devolution that transpired in 1993 explains the dramatic drop of approximately P.4 billion in the DOH budget that year. Approximately 45,000 health personnel have been transferred to the local governments and an estimated P. 4.2 billion in expenditures that has been shifted to local government units (LGUs) (Republic Act, 7610, 1992). Recent data from the 2001 National Health Accounts show that LGU spending on health has reached P. 24.9 billion, thus comprising 21% of the country's total health spending. As of 2007, this stands at 13% of total health spending at P.31 billion (NSCB, 2007).

Weak legal regimes: non-compliance by physicians, collusion by lay public

Because the Generics Act of 1988 (Republic Act No., 6675, 1988) (upheld by the Supreme Court (*Del Rosario, S.A. & et al.* v. *Secretary of Department of Health*, 1989)) was ineffective in promoting affordable medicine due to widespread non-compliance (Molino, 2001), an omnibus bill entitled the 'Cheap Medicines Act of 2007' was brought before Congress that would plug a perceived loophole in the previous legislation. Specifically, the Generics Act required all physicians to 'write prescriptions using the generic name [but t]he brand name may be included if so described' (Republic Act No. 6675, 1988). The Cheap Medicines legislation negated the option to indicate the brand name and would allow this only 'if the prescribed drug or medicine is an innovator, pioneer, or ethical drug that has no known generic counterpart' (House Bill No., 2844, 2008). The Cheap Medicines legislation likewise aimed to carve out exceptions to intellectual property laws that protect local pharmaceutical patents for their products by preventing the 'parallel importation' of such drugs from countries where they are sold more cheaply (AGAP, 2007). However, under its intellectual property laws, the Philippines does not allow importation of cheaper versions of patented medicines until the Philippine patent expires (Intellectual Property Code §71.1.a., 1997). The Cheap Medicines legislation was later passed as Republic Act No. 9502 or the 'Universally Accessible Cheaper and Quality Medicines Act of 2008' (Republic Act No. 9502, 2008). While more emphasis was given to the use of generic terminology, practitioners were still left with an option to include the brand name of prescribed drugs if desired. The Act, however, was successful in amending the Intellectual Property Code of the Philippines, specifically those sections concerning patent protection and compulsory licensing (Republic Act No., 9502, 2008).

Resistance to these reforms is found both externally and internally. In 2006, in *Pfizer* v. *Bureau of Food and Drugs Director*, the multinational pharmaceutical company Pfizer Inc. filed a patent infringement suit to stop a government corporation from importing Norvasc®, a hypertension drug, in a generic formulation from India, citing an extant patent issued in the Philippines (*Pfizer* v. *Bureau of Food and Drugs Director*, 2006). The trial court has issued an order containing a settlement of the case, so that parallel importation into the country will commence only after the Philippine patent of the drug has expired (*Pfizer* v. *Bureau of Food and Drugs Director*, 2006). Cases such as this demonstrate the countervailing source of power working against accessible medicines, namely, the huge pharmaceutical transnational corporations that have asserted their intellectual property rights even against well-defined legal exceptions. The second source of resistance, however, is the Filipino medical establishment itself that has jealously guarded its own interests, in collusion with a willing, uninformed Filipino public who, given the choice between generic and branded drugs, still claim to prefer the latter. The pervasive power of elite professionals in medicine is best demonstrated by the failure of periodic attempts to legislate in favour of 'patients' rights' and medical malpractice laws, which have been resisted by professional organizations (House Bill No. 226, 2002). The failure to include the strict clauses into the new Republic Act reflects this pervasive power of both the pharmaceuticals and the local medical establishment.

Lack of effective health insurance coverage: non-actuarialization and privatization of health costs

One determining element of the reform of healthcare delivery in the Philippines is the lack of an effective public health insurance system. To address this problem, the Philippine Congress established in 1995 a National Health Insurance Program (or PhilHealth) to provide universal and compulsory health coverage to all Filipino citizens (Republic Act No. 7875, 1995). It created the Philippine Health Insurance Corporation to administer the former Medicare (Republic Act No. 6111, 1969) programme, and to take over the management of the existing health insurance services for both public (Presidential Decree No. 1146, 1977) and private (Republic Act No. 1161, 1954) employees.

Two subsequent developments reveal the fundamental weaknesses of the PhilHealth system. The first was the finding by a Citizens' Congress for Truth and Accountability that then-President Gloria Macapagal-Arroyo distributed free PhilHealth insurance cards as part of her campaign for a fresh mandate in the 2004 presidential elections and paid for the cards using public funds (The PCJI Blog, 2006). The second was the passage by Congress in 2007 of the Hospital Detention Law (Republic Act No. 9439, 2007), which aimed to stop the practice of detaining absconding patients (House Bill No. 00068, 2004). It is significant that the problem of absconding patients warranted legislation 38 years after the Medicare law was passed, and 12 years after universal and compulsory coverage was mandated (DOH & Padilla, 2009). The Hospital Detention Law, together with the No-Deposit Law (Republic Act No. 8344, 1997), which stops hospitals from requiring patients to put up an initial deposit before they are given admission or emergency care, shows the difficulties of prescribing the right to health in the absence of a comprehensive health insurance system.

The privatization of erstwhile public hospitals has reduced the need for public money for these hospitals. Indeed, a major component of the HSRA, apart from devolution, is the planned privatization or corporatization of certain DOH-managed hospitals and the conversion of others into fiscally autonomous entities (DOH, 2010c). This plan entails the gradual reduction of direct subsidies (and the outright elimination of the subsidies in the case of full privatization) to these institutions with the objective of making them self-supporting and financially stable. To this end, these public hospitals will be allowed and encouraged to collect, retain, and allocate revenues from socialized user fees (HSRA, 2010).

While the ultimate goal of creating and maintaining self-sustaining public hospitals may seem desirable in the long-term interest of government efficiency, implementation of this policy has had a deleterious impact on the access of citizens, particularly the indigent, to crucial health services. Reduced subsidies have led some hospitals to start taking steps to increase revenues, by limiting the number of charity patients via stricter screening procedures, requiring some of these charity patients to pay for medical supplies needed in their treatment, and imposing a ceiling amount of allowable expense for those classified as indigent patients (Simbulan, 2001). Indeed, NGOs have noted that the policy of privatization and the focus on attaining fiscal autonomy for State-run hospitals has resulted in 'passing more burden on [an] already impoverished people' who, already saddled with the pernicious effects of an economic crisis, are now forced 'to shoulder [their] health needs' (Molino, 2001).

The present universal healthcare agenda seeks to address these issues by expanding the National Health Insurance Program coverage, while simultaneously enhancing health facilities. A pending bill will amend the universal healthcare law to provide 'socialized' healthcare for the 'underprivileged, sick, elderly, disabled, women and children' and 'free' healthcare for 'indigents' (House Bill No. 6048, 2012).

Recognizing its limitations, PhilHealth has been undertaking many reforms in its policies and benefits design. Recently, PhilHealth implemented the Case Payment Scheme and No Balance Billing (NBB) Policy in 2011. The NBB policy stipulates that 'no other fees or expenses shall be charged or paid for by the patient-member above and beyond the packaged rates' for indigents confined in government hospitals (Philippine Health Insurance Corporation, 2011). While this is a promising policy for promoting financial risk protection, its implementation is being met with resistance and is yet to be held acceptable in private facilities.

Conclusion: health as both a normative and international claim

The first lesson to be drawn from the Philippine experience is that, in a fragile democracy like the Philippines, where State institutions are weak, health is best advanced as an internationally protected human right, normativized and internationalized, and thus insulated from elite-dominated domestic politics. Accordingly, the capacity of the Philippines to fulfil its international obligation to realize the right to health depends, in large part, on its own domestic constitutional set-up. Second, the indicia of compliance with treaty obligations demonstrate the competing tension between progressive realization and justiciability, the first of which recognizes the multifaceted and programmatic character of economic, social, and cultural rights claims. Even when these claims are advanced through domestic legislation, these have rarely given rise to justiciable rights except to the extent that norms related to non-discrimination norms are implicated. Finally, by establishing these principles as norms and internationalized health claims, we likewise force a recalibration of the domestic public/private distinction. Health was hitherto a family matter, and its burdens absorbed by the private sphere. The international indicia assume that costs are borne through social security and health insurance, and properly shift them to the public sphere. In this sense, the international right to health extends to attitudes and relations most deeply embedded within the domestic sphere, and therein lies both its greatest challenge as well as its truly transformative power.

References

Ayos na Gamont Sa Abot-kayang Presyo (AGAP). (2007). *Position Paper of Ayos na Gamot sa Abot-Kayang Presyo (Good Medicine at Affordable Prices)*. Submitted 20 September 2007 during the Public Hearing, Committee on Trade and Industry. House of Representatives: Philippines.

Batalla, E. (2000). *Corruption in the Philippines: Identifying Strategic Requirements for Reinventing Institutions*. De La Salle University: Manila.

Bernas, J. (1988). *The Constitution of the Republic of the Philippines: A Commentary 497*. Rex Printing Company, Inc: Manila.

CESCR. (2000). *General Comment No. 14: The right to the Highest Attainable Standard of Health (article 12 of the International Covenant on Economic, Social and Cultural Rights)*. Committee on Economic, Social, and Cultural Rights (CESCR): Geneva.

Del Rosario, S.A. et al. v. *Secretary of Department of Health*. (1989). General Rule No. 88265, Supreme Court of Manila, 21 December 1989.

Demeterio-Melgar, J. and Pacete, J.C. (2007). *Imposing Misery: The Impact of Manila's Ban on Contraception*. Likhaan: Manila.

Department of Health v. *Honorable Tamayo*. (2010). G.R. 193414, filed 10 July.

DOH. (2005). *Philippine Health Statistics*. Department of Health, Government of the Philippines: Manila.

DOH. (2010a). *National Objectives for Health: 2011–2016*. Department of Health (DOH): Manila. Available at: <http://www.doh.gov.ph/sites/default/files/1%20table%20of%20contents,%20foreword,%20preface.pdf> (accessed 9 November 2012).

DOH. (2010b). *Administrative Order No. 0036*. Department of Health (DOH): Manila.

DOH. (2010c). *Toward Financial Risk Protection: Health Care Financing Strategy of the Philippines 2010–2020, Health Sector Reform Agenda—Monograph No. 10*. Government of the Philippines: Manila.

DOH. (2011). *Department Order No. 0188*. Department of Health (DOH): Manila.

DOH. (1987). *Order No. 196*. Department of Health (DOH): Manila.

DOH and Padilla, A. (2009). *Interview with DOH USec. Alex Padilla on Hospital Holiday*. Philippine Department of Health: Manila. Available at: <http://www.gmanetwork.com/news/video/46148/unanghirit/interview-with-doh-usec-alex-padilla-on-hospital-holiday> (accessed 8 November 2012).

DOH. (1992b). *Order No. 182-C.* Department of Health (DOH): Manila.

DOH. (1992a). *Order No. 105-F.* Department of Health (DOH): Manila.

Executive Order No. 003. (2000). *Declaring Total Commitment and Support to the Responsible Parenthood Movement in the City of Manila and Enunciating Policy Declarations in Pursuit Thereof.* Office of the Mayor: Manila.

Executive Order No. 292. (1987). *Section 13, Title IX, Chapter 1.* Office of the President: Manila.

Field Health Service Information System (FHSIS). (2009). *Annual Report: Department of Health.* National Epidemiology Center, Department of Health: Manila.

Health Sector Reform Agenda (HRSA). (2010). *Health Sector Reform Agenda.* Department of Health: Manila. Available at: <http://erc.msh.org/hsr/linksites/otherreports/hsra.pdf> (accessed 8 November 2012).

House Bill 226. (2002). *An Act Establishing a Medical and Health Care Liability Law, Providing Penalties Therefore and For Other Purposes.* 13th Congress.

House Bill No 2844. (2008). *An Act Providing for Cheaper Medicines and For Other Purposes.* 14th Congress, §29.magna.

House Bill No. 00068 (2004). *An Act Prohibiting the Detention of Live or Dead Patients in Hospitals and Medical Clinic on Grounds of Nonpayment of Hospital Bills or Medical Expenses.* 15th Congress.

House Bill No. 4244. (2011). *An Act Providing For A Comprehensive Policy On Responsible Parenthood, Reproductive Health, And Population And Development, And For Other Purposes.* 15th Congress.

House Bill No. 6048. (2012). *Universal Health Coverage.*

Intellectual Property Code §71.1.a. (1997). *Rights of Patentees and Infringement of Patents.*

International Code of Marketing of Breastmilk Substitutes (ICBMS). (1981). A code adopted by the WHO on 21 May 1981, WHA Resolution 34.22. World Health Organization: Geneva.

International Council on Human Rights Policy. (2002). *Local Rule: Decentralisation and Human Rights.* International Council on Human Rights Policy (ICHRP): Geneva.

Manila Times. (2007, 29 June). Family-planning advocates plan to Sue Lito Atienza. *Manila Times.* Available at: <http://newsinfo.inquirer.net/topstories/topstories/view/20070929-91513/Family_planning_advocates_plan_suit_vs_Atienza> (accessed 8 November 2012).

Mayor Simon v. *Commission on Human Rights.* (1994). G.R. No. 100150.

Medium Term Philippine Development Plan. (2004). *Medium-Term Philippine Development Plan, 2004–2010.* Philippine Government: Manila. Available at: <http://www.neda.gov.ph/ads/mtpdp/MTPDP2004-2010/PDF/MTPDP2004-2010.html> (accessed 8 November 2012).

Melgar, J. (1999). Ailing Philippine health: proof of market failings. *Development,* 42, 138–141.

Melgar, J. (2005). Barriers to reproductive health and rights: what should be done? In E.A. Pangalangan (Ed.), *Ten Years after Cairo: Between Commitment and Realization of Reproductive Health in the Philippines,* No. 6, pp. 126–130. Reproductive Health, Rights and Ethics Center for Studies and Training, Special Publication Series: Philippines.

Millennium Development Goals Indicators. (2011). *UN Inter-Agency and Expert Group on MDG Indicators, 2011.* United Nations: New York, NY. Available at: <http://mdgs.un.org/unsd/mdg/Host.aspx?Content=Indicators/OfficialList.htm> (accessed 8 November 2012).

Molino, B.E. (2001). *Right to Health 2001.* Medical Action Group (MAG): Manchester.

National Center for Disease Prevention and Control. (2011). *Malaria Medium Term Development Plan 2011–2016.* Department of Health: Manila. Available at: <http://www.doh.gov.ph/sites/default/files/Final%20Malaria%20Medium%20Term%20Development%20Plan_0.pdf> (accessed 9 November 2012).

National Statistic Coordination Board. (2007). *Philippine National Health Accounts.* National Statistical Coordination Board: Makati City.

National Statistic Coordination Board. (2012). *NSCB Fact Sheet: Updates on Women and Men in the Philippines.* NSIC: Makati City.

National Statistics Office. (2008). *National Demographic and Health Survey 2008.* National Statistics Office: Manila.

Pfizer Limited (United Kingdom) and Pfizer Inc. (Philippines) v. *Philippine International Trading Company and Bureau of Food and Drug Director, et al.* (2006). Regional Trial Court, Branch 149, Civil Case No. 06-172.

Pharmaceutical and Health Association of the Philippines v. *Health Secretary Francisco T. Duque III.* (2007). G.R. No. 173034.

Philippine Constitution. (1987). art. II § 15.

Philippine Health Insurance Corporation. (2011). *Circular No. 011: New PhilHealth Case Rates for Selected Medical Cases and Surgical Procedures and the No Balance Billing Policy*. Philhealth: Manila.

Philippine Health Insurance Corporation. (2012). *Database of the Philippine Health Insurance Corporation*. Philhealth: Manila.

Presidential Decree No. 996. (1976). Amended by Republic Act No. 7846, *Providing for compulsory basic immunization for infants and children below eight years of age*. Government of the Philippines: Manila.

Presidential Decree No. 1146. (1977). *Government Service Insurance System Act of 1977, Amending, Expanding, Increasing and Integrating the Social Security and Insurance Benefits Of Government Employees*. Government of the Philippines: Manila.

Reproductive Health Care Act. (2002). *House Bill 4110*, 12th Congress. Government of the Philippines: Manila.

Republic Act No. 10070. (2009). *An Act Establishing An Institutional Mechanism To Ensure the Implementation Of Programs And Services For Persons With Disabilities In Every Province, City And Municipality, Amending Republic Act No. 7277*. Government of the Philippines: Manila.

Republic Act No. 10155. (2012). *General Appropriations Act*. Government of the Philippines: Manila.

Republic Act No. 1161. (1954). *Social Security Act, To Create A Social Security System Providing Sickness, Unemployment, Retirement, Disability And Death Benefits For Employees*. Government of the Philippines: Manila.

Republic Act No. 3815. (1930). *Penal Code Criminalizing Abortion*. Government of the Philippines: Manila.

Republic Act No. 6111. (1969). *Philippine Medical Care Act of 1969, Establishing the Philippine Medical Care Plan and Creating The Philippine Medical Care Commission*. Government of the Philippines: Manila.

Republic Act No. 6675. (1988). *§6.b. An Act to Promote and Ensure the Production of an Adequate Supply, Distribution, Use and Acceptance of Drugs and Medicines Identified by their Generic Names*. Government of the Philippines: Manila.

Republic Act No. 6972. (1990). Section 3. *An Act Establishing a Daycare Center in Every Barangay*. Government of the Philippines: Manila.

Republic Act No. 7609. (1992). *An Act Providing for the Conversion of Selected Municipal Main Health Centers*. Government of the Philippines: Manila.

Republic Act No. 7610. (1992). *An Act Providing for Stronger Deterrence and Special Protection Against Child Abuse, Exploitation and Discrimination, and for Other Purposes*. Government of the Philippines: Manila.

Republic Act No. 7875. (1995). *National Health Insurance Act*. Government of the Philippines: Manila.

Republic Act No. 7883. (1995). *Brgy. Health Workers Benefits and Incentives Acts*. Government of the Philippines: Manila.

Republic Act No. 8172. (1995). *Act for Salt Iodization Nationwide*. Government of the Philippines: Manila.

Republic Act No. 8191. (1996). *National Diabetes Act*. Government of the Philippines: Manila.

Republic Act No. 8344. (1997). *An Act Penalizing the Refusal Of Hospitals and Medical Clinics To Administer Appropriate Initial Medical Treatment and Support in Emergency Or Serious Cases*. Government of the Philippines: Manila.

Republic Act No. 8423. (1997). *Traditional and Alternative Medicine Act*. Government of the Philippines: Manila.

Republic Act No. 8584. (1998). *An Act Converting the Pilar National High School in Barangay Pilar, Oquendo District, Calbayog City, into an Agricultural High School to Be Known as the Pilar National Agricultural High School*. Government of the Philippines: Manila.

Republic Act No. 8976. (2000). *Philippine Food Fortification Act*. Government of the Philippines: Manila.

Republic Act No. 9439. (2007). *Prohibiting the Detention Of Patients In Hospitals And Medical Clinics On Grounds Of Nonpayment Of Hospital Bills Or Medical Expenses*. Government of the Philippines: Manila.

Republic Act No. 9502. (2008). *Universally Accessible Cheaper and Quality Medicines Act of 2008*. Government of the Philippines: Manila.

Republic Act No. 9710. (2009). *An Act Providing For The Magna Carta Of Women*. Government of the Philippines: Manila.

Rights of Conscience Act. (2006). *House Bill No. 5028*, 12th Congress. Government of the Philippines: Manila.

Senate Bill No. 2865. (2011). *Reproductive Health Act*. Government of the Philippines: Manila.

Simbulan, N.P. (2001). The impact of structural adjustment programs on the Philippine health delivery system. *Public Policy*, 5, 43–74.

Tadiar, F.L.M. (2002). *Improving Maternal Health Care Services in the Philippines*. UP University Center for Women's Studies: Manila.

The PCIJ Blog. (2006). *Arroyo Deliberately Cheated Her Way to the Presidency in 2004*. Philippine Center Investigative Journalism Blog (PCIJ): Philippines. Available at: <http://www.pcij.org/blog/?p=910> (accessed 8 October 2012).

UN. (2012). *United Nations Treaty Collection: Chapter IV, Human Rights*. Available at: <http://www2.ohchr.org/english/bodies/ratification/index.htm> (accessed 8 November 2012).

UNDP. (2012). *Philippines Country Profile: Human Development Indicators*. United Nations Development Programme: New York, NY. Available at: <http://hdrstats.undp.org/en/countries/profiles/phl.html> (accessed 30 October 2012).

USAID. (2012). *Overview of Health Programs: Philippines*. US Agency of International Development: Washington, DC. Available at: <http://philippines.usaid.gov/programs/health> (accessed 8 November 2012).

WHO. (1998). *Emergency Contraception: A Guide for Service Delivery*. World Health Organization (WHO): Geneva.

World Bank. (2012). *Projects and Operations: National Sector Support for Kalusugan Pangkalahatan*. World Bank: Washington DC. Available at: <http://www.worldbank.org/projects/P119069/national-sector-support-universal-health-care-project?lang=en> (accessed 8 November 2012).

Chapter 11

China's evolution in progressively realizing the right to health

Philip D. Chen and Di Wu

Introduction

China's health challenges today are a function of the complex relationship between its rapid development, vast population, and governance system. Although the government has undertaken significant reforms to expand availability and access in both areas, people affected by new reforms will continue to face difficulties in realizing their rights on an individual basis because of structural and systemic obstacles to open governance.

Overview

China's health status

When Peng-chun Chang participated in the drafting of the Universal Declaration of Human Rights (UDHR) in the late 1940s, he would likely not have recognized the China of today. In 1948, the population of mainland China was reportedly at least 464 million—today that figure is 1.34 billion (Taeuber, 1957; Xinhua News Agency, 2011). Average life expectancy in China in the 1940s was approximately 35 years; today it has reached 73 years (Shi, 1993; World Bank, 2012). Other major health indicators show a similarly dramatic improvement. The maternal mortality ratio declined from 1,500 to 30 deaths per 100,000 live births and infant mortality rates dropped from 200 to 13.1 per 1,000 live births between 1949 and 2010 (MOH, 2011).

These improvements were in part due to the development of an expansive public health system, and the country's rapid economic growth beginning in 1978, when the Chinese leadership introduced significant economic reforms. The resulting growth triggered changes in society, the legal structure, and the national health system, creating new challenges for advancing the right to health.

Urbanization is one of the clearest consequences of development that profoundly affects how China's population accesses healthcare. The growth in the export economy led to greater manufacturing in urban areas along the coast. Unskilled labour migrated from rural areas to the city to take advantage of these new work opportunities. By the end of 2011, urbanites outnumbered the rural population for the first time (National Statistics Bureau of China, 2012). Urbanization placed greater strain on a health system already contracting from the decline of State support.

Because of the improvement in the overall health of the general population, the disease map changed. Today, non-communicable diseases, such as cardiovascular diseases and cancer, account for more than 80% of China's deaths (WHO, 2011). Longer life expectancy can increase the demand for healthcare dramatically in ways that the existing supply of healthcare facilities and professionals may not be adequate to meet. Changes to the economic structure gave rise to new health concerns, such as food safety and quality.

Legal and accountability framework

China is officially a country organized according to a 'socialist system of laws with Chinese characteristics' (People's Republic of China, 2011). Although the Chinese Constitution does not explicitly refer to the right to health, it provides that 'the State respects and protects human rights' (Chinese Constitution, 1982). The General Principles of Civil Law, which is a core component of China's legal system, state: 'Citizens shall enjoy the rights of life and health' (People's Republic of China, 2012a, Article 98). In 2001, China ratified the International Covenant on Economic, Social and Cultural Rights (ICESCR, 1966); however, those provisions, like those of China's Constitution itself, are not practicably enforceable in the courts (Hand, 2011).

China's most recent major legislative enactments tackle core issues in the health sector and social safety net: for example, the Food Safety Law (2009), the Social Insurance Law (2010), and the revised Law on Occupational Disease Prevention and Treatment (2011). China is adopting a more administrative process for reform of the health system, and so the critical decision documents are less statutory in nature. The overall trend of legislation and administrative reform in this recent period is towards an expansion of government coverage and greater regulatory supervision over these areas.

In practice, the implementation of these laws and policies cannot be fully understood without reference to the role of the Communist Party, which ultimately determines both macro-level policy and even micro-level outcomes in some cases. With respect to the law, the Party's approach has been to see it as orders that preserve its control, rather than as an enforceable restraint on its own actions (Peerenboom, 2002). As a result, the outcomes of both policy and individual cases can turn heavily on non-legal factors, such as whether the situation is deemed sensitive to the Party's maintenance of its control and its legitimacy. For example, individuals that find it difficult to challenge the sufficiency of reimbursement of particular healthcare costs by the government health insurance payer might have significant problems in resolving a dispute, due to the overall system's focus on stability.

As a result of the Party-State system, the administrative and Party apparatus are fundamental drivers of policy. Incentivizing these large bureaucracies to undertake significant reforms is difficult. Because the leadership is not accountable at the ballot box and media is constrained, a key factor for policy implementation is the formal performance review structure for key officials, in which promotion depends upon meeting policy metrics (Minzner, 2009).

A third layer of complexity is the relationship between central institutions and their local counterparts at the provincial, municipal, and county level. Although China's system is unitary and not federal in formal terms, in practice, the relationship between national and local government institutions can approximate these intergovernmental dynamics (Ho, 2010). While government agencies at lower levels take instruction from their higher-level departments, in many cases, those same local agencies are funded by the local government treasury (Mertha, 2005). As a result, such entities face mixed incentives when implementing central directives.

In the following sections, we discuss how these legal and accountability frameworks intersect with issues arising in the health sector.

Right to health in China

China's rapid economic growth has created the background financial, technological, and human resources available to significantly raise the standard of health. Yet the State's weak regulatory oversight structure and closed, controlled governance often frustrate efforts by individuals to realize this standard.

Healthcare

The Chinese healthcare system experienced dramatic changes as a result of the broader economic reforms instituted in 1979. While the supply and quality of healthcare services increased, the country is wrestling with the twin challenges of providing accessible and affordable care in a changing regulatory and demographic environment.

Healthcare challenges prior to the 2009 reform

Under the planned economy system, in which the central government controls the market, healthcare services were basic but affordable. Urban residents accessed care through their affiliation with their work unit affiliation (*dan wei*), which rationed access to higher levels of care (Dong, 2001/2002). Rural residents depended upon care provided by the so-called 'barefoot doctors'. These were people living in the village collective with basic educations and several months' medical training (Zhang & Unschuld, 2008). This segregated healthcare structure was held together by rigid control of internal migration through the residential permit (*hukou*) system, which prevented persons of either rural or urban status from relocating. Healthcare was also rationed by a relatively fixed status: those with special privileges by virtue of employment as an official or cadre had access to better care.

Starting in 1979, China's leaders began to transform the country's economic model by introducing a number of market mechanisms into the rural and urban economy. In particular, the State implemented two decisions with negative effects on healthcare access and affordability. First, by de-collectivizing agriculture, barefoot doctors no longer had a guaranteed financial base from which to practise. By 1993, less than 10% of rural residents were covered by any insurance provided by the government, employers, or the collective economy (Wagstaff et al., 2009). In urban areas, similarly, many enterprises were moved to a profit–loss model, and employees no longer had any third party to assume financial responsibility for healthcare. The result was that personal healthcare costs were paid on an out-of-pocket basis.

Second, the State drastically cut funding to hospitals, while maintaining price controls for certain medical services (World Bank, 2010). It directed medical providers to find revenue in the new marketplace. The funding hole left by the State's retreat was filled by medical providers through creative revenue generation, the most common being overutilization of pharmaceuticals and excessive medical care, paid for out-of-pocket by the patient. These policy decisions effectively shifted the burden of healthcare costs to individuals.

Public discontent with this system ran high. One disturbing indicator is the increase in hospital-related violence, leading in many instances to attacks on physicians (Ho & Gostin, 2009). Underlying these incidents is distrust in the motivations of the hospital and the medical practitioners (Liebman, 2013) because the public perceives the problematic incentives at work in the system. After reviewing a decade of failed experiments that included the introduction of more market mechanisms and the creation of a new health insurance system, the government's lead research centre in 2005 candidly declared that the healthcare reform since 1979 was 'unsuccessful' (State Council, 2005).

Rebuilding availability and accessibility in healthcare

In 2009, the State Council released a new policy that aimed at providing 'safe, effective, convenient, and affordable' (*anquan, youxiao, fangbian, jialian*) healthcare services for both urban and rural residents (China Communist Party and State Council, 2009; State Council, 2009a). The State committed to spend an additional 850 billion RMB (approximately US$135 billion) in three years to prioritize expansion of medical insurance coverage, creation of an essential drug system, health professionals' capacity building, equalization of basic public health services, and public hospital reform (State Council, 2009b). The roadmap aims to increase people's availability and accessibility to health services.

Availability

The State invested heavily in building basic healthcare facilities in villages and communities to increase the supply of public health and medical services. From 2009 to mid-2012, 47 billion RMB in local and central government funds supported 2,233 county hospitals; 6,213 township clinics; and 25,000 village clinics (Zhang, 2012). According to China's Ministry of Health (MOH), more than 80% people can arrive at a healthcare facility within 15 minutes (MOH, 2012a). In addition, free public health services were expanded to include benefits such as access to more childhood vaccines and pre-natal medical visits (People's Republic of China, 2012b).

While emphasis on building institutional capacity appears to address the problem of availability, effectiveness remains to be seen. Because of the varying quality in medical providers and the generalized belief that better medical care resides in large urban hospitals, the government cannot simply rely on creating new supply—it will need to show that the care provided in these new institutions will be the same, if not better, than in large urban hospitals.

Accessibility

The development of voluntary basic health insurance plans for rural residents and unemployed urban residents improves equality and the ability of these vulnerable groups to afford healthcare. Previously, only urban employees of enterprises were covered by a mandatory contribution insurance plan (Liu, 2002). Rural and urban unemployed largely paid out of their own pockets for healthcare services, which placed families at considerable financial risk (World Bank, 2005).

Under these new programmes, central and local governments co-fund the insurance pool to which rural residents voluntarily contribute approximately US$10 annually (MOH, 2012b). Unemployed urban residents can participate in a similar plan (MOF, 2011). These new structures, however, still inhibit accessibility. For instance, insured rural residents must keep receipts for reimbursement of medical services outside their designated area (People's Republic of China, 2012c). The slow reimbursement process burdens migrants living in one locality but whose health insurance is based in another province (Li & Wang, 2012).

In addition, the supply of advanced medical services is limited. Local clinics in rural areas only provide basic services. Rural residents requiring advanced treatment usually travel long distances to an urban centre, where they encounter long lines and higher costs. For rural residents, the costs can be exorbitant: the World Bank found that the average inpatient care out-of-pocket payment 'associated with a single average hospitalization episode exceeded 140% of annual per capita income in the poorest quintile compared to about 10% in the richest quintile' (emphasis in original, Brixi et al., 2011).

The allocation of medical resources generally favours more select groups. For example, 70% of healthcare providers are located in urban areas (*Beijing News,* 2012a). Most providers with advanced technology are based in a handful of large cities. Top-tier hospitals have special wards for high-ranking officials (in office or retired) that are not publicly accessible (Brixi et al., 2011). Those special wards have better facilities and care, all covered by the public budget. Such special systems make healthcare less available to society at large, raising concerns about non-discrimination and equal treatment.

Vulnerable populations with HIV/AIDS often suffer discrimination and denial of access to healthcare (Yang, 2002). Most hospitals do not want to accept HIV-positive patients because health professionals fear potential occupational exposure. HIV-positive patients typically transfer to specialized hospitals for patients with contagious diseases. However, these institutions are not as comprehensive and may only be able to treat certain conditions (*Phoenix Report,* 2010).

Food safety

While China has made great strides in ensuring that sufficient quantities of food are available and accessible, the country's major challenge is to establish a regulatory system that protects the general population's food supply from contamination and economic adulteration.

Availability: from food security to food safety

Food that is 'adequate' for purposes of Article 25 of the UDHR must be available in 'quantity and quality sufficient to satisfy the dietary needs of individuals, free from adverse substances, and acceptable within a given culture' (CESCR, 1999). Between 1949 and 1979, one of the abiding challenges in China was to ensure food security for an expanding population. The emphasis was on quantity and self-sufficiency.

Today, the emergence of a profit-seeking food production and processing industry has resulted in more public incidents of economic adulteration. The most tragic of these incidents involved the dairy industry. In 2003 and 2004 in Anhui province, watered-down infant formula was widely sold, evading regulators and resulting in more than a dozen deaths (Yardley, 2004). A few years later, in an attempt to reduce costs, producers again diluted infant formula and exposed the product to hundreds of thousands of children. To hide the fact that it was diluted, producers added the chemical melamine, which resulted in hundreds of thousands of exposures and caused the death of at least six infants (WHO, 2009). Besides cases of economic adulteration, China faces the challenge of environmental pollution leaching into the water and food supply, as well as the overuse of products such as pesticides (Ellis & Turner, 2008).

Incidents such as these generated public pressure on China's leadership to tackle weaknesses in the regulatory system. Before 2009, existing food safety laws and regulations primarily focused on issues related to hygiene, and not on the process of ensuring quality through each link in the supply chain from farm to kitchen table (Tam & Yang, 2005). The new legislation created a system of risk assessment and food safety standards uniformity (Food Safety Law, 2009). On the implementation side, bureaucratic inertia and a highly segmented administrative system complicate matters. Prior to the new law, at least six agencies were tasked with regulating food, which led to agencies passing the buck and failing to take the initiative to enforce when necessary (Tam & Yang, 2005). Today, the problem still remains, although some rationalization has occurred—currently, five central government agencies are primarily responsible for oversight of the food supply chain, together with local government (Food and Safety Law, 2009). Other accountability issues are being addressed administratively: metrics on food safety law implementation are being integrated into key officials' performance reviews (State Council, 2012).

Despite campaigns to prosecute violators of the Food Safety Law and significant effort to modernize the administrative apparatus, food safety incidents continue to materialize. The public is sceptical that the government's effort is effective and that the public is being informed of the true scope of the problem. For example, it was discovered shortly after the conclusion of the melamine contamination incident noted earlier that seized products were not destroyed by authorities, and that tainted product had found its way back into the marketplace (Areddy, 2010).

Moreover, the leader of a group of parents of children injured by melamine contamination was imprisoned for 'inciting social disorder' by attempting to organize protests against officials and industry (Jacobs, 2010). As a result, despite a widespread government and industry campaign to reassure the public that dairy products are safe, Chinese parents continue to purchase imported milk or to travel to Hong Kong expressly for the purpose of purchasing infant formula (Pomfret, 2011). As a general matter, consumer litigation has not been effective for addressing these food safety issues because the political leadership fears they may have a destabilizing effect (Wong, 2009).

Accessibility

Accessibility to food includes both 'economic and physical accessibility'. In China, while incomes have risen substantially, poorer populations still face significant barriers to food. The concern in recent years has been on poor populations living in urban centres. Because of the threadbare nature of social insurance, particularly the subsistence aid (or *dibao*) programme, economically marginalized persons face spiking food prices. The 2010 visit to China by the UN Special Rapporteur on the right to food highlighted these issues, noting the significant 11.7% rise in food prices (De Schutter, 2012).

Another problematic trend is the development of special food supply chains for special groups. The emergence of these special supply chains was a response in part to anxiety over the safety of food. Chinese media publicized the existence of special organic farms for particular classes of government officials and other special categories of persons such as high-level athletes and astronauts (*Beijing News,* 2012b). This special treatment raises issues of equity. Special efforts are also made for major international events hosted in China. In recent years, China held the Olympic Games, the World Expo, and the Asian Games. In each of these instances, a very stringent and effective food safety monitoring system was established for visitors and participants. It remains to be seen how those experiences can translate on a national scale.

In sum, in China, the right to health with respect to food in large part has transitioned from a concern over quantity to one over quality and safety. While the government has instituted broad ranging administrative reforms to the food safety system, it still relies on traditional, government-driven methods of deterrence: inspection, arrests, and imprisonment. It has not adopted a general policy of transparency, stakeholder and civil society organization, product liability, and stakeholder engagement.

Systemic challenges to the right to health

Remedial structures

The term 'remedial structures' is used here to mean avenues through which individuals or groups can seek satisfaction of claims for compensation or can challenge policies or limitations on rights enforced by the State in the name of public health. In many countries, courts typically serve as the forum for the handling of individual claims. While China has an extensive formal court system, in practice, the realization of rights through litigation is challenging because of the political imperative to maintain social stability.

During the Hu-Wen Administration (from 2003 to 2012), political authorities emphasized the need to maintain a 'harmonious society' (*hexie shehui*), which was taken as a directive to minimize formalized conflict in the court system and to resolve disputes through mediation. Courts were encouraged to meet quotas for successfully mediated cases, and individual judges were to be assessed according to their ability to achieve these targets (Minzner, 2011). One criticism of this practice is that such pressure to mediate may result in parties relinquishing legitimate claims.

Even civil disputes can run afoul of political authorities because of the fear that such disputes might trigger political instability. For example, in the case of melamine-contaminated infant formula, a group of parents planning to sue the responsible milk companies in court were deterred by authorities and the group's leader was imprisoned. If issues within the scope of the right to health raise fears in the mind of political authorities, then the government will structure the terms of the dispute's resolution.

Internal administrative processes are similarly difficult. One traditional method of seeking remedies is through a system of letter petitions (*xinfang*) (Minzner, 2005). Under this system, an individual submits a complaint to an internal bureau of the agency with jurisdiction over the issue. The petition is supposed to be reviewed and then handled in due course. However, most petitioners are unsuccessful. In many instances, petitioners that complain to higher-level authorities of government inaction or abuse at a local level are often prevented from submitting complaints by agents of local authorities and detained (Bristow, 2011).

Often it is only through indirect methods, such as strategic use of the media, that disputes can be resolved effectively within the legal framework (Liebman, 2005). Although the State interferes heavily in formal and social media, publicity through particular outlets can generate impact and official action (Liebman, 2005). Often, once a story is initially published and attracts public interest, complainants with health claims may get a more effective settlement (Fu, 2010).

There is momentum towards increasing transparency and public input in the formulation of health policy. Government agencies at all levels, including ministries and local governments, publish drafts of laws and regulations for public comment in paper and on the Internet, typically for periods between two and four weeks. In the health law area, a recent example is the draft Shenzhen regulations on social medical insurance. In some instances, public comment is considered. For example, in a 20-day period in early 2012, the local government in Shenzhen received more than 20,000 individual comments on key terms related to municipal health insurance legislation. Because the draft attracted such intense response, the government extended the public comment period to ensure that it had taken into account all of the public's concerns (*China Youth Daily*, 2012).

Formal remedial mechanisms in China exist, but often are very difficult for individuals to employ because of the State's overriding concern to maintain social stability. Often indirect methods must be used to resolve problems effectively. However, the developments in legislative and regulatory notice-and-comment procedures are an indicator that some limited space exists for public participation.

Identities based on the Residential Registration (Hukou) System and special occupational status

The State has the obligation to respect, protect, and fulfil an individual's right to health. Yet the Residential Registration (*Hukou*) System and treatment based on special occupational status turn out to be restrictive measures that prevent persons from receiving equitable health-related benefits.

Household registration (Hukou)

China's household registration (*hukou*) system, which restricts movement and migration of individuals (Chan & Zhang, 1999), exacerbates inequality between urban and rural populations, by preventing persons from accessing equal social and economic benefits such as healthcare insurance and pensions. A person's *hukou* status can also be a barrier in obtaining work in a preferred place, in obtaining title to real property, and to access to education (Treiman & Zhang, 2011).

The *hukou* system divides people into two categories at birth: agricultural and non-agricultural, and requires people to register at only one place as a permanent residence (Chan & Buckingham, 2008). Only a few limited ways exist to change one's *hukou* status formally from agricultural to non-agricultural, or from the original local permanent residence to a larger city, such as enrolment in a university, employment by certain large corporations, or government employment.

The design of the social welfare system was based on *hukou* status. For example, basic healthcare insurance plans and pension plans are categorized based on one's *hukou* and employment status. As a general matter, those with a non-agricultural *hukou* have access to more and higher quality benefits, and those who have *hukou* registered in the top tier-eastern cities like Beijing and Shanghai have even greater access.

Generally speaking, the *hukou* system has a direct adverse impact on people on agricultural status regarding access to healthcare services and pensions. Rural residents face severe difficulties in obtaining high-quality care, particularly for catastrophes. As discussed earlier, in practice, they must seek care in large urban centres, pay their expenses out-of-pocket, and then seek reimbursement for costs under the rural system. Migrant workers, usually registered with an agricultural *hukou*, have moved to the metropolises. They cannot transfer their *hukou* to where they work, so even though they remit payroll taxes to the local municipal government, their health-related rights and privileges may still be restricted.

Stratification within the social insurance system

The Chinese government is establishing a social insurance system including health insurance and pension components for all citizens, yet legacy systems of privilege still exist. The current social insurance system could be thought of as a pyramid. At the top are public employees, including civil servants and employees of public institutions (*shiye danwei*) (State Council, 1998). The numbers of public employees relative to the general population is small. On the second tier are employees of State- and privately-owned enterprises that contribute jointly to the basic health insurance pool and pension plans. The third and largest tier is comprised of peasants and migrant workers who are registered as rural residents and urban residents who do not have a formal employer. As a general matter, those at the top of the pyramid receive more generous levels of funding support and coverage.

Such distinctions raise equity concerns, and the government proposed to merge the health insurance and pension plans for public employees with the ones for enterprise employees. In the past, public employees as well as retired Party cadres and students at State universities received access to higher-quality, free medical services (*gongfei yiliao*). By the end of 2011, 24 of 31 provinces had transferred students at State universities, as well as employees of government and public institutions, from the 'public employee' category to the new basic urban health insurance plan, which used to only apply to employees of enterprises (*People's Daily*, 2012). The media has reported that civil servants at the central level will join the basic urban health insurance plan in 2013 (Wei, 2012). At this point in time, the trend is towards fewer categories in the provision of health insurance, a progressive realization of non-discrimination in healthcare.

However, this trend is lagging in pensions, a key element in ensuring elderly health and security. Currently, civil servants and employees of public institutions do not contribute to a pension pool. However, when those employees retire, the State provides a monthly pension equal to

80% of their working salary (Xiong, 2012a). The pensions of non-public employment retirees are approximately 44% of the retirees' working salary, based on a joint monthly contribution of 28% of the employees' salary to the pension pool (Xiong, 2012b). A retired public employee in Beijing can probably receive 4,000 RMB/month to 5,000 RMB/month, (Caijing, 2012) depending on his or her rank, whereas by the end of 2011, the national average monthly pension for someone retired from an enterprise is 1,511 RMB (CNCA, 2011). The monthly pension for rural residents is 74 RMB, and only 34.6% of rural elderly people are covered by such a pension plan (CNCA, 2010).

Given these significant monetary differences, public employee stakeholders in the system unsurprisingly resist reform to their pensions. For example, the central government launched a reform in 2009 in five designated provinces to mandate that public institutions and their employees contribute to the pension pool (State Council, 2008), but localities resisted (*China Economics Weekly*, 2009). Current employees of public institutions, especially those in the educational sector, are concerned that the reform will reduce their pensions (*China Economics Weekly*, 2009). The pilot plan was published without a period of open comment (*China Economics Weekly*, 2009). It is possible that a more open process could have pressured policymakers that are currently benefitting from the existing allocation of resources to agree to a reallocation.

With respect to retirement security for rural elderly, much work remains. The current wave of reforms started in 2009, with the goal of covering all rural residents by 2020 (State Council, 2009b). It creates a general funding pool that combines individual contributions with national and local subsidies. However, the plan requires that a beneficiary have contributed for 15 years in order to yield a national baseline 55 RMB payment (State Council, 2009b) (which can be supplemented by local government programmes), a discouragingly small sum.

Stratification in the social insurance system directly affects the ability of individuals to access health resources. Some aspects of stratification are reinforced because of other systems of social control (such as the *hukou* system), while others are perpetuated by barriers to economic mobility (access to public employment). While the trend is towards the creation of a more uniform system, the final outcome is yet to be determined.

Conclusion

In recent years, China has undertaken the significant challenge of progressively realizing the right to health by reforming its complex healthcare and food safety systems. The reforms were necessary to adjust to the advances made in economic growth and to increase the standard of health in the general population. Although economic and market conditions changed, China's governance model and legacy systems have not kept pace. Systems based upon special privilege entrench inequities based on geography and occupational status. At the same time, individuals that may encounter difficulties in accessing their benefits under the new healthcare plan or who wish to protect themselves from injurious food have limited options to raise their concerns before impartial decision-makers. This tension between macro-level reform and micro-level remedies is at the core of China's dilemma in progressively realizing the right to health.

References

Areddy, J.T. (2010, 4 January). China reports new milk scare. *Wall Street Journal*. Available at: <http://online.wsj.com/article/SB126255525849313997.html> (accessed 29 August 2012).

Bristow, M. (2011, 2 December). Beijing to crackdown on 'black jails'. *BBC News*. Available at: <http://www.bbc.co.uk/news/world-asia-china-15998076> (accessed 29 August 2012).

Brixi, H., Mu, Y., Targa, B., *et al.* (2011). *Equity and Public Governance in Health System Reform: Challenges and Opportunities for China.* World Bank Policy Research Working Paper 5530. Available at: <http://www-wds.worldbank.org/external/default/WDSContentServer/WDSP/IB/2011/01/13/000158349_20110113134311/Rendered/PDF/WPS5530.pdf> (accessed 29 August 2012).

Caijing. (2012, 18 June). [*Civil Servants' Pensions are 3 Times Higher than Enterprise Employees and They will Benefit from the Delay of Retirement the Most.*] Available at: <http://economy.caijing.com.cn/2012-06-18/111898544.html> (accessed 29 August 2012).

CESCR. (1999). *General Comment No. 12: The Right to Adequate Food.* E/C.12/1999/5. Committee on Economic, Social and Cultural Rights (CESCR): Geneva.

Chan, K.W. and Buckingham, W. (2008). Is China abolishing the *Hukou* system?*China Quarterly*, 195, 582–606.

Chan, K.W. and Zhang, L. (1999). The *Hukou* system and rural-urban migration in China: processes and changes. *The China Quarterly* 160, 818–855.

China Communist Party Central Committee and State Council. (2009). *Views of the CPC Central Committee and the State Council on deepening medical and health system.* Available at: <http://www.gov.cn/jrzg/2009-04/06/content_1278721.htm> (accessed 29 August 2012).

China Economics Weekly. (2009, 26 September). The pension reform for public institutions started 9 months ago but the five pilot project provinces such as Guangdong did not make substantial changes. *Zhongguo Jingji Zhoukan.* Available at: <http://finance.ifeng.com/news/special/yanglaogaige/bgt/20091026/1384396.shtml> (accessed 29 August 2012).

Chinese Constitution. (1982). *The Constitution of the People's Republic of China*, 4 December 1982, Art. 33.2 (China). Available at: <http://www.gov.cn/gongbao/content/2004/content_62714.htm> (accessed 31 August 2012).

CNCA. (2010). *2010 Main Data Report on the Status of China's Elderly People in Urban and Rural Areas.* China National Committee on Aging: China. Excerpt available at: <http://caijing.iqilu.com/guancha/2012/0711/1268822.shtml> (accessed 29 August 2012).

CNCA. (2011). *The 2011 Statistical Communique on China's Aging Development.* China National Committee on Aging: China.

De Schutter, O. (2012). *Report of the Special Rapporteur on the Right to Food.* United Nations Human Rights Council A/HRC/19/59/Add.1. Available at: <http://www.srfood.org/images/stories/pdf/officialreports/20120306_china_en.pdf> (accessed 29 August 2012).

Dong, W. (2001/2002). *Health Care Reform in Urban China. Comparative Program on Health and Society.* Working Paper 2001/2. Munk Centre for International Studies at University of Toronto: Toronto. Available at: <http://www.utoronto.ca/cphs/WORKINGPAPERS/CPHS2001_Weizhen_Dong.pdf> (accessed 31 August 2012).

Ellis, L.J. and Turner, J.L. (2008). *Sowing the Seeds: Opportunities for U.S.–China Cooperation on Food Safety.* Woodrow Wilson Center: Washington, DC. Available at: <http://www.wilsoncenter.org/publication-series/sowing-the-seeds-opportunities-for-us-china-cooperation-food-safety> (accessed 29 August 2012).

Food Safety Law. (2009). *Food Safety Law art. 2 and 4 (China).* Available at: <http://www.gov.cn/flfg/2009-02/28/content_1246367.htm> (accessed 29 August 2012).

Fu, H. (2010). *From Online Mobilization to Offline Action: Yirenping and Public Interest Litigation.* Working paper, University of Hong Kong. Available at: <http://dx.doi.org/10.2139/ssrn.1730122> (accessed 29 August 2012).

Hand, K. (2011). Resolving constitutional disputes in contemporary China. *University of Pennsylvania East Asia Law Review*, 7(1), 51–159.

Ho, C.S. (2010). Health reform and de facto federalism in China. *China: An International Journal*, 8(1), 33–62.

Ho, C. and Gostin, L. (2009). The social face of economic growth: China's health system in transition. *Journal of the American Medical Association*, 301(17), 1809–1811.

ICESCR (1966). *International Covenant on Economic Social and Cultural Rights*. Available at: <http://treaties.un.org/Pages/ViewDetails.aspx?src=TREATY&mtdsg_no=IV-3&chapter=4&lang=en> (accessed 31 August 2012).

Jacobs, A. (2010, 10 November). China sentences activist in milk scandal to prison. *New York Times*. Available at: <http://www.nytimes.com/2010/11/11/world/asia/11beijing.html> (accessed 29 August 2012).

Li, H. and Wang, Y. (2012, 17 May). What are the barriers to use the medical insurance stemmed from the same national plan outside the designated area? *Renmin Ribao* [People's Daily]. Available at: <http://www.hup.harvard.edu/resources/authors/pdf/notes.pdf> (accessed 29 August 2012).

Liebman, B.L. (2005). Watchdog or demagogue? The media in the Chinese legal system. *Columbia Law Review*, 105(1), 118–120.

Liebman, B.L. (2013). Malpractice mobs: medical dispute resolution in China. *Columbia Law Review*, *113*, 181–264.

Liu, Y. (2002). Reforming China's urban health insurance system. *Health Policy*, 60, 133–150.

Mertha, A.C. (2005). China's 'soft' centralization: shifting Tiao/Kuai authority relations. *China Quarterly*, 184, 791–810.

MOF. (2011). *Ministry of Human Resource and Social Security and Ministry of Health's Announcement on Adjusting Central Budget for Subsidies of Urban Resident Health Insurance and New Cooperative Medical Insurance, No. 285, 2011*. Ministry of Finance. Available at: <http://hlj.mof.gov.cn/lanmudaohang/zhengcefagui/201206/t20120605_656901.html> (accessed 29 August 2012).

MOH. (2011). *2011 Report on China's Maternity and Infant Health Development*. Available at: <http://www.gov.cn/gzdt/att/att/site1/20110921/001e3741a4740fe3bdab01.pdf> (accessed 29 August 2012).

MOH. (2012a). 卫生事业发展概况 *Weisheng shiye fazhan gaikuang* [Overview of China's Health Affairs Development]. Ministry of Health. Available at: <http://www.gov.cn/test/2012-04/18/content_2116000.htm> (accessed 29 August 2012).

MOH. (2012b). 新农合工作 2011 年进展和 2012 年重点 *Xinnonghe gongzuo 2011nian jinzhan he 2012nian zhongdian* [The Progresses of New Cooperative Medical System in 2011 and Key Issues in 2012]. Ministry of Health. Available at: <http://www.moh.gov.cn/publicfiles/business/htmlfiles/mohbgt/s3582/201202/54209.htm> (accessed 29 August 2012).

Minzner, C.F. (2005). Xinfang: an alternative to formal Chinese legal institutions. *Stanford Journal of International Law*, 42, 103–179.

Minzner, C.F. (2009). Riots and cover-ups: counterproductive control of local agents in China, *University of Pennsylvania Journal of International Law*, 31(1), 53–133.

Minzner, C.F. (2011). China's turn against law. *American Journal of Comparative Law*, LIX(4), 935–984.

National Statistics Bureau of China. (2012). 金砖国家联合统计手册 *2012 Jinzhuan guojia lianhe tongji shouce 2012* [BRICS Countries United Statistical Handbook 2012]. Available at: <http://www.stats.gov.cn/tjsj/qtsj/JZSC2012/P020120329599266710333.pdf> (accessed 29 August 2012).

Peerenboom, R. (2002). *China's Long March Toward Rule of Law*. Cambridge University Press: New York, NY.

People's Republic of China. (2011). *Information Office of the State Council, 'The Socialist Legal System with Chinese Characteristics'*. Available at: <http://www.china.org.cn/government/whitepaper/node_7137666.htm> (accessed 29 August 2012).

People's Republic of China. (2012a). *General Principles of the Civil Law of the People's Republic of China, Article 98 (China)*. Available at: <http://www.china.com.cn/policy/txt/2012-01/14/content_24405953_5.htm> (accessed 31 August 2012).

People's Republic of China. (2012b). *China Initiated and Deployed 9 National Basic Public Health Service Projects*. Available at: <http://www.gov.cn/jrzg/2009-07/10/content_1362010.htm> (accessed 29 August 2012).

People's Republic of China. (2012c).*The Reimbursement Approval Process for Outpatient Services that People with New Cooperative Medical Insurance Plan Receive Outside the Designated Area*. Available at: <http://www.scwst.gov.cn/index.php/2012-01-31-09-49-50/4084-2012-05-10-08-02-16> (accessed 29 August 2012).

People's Daily. (2012, 19 January).Civil servants' free medical service benefit was eliminated in 80% provinces. *Renmin Ribao*. Available at: <http://cpc.people.com.cn/GB/64093/82429/83083/16917529.html> (accessed 29 August 2012).

Phoenix Report (*Kucao Gongzuoshi*). (2010). *Medical Discrimination Against People Living with HIV/AIDS*. Available at: <http://asiacatalyst.org/news/Phoenixreport1110.pdf> (accessed 29 August 2012).

Pomfret, J. (2011, 1 February). China milk powder demand leaves Hong Kong shelves bare. *Reuters*. Available at: <http://www.reuters.com/article/2011/02/01/idINIndia-54556620110201> (accessed 29 August 2012).

Shi, L. (1993). Health care in China: a rural-urban comparison after the socioeconomic reforms. *Bulletin of the World Health Organization*, 71(6), 723–736. Available at: <http://www.ncbi.nlm.nih.gov/pmc/articles/PMC2393531/?page=1> (accessed 29 August 2012).

State Council. (1998). [*Interim Regulation on the Registration of Public Institutions*], Order No. 252 issued on 25 October 1998, amended on 27 June 2004, translated by lawinfochina.

State Council of the People's Republic of China. (2005). An evaluation of and recommendations on the reforms of the health system in China. *China Development Review*, 7(1), Report no. 6.

State Council. (2008). [*Announcement on pilot project plan on the reform of public institution's employees' pension*]. Available at: <http://www.law-lib.com/law/law_view.asp?id=305811> (accessed 29 August 2012).

State Council. (2009a, 18 March). *2009–2011 Implementation Plan for Recent Key Issues in the Health Care Reform*. Available at: <http://www.gov.cn/zwgk/2009-04/07/content_1279256.htm> (accessed 29 August 2012).

State Council. (2009b, 1 September). *Guidance Opinion on Developing Pilot Projects for the New Rural Social Pension Insurance Plan, No. 32 in 2009*. Available at: <http://www.gov.cn/zwgk/2009-09/04/content_1409216.htm> (accessed 29 August 2012).

State Council. (2012). Decision on Strengthening Food Safety, No.20 in 2012, Part VIII (28), 23 June 2012. Available at: <http://www.gov.cn/zwgk/2012-07/03/content_2175891.htm> (accessed 29 August 2012).

Taeuber, I. (1957). China's population: riddle of the past, enigma of the future. *Antioch Review* 17(1), 7–18. Available at: <http://www.jstor.org/stable/4609926?seq=7> (accessed 31 August 2012).

Tam, W. and Yang, D. (2005). Food safety and the development of regulatory institutions in China. *Asian Perspective*, 29(4), 5–36. Available at: <http://www.asianperspective.org/articles/v29n4-a.pdf> (accessed 29 August 2012).

The Beijing News. (2012a, 15 June). 70% of medical resources are concentrated in big cities. *Xin Jing Bao*, p. A21. Available at: <http://epaper.bjnews.com.cn/html/2012-06/15/content_347782.htm?div=-1> (accessed 29 August 2012).

The Beijing News. (2012b, 13 June). [Free-range cattle and sheep and cage-free duck eggs as special supply for astronauts], *Xin Jing Bao*. Available at: <http://www.bjnews.com.cn/news/2012/06/13/204393.html> (accessed 29 August 2012).

Treiman, D.J. and Zhang, Z. (2011). *Social Origins, Hukou Conversion, and the Wellbeing of Urban Residents in Contemporary China*. California Center for Population Research, On-line Working Paper Series PWP-CCPR-2011-009, University of California, Los Angeles: Los Angeles, CA. Available at: <http://papers.ccpr.ucla.edu/papers/PWP-CCPR-2011-009/PWP-CCPR-2011-009.pdf> (accessed 31 August 2012).

Wagstaff, A., Lindelöw, M., Wang, S., *et al.* (2009). *Reforming China's Rural Health System*. World Bank: Washington, DC.

Wei, M. (2012, 15 January). Civil servants at the central level will join basic urban employee health insurance plan next year. *Xin Jing Bao* [The Beijing News], p. A12. Available at: <http://epaper.bjnews.com.cn/html/2012-01/15/content_310387.htm?div=-1> (accessed 29 August 2012).

WHO. (2009). *Toxicological and Health Aspects of Melamine and Cyanuric Acid*. World Health Organization (WHO): Geneva. Available at: <http://www.who.int/foodsafety/publications/chem/Melamine_report09.pdf> (accessed 29 August 2012).

WHO. (2011). *Non-Communicable Disease Country Profiles, 2011 – China*. Available at: <http://www.who.int/nmh/countries/chn_en.pdf> (accessed 29 August 2012).

Wong, E. (2009, 20 January). Families file suit in Chinese tainted milk scandal. *New York Times*. Available at: <http://www.nytimes.com/2009/01/21/world/asia/21milk.html> (accessed 29 August 2012).

World Bank. (2005). *China's Health Sector: Why Reform is Needed, Rural Health in China: Briefing Notes Series, Note No. 3*. Available at: <http://www-wds.worldbank.org/external/default/WDSContentServer/WDSP/IB/2005/08/11/000090341_20050811151809/Rendered/PDF/332320ENGLISH0CHA0BN31en.pdf> (accessed 29 August 2012).

World Bank. (2010). Fixing the public hospital system in China. *China Health Policy Notes*, 2, 1–84.

World Bank. (2012). *Country Databank*. Available at: <http://data.worldbank.org/country/china> (accessed 31 August 2012).

Xinhua News Agency. (2011, 28 April). China's mainland population grows to 1.3397 billion in 2010: census data. *English.news.cn*. Available at: <http://news.xinhuanet.com/english2010/china/2011-04/28/c_13849795.htm> (accessed 29 August 2012).

Xiong, T. (2012a, 27 June). *Chinese Civil Servants have the Best Pension Package in the World*. Available at: <http://www.21cbh.com/HTML/2012-6-27/yMMDY5XzQ2MTgyMw.html> (accessed 29 August 2012).

Xiong, T. (2012b, 25 June). *An Explanation of Inequality in the Current Double-Track Pension System*. Available at: <http://www.21cbh.com/HTML/2012-6-25/zOMDY5XzQ1OTgzOQ.html> (accessed 29 August 2012).

Yang, Y. (2002). Entering wards for cadres. *Zhongguo Zhoukan* [China Weekly], 12, 50–52. Available at: <http://www.chinaweekly.cn/bencandy.php?fid=63&id=5826> (accessed 31 August 2012).

Yardley, J. (2004, 5 May). Infants in Chinese city starve on protein-short formula. *New York Times*. Available at: <http://www.nytimes.com/2004/05/05/world/infants-in-chinese-city-starve-on-protein-short-formula.html?pagewanted=all&src=pm> (accessed 29 August 2012).

Zhang, D. and Unschuld, P.U. (2008). China's barefoot doctor: past, present, and future. *Lancet*, 372(9653), 1865–1867.

Zhang, M. (2012, 1 August). Deepening the health reform and promoting the development of health science. *Qiushi*, 15. Available at: <http://www.qstheory.cn/zxdk/2012/201215/201207/t20120727_172655.htm> (accessed 31 August 2012).

Chapter 12

Brazil: a long journey towards a universal healthcare system

Armando De Negri Filho

Introduction: history of Brazil and overview of the nation's health

Brazilian unified health system

Brazil's unified national health system, known as the *Sistema Único de Saúde* (SUS), was created by Article 198 of the Federal Constitution adopted in 1988 (Brazil, 1988). It was the result of an important social mobilization that was conceived during the dictatorial period (1964–1985) as part of the civilian struggles for democracy in the country. Its final implementation represented a plurality of interests that generated a political agenda able to lead to the constitutional text on the universal right to social security and health, including: a critical approach to the social determinants of health-disease that was built by academics in the social medicine field, political activists that were deeply influenced by the Italian health reform of 1978, Catholic ecclesiastical community movements that inspired a popular movement for health, and many groups of university students, labour union activists, and other political leaders.

Population and health statistics

Brazil's population exceeds 190 million inhabitants over 8.5 million square kilometres (IBGE, 2010). Brazil is a Federal Republic with a national government, 27 states, and 5,565 municipalities (IBGE, 2010). Since slavery was abolished in 1888, Brazil has remained deeply socially divided with tremendous levels of inequity.

Nevertheless, Brazil's infant mortality rate (IMR) has dropped by 73% in the past two decades. According to the United Nations Children's Fund (UNICEF), the IMR per thousand live births fell from 58 in 1990 to 36 in 2000, and to 16 in 2011 (UNICEF, 2011).

As with many industrialized nations, cardiovascular diseases are the leading causes of death in Brazil, followed by cancer as well as external causes such as homicides and traffic accidents (WHO, 2008). As chronic diseases are increasingly contributing to the burden of disease, communicable diseases are decreasing, but they still affect a sizable portion of the population. It is estimated that 40% to 50% of Brazilians over the age of 40 suffer from hypertension, and as many as 6 million have diabetes (WHO, 2008).

The health system

According to the World Health Organization (WHO), Brazil ranks 72nd among countries in terms of government spending on health—US$317 per capita (WHO, 2008). Although Brazil has the largest economy in South America, its government spends less on health than Argentina, Chile, and Uruguay (WHO, 2008).

According to the Brazilian Ministry of Health (Brazil, 2012a), SUS includes more than 73,000 outpatient services, including 32,000 family health teams with a medical doctor, a nurse, one or two nurse technicians, and four to six community health agents. Those teams are the basic module of a national strategy of primary healthcare, and each one is charged to take care of around 3,500 people, reaching more than 106 million people throughout the country. The impact on child mortality and the reduction of in-hospital care for primary healthcare-sensitive conditions in Brazil, as hypertension, heart failure, diabetes, among others, are noteworthy—between 1999 and 2007, there was a 24% decrease in the hospitalization rates, from 183.9 to 143.3 hospitalizations per 10,000 inhabitants (NESCON, 2012). Each year, SUS provides nearly 24,000 transplantations, over 84,000 cardiac surgeries, 62,000 cancer surgeries, and care to over 11 million in-hospital patients (CFM/CREMESP, 2011). However, there is a persistent shortage on access to complex care needs (Brazil, 2008).

Approximately 144 million Brazilians are exclusively users of SUS; the remaining 46 million are still considered partial users because the entire population is covered by health surveillance procedures such as vaccines and the protection of food, water, health-related products, and waste services (CFM/CREMESP, 2011). Many of these partial users also selectively use services that are not fully covered by their private health insurance. Approximately 94% of the privately insured have collective insurances provided through collective agreements with employers, including many civil servants, and those insurance plans are not able to cover a complete range of services, such as transplantations, special and expensive drugs, intensive care, and renal therapy, among others.

Human rights and accountability in Brazil

Brazil did not accede to the International Convention on Economic, Social and Cultural Rights (ICESCR) until 1992. Before this, Brazil ratified the Convention on the Elimination of All Forms of Racial Discrimination (CERD) in 1968, the Convention on the Elimination of All Forms of Discrimination against Women (CEDAW) in 1984, the Convention on the Rights of the Child (CRC) in 1990, and the Inter-American Convention on Human Rights in 1996. Brazil also ratified the Convention on the Rights of Persons with Disabilities (CRPD) in 2008.

In practice, however, it is Article 196 of the Brazilian Federal Constitution of 1988 that implements health as a human right and a duty of the State. The 1988 Constitution, representing a human rights perspective and advocating for socioeconomic rights such as health and social security (Article 6), was a big change in Brazilian history. To this extent, it faced strong resistance from politically conservative and liberal economic sectors favouring a privatization of the healthcare system. Immediately following the adoption of the new Constitution, a neoliberal government was elected in 1989, which presented significant barriers for the implementation of legislation and regulation necessary for the financing of the new universal health system. The implementation of SUS was therefore delayed until the end of 1992, with the impeachment of Brazil's President, Collor de Mello.

Decentralization

When decentralization was implemented in 1993 (Basic Operational Rule—NOB-SUS 01/1993/ Ministry of Health Ordinance No. 545, 1993), a direct transfer from national to municipal health funds made it possible for local governments to fulfil their responsibilities for primary healthcare and health surveillance. As a result, the family health strategy was adopted as a modality of primary healthcare (since 1994) (Brazil, 1993, 1994).

The Constitutional Amendment No. 29/2000 permitted the rescue of a constitutional rule that had been eliminated by President Collor's government, that is, to guarantee a minimum amount of funds to finance health actions and public services. It earmarked federal, State, and municipal revenues for joint financing of basic health services and medical care. Each year, federal government expenditures must increase by an amount equal to the nominal gross domestic product growth rate on previous fiscal year expenditures. Municipal government must spend 15% and states and federal districts 12% of their own revenues (Brazil, 2000a).

It was expected by civil society that the regulation of Constitutional Amendment No. 29/2000 would establish that the federal government would spend 10% of its own revenue. However, in a new chapter of this constant struggle between a socializing approach promoted by the health policy and the restrictions promoted by the neoliberal economic policies, its regulation by the Complementary Law No. 141/2012 did not approve, in case of Union, the minimum of 10%, but maintained that as set forth by the Constitutional Amendment (Brazil, 2012b). A dedicated advocacy movement in favour of 10% of the federal budget for health continues in late 2012.

Despite the progress achieved in advancing universal access and comprehensiveness as promoted by SUS, significant challenges remain. In particular, those related to the clashes with the hegemony of economic liberalism in terms of private sector interests, government contradictions and the influence in public opinion regarding the tax system, and the need for a solidarity-based social protection system.

Social control

According to Federal Law No. 8.142/1990, the system must be socially controlled by means of health councils at each level of the federation—nation, states, and municipalities, with decision-making powers over the health plans and budget, and accountability of policies, plans, and financial resources, making accessible to people the decisions and process of the public management. Citizens' representatives compose half of the membership on these councils, and the other half is divided among representatives for government, health workers, and health providers. Additionally, periodically organized national health conferences, which define the strategic pathway of the system every four years, mobilize delegates from municipalities to the nation (Brazil, 1990b). So the radical decentralization that characterizes SUS is very much related to the aim of a radical democratization of society and government relationships after the long dictatorship, bringing the policymaking process and the control of public management closer to the people. This participatory concept recently inspired the design of the national social assistance system, SUAS, and the national public security policy and system, SENASP.

Judicialization of the right to health

While feeling the scarcity of health resources via long waiting times and delayed answers from the health system regarding access and quality of care, citizens have become increasingly conscious of their right to health. This realization, combined with improved access to courts and attorneys specially dedicated to defend the right to health, as well as the Brazilian Constitution's recognition of health as a right, allowed the courts to start interpreting the Constitution as giving rise to individually enforceable social rights and health as a legal right which can be judicially demanded. We thus have observed an increasing quantity of health rights-related litigation in Brazil. As Biehl notes, 'Across Brazil, at the federal, State and municipal level, there is a growing trend of health-related lawsuits by citizens seeking and realizing access to health actions and services from SUS through the courts, though patients are suing the government for everything from baby formula to complex surgeries, a large portion of lawsuits are for drugs' (Biehl, 2009). With the quantity of health-related lawsuits reaching the hundreds of thousands, the National Council of Justice established the National Forum of Health to promote greater efficiency in the settlement of these claims (Resolution no. 107/2010; Recommendation no. 31/2010). Yet increased litigation has also shifted decision-making power to the courts. As Lunes and colleagues note:

> It is evident that right-to-health litigation has held governments accountable for their constitutional duties and provided access for thousands of individuals to administrative or judicial mechanisms to enforce their rights. Litigation has raised citizen awareness of individual rights and the government's responsibilities. Increased transparency and accountability will improve human rights protection as well as strengthen SUS . . . On the other hand, however, access to justice, like access to health, is unequally distributed because is conditioned by socio-economic factors. Furthermore, some court rulings have systematically favored the concept of the treating physician over the opinion of peer clinical experts or the clinical protocols of the health authority. This may force the System to deliver drugs/services for which there is no evidence of its clinical effectiveness. The limited technical capacity of the courts might lead to suboptimal decisions for society as a whole, given the opportunity cost of no delivery of other services. (Lunes et al., 2012)

Similarly, the high volume of health rights litigation has blurred the distinction between the adjudication of rights and public deliberation regarding the content of these rights. As de Oliveira and Noronha explain:

> The Law debates frames the problem as one of positive constitutional rights, whereas the debate in the area of public health argues that the matter is a technical one, which needs to be addressed through a public health perspective based on risks and priorities. Aside from these perspectives, this problem has captured the attention of political and social scientists for a simple reason: it entails a political issue that involves decisions taken by political actors – be they members of the Executive, Legislative or Judiciary branch – with consequences for governmental policy agendas, management of public policies and social justice. (de Oliveira & Noronha, 2011)

The right to health in Brazil: availability, accessibility, acceptability, and quality

Availability

While the availability of comprehensive services has always been a key provision of SUS, the availability of high-cost medicines has incrementally progressed—both as a result of political advocacy and litigation—in accordance with progressive realization of the right to health. An important step towards achieving the right to health for all Brazilians occurred in 1996 with the executive decision to provide free antiretroviral drugs to persons living with HIV/AIDS (Brazil, 2002a).

Despite the improved access to specialized care through SUS, there is a long way to go. For instance, while there are 356,000 hospital beds (1.85 beds per 1,000 people) in the public system, in order to achieve a minimum of four beds per 1,000 inhabitants (Spain's rate), Brazil would need almost 335,000 new hospital beds. While this is not officially considered an urgent need, lack of sufficient qualified public beds leads to a search for beds in the private sector, which reinforces the market dimensions, generating an increase in waiting times in emergency rooms and for programmed procedures. As this example shows, improved and more equitable funding is necessary to break the dynamics of the scarcity that continue to block the full development of SUS (DATASUS, 2012).

Accessibility

With the implementation of SUS, health has become universally accessible because the national, State, and municipal services operate in an integrated manner through a single payer system financed by the general tax system. According to Federal Law No. 8.080/1990, healthcare must be: provided everywhere, with the same universal coverage and qualified assistance, with no service restrictions except purely cosmetic procedures; provided for free at the point of service; and egalitarian, with no restrictions to any person in terms of access or kinds of treatment, ranging from basic health surveillance actions to more sophisticated transplantation procedures or special drugs access (Brazil, 1990a). Although SUS has integrated all government facilities as part of the universal system, many private services, mostly non-profit institutions, remain a complementary part of the public system in order to more comprehensively address all health needs.

Acceptability and quality

At the drafting of the 1988 Constitution, lobbyists pushed for the exclusion from SUS of the high-quality health services for the military, civil servants, and State-owned enterprise employees. In particular, because the legislators and government employees are generally not regular users of SUS, they reflect a widespread understanding that high-quality care is found in the private sector, while the public system is simply a solution for the more 'vulnerable'. While SUS serves as a lifeline for the poor, it is not seen as acceptable to a large proportion of middle- and high-income individuals, whose participation in the system is necessary for its success.

Nevertheless, the Brazilian government has taken steps to improve the quality of public services. The field of emergency services, which has historically been overcrowded, presents a good example of Brazil's progress in improving the quality of care. In 2003, the federal government gave priority to mobile emergency care (SAMU) (Machado et al., 2011)—a pre-hospital ambulance system with advanced life support has been installed with more than 1,600 vehicles and 170 medical regulation centres, as well as a network of emergency ambulatory facilities as an alternative for the saturated hospital emergency rooms. Despite these advancements, the already crowded emergency hospital services reflect the lack of access to acute care in the public system, generating a spread of overcrowding throughout the country. In response, a coalition of movements and institutions has developed a national campaign calling for Human Rights at the Emergency Services (Brazil, 2002b, 2003a, 2003b, 2011).

Limitations on rights under domestic laws to protect the public health

The main accomplishment of SUS has been to make health a right for all. Until 1988, only formal workers and their families were covered by social insurance, while the rest, the 'indigents' that represented around 85% of the population, received care at the charity and public services of some cities and states, as well as in some of the federal hospitals dedicated to certain pathologies. Yet while the health sector represents around 8.8% of all economic activity in the country, public expenditure only represents 45% of the total health expenditure, with private expenditures reaching US$44,300 per capita per year (IBGE, 2010). As health costs rise while public expenditures remain relatively constant, individuals are paying more out-of-pocket than in the late 1990s.

The private sector is also imperfect. This sector is mostly made accessible through private insurance companies (such as big State-owned companies' self-managed funds of social security), and a variety of service providers that can be managers as well (as in the case of medical cooperatives); all of which are under the supervision of the National Agency of Supplementary Health, designated by the Minister of Health. Around 46 million Brazilians are covered by supplementary health, and despite the Agency's activity and advancements in respect of users' rights, there are many failures at the effective regulation of the private system (CFM/CREMESP, 2011).

History of failures with respect to the human right to health

The SUS has been systemically underfinanced. Comprehensive universalism has not been fully possible because there is a persistent difficulty in making the need to address underfunding politically valuable. This misunderstanding is very useful for conservative interests that oppose the building of a powerful public system able to regulate the market and establish the public interest as the main organizer of the health agenda.

Despite its commitment to the right to health, Brazil has historically faced a contradiction imposed by a law of 'fiscal responsibility' (Complementary Law No. 101/2000) approved in the 1990s that imposed a limit on personnel expenditures of 53% of the total budgets for public administration (Brazil, 2000b). That law generated a barrier for the full provision of health services, generating a dilemma for public authorities under the pressure of people's needs: either satisfy social demands or respect the law. That typical neoliberal legislation generated a very complex arrangement, whereby in order to respect the fiscal law and people's constitutional rights, public authorities have to contract personnel using cooperatives or enterprises as intermediaries. This process generates substantial discontinuity in the provision of public services and exacerbates corrupt practices. The complexity of the health workforce necessitates a thorough reorganization of employment contracts that promote a permanent health workforce that can be sustainably financed by SUS. In order to fully achieve the right to health, Brazil's social rights and fiscal policies must be harmonized.

Importantly, the large number of middle-class and high-profile employees outside of SUS has resulted in political fragility in the continued implementation and promotion of SUS. In the arrangements that were made to approve SUS, it was accepted that personal expenditures on private health and education could be deducted from personal income taxes. In effect, this means that the vulnerable populations who rely on public systems ultimately subsidize the richer sectors of the country who can save their tax credits for private assistance on health and education—this could represent almost 10% of the total public health budget. This example demonstrates the extent to which structural inequities serve as barriers to the SUS operating in a way that fully respects the right to health. The SUS, despite its accomplishments, remains in a scenario of permanent conflict with unfavourable power structures that must be directly confronted in order to achieve real universal coverage.

Evolving responses and obligations: future national directions towards the right to health

After 22 years of social participation at the health councils, it is time in Brazil to make a radical reflection on the need for political education and the constructive power of society to overcome the structural barriers that prevent the full implementation of SUS. In order for SUS to achieve full availability, accessibility, acceptability, and quality of services, government expenditures on health should be increased from US$367 per capita per year to US$1000, reaching around 10% of gross national product, and radically more effective public management standards implemented in order to eliminate gaps in access and quality. At its core, this will require the promotion of a progressive tax reform, a political reform that could ensure participatory democracy as a qualifier of representative democracy, and a rights-based approach to State reform.

Moreover, it is necessary for Brazil to establish the public regulation of the private-public provider contracts as a complement to the State-owned services. The planning process of SUS must be reinforced by a sustained effort to make State-owned services the majority in the system, which requires planning for an expansion of investments on State-owned facilities. Similarly, it is necessary to reinforce the public interests of government-contracted private providers to eliminate the ambiguity of services being provided for SUS and the private market at the same time.

Despite the limitations and structural imbalances in SUS functioning, the system has promoted a change in social perception of health. It is noteworthy that all presidential candidates in the past three elections talked about how to reinforce the system and no longer oppose it.

Conclusion: present and future challenges

Brazil's efforts in progressively realizing the right to health through SUS have had clearly discernible impacts on the health of the population. However, many challenges still lie ahead. 'Densifying' the law by fully applying constitutional principles towards the fundamental respect for rights, is the main political challenge of both society and government in Brazil in achieving the right to health. Achieving complete availability, accessibility, acceptability, and quality of care will require continuing building upon the foundation of SUS based on the satisfaction of social needs, defining the quantity and quality standards of services, adopting regional systems with needs-based benefits that are not based on historical limits. In turn, this progressive reform of SUS necessitates political education of the population and its political leaders about the meaning of the right to health as a constitutive part of the right to full social protection, which requires the creation of a positive environment for the progress and stability of SUS.

References

Biehl, J. (2009). *Right to Health Litigation*. Available at: <http://joaobiehl.net/global-health-research/right-to-health-litigation/> (accessed 24 October 2012).

Brazil. (Constituição). (1988). *Constituição da República Federativa do Brazil*. Brasília: Senado Federal.

Brazil. (Governo Federal). (1990a). *Lei Federal nº 8.080, de 19 de Setembro de 1990*. Available at: <http://www.planalto.gov.br/ccivil_03/leis/L8080.htm> (accessed 10 October 2012).

Brazil. (Governo Federal). (1990b). *Lei Federal nº 8.142, de 28 de Dezembro de 1990*. Available at: <http://www.planalto.gov.br/ccivil_03/leis/L8142.htm> (accessed 10 October 2012).

Brazil. (Ministério da Saúde). (1993). *Portaria nº 545, de 20 de Maio de 1993*. Available at: <http://siops.datasus.gov.br/Documentacao/Portaria%20545_20_05_1993.pdf> (accessed 10 October 2012).

Brazil. (Ministério da Saúde). (1994). *Programa Saúde da Família: Dentro de Casa*. Brasília: Editora do Ministério da Saúde.

Brazil. (Governo Federal). (2000a). *Emenda Constitucional nº 29, de 13 de Setembro de 2000*. Available at: <http://www.planalto.gov.br/ccivil_03/constituicao/Emendas/Emc/emc29.htm> (accessed 10 October 2012).

Brazil. (Governo Federal). (2000b). *Lei Complementar nº 101, de 4 de Maio de 2000*. Available at: <http://www.planalto.gov.br/ccivil_03/leis/LCP/Lcp101.htm> (accessed 10 October 2012).

Brazil. (Ministério da Saúde). (2002a). *National AIDS drug policy*. Brasília: Coordenação Nacional de DST e AIDS.

Brazil. (Ministério da Saúde). (2002b). *Portaria No. 2048, de 5 de Novembro de 2002*. Available at: <http://www.saude.mg.gov.br/atos_normativos/legislacao-sanitaria/estabelecimentos-de-saude/urgencia-e-emergencia/portaria_2048_B.pdf> (accessed 10 October 2012).

Brazil. (Ministério da Saúde). (2003a). *Portaria No. 1863, de 29 de Setembro de 2003*. Available at: <http://dtr2001.saude.gov.br/sas/PORTARIAS/Port2003/GM/GM-1863.htm> (accessed 10 October 2012).

Brazil. (Ministério da Saúde). (2003b). *Política Nacional de Atenção às Urgências*. Brasília: Editora do Ministério da Saúde. Available at: <http://bvsms.saude.gov.br/bvs/publicacoes/politica_nac_urgencias.pdf> (accessed 10 October 2012).

Brazil. (Ministério da Saúde). (2008). *Mais Saúde: Direito de Todos: 2008—2011*. Brasília: Editora do Ministério da Saúde. Available at: <http://bvsms.saude.gov.br/bvs/publicacoes/mais_saude_direito_todos_2ed.pdf> (accessed 10 October 2012).

Brazil. (Ministério da Saúde). (2011). *Portaria nº 1.600, de 7 de Julho de 2011*. Available at: <http://bvsms.saude.gov.br/bvs/saudelegis/gm/2011/prt1600_07_07_2011.html> (accessed 10 October 2012).

Brazil. (Governo Federal). (2012b). *Lei Complementar nº 141, de 13 de Janeiro de 2012*. Available at: <http://www.planalto.gov.br/ccivil_03/leis/LCP/Lcp141.htm> (accessed 10 October 2012).

Brazil. (Ministério da Saúde). (2012a). *Saúde da Família*. Available at: <http://dab.saude.gov.br/abnumeros.php> (accessed 10 October 2012).

CFM/CREMESP. (2011). *Demografia Médica no Brazil*. Available at <http://www.cremesp.org.br/pdfs/demografia_2_dezembro.pdf> (accessed 10 October 2012).

DATASUS. (2012). *CNES—Recursos Físicos—Hospitalar—Leitos de internação—Brazil*. Available at: <http://tabnet.datasus.gov.br/cgi/tabcgi.exe?cnes/cnv/leiintbr.def> (accessed 10 October 2012).

de Oliveira, V. and Noronha, L. (2011). Judiciary-executive relations in policy making: the case of drug distribution in the state of São Paulo. *Brazilian Political Science Review*, 5(2), 10–38. Available at: <http://bpsr.org.br/english/arquivos/BPSR_v5_n2_artigos/Article_vanessa.pdf> (accessed 10 October 2012).

IBGE. (2010). *Censo Demográfico 2010*. Available at: <http://www.ibge.gov.br> (accessed 10 October 2012).

Lunes, R., Cubillos-Turriago, L. and Escobar, M.L.2012. *Universal Health Coverage and Litigation in South America*. Available at: <http://api.ning.com/files/ldLkAktbGtZiZS3*CemHt3dKwQBwYn9GPw3SLLCumE7CNJ3-66GEpPi8zz60z1ejgLg511Si69sUNS7R6go0-wJuXgi0aIB1/EnBreve_178_English_Web.pdf> (accessed 10 October 2012).

Machado, C.V., Gonçalves, F., Salvador, F., *et al.* (2011). Mobile emergency care service: analysis of Brazilian policy. *Revista de Saúde Pública*, 45(3), 519–598.

NESCON. (2012). *Avaliação do impacto das ações do programa de saúde da família na redução das internações hospitalares por condições sensíveis à atenção básica em adultos e idosos*. Available at: <http://www.nescon.medicina.ufmg.br/biblioteca/imagem/3261.pdf> (accessed 8 November 2012).

UNICEF. (2011). *Situação mundial da infância 2011—Adolescência uma fase de oportunidades*. Available at: <http://www.unicef.org/brazil/pt/br_sowcr11web.pdf> (accessed 10 October 2012).

WHO. (2008). *World Health Statistics 2008*. World Health Organization (WHO): Geneva. Available at: <http://www.who.int/gho/publications/world_health_statistics/2008/en/> (accessed 10 October 2012).

Chapter 13

The right to health in Peru

Ariel Frisancho

Background

Peru is an upper-middle-income country with a population of 30 million people (UNDP, 2011; World Bank, 2012). Political divisions exist along the borders of 24 provinces (currently called 'regions') and more than 1,000 districts. In the Andean area of the country, a district can consist of 20 to 30 rural communities, each one with elected community leaders, but with no power to manage public resources, thus making the district the basic unit for Peruvian political and geographical ordering.

The distribution of wealth and resources in Peru is highly unequal, with many people suffering from deprivation. The country's interior still displays major inequities, discrimination, and poverty, resulting in a high incidence of preventable disease and mortality among the poorest and most excluded, but also in the rural population living in the regions with little social and economic development. Life expectancy in Peru in the time period 2005 to 2010 reached 71.2 years, but ranges from 63 (among the poorest income quintiles) to 78 (UNDP, 2011).

In 2011, approximately 35% of all Peruvians lived in poverty, and an estimated 10% lived in extreme poverty (National Institute of Statistics and Informatics, 2008a). The majority of the extreme poor are indigenous people who live in isolated Andean or tropical rainforest communities (Eyben, 2004). Thirty per cent of the urban population and 60% of the rural population still do not have access to safe water and adequate sanitation (Peruvian MOH, 2002).

Structure of the Peruvian healthcare system

Since 2006, responsibility for healthcare has been decentralized and assumed by regional governments, with financing and services offered by three main providers. The largest of these providers is the Peruvian Ministry of Health (MOH), which is also in charge of national stewardship, and the regional governments, which obtain their funds from tax revenues and co-payments from patients, providing services primarily oriented towards those who are informally employed (75% of the population) and the poor (Peruvian MOH, 2002). Those subpopulations together comprise almost 67% of the Peruvian population and depend entirely upon the network of public health: posts, clinics, and hospitals that are overseen by the MOH and decentralized regional authorities (Peruvian MOH, 2002). The second largest healthcare provider is the Social Security Institute (ESSALUD), financed by a 9% payroll tax and responsible for covering all the healthcare needs of its formal-sector contributors who comprise about 20% of the total population (Peruvian MOH, 2002). The private sector constitutes the third major provider (3% to 5%, of the total population and increasing) and is financed almost entirely by out-of-pocket expenditures from households (Peruvian MOH, 2002). Private insurance coverage is still reduced. There is a growing 'informal' health system that includes direct consultation by poor people at drug stores. In the mid-2000s,

Lima's local government implemented 'Solidarity Hospitals', where people pay for low-cost health consultation, auxiliary exams, and treatment. This model has evidenced increasing demand and has been replicated throughout the country (World Bank, 2012).

A 1999 World Bank study noted that:

> . . . most of the inequality in [healthcare] consumption results from the assignment of greater amounts of private expenditure to healthcare by the rich than by the poor. This is reinforced by *Instituto Peruano de Seguridad Social* (*IPSS*) [former name of ESSALUD], which serves only formal sector employees and their families, who are concentrated in the higher echelons of the income distribution. [MOH] expenditures reduce the overall inequality, but are not large enough or sufficiently well targeted among the poor to equalize expenditures. The importance of [the MOH] is largest for the bottom 20%, who obtain 70% of their health benefits from this source as compared to 20% for the richest quintile. (World Bank, 1999)

These figures have not changed significantly in recent years, resulting in a highly unequal distribution of funding for health services.

Social and economic inequalities within Peru increased starkly in the 1980s, due to the governments' severe mismanagement of the country's financial crisis, which caused annual inflation rates to soar as high as 7,650% (end of Alan García's government, 1985 to 1990), but also due to persistent domestic political threats from violent rebel terrorist groups (Ewing, 2004). Although successful in stabilizing and remarkably improving the Peruvian economy and controlling terrorist threats, the government of Alberto Fujimori (1990 to 2000) became increasingly authoritarian and populist. Macroeconomic adjustment measures taken in the early 1990s to control the previous decade's hyperinflation left wealth concentrated in a smaller portion of the population (Grupo Cuánto S.A., 1991, 1994, 1997, 2000).

Following the dramatic 'functional collapse' of the health system in the 1980s, especially in rural areas, the 1990s saw a substantial increase in publicly funded health services and a strengthening of key national health programmes, especially those related to immunizations, maternal and perinatal health, family planning, paediatric care, HIV/AIDS, and other infectious diseases, thus improving health indicators. In addition, innovative pro-poor initiatives were launched, such as a national programme increasing financial and human resources for targeted rural poor communities (Basic Health for All, PSBT); another national programme which sought to improve citizen participation in the provision of publicly funded health services (the Shared Administration Program, PAC); and two national insurance programmes offering, for the first time, integral healthcare subsidies to assist the poor in overcoming cost barriers to accessing healthcare (transferring to the public hospitals and health networks, the costs of consultancy, treatment, auxiliary tests, and transport for the patient and family, in a fee-for-services scheme). These two programmes were the Free School Health Insurance programme, and the Maternal and Child Health Insurance programme (Ewing, 2004; Pollarolo, 2000). Throughout the 1990s, technical teams from the Peruvian MOH implemented innovations that improved the organization and management of healthcare facilities (turning them into healthcare networks); strategies to address physical/geographical barriers to healthcare access through the creation of itinerant brigades (mobile health teams) to provide access to isolated populations scattered around the rural Andean and rainforest regions; and to assess intercultural appropriateness of healthcare. In spite of these improvements, Fujimori's government suffered under corruption and ultimately failed to achieve the vision of 'equity, efficiency, and quality' in the health sector, as promised by the 1995 Policy Guidelines of the Peruvian MOH (Peruvian MOH, 1995).

In 2002, the MOH established National and Regional Health Councils that offered representatives of health organizations and civil society the opportunity to gather and coordinate their efforts to contribute to health policies design and implementation. The MOH in Alejandro Toledo's administration also emphasized the reduction of maternal and infant mortality, combining both Free School Health Insurance and Maternal and Child Health Insurance into the more comprehensive Integral Health Insurance (SIS), increasing the nearly four million individuals covered by both schemes in 2000 to approximately 6.5 million individuals in 2004 (World Bank, 2006). However, that political decision brought serious concerns regarding its financial sustainability, operational management, and true capacity for reaching the extreme poor and excluded population (*Gestion Medica*, 2003). While the right to health was an explicit commitment of the Toledo administration's last Minister of Health, rights-based approaches were abandoned by the successive government and only partially re-visited in 2008.

Overall, although it made advances, the Toledo government failed to effectively redistribute the country's increased financial resources and Peru's welfare to most of the poor and poorest rural people. In early 2006, the government launched a cash-conditioned transfer programme (JUNTOS). That programme was strengthened by President García's second government (2006 to 2011) and the current regime of Ollanta Humala (2011 to 2016), becoming one of the main mechanisms to support and mobilize poor and extremely poor people living in rural areas and increasing demand for health and education services. President Garcia's government prioritized the improvement of maternal health, the reduction of chronic infant malnutrition, evidence-based strategies to improve neonatal health, and initial attempts to promote the role of citizen oversight of health services quality (Peruvian MOH, 2008a, 2011).

Despite deep inequalities in access to high-quality health services for the poor and rural areas, Peru has made progress towards universal health insurance, through increasing the number of people covered—or, at least, registered within this public financing system—by the SIS (subsidized reimbursements of healthcare services for the poor) (Law No. 29344, 2010). Since 2008, SIS enrolment has increased from 8.7 million (National Institute of Statistics & Informatics, 2007a) to more than 12.7 million (Peruvian MOH, 2012); insurance coverage has similarly increased from 42.3% to 55% (Peruvian MOH, 2012).

Health in Peru: the complex challenges of achieving the right to health in the face of poverty

Maternal mortality has decreased from 183 to 98 maternal deaths per 100,000 live births between 2000 and 2010 (National Institute of Statistics and Informatics, 2001, 2005, 2011). However, maternal mortality and neonatal death rates among indigenous populations can be up to twice as high as national averages in rural areas (Watanabe Varas, 2002), reflecting profound inequalities in the right to health. Women are especially vulnerable to sexual and reproductive health (SRH) issues, due largely to high rates of sexual violence and high incidence of sexually transmitted infections, particularly in the rural regions. Chronic malnutrition affects nearly 20% of children under the age of five, but disaggregated by quintiles, this rate ranges from 2% to 44% (National Institute of Statistics and Informatics, 2011). Similarly the infant mortality and under-five mortality rates are nearly four times as high in the lowest quintile (27% and 36%, respectively,) than the highest quintile (7% and 9%, respectively) (National Institute of Statistics and Informatics, 2011).

Twenty-five years ago there was a resurgence of communicable diseases, once thought to be under control, accompanied by the appearance of new diseases. Beginning in the mid-1980s the incidence of diseases such as malaria (*Plasmodium falciparum*), multi-drug resistant tuberculosis (MDR-TB), yellow fever, dengue, cholera, wild rabies, and HIV/AIDS increased (World Bank, 1999). Compared to its South American neighbours, Peru has an especially high incidence of MDR-TB and HIV/AIDS (Hunt, 2005).

Much of Peruvian society has only limited knowledge about the implications of the right to health, resulting in low accountability and participation. For example, although civil society advocacy compelled the passage of the Law on Health Services Users' Rights in 2009 (Law No. 29414, 2009), the MOH has yet to finalize its implementing norms and regulations. Little visibility and commitment from duty-bearers is associated with high levels of 'social tolerance': many poor Peruvians are significantly excluded from mainstream society and frequently suffer discrimination and poor access to public social services. Moving towards a situation in which the right to health can be translated into inclusive strategies and actions that contribute decisively to the realization of universal access to good quality healthcare demands increasingly effective, legitimate, and sustainable social policies (Frisancho, 2005a).

Fulfilment of State obligations regarding the right to health in Peru

The Government of Peru has ratified a range of international and regional human rights treaties recognizing the right to health and other health-related rights. The ratification of these international and regional human rights treaties gives rise to national obligations that are binding under international law. However, monitoring of these obligations remains minimal; Peru's last report to the Committee on Economic, Social, and Cultural Rights (CESCR) was submitted nearly 20 years ago.

Article 7 of the Constitution of Peru (1993) recognizes the right of every person to protection of their health. In addition, Article 9 emphasizes the responsibility of the State for developing national health policies as well as the responsibility of the executive branch for designing and administering the implementation of those policies in a decentralized and pluralistic manner. The explicit goal of these articles is to ensure equal access to health services for all. Hunt's report noted that inclusion of the right to health within the 'Directive Principles' as opposed to 'Fundamental Rights' runs contrary to 'the fundamental principle reaffirmed by all States at the World Conference on Human Rights (1993) that all human rights must be treated in a fair and equal manner, on the same footing and with the same emphasis' (Hunt, 2005).

Peru's General Health Law proclaims that the State has a duty to regulate, safeguard, and promote health and that public health is primarily the responsibility of the State, although it is shared by society and the individual (Law No. 26842, 1997). This has been understood by some as a lack of a State guarantee to the right to health. The drafters of the General Health Law raised the concern of limited, scarce resources when addressing the failure of the State to completely fulfil its obligations (Peruvian MOH, 1997). As stated previously, this ideal vision has never been realized and the pace of the 'progressive' realization of the right to health thus raises legitimate concerns.

Nevertheless, the 1997 General Health Law defined the relationship between the rights of people and State obligations, recognizing, among others, the right to qualified healthcare, the right to appropriate and confidential information about one's health status, the right to emergency health services, contraceptive choice, rehabilitation, mental health promotion, and healthy and sufficient nutrition.

The General Health Law also formalized what constitutes the right to health and its fulfilment in Peru, including the right to be treated with respect and dignity, confidentiality when using health facilities, give informed consent before performance of medical procedures, be adequately informed about one's health status, and not be discriminated against while receiving health services (Law No. 26842, 1997). Again, these aims are weakened by the 15-year absence of the complementary norms to clarify accountability and enforcement mechanisms for many of its chapters, including those of health services users' rights.

Analysing the fulfilment of the right to health and General Comment 14 in Peru

In 2004, Paul Hunt, the former Special Rapporteur on the right of everyone to the enjoyment of the highest attainable standard of physical and mental health, visited Peru to enhance the dialogue between government and civil society organizations on critical issues related to the right to health. His report (Hunt, 2005) constituted a key strategic tool for analysing the current status of the health system in Peru, advancing the right to health in Peru, and effectively surveying actions taken based on his recommendations.

The impact of poverty, discrimination, and inequity

In the opinion of the Special Rapporteur, the primary challenges facing Peru are poverty, discrimination, and inequity. There is great inequity among Peruvians with regard to health status, including starkly different environmental conditions, morbidity and mortality rates, and a high concentration of avoidable illnesses and deaths among poor, indigenous populations and excluded groups (Francke, 2005; Hunt, 2005).

An unacceptable reality in Peru is that indigenous populations have demonstrably inferior access to healthcare services, especially due to poverty, geographical access barriers, and the significant linguistic and cultural inappropriateness within healthcare. By 2009, the greater percentage of people excluded from having any kind of health insurance were those whose maternal language was Quechua (61%) or Aymara (80%) (World Bank, 2012). Similarly, the higher percentage of non-institutional birth deliveries belong to those groups (32.3% and 60.3% among Quechua and Aymara speakers, respectively, compared to 21.6% of Spanish-speakers) and is highest among speakers of other native languages (89.9%) (World Bank, 2012). Exclusion also includes access to clinical procedures: although 90% of women had at least one prenatal visit with health personnel, only half of those women belonging to the poorest income quintile had a blood test compared with 93.1% of those women belonging to the richest quintile (National Institute of Statistics and Informatics, 2009).

Lack of financial resources and budgetary allocations for health services is contrary to the National Agreement (*Acuerdo Nacional*), which states a national commitment to progressively increase budgetary allocations to the health sector. Measured as per cent of gross domestic product (GDP), the 4.5% of total expenditure in health—sustained, with some little variations along the last 15 years—places Peru far behind the average total expenditure in health of Latin American countries (approximately 7% to 8% of their GDP); public expenditure for health (1.34% of GDP) is less than half of the Latin American average (3.5% of GDP in 2012) (Hunt, 2005). The Peruvian MOH's budget has increased somewhat in recent years (Peruvian MOH, 2008b). Limited availability of financial resources has resulted in increasing inequity in impoverished regions such as Huancavelica and Ayacucho, which require additional financial support to ensure effective health service delivery. This unequal allocation of already scarce financial resources affecting the poorest regions is at the root of Peru's lack of fulfilment of its right to health obligations (Francke, 2005).

During recent years it has been estimated that nearly half of the population lacked access to a health facility or proper health service (National Institute of Statistics and Informatics, 2009). Until the launch of Maternal and Child Public Insurance in 1998, there was no attempt to limit the direct and indirect economic cost for patients seeking obstetric and paediatric services, turning birth coverage by skilled personnel into a serious problem, particularly in rural areas. However, in 2012, only 30.9% of poor people affiliated to the SIS had access to a health facility or proper health service when faced with injury or illness, and only half of those received all their diagnostic procedures and medicines for free; to be registered at SIS neither ensures effective access, nor the subsidy itself (Petrera, 2012).

Availability of health professionals is very limited, with only 9.4 physicians per 10,000 inhabitants at the national level (and fewer in rural areas) (WHO, 2006). The disparity in availability of physicians in rural areas clearly tracks the disparities in health indicators that occur in those parts of the country (Peruvian MOH, 2008c).

Comparing the poorest and richest quintiles, access to health services varies starkly in key areas: full immunization coverage (62.5% to 81.1%), medical treatment of diarrhoea amongst children under five (32.6% to 70.5%), treatment of acute respiratory infection in children under five (59.2% to 78.1%), antenatal care visits by a physician (11.9% to 69.5%), and delivery attendance at a home instead of a facility (42.6% to 0.1%) (National Institute of Statistics and Informatics, 2011).

Critical health issues related to the progressive realization of the right to health

Ten years after the International Conference on Population and Development (ICPD) in Cairo (ICPD, 1993), a civil society follow-up report noted limited progress in promoting SRH rights (Centro de la Mujer Peruana Flora Tristán, 2003a). Between 2001 and 2003, the Government of Peru sought to further the 'rights of the unborn child' and placed them in opposition to SRH rights, promoting sexual abstinence outside marriage (at the cost of access to safe and effective birth control, particularly in rural areas); (National Institute of Statistics & Informatics, 2007b) and eliminating any reference to gender equity in official policy documents (Centro de la Mujer Peruana Flora Tristán, 2003a, 2003b; Chavez & Cisneros, 2004). Nevertheless, Pilar Mazzetti, former Minister of Health (2004–2006), made efforts to reinstate policies based on scientific evidence and in compliance with national and international human rights law in spite of considerable pressure from the powerful fundamentalist minority groups (Hunt, 2005). Non-therapeutic abortion is considered a crime under Peruvian law. For these reasons, abortion is very much a secret practice, and it is estimated that of approximately one million pregnancies in Peru each year, 25% result in the birth of an undesired child while 35% result in induced abortions (which implies 350,000 secret abortions each year) (Yamin, 2000). Furthermore, it is estimated that 85% of rural women have this performed by an unskilled friend or family member or try to do it themselves, increasing their health risk (Yamin, 2000). This is particularly problematic considering that gender-based violence is widespread: one of the largest studies in the country found that more than half of all women living in Lima (Pacific coast) and two-thirds of those living in Cusco (Andes) had suffered from physical or sexual violence (Guezmes et al., 2002). Access to reproductive health services and modern contraception methods remain restricted, especially for rural women, and attempts have been made to strengthen punitive legal provisions against women who undergo abortions.

Recent studies have demonstrated that health services for people living with TB has markedly decreased, with respect to both detection and treatment, largely due to the removal of technical teams (who led institutions involved in the programme during the 1990s) as well as the limited capacities of newly appointed staff (Francke, 2005). The cumulative incidence of HIV/AIDS cases decreased from 5.0 cases per 100,000 people in 1996 to a cumulative incidence rate of 3.37 per 100,000 people in 2005 (Peruvian MOH, 2006a). Nevertheless, recent surveys indicate great disparity in knowledge about HIV: only 47% of illiterate women have heard about HIV/AIDS, as opposed to 91% of women who have completed primary education (National Institute of Statistics and Informatics, 2009).

Mental health problems have also become a key challenge in the realization of the right to health. In the late 1990s, the first mental health policy guidelines were designed with a National Mental Health Plan, followed by the launch of the country's National Institute for Mental Health. In spite of these institutional developments, few resources are currently available for mental health, particularly in rural areas. As Professor Hunt noted:

> The provision of mental health is largely centralized, making it inaccessible for much of Peru's population. Where it exists, mental health care predominantly consists of large psychiatric institutions. There is an almost universal lack of rehabilitation services and community-based mental health and support services . . . [This] denies those with mental disabilities the rights to be treated and cared for in the community in which they live . . . as far as possible. (Hunt, 2005)

Professor Hunt's report paid particular attention to internal armed conflict and its impact on mental health. Despite his recommendations, by 2010, neither the National Mental Health Plan nor the Mental Health Direction within the MOH had significant public budget allocation (Alegre et al., 2006). However, progress has recently been made with the creation of the Committee on Social Inclusion and Persons with Disabilities, which seeks to reorient mental health services towards community-based care (PAHO, 2012).

The costs of medicines and other healthcare supplies, such as equipment and services, are one of the most critical barriers preventing poor people from accessing effective, quality healthcare services. Medicines and other medical supplies constitute 71% of direct health expenditures (81% among the poorest quintile) (World Bank, 1999). Although essential to healthcare access, the Peruvian drug market provides a serious challenge to the realization of the right to health. Imperfect competition due to information asymmetry, irrational use of medicines (in 2008, 14.5% of people bought their medicines without prescriptions) (National Institute of Statistics & Informatics, 2008b), and an extremely flexible drug registration system have led to a lack of access to affordable medicines. The lack of State quality control mechanisms has only exacerbated this problem (Peruvian MOH, 2008d). Moreover, a lack of State regulation of private practices by pharmaceutical companies has meant that the prices of key drugs are neither related to their actual production costs, nor to inflation, but rather to commercial strategies that aim to compensate reductions in selling volumes with unjustified increases in the prices of medicines (Peruvian MOH, 2008d). In 2005, the Minister of Health condemned the increase in the prices of antiretroviral drugs and drugs for cancer therapy despite the tax exemptions from which they had previously benefited (*Diario Correo*, 2005).

Facing this complex and unregulated system, it is possible to understand the deep concern expressed by the Special Rapporteur regarding the likely consequences of the US–Peru Free Trade Agreement (FTA) 'TRIPS-plus' restrictions, including new patent and registration regulations that would significantly impede access to essential medicines for those living in poverty (Hunt, 2005). In 2005, the Peruvian MOH estimated that the US–Peru FTA would result in an additional 700,000 to 900,000 people being unable to access medicines without an increase in the budget of the MOH or an increase in household income for the poor and the first year of the FTA would require an additional increase in spending of US$34.4 million (MOH et al., 2005).

State responsiveness in the fulfilment of its obligations on the right to health

Among the policies incorporated into the National Agreement (Acuerdo Nacional) is the one that claims poverty reduction and the reduction of social inequalities to be a government priority (Peruvian Government, 2001). Additionally, there is a commitment to achieving universal access to free, high-quality health services and this commitment claims that priority in this respect should be given to impoverished areas and vulnerable populations. Accordingly, the MOH Health Sector Plan and Policy Guidelines for 2002 to 2012 include a commitment to address inequalities in health (Peruvian MOH, 1995).

In an attempt to offer universal access to health services and overcome the cost barrier for poor people and vulnerable groups, the government established new mechanisms in 1997 for financing a range of key health services for vulnerable groups, deemed 'public insurance schemes'. Those schemes eliminated co-payments by patients at the point of service utilization and, for the first time, covered prescription drugs and transport costs. A predefined package of services was provided to any member of the stipulated vulnerable groups and the government reimbursed providers for those services. Specifically, the Free School Health Insurance programme included all children aged 3 to 17 who attended public schools and Maternal and Child Health Insurance programme covered mothers and children under the age of 3. In 2001, the government consolidated both schemes into the SIS and extended these benefits to adults in emergency situations, though at this point the programme began to lose its focus on coverage of poorer geographic areas as it was run under a nationwide system (PHRplus, 2005).

Despite the 2010 expansion of 'universal insurance', there are challenges related to the quality of care that have not been resolved. Many indigenous women still reject SIS healthcare services as culturally unacceptable (Amnesty International, 2006). The reluctance to go to these health facilities is accentuated by frequent episodes of mistreatment of patients; particularly for females, the poor, indigenous peoples, and non-Spanish speakers. Various studies have documented abuse and illegal charges—i.e. 'fines' for not giving birth in the facility (Amnesty International, 2006) or charges for medicines and transport that the 'insurance' should cover—as serious problems that threaten the dignity and rights of these people, and that limit or deny the acceptability of healthcare services (Amnesty International, 2006; Peruvian MOH, 2006b; Physicians for Human Rights, 2007). The lack of choice that the poorest individuals have regarding their healthcare providers, and the unequal and inequitable power relations that exist between healthcare workers and the users of such services, aggravate this situation.

A Ministry of Health trying to incorporate a rights-based approach

In spite of previous 'relapses' and institutional MOH limitations and challenges for the fulfilment of its obligations for realizing the right to health, Dr Mazzetti, former Peruvian Minister of Health, after consultation with civil society and international agencies (e.g. the Pan American Health Organization [PAHO], US Agency for International Development [USAID], and CARE Peru), became interested in cultivating institutional engagement with rights-based principles. The first orientation guidelines for an institutional approach to the right to health were developed and released in 2004, highlighting: national dissemination and sensitization on the contents and meaning of the right to health, universal access to qualified health services, social participation, SRH rights, and the cultural adaptation of health strategies to reach the indigenous people.

Based on the proposals developed, Dr Mazzetti publicly formulated a National Mobilization around Rights and Responsibilities in Health, which resulted in three main processes (Forosalud, 2004). The first deals with various joint activities meant to demonstrate the improvement in the relationship between the MOH and civil society organizations such as the Peruvian ForoSalud and other feminist organizations that were previously excluded as a result of ideological intolerance by previous Ministers of Health (Frisancho, 2008). The other two processes selected in the beginning of the institutional campaign were: (1) education around and sensitization about rights and responsibilities in health; and (2) strengthening of citizen participation to improve health governance. In 2004, the MOH issued a 'Health Letter' inviting people to present their perceptions of major health needs in order to enhance State responsiveness in this area. Thousands of letters were received, systematized, and 'responded to' in a public ceremony in 2005 (UN, 2005). In early 2006, those results were presented to all regional health directors. Nationally, the people expressed concern in three areas: limited quality of health services, mistreatment within health facilities, and lack of availability of medicines. Additionally, through national regional workshops, high-level MOH representatives, along with civil society representatives, made an initial analysis of the best ways to further the right to health and the fulfilment of responsibilities at the regional and local levels (Frisancho, 2008).

Among the several promising steps taken by the MOH was the establishment, in March 2005, of a Unit on Health Rights, Gender Equity, and Cultural Appropriateness of Healthcare. In 2005 and 2006, with support from CARE Peru, PAHO, the European Commission Health Programme, and the World Bank Health Programme, this Unit defined national norms related to the incorporation of a rights-based approach to health into the public analysis and implementation of health programmes—a clear attempt by the MOH to ground conceptual guidelines into concrete practices (MOH et al., 2005). Additionally, the institutional Transparency Office began the design of 'health rights-defending offices', which were installed in some regions to respond to claims from public health services users. Moreover, the MOH sanctioned norms to include cultural appropriateness within healthcare practices and restored the norms and internal policies for the MOH to support SRH rights. Additionally, the MOH designed a Health Reparations Plan, oriented towards people affected by internal armed conflict and paying special attention to mental health issues, the quality of mental health services, and compensating for SRH rights violations (UN, 2005). Finally, the MOH decided to initiate, together with civil society organizations, a national social communication campaign to disseminate and sensitize the public opinion and common people on the contents and meaning of the right to health.

However, by 2006, other political priorities and limited understanding and political will of intermediate MOH representatives slowed the pace of these changes. The Unit on Health Rights, Gender Equity, and Cultural Appropriateness of Healthcare, lost support, institutional visibility, and resources to implement its plans. The 'health-rights defending offices' were progressively deactivated due to lack of support from both national and regional authorities, and the Health Reparations Plan was poorly implemented. While a dynamic public health rights dialogue has not been maintained, in recent years the MOH political messaging has presented universal health insurance as almost synonymous with the realization of health rights. In truth, it neither ensures access nor quality.

There is still limited capacity and understanding within the Peruvian MOH to implement a rights-based approach in the health sector. Such an effort would demand from health workers the construction of a common view of their current practices and the acceptance of changes to institutional culture, including the acceptance of equal dialogue and negotiation between decision-makers and people's representatives (Goulden et al., 2010). Furthermore, this would mean both increasing accountability on public health policies and in service delivery and demonstrating adequate responsiveness to complex health problems. Ultimately this also means finding a way to overcome (1) the 'non-rational' policy-making cycles within Peruvian public sectors, which generate mostly under-resourced health plans, (2) the historic indifference in allocating sufficient resources and demonstrating political will and technical capacities to 'formulate a comprehensive health strategy that furthers realization of the right to health and addresses inequity, discrimination, and poverty' (Hunt, 2005) and to implement it accordingly, at national, regional, and local level.

Citizen participation: a critical issue in the realization of the right to health

Importantly, Peru's historical social dynamic and rich legacy of participatory experiences has led to many organized initiatives and inter-related civil society networks. Four of the five rights-based principles shared and discussed with the MOH at the 2004 Health Rights workshops were all related to a vision of enhanced participation in the policymaking process. Specifically, the principles mentioned were inclusion (needed to build societies based on the values of equity and non-discrimination); participation (as a right, but also as a transformative process to ensure empowerment and citizenship building); democratic deliberation in the public sphere (required to build consensus between public policymakers and individual representatives and to strengthen mechanisms for dialogue and debate); shared responsibility (necessary to secure the fulfilment of obligations at the level of the State and collective society); and collective action at the local level (to ensure respect for the cultural diversity of the population). On the occasion of the III National Health Conference organized by ForoSalud in 2006, Professor Hunt issued a public statement highlighting that: 'The right to health not only emphasizes the importance of reducing the burden of disease and damage to health and the conditions for a healthy life, but also involves the importance of this goal being achieved through processes that are democratic and inclusive' (Hunt, 2006).

In the 1990s, together with the approval of a Law on Rights to Citizen Participation and Control (Law No. 26300, 1994), the Peruvian Government initiated a model that looked for active participation of health services' users on the administration of health facilities' resources and personnel called Comunidades Locales de Administracion de Salud (CLAS) ('Local Health Management Communities'). In 1994, the MOH launched a Shared Administration Program (SAP) that allowed for the election of six community representatives who would, along with the district health facility manager, constitute a CLAS. However, the MOH, medical associations, unions, and related government agencies resented the loss of direct control over administration of the health facilities and thus did not provide the necessary technical support to the communities participating in CLAS (Frisancho, 2005b; World Bank, 1999). Nevertheless, several studies have shown CLAS to be successful as a means of increasing the effectiveness of primary care delivery. After visiting Peru, the UN Special Rapporteur on the right to health commended CLAS 'as a good practice concerning health-related community participation, which is an integral element of the right to health' (Hunt, 2005). He went on to encourage the government of Peru 'to take measures to improve and refine CLAS and to extend the scheme throughout the country' (Hunt, 2005). Three additional challenges have decreased CLAS performance possibilities: lack of political support by the different national health authorities since 2001 reflected in almost a static budget allocated for its development, few resources and political support to officers in charge of the programme, limited support from the regional authorities, and the inclusion of most of the medical doctors temporarily contracted by CLAS in a permanent State contract (World Bank, 2006).

After significant consultation with Future Generations, CARE Peru, and PAHO, the Peruvian Congress sanctioned a Law on Health Services Co-Management and Citizen Participation in 2009, intended to strengthen and extend the CLAS co-management model and other possible citizen participation mechanisms. However, despite the fact the implementation rules for this law were completed after a nine-month participatory process, they have yet to be carried out by the MOH and regional governments.

In 2008, an enabling environment for new participatory, de-centralized mechanisms and institutions re-emerged (Cortez & Phumpiu, 1999). A key feature of the decentralization process has been the emphasis on enhancing opportunities and 'invited spaces' for citizens and civil society representatives to participate. Accordingly, the ongoing decentralization process in Peru has led to the presence of 'more chairs at the regional and local decision-making tables' (Frisancho, 2008). As noted previously, this is also happening in the Peruvian health sector, through the National and Regional Health Councils, where representatives of health organizations and civil society gather, coordinate, and discuss regional health policy proposals. However, the development of these 'invited spaces' raises some problems. The overwhelming presence of health providers (seven of a total of eight council representatives) raises concerns about how professional or group interests potentially limit a democratic decision-making process (Frisancho, 2008). Nevertheless, there have been some achievements in this area, as participation by ForoSalud has influenced the design of policy proposals in preventative health, medicine, mental health, youth, and health investment within the technical committees of National Health Council. Some Regional Health Forums have initiated promising practices of public consultation in health prioritization driven by regional governments. Though promising in some respects, the decentralization process and the newly created participatory mechanisms have failed to promote either increased quantity or improved quality of citizen participation (Frisancho, 2008).

Over the last decade, civil society health networks have been strengthened in both conceptual and organizational terms. A key civil society actor in these issues has been ForoSalud. Formally founded in 2001, ForoSalud is an independent channel for sustaining a policy dialogue about issues facing the health sector at the national, regional, and local levels and as a means of facilitating independent citizen participation in the formation of policies, management strategies, and evaluation techniques (World Bank, 2006). ForoSalud launched its first National Health Conference in 2002, where 1500 participants convened and elected the first General Assembly members. In spite of initial opposition from State representatives, during the next two years ForoSalud decentralized its structure, creating 15 Regional Health Forums, and contributed to bringing 'the voice of the poor' to the process of policy design and public debate. This organization has catalysed more than 40 regional meetings for the construction of health policy proposals using a 'bottom-up approach' that has strengthened local civil society networks and promoted public policy dialogue in 15 regions of Peru. Additionally, ForoSalud has secured formal inclusion in the National Health Council as well as several Regional Health Councils. Representation of diverse voices is an ongoing challenge as it brings together actors from diverse professional and personal backgrounds (Frisancho, 2008). Working with a range of partners, ForoSalud emphasizes the importance of citizen participation as a means for the construction of more inclusive public policy contents, but also participation as an end in itself, for empowerment and building citizenship. Major advances have been achieved through the efforts of thousands of volunteers gathered by ForoSalud and allies, including: (1) the long term process of successful advocacy and social mobilization—which took four years—for the enactment of the Law on Health Services Users' Rights (Law No. 29414, 2009); (2) approval (2008–2012) of a law proposal to ensure a more equitable composition of the National Health Council, Regional Health Councils, Province Health Councils and the realization of National Health Conventions, with a bottom-up approach for the participatory presentation and discussion of the new government health policy and commitments, and a second convention for holding government officers accountable for the achievements and pitfalls (Backman et al., 2008); and (3) the implementation, with CARE Peru, of mechanisms for citizen surveillance to promote health services' quality and accountability which has provided lessons that can be transferred to the monitoring of the implementation of Universal Health Insurance, the actual benefits (in service) of conditional cash transfers, the implementation of participatory budgeting, and the monitoring of outputs-oriented budgets (Frisancho, 2013).

Although national and regional authorities, media, and public opinion recognize ForoSalud as a both political and technical key actor within the Peruvian health sector, it is important to analyse the challenges civil society faces to effectively influence health policy processes and the evidence gained when overcoming those challenges to propel sustainable change. These challenges include lack of: five-year policies or medium-term plans, long-term public health positions, real and sustained political will towards good governance, and financial resources for new policy implementation.

International cooperation

As previously mentioned, the UN Special Rapporteur on the right to health played a key role in enhancing and supporting the Peruvian government's interest in realizing the right to health, highlighting the need for increased attention to the role of the international community in this process, as this could become very influential in terms of increasing the government's willingness to fulfil its obligations or choose to continue 'business as usual'. Additionally, as previously described, the MOH has often collaborated with various international NGOs. However, strong economically oriented visions and measures of 'efficiency' developed in the health sector reform process and promoted by many multilateral organizations offer an example of the influence of donors in shaping health sector development (Ewing, 2004) and the policymaking environment. Thus, support from international organizations has proven beneficial—or harmful—to the realization of the right to health in different situations. Influence of donors and international community agents over the government performance thus requires further investigation, especially with respect to the true ability for governments to fulfil their obligations while still honouring their international commitments towards the realization of health rights and their accountability to donors and global community, but also to those they have obligations to, especially the poor and other vulnerable members within their societies.

Conclusion

Significant and sustainable change in Peru's highly unequal society will only be achieved if people have a greater involvement in the design and adjustment of social policies and programmes and in their implementation. Peruvian civil society initiatives, supported by the efforts of the first UN Special Rapporteur on the right to health, have shown that it is possible to promote accountability based on dialogue and the promotion of good governance, rather than on 'naming and shaming'—building mutual understanding and increasing trust and credibility among healthcare authorities, representatives, professionals, and citizen representatives. Nevertheless, there are still major challenges. The low quality of local health management—in which leadership, as well as skills to manage and monitor the national and regional policies and their enforcement have been mostly lost—and the lack of definition of performance indicators are but two such challenges. The situation is worsened by evidence of discrimination, the undervaluation of citizens' capacity for dialogue and negotiation, and the high turnover of healthcare representatives and public authorities in the region (Frisancho, 2013).

Progressive realization of the right to health in Peru will require sustained government efforts to allocate resources, use them effectively, and continue democratizing the provision of health, with particular attention to the vulnerable populations in indigenous and rural areas.

Acknowledgements

The author wants to thank Sara Green, Jennifer Manne and very specially Adriana Benedict for their invaluable support in editing this chapter for publication.

References

Alegre, M., Frisancho, A., Jugo, P., *et al.* (2006). *Health Rights in Peru: Balance 2004–2006 from Civil Society, Two Years After the Visit of Paul Hunt, United Nations Special Rapporteur, on Everyone's Right to the Highest Attainable Standard Of Health.* Sinco Editores: Lima.

Amnesty International. (2006). *Peru: Poor and Excluded Women—Denial of the Right to Maternal and Child Health.* Available at: http://www.amnesty.org/fr/library/info/AMR46/004/2006/en (accessed 1 November 2012).

Backman, G., Hunt, P., Khosla, R., *et al.* (2008). Health systems and the right to health: an assessment of 194 countries. *Lancet*, 372, 2047–2085.

Centro de la Mujer Peruana Flora Tristán. (2003a). *El Peru a Diez Años de la Conferencia Internacional de Poblacion y Desarrollo de el Cairo. Situation y Compromisos Pendientes. Informe de la Sociedad Civil Cairo Mas Diez.* Informally published: Lima.

Centro de la Mujer Peruana Flora Tristán. (2003b). *Violencia Familiar, Violencia Sexual, Aborto, Derechos Reproductivos: Informe 2003.* Centro de la Mujer Peruana Flora Tristán: Lima.

Chávez, S. and Cisneros, R. (2004). *When Fundamentalisms Take over Public Policies.* Centro de la Mujer Peruana Flora Tristán: Lima.

Cortez, R. and Phumpiu, P. (1999). *The Delivery of Health Services in Centres Jointly Administered by the Community and the State: the Case of Peru.* Inter-American Development Bank and Canadian International Development Research Centre: Washington, DC.

Diario Correo. (2005, 7 September). Minister Mazzetti: laboratories that did not reduce their prices are immoral. *Diario Correo*, p. 14.

Ewig, C. (2004). *Piecemeal but Innovative: health sector reform in Peru.* In R. Kaufman and J. Nelson (Eds.), *Crucial Needs, Weak Incentives: Social Sector Reform, Democratization and Globalization in Latin America*, pp. 217–243. Johns Hopkins University Press: Baltimore, MD.

Eyben, R. (2004). *Alliances against Poverty. DFID's Experience in Peru 2000–2005.* Department for International Development: Lima.

ForoSalud. (2004). *Minister of Health Opening Speech at the II Health National Conference.* ForoSalud: Lima.

Francke, P. (2005). *Draft on Health Rights Situation, Prepared for Discussion with the Public Ombudsman Office.* Unpublished: Lima.

Frisancho, A. (2005a). *Promoting Health Rights Engagement: Strengthening 'Voice' is Not Enough.* CARE: Lima.

Frisancho, A. (2005b). *Feasibility of Citizen Participation Programs on Shared Health Management: The Health Facilities Shared Management Program (Peru 1994–1999).* Inter-American Institute for Social Development: Washington, DC.

Frisancho, A. (2008). Looking for more inclusive and sustainable health policies: the role of participation. In P. Cholewka and M. Motlagh (Eds.), *Health Capital and Sustainable Socioeconomic Development*, pp. 323–342. CRC Press: New York, NY.

Frisancho, A. (2013). Citizen monitoring to promote the right to health care and accountability. In P. Hunt and T. Gray (Eds.), *Maternal Mortality, Human Rights and Accountability*, p. 13–30. Routledge: Taylor & Francis Group.

Gestión Medica. (2003). SIS needs additional 127,000,000 new souls to ensure increased coverage. *Gestion Medica Magazine* (currently out of print).

Goulden, J., Gayle, H., and Frisancho, A. (2010). Working with right holders and duty bearers to operationalize rights-based approaches to health: the experience of CARE in Peru. In E. Beracochea, C. Weinstein, and D. Evans (Eds.), *Rights-Based Approaches to Public Health*, pp. 271–292. Springer Publications: New York, NY.

Grupo Cuánto S.A. (1991). *National Survey of Household Living Levels, 1991.* Grupo Cuanto S.A.: Lima.

Grupo Cuánto S.A. (1994). *National Survey of Household Living Levels, 1994.* Grupo Cuanto S.A.: Lima.

Grupo Cuánto S.A. (1997). *National Survey of Household Living Levels, 1997.* Grupo Cuanto S.A.: Lima.

Grupo Cuánto S.A. (2000). *National Survey of Household Living Levels, 2000.* Grupo Cuanto S.A.: Lima.

Guezmes, A., Palomino, N., Ramos, M. (2002). *Sexual and Physical Violence against Women in Peru: Multi-Centric Study of the World Health Organization on Gender-Based Violence and Women's Health.* Ediciones Flora Tristán, Universidad Peruana Cayentano Heredia, Organization Mundial de la Salud: Lima.

Hunt, P. (2005). *Report of Paul Hunt, Special Rapporteur on the Right of Everyone to the Enjoyment of the Highest Attainable Standard of Physical and Mental Health: Mission to Peru.* UN Doc. E/CN.4/2005/51/Add.3. United Nations: New York, NY.

Hunt, P. (2006). *Public Statement for the Third National Health Care Conference*, read at the Opening Ceremony of ForoSalud's III National Health Conference, Lima.

ICPD . (1994). *International Conference on Population and Development (ICPD)*, Cairo, Egypt, 5–13 September 1994.

Law No. 26300. (1994). *Law on Participation and Social Control.* Peruvian Government: Lima Peru. (Published in Official Government Newspaper *El Peruano*.)

Law No. 26842. (1997). *General Health Law.* Peruvian Government: Lima.

Law No. 29344. (2010). *Law 29344, Framework Law on Universal Health Insurance.* Peruvian Government: Lima. (Published in Official Government Newspaper *El Peruano*.)

Law No. 29414. (2009). *Health Services Users' Rights.* Peruvian Government: Lima.

MOH, PAHO, and CARE Peru. (2005). *Workshop on Health Rights, Gender Equity and Intercultural Issues.* Peruvian Ministry of Health: Lima.

National Institute of Statistics and Informatics. (2001). *Demography and Family Health Survey 2000.* Peruvian Government: Lima.

National Institute of Statistics and Informatics. (2005). *Demography and Family Health Survey 2004.* Peruvian Government: Lima.

National Institute of Statistics and Informatics. (2007a). *National Census, 2007: XI of Population and VI of Housing.* Peruvian Government: Lima, Peru. Available at: <http://censos.inei.gob.pe/Anexos/libro.pdf> (accessed 07 October 2012).

National Institute of Statistics and Informatics. (2007b). *Main Report: National Household Health & Demographic Survey, 2004–2006.* Peruvian Government: Lima.

National Institute of Statistics and Informatics. (2008a). *Technical Report: Poverty in Peru in 2008*). Peruvian Government: Lima.

National Institute of Statistics and Informatics. (2008b). *Technical Report on the National Households Survey on Life Conditions.* Peruvian Government: Lima.

National Institute of Statistics and Informatics. (2009). *National Household Health & Demographic Survey, 2009 (Encuesta Demográfica y de Salud Familiar 2009).* Peruvian Government: Lima.

National Institute of Statistics and Informatics. (2011). *Main Report. National Household Health & Demographic Survey, 2011 (Encuesta Demografica y de Salud Familiar 2011).* Peruvian Government: Lima.

PAHO. (2012). *Advances in Peru.* Pan-American Health Organization (PAHO). Available at: <http://new.paho.org/bulletins/index.php?option=com_content&task=view&id=1120&Itemid=306> (accessed 30 September 2012).

Peruvian Government. (2001). *National Agreement, Policies 10 and 11.* Peruvian Government: Lima.

Peruvian MOH. (1995). *The Challenge of the Millennium Ending: A Health Sector with Equity, Efficiency and Quality, Health Sector Policy Guidelines 1995–2000.* Peruvian Ministry of Health: Lima.

Peruvian MOH. (1997). *Institutional Task Force in Charge of the Formulation of the General Health Law Project, Opinion Project Presented to the National Congress of the Republic.* Presented by Ministry of Health to the Peruvian Congress of the Republic. Peruvian Ministry of Health: Lima.

Peruvian MOH. (2002). *Health Sector Policy Guidelines 2002—2012 and Main Principles for the Health Sector Strategic Plan for 2001-2006*. Peruvian Ministry of Health: Lima.

Peruvian MOH. (2006a). *HIV/AIDS Epidemiological Situation in Peru*. Peruvian Ministry of Health: Lima.

Peruvian MOH. (2006b). *Health Care Letter: Listening to the Voice of People. National Crusade for Citizenship Rights and Responsibilities in Health Care*. Peruvian Ministry of Health: Lima.

Peruvian MOH. (2008a). *Ministry of Health Official Document of Recognition for Health Surveillance Committees*. Peruvian Ministry of Health: Lima.

Peruvian MOH. (2008b). *National Health Account*. Peruvian Ministry of Health: Lima.

Peruvian MOH. (2008c). *Technical Report from the High-Level Multisectoral Commission in Charge of Proposing the Mechanisms to Form a National Health System*. Peruvian Ministry of Health: Lima.

Peruvian MOH. (2008d). *Final Report of the High-Level Commission in Charge of Reinitiating the Process of Organizing the National Health System*. Peruvian Ministry of Health: Lima.

Peruvian MOH. (2011). *Policy Guidelines to Promote Health Surveillance*. Peruvian Ministry of Health: Lima.

Peruvian MOH. (2012). *Ensuring Integral Health: 10 Years of Financing the Peruvian People's Health*. Peruvian Ministry of Health: Lima.

Petrera, M. (2012). *Health Insurance in Peru—Analysis of 2007-2011 Results and Trends. Health Indicators Framework from Civil Society*. Available at: <http://www.observatorio.cies.org.pe> (accessed 30 September 2012).

PHRplus. (2005). *Working Breakfast on Insurance Schemes and Alternatives*. Unpublished: Lima.

Physicians for Human Rights. (2007). *Fatal Delays: Maternal Mortality in Peru: A Human Rights Approach To Safe Motherhood*. Available at: <http://www.care.org.pe/pdfs/cinfo/libro/Demoras%20Fatales%20PHR.pdf> (accessed 25 October 2012).

Pollarolo, P. (2000). Health sector reform. In R. Abusada, F. Du Bois, E. Morón, *et al.* (Eds.), *The Incomplete Reform: Rescuing the Nineties*, pp. 239–334. Centro de Investigación de la Universidad del Pacífico e Instituto Peruano de Economía: Lima.

UNDP. (2011). *Human Development Report 2011*. United Nations Development Programme (UNDP): New York, NY.

United Nations. (2005). *Answer of Peruvian Government to the Report of the UN Special Rapporteur on the Right to Health from his Mission to Peru*. United Nations: Geneva.

Watanabe Varas, T. (2002). *Trends, Levels and Structure of Maternal Mortality in Peru. 1992—2000*. National Institute of Statistics and Informatics: Lima.

WHO. (2006). *World Health Report 2006: Working Together for Health*. World Health Organization (WHO): Geneva.

World Bank. (1999). *Improving the Health of the Poor*. World Bank: Washington, DC.

World Bank. (2006). *A New Social Contract for Peru: An Agenda for Improving Education, Healthcare, and the Social Safety Net*. World Bank: Washington, DC.

World Bank. (2012). *Peru at the Edge of a New Era—Policy Notes, Volume II*. World Bank: Lima.

Yamin, A. (2000). *Citizen Surveillance on the Right to Health: Addressing Inequities*. Centro de Asesoría Laboral del Perú (CEDAL): Lima.

Chapter 14

Realizing the right to healthcare in Mexico

Julio Frenk and Octavio Gómez-Dantés

Introduction

In 2003, the Mexican Congress approved a reform to the General Health Law which established the System of Social Protection in Health (SSPH). Among other things, this system has increased public funding in order to provide universal health insurance. This chapter builds upon previous work on the ethical basis of the recent health reform to examine the process carried out in Mexico to extend the right to healthcare to all (Frenk & Gómez-Dantés, 2001, 2009a, 2009b; Secretaría de Salud & Comisión Nacional de Bioética, 2009).

General demographic and health data

Mexico is an upper-middle-income country with a population of 112.3 million (Consejo Nacional de Población, 2010). Around 10% of its population is indigenous. Its Human Development Index (HDI) ranking is 0.770, which makes Mexico 57 out of 187 countries; it is the fifth highest HDI-ranked country in the Latin American and Caribbean region (UN Development Programme, 2011). Life expectancy at birth is 76.6 years (in 2010) and under-five mortality, is 15.7 per 1,000 live births, down from 47.1 in 1970 (Consejo Nacional de Población, 2010; Secretaría de Salud, 2011). Its gross domestic product (GDP) based on purchasing power parity (PPP) is US$$_{ppp}$1.6 trillion (2011) with a per capita GDP of US$$_{ppp}$15,100 (World Bank, 2012). Close to one-fifth of the population lives below the poverty line (World Bank, 2012). Inequality as measured by the Gini index (a Gini coefficient value of zero represents perfect equality, and a value of 100 perfect inequality) was 51.7 in 2008, which ranks the country 19th in the world (World Bank, 2012).

Mexico is facing an epidemiological transition characterized by a double burden of ill health (Gómez-Dantés et al., 2011). On the one hand, there is the unfinished agenda of common infections, under-nutrition, and reproductive health problems, affecting mostly the rural poor. This burden is mostly prevalent in the southern states of the country, such as Chiapas or Oaxaca, where diarrheal disease, respiratory infections, and reproductive ailments are still important causes of mortality. On the other hand, the country is facing the emerging challenges represented by non-communicable diseases, mental disorders, and injury. The leading causes of death are diabetes and ischaemic heart disease (Gómez-Dantés et al., 2011).

Total spending on health in Mexico is 6.3% of GDP (2010), up from 5.1% in 2000 but still lower than that of other upper-middle-income countries of the Latin American region (WHO, 2012a, 2012b). Health spending per capita is US$$_{ppp}$959 (2010), up from US$$_{ppp}$508 in 2000 (WHO, 2012b). Mexico's public expenditure on health as a percentage of total expenditure is 48.9% (2010), up from 46.6% in 2000 (WHO, 2012a, 2012b). And, in Mexico, there are two physicians and 2.5 nurses per 1,000 population (OECD, 2011; WHO, 2011).

Mexican health reform

Since the first half of the past decade, a major evidence-based health reform has been implemented in Mexico. National health account studies developed in the 1990s revealed that more than half of total health expenditure in Mexico was out-of-pocket, due to the fact that approximately half of the population lacked health insurance, exposing many Mexican families to financial shocks (Secretaría de Salud, 2011). In 2000, around three million Mexican households suffered catastrophic health expenditures (Secretaría de Salud, 2001). Not surprisingly, Mexico performed poorly on the international comparative analysis of fair financing developed by the World Health Organization (WHO) as part of the World Health Report 2000 (WHO, 2000). These poor results encouraged additional analysis which showed that catastrophic and impoverishing health expenditures were concentrated among the poor and uninsured households, which in turn was used to promote a legislative reform that established the SSPH in 2004. This system has mobilized public resources to provide health insurance through *Seguro Popular* to all those ineligible for employment-based social insurance, which represented half of the population. The financial reform is being complemented by a management reform that seeks to strengthen the capacity to deliver safe, effective, and efficient health services through long-term planning of new facilities, improved drug-delivery systems, outcome-oriented information systems, facility accreditation, quality assurance programmes, and performance benchmarking among States and organizations.

External evaluations of the initial results of this reform have shown:

- increased outpatient and inpatient service utilization rates among those enrolled in *Seguro Popular*;
- improvements in the supply of drugs in ambulatory health facilities offering services to these beneficiaries;
- better effective coverage figures for several interventions in the population as a whole in 2005 than in 2000; and
- positive changes in financial protection indicators among households affiliated to the new insurance scheme, including out-of-pocket expenditures as well as impoverishing and catastrophic health expenditures (Gakidou et al., 2006; Lozano et al., 2006; Secretaría de Salud, 2007).

A 35,000-household impact evaluation carried out in 2006 also showed positive changes in financial protection indicators that could be reasonably attributed to the implementation of *Seguro Popular* (King et al., 2009).

The expansion of the right to healthcare

Health reform in Mexico made use of technical evidence, but it also had a strong ethical foundation, promoting health as a non-discriminatory social right (Beauchamps & Childress, 1983). In fact, the guiding concept underlying the Mexican health reform of 2003 was the 'democratization of health' (O'Donnell & Schmitter, 1991).

In the Mexican Constitution of 1917, healthcare was included as a labour right, limited to occupational accidents and diseases (de la Selva, 1961). The range of health benefits associated to formal employment was expanded with the creation of the Mexican Institute for Social Security

(IMSS) in 1943. But it was not until 1983 that healthcare was recognized in the Constitution as a social right. However, only workers of the formal sector of the economy and their families, which represented half of the total population, received comprehensive health services through social security institutions (Gómez-Dantés et al., 2011). The other half of the population, in contrast, was left without any form of social protection in health. A large fraction of this population received healthcare at units of the Ministry of Health (MOH), but healthcare was delivered under a public assistance scheme with huge variations in benefits: from a reasonable package of services in the big cities of the wealthy states to a minimal set of preventive interventions for the rural poor of the southern states of the country. What was missing was an explicit pledge of access to the concrete benefits derived from such a claim, and the legal, financial, and organizational tools to translate it into comprehensive healthcare services for all (Daniels, 2008). Brachet-Márquez states that the transformation of healthcare into a social right demands the definition of the benefits that all citizens should receive and can legally demand, and the definition of the mechanisms through which the costs of these benefits will be distributed to guarantee their financial viability and sustainability (Brachet-Márquez, 2001).

The starting point of *Seguro Popular* was precisely the definition and costing of those entitlements that would give operational meaning to the right to health. Thus, the General Health Law now stipulates a budgetary obligation for the federal and State governments in order to meet the expected demand from each individual that enrols in *Seguro Popular*. Government contributions are complemented by personal contributions that are a function of the income level of the beneficiary (individuals in the first four income deciles make no contributions to *Seguro Popular*). In order to meet the resource requirements of the new scheme, between 2000 and 2010 the budget of the MOH increased in real terms by 142%, thanks mostly to the resources devoted to *Seguro Popular* (Recursos Financieros, 2011). This important mobilization of fresh resources will contribute to the sustainability of the reform, although it is almost certain that further financial requirements will arise as new health challenges continue to emerge.

The entitlements comprise two sets of benefits: a package of 275 preventive and curative interventions, which account for more than 95% of the demand for services in public ambulatory units and general hospitals; and a package of 57 high-cost interventions, including treatment for critical neonatal conditions, cancer in children, cervical, breast and testicular cancer, and HIV/AIDS, among others (Secretaría de Salud, 2001). These packages must be updated annually on the basis of changes in the epidemiological profile, social preferences, technological developments, and the availability of resources.

In response to concerns for priority setting in the design of the packages, cost-effectiveness studies were developed alongside other criteria. Cost-effectiveness analyses were used to identify those interventions that could be included in the package of high-cost benefits, but social preferences criteria were also utilized to select the interventions through a fair and transparent process (Daniels & Sabin, 2007). The package of essential services was also designed to serve as a quality assurance tool to guarantee that all the benefits are offered in accordance with standardized protocols. In fact, the new law requires that every health facility be accredited to participate in the insurance scheme, and accreditation is partly based on having the required resources to provide the stipulated interventions.

Finally, both packages have been used to empower citizens by making them conscious of their entitlements, turning them into effective recipients of a social right. In fact, at the moment of affiliation, all individuals receive a Charter of Rights and Duties that lists the health interventions and drugs to which they are legally eligible. Thus the Mexican approach to the use of packages of healthcare services may be viewed as an option to reconcile the technocratic approach to the distribution of healthcare, which provides practical alternatives but pretends to be morally neutral, and the rights-based approach, which has a strong value foundation but has lacked operational support.

International commitments to guarantee the right to healthcare

Mexico acceded to the International Covenant on Economic, Social and Cultural Rights (ICESCR) in March 1981 (Office of the High Commissioner for Human Rights, 2012), and has also ratified the Convention of the Elimination of All Forms of Discrimination against Women (CEDAW); the Convention on the Rights of the Child (CRC); the Convention on the Elimination of All Forms of Racial Discrimination (CERD); the Additional Protocol to the American Convention on Human Rights in the Area of Economic, Social and Cultural Rights ('Protocol of San Salvador'); and Convention 169 of the ILO Concerning Indigenous and Tribal Peoples in Independent Countries.

In 2003, the Office of the UN High Commissioner for Human Rights published a report on the situation of human rights in Mexico that included a chapter on health devoted to monitoring the fulfilment of the obligations established in the earlier mentioned treaties (Office of the High Commissioner for Human Rights, 2003). Salient among the specific challenges relevant to health were:

- the existence of geographical, institutional, financial, and organizational barriers to healthcare, especially among the uninsured
- chronic lack of financial resources that has influenced the regular operation of public facilities and limited the possibility of investments in infrastructure and equipment
- quality problems reflected in the lack of basic inputs, such as drugs, and the low levels of satisfaction among both the users and providers of health services
- the lack of a comprehensive and transparent evaluation system.

However, the report's analysis occurred before the approval of the recent reforms to the General Health Law, and most of the critical problems described are being addressed by the SSPH, most notably those related to the lack of budgetary resources and the existence of barriers to healthcare, specifically among the uninsured.

On the evaluation side, *Seguro Popular* counts on several external assessments, including a quasi-experimental community trial which measured changes in service utilization, responsiveness, effective coverage, financial protection, and health conditions (King et al., 2009). For the health system as a whole, the reform designed a comprehensive evaluation model that includes the comparative monitoring of State and institutional health systems performance; external evaluations of the main policies and programmes; and monitoring and evaluation of personal and public health services. Part of the results of these monitoring and evaluation procedures are published in an annual report, previously called *Salud:México* (Health: Mexico) and now called *Rendición de Cuentas en Salud* (Accountability in Health) (Dirección General de Evaluación del Desempeño, 2012). The National Human Rights Commission of Mexico (CNDH, Comisión Nacional de los Derechos Humanos) has created a Programme on HIV/AIDS and Human Rights and maintains a programme focused on the rights of Women, Children and the Family (Comisión Nacional de Derechos Humanos, México, 2012). In this work, the CNDH is joined by the *Academia Mexicana de Derechos Humanos* (Mexican Academy of Human Rights), which identified both the attainment of the right to health as well as the promotion of economic, social and cultural rights as two areas of particular concern to the *Academia Mexicana de Derechos Humanos*.

Finally, the recent reform has also made important progress regarding the possibility of extending the legal effects of the constitutional right to health. At the turn of the past century, the right to health could be legally demanded only by those covered by social security institutions and appealing to the content of the social security laws. Now the General Health Law also contains articles applied to those affiliated to *Seguro Popular* that are justiciable in the common courts of justice, including those articles that refer to the guaranteed access to the package of essential health interventions and the package of costly interventions.

Impact of the health system reform from a human rights perspective

While Mexico's health system reform did increase the availability, accessibility, acceptability, and quality of care (CESCR, 2000), the three biggest challenges that the recent reform intended to address were equity, quality, and financial protection.

Availability

As mentioned earlier, Mexico faces a double burden of disease: the backlog represented by malnutrition, common infections and ailments related to reproductive events, and the challenge represented by an increasing prevalence of non-communicable diseases and injuries. Although common infections and illnesses related to malnutrition and reproduction have decreased, they continue to be an unacceptable burden for a middle-income country such as Mexico. This health backlog is concentrated in the poorest sectors of the population and is responsible for the high levels of inequality. Infant mortality rate in the southern state of Chiapas is 19.5 per 1,000 live births, while in the northern state of Nuevo León is only ten (Secretaría de Salud, 2011). Maternal mortality ratio in the southern state of Oaxaca is 88.7 per 100,000 live births, in contrast with 18.6 in Nuevo León (Secretaría de Salud, 2011).

Recent efforts have been developed to improve the availability of these resources and services, and to close the gaps that their inequitable distribution generates. Between 2000 and 2010 the percentage of the population with regular access to drinking water increased from 90% to 96% (WHO & UNICEF, 2012). The percentage of households with sanitation reached 96% in 2010, up from 84% in 2000 (WHO & UNICEF, 2012). The number of physicians per 1,000 population increased from 1.6 in 2000 to 2.0 in 2010, while the number of nurses per 1,000 population increased from 2.2 to 2.5 in that same period of time (WHO, 2011). Between 2001 and 2011, more than 2,000 new health facilities were built, including 15 specialty centres, over 200 hospitals, and almost 2,000 ambulatory clinics (Gobierno de los Estados Unidos Mexicanos, 2012; Presidencia de la República, 2006).

Major efforts have also been made to increase access to medicines. In 2002, 55% and 70% of prescriptions in ambulatory clinics of the MOH and social security institutions, respectively, were fully filled (Secretaría de Salud, 2008). By 2008, the figure for all public institutions had increased to 87.2% (Presidencia de la República, 2008). Improvements in prescriptions fully filled for in-patients at the moment of discharge are less impressive: 97% for social security hospitals but only 56% for MOH hospitals (Sesma-Vázquez et al., 2011).

Health service utilization has also increased. A study based on the 2006 National Health and Nutrition Survey concluded that *Seguro Popular* enrollees have a higher probability of service use conditional on perceived need than uninsured individuals (Gakidou et al., 2006). A study based on data generated by a survey carried out in 74 hospitals nationwide showed that *Seguro Popular* enrollees have a higher probability of using hospital services for elective surgeries, diabetes, and hypertension than the uninsured (Secretaría de Salud, 2006). The effect of this insurance scheme is even higher on service utilization for leukaemia in children, one of the costly interventions covered by *Seguro Popular.*

Progress in the availability of health resources and services is due to the mobilization of public expenditure. Between 2000 and 2012, total health expenditure in Mexico increased 1.2 GDP points (WHO, 2012a), while the MOH's budget increased over 140% in real terms (Recursos Financieros, 2011). In contrast, the budget of the main social security agency, IMSS, only increased 42% in that same period (Recursos Financieros, 2011). This differential increase helped to narrow the gaps in the distribution of public resources for health between those covered by social security and those previously uninsured and now covered by *Seguro Popular* (Knaul et al., 2011).

Accessibility

The recent health reform has extended social protection in health by expanding access to a package of comprehensive healthcare services with financial protection. In 2002, there were 38.7 million Mexicans affiliated to social security agencies and 3.6 million persons covered by private health insurance (Asociación Mexicana de Instituciones de Seguro, 2012; Puentes-Rosas et al., 2005). If we consider that half of the population covered by private insurance was also covered by social security, the total number of Mexicans with health insurance that year was 41.5 million. This means that 62 million Mexicans (of a total population of 103.4 million in 2002) had no access to any form of financial protection in health.

These coverage figures have improved. In 2010, the population covered by social security institutions increased to 47.3 million, *Seguro Popular* enrollees reached 43.5 million and the number of individuals covered by private health insurance grew to 6.8 million (Comisión Nacional de Protección Social en Salud, 2012; Consejo Nacional de Población, 2010; Sesma-Vázquez et al., 2011). If we assume that half of the population covered by private insurance is also covered by a public insurance scheme, the population with health insurance in Mexico in 2010 reached 94.2 million, which represents 84% of the total population for that year (112.3 million). If we add the 8.5 million people enrolled to *Seguro Popular* in 2011, we can conclude that Mexico will reach universal health coverage in the near future.

One critical achievement of the Mexican reform is the substantial increase in coverage of the poorest population by *Seguro Popular*. In fact, the largest fraction of beneficiaries falls into the second lowest decile of the national income distribution and the second-largest fraction into the poorest decile (Secretaría de Salud, 2006). While some critics suggest that the poorest should have been enrolled in greater numbers, the law specified preferential coverage in communities with a certain level of health infrastructure to ensure that local healthcare systems were sufficiently prepared to provide all the services included in the package of benefits offered by the insurance plan.

The ICESCR defines economic accessibility in terms of equity. This means that poorer households should not be disproportionately burdened with health expenses as compared to richer households. This principle is respected both in the social security institutions and in *Seguro Popular*. Employee contributions to social security are dependent upon income. In addition, workers earning three minimum salaries or less are exempted from any contribution. As mentioned earlier in this chapter, *Seguro Popular* is financed mostly with federal and State resources, complemented by a small family contribution that is dependent on income. Families in the lowest four deciles of income distribution are exempted from payment.

However, out-of-pocket expenditures, which show very high figures in Mexico (around 50% of total health spending), generate frequent financial emergencies on the population. Fortunately, the implementation of *Seguro Popular* seems to be reducing the financial burden of the poor and previously uninsured families. In 2000, the proportion of households that suffered catastrophic or impoverishing health expenditure was 3.1% and 3.3%, respectively. In 2004 these figures dropped to 2.7% and 1.3%, respectively. By 2010, they had decreased to 2% and 0.8% (Knaul et al., 2011). Furthermore, the gap between households with and without social security is closing.

The Health Infrastructure Master Plan, designed with the participation of the federal and the 32 state ministries of health, began to address problems of geographical access to health services in 2004. This plan rationalizes the location of new health facilities in order to avoid duplication in the supply of public services and extend the access both to ambulatory and hospital care. However, regular geographical access of rural populations to comprehensive healthcare is still a major challenge, especially among the dispersed indigenous communities.

To address access to information, the Mexican Congress approved the Federal Transparency and Access to Public Government Information Law in 2002. This law guarantees access to all persons to the information held by the government. Some of the measures adopted by the recent health reform are consistent with this law. The national information system has been strengthened through several initiatives intended to increase its reliability and transparency, including the dissemination of all relevant information through the MOH's Internet site. The reform has also expanded the nature and scope of monitoring and evaluation. As mentioned above, annual benchmark reports have been published since 2001 using performance indicators at the national, State, institution, and hospital levels. At the clinical level, the National Crusade for Quality in Healthcare promoted the participation of patients in all decisions related to their health, which requires the access to all relevant clinical information.

Finally, families affiliated to *Seguro Popular* receive written information on the diseases and treatments that are covered by their insurance. The fact that there is a defined list of services that *Seguro Popular* is obliged to provide with no cost at the moment of utilization of services, and that citizens have access to that list, goes a long way in terms of empowerment. Once patients know what they are entitled to access, they acquire the ability to claim for these services. In this way, access to health becomes a true right, since duty-holders have been identified and clear obligations in service are defined.

Acceptability

An explicit objective of the Mexican reform was to strengthen responsiveness, comprised of respect for persons and client orientation (Murray & Frenk, 2000), of the national health system. Respect for persons includes treating patients with dignity, stimulating their participation in decisions about their care, providing clear communication with their healthcare providers, and ensuring that medical encounters are kept confidential. Both elements of responsiveness were promoted by the National Crusade for Quality in Healthcare, which operated in all public institutions. National satisfaction and responsiveness surveys were also implemented to monitor, among other things, State, institutional, and hospital performance in both elements of responsiveness (Dirección General de Evaluación del Desempeño, 2005).

The cultural acceptability element creates a special challenge for Mexico given the fact that around six million Mexicans are considered indigenous (Consejo Nacional de Población, 2010). Initiatives addressing this issue include: implementation of workshops at the units of the MOH to introduce the cultural perspective among public healthcare providers; the inclusion of the subject of intercultural healthcare in the curricula of medical and nursing schools; and the addition of cultural variables to the requirements for health units accreditation (Almaguer-González & Mas-Oliva, 2009). An important challenge is to guarantee a culturally sensitive approach in the ongoing expansion of *Seguro Popular* to all the indigenous communities of the country.

Finally, the reform implemented a comprehensive strategy to promote maternal, reproductive, and women's health and extend the gender perspective. Regarding maternal health, the programme 'Fair Start in Life' was designed. It aimed to strengthen healthcare networks with equipment, drug supplies, and training programmes, to improve antenatal care and delivery with emphasis in early identification of high-risk pregnancies and obstetric emergencies, and to promote breastfeeding. In a separate effort, sexual and reproductive rights were promoted, new family planning methods were incorporated to the list of essential drugs used in the public sector, including subdermic implants, the female condom, and emergency contraception, and a National Reproductive Health Survey was implemented. Moreover, several initiatives were developed to meet health needs that are gender-specific (cervical and breast cancer) or more common (depression, sexual and domestic violence) in women. Finally, a number of measures were undertaken to strengthen the gender perspective, including the establishment of the National Center for Gender Equity and Reproductive Health within the MOH, the implementation of gender-sensitive budgets, the generation of health information disaggregated by sex, and the follow-up of gender inequities in health.

Quality of care

Prior to the reform, there were serious problems with waiting times and waiting lists; drug supply and prescription practices were poor both in ambulatory and hospital settings; equipment in hospitals was insufficient or obsolete; and there was a deficient use of medical records (Secretaría de Salud, 2001). The reform's main quality assurance instrument was the National Crusade for Quality in Healthcare, launched in 2001 to improve technical and interpersonal quality of care. The campaign was designed to address the problems of public health agency monopolies and inadequate responsiveness and quality by focusing on improving standards of quality in service delivery, while at the same time enhancing the capacity of citizens to demand accountability. The campaign also strengthened the accreditation process to achieve *Seguro Popular*'s new accreditation requirements. Additionally, indicators were developed and implemented to monitor quality, such as waiting times for ambulatory and emergency care, waiting times for elective interventions, and distribution and dispensing of pharmaceuticals. Furthermore, arbitration commissions, aimed at offering protection to healthcare consumers while containing malpractice litigation, were established in all States.

International cooperation for the realization of the right to healthcare

Mexico has cooperated with the Pan-American Health Organization (PAHO), the World Bank, and the Inter-American Development Bank to improve access to healthcare in Mexico. The specific themes of focus for PAHO in Mexico include migration and health, influenza, promotion of adolescent health, and health system evaluation. Similarly, in the case of Mexico the World Bank and Inter-American Development Bank have addressed healthcare projects in the context of social sector modernization and poverty reduction. Total programme funds from the US Agency for International Development (USAID) for Mexico in US fiscal year 2010 amounted to more than US$28 million (USAID, 2012), some of which was designated to the prevention and control of infectious disease. The Mexico programme focuses on HIV and tuberculosis (TB) prevention, particularly in vulnerable populations.

The Canadian International Development Agency (CIDA), which explicitly adopted a human rights approach in 1996 (CIDA, 2006), currently supports limited, short-term assistance programmes in Mexico. Pursuing this strategy, the CIDA works with a wide range of programme partners, including grassroots non-governmental organizations (NGOs) working at the community level. At the governmental level, Canada supports national human rights institutions through the Canadian Human Rights Commission, which has signed cooperative agreements with several national human rights commissions, including Mexico (Cárdenas, 2003).

A few NGOs work in Mexico with local partners to advance the right to health. For example, Partners in Health (PIH), a Boston-based health-focused NGO, maintains a team which seeks to improve access to healthcare for the indigenous population in Chiapas, a particularly resource-poor State in the South of Mexico (PIH, 2012). The programme is specifically focused on training and empowering community health promoters to provide health education and basic health services to local communities. Similarly, Physicians for Human Rights (PHR) has focused extensively on the health of people living in extremely resource-poor settings within Mexico (PHR, 2012). An international NGO called Ipas works to incorporate human rights, including sexual and reproductive rights, into the training of future healthcare professionals (Ipas, 2012). And, the International Association of Providers of AIDS Care (IAPAC) has partnered with the Grupo de Estudios de VIH/SIDA del Sureste (GEVIHSS) since 2004 to increase the capacity of clinicians throughout Mexico to deliver quality HIV care and treatment (IAPAC, 2012).

Future directions

While significant strides have been made towards increasing the accessibility and affordability of healthcare to a greater number of Mexicans, while also improving the quality of the available services, Mexico continues to face difficulties, mostly related to the challenges posed by emerging diseases. Efforts towards controlling communicable diseases and reproductive health issues yielded significant improvements. However, as benchmarks such as increased immunization coverage and reductions in deaths due to diarrhoea were achieved, non-communicable diseases began to take an increasingly large toll on the health of the population and the health system. Salient among the challenges related to the new epidemiological profile is a critical need for additional public funding to extend access to costly interventions for non-communicable ailments, such as cardiovascular diseases, cancer, mental health problems, and the complications of diabetes. Another challenge facing the reformed system is to achieve the right balance between additional investments in health promotion and disease prevention, on the one hand, and personal curative health services, on the other. Finally, additional improvements in the quality of care require strengthening: technical quality of care, availability of drugs, availability of after-hours care, and waiting times for ambulatory emergency care and elective interventions. Narrowing the health gaps affecting the rural, dispersed communities also remains a challenge (Sepúlveda et al., 2006).

References

Academia Mexicana de Derechos Humanos. (2012). *Academia Mexicana de Derechos. Humanos.* [Website.] Available at: <http://www.amdh.org.mx/portal> (accessed 3 May 2012).

Almaguer-González, J. and Mas-Oliva, J. (coordinators). (2009). *Interculturalidad en Salud. Experiencia y Aportes para el Fortalecimiento de los Servicios de Salud.* UNAM and Secretaría de Salud: Mexico City.

Asociación Mexicana de Instituciones de Seguro. (2012). *Accidentes y Enfermedades Comprende.* Available at: <https://www.amis.com.mx/InformaWeb/IndexDocs.jsp?idRamo=4> (accessed 4 May 2012).

Beauchamps, T. and Childress, J. (1983). *Principles of Biomedical Ethics.* Oxford University Press: New York, NY.

Brachet-Márquez, V. (2001). Ciudadanía para la salud: una propuesta. In M. Uribe and M. López-Cervantes (Eds.), *Reflexiones Acerca de la Salud en México*, pp. 43–47. Editorial Panamericana: Mexico City.

Cárdenas, S. (2003) Transgovernmental activism: Canada's role in promoting national human rights commissions, *Human Rights Quarterly*, 25, 775–790.

CESCR. (2000). *General Comment 14: The Right to the Highest Attainable Standard of Health (Article 12 of the International Covenant on Economic, Social and Cultural Rights).* Committee on Economic, Social and Cultural Rights (CESCR): Geneva.

CIDA. (2006). *Government of Canada Policy for CIDA on Human Rights, Democratization, and Good Governance.* Canadian International Development Agency (CIDA): Gatineau.

Comisión Nacional de Derechos Humanos, México. (2012). *Comisión Nacional de Derechos Humanos.* [Website.] Available at: <http://www.cndh.org.mx> (accessed 4 May 2012).

Comisión Nacional de Protección Social en Salud. (2012). *Comisión Nacional de Protección Social en Salud.* [Website.] Available at: <http://www.seguro-popular.gob.mx> (accessed 4 May 2012).

Consejo Nacional de Población (2010). *Censo de Población y Vivienda.* Available at: <http://www3.inegi.org.mx/sistemas/TabuladosBasicos/Default.aspx?c=27302&s=est> (accessed 8 April 2012).

Daniels, N. (2008). *Just Health. Meeting Health Needs Fairly.* Cambridge University Press: New York, NY.

Daniels, N. and Sabin, J. (2007). Limits to health care: fair procedures, democratic deliberation, and the legitimacy problem for insurers. *Philosophy and Public Affairs*, 26, 303–350.

de la Selva, M. (1961). *La Seguridad Social, el Seguro Social y Sus Realizaciones en México.* Cuadernos Americanos México: Mexico City.

Dirección General de Evaluación del Desempeño. (2005). *Salud: México 2004: Información para la Rendición de Cuentas.* Available at: <http://www.dged.salud.gob.mx/opencms/opencms/contenidos/dedss/descargas/rcs/sm2004.pdf> (accessed 15 August 2012).

Dirección General de Evaluación del Desempeño. (2012). *Rendición de Cuentas en Salud.* Available at: <http://www.dged.salud.gob.mx/contenidos/dedss/rcs.html> (accessed 15 August 2012).

Frenk, J. and Gómez-Dantés, O. (2001). *La democratización de la salud. Gaceta Médica de México*, 137, 281–287.

Frenk, J. and Gómez-Dantés, O. (2009a). Ideas and ideals: ethical basis of health reform in Mexico. *Lancet*, 373, 1406–1408.

Frenk, J. and Gómez-Dantés, O. (2009b). The democratization of health in Mexico: extending the right to health care. In A. Clapham and M. Robinson (Eds.) *Realizing the Right to Health*, pp. 463–471. Ruffer & Rub: Zurich.

Gakidou, E., Lozano, R., González-Pier, E., *et al.* (2006). Assessing the effect of the 2001-06 Mexican health reform: an interim report card. *Lancet*, 368, 1920–1935.

Gobierno de los Estados Unidos Mexicanos. (2012). *El Plan Nacional de Desarrollo.* Available at: <http://pnd.calderon.presidencia.gob.mx> (accessed 3 May 2012).

Gómez-Dantés, O., Sesma, S., Becerril, O., *et al.* (2011). Sistema de salud de México. *Salud Pública de México*, 53, S220–S232.

International Association of Physicians in AIDS Care. (2012). *IAPAC Annual Report.* Available at: <http://www.iapac.org> (accessed 2 May 2012).

Ipas. (2012). *Ipas.* [Website.] Available at: <http://www.ipas.org/en/pages/contact-us.aspx> (accessed 2 May 2012).

King, G., Gakidou, E., Imai, K., *et al.* (2009). Public policy for the poor? A randomized assessment of the Mexican universal health insurance programme. *Lancet*, 373, 1447–1454.

Knaul, F., Arreola-Ornelas, H., Méndez, O., *et al.* (2011). *Financiamiento y Sistema de Salud en México: Evolución en la Desigualdad en la Carga Financiera entre Población Afiliada a la Seguridad Social y Afiliados al Seguro Popular de Salud y no Asegurados en México, 1992–2010.* FUNSALUD: Mexico City.

Lozano, R., Soliz, P., Gakidou, E., *et al.* (2006). Benchmarking of performance of Mexican states with effective coverage. *Lancet*, 368, 1729–1741.

Murray, C. and Frenk, J. (2000). A framework for assessing the performance of health systems. *Bulletin of the World Health Organization*, 78, 717–731.

O'Donnell, G. and Schmitter, P. (1991). *Transiciones desde un Gobierno Autoritario*. Paidos: Buenos Aires.

Office of the High Commissioner for Human Rights. (2003). *Diagnóstico Sobre la Situación de los Derechos Humanos en México*. Office of the High Commissioner for Human Rights, Mundi-Prensa México: Mexico City.

Office of the High Commissioner for Human Rights. (2012). *United Nations Human Rights: Office of the High Commissioner for Human Rights*. Available at: <http://www.ohchr.org/EN/Pages/WelcomePage.aspx> (accessed 3 May 2012).

Organization for Economic Cooperation and Development. (2011). *OECD Health Data 2011*. Available at: <http://www.oecd.org/document/16/0,3746,en_2649_33929_2085200_1_1_1_1,00.html> (accessed 3 May 2012).

Physicians for Human Rights. *Physicians for Human Rights: Using Science and Medicine to Stop Human Rights Violations*. Available at: <http://physiciansforhumanrights.org> (accessed 2 May 2012).

PIH. (2012). *Mexico/Companeros en Salud*. Partners in Health (PIH): Boston, MA. Available at: <http://www.pih.org/pages/Mexico> (accessed 2 May 2012).

Presidencia de la República. (2006). *Sexto Informe de Gobierno, Presidencia de la República*. Presidencia de la República: Mexico City.

Presidencia de la República. (2008). *Segundo Informe de Ejecución, Presidencia de la República*. Presidencia de la República: Mexico City.

Puentes-Rosas, E., Sesma, S., and Gómez-Dantés, O. (2005). Estimación de la población con seguro de salud en México mediante una encuesta nacional. *Salud Pública de México*, 47(Suppl 1), 22–26.

Recursos Financieros. (2011). *Dirección General de Información en Salud, Secretaría de Salud: Gasto Público*. Available at: <http://www.sinais.salud.gob.mx/recursosfinancieros/gastopublico.html> (accessed 2 May 2012).

Secretaría de Salud. (2001). *Programa Nacional de Salud 2001–2006, La Democratización de la Salud en México*. Hacia un Sistema Universal de Salud, Secretaría de Salud: Mexico City.

Secretaría de Salud. (2006). *Sistema de Protección Social en Salud. Evaluación de Procesos*. Secretaría de Salud: Mexico City.

Secretaría de Salud. (2007). *Sistema de Protección Social en Salud. Evaluación de Efectos*. Secretaría de Salud: Mexico City.

Secretaría de Salud. (2008). *Sistema de Protección Social en Salud. Evaluación del Surtimiento de Medicamentos a la Población Afiliada al Seguro Popular de Salud*. Secretaría de Salud: Mexico City.

Secretaría de Salud. (2011). *Rendición de Cuentas en Salud 2010*. Secretaría de Salud: Mexico City.

Secretaría de Salud and Comisión Nacional de Bioética. (2009). *Bioética en Acción: Fundamentos Éticos de las Políticas Públicas en Salud. Aspectos Sociales de la Bioética*. Secretaría de Salud: Mexico City.

Sepúlveda, S., Bustreo, F., Tapia, F., *et al.* (2006). Improvement of child survival in Mexico: the diagonal approach. *Lancet*, 368, 2017–2027.

Sesma-Vázquez, S., Gómez-Dantés, O., Wirtz, V., *et al.* (2011). *Abasto, Surtimiento y Gasto de Bolsillo en Medicamentos en Hospitales Públicos de México en 2009*. Salud Pública de México: Mexico City.

UN Development Programme. (2011). *International Human Development Indicators; Mexico*. Available at: <http://hdrstats.undp.org/en/countries/profiles/MEX.html> (accessed 8 April 2012).

USAID. (2012). *Country Overview—Mexico*. Available at: <http://transition.usaid.gov/mx/> (accessed 8 November 2012).

WHO. (2000). *World Health Report 2000, Health Systems: Improving Performance*. World Health Organization (WHO): Geneva.

WHO. (2011). *World Health Statistics 2011*. World Health Organization (WHO): Geneva.

WHO. (2012a). *Table of Key Indicators, Sources and Methods by Country: Mexico*. Available at: <http://apps.who.int/nha/database/StandardReport.aspx?ID=REP_WEB_MINI_TEMPLATE_WEB_VERSION&COUNTRYKEY=84027> (accessed 2 May 2012).

WHO. (2012b). *Global Health Expenditure Database*. Available at: <http://apps.who.int/nha/database/DataExplorerRegime.aspx> (accessed 3 May 2012).

WHO and UNICEF. (2012). *Progress on Drinking Water and Sanitation: 2012 Update*. World Health Organization (WHO), United Nations Children's Fund (UNICEF): Geneva.

World Bank. *Data: Mexico*. Available at: <http://data.worldbank.org/country/mexico> (accessed 8 April 2012).

Chapter 15

The United Kingdom: the right to health in the context of a nationalized health service

Matthew Weait

Introduction

The principal provider of healthcare in the United Kingdom is the National Health Service (NHS), the world's largest publicly funded healthcare system. Grounded in the welfare principles articulated in the Beveridge Report of 1942 (Abel-Smith, 1992), established by the National Health Service Act of 1946, and funded from general taxation, its budget has risen from £437 million (approximately £9 billion at today's value) to £106 billion in 2011/2012 (NHS, 2012). Some 3 million people per week are treated by the NHS, and it employs 1.7 million people. Overall responsibility for the NHS (and its management in England) lies with the Department of Health, while delivery of services in Scotland, Wales, and Northern Ireland is the responsibility of the devolved administrations. The Health and Social Care Act 2012 (Department of Health, 2012a), an initiative of the Conservative–Liberal Democrat coalition government that was formed in 2010, provides for a fundamental restructuring of the NHS, and will bring about the most significant changes in the delivery of services since its inception. Primary Care Trusts and Strategic Health Authorities, which have had primary responsibility for commissioning healthcare services at a regional level, will be abolished under the legislation and this function will be transferred in large part to a far larger number of local consortia led by general medical practitioners. Equally momentous, the legislation no longer imposes upon the Secretary of State for Health a duty to 'provide or secure' health services in England (a duty re-affirmed in NHS legislation since 1948), but rather one to promote a comprehensive health service 'designed to secure improvement' in physical and mental health, and in prevention, diagnosis, and treatment of physical and mental illness (Health and Social Care Act 2012, s. 1 (Department of Health, 2012a)). The Secretary of State does, however, have a positive obligation under the Health and Social Care Act to take such steps as he considers appropriate to protect public health.

National improvements in mortality and morbidity in recent years suggest that concerns with these indicators are not the primary reason for these changes. In the decades 1999–2001 to 2008–2010, life expectancy for men increased by 3.6% (from 75.6 to 78.4 years) and for women by 2.8% (from 80.3 to 82.4 years). In the same period, deaths from cancer among those aged below 75 fell by 14% to 110 deaths per 100,000 population; and from circulatory diseases for the same age group by 41% (67 deaths per 100,000) (Department of Health, 2011a). Rather, these changes, which the government argues will lead to greater efficiency and responsiveness to local needs, are seen by some as a move towards privatization (Peedell, 2012), to undermine the national quality of the NHS, reduce political accountability, and to increase the risk of disparity and inequality in healthcare provision (Cragg, 2011). It remains the case, however, that—subject to specified and limited exceptions—health services delivered under the new arrangements will continue to be free of charge to those ordinarily residing in the United Kingdom. It is against the backdrop of this history of publicly funded healthcare and—as yet untested legislative revolution in its delivery—that the meaning of 'the right to the highest attainable standard of physical and mental health' (Universal Declaration of Human Rights (UDHR) Article 25, International Covenant for Economic, Social and Cultural Rights (ICESCR) Article 12) in the United Kingdom has to be understood.

Human rights and health in the United Kingdom

The United Kingdom has ratified the ICESCR, but has not incorporated it into national law, so the right to health is not legally enforceable in domestic courts. It is a similar case with the health provisions of other relevant ratified treaties (such as the International Covenant for Civil and Political Rights (ICCPR), Article 7; International Covenant on the Elimination of All Forms of Racial Discrimination (ICERD), Article 5(e)(iv); Convention on the Elimination of All Forms of Discrimination against Women (CEDAW), Articles 11.1(f), 12, 14.2(b); Convention on the Rights of the Child (CRC), Articles 3, 23, 24, 26, 33; and Convention on the Rights of Persons with Disabilities (CRPD), Art 25). Instead, the right to the highest attainable standard of health is secured through the provision of free healthcare through the NHS for those entitled to it, judicial review, and via certain rights contained in the European Convention on Human Rights (ECHR), which were incorporated into domestic UK law through the Human Rights Act 1998. This legislation made it unlawful for bodies exercising public functions to act in a manner incompatible with ECHR rights (section 6) unless the specific wording of the legislation makes that impossible, and courts are required to interpret legislation, wherever possible, compatibly with those rights (section 3). Those who satisfy the definition of actual or potential 'victim' of a human rights violation (a patient, a care provider, or a parent on behalf of a child) may bring proceedings directly under the Human Rights Act 1998 (section 7(1)(a), or they may seek to rely on their convention rights in any other legal proceedings (such as a claim for clinical negligence, or for judicial review of the exercise of a statutory power) (section 7(1)(b)). In addition to the Human Rights Act 1998, the Equality Act 2010, which makes it unlawful to treat people with a 'protected characteristic' less favourably than those without that characteristic, may be relevant for those discriminated against in access to health services (whether free or paid for privately) (EHRC, 2011). The 'protected characteristics' are age, disability, gender and gender reassignment, marital or civil partnership status, pregnancy and maternity, race, religion or belief, sex, and sexual orientation (EHRC, 2011).

Specific examples of the ways in which the right to treatment and care has (and has not) been secured within this legislative framework, are discussed below, but it is first important to recognize that, fully realized, the right is one achieved not only through diagnosis, treatment, and the delivery of services to those in need. Just as important are efforts taken by the State to prevent disease and to minimize the risk of ill-health to members of vulnerable and at-risk populations.

Public health and prevention

A focus on preventing diseases, whether communicable or non-communicable, environmental or occupational, or physical or mental, has a long history in the United Kingdom and one that has spawned a complex regulatory infrastructure. From the first Public Health Act in 1848 (Calman, 1998; Hamlin & Sheard, 1998) and early legislative responses to impure food (Paulus, 1974), factory conditions (Carson, 1974) and pollution (Gunningham, 1974; Hawkins, 1984), through to more recent interventions in the areas of communicable disease screening, notification, and control (Coker, 2000, 2004), tobacco marketing (Gilmore & McKee, 2002), and genetic screening (Hervey and McHale, 2004; Martin, 2001), British governments have legislated to improve the health of specific groups and the public in general. These legislative measures have not, it should be emphasized, always had as their aim—whether implicitly or explicitly—the securing of the right to health as such (the very notion would, of course, have been alien to 19th- and early 20th-century policymakers in the way that it is understood today). The origins of public health legislation, as well as its interpretation and enforcement, have just as often reflected a compromise between a liberal political tradition that respects a person's right to make choices (and the property owner's/manufacturer's right to make a profit) and the wider public interest (see, e.g. Hutter, 1988). Indeed, the British liberal political tradition of respecting individual autonomy—and its correlate (individual responsibility for decisions taken, even if unhealthy ones) is one that has had a significant impact on securing public health, whether that be in the field of childhood vaccination and immunization (which is strongly recommended, but not legally required (Pywell, 2001)), to information for consumers on guideline daily allowances for certain kinds of food (which is currently voluntary) (House of Commons, 2012). (From 2015, European Union Regulations will require certain nutritional information to be provided (European Union, 2011)).

While it is true that there remain vestiges of this liberal tradition in the United Kingdom, recent years have witnessed a far greater emphasis on reducing opportunities to make unhealthy choices. Examples include a ban on cigarette vending machines (which, though challenged by the tobacco industry, has been upheld: *Sinclair Collis Ltd and Nacmo* v. *The Secretary of State for Health*, 2011), outlawing the display of tobacco products (Health Act 2009; Tobacco Advertising and Promotion (Display) (England) Regulations 2010), and the introduction in Scotland of a minimum unit price for alcohol (Christie, 2012), a policy that is anticipated will be followed in England and Wales in due course (Kmietowicz, 2012). These specific initiatives, which are intended both to improve the health of individuals and to reduce the costs associated with care for tobacco- and alcohol-related disease, are part of a more fundamental rethinking of public health. Responsibility for the protection and promotion of these initiatives will be returned to local authorities in 2013 on the basis that they are best placed to address and respond to local health needs (Department of Health, 2011b).

Vulnerable and at-risk populations: the problem of acceptability

The right to the highest attainable standard of health is a right to which all people, irrespective of their personal circumstances and behaviours, are entitled. This means that individuals who are particularly vulnerable to ill health or disease, or whose circumstances render them especially susceptible to discrimination in healthcare settings, should be accorded the same human rights protections as anyone else, irrespective of any moral judgement that others may have of them or what they do (International Harm Reduction Association, 2008). Indeed, it may be argued that it is of even greater importance that the right to health of vulnerable people is secured, given the environmental and other constraints that they face in maintaining their own physical and psychological health and well-being.

The situations of drug users and incarcerated individuals provide good examples. The United Kingdom, in common with many other high-income countries, has embraced some, if not all, measures that reduce the risk of harm for injection drug users including needle and syringe exchange programmes and opioid substitution therapy. These measures are acknowledged to reduce the risk of infection with blood-borne viruses and to provide a route into other treatment services, especially for those who may experience particular health inequalities (such as women who inject drugs and homeless people) (National Institute for Health and Clinical Excellence (NICE), 2012). At the same time, and despite their proven health benefits, these measures are controversial and operate within a political environment in which getting people off drugs or 'full recovery' is a recently reaffirmed policy goal (Department of Health et al., 2010). The negative impact on the health of drug users of pursuing this policy has been strongly criticized (UKHRA, 2012). Similar criticisms have been made of prisons in the United Kingdom where, despite a higher than average prevalence of blood-borne viruses and sexually transmitted infections, the availability of condoms and bleaching tablets (to sterilize needles) has historically been subject to regional and institutional variation (National AIDS Trust, 2011; Prison Reform Trust and National AIDS Trust, 2005).

The acceptability of these interventions, impacted primarily by domestic political considerations, may be contrasted with the approach taken to another potentially vulnerable population—individuals seeking gender-reassignment, where human rights challenges and medical expertise have proven influential and persuasive. The Gender Recognition Act 2004 was passed despite vocal opposition in the UK Parliament in the wake of a ruling by the European Court of Human Rights that the United Kingdom's failure fully to recognize in law the rights of transgendered persons (*Christine Goodwin* v. *UK*, 2002). The Act provides such persons with the right to have a new birth certificate issued to reflect their acquired gender. Provided they have transitioned (lived in their acquired gender) for a minimum of two years and satisfy the Gender Recognition Panel of their permanent commitment to this, a certificate may be issued without a requirement of having undergone gender reassignment surgery (Sharpe, 2007). Furthermore, gender dysphoria has been recognized as a medical condition by the Court of Appeal since 1999, thus enabling those seeking care and treatment to access these on the NHS in appropriate cases (*R* v. *North West Lancashire Health Authority ex parte A, D, and G*, 2000).

Securing the right to health

As explained above, eligibility for free treatment under the NHS is relatively comprehensive (House of Commons, 2011). Some hospital services, including outpatient emergency treatment and treatment for certain communicable diseases, as well as family planning, are free irrespective of a person's residency status. The availability without charge of other hospital treatment will depend on whether a person is 'ordinarily resident'. As far as free primary care is concerned, general practitioners have some flexibility as to whether they accept a patient at their practice, and may or may not accept someone who is resident—they may, for example, refuse to register someone who does not live in the practice's catchment area, or if they have formally closed their books because they have reached capacity. (It is important to recognize that because healthcare is a 'devolved matter', eligibility and entitlements vary in certain respects as between England, Wales, Scotland, and Northern Ireland.) (See, generally, Montgomery, 2009.)

There can be little doubt that the NHS and its legal framework has ensured, and continues to ensure, that people in need of healthcare services receive them, and that the provision is generous and comprehensive compared with that in many other developed countries. This does not mean, however, that disputes have not arisen as to eligibility, availability, or the type of treatment that is provided. It is in these situations that the courts have had to address the competing interests of patients and providers, balancing in many cases wider economic and political considerations against professional medical and clinical opinion, individual rights and expectations, and fundamental human rights principles. In the area of eligibility, HIV treatment for those not 'ordinarily resident' provides a good illustration of the issues at stake (Anderson, 2008). Many people living with HIV in the United Kingdom contracted the virus outside the country, often in sub-Saharan Africa (Health Protection Agency, 2011). Many of those individuals are non-nationals who have entered the United Kingdom as asylum-seekers or irregular (undocumented) migrants (National AIDS Trust, 2008). While asylum-seekers have been eligible for HIV treatment pending determination of their application, undocumented migrants and those who have failed in their application have not been. One consequence of this situation has been that people responding well to life-saving antiretroviral therapy (ART) may find themselves at risk of deportation to their home country where treatment may be unavailable or less efficacious. The question then arises as to whether their deportation amounts to inhuman and degrading treatment, contrary to Article 3 of the ECHR. The UK courts—supported by the ECtHR—have held that this will only be the case in the most exceptional of circumstances (*N* v. *UK*, 2008; *N (FC)* v. *Secretary of State for the Home Department*, 2005). It is only where the applicant is extremely, or terminally, ill that there will be a violation of Article 3 such that deportation would be unlawful (*D* v. *UK*, 1997).

This approach reflects the courts' recognition of the need to protect the legitimate interests of the State in determining who should be entitled to remain in its territory (and take advantage of the treatment benefits of doing so) and the right to health of individuals, and has been criticized as favouring the former at the expense of the latter (Devillard, 2009). At the same time there has been recognition that because treatment for HIV reduces infectiousness (and hence constitutes an important public health benefit) (Cohen et al., 2011) the United Kingdom's restrictions on eligibility are being lifted and extended to all people, irrespective of their immigration status (Department of Health, 2012b; Pebody, 2012). A recent decision of the High Court has recognized that scarcity of resources resulting in the denial of care and assistance for a person in the late stages of AIDS-related illness may (and did in the particular case) amount to a violation of both Article 3 and Article 8 of the ECHR (*R (on the application of Adalberto Jesus de Almeida)* v. *RBKC*, 2012).

Where questions concerning eligibility for medical treatment will typically turn on the status of the applicant (whether he is 'ordinarily resident', for example), those concerned with the availability of treatment for a person who is in fact eligible will often centre on clinical judgement and the allocation of scarce resources (Jackson, 2010; Newdick, 2005). Each of these is a concern of the NICE, an agency charged both with assessing the efficacy of a particular treatment and whether it should be funded by the NHS. The appraisals conducted by the NICE can result in a recommendation for unrestricted use, use for certain categories of patient, use only in clinical trials or that it should not be used (NICE, 1999). Although recommendations for a certain treatment's use mean that there is a duty, in effect if not strictly in law, on the NHS to fund such treatment, there is no obligation on physicians to prescribe the treatment (Rawlins, 2005). As a body exercising a public function, the NICE's recommendations are subject to judicial review, both on the application of pharmaceutical companies (who may lose financially if a drug is not approved) and patients (*R (on the application of Eisai Limited)* v. *National Institute for Health and Clinical Excellence*, 2008; Syrett, 2002). More often, however, judicial review cases have centred on the decisions of physicians and treatment providers to refuse treatment. Claimants will only be successful if they are able to establish that the refusal was unlawful in the sense that the decision was made *ultra vires* (outside the decision-maker's statutory powers) or was irrational, and the most they can realistically hope for even if they are successful is that the court will require the treatment provider to revisit its decision. Claimants may also, as explained above, argue that the decision violates their human rights under the Human Rights Act 1998, either in judicial review proceedings, or as a free standing application.

It will not come as a surprise that the courts have generally shown great reluctance to interfere with clinical judgement—not only because of deference to the expertise of physicians, but because they recognize that limited resources mean that difficult (and sometimes tragic) decisions have to be made. Thus Sir Thomas Bingham MR, who gave the leading judgment, explained why the Court of Appeal would not interfere with the decision of a health authority not to fund the treatment of a child with acute myeloid leukaemia:

> I have no doubt that in a perfect world any treatment which a patient, or a patient's family, sought would be provided if doctors were willing to give it, no matter how much it costs, particularly when a life was potentially at stake. It would however, in my view, be shutting one's eyes to the real world if the court were to proceed on the basis that we do live in such a world. It is common knowledge that health authorities of all kinds are constantly pressed to make ends meet. They cannot pay their nurses as much as they would like; they cannot provide all the treatments they would like; they cannot purchase all the extremely expensive medical equipment they would like; they cannot carry out all the research they would like; they cannot build all the hospitals and specialist units they would like. Difficult and agonising judgments have to be made as to how a limited budget is best allocated to the maximum advantage of the maximum number of patients. That is not a judgment which the court can make. In my judgment, it is not something that a health authority such as this authority can be fairly criticised for not advancing before the court. (*R* v. *Cambridge Health Authority & ex parte B*, 1995)

This approach still holds true, though there have been cases where courts have required healthcare providers to ensure that where a patient falls into the category of those eligible for a particular treatment (on the basis of clinical need), decisions as to availability of the treatment for that patient must be based on rational and defensible policy. Thus, where a woman fell into the category of patients eligible for the cancer drug, Herceptin®, it was unlawful to deny it to her on the basis that it was only available in exceptional cases without any clear policy on what 'exceptional' meant (*R (on the application of Rogers)* v. *Swindon NHS Primary Care Trust & Anor*, 2006).

Although an appeal to human rights arguments will not always be necessary, the fact that the human rights of a patient are engaged by a decision will result in more intensive scrutiny of that decision, and the according of a narrower 'margin of appreciation' as regards the exercise of discretion. This does not mean, however, that the human rights in the ECHR are necessarily treated as relevant. The right to respect for private and family life in Article 8, for example, is not something that the English courts have seen as the basis for an argument to fund a particular procedure, even where a patient's condition without treatment impacted adversely on the enjoyment of that right (*North West Lancashire Health Authority* v. *A & Ors*, 1999; *Sheffield and Horsham* v. *UK*, 1999). This is the case whether the procedure or treatment is for a potentially life-saving operation, such as gastric bypass surgery to address morbid obesity (*R (on the Application of Condliff)* v. *North Staffordshire Primary Care* Trust, 2011) or not (such as breast augmentation for a male to female transgendered person (*R (on the Application of AC)* v. *Berkshire West Primary Care Trust*, 2011)). Similarly, it will rarely be possible for a patient to argue successfully that having to wait an extended period in severe pain for surgery will constitute inhuman or degrading treatment within the meaning of Article 3 (*R (on the application of Watts)* v. *Bedford Primary Care Trust*, 2003).

Concluding observations: availability, accessibility, acceptability, quality

The intention of this chapter was to provide an overview of the ways in which, and extent to which, the highest attainable standard of health is achieved in the United Kingdom. Such a brief account can neither hope to do full justice to such a complex area, nor identify all the issues at stake (see, generally, Montgomery, 2009). Focusing on the literature and decided cases in this area, the role of the NHS, and emphasizing treatment eligibility and availability, has meant that areas such as patient confidentiality and the right to life (which though important, are of limited significance in domestic right to health jurisprudence) have not been discussed (see Jackson, 2010). What should be clear is that the right enshrined in Article 25 of the UDHR and Article 12 of the ICESCR is one that, in the United Kingdom, finds relatively full expression in the operation and scope of the NHS. This institution, governed by a comprehensive Constitution (Department of Health, 2012c), has ensured that primary and critical healthcare is available and accessible to the vast majority of those who need it, when they need it. Furthermore, the existence of the NICE has guaranteed that treatments are subjected to rigorous evaluation with respect both to quality and cost-effectiveness. There have always been legal challenges to treatment, or non-treatment, decisions which impact negatively on specific individuals, whether those decisions be based on either clinical or financial grounds (or both); and it is not unlikely that the combination of increasingly scarce resources, ever more costly and innovative medical technologies, and a growing and ageing population who want to live for long as possible as healthily as possible, that challenges concerning availability and accessibility will continue. Political considerations, such as those discussed above in the context of treatment for vulnerable and stigmatized populations, will continue to have an impact, mediated and moderated by the judgments of domestic courts and the ECtHR. Less clear is the potential impact of the recent and radical changes in the structure and commissioning processes of the NHS. Although these are intended, at least in part, to increase efficiency and competitiveness, they may result in challenges and problems of a kind and magnitude that cannot at the time of writing be anticipated. Private companies, enabled under the legislation to provide healthcare services, will—despite having to meet quality thresholds—be concerned as much with profit and shareholder dividend, and commercial considerations may undermine the principles of social solidarity and best possible care upon which the NHS were based. The British Medical Association, the professional body representing UK physicians, has been especially critical, calling the reforms 'complex, incoherent and not fit for purpose', drawing particular attention to the fact that elected local authorities will henceforth have responsibility for public health, but have no statutory duty to reduce health inequalities (Campbell, 2012).

It is questionable whether legislating a right to health as such in UK domestic law would have the effect of securing it in practice (Joint Committee on Human Rights, 2003/2004), and in any event is barely conceivable the current economic and political climate. For as long as treatment and care under the NHS remain free at the point of delivery for those in need, and provided it continues to be recognized that eligibility for that treatment and care constitutes a public benefit to the long term advantage of everyone, not merely its immediate beneficiaries, the right to health in the United Kingdom will be realized in effect, if not in principle. What is not clear is whether the reforms currently being implemented will have the effect of reversing this reality, and if so to what extent, and in what ways.

References

Abel-Smith, B. (1992). The Beveridge report: its origins and outcomes. *International Social Security Law Review*, 45(1–2), 5–16.

Anderson, J. (2008). Coming and going: some aspects of care for migrants with HIV in the UK. *Journal of Infection*, 57(1), 11–15.

Calman, K. (1998). The 1848 Public Health Act and its relevance to improving public health in England now. *British Medical Journal*, 317(7158), 596–598.

Campbell, D. (2012, 1 March). NHS reform bill 'complex, incoherent and not fit for purpose', say doctors. *Guardian Online*. Available at: <http://www.guardian.co.uk/politics/2012/mar/01/nhs-reform-bill-incoherent-doctors> (accessed 27 August 2012).

Carson, K. (1970). Some sociological aspects of strict liability and the enforcement of factory legislation. *Modern Law Review*, 33, 396–412.

Christie, B. (2012). Cheap alcohol is to be outlawed in Scotland. *British Medical Journal*, 344, e3425.

Christine Goodwin v. *UK*. (28957/95) (2002). ECHR 588 (11 July 2002).

Cohen, M., Chen, Y., McCauley, M., *et al.* (2011). Prevention of HIV-1 infection with early antiretroviral therapy. *New England Journal of Medicine*, 365, 493–505.

Coker, R. (2000). For debate: the law, human rights, and the detention of individuals with tuberculosis in England and Wales. *Journal of Public Health*, 22(3), 263–267.

Coker, R. (2004). Compulsory screening of immigrants for tuberculosis and HIV. *British Medical Journal*, 328(7435), 298–300.

Cragg, S. (2011). *In the matter of the Health and Social Care Bill 2011, and in the matter of the duty of the Secretary of State for Health to provide a National Health Service*. Available at <http://38degrees.3cdn.net/75856a0564e9244f2a_rum6i66sh.pdf> (accessed 9 May 2012).

D v. *UK*. (30240/96) (1997). ECHR 25.

Department of Health. (2011a). *Mortality Monitoring Bulletin: Life expectancy, All-Age-All-Cause Mortality, and Mortality from Selected Causes, Overall and Inequalities*. Available at: <http://www.dh.gov.uk/en/Publicationsandstatistics/Publications/PublicationsStatistics/DH_130282> (accessed 4 September 2012).

Department of Health. (2011b). *Public Health in Local Government*. Department of Health: London. Available at: <http://www.dh.gov.uk/prod_consum_dh/groups/dh_digitalassets/documents/digitalasset/dh_131904.pdf> (accessed 15 May 2012).

Department of Health. (2012a). *Health and Social Care Act 2012*. The Stationery Office: London.

Department of Health. (2012b). *HIV Treatment for Overseas Visitors: Guidance for the NHS*. Department of Health: London. Available at: <https://www.wp.dh.gov.uk/publications/files/2012/09/DH-Guidance-HIV-and-NHS-Charging-fORMATED.pdf> (accessed 28 September 2012).

Department of Health. (2012c). *The NHS Constitution*. Department of Health: London. Available at: <http://www.dh.gov.uk/prod_consum_dh/groups/dh_digitalassets/@dh/@en/documents/digitalasset/dh_132958.pdf> (accessed 28 August 2012).

Department of Health, Department of Work and Pensions, Ministry of Justice, *et al.* (2010). *Putting Full Recovery First*. Available at: <http://www.homeoffice.gov.uk/publications/alcohol-drugs/drugs/recovery-roadmap?view=Binary> (accessed 15 May 2012).

Devillard, A. (2009). The principle of non-discrimination and entry, stay and expulsion of foreigners living with HIV/AIDS. *International Journal on Multicultural Societies*, 11(1), 91–102.

Equality and Human Rights Commission. (2011). *Your Rights to Equality from Healthcare and Social Care Service*. Equality and Human Rights Commission: London. Available at: <http://www.equalityhumanrights.com/uploaded_files/EqualityAct/service_users_healthcare_and_social_care.pdf> (accessed 8 May 2012).

European Union. (2011). *European Parliament Regulation (EU) no. 1169/2011 of the European Parliament and of the Council (25/10/2011)*. Available at: <http://eur-lex.europa.eu/LexUriServ/LexUriServ.do?uri=OJ:L:2011:304:0018:0063:EN:PDF> (accessed 15 May 2012).

Gilmore, A. and McKee, M. (2002). Tobacco control policy: the European dimension. *Clinical Medicine*, 2(4), 335–342.

Gunningham, N. (1974). *Pollution, Social Interest and the Law*. Martin Robertson: London.

Hamlin, C. and Sheard, S. (1998). Revolutions in public health 1848 and 1998. *British Medical Journal*, 317, 587.

Hawkins, K. (1984). *Environment and Enforcement: Regulation and the Social Definition of Pollution*. Oxford University Press: Oxford.

Health Protection Agency. (2011). *HIV in the United Kingdom, 2011 Report*. Health Protection Services, Colindale: London. Available at: <http://www.hpa.org.uk/webc/HPAwebFile/HPAweb_C/1317131685847> (accessed 28 September 2012).

Hervey, T.K. and McHale, J.V. (2004). *Health Law and the European Union*. Cambridge University Press: Cambridge.

House of Commons. (2011). *Standard Note: NHS Charges for Overseas Visitors (SN/SP/3051)*. House of Commons: London. Available at: <http://www.parliament.uk/briefing-papers/SN03051.pdf> (accessed 22 May 2012).

House of Commons. (2012). *Food Labelling Nutrition—Voluntary Schemes (Standard Note SN/SC/4019)*. Available at: <http://www.parliament.uk/briefing-papers/SN04019> (accessed 22 May 2012).

Hutter, B. (1988). *'The Reasonable Arm of the Law?': The Law Enforcement Procedures of Environmental Health Officers*. Clarendon Press: Oxford.

International Harm Reduction Association. (2008). *Harm Reduction and Human Rights: The Global Response to Injection-Driven HIV Epidemics (Submission to the Office of the High Commissioner for Human Rights for the Biennial Report on HIV/AIDS Requested by Commission on Human Rights) Resolution E/CN.4/RES/2005/84*. Available at: <http://www.ttag.info/pdf/HR2SubmissiontoOHCHR.pdf> (accessed 22 May 2012).

Jackson, E. (2010). *Medical Law: Text, Cases and Materials* (2nd Ed.). Oxford University Press: Oxford.

Joint Committee on Human Rights. (2003/2004). *Twenty-First report*. House of Lords/House of Commons: London. Available at: <http://www.publications.parliament.uk/pa/jt200304/jtselect/jtrights/183/18302.htm> (accessed 22 May 2012).

Kmietowicz, Z. (2012). Minimum unit price for alcohol is planned for England and Wales. *British Medical Journal*, 344, e2295.

Martin, P. (2001). Genetic governance: the risks, oversight and regulation of genetic databases in the UK. *New Genetics and Society*, 20(2), 157–183.

Montgomery, J. (2009). *Health Care Law* (3rd Ed.). Oxford University Press: Oxford.

N (FC) v. *Secretary of State for the Home Department*. (2005). UKHL 31.

N v. *UK*. (2008). (Application no. 26565/05), 27 May 2008.

National AIDS Trust. (2008). *HIV and the UK Asylum Pathway*. NAT: London. Available at: <http://www.nat.org.uk/Media%20library/Files/PDF%20documents/HIV-and-the-UK-Asylum-Pathway.pdf> (accessed 28 September 2012).

National AIDS Trust. (2011). *Tackling Blood-Borne Viruses in Prisons—A Framework for Best Practice in the UK*. NAT: London. Available at: <http://www.nat.org.uk/Media%20library/Files/Policy/2011/NATBlood%20Borne%20VirusesPrisonsMay2011.pdf> (accessed 20 May 2012).

Newdick, C. (2005). *Who Should We Treat? Rationing and Resources in the NHS* (2nd Ed.). Oxford University Press: Oxford.

NHS. (2012). *About the NHS*. Available at: <http://www.nhs.uk/NHSEngland/thenhs/about/Pages/overview.aspx> (accessed 21 May 2012).

NICE. (1999). *A Guide to Our Work*. National Institute for Health and Clinical Excellence: London. Available at: <http://www.nice.org.uk/niceMedia/pdf/guide_to_work.pdf> (accessed 12 May 2012).

NICE. (2012). *Commissioning Needle and Syringe Programmes*. National Institute for Health and Clinical Excellence: London. Available at: <http://www.nice.org.uk/usingguidance/commissioningguides/nsp/commissioning.jsp> (accessed 12 May 2012).

North West Lancashire Health Authority v. *A & Ors*. (1999). EWCA Civ 2022.

Paulus, I. (1974). *The Search for Pure Food: A Sociology of Legislation in Britain*. Martin Robertson: London.

Pebody, R. (2012). *HIV Treatment to be Free for Undocumented Migrants and Non-UK Citizens*. AIDSMAP: London. Available at: <http://www.aidsmap.com/page/2271302/> (accessed 21 May 2012).

Peedell, C. (2012). Further privatisation is inevitable under the proposed NHS reforms. *British Medical Journal*, 342, d2996.

Prison Reform Trust and National AIDS Trust. (2005). *HIV and Hepatitis in Prisons: Addressing Prisoners' Healthcare Needs*. Prison Reform Trust/National AIDS Trust: London. Available at: <http://www.nat.org.uk/media/Files/Policy/2011/Blood_Borne_Viruses_updateSept2011.pdf> (accessed 21 May 2012).

Pywell, S. (2001). Particular issues of public health: vaccination. In R. Martin and L. Johnson (Eds.), *Law and the Public Dimension of Health*, pp. 209–327. Cavendish: London.

R (on the Application of AC) v. *Berkshire West Primary Care Trust*. (2011). EWCA Civ 247.

R (on the application of Adalberto Jesus de Almeida) v. *RBKC*. (2012). EWHC 1082 (Admin).

R (on the Application of Condliff) v. *North Staffordshire Primary Care Trust*. (2011). EWHC 872 (Admin).

R (on the application of Eisai Limited) v. *National Institute for Health and Clinical Excellence*. (2008). EWCA Civ 438.

R (on the application of Rogers) v. *Swindon NHS Primary Care Trust & Anor*. (2006). EWCA Civ 392.

R (on the application of Watts) v. *Bedford Primary Care Trust*. (2003). EWHC 2228 (Admin).

R v. *Cambridge Health Authority*, ex parte *B*. (1995). 1 WLR 898.

R v. *North West Lancashire Health Authority*, ex parte *A, D, and G*. (2000). 53 BMLR 148.

Rawlins, M. (2005). Five NICE years. *Lancet*, 365, 904–908.

Sharpe, A. (2007). Endless sex: the Gender Recognition Act and the persistence of a legal category. *Feminist Legal Studies*, 15(1), 57–84.

Sheffield and Horsham v. *UK*. (1999). 27 EHRR 163.

Sinclair Collis Ltd and Nacmo v. *The Secretary of State for Health*. (2011). EWCA Civ 437.

Syrett, K. (2002). Nice work? Rationing, review and the 'legitimacy problem' in the new NHS. *Medical Law Review*, 10(1), 3–5.

UK Harm Reduction Alliance (2012). *Putting Public Health First*. Available at: <http://www.ukhra.org/putting_public_health_first/resources/covering_letter_and_statement.pdf> (accessed 22 May 2012).

Chapter 16

The right to health in Japan: challenges of a super-ageing society and implications from its 2011 public health emergency

Hiroaki Matsuura and Eriko Sase

Introduction

An unprecedented natural disaster struck Northeastern Japan on 11 March 2011. The hardest-hit places were primarily remote areas populated by a relatively high proportion of elderly people, not too remarkably different from the makeup of Japan's other remote regions given it is the fastest ageing country in the world. Historically, the country has been recognized for good population health outcomes achieved with the context of a universally accessible and equitable healthcare system. However, the public health emergency provoked by the magnitude 9.0 Great East Japan Earthquake of 2011 revealed Japan's human rights challenges in the field of health. Using a human rights-based approach, this chapter reviews the country's healthcare system, identifying the achievements and challenges, with emphasis on the ageing population. The results suggest the necessity of embedding the right to health in practices, grounded upon a clearly guaranteed right to health for all populations.

General description of Japan

Japan is ruled by a constitutional monarchy with a parliamentary government (Lansford, 2012). The country has approximately 127.6 million inhabitants and the population growth started to stagnate from 2007 (Statistics Bureau of Japan, 2012). The population is ageing significantly because of long life expectancy rates and a low birth rate. The proportion of the population aged 65 and older rose to 24% in 2012 from 7.1% in 1970 (Statistics Bureau of Japan, 2012). The 2010 census also revealed that there were 4.8 million elderly living in the country. Their social isolation has become a significant national social issue (Statistics Bureau of Japan, 2010).

The country ranked 10th in the 2012 Human Development Index (HDI) ranking (UNDP, 2012). In terms of economy, Japan is one of the leading industrial countries that make up the Group of 8 (G-8) countries. Its 2011 gross domestic product (GDP) of US$5.869 billion made its economy the third largest in the world (IMF, 2012). Japan has experienced rapid economic growth since the last half of the 20th century. The share of employment in the agricultural sector declined from 26.3% in 1960 to 4.2% in 2008, while the share of employment in the service sector increased from 42.2% to 67.3% (MHLW, 2012a). In response to a 'lost decade' of economic stagnation in the 1990s, the Japanese government introduced a series of economic stimulus programmes and various bank bailouts. A 2.3% budget surplus in 1991 turned into a deficit of 2.9% by 1997, as the national-debt-to-GDP ratio reached 100% (Cabinet Office, 2011b; IMF, 2012). Since then, Japan has increased its debt-to-GDP ratio and, by 2005, was the world's most-indebted country (IMF, 2012).

Health system characteristics and its challenges

Japan's health system is organized according to the model of social health insurance. The current healthcare system is characterized by universal coverage; free choice of health providers by patients; a multi-payer, employment-based system of financing; a predominant role for not-for-profit hospitals; and fee-for-service practice (Tatara & Okamoto, 2009). Healthcare costs are well controlled by the central government and were about 8.5% of GDP as of 2011, approximately half of the cost in the United States (OECD, 2012).

Since 1986, Japan has ranked first in the world in terms of female life expectancy at birth; in 2009, the country marked the highest recorded life expectancy ever at 86 years (WHO, 2011a). The country has also maintained the best healthy life expectancy (HALE) (73 years for men and 78 years for women) (WHO, 2011a). The country's infant mortality rate was also 2.3 per 1,000—one of the lowest in the world (MHLW, 2011c).

The Japanese health system has achieved good population health outcomes at relatively low cost through tight control of healthcare prices and a market-based approach to service delivery (Shibuya et al., 2011). At the same time, the Japanese healthcare system has maintained an adequate quality of healthcare compared to other developed countries, as evidenced by treatment outcomes such as postsurgical mortality rates (Hashimoto et al., 2011). On the other hand, the process dimensions of quality seem to be poor, reflected in low scores for 'client orientation' and 'respect for patient' (WHO, 2000).

Japan's enormous government debt and its ageing population are two of the biggest challenges to its healthcare system. In response, the Japanese government increased the co-payment from 10% to 20% in 1997 and further increased to 30% in 2003. The co-payment is now 30% for all residents, except for people aged 70 and older with below-average incomes, who pay 10%, and children younger than age six, whose guardians usually pay 20%. However, Japan has also had a system of catastrophic coverage since 1973. Once a monthly co-payment reaches the set cap, no additional co-payment is required (*Kogaku Ryoyohi Seido*). This mechanism has kept the level of household out-of-pocket health expenditures relatively lower than other Organization for Economic Cooperation and Development (OECD) countries (OECD, 2012).

In addition, changes in working patterns and the economic structure have resulted in rising income inequality, which has created the emerging issue of uninsured people. Using the Comprehensive Survey of People's Living Conditions data for 2007, the *Lancet* Japan Team estimated that 1.3% of the Japanese population was not paying social health insurance premiums even though their incomes were high enough to be taxable (Ikegami et al., 2011). The researchers also reported that if this proportion could be extrapolated, about 1.6 million people would not have insurance, a situation which, if true, would bring into serious question Japan's status as a country with universal coverage (Ikegami et al., 2011).

The increasing rate of suicide is one of the biggest challenges of population health in Japan. In 2012, a total of 27,766 people committed suicide in the country (National Police Agency, 2013a). According to 2011 statistics, suicide is the leading cause of death among men aged 20 to 44 and women aged 15 to 34 (MHLW, 2011c).

Constitution, ratification of international treaties, and other legal foundations of the right to health and healthcare

Arguments on the right to health and healthcare in Japan have centred on the rights of existence stipulated in Article 25 of the Japanese Constitution (Kegan, 2008). Article 25 of the 1946 Constitution obligates the State to 'maintain the minimum standards of wholesome and cultured living', which might imply the right to health of all citizens. The Constitution's framers intended Article 25 to provide an enforceable, positive right, but within two years the Supreme Court had interpreted Article 25 as merely a programmatic declaration (Tonosaki, 2007). In 1980, the Japanese Bar Association declared that, based upon Article 25, health rights are fundamental human rights, the government is obligated to fulfil citizens' healthcare needs equally, and people have positive rights to demand that the government, public hospitals, and physicians provide adequate healthcare services (Japanese Bar Association, 1980). The 1984 'Drafting Committee of Patients' Bill of Rights' in Japan also contains similar language about rights to healthcare (Drafting Committee of Patients' Bill of Rights, 1984). However, in the history of Japan, the courts have never cited these draft declarations and have never interpreted Article 25 as demonstrating an enforceable right to healthcare.

Japan has adopted the Constitution of the World Health Organization (WHO) and ratified major international human rights instruments, which encompasses right to health and healthcare, including the International Covenant for Civil and Political Rights, the International Covenant for Economic, Social, and Cultural Rights, the International Convention on the Elimination of All Forms of Racial Discrimination, the Convention on the Elimination of All Forms of Discrimination against Women, and the Convention on the Rights of the Child.

The courts have sometimes used international human rights law to aid in the interpretation of the Japanese Constitution, but they have not used these international human rights instruments to interpret Article 25 (Buraku Liberation and Human Rights Research Institute, 2004). As of August 2012, the country also does not yet have a national human rights institution in line with the Paris Principles, which recommend seven responsibilities to promote and protect human rights (OHCHR, 1993).

On the legislative level, Article 19 of the nation's 1948 Medical Practitioners Law, as well as Article 19 of the Dentists Law (1938), stipulates that physicians and dentists cannot refuse to care for patients if requested to do so, although no punishment for violations is specified (Medical Practitioners Law, 1948). Similarly, Article 39 of the Public Health Nurses, Midwives, and Nurses Law imposes the same obligation on a wide range of health professionals beyond physicians and dentists (Public Health Nurses, Midwives, and Nurses Law, 1948). These three pieces of legislation provide a legal foundation to guarantee access to healthcare for the growing uninsured population in Japan. Uninsured patients are still responsible for their entire medical bill, but national health insurance will cover the bill retrospectively after the patients pay a sufficient premium to the National Health Insurance Fund. Uninsured patients who cannot afford the premium also have the option of participating in the public assistance programme (MHLW, 2009).

Japan's health insurance system does not have a reimbursement mechanism for primary care physicians or gate-keeping by general practitioners. The recent reform in 2008 aimed to integrate primary care into the health insurance systems by requiring all insurers to provide health checkups to detect lifestyle-related diseases for the people aged 40 or over and to provide appropriate guidance for those who are at elevated risk of developing diseases (Health Services for the Elderly Act, 2008). In addition, the Health Promotion Law of 2002 replaced the traditional Nutrition Improvement Law, which supports comprehensive promotion of population health beyond the traditional healthcare system (Health Promotion Law, 2002). This law uniquely imposes responsibilities not only on the government but also on citizens and health-related businesses (Articles 2, 3, and 4).

The law explicitly obligates State and local authorities to:

> disseminate accurate information about health promotion through educational and public relations activities; collect, organize, analyse, and provide health-related information; promote studies on health improvement; cultivate human resources and working for the public health workforce improvement (and enhance the quality of such personnel); and provide the technical support needed for health-promoting business operators and other interested parties. (Health Promotion Law, 2002, Article 4)

Japan's efforts to realize the right to health in international cooperation

Japan has been a global leader in the realization of human rights. It has actively participated as a member of the United Nations (UN) Human Rights Council, formerly the UN Commission on Human Rights, since 1982. Japan has increased to US$1 million its annual contribution to the Voluntary Fund for advisory services and technical assistance in the fields of human rights in order to encourage cooperation in building legal systems and raising awareness to promote human rights (MOFA, 2000). To fulfil human rights to health, the Japan International Cooperation Agency (JICA) collaborates with the WHO and the international community in order to improve maternal, newborn and child health, combat infectious diseases, and strengthen health systems (JICA, 2012).

At the same time, Japan has positioned human security as one of the pillars of its foreign policy. Since 1998, the Japanese government has funded the Grant Assistance for Grassroots Human Security Projects to the benefit of 140 countries (MOFA, 2011). Along this line, Japan initiated the establishment of the Trust Fund for Human Security in the United Nations in 1999 and funded a grand total of approximately US$346.58 million for 199 projects (MOFA, 2010b). In 2003, Japan's official development assistance (ODA) charter was revised to include human security as a fundamental policy tool. In 2008, the 34th G-8 Summit was held in Hokkaidō, Japan, and human security was emphasized to promote global health and other measures towards the achievement of the Millennium Development Goals (MDGs) (MOFA, 2008). Mobilizing US$5 billion over five years from 2011, Japan will work to achieve the health-related MDGs in cooperation with other development partners around the world (MOFA, 2010a).

Right to health in Japan's health system: implications from the 2011 public health emergency

As noted in the introduction to this chapter, the magnitude 9.0 Great East Japan Earthquake struck Japan on 11 March 2011. The earthquake and a subsequent tsunami killed 15,882 people (National Police Agency, 2013b). The Fukushima Daiichi Nuclear Power Plant subsequently exploded and released radiation. The accident was categorized as a Level 7, the highest level on the International Nuclear and Radiological Event Scale (IAEA, 2011).

The estimated damage caused by the 2011 disaster ranged from US$195 billion to US$305 billion (Cabinet Office, 2011a). In response, the Japanese government published the Basic Guidelines for Reconstruction in July 2012, which constituted a template for the government and other actors to tackle numerous challenges in the reconstruction process. Government expenditure for reconstruction is expected to be about 23 trillion yen over the next ten years (Reconstruction Agency, 2011).

After the disaster, the whole system, including health facilities, as well as goods and services in the affected area, was overwhelmed and unable to respond promptly to local demand. As a result, the elderly were disproportionately affected. People aged 60 and older accounted for 63.6% of the total deaths due to the earthquake (MHLW, 2011c). The government also reported that people aged 66 and older accounted for 89.8% of the 2,302 additional deaths indirectly linked to the earthquake (Reconstruction Agency, 2013).

In this section, we examine the robustness and weaknesses of Japan's half-century old universal healthcare system by applying a human rights-based approach to the situations during and after the 2011 public health emergency, as well as in non-emergency settings. We also consider the governmental obligation to respect, protect, and fulfil the human rights of all the people in a non-discriminatory manner under any circumstance (CESCR, 2000).

Availability of healthcare

Non-emergency

In Japan, the number of physicians is 2.2 per 1,000 population, lower than the OECD average (3.4 per 1,000) (OECD, 2012). Physicians are also unequally distributed across regions. The mismatch between high healthcare demand among the elderly and lack of human resources in healthcare in remote and rural areas has become the country's major health system concern. The three prefectures worst hit by the earthquake and tsunami are no exception. Iwate is one of the three prefectures, and is considered to have a serious health worker shortage crisis. As of 2010, there were only 178.3 physicians per 100,000 people, in comparison with the national average of 212.9 physicians; and only 129.5 pharmacists versus the national average of 154.3 pharmacists (MHLW, 2012b).

Emergency

The disruption of healthcare facilities and infrastructure after the disaster exacerbated the already existing problems of the health service shortage. Seventy-eight per cent (380) of hospitals, 31% (1,256) of clinics, and 34% (903) of dental clinics in the three affected prefectures were completely or partially destroyed (MHLW, 2011b). The health-related facilities outside of the affected areas, such as nursing homes, became available for 53,405 persons. However, only 1,785 persons actually used the facilities (MHLW, 2011b).

A good practice in response to the 2011 public health emergency would be prompt coordination to assist patients in the severely affected areas. Immediately after the earthquake, the Cabinet Office of Japan declared a state of emergency and began overseeing and coordinating relief and recovery activities. The MHLW set up a Disaster Response Headquarters and established local headquarters in the three affected prefectures on the following day to enhance communication between local and central governments. Over the next six months, approximately 30,000 health workers; 1,915 pharmacists; and 1,580 caregivers had been dispatched to the affected areas in order to meet the local demand (MHLW, 2011b).

Accessibility of healthcare

Non-emergency

Since 1961, all people in Japan have been covered by some form of health insurance, which allows them to visit a physician of their choice. However, relatively high rates of co-payment (30%) and a growing number of the uninsured may constitute a potential financial barrier to accessing healthcare for many individuals. The United Nations recently expressed concerns about Japan's access to healthcare, in response to increasingly high health insurance premiums and healthcare-related budget cuts (CESCR, 2012).

Although Article 19 of the country's Medical Practitioners Law stipulates that physicians cannot refuse to care for patients if requested, emergency hospitals in reality decline to accept patients because of limitations in resources. The Ministry of Internal Affairs and Communication (MIAC) reported that 16,381 emergency patients were rejected by at least three Japanese hospitals before getting treatment in 2010 (MIAC, 2011). The risk of refusal was high for critical, obstetric and paediatric patients (Hori, 2010).

Emergency

Grounded upon the universal healthcare system, Japan has responded to the 2011 public health emergency by successfully assuring survivors' access to healthcare. The MHLW ensured financial accessibility and temporarily allowed the disaster victims and the evacuees from Fukushima to receive free health services (MHLW, 2011a). The government also temporarily exempted the regulation imposed by the Pharmaceutical Affairs Act of Japan. More than 70% of the drug delivery system was recovered within three days. The disaster victims in three prefectures were able to receive medication without presenting a medical booklet that contains the prescription history (Japan Pharmaceutical Association, 2012). Lifelong health check-up services are also provided for children free of charge in the radiation-affected area (Fukushima Prefecture, 2011).

Only limited information was accessible regarding the radiation from the Fukushima Daiichi Nuclear Power Plant in the early stage of the nuclear disaster. As a result, numerous Fukushima residents evacuated towards the higher radiation zones and remained there for a month (Nuclear Accident Independent Investigation Commission, 2012). Although some improvements had been made in the improvement of health information access and transparency of operations, the public displayed a growing distrust of the government and mass media. Repeated public demonstrations against nuclear power plants in Tokyo have occurred despite the governmental and Tokyo Electric Power Company (TEPCO)'s statements of assurance that the amount of radiation had little effect on health outcomes.

Emergency information was not necessarily accessible to the elderly and disabled. Elderly people tend to receive information, assistance, and support from their families, friends, and neighbours. The breakdown in the community's support networks could act against their normal way of accessing information and support. Thus, their departure from the shelters and temporary houses could also mean departure from information and social support for these elderly evacuees. There is also a limited capacity to track people with disabilities who need assistance and support. In the tsunami-affected parts of Miyagi Prefecture, 53,511 people had been identified as having disabilities, but the Japan Disability Forum had only been able to contact 1,386 of them in the three months following the earthquake (Japan Disability Forum, 2011). This makes it difficult to estimate the potential need for support.

Acceptability of healthcare

Non-emergency

Concerning the respectfulness of medical ethics in Japan, the physician–patient relationship has been historically paternalistic, which allows patients little autonomy. In recent years, however, patient rights are increasingly drawing public attention (Neary, 2002). Japan has long been regarded as a non-litigious society, but an alarming increase in medical malpractice litigation indicates a rapid change of both social atmosphere and patient attitude (Leflar, 2009). During the past two decades, there has been substantial progress in the legislation of informed consent and patients' right to access medical records. In 1997, the MHLW revised the country's Medical Care Act and the concept of informed consent was formally introduced in the Japanese health system. In 2003, Japan passed the Act on the Protection of Personal Information that regulates the use of personal data (Cabinet Secretariat, 2003). This law also allowed patients to access their own medical records. In practice, however, such rights are rarely enforced by patients and medical records are rarely transferred to another healthcare institution (Patient's Rights Ombudsman Tokyo, 2010). The Japanese Medical Association (JMA)'s Code of Medical Ethics also encompasses patients' autonomy, beneficence, and fairness to respect patient rights (JMA, 1951, revised in 2000, 2004, and 2008).

Regarding mental health, in the 1980s, Japan faced international criticism for treatment in this area and has implemented a number of mental health law reforms. Although the exact number of people with mental disorders is still unknown, the proportion of employees who find their working life stressful was approximately 58% (MHLW, 2008). Another report found that one in five adults had considered killing themselves, with actual suicide rates at 51 per 100,000 people (Cabinet Office, 2011c). Yet, the Japanese are found to be reluctant to use psychiatric labels, particularly for cases of depression, and to discuss mental disorders with others outside the family (Jorm et al., 2005).

Emergency

The priorities of mental health practice during the disaster were to transfer psychiatric patients to hospitals outside the affected area and to re-establish mental health services in the disaster zone to increase acceptability of the patients (Yamazaki et al., 2011). Sixty per cent of 73 shelters in Iwate prefecture were found to have patients who needed immediate psychosocial support (WHO, 2011b). The disaster is likely to increase the long-term incidence of mental disorders and mental distress in the region. An increase in isolated deaths among the elderly is also expected due to the breakdown in community support networks. The anxiety surrounding the nuclear disaster also increased the need for psychosocial care, not only in the affected area, but in wider areas, including Tokyo (Yamazaki et al., 2011).

Quality of healthcare

Non-emergency

An important shortcoming of Japan's health system is the poor measurement and evaluation of quality, with very few hospitals undergoing formal quality assurance programmes. In 1995, the Japan Council for Quality Health Care (JCQHC) was established and an accreditation programme for good hospital management supported by the government was introduced. However, the accreditation is voluntary and only 2,409 hospitals out of 8,580 were accredited as of 2013 (JCQHC, 2013). In addition, the JCQHC's survey items were concerned more with managerial aspects, such as patient satisfaction, and less with quantitative aspects of performance, such as the postoperative mortality rate.

Emergency

Remarkable achievements were made in guaranteeing patient access to healthcare even during the emergency. Yet, some issues remain to be improved in terms of quality. For example, over a more than one-month period, 1,782 elderly and disabled people in Iwate, Fukushima, and Miyagi were transferred to other prefectures (WHO, 2011b). The quality of the patient transfer process was not necessarily ensured in all of these hospitals. It was reported that 21 of 435 elderly at Futaba Hospital (and at a related senior care centre) in Fukushima Prefecture died either in buses en route to shelters, or in the centres themselves, before they could be admitted to another medical facility outside of the affected region (Yamaguci, 2009).

In addition, the lack of clean water, essential medicines, and other relief materials led to deteriorating sanitary conditions at shelters. For example, there were two post-tsunami influenza A outbreaks in evacuation centres in the Miyagi Prefecture (Hatta et al., 2012). And at the Tohoku University Hospital, patient visits for infectious diseases, especially elderly patients reporting with pneumonia, increased in the first week following the disaster (Aoyagi et al., 2013).

Discussion

Japan's 2011 public health emergency revealed new challenges for health and human rights in the country, but also exacerbated existing problems with the country's health-related legislation, health system, and demographic make-up. The result of our human rights-based analysis of the country's implementation of the right to health in emergency and non-emergency situations suggests that the right to health enshrined in statutory laws, international treaties, and other declarations needs to be thoroughly embedded into practices, especially for the elderly who represent approximately a quarter of the nation's citizenry and were disproportionately affected by the 2011 disaster. High demand exists for explicit and clearly written right to health and healthcare policies for vulnerable populations, especially with respect to protecting the elderly impacted by public health emergencies. In addition, many in the right to health movement argue that the Japanese government would benefit from reconsidering how to systematically comply with its domestic and ratified international laws during a public health emergency and its aftermath.

A growing body of literature outlines steps that must be taken to improve disaster preparedness for the elderly during public health emergencies (Aldrich & Benson, 2008; Fernandez et al., 2002). The areas affected by the complex disaster that befell Japan in 2011 need comprehensive and long-term approaches focused upon community empowerment and building community resilience, along with strengthening the protection of the people from multiple threats (Jimba et al., 2011). Building social and health systems that ensure the availability, accessibility, acceptability, and quality of healthcare facilities, services, and goods for vulnerable populations, would position society for a rapid response to, and recovery from, future disasters.

Acknowledgements

The authors would like to thank Tokuko Munesue and Christopher Eddy for their valuable comments on the manuscript.

References

Aldrich, N. and Benson, W. (2008). Disaster preparedness and the chronic disease needs of vulnerable older adults. *Preventing Chronic Disease*, 5(1), A27.

Aoyagi, T., Yamada, M., and Kunishima, H. (2013). Characteristics of infectious diseases in hospitalized patients during the early phase after the 2011 Great East Japan earthquake: pneumonia as a significant reason for hospital care. *Chest*, 143(2), 349–356.

Buraku Liberation and Human Rights Research Institute. (2004). *International Human Rights Law and Domestic Case Law: 20 Cases (Japanese)*. Buraku Liberation and Human Rights Research Institute: Osaka.

Cabinet Office. (2011a). *Analysis of the Macroeconomic Impact of the Tohoku-Pacific Ocean Earthquake*. Cabinet Office: Tokyo.

Cabinet Office. (2011b). *Annual Report on National Accounts*. Cabinet Office: Tokyo.

Cabinet Office. (2011c). *Whitepaper of Suicide Measures*. Cabinet Office: Tokyo.

Cabinet Secretariat. (2003). *Act on the Protection of Personal Information, Law No. 57 2003*, Japan. Available at: <http://www.cas.go.jp/jp/seisaku/hourei/data/APPI.pdf> (accessed 9 November 2012).

CESCR. (2000). *General Comment 14: The Right to the Highest Attainable Standard of Health (Article 12 of the International Covenant on Economic, Social and Cultural Rights)*. Committee on Economic, Social, and Cultural Rights (CESCR): Geneva.

CESCR. (2012). *Implementation of the International Covenant on Economic, Social and Cultural Rights : list of issues in connection with the consideration of the 3rd periodic report of Japan concerning articles 1 to 15 of the International Covenant on Economic, Social and Cultural Rights: Japan*. E/C.12/JPN/Q/3. Committee on Economic, Social and Cultural Rights (CESCR): Geneva.

Dentists Law. (1938). *Law No. 202*, Japan.

Drafting Committee of Patients' Bill of Rights. (1984). *Patients' Bill of Rights: Draft* (Japanese).

Fernandez, L., Byard, D., Lin, C., *et al.* (2002). Frail elderly as disaster victims: emergency management strategies. *Prehospital and Disaster Medicine*, 17(2), 67–74.

Fukushima Prefecture. (2011). *Fukushima Health Management Survey*. Fukushima Prefecture: Fukushima.

Hashimoto, H., Ikegami, N., Shibuya, K., *et al.* (2011). Cost containment and quality of care in Japan: is there a trade-off? *Lancet*, 378, 1174–1182.

Hatta, M., Endo, S., Tokuda, K., *et al.* (2012). Post-tsunami outbreaks of influenza in evacuation centers in Miyagi Prefecture, Japan. *Clinical Infectious Diseases*, 54(1), e5–e7.

Health Promotion Law. (2002). *Law No. 103*, Japan.

Health Services for the Elderly Act. (1982). *Law No. 80* (revised 2008), Japan.

Hori, S. (2010). Emergency medicine in Japan. *Keio Journal of Medicine*, 59(4), 131–139.

IAEA. (2011). *Briefing on Fukushima Nuclear Accident*. Available at: <http://www.iaea.org/newscenter/news/tsunamiupdate01.html> (accessed 27 August 2012).

Ikegami, N., Yoo, B.K., Hashimoto, H., *et al.* (2011). Japanese universal health coverage: evolution, achievements, and challenges. *Lancet*, 378, 1106–1115.

IMF. (2012). *World Economic Outlook Database: April 2012 Edition*. International Monetary Fund (IMF): Washington, DC.

Japan Disability Forum. (2011). Miyagi Support Center News 'Yui.' Miyagi Support Center: Miyagi.

Japan Pharmaceutical Association. (2012). *Activities Report in the Great East Japan Earthquake*. Japan Pharmaceutical Association: Tokyo.

Japanese Bar Association. (1980). *Declaration toward the Establishment of Health Rights*. Japanese Bar Association. Available at: <http://www.nichibenren.or.jp/activity/document/civil_liberties/year/1980/1980_1.html> (accessed 9 November 2012).

JCQHC. (2013). *Information on Hospital Accreditation*. Japan Council for Quality Health Care (JCQHC): Tokyo. Available at: <http://www.report.jcqhc.or.jp/index.php> (accessed 7 March 2013).

JICA. (2012). *Health: JICA Activities*. Japanese International Cooperation Agency (JICA): Tokyo. Available at: <http://www.jica.go.jp/english/operations/thematic_issues/health/activity.html> (accessed 27 August 2012).

Jimba, M., Hubbard, S., Sase, E., *et al.* (2011). Human security approaches for disaster recovery and resilience. *Japan Medical Association Journal*, 54(5), 338–341.

JMA. (2008). *The JMA Guidelines for Physician's Professional Ethics*. Japanese Medical Association (JMA): Tokyo. (Original work published in 1951.)

Jorm, A. F., Nakane, Y., Christensen, H., *et al.* (2005). Public beliefs about treatment and outcome of mental disorders: a comparison of Australia and Japan. *BMC Medicine*, 3(12), doi: 10.1186/1741-7015-3-12.

Kegan, A.S. (2008). As a negative right, Article 25 can have a positive effect combating Japan's poverty. *Pacific Rim Law & Policy Journal Association*, 17(3), 735–765.

Lansford, T. (2012). *Political Handbook of the World 2012*. CQ Press: Washington, DC.

Leflar, R.B. (2009). The regulation of medical malpractice in Japan. *Clinical Orthopaedics and Related Research*, 467, 443–449.

Medical Practitioners Law. (1948). *Law No. 201*, Japan.

MHLW. (2008). *Survey on Japanese Employee Health Issues*. Ministry of Health, Labour and Welfare (MHLW): Tokyo.

MHLW. (2009). *Guidance for Response to National Health Insurance Beneficiaries Who Cannot Afford Their Health Care Bills*. Ministry of Health, Labour and Welfare (MHLW): Tokyo.

MHLW. (2011a). *Information for Individuals Regarding the Great East Japan Earthquake*. Ministry of Health, Labour and Welfare (MHLW): Tokyo.

MHLW. (2011b). *On Recovery from the Great East Japan Earthquake Tokyo*. Ministry of Health, Labour and Welfare (MHLW): Tokyo.

MHLW. (2011c). *Vital Statistics*. Ministry of Health, Labour and Welfare (MHLW): Tokyo.

MHLW. (2012a). *Outline of the Labour Force Survey*. Ministry of Health, Labour and Welfare (MHLW): Tokyo.

MHLW. (2012b). *Survey of Physicians, Dentists and Pharmacists*. Ministry of Health, Labour and Welfare (MHLW): Tokyo.

MIAC. (2011). *Survey of Hospital Acceptance of Patients Transported by Ambulance*. Ministry of Internal Affairs and Communications: Tokyo.

MOFA. (2000). *UN Activities on Human Rights*. Ministry of Foreign Affairs of Japan (MOFA): Tokyo. Available at: <http://www.mofa.go.jp/policy/un/pamph2000_archive/human.html> (accessed 27 August 2012).

MOFA. (2008). *G8 Hokkaido Toyako Summit Leaders Declaration*. Ministry of Foreign Affairs of Japan (MOFA): Tokyo.

MOFA. (2010a). *Japan's Global Health Policy 2011–2015*. Ministry of Foreign Affairs of Japan (MOFA): Tokyo.

MOFA. (2010b). *The Trust Fund for Human Security*. Ministry of Foreign Affairs of Japan (MOFA): Tokyo.

MOFA. (2011). *The Recipients of the Grant Assistance for Grassroots Human Security Projects*. Ministry of Foreign Affairs of Japan (MOFA): Tokyo.

National Police Agency. (2013a). *Statistics of Suicide Victims in Japan*. National Policy Agency: Tokyo.

National Police Agency. (2013b). *Damage Situation and Police Countermeasures*. National Policy Agency: Tokyo.

Neary, I. (2002). *Human Rights in Japan, Korea and Taiwan*. Taylor and Francis: Oxford.

Nuclear Accident Independent Investigation Commission. (2012). *Survey of the Evacuees from the Fukushima Nuclear Power Plant Accident*. Available at: <http://warp.da.ndl.go.jp/info:ndljp/pid/3856371/naiic.go.jp/en/index.html> (accessed 9 November 2012).

OECD. (2012). *OECD Health Data 2012*. Organization for Economic Cooperation and Development (OECD): Paris.

OHCHR. (1993). *Principles Relating to the Status of National Institutions (The Paris Principles)*. Office of the High Commissioner for Human Rights (OHCHR): Geneva. Available at: <http://www2.ohchr.org/english/law/parisprinciples.htm> (accessed 27 August 2012).

Patient's Rights Ombudsman Tokyo. (2010). *On the Medical Information System and Records*. Patient's Rights Ombudsman Tokyo: Tokyo.

Public Health Nurses, Midwives, and Nurses Law. (1948). *Act No. 203*, Japan.

Reconstruction Agency. (2011). *Basic Guidelines for Reconstruction in response to the Great East Japan Earthquake*. Reconstruction Agency: Tokyo.

Reconstruction Agency. (2013). *Deaths Indirectly Linked to the Great East Japan Earthquake*. Reconstruction Agency: Tokyo.

Shibuya, K., Hashimoto, H., Ikegami, N., *et al.* (2011). Future of Japan's system of good health at low cost with equity: beyond universal coverage. *Lancet*, 378, 1265–1273.

Statistics Bureau of Japan. (2010). *Census of Japan*. Statistics Bureau of Japan: Tokyo.

Statistics Bureau of Japan. (2012). *Annual Report on Current Population Estimates*. Statistics Bureau of Japan: Tokyo.

Tatara, K. and Okamoto, E. (2009). *Japan: Health System Review. Health Systems in Transition*. World Health Organization (European Regional Office): Copenhagen.

Tonosaki, K. (2007). Drafting process of the current Japanese Constitution and thought on human rights (Japanese). *Bulletin of the Junior College Division, University of Aizu*, 64. Available at: <http://ci.nii.ac.jp/vol_issue/nels/AN10448031/ISS0000430861_en.html> (accessed 9 November 2012).

UNDP. (2012). *Human Development Report*. United Nations Development Programme (UNDP): New York, NY.

WHO. (2000). *The World Health Report 2000: Health Systems: Improving Performance*. World Health Organization (WHO): Geneva.

WHO. (2011a). *World Health Statistics*. World Health Organization (WHO): Geneva.

WHO. (2011b). *Japan Earthquake and Tsunami. WHO Situation Report No. 5*. World Health Organization (Western Pacific Region): Manila.

Yamaguci, M. (2009, 4 February). *Injured Man Dies After Rejection by 14 Hospitals*. Associated Press: Tokyo.

Yamazaki, M., Minami, Y., Sasaki, H., and Sumi, M. (2011). The psychosocial response to the 2011 Tohoku earthquake. *Bulletin of the World Health Organization*, 89(9), 623.

Chapter 17

The United States: right to health obligations in the context of disparity and reform

Alicia Ely Yamin and Jean Connolly Carmalt

Introduction

The United States has long eschewed the concept of a right to health and the implications of applying a human rights framework to health policy and programming. As a consequence, it continues to face significant barriers to the full realization of the right to health for a substantial portion of its population. This is true despite the fact that the United States not only ranks 'very high' on the United Nations (UN) Development Programme's Human Development Index, but also spends more on healthcare per capita than any other country in the world (OECD, 2012). Many millions of US citizens and legal residents can access care that is ethically and culturally acceptable, and some of the care is among the highest quality in the world. Many millions also comfortably enjoy the underlying preconditions to health and well-being, such as adequate housing, food, clothing, and stable employment. The leading cause of death for people between the ages of five and 34 in the United States is not infectious disease, contaminated water, lack of available treatment, or other dimensions of nationwide poverty: it is motor vehicle accidents (CDC, 2011). Nonetheless, the structure of the American healthcare system both reflects and exacerbates deeply embedded inequities based on race, ethnicity, gender, socioeconomic status, and place of residence.

The US health system is extremely complex. For most Americans (58.7% in 2010), access to care is governed by private health insurance plans which are paid for by their employers (Fronstin, 2011). However, since health insurance is primarily provided through employers, the number of people without health insurance has grown as the economy has contracted and unemployment has increased. Some of these newly uninsured have been absorbed into government-provided insurance plans, one of which is focused on the elderly (the Medicare entitlement provides coverage for Americans who are over the age of 65) and one of which provides insurance for those living in poverty (the Medicaid entitlement, which provides coverage through a State–federal partnership to individuals making less than US$15,000 annually). This estimate is high, and will vary significantly by State. It reflects an increase in Medicaid coverage introduced by the Patient Protection and Affordable Care Act of 2010 (Affordable Care Act) to individuals under age 65 with an income below 133% of the federal poverty level (PPACA, 2010); in 2012, that level for an individual was US$11,170. However, in 2012, the US Supreme Court held that this increase would not be binding on States. In addition, a 1997 law known as CHIP provides for State-administered programmes of health insurance for children whose families are low-income but not impoverished enough to qualify for Medicaid. The Centers for Medicare and Medicaid Services (which also service CHIP) currently provide health coverage for approximately 100 million people, which is nearly one-third of the total US population (Centers for Medicare and Medicaid Services, 2012).

Despite significant coverage by government programmes for the elderly and the very poor, as of 2010 there were 49.9 million people in the United States with no form of health insurance (US Census Bureau, 2011). Because the system is designed around employment-based health insurance, this lack of coverage translates into a nearly insurmountable barrier to accessing adequate health services. Since 2000, the number of uninsured has increased by approximately 13 million people (DeNavas-Walt et al., 2011). Moreover, this barrier to access is not equally distributed across the population: instead, those without insurance reflect the racial-, ethnic-, and income-based inequalities that permeate US society. The financial burden, if not the ethical implications, of the uninsured problem provided political will to enact a major healthcare reform bill in 2010—the Affordable Care Act (PPACA, 2010).

Human rights and accountability in the United States

The equal dignity of all human beings and non-discrimination are among the most important principles of all human rights, including the right to health (UDHR, 1948). However, racial disparities are prevalent throughout the US healthcare system, as well as the broader society, and affect virtually every component of health (Gee, 2002; Williams, 2002; Williams et al., 2008). For example, infant mortality and maternal mortality—two indicators that are highly sensitive to the functioning of health systems—reflect these gaping inequalities; infant mortality is three times as high among African Americans and Latinos than among white people in some cities; maternal mortality is four times as high and five and a half times as high among high-risk pregnancies (Amnesty International, 2010; Maryland Department of Health and Mental Hygiene, 2008). Poverty illustrates another dimension of health inequality: three-quarters (75.5%) of the people who do not have health insurance (which is generally a prerequisite for affordable access to the provision of non-emergency care) in the United States are those who are classified as 'poor' or 'near-poor' (DeNavas-Walt et al., 2011). For those who face double or triple burdens of discrimination based on race, class, and gender, health statistics mirror intersecting forms of exclusion: for example, the prevalence of obesity (which is linked both to poor health outcomes and social determinants of health) in non-Hispanic black women is higher than non-Hispanic black men or than white women (CDC, 2011).

The Affordable Care Act includes some substantial improvements but leaves in place structural failures to address inequalities based upon income. Although it sets some floor with respect to 'health exchanges' (which provide access to subsidized health insurance plans) and contains some progressive tax financing, it essentially leaves in place a system that differentiates access and quality of care according to the ability to mobilize financial resources, and in so doing perpetuates a health system that endorses the exclusion of the poor (PPACA, 2010). Recent examples of State-based cuts to the Medicaid programme—which provides health insurance to indigent Americans—illustrate the consequences of a system that fails to prioritize access to health services. In Arizona, for instance, cuts were made to Medicaid in 2010 that restrict access even to life-saving organ transplants (Sack, 2010). Similarly, cuts to Medicaid coverage in Nebraska have resulted in significant barriers to prenatal care and a consequent rise in premature births, infant deaths, and other negative health outcomes for low-income women living in that state (Benen, 2011). In other countries, cuts in programmes that are targeted at low-income people have been found to constitute retrogression with respect to the right to health, which is presumptively inconsistent with State obligations unless it is narrowly tailored and justified in accordance with legitimate reasons—something which appears not to have been done in these cases.

Perhaps more disturbing than the failure to undertake meaningful deliberation regarding which cuts were truly necessary was that these cuts were applied solely to Medicaid recipients—i.e. people below a certain income threshold. Since Medicaid recipients already tend to have poorer care and fewer options than those with private insurance coverage, Arizona's Medicaid cuts highlight the depths of inequality that the US health system is willing to tolerate (Landon et al., 2007). The Affordable Care Act expands the coverage for Medicaid by requiring states to provide Medicaid to those below 133% of the federal poverty level, but that expansion was limited by the US Supreme Court's 2012 holding that this expansion would be voluntary for states. Even where it is enacted, this expansion also deepens the schism between the ways poorer individuals gain access to care as compared to wealthier individuals. Since there have been studies showing a relationship between poor quality care and the low payment rates by the Medicaid programmes, this schism is of significant concern from a rights-based perspective (O'Brien & Elias, 2004). In terms of both racial and income inequalities, the Affordable Care Act fails to treat health and healthcare as a basic right, as opposed to a market commodity, and as a consequence, perpetuates the current structural failure to address the underlying causes of inequalities in the system.

The failure to address health and healthcare as a right is also reflected in a lack of meaningful participation in the US health system. The right to health requires meaningful participation at all levels of decisions regarding the health system (CESCR, 2000). Meaningful participation requires more than the prerequisites of access to information and opportunities to express one's preferences in a liberal democratic democracy. In the United States, some interests, such as providers and insurers, are highly organized, while others, such as the majority of patients, are not. Sociologists and political theorists have recognized that all organization involves 'a mobilization of bias . . . in favour of the exploitation of certain kinds of conflict and the suppression of others . . . some issues are organized into politics and others are organized out' (Schattschneider, 1960; NESRI and NHELP, 2009). For example, during the extensive discussion of how to reform health policy under US President Barack Obama, several legislative proposals were made for single-payer plans, but only one subcommittee hearing was held, and it never came up for a vote (Govtrack.us, 2011). The universe of possibilities for healthcare reform was established outside of the political process; the only outstanding question in the reform process was whether organized industries and associations would succeed in defeating a robust public option to be offered alongside the private insurance option—which in the end, they did.

In addition to the scope and nature of the reform, a rights-based approach to health reform would incorporate meaningful participation into systematic priority-setting exercises. Such an approach to priority-setting calls for a participatory process that is transparent and public, based on relevant reasons and current epidemiological information, subject to revision in light of new information or atypical cases, and subject to regulation and enforcement (Daniels, 2000, 2008; Gruskin & Daniels, 2008). In a rights framework, it is not only 'experts' who should make priority-setting decisions behind closed doors, as though the technical criteria being applied were value-free; there should be meaningful opportunities for the people affected by policies and programmes to deliberate about the criteria and values used to determine priorities as well as how they are applied, in order to reach democratically legitimate and sustainable decisions.

In the United States, however, the discourse around healthcare has changed very little since the failed attempts of the early 1990s at structural overhaul. In the recent reform process, issues of fairness, social justice, and equity were not central to the debate. Indeed, even discussions around cost centred on projections of gross national product spent on healthcare, with minimal attention on the relatively low percentage of public expenditures on health compared with private financing of healthcare compared to other Organization for Economic Cooperation and Development (OECD) countries, which is a more accurate indicator of government commitment to health (OECD, 2012). It was as true in 2010 as it was during the last US healthcare reform debate in 1993, as the late Virginia Leary noted then, that 'discussions of [healthcare] reform in the United States have devoted little or no attention to the concept of the right to healthcare in international instruments *or in the constitutions or legislation of other countries*' (emphasis added; Leary, 1995), as they have in all other nations in the industrialized world (Leary, 1995).

The right to health in the United States: availability, accessibility, acceptability, and quality

In 2009, the United States spent US$7,960 per capita on healthcare (OECD, 2012). This was approximately one and a half times the amount of the second next highest per capita spender (Switzerland) according to the health data kept by the OECD. This difference is unsurprising since the United States has spent more on healthcare than other OECD countries since 1975 (OECD, 2012). Indeed, the amount of money devoted to healthcare spending in the United States is so dramatic that it has long occupied the focal point of most domestic debates over health in the United States. That focus on cost has, in turn, eclipsed other perspectives on health in the United States, including a perspective rooted in human rights.

Despite the Affordable Care Act, there is a continuing disconnect between the United States and the rest of the world with respect to treating health, including healthcare, as an issue of fundamental rights. Although the Affordable Care Act should result in significant improvements in insurance coverage over the next few years, it fails to address entrenched inequities that continue to characterize the US health system.

Under international standards, healthcare should be available both in terms of different geographic regions and in terms of the type of medical care that is required (CESCR, 2000). At the moment, for example, the United States faces a significant shortage of primary care physicians, as well as a shortage of providers in rural areas and underserved communities (Carmalt et al., 2011; Cooper, 2004; Lakhan & Laird, 2009). The Affordable Care Act addresses these issues through incentives to help existing physicians survive and an expanded stream of funding for community health centres (PPACA, 2010). These are both very positive changes. However, focused incentives and expansion to community health do little to tackle complex issues relating to medical education costs and reimbursement incentives that lead many physicians to pursue specialty practice instead of primary care (Iglehart, 2008; Lakhan & Laird, 2009). While the Affordable Care Act's incentives are welcome, they do not go nearly far enough in addressing the underlying problem of a system that is designed to focus on lucrative specialty care instead of more broadly needed primary care.

Second, care needs to be accessible under international law (CESCR, 2000). Accessibility includes physical access, geographic access (which overlaps with availability), and economic access, or affordability. International standards also require equality of access or non-discrimination, and access to health-related information. While the United States does well on some of these dimensions (physical access to medical facilities tends to be excellent, for example), it fails on others. The Affordable Care Act's expansion of insurance coverage to an estimated 31 million additional people is to be applauded, but it falls short of ensuring economically accessible care to all, including those without documentation (Healthcare.gov, 2010).

Moreover, insurance coverage does not equal access to care (California Nurses Association, 2009; National Nurses United, 2010). For example, denial rates for first-time claims are as high as 40% for some insurance companies (National Nurses United, 2010). Although the Affordable Care Act encourages regulation and oversight, insurance companies will likely maintain the flexibility to eliminate some important coverage and establish high deductibles (Cooper, 2004). For example, a study of a similar plan in the state of Massachusetts demonstrates a shift from un-insurance to under-insurance, and as a result medical bankruptcies were unaffected by statutory requirements to hold insurance (Himmelstein et al., 2011).

In addition, given the complexity of the US health system, one of the most persistent barriers to access (even among those with insurance) is bureaucracy and lack of information. Mandating Patients' Bills of Rights is an important gesture; however, the Affordable Care Act does not address the structural reasons for the complexity, bureaucracy, or opacity of the healthcare system in a comprehensive way (PPACA, 2010).

Under international law, care must also be acceptable, which entails both cultural and ethical standards (CESCR, 2000). While the United States has developed stringent, well-enforced ethical standards for medical professionals, care is not always culturally appropriate (Betancourt & Green, 2010). Given the diverse population, this point speaks to a broader need to create institutions and systems that allow for trusting, care-based relationships between patients and their providers, rather than addressing cultural inadequacies through provider training about 'cultural competency' of variable effectiveness.

Finally, the right to health requires that healthcare be of adequate quality (CESCR, 2000). The Affordable Care Act takes important steps in this regard, for example by adopting evidence-based practices and establishing Accountable Care Organizations (PPACA, 2010) and decreasing the number of uninsured who need to rely on emergency room care, which evidence shows often heightens cultural miscommunication and clinical uncertainty. Nevertheless, the Affordable Care Act's welcome improvements in quality fall short of providing a systemic change that would address some of the most important root causes of these problems, such as structural incentives to maximize the number of patients seen by a given provider in a given time, and the variable quality of care based upon de facto segregation in neighbourhoods and cities.

Limitations on rights under domestic laws

The US Constitution does not include the human right to health. Moreover, the United States has consistently resisted any attempt to recognize that right at the federal level, or indeed, to recognize economic and social rights more generally, except for certain classes of people or for isolated types of care (Sunstein, 2004; Yamin, 2005). In response to enormous disparities in State tort law interpretations of common law rights to care, the United States did enact federal legislation that provides for emergency care, the Emergency Medical Treatment and Active Labor Act (EMTALA, 1986). However, EMTALA provides limited rights of care until conditions are stabilized and does not relieve a patient of paying for care once the emergency has passed.

The US Constitution does grant Congress power to regulate interstate commerce (US Constitution, 1787). In 1937, the Supreme Court held that this includes the power to regulate things that indirectly effect interstate commerce, which has resulted in a long history of Congressional power to pass laws that relate to everything from minimum wage to racial discrimination, including issues related to health such as the EMTALA (*National Labor Relations Board* v. *Jones & Laughlin Steel Corp.*, 1937).

Although commerce clause jurisprudence provides some legal basis for national legislation that upholds economic and social rights, such legislation has not typically been forthcoming. National legislation pertaining to health policy has not only failed to recognize health as a human right, it has also consistently failed to prioritize health and well-being over other policy-related concerns. Nonetheless, the commerce clause does provide a legal basis for national health legislation, and it was the legal grounding for the Affordable Care Act. Framing health as an issue of interstate commerce is what prompted the US Supreme Court to review the Affordable Care Act's constitutionality in March 2012, and the primary question before the Supreme Court (along with much of the questioning) focused on whether Congress has the authority to require all individuals to purchase a private product (health insurance) in order to make that product more affordable for everyone. On 28 June 2012, the Supreme Court held that the Affordable Care Act is constitutional, but decided the issue on the grounds that the legislation imposes a tax—because people have a choice of whether to buy insurance or pay a penalty—and Congress is within its authority to impose such a tax under the enumerated powers. The Supreme Court (surprisingly, given past decisions) struck down the commerce clause arguments, holding that Congress does not have the power to force individuals to '*become* active in commerce by purchasing a product, on the ground that their failure to do so affects interstate commerce' (emphasis in original; *National Federation of Independent Business et al.* v. *Sebelius, Secretary of Health and Human Services*, 2012).

From a rights-based perspective, however, it is worth noting that the legal arguments surrounding the Affordable Care Act mirrored the political debates, in that they focused on the structure and distribution of costs instead of on the health of the population. This indicates the degree to which the Affordable Care Act is expanding upon an existing system based upon market allocation of healthcare instead of approaching health as a public good and healthcare as a right. For example, one of the foremost goals of the Affordable Care Act is to ensure that 'consumers get value for their dollars' when it comes to health expenditures (PPACA, 2010).

The United States also has a narrow legal interpretation of prohibited forms of discrimination. Although the Civil Rights Act of 1964 prohibits intentional discrimination, the Supreme Court has long held that the Civil Rights Act does not include a prohibition against disparate impact discrimination (*Alexander* v. *Sandoval*, 2001; *Washington, Mayor of Washington, D.C. et al.* v. *Davis et al.*, 1976). This legal interpretation continues to govern discrimination law in the United States despite the fact that it directly contradicts the legal definition of discrimination articulated by numerous international legal instruments, including treaties ratified by the United States (ICCPR, 1966; ICERD, 1965). In terms of the right to health, this narrow legal definition for discrimination means that the disparate impact discrimination that exists in terms of the preconditions to health, access to quality healthcare, and availability of acceptable care are considered policy concerns instead of an abrogation of the Government's duty to respect, protect, and fulfil the right to health. Unlike under international law, under US law, however, there is neither a private right of action against discrimination nor can enforcement actions brought pursuant to the Civil Rights Act be based upon disproportionate impact, as would be required under international law (Civil Rights Act, 1964; Watson, 1994). Thus, for example, funding allocations that had a disproportionate racial impact would violate international law, but would only violate US law if there were intent to discriminate 'on the ground[s] of race, colour, or national origin' (Civil Rights Act, 1964).

The United States' focus on civil and political rights—and concomitant neglect of economic, social, and cultural rights—has resulted in a lack of recognition at the state level in addition to the federal level. Consequently, to the extent that certain aspects of the right to health are legally protected, it is most often under laws that are framed in terms other than health. For example, reproductive rights for women in the United States are, legally speaking, considered part of the right to privacy instead of the right to health. In the case of reproductive rights in particular, that legal framing has politicized aspects of reproductive decisions that might not otherwise be as open to politicization, such as the permissibility of terminating a pregnancy, and, as it has precluded governmental funding of certain services, has meant that in practice poor women do not have the same rights to abortion that wealthier women do (*Griswold* v. *Connecticut*, 1965; *Harris* v. *McRae*, 1980; *Roe* v. *Wade*, 1973).

Thirteen of the 50 states have specific references to health in their state constitutions, and another two states have provisions that have been interpreted in ways that recognize the importance of health on some level (Leonard, 2009). However, these provisions have been interpreted narrowly, with the result that none of the states recognize a human right to health as it is interpreted under international law (Leonard, 2009). That narrow interpretation arises in part thanks to pre-emption issues—the concept that under the US Constitution and federal law (i.e. the Employee Retirement Income Security Act of 1974) pre-empts conflicting State law—which have posed greater challenges to the local advancement of the right to healthcare than, for example, the right to education (ERISA, 2012; United States Constitution, 1787).

Taken together with the failure to provide a right to health at the federal level and the failure to recognize the legal legitimacy of disparate impact discrimination, the failure of states to recognize the right to health has resulted in a country that spends a great deal of money on health while constantly side-stepping the implications of what a right to health would mean for the organization of its system.

History of failures with respect to the human right to health

When US President Franklin D. Roosevelt delivered his famous 1941 speech on the 'four freedoms'—freedom of speech and belief and freedom from fear and want—he advanced two ideas that would become an indispensable part of the UDHR: first, that freedoms include not only civil and political rights, but also economic, social, and cultural rights, and second, that these different types of rights are interdependent and inseparable (Glendon, 2001). In the United States, however, both the importance of interdependent rights and the role of economic and social rights were subsumed by Cold War politics.

In 2010, as in earlier reform efforts, the enduring power of the libertarian rejection of a 'government take-over' of healthcare has proven to have broad public appeal (Epstein, 1997). In countries where there has been a mass movement for comprehensive healthcare reform, the organized labour movement has played a pivotal role (Epstein, 1997). However, the United States has a relatively eviscerated labour movement and, as scholars from Emile Durkheim on have noted, 'cross-cutting cleavages' among race, class, religion, and ethnicity in this country have led to a lack of consciousness of even being 'working class' (Durkheim, 1933). By contrast, the United States has extremely well-organized insurance and pharmaceutical industries which were largely able to control which issues were placed into public debate during the reform process (Navarro, 2003).

The public perception of health as divorced from basic human rights dovetails with both libertarianism and the relative lack of social solidarity in the United States (Epstein, 1997). That is, there is a widespread notion that sickness is somehow a moral failing, so that those who eat right, regularly exercise, avoid smoking and transfats, and the like should not subsidize 'them'—who do not. This perspective was most recently argued in front of the Supreme Court as a reason to strike down the constitutionality of the Affordable Care Act's requirement that all individuals be required to purchase health insurance. That argument focused a great deal of attention on the fact that young, relatively healthy people may not have health insurance, and argued that it would be inappropriate to make those individuals 'subsidize' those who were in more immediate need of health services (*Department of Health and Human Services et al.*, v. *Florida et al.*, 2012). The idea that individuals are instead cut off from each other and that—as an extension—dependency on healthcare provision is a moral failing instead of a natural part of humanity, are also continually reinforced by disproportionate emphasis by popular media on dramatized individual cases that distract from the social determinants of poor health (McCann et al., 2001–2002).

Finally, in relation to the 2010 reform effort specifically, there were arguably shortfalls in political leadership that prevented a right to health from being more present in the political discourse around healthcare reform. Despite a rhetorical reference to healthcare as a right by then-Presidential candidate Obama in one political debate with US Senator John McCain, the elected President Obama did not appear committed to that ideal throughout the process, and neither did many legislators (*Wall Street Journal*, 2008). The continued lack of public understanding that popular provisions in the Affordable Care Act (e.g. stopping the insurance industry's discriminatory and exclusionary practices) are linked to universal coverage again reflect a lack of leadership regarding the issue of healthcare as an issue of democracy in the United States.

Evolving responses and obligations: future national directions towards the right to health

In June 2012, the US Supreme Court found that the individual mandate contained in the Affordable Care Act was constitutional, thus ending a long legal debate over whether it would be struck down. From a right to health perspective, the decision is welcome. The Affordable Care Act enacts a number of changes that are in line with a rights-based approach to health, such as expanding access to insurance to many millions of people and requiring insurance companies to provide coverage for people who have pre-existing conditions, and its implementation will therefore move the country forward in terms of providing the highest attainable standard of health for many Americans. However, since the Affordable Care Act was not rooted in a rights-based approach, it also falls short of what would be required to ensure the right to health for those living in the United States. Moreover, opponents of the law have vowed to continue the political battle for repeal.

Even if this political battle does not succeed, the legal trends in the United States suggest that there will continue to be a narrow definition of discrimination, and that there will be continued tolerance for those living in poverty, women, and people of colour to experience a disproportionate burden of health-related problems. The Supreme Court's emphatic denial that the commerce clause would provide valid constitutional grounding for the Affordable Care Act is also an indication that future legislation that governs health rights will need to be couched in terms of other enumerated powers, which means that new legal arguments will need to be developed in order to provide support to rights-based initiatives. Therefore, although there is reason to expect some of the health indicators in the United States to improve as a result of the Affordable Care Act's implementation, there is still a great need for a rhetorical shift surrounding issues of health, if the United States is to respect, protect, and fulfil the human right to health.

Conclusion

Although the United States is not party to the treaties explicitly articulating health as a right, it has ratified the International Convention on the Elimination of all Forms of Racial Discrimination (Race Convention), which contains provisions related to health, as well as the International

Covenant on Civil and Political Rights (ICCPR), in which the right to life includes health-related elements (Human Rights Watch, 2009; ICCPR, 1966; ICERD, 1965). Thus, the United States has undertaken some legal obligations regarding health and the provision of care. Moreover, the right to health has been so widely enshrined in international and domestic laws that it signals an ethical consensus regarding at least some general principles. Without question, the United States is currently an outlier. However, it can—and should—join the rest of the world in embracing a rights-based approach to health and healthcare.

References

Alexander v. *Sandoval*. (2001). 532 U.S. 275; 121 S. Ct. 1511; 149 L. Ed. 2d 517.

Amnesty International. (2010). *Deadly Delivery: The Maternal Health Care Crisis in The USA*. Available at: <http://www.amnestyusa.org/dignity/pdf/DeadlyDelivery.pdf> (accessed 10 November 2010).

Benen, S. (2011). *Cuts and Consequences*. Available at: <http://www.washingtonmonthly.com/archives/individual/2011_03/028657.php> (accessed 29 March 2011).

Betancourt, J.K. and Green, A.R. (2010). Commentary: linking cultural competence training to improved health outcomes: perspectives from the field. *Academic Medicine*, 85, 583–585.

California Nurses Association. (2009). *California's Real Death Panels: Insurers Deny 21% of Claims*. Available at: <http://www.calnurses.org> (accessed 10 November 2010).

Carmalt J., Zaidi, S., and Yamin, A.E. (2011). Entrenched inequity: health care in the United States of America. In S. Hertel and K. Libal (Eds.), *Human Rights in the United States*, pp. 153–174. Cambridge University Press: Cambridge.

CDC. (2011). CDC health disparities and inequalities report—United States, 2011. *MMWR 2011*, 60(Suppl), 1–114. Available at: <http://www.cdc.gov/mmwr/pdf/other/su6001.pdf> (accessed 5 April 2012).

Centers for Medicaid and Medicare Services. (2012). *Home: Centers for Medicaid and Medicare Services*. Available at: <http://www.cms.gov/> (accessed 5 April 2012).

CESCR. (2000). *General Comment 14: The Right to the Highest Attainable Standard Health. (Article 12 of the International Covenant on Economic, Social and Cultural Rights)*. United Nations: UN Doc E/C.12/2000/4. Committee on Economic, Social, and Cultural Rights (CESCR): Geneva.

Civil Rights Act. (1964). 24 USC 2000d.

Cooper, R.A. (2004). Weighing the evidence for expanding physician supply. *Annals of Internal Medicine*, 141, 705–714.

Daniels, N. (2000). Accountability for reasonableness. *British Medical Journal*, 321, 1300–1301.

Daniels, N. (2008). *Just Health: Meeting Health Needs Fairly*. Cambridge University Press: New York, NY.

DeNavas-Walt, C., Proctor, B., and Smith, J. (2011). *US Census Bureau. Current Population Reports, P.60-239, Income, Poverty, and Health Insurance Coverage in the United States: 2010*. US Government Printing Office: Washington, DC.

Department of Health and Human Services, et al. v. *Florida, et al.* (2012). US Supreme Court Docket No. 11-11021, 11-11067.

Durkheim, E. (1933). *The Division of Labor in Society*. The MacMillan Co: New York, NY.

Emergency Medical Treatment and Active Labor Act (EMTALA). (1986). 42 U.S.C. § 1395dd.

Epstein, R. (1997). *Mortal Peril? Our Inalienable Right to Health Care*. Addison-Wesley: New York, NY.

ERISA. (2012). *Employee Retirement Income Security Program*. 29 U.S.C. 1001 et seq.

Fronstin, P. (2011). *Sources of Health Insurance and Characteristics of the Uninsured: Analysis of the March 2011 Current Population Survey*. Available at: <http://www.ebri.org/pdf/briefspdf/EBRI_IB_09-2011_No362_Uninsured1.pdf> (accessed 17 April 2012).

Gee, G.C. (2002). A multilevel analysis of the relationship between institutional and individual racial discrimination and health status. *American Journal of Public Health*, 92, 615–623.

Glendon, M.A. (2001). *A World Made New: Eleanor Roosevelt and the Universal Declaration of Human Rights*. Random House Paperbacks: New York, NY.

Govtrack.us. (2011). *A Civic Project to Track Congress. H.R. 676: Expanded and Improved Medicare for All Act*. Available at: <http://www.govtrack.us/congress/bill.xpd?bill=h111-676> (accessed 3 February 2011).

Griswold v. *Connecticut*. (1965). 381 U.S. 479; 85 S. Ct. 1678; 14 L. Ed. 2d 510.

Gruskin, S. and Daniels, N. (2008). Process is the point: justice and human rights: priority setting and fair deliberative process. *American Journal of Public Health*, 98, 1573–1577.

Harris v. *McRae*. (1980). 448 U.S. 297; 100 S. Ct. 2671; 65 L. Ed. 2d 784.

Healthcare.gov. (2010). *Newsroom: Affordable Care Act and Immunization*. Available at: <http://www.healthcare.gov/news/factsheets/affordable_care_act_immunization.html> (accessed 29 January 2011).

Himmelstein, D., Thorne, D., and Woolhandler, S. (2011). Medical bankruptcy in Massachusetts: has health reform made a difference? *American Journal of Medicine*, 124, 224–228.

Human Rights Watch. (2009). *United States Ratification of International Human Rights Treaties*. Available at: <http://www.hrw.org/sites/default/files/related_material/Treaty%20Ratification%20Advocacy%20document%20-%20final%20-%20Aug%202009.pdf> (accessed 10 November 2010).

ICCPR. (1966). *International Covenant on Civil and Political Rights*. GA res 2200A (XXI), 21 UN GAOR Supp (No 16) at 52, UN Doc A/6316, 999 UNTS 171.

ICERD. (1965). *International Convention on the Elimination of All Forms of Racial Discrimination*. GA res 2106 (XX), Annex, 20 UN GAOR Supp (No 14) at 47, UN Doc A/6014, 660 UNTS 195.

Iglehart, J.K. (2008). Medicare, graduate medical education, and new policy directions. *New England Journal of Medicine*, 359, 643–650.

Lakhan, S.E. and Laird, C. (2009). Addressing the primary care physician shortage in an evolving medical workforce. *International Archives of Medicine*, 2, 1–4.

Landon, B., Schneider, E., Normand, S., *et al.* (2007). Quality of care in Medicaid managed care and commercial health plans. *Journal of the American Medical Association*, 298, 1674–1681.

Leary, V. (1995). Defining the right to health care. In A. Chapman (Ed.), *Health Care Reform: A Human Rights Approach*, pp. 87–99. Georgetown University Press: Washington, DC.

Leonard, E.W. (2009). State constitutionalism and the right to health care. *University of Pennsylvania Journal of Constitutional Law*, 12. Available at: <http://ssrn.com/abstract=1421504> (accessed 25 October 2012).

Maryland Department of Health and Mental Hygiene. (2008). *Plan Reducing Infant Mortality in Maryland*. Available at: <http://fha.maryland.gov/pdf/mch/GDU_IM_Plan.pdf> (accessed 10 November 2010).

McCann, M., Halton, M., and Bloom, A. (2001–2002). Java jive: genealogy of a juridical icon. *University of Miami Law Review*, 56, 113–178.

NESRI and NHELP. (2009). *A Human Rights Assessment of Single Payer Plans: Toward the Human Right to Healthcare: The Contributions of Single Payer Plans*. Available at: <http://www.nesri.org/sites/default/files/Single_Payer_Human_Rights_Analysis.pdf> (accessed 17 April 2012).

National Federation of Independent Business et al. v. *Sebelius, Secretary of Health and Human Services*. (2012). 567 U.S. __; 132 S. Ct. 2566; 183 L. Ed. 2d 450.

National Labor Relations Board v. *Jones & Laughlin Steel Corporation*. (1937). 301 U.S. 1; 57 S. Ct. 615; 81 L. Ed. 893.

National Nurses United. (2010). *Press Release: California Insurers Denied over 26% of all Claims in 2009*. Available at: <http://www.nationalnursesunited.org/press/entry/california-insurers-denied-over-26-of-all-claims-in-2009/> (accessed 10 November 2010).

Navarro, V. (2003). Policy without politics: the limits of social engineering. *American Journal of Public Health*, 93, 64–67.

O'Brien, E. and Elias, R. (2004). *Medicaid and Longterm Care*. Available at: <http://www.kff.org/medicaid/loader.cfm?url=/commonspot/security/getfile.cfm&pageid=36296> (accessed 6 April 2012).

OECD (2012). *OECD Health Data 2011—Frequently Requested Data*. Available at: <http://www.oecd.org/dataoecd/52/42/49188719.xls> (accessed 5 April 2012).

PPACA (2010). *Patient Protection and Affordable Care Act, 42 USC 18001*. Available at: <http://www.gpo.gov/fdsys/pkg/PLAW-111publ148/pdf/PLAW-111publ148.pdf> (accessed 17 April 2012).

Roe v. *Wade*. (1973). 410 US 113.

Sack, K. (2010, 5 December). Arizona Medicaid cuts seen as a sign of the times. *The New York Times*, p. A26.

Schattschneider, E.E. (1960). *The Semi-Sovereign People: A Realist's View of Democracy in America*. Holt, Reinhart & Winston: New York, NY.

Sunstein, C. (2004). *The Second Bill of Rights: FDR's Unfinished Revolution and Why We Need It More Than Ever*. Basic Books: New York, NY.

UDHR. (1948). *Universal Declaration of Human Rights*. GA Res 217A (III), UN Doc A/810 at 71. United Nations General Assembly: New York, NY.

UNHRC. (2011). *Preventable maternal mortality and morbidity and human Rights*. Resolution 18/2. United Nations Human Rights Council (UNHRC): Geneva.

United States Constitution. (1787). Article 1, §8.

US Census Bureau. (2011). *Income, Poverty, and Health Insurance Coverage in the United States: 2010*. Available at: <http://www.census.gov/prod/2011pubs/p60-239.pdf> (accessed 17 April 2012).

Wall Street Journal. (2008, 7 October). Transcript of the second presidential debate. *Wall Street Journal*. Available at: <http://online.wsj.com/article/SB122344363678714595.html> (accessed 10 November 2010).

Washington, Mayor of Washington, D.C. et al. v. *Davis et al.* (1976). 426 U.S. 229; 96 S. Ct. 2040; 48 L. Ed. 2d 597.

Watson, S.D. (1994). Minority access and health reform: a civil right to health care. *Journal of Law & Medical Ethics*, 22, 127–137.

Williams, D.R. (2002). Racial/ethnic variations in women's health: the social embeddedness of health. *American Journal of Public Health*, 92, 588–597.

Williams, D.R., Neighbors, H.W., and Jackson, J.S. (2008). Racial/ethnic discrimination and health: findings from community studies. *American Journal of Public Health*, 98, S29–S37.

Yamin, A.E. (2005). The right to health under international law and its relevance to the United States. *American Journal of Public Health*, 95, 1156–1161.

Section 3

The right to health: challenges and opportunities

Chapter 18

Human rights-based approaches to HIV, tuberculosis, and malaria

Britta Baer, Andrew Ball, Helena Nygren-Krug, Aafje Rietveld, and Diana Weil

Introduction

This chapter will examine the interface between human rights and HIV/AIDS, tuberculosis (TB), and malaria. While attention to human rights has been explicit from the outset of the HIV response, the nature of the TB epidemic has brought to the forefront concerns about the determinants of disease, barriers to accessing prevention and care, and the special needs of marginalized groups affected by the disease. Of the three health issues, the connection with human rights has been least explicit to date in the context of malaria. Nonetheless, analysis of the varying incidence of malaria among different population groups underscores the potential for applying a human rights-based approach. This chapter will explore to what extent human rights efforts have challenged or strengthened responses to HIV, TB, and malaria. It will look at how the search for the most effective public health response has been informed by taking into account human rights principles, such as non-discrimination, participation and accountability, as well as the right to health.

Background

Sixty-five years ago, the Universal Declaration of Human Rights (UDHR) enshrined the right to a standard of living adequate for health and well-being of everyone, including medical care. During the same time, the Constitution of the World Health Organization (WHO) recognized the enjoyment of the highest attainable standard of health as a fundamental right of every human being. For decades, however, efforts to prevent, control, and treat diseases were disconnected from the human rights discourse. HIV can be seen as a milestone, an 'eye opener' in forging the link between public health and human rights.

The history of HIV

The early years of the HIV epidemic were characterized by silence, fear, and uncertainty (Mann, 1989). When the first cases of AIDS were identified in the 1980s, society was confronted with an infection that was fatal with no effective treatment, resulting in a disease with obvious physical and disfiguring signs and complications including wasting and Kaposi's sarcoma. Uncertainties about how HIV could be transmitted fuelled fear and stigma. Even more so, HIV became increasingly associated with already stigmatized behaviours and groups, including unprotected sex with multiple partners, sex workers, men who have sex with men (MSM), and people who inject drugs.

At a time when there was limited information and no treatment available, knowledge of one's HIV status offered little hope. It often came with numerous social, economic, and other risks as affected people were faced with exclusion from schools, communities, and families, loss of employment, insurance, and housing, and, in extreme cases, violence (Gostin, 2009). Proposed health measures in the early years, such as mandatory testing, were often in direct conflict with human rights (Golenski & Lo, 1990). Stigma and discrimination associated with HIV not only resulted in human rights violations but soon proved unproductive for public health efforts. As people began to avoid testing for fear of discrimination and stigma, WHO Member-States recognized in 1988 that tackling discrimination was a key element of an effective response to HIV (World Health Assembly, 1988). By the 1990s, it had become clear that a traditional public health approach, combining information and education with specific health services, while necessary and helpful, was clearly insufficient for HIV (Crewe, 2009). This transformation was helped along by efforts stressing the linkages between a lack of respect for human rights and increased vulnerability to HIV. There was growing awareness among health professionals that it was important to look at the determinants of risk and transmission, especially among key population groups including MSM, people who inject drugs, transgender people, sex workers, and prisoners.

Tackling discrimination—a necessary and effective public health strategy

Recognition that specific attention is required for marginalized groups has by now become common practice in public health—the WHO has, for example, developed specific guidelines for HIV interventions and services for sex workers, prisoners, MSM, transgender people, people who inject drugs, and other groups vulnerable to and at higher risk of HIV (WHO et al., 2010). The vulnerabilities of particular groups such as MSM and sex workers, and related human rights violations have also been highlighted by the United Nations (UN) Special Rapporteur on the right to the highest attainable standard of health (Grover, 2010). Men who have sex with men, for example, are estimated to be nearly 20 times more likely to be infected with HIV (WHO, 2011a; 2012a). The ability of MSM to access healthcare is complicated by the fact that in many countries they continue to face punishment, violence, and discrimination (Grover, 2010; Moody, 2009). A 2011 report revealed that same-sex sexual relations between consenting adults are criminalized by law in almost 80 countries (UNAIDS, 2012). Where such laws are in place, governments are unlikely to promote any sort of HIV interventions aimed at MSM. Moreover, non-governmental organizations (NGOs) or individuals who do try to carry out such services might also be at risk of violence or arrests, thus making HIV prevention efforts difficult to implement. Similar challenges exist in relation to HIV and sex work. In 2009, an estimated 43% of the number of people newly infected with HIV was associated with paid sex in Morocco (WHO et al., 2011a). In many countries, sex work is ignored by society, if not considered morally corrupt or criminal. This has created huge barriers of access for sex workers, who avoid contact for fear of discrimination, violence, or criminal proceedings (Crago et al., 2010; WHO, 2012b). Sex workers are not a homogenous group and might face multiple forms of risk and discrimination. For example, migration, sex work, and HIV are often interlinked, as migrants may turn to sex work as a means of making money (AVERT, 2011a; UNAIDS, 2002). Evidence also suggests that sex workers, particularly those who are trafficked, might be especially vulnerable to HIV infection as they can rarely negotiate condom use, they are often forced to endure multiple sex partners, and they may be subjected to violent sex (AVERT, 2011a; WHO, 2012b). Sex work and injecting drug use and HIV risk are often positively correlated (AVERT, 2011a; UNAIDS, 2002). For example, in the Ukraine, HIV prevalence has been estimated at 43% among sex workers who inject drugs versus 8.5% among those who do not (WHO et al., 2011a). Historically, injecting drug users were one of the first groups affected by HIV. Today, people who inject drugs remain perhaps the most marginalized group at risk of HIV infection (AVERT, 2011b). This is evidenced by the fact that on average 49% of sex workers, 32% of MSM, and only 23% of people who inject drugs received HIV testing and counselling in 2010 (WHO et al., 2011a).

Gender equality and women's empowerment is now central to any effort to effectively tackle HIV. In sub-Saharan Africa, six in ten adults living with HIV are women (UNAIDS, 2012). As far back as the 1990s, Jonathan Mann reflected that a woman's vulnerability to HIV was fundamentally linked to the extent to which her rights were respected and protected (Mann et al., 1999). Effective health sector responses to HIV, such as condom promotion, would thus need to go hand in hand with the promotion and protection of human rights, empowering women and girls to negotiate safer sex and protect their health from HIV (Mann et al., 1999).

To ensure equality and address discrimination, an important entry point is national legislation. Legislation can protect the human rights of those living with HIV as well as lead to successes in mitigating the causes and consequences of HIV (Global Commission on HIV and the Law, 2012). For example, some countries have legislation protecting certain groups against discrimination in various contexts, including when accessing health services. Sweden's Discrimination Act specifically refers to health and medical care and other medical services in the context of combating discrimination with respect to sexual orientation and disability, including mental, and drug dependence (Sweden Discrimination Act, 2008). The United Kingdom's Equality Act 2010 includes HIV infection in its definition of 'disability', which may protect individuals living with HIV from discrimination and harassment (United Kingdom Equality Act, 2010). Health service providers may not refuse to serve HIV-positive patients, nor may they give HIV-positive patients service of lower quality than usual (United Kingdom Equality Act, 2010). The beginnings of this positive trend of protective legislation contrasts, however, with the recent wave of disease-specific laws, usually focusing on punitive measures. This has reinforced concerns about the risks associated with law-making, as potentially increasing discrimination and vulnerability of marginalized groups. There have been a number of prosecutions for HIV exposure, non-disclosure, and transmission in North America, Western Europe, and Australasia (Cameron & Reynolds, 2010). In sub-Saharan Africa, some 20 countries have passed HIV-specific criminal statutes in the last five years (Eba, 2008). In practice, these laws have created an adverse incentive for people to avoid HIV testing and disclosure for fear of prosecution, stigma, and violence (UNAIDS, 2008). Moreover, the cases that have been prosecuted so far, have disproportionately focused on people from ethnic minorities, migrants or MSM, thus adding to the discrimination and stigma faced by vulnerable groups (UNAIDS, 2008).

HIV, community involvement, and GIPA

The history of HIV has highlighted the importance of empowerment of affected communities as a central component of an effective response to the epidemic. The beginnings of HIV were strongly intertwined with community activism and involvement. Before HIV became a concern, gay movements had already mobilized around a gay rights agenda in many countries (predominantly high-income countries). When HIV emerged, there were already established networks and structures driven by a human rights agenda, which could now be used to mobilize, understand, and deal with what was happening in their communities. For example, gay entertainment venues provided opportunities to reach marginalized groups, provide information, and change community norms. Important civil society organizations emerged all around the world—for example, the Gay Men's Health Crisis in the United States, the Terrence Higgins Trust in the United Kingdom, and the AIDS Support Organization (TASO) in Uganda—that began to combat discrimination and stigma and advocate for the rights of people affected by HIV. In clear contrast to earlier attempts to isolate or quarantine people, there was growing recognition that effective responses to HIV strongly depended upon the participation of people living with HIV. The idea that personal experiences were essential to the public health response to HIV was first voiced by people living with HIV in Denver in 1983 (UNAIDS, 2007). What developed into a core principle of Greater Involvement of People living with HIV (GIPA) was formalized in 1994 in Paris, where countries committed to 'fully involve non-governmental and community-based organizations as well as people living with HIV/AIDS in the formulation and implementation of public policies' and to 'support a greater involvement of people living with HIV/AIDS [. . .] in our common response to the pandemic at all—national, regional and global—levels' to promote and establish 'supportive political, legal and social environments' (Paris Declaration, 1994). What we know now is that communities affected by HIV can help to strengthen responses, that communities should be involved in the design, implementation, *and* evaluation of programmes, and that that the best way to ensure people are empowered and supported to protect themselves and others, is by protecting their human rights.

Access to medicines

With the Cold War ending, and antiretroviral therapy (ART) becoming available, the human rights discourse in relation to HIV extended to embrace economic and social rights. Central among these is the right to health. At the international level, the Committee on Economic, Social and Cultural Rights (CESCR) recognized access to essential medicines as a core obligation of the right to health in 2000 (CESCR, 2000). An important trend has been that of national constitutions across the world enshrining the right to health (WHO, 2012c). The WHO has also analysed constitutions worldwide and found that 135 of 186 national constitutions included provisions relating to health or the right to health (WHO, 2012c). Of these, 95 mentioned the right to access to health facilities, goods, and services, while only four recognized access to essential medicines as a fundamental right (Mexico, Peru, the Philippines, and the Syrian Arab Republic) (WHO, 2012c). The constitutionalization of the right to health has given rise to extensive litigation, particularly in the area of access to medicines. For example, in *Minister for Health* v. *Treatment Action Campaign*, the South African Constitutional Court held that the Constitution required the government to devise and implement a comprehensive and coordinated programme to progressively realize the right of pregnant women and their newborn children to have access to treatment and care in order to combat mother-to-child transmission of HIV (*Minister of Health* v. *Treatment Action Campaign*, 2002).

Brazil is one example of the many countries with a constitution that enshrines the right to health. It is frequently being used as an example for the 'judicialization of health' (Biehl et al., 2009) characterized by an explosion of right to health litigation, initially focusing on HIV-related treatment. The success of these court challenges led the Brazilian government to adopt a wide-ranging policy of universal access to ART. The notion of health, as an individual enforceable right with corresponding duties of the State to generate the conditions for its realization, has also influenced the country's trade policy. The adoption of the new policy on HIV drugs, informed by constitutional guarantees and domestic courts, and combined with obvious resource constraints led Brazil to explore new flexibilities in terms of health and intellectual property law. As a result, the government introduced a new approach to patents, allowing for 'compulsory licensing' and 'parallel importing', leading to a US complaint against Brazil under the World Trade Organization (WTO) agreement on Trade-Related Aspects of Intellectual Property Rights (TRIPS) ('t Hoen, 2003). Spearheaded by Brazil, the UN Human Rights Commission (now UN Human Rights Council) adopted a resolution on the right to access affordable medicines in the context of the HIV pandemic in 2001 (UNHRC, 2001). The same year, the WTO conference in Doha, Qatar, asserted that that TRIPS 'does not and should not prevent Members from taking measures to protect public health', including 'medicines for all' (WTO, 2001). Developing countries are now actively encouraged to make full use of flexibilities built into trade agreements such as TRIPS, allowing them to overcome patent barriers and thus ensure access to essential medicines, in particular in the context of HIV/AIDS.

The example of Brazil illustrates how incentives to produce essential medicines inside the country may be established, advancing the development of a domestic pharmaceutical industry. It also served as an essential negotiating tool to pressure companies to reduce the high price of imported medicines in general, allowing for wider access to treatment. In 2001, when the HIV crisis was at its peak, prices for antiretroviral medicines dropped from US$15,000 to less than US$400 per patient per year (Grover, 2011).

Ongoing and new challenges ahead

Today, an estimated 34.2 million persons live with HIV worldwide (UNAIDS, 2012). Epidemic patterns and responses have varied greatly across countries and regions. Since 2001, annual HIV incidence has fallen in 33 countries, 22 of them in sub-Saharan Africa, while the incidence in Eastern Europe and Central Asia has accelerated since 2008 (WHO et al., 2011).

Challenging issues relating to sexuality, gender and gender identity, drug use, migration, detention/imprisonment, involvement of marginalized groups, and discrimination and financial inequalities remain central to the HIV response (Piot et al., 2009). Meanwhile, the diversity of HIV testing approaches (including mandatory testing, provider- and client-initiated voluntary testing and counselling, family testing, and self-testing) have generated a whole host of concerns. While the move from mandatory to voluntary testing was welcomed by the human rights community, the promotion of provider-initiated approaches initially met significant resistance (Bayer & Edington, 2009). It was first launched as a way to increase global coverage of HIV testing and counselling. However, it was being introduced in environments where laws and policies did not always guarantee human rights protections. In particular, the human rights community highlighted the need to ensure informed consent, privacy, confidentiality, and subsequent protections against discrimination based on HIV status (UNAIDS, 2009).

Growing evidence on the effectiveness of ART in reducing HIV transmission has paved the way for treatment as a form of prevention (WHO, 2012d). This raises a range of ethical and human rights issues, particularly in settings where people in need of ART for their own health lack access to treatment. How to maximize on this new scientific success without increasing inequities, how to move from HIV 'exceptionalism' without compromising HIV gains and momentum, and how to build a supportive and enabling environment consistent with human rights, are at the top of the HIV agenda today. A growing number of bilateral and multilateral development actors have recognized this challenge and have adopted strategies and policies which include human rights as part of their strategic objectives. This reinforces the aid effectiveness agenda which is about ensuring national ownership and alignment with national priorities (OECD, 2005), including health-related human rights as enshrined in national legislation and constitutional provisions. National health sector plans and strategies are considered the roadmap for the realization of the right to health under which programmes aimed at tackling HIV, TB, and malaria must be aligned.

TB and human rights

There were 8.8 million new cases of TB and 1.4 million deaths caused by TB in 2010 (WHO, 2011b). Over 25% of HIV deaths are attributable to TB (WHO, 2011b). Although TB occurs in every part of the world, over 95% of cases are in developing countries (WHO, 2012e). Risk of TB infection and disease is associated with lack of enjoyment of a range of civil, cultural, economic, political, and social rights (Stop TB Partnership, 2011; UNAIDS Reference Group on HIV and Human Rights, 2010; WHO, 2005a, 2011c). Historically, the link between TB and poverty at the societal, community, and patient level has been well established (WHO, 2005a). People who face overcrowding, poor ventilation, inadequate sanitation, and poverty or low income are more vulnerable to TB infection and disease (UNAIDS Reference Group on HIV and Human Rights, 2010; WHO, 2005a). Rapid urbanization and migration has led to higher TB incidence in urban areas that are characterized by high population density, crowded living and working conditions, as well as lifestyle changes such as smoking, high alcohol consumption, and substance abuse (Lonnroth et al., 2009). Also at risk are persons who are undernourished, persons with immune-compromising illnesses such as HIV/AIDS or diabetes, or vulnerable groups facing marginalization and deprivation (Lonnroth et al., 2010).

Conversely, falling ill with TB or facing TB in the family, can lead to impoverishment, for example, due to loss of employment (WHO, 2005a). The direct and indirect costs of seeking diagnosis and care can also lead to catastrophic expenses (Hanson et al., 2006). Moreover, those individuals and groups at risk for TB can face other challenges in accessing high-quality TB care: while TB medicines and follow-up visits are free of charge in most countries, the diagnostic process can be costly, due to delays in referral for testing, charging for tests, and indirect costs of returning for results (Hanson et al., 2006). This is also highly relevant in the context of the recent political push for universal coverage which aims to ensure that 'all people have access to services and do not suffer financial hardship paying for them' (Resolution WHA58.33, 2005). By helping to overcome financial barriers to access health services, universal coverage can be an important building block towards the realization of every person's right to health. Marginalized populations, such as migrants, indigenous populations, women in some settings, and intravenous drug users often face legal, social, and cultural barriers to accessing and fully utilizing TB treatment and care, including stigma and lack of information (UNAIDS, 2010). Prisoners and other persons in detention often face high relative risks of TB infection and illness (Baussano et al., 2010). The European Court of Human Rights has gone as far as linking prison conditions and exposure to TB to a breach of Article 3 (freedom from torture, inhuman or degrading treatment, or punishment) of the European Convention on Human Rights.

TB, social mobilization, and conflicts of rights

Building on progress in the HIV community, social mobilization efforts have increased among communities affected by TB. The *Patients' Charter for Tuberculosis Care*, which was developed by TB patients from around the world, has been endorsed by the WHO and is a subcomponent of the recommended Stop TB Strategy (WHO, 2007). It is designed to address the interlinked rights and responsibilities of TB patients (World Care Council, 2006). The charter enumerates rights and responsibilities of patients and the community in relation to care, dignity, information, choice, confidence, justice, organization, and security, and solidarity. It underscores the link between the human rights of individuals and the public health responsibilities of the community. Importantly, it supports the development of a mutually beneficial relationship between patients and healthcare providers by empowering TB patients and their communities through knowledge. It is meant to be adapted for use at country, local, and institutional levels. For example, one of the six strategic action points of Nepal's National Tuberculosis Center is to empower communities and people with TB in accordance with the rights and responsibilities established in the Charter (Government of Nepal, 2011). Still, scaled-up use has not yet been documented (WHO, 2011b).

There has been growing concern regarding multi-drug resistant (MDR) TB and extensively drug resistant (XDR) TB. In response to public fears, even sometimes before developing appropriate diagnostic, care, and infection control practices, several countries have adopted controversial policies and/or legislation enabling the involuntary hospitalization and/or isolation of persons with suspected or known drug-resistant disease (WHO, 2007). The Siracusa Principles lay out limited circumstances when limitations on personal freedom may be justified, including public health grounds, but also require that certain conditions are met: the rights restriction is provided for and carried out in accordance with the law, is in the interest of a legitimate objective or general interest, and is strictly necessary in a democratic society to achieve the objective; there are no less intrusive and restrictive means available to reach the same objective; and the restriction is based on scientific evidence and not drafted or imposed arbitrarily (UNCHR, 1984). The WHO and others have noted that grounds invoked to restrict individual liberty are rarely justified. There are other means to reduce the risk of infection in the community through varying approaches to early diagnosis and ambulatory care, to enable patients to take their treatment. There is also a duty to ensure infection control in any hospital or other setting, and fulfilling this duty can be challenging (WHO, 2007). New diagnostics and support for community-based care models as well as novel strategies to increase early TB diagnosis and appropriate care in and/or close to the home are opening up new means to better fulfil the rights to prevention from illness, to healthcare and to elimination of the stigma and discrimination that can come with disease.

The WHO, the Stop TB Partnership, and the Joint United Nations Programme on HIV/AIDS (UNAIDS) are coordinating a Stop TB Partnership Task Force on TB and Human Rights with a range of partner agencies including the Office of the UN High Commissioner for Human Rights (OHCHR), the Global Fund to Fight AIDS, Malaria, and Tuberculosis (Global Fund), and constituencies representing affected communities and groups and human rights expertise (WHO, 2012f). The group is developing policy guidance for a human rights-based approach to TB prevention, care, and control—building on the principles of participation and empowerment of those affected, access to care, legal and policy enablers, and engaging with development and rights agendas. The approach combines lessons learnt from HIV and also from a long evolution of large-scale TB prevention and treatment practice and adaptation in different settings and the momentum of new resources and tools brought to the fight against TB.

A human rights framework cannot only help to strengthen health advocacy and social mobilization in a specific disease area, but it also provides activists and advocates and civil society representatives with a common set of vocabulary based on universally accepted legal norms that can strengthen advocacy and awareness-raising activities. This does not necessarily need to be limited to collaboration between HIV and TB but can also be expanded to other major health challenges such as malaria. There is a major opportunity for different disease communities to inform each other on their best practices and problem-solving in adopting a human rights-based approach, as well as to interact further with human rights advocates. The Global Fund has laid out the promotion and protection of human rights as the fourth of its five elements of its strategy framework for 2012–2016, entitled 'Investing for Impact' (The Global Fund, 2012a). The Global Fund, stimulated by the strong constituency of affected communities/civil society represented in its Board, is working with disease partnerships, UNAIDS, the WHO, the United Nations Development Programme (UNDP), and others to develop associated tools to fulfil the promise of the strategy in its grant-making, support, and monitoring.

Malaria: making explicit the link with human rights

More than half of the world's population is at risk of malaria (WHO, 2012g), which is endemic in 99 countries. In 2010, there were an estimated 216 million cases of malaria (uncertainty interval: 149–274 million) and 655,000 malaria deaths (uncertainty interval: 537,000–907,000) (WHO, 2011d). Children, pregnant women, and those with compromised immune systems, such as people living with HIV/AIDS, are especially vulnerable to malaria (WHO, 2012g). Over 80% of malaria cases and 90% of malaria deaths occur in tropical sub-Saharan Africa (Hay et al., 2004). In an 'unmistakable correlation' with lower per capita gross domestic product (Sachs & Malaney, 2002), 58% of all malaria deaths occur among the poorest 20% of the global population (Barat et al., 2004). Eighty-six per cent of malaria deaths globally in 2010 were among children under five years of age (WHO, 2011d), and an estimated 10,000 pregnant women and 200,000 newborn babies die annually due to malaria during pregnancy (Dellicour et al., 2010).

Looking at malaria through a human rights lens highlights the linkages between health and the rights to housing, food, water, and sanitation, which play a central role in the disease's incidence. Adequate living conditions also include access to nutritious food, safe water, and sanitation (ICESCR, 1966; UN General Assembly, 1948). Without access to adequate food and nutrition, the health consequences of the destruction of red blood cells by malarial parasites are greatly exacerbated (Latham, 2007). While malaria may contribute directly and indirectly to malnutrition, malnutrition in turn has been found to be a separate and fundamental contributing factor to malarial morbidity and anaemia in children (Ehrhardt et al., 2006). Addressing the right to adequate food may play a pivotal role in reducing malaria-associated morbidity in children (Ehrhardt et al., 2006). The right to safe and potable water and adequate sanitation is also central due to the correlations between waterborne parasitic diseases and malarial mortality. Studies in Africa and Asia have demonstrated that malnutrition caused by parasitic worm infections in children is positively linked to malarial morbidity and mortality (Druilhe et al., 2005). As a result, treating such infections has been demonstrated to improve the health outcomes of children with malaria (Druilhe et al., 2005). The fact that some studies have demonstrated improved malarial clinical outcomes for children infected with parasitic worms points to the need to deliver integrated disease control programmes at community level (Brutus et al., 2006). Addressing the right to water and sanitation thus has the potential to improve the disease impact of malaria, especially in children. The right to adequate housing also plays an important role in the success of antimalarial interventions. In studies in Eritrea, the incidence of malaria significantly increased in people living in mud-walled houses (Sintasath et al., 2005). Studies have concluded that these mud-walls resulted in a low adherence of the insecticides used for indoor residual spraying against malaria, while the poor construction of the homes made it easier for mosquitoes to have access to sleeping quarters (Brentlinger, 2006).

The rights of migrants, refugees, and internally displaced persons also play an important role in reducing malaria-related morbidity and mortality. Groups that are particularly vulnerable to and at risk of malaria include those that have been forced to move for reasons such as conflict and humanitarian emergencies, environmental degradation, natural disasters, and poverty (WHO, 2005b). Increased malarial incidence among displaced persons has been demonstrated in a number of cases. In the 1980s, Afghan refugees in Pakistan were located in refugee camps sited on marginal land adjacent to rice-fields and water-logged farmland (Rowland & Nosten, 2001). Due to a highly successful malarial intervention programme in Afghanistan prior to the conflict, the refugees had no malarial immunity upon arrival (Suleman, 1988), and as a result, malaria rapidly became a health concern with over 150,000 cases diagnosed and treated each year. The circumstances leading to displacement, such as conflict or humanitarian crises, often make implementation of antimalarial strategies particularly difficult.

The inherent link between the right to housing and the right to life has been raised in connection to a recent case in front of the African Commission on Human and Peoples' Rights. In December 2008, the Social and Economic Rights Action Center filed a communication against the government of Nigeria (Social and Economic Rights Action Center, 2008). While as of June 2012, the Commission had not yet made a determination, the grounds upon which the communication was made provide insight into the interconnections between socioeconomic rights and malaria. In 1990, the government of Nigeria allegedly evicted 300,000 residents of the Maroko community from their homes, demolishing residential, medical, community, business, and education buildings. Eighteen years later, the government had not yet provided adequate resettlement or assistance to remedy the extreme state of poverty the Maroko residents were now living in. Out of the 300,000 Maroko evictees, only 3,000 property owners were provided with housing allotments by the government. These allotments either had no housing, or were uninhabitable, lacking electricity, toilets, potable water, as well as windows and roofs. The communication alleges multiple breaches of the African Charter on Human and Peoples' Rights, including the right to housing and the right to life (Organization of African Unity, 1981). Under the jurisprudence of the Commission, the right to life is violated not only by intentional deprivation, but also by subjecting individuals to conditions that will predictably lead to their deaths (Malawi African Association Communications, 2000; Social and Economic Rights Action Center, 2001). The communication alleges that the living conditions to which the Maroko evictees were exposed will predictably lead to their deaths through diseases such as malaria. It alleges express breaches of the right to health under Article 16 of the African Charter by destroying medical facilities upon which the Maroko community relied, failing to remedy the disease-ridden living conditions in which the homeless Maroko evictees were forced to live, and for those that were resettled, resettling them in areas prone to flooding and disease such as malaria. The Commission has held that Article 16 of the African Charter also imposes a positive obligation on governments to provide the basic essentials for health, such as safe drinking water, electricity, and medicines (Social and Economic Rights Action Center, 2001). In addition to these rights expressly connected with health, socioeconomic rights, such as the right to housing, clearly play an important role in the realisation of the right to health in the context of malaria.

Population groups such as displaced persons that are already marginalized, may be further ostracized by singling them out as 'cause' of disease outbreaks, as was seen with the Afghan refugees in Pakistan who were incorrectly blamed for 'bringing' malaria to Pakistan (Rowland & Nosten, 2001). The tendency to relegate population groups that are already marginalized due to circumstance can have detrimental effects on public health outcomes, as has also been seen in HIV/AIDS and TB strategies. An essential element of a human rights-based approach is to empower those that have been marginalized. In this context, it is impossible to ignore that malaria has not yet experienced the same empowerment movements as seen with HIV and TB. This may be due to the fact that malaria is limited to certain geographical regions, rather than a global concern, or that affected communities have been less organized than, for example, lesbian, gay, bisexual, and transgender communities at the start of the HIV epidemic. Or it could be due to the transmission of malaria via a mosquito vector, rather than human-to-human transmission.

The interdependence of the rights to education and health is clear in relation to education and cultural acceptability for malaria control and elimination. In Laos, school education programmes on malaria control have been shown to significantly increase community-wide understanding and knowledge regarding the control of malaria (Nonaka et al., 2008). Information accessibility also requires acknowledgement of limited literacy, commonly experienced in malaria endemic areas, requiring innovative educational strategies. In rural India, community theatre has been successful in communicating local solutions for bio-environmental control, enabling community-based problem solving, such as releasing mosquito-larvae eating fish into water sources, rather than indoor residual spraying with DDT (dichlorodiphenyltrichloroethane), which had previously raised agricultural and economic concerns in the local silk industry (Ghosh et al., 2006). Studies have noted the impact of local customs on the use of bed-nets. While previously considered only anecdotal, a study in Kenya found that local villagers chose to use their nets for fishing, rather than malaria protection, due to the perceived relative importance of food (Minakawa et al., 2008). Similarly, a study undertaken in Burkina Faso found that communities were not using bed-nets during the dry season due to a perceived decreased risk of mosquitoes and the cultural practice of sleeping outdoors (Frey et al., 2006). Empowering communities through education with the correct information on the use and purpose of bed-nets is essential to the success of antimalarial intervention programmes. In Ghana, some observers have warned about superstition about sleeping under white-coloured bed-nets by communities who claim to see ghosts or shadows standing over them when they sleep (Addul-Rahaman, 2009). Aside from education, another more culturally acceptable option might be the provision of bed-nets in colours other than white, based on consultations with the communities themselves. Acknowledgement and consideration of cultural sensitivities can lead to innovative approaches to acceptability of health treatment, and in turn, may provide much more efficient and effective solutions than education alone. The right to participation, which requires affected communities to be actively involved in health-related decision-making at the community, national, and international levels, is integral to the right to health (CESCR, 2000). Moreover, community participation in the management of malaria has shown to be effective in reducing morbidity and mortality (WHO et al., 2012). Examples of the successes of community empowerment for malarial interventions include volunteer collaborator programmes in Latin America (Guatemala) (Ruebush & Godoy, 1992), community-based control programmes in the Andean Region (Global Fund, 2012b), and *Salud Mesoámérica 2015*, which finances projects to reduce health inequities affecting the poorest 20% of the Central American population (Inter-American Development Bank, 2010).

Conclusion

Applying a human rights-based approach to HIV, TB, and malaria can be a powerful means to advance towards 2015 Millennium Development Goal targets and beyond, offering 'a dramatic way to challenge the status quo and the prevailing patterns of discrimination and prejudice'

(Crewe, 2009). In order to effectively combat HIV, TB, and malaria, we must move beyond clinical and public health interventions and address the underlying determinants of health, including health-related rights such as non-discrimination and participation. This chapter has illustrated that human rights are inherently linked to good public health practice. HIV has in many ways been a forerunner in forging the relationship between health and human rights, including highlighting the vulnerabilities and risks faced by specific groups. With scientific progress and new effectiveness of treatment, there is now an opportunity to move away from HIV 'exceptionalism' while maintaining the momentum for action.

While the history of TB has demonstrated that efforts to control its spread depend much more on the enjoyment of the right to an adequate standard of living than on specific medical interventions, the explicit use of human rights in the TB agenda is fairly recent. Collaboration across HIV and TB communities has created new ways of mobilizing communities and demanding and informing action. For the first time in decades, there are new diagnostic and treatment tools and approaches for malaria, TB, and HIV that can make a dramatic difference in early identification of those affected, increasing prevention and expanding early and effective treatment. But with limited resources, such new tools are in short supply and vulnerable and marginalized communities and groups may be among the last to receive support, despite their burden of disease, unless rights-based approaches to expanding access are adopted early as these tools become available. Monitoring of access and use is critical to ensure that such approaches fulfil their potential to drive down disease, especially for those most at risk of poor health outcomes.

Human rights mainstreaming is high on the agenda in the context of the recent reform of the WHO (Bustreo, 2012), and human rights are increasingly being included in WHO strategy papers in specific health areas, including, for example, the WHO Global Health Sector Strategy on HIV/AIDS and the ongoing work of the Stop TB Partnership taskforce on TB and human rights on a human rights-based approach on TB (WHO, 2012h). More recently, WHO Director-General Margaret Chan has called for universal coverage as 'the single most powerful concept that public health has to offer' (Chan, 2012). The growing political momentum for universal coverage as a central vehicle towards the realization of the right to health provides another welcome push for enhancing access to prevention, treatment, and care for HIV, TB, and malaria (World Health Assembly, 2005). This overarching political support for universal coverage and human rights will help ensure that existing and underlying structural barriers continue to be addressed; including promoting the adoption of policies, practices, and laws that protect human rights and eliminate discrimination in the health and related development sectors. Human rights-based approaches result in not only good public health but also are underpinned by international legal obligations that must be respected, protected, and fulfilled. Cooperation between the human rights and disease communities will be essential in order to learn from each other and build upon past achievements. Together, they can generate stronger leadership from governments and international organizations to scale up action to address HIV, TB, and malaria.

Note and acknowledgement

The authors are staff members of the World Health Organization (WHO). The authors alone are responsible for the views expressed in this publication and they do not necessarily represent the decisions, policy, or views of the WHO. The authors would like to thank Jaime Cardy, Josefin Mattsson, and Alexandra Phelan who, at the time of this writing, were health and human rights interns at the WHO.

References

Addul-Rahaman, S. (2009). *When Bednets Become Coffins*. Available at: <http://www.eyesonmalaria.org/thirdstories/whenbednetbecomecoffins.html> (accessed 22 June 2012).

AVERT. (2011a). *Sex Workers and HIV Prevention*. AVERT: West Sussex, England. Available at: <http://www.avert.org/sex-workers.htm> (accessed 28 June 2012).

AVERT. (2011b). *Injecting Drugs, Drug Users, HIV & AIDS*. AVERT: West Sussex, England. Available at: <http://www.avert.org/injecting.htm> (accessed 25 June 2012).

Barat, L.M., Palmer, N., Basu, S., *et al.* (2004). Do malaria control interventions reach the poor? A view through the equity lens. *American Journal of Tropical Medicine and Hygiene*, 71, 174–178.

Baussano, I., Williams, B.G., Nunn, P., *et al.* (2010). Tuberculosis incidence in prisons: a systematic review. *PLoS Medicine*, 7, 1–10.

Bayer, R. and Edington, C. (2009). HIV testing, human rights, and global AIDS policy: exceptionalism and its discontents. *Journal of Health Politics, Policy and Law*, 34, 301–323.

Biehl, J., Amon, J.J., Socal, M.P., *et al.* (2009). Judicialisation of the right to health in Brazil. *Lancet*, 373, 2182–2184.

Brentlinger, P.E. (2006). Health, human rights, and malaria control: historical background and current challenges. *Health and Human Rights*, 9, 10–38.

Brutus, L., Watier, L., Briand V., *et al.* (2006). Parasitic co-infections: does *Ascaris lumbricoides* protect against *Plasmodium falciparum* infection? *American Journal of Tropical Medicine and Hygiene*, 75, 194–198.

Bustreo, F. (2012). *Statement by the World Health Organization: the 19th Session of the UN Human Rights Council*, 28 February, Geneva, Switzerland.

Cameron, S. and Reynolds, L. (2010). *Global Criminalisation Scan Report*. Global Network of People Living with HIV: Amsterdam.

CESCR. (2000). *General Comment 14: The Right to the Highest Attainable Standard of Health (Article 12 of the International Covenant on Economic, Social and Cultural Rights)*. Committee on Economic, Social and Cultural Rights (CESCR): Geneva.

Chan, M. (2012). *Universal Coverage is the Ultimate Expression of Fairness*. Acceptance speech at the Sixty-fifth World Health Assembly, 23 May, Geneva, Switzerland.

Crago, A.L., Rakhmetova, A., and Shields, A. (2010). The police beat you up, demand money and will detain you until you pay—police violence against sex workers in eleven countries in Europe and Central Asia. *Research for Sex Workers*, 12, 3–5.

Crewe, M. (2009). The HIV/AIDS epidemic and human rights responses. In A. Clapham and M. Robinson (Eds.), *Swiss Human Rights Book, Volume 3: Realizing the Right to Health*, pp. 277–286. Rüffer & Rub: Zurich.

Dellicour, S., Tatem, A.J., Guerra, C.A., *et al.* (2010). Quantifying the number of pregnancies at risk of malaria in 2007: a demographic study. *PLoS Medicine*, 7, 1–10.

Druilhe, P., Tall, A., and Sokhna, C. (2005). Worms can worsen malaria: towards a new means to roll back malaria? *Trends in Parasitology*, 21, 359–362.

Eba, P. (2008). *One Size Punishes All: A Critical Appraisal of the Criminalization of HIV Transmission*. AIDS Legal Network: Cape Town.

Ehrhardt, S., Burchard, G., Mantel, C., *et al.* (2006). Malaria, anemia, and malnutrition in African children—defining intervention priorities. *Journal of Infectious Diseases*, 194, 108–114.

Frey, C., Traore, C., De Allegri, M., *et al.* (2006). Compliance of young children with ITN protection in rural Burkina Faso. *Malaria Journal*, 5, 70–75.

Ghosh, S.K., Patil, R.R., Tiwari, S., *et al.* (2006). A community-based health education programme for bio-environmental control of malaria through folk theatre (*Kalajatha*) in rural India. *Malaria Journal*, 5, 123–128.

Global Commission on HIV and the Law. (2012). *HIV and the Law: Risks, Rights and Health*. Available at: <http://www.hivlawcommission.org/> (accessed 13 August 2012).

Global Fund. (2012a). *The Global Fund Strategy 2012-2016: Investing for Impact*. Global Fund to Fight AIDS, Malaria and Tuberculosis (Global Fund): Geneva. Available at: <http://www.theglobalfund.org/en/about/strategy/> (accessed 7 October).

Global Fund. (2012b). *Grant Summary: Malaria Control on the Cross Border Areas of the Andean Region: A Community-Based Approach*. Global Fund to Fight AIDS, Malaria and Tuberculosis (Global Fund): Geneva. Available at: <http://portfolio.theglobalfund.org/en/Grant/Index/MAA-305-G01-M> (accessed 19 July 2012).

Golenski, J., and Lo, B. (1990). *AIDS, Privacy and the Community: Ethics of Mandatory AIDS Testing and Disclosure*. Available at: <http://www.scu.edu/ethics/publications/iie/v3n3/AIDS.html> (accessed 7 November 2012).

Gostin, L. (2009). HIV screening in health care settings: public health and civil liberties in conflict? *Public Health*, 123, 260–264.

Government of Nepal. (2011). *National Tuberculosis Center Strategy*. Available at: <http://nepalntp.gov.np/> (accessed 22 June 2012).

Grover, A. (2010). *Report of the UN Special Rapporteur on the Right of Everyone to the Enjoyment of the Highest Attainable Standard of Physical and Mental Health: A/HRC/14/20*. United Nations: New York, NY.

Grover, A. (2011). *Report of the UN Special Rapporteur on the Right of Everyone to the Enjoyment of the Highest Attainable Standard of Physical and Mental Health – Expert Consultation on Access to Medicines as a Fundamental Component of the Right to Health*. A/HRC/17/43. United Nations Human Rights Council: Geneva.

Hanson, C.L., Weil, D.E.C., and Floyd, K. (2006). Tuberculosis in the poverty alleviation agenda. In Raviglione MC (Ed.), *Reichman and Hershfield's Tuberculosis: A Comprehensive, International Approach (Lung Biology in Health and Disease), Volume 219*, pp. 1097–1114. Informa Healthcare USA: New York, NY.

Hay, S.I., Guerra, C.A., Tatem, A.L., *et al.* (2004). The global distribution and population at risk of malaria: past, present and future. *Lancet: Infectious Diseases*, 4, 327–336.

ICESCR. (1966). *International Covenant on Economic, Social and Cultural Rights, Art. 11(2), 993 UNTS 3*. International Covenant on Economic, Social and Cultural Rights (ICESCR): Geneva.

Inter-American Development Bank. (2010). *Bill & Melinda Gates Foundation, Carlos Slim Health Institute, Spain, and the IDB Collaborate to Improve the Health of the Poor in Mesoamerica*. Available at: <http://www.iadb.org/en/news/news-releases/2010-06-14/salud-mesoamerica-2015-initiative-launched-idb,7317.html> (accessed 13 August 2012).

Latham, M.C. (2007). Global action against worm infections, measles and malaria. In G. Kent (Ed.), *Global Obligations of the Right to Food*, pp. 145–149. Rowman and Littlefield: Lanham, MD.

Lonnroth, K., Castro, K.G., Chakaya, J.M., *et al.* (2010). Tuberculosis control and elimination 2010–50: cure, care and social development. *Lancet*, 375, 1814–1829.

Lonnroth, K., Jaramillo, E., Williams, B.G., *et al.* (2009). Drivers of tuberculosis epidemics: the role of risk factors and social determinants. *Social Science & Medicine*, 68, 2240–2246.

Malawi African Association Communications. (2000). *13th Annual Activity Report of the African Commission on Human and Peoples' Rights*, 54/91, 61/91, 98/93, 164-96/97 and 210/98, 120. African Commission on Human and Peoples' Rights: Banjul.

Mann, J.M. (1989). AIDS: a worldwide pandemic. In M.S. Gottlieb, D.J. Jeffries, D. Mildvan, *et al.* (Eds.), *Current topics in AIDS, Volume 2*, pp. 1–10. John Wiley & Sons: Chichester.

Mann, J.M., Grodin, M.A., Gruskin, S., *et al.* (1999). *Health and Human Rights: A Reader*. Routledge: New York, NY.

Minakawa, N., Dida, G.O., Sonye, G.O., *et al.* (2008). Unforeseen misuses of bed nets in fishing villages along Lake Victoria. *Malaria Journal*, 7, 165–168.

Minister of Health v. *Treatment Action Campaign*. (2002). 5 SA 721 (CC).

Moody, K. (2009). Ensuring human and sexual rights for men who have sex with men living with HIV. *Bulletin of the World Health Organization*, 87, 875–876.

Nonaka, D., Kobayashi, J., Jimba, M., *et al.* (2008). Malaria education from school to community in Oudomxay province, Lao PDR. *Parasitology International*, 57, 76–82.

OECD. (2005). *Paris Declaration on Aid Effectiveness*. Organization for Economic Cooperation and Development (OECD): Paris, France. Available at: <http://www.oecd.org/development/aideffectiveness/34428351.pdf> (accessed 8 October 2012).

Organization of African Unity. (1981). *African Charter on Human and Peoples' Rights ('Banjul Charter')*. Available at: <http://www.unhcr.org/refworld/docid/3ae6b3630.html> (accessed 14 August 2012).

Paris Declaration. (1994). Adopted 1 December 1994 by the Paris AIDS Summit of the European Coalition of Positive People.

Piot, P., Timberlake, S., and Sigurdson, J. (2009). Governance and the response to AIDS: lessons for development and human rights. In A. Clapham and M. Robinson (Eds.), *Swiss Human Rights Book, Volume 3: Realizing the Right to Health*, pp. 331–569. Rüffer & Rub: Zurich.

Rowland, M. and Nosten, F. (2001). Malaria epidemiology and control in refugee camps and complex emergencies. *Annals of Tropical Medicine and Parasitology*, 95, 741–754.

Ruebush II, T.K. and Godoy, H.A. (1992). Community participation in malaria surveillance and treatment: The Volunteer Collaborator Network of Guatemala. *American Journal of Tropical Medicine and Hygiene*, 46, 261–271.

Sachs, J. and Malaney, P. (2002). The economic and social burden of malaria. *Nature*, 415, 680–685.

Sintasath, D.M., Ghebremeskel, T., Lynch, M., *et al.* (2005). Malaria prevalence and associated risk factors in Eritrea. *American Journal of Tropical Medicine and Hygiene*, 72, 682–687.

Social and Economic Rights Action Center. (2001). *Center for Economic and Social Rights* v. *Nigeria*. Communication 155/96, 15th Annual Activity Report of the African Commission on Human and Peoples' Rights (the Ogoni Case). ACHPR: Banjul.

Social and Economic Rights Action Center. (2008). *Social and Economic Rights Action Center v. Nigeria*. Communication to the African Commission on Human and Peoples' Rights, Lagos, Nigeria, 3 December 2008. Available at: <http://www.serac.org/Pages.asp?id=301> (accessed 22 June 2012).

Stop TB Partnership. (2011). *TB and Human Rights*. Stop TB Partnership: Geneva. Available at: <http://www.stoptb.org/assets/documents/global/hrtf/Briefing%20note%20on%20TB%20and%20Human%20Rights.pdf> (accessed June 2012).

Suleman, M. (1988). Malaria in Afghan refugees in Pakistan. *Transactions of the Royal Society of Tropical Medicine and Hygiene*, 82, 44–47.

Sweden Discrimination Act. (2008). Swedish Code of Statutes SFS, 25 June 2008: 567, Chapter 2, Section 13.

'T Hoen, E. (2003). TRIPS, pharmaceutical patents and access to essential medicines: Seattle, Doha and beyond. In J.P. Moatti, B. Coriat, Y. Souteyrand, *et al.* (Eds.), *Economics of AIDS and Access to HIV/AIDS Care in Developing Countries, Issues and Challenges (ANRS)*, pp. 39–67. ANRS: Paris.

UNAIDS. (2002). *Sex Work and HIV/AIDS: UNAIDS Technical Update*. Joint United Nations Programme on HIV/AIDS (UNAIDS): Geneva.

UNAIDS. (2007). *The Greater Involvement of People living with HIV/AIDS (GIPA)*. Joint United Nations Programme on HIV/AIDS (UNAIDS): Geneva. Available at: <http://data.unaids.org/pub/BriefingNote/2007/jc1299_policy_brief_gipa.pdf> (accessed 22 June 2012).

UNAIDS. (2008). *Criminalization and HIV Transmission: Policy Brief*. Joint United Nations Programme on HIV/AIDS (UNAIDS): Geneva. Available at: <http://data.unaids.org/pub/basedocument/2008/20080731_jc1513_policy_criminalization_en.pdf> (accessed 22 June 2012).

UNAIDS. (2009). *Reference Group on HIV and Human Rights: Statement and Recommendations on Scaling Up HIV Testing and Counseling*. Joint United Nations Programme on HIV/AIDS (UNAIDS): Geneva. Available at: <http://data.unaids.org/pub/ExternalDocument/2007/20070905_rghr_statement_testing_en.pdf> (accessed 5 October 2012).

UNAIDS. (2012). *Together We Will End AIDS.* Joint United Nations Programme on HIV/AIDS (UNAIDS): Geneva.

UNAIDS Reference Group on HIV and Human Rights. (2010). *HIV and Tuberculosis: Ensuring Universal Access and Protection of Human Rights.* Joint United Nations Programme on HIV/AIDS (UNAIDS): Geneva.

UN General Assembly. (1948). *Universal Declaration of Human Rights.* Adopted by the UN General Assembly, 217 A(III), 10 December 1948, article 25. UN General Assembly: Paris.

UNHCHR. (2001). *Access to Medication in the Context of Pandemics Such as HIV/AIDS: Commission on Human Rights Resolution 2001/33.* United Nations High Commissioner for Human Rights (UNHCHR): Geneva.

UNCHR. (1984). *Siracusa Principles on the Limitation and Derogation Provisions in the International Covenant on Civil and Political Rights.* Adopted by the UN Commission on Human Rights, U.N. Doc. E/CN.4/1985/4 (annex), 28 September 1984.

United Kingdom Equality Act. (2010). *Equality Act 2010.* Available at: <http://www.legislation.gov.uk/ukpga/2010/15/introduction> (accessed 13 August 2012).

World Care Council. (2006). *The Patients' Charter for Tuberculosis Care: Patients' Rights and Responsibilities.* Available at: <http://www.who.int/entity/tb/publications/2006/patients_charter.pdf> (accessed 22 June 2012).

World Health Assembly. (1988). *Avoidance of Discrimination against HIV-Infected Persons and Persons with AIDS.* Adopted by the World Health Assembly at its 41st meeting, on 13 May 1988, Resolution 41.24. World Health Assembly (WHA): Geneva.

World Health Assembly. (2005). *Sustainable Health Financing, Universal Coverage and Social Health Insurance.* Adopted by the World Health Assembly at its 58th meeting, on 16–25 May 2005, Resolution WHA 58.33. World Health Assembly (WHA): Geneva.

WHO. (2005a). *Addressing Poverty in TB Control: Options for National TB Control Programmes.* World Health Organization (WHO): Geneva.

WHO. (2005b). *Malaria Control in Complex Emergencies: An Inter-Agency Field Handbook.* World Health Organization (WHO): Geneva.

WHO. (2007). *WHO Guidance on Human Rights and Involuntary Detention for XDR-TB Control.* World Health Organization (WHO): Geneva. Available at: <http://www.who.int/tb/features_archive/involuntary_treatment/en/> (accessed 22 June 2012).

WHO. (2011a). *Prevention and Treatment of HIV and Other Sexually Transmitted Infections Among Men Who Have Sex With Men and Transgender People: Recommendations For a Public Health Approach 2011.* World Health Organization (WHO): Geneva.

WHO. (2011b). *Report on Global TB Control.* World Health Organization (WHO): Geneva.

WHO. (2011c). *Ethical Issues in TB Prevention, Care and Control.* World Health Organization (WHO): Geneva.

WHO. (2011d). *World Malaria Report 2011.* World Health Organization (WHO): Geneva.

WHO. (2012a). *Scaling-up HIV Services for Men who have Sex with Men and Transgender People: New Public Health Approaches Aim to Reduce the Spread of HIV and Save Lives of Men who have sex with Men and Transgender People.* World Health Organization (WHO): Geneva. Available at: <http://www.who.int/mediacentre/news/releases/2011/hiv_20110621/en/> (accessed 30 June 2012).

WHO. (2012b). *The Public Health Rationale for HIV Interventions in Sex Work Settings.* World Health Organization (WHO): Geneva. Available at: <http://www.who.int/hiv/topics/vct/sw_toolkit/context/en/index.html> (accessed 28 June 2012).

WHO. (2012c). *Access to Essential Medicines as Part of the Right to Health.* World Health Organization (WHO): Geneva. Available at: <http://www.who.int/medicines/areas/human_rights/en/index.html> (accessed 5 October 2012).

WHO. (2012d). *The Strategic Use of Antiretrovirals to Help End the HIV Epidemic.* World Health Organization (WHO): Geneva.

WHO. (2012e). *Tuberculosis: Fact Sheet No. 104*. World Health Organization (WHO): Geneva. Available at: <http://www.who.int/mediacentre/factsheets/fs104/en/> (accessed 22 June 2012).

WHO. (2012f). *TB and Human Rights Task Force*. World Health Organization (WHO): Geneva. Available at: <http://www.stoptb.org/global/HRTF> (accessed 13 July 2012).

WHO. (2012g). *Malaria: Fact Sheet No. 94*. World Health Organization (WHO): Geneva. Available at: <http://www.who.int/mediacentre/factsheets/fs094/en/index.html> (accessed 22 June 2012).

WHO. (2012h). *Working Document on TB and Human Rights*. World Health Organization (WHO): Geneva. Available at: <http://www.stoptb.org/assets/documents/global/hrtf/Briefing%20note%20on%20TB%20and%20Human%20Rights.pdf> (accessed 5 October 2012).

WHO, TDR, and Malaria Eradication Research Agenda (malERA) Initiative. (2012). *Community-based reduction of malaria transmission*. World Health Organization (WHO): Geneva.

WHO, UNAIDS, and UNICEF. (2010). *Toward Universal Access: Scaling Up Priority HIV/AIDS Interventions in the Health Sector, Progress Report 2010*. World Health Organization (WHO): Geneva.

WHO, UNAIDS, and UNICEF. (2011). *Global HIV/AIDS Response Epidemic, Update Health Sector Progress toward Universal Access, Progress Report 2011*. World Health Organization (WHO): Malta.

World Trade Organization (WTO). (2001). *World Trade Organization Declaration on the TRIPS Agreement and Public Health: Adopted by the Doha WTO Ministerial on 14 November 2001*. World Trade Organization (WTO): Geneva.

Chapter 19

Global tobacco control: a vital component of the right to health

Oscar A. Cabrera and Lawrence O. Gostin

Introduction

The end of the 20th century marked a shift in public and political perceptions about tobacco consumption. Litigation in North America exposed the industry's attempts to conceal the harmful effects of tobacco smoking, the deliberate manipulation of nicotine content, and the toxicity of tobacco products. In reaction, developed countries in North America and Western Europe ramped up regulation. Although tobacco consumption still poses a major public health threat in these regions, the tobacco industry's response to increased regulation in developed countries has been to shift its focus to poorer regions in the world—to unexplored markets in Africa, Asia, Eastern Europe, and Latin America (Bollyky & Gostin, 2010; Gostin, 2007a). This strategy has had devastating effects, as these are the world's poorest regions and are ill-equipped either to prevent smoking, or to cope with its major health consequences.

The burden of the tobacco pandemic is not fairly distributed—tobacco consumption rates are much higher among poor communities both within and among States. According to the World Health Organization (WHO), 'it is the poorer and the poorest who tend to smoke the most. Globally, 84% of smokers live in developing and transitional economy countries' (WHO, 2004). These communities also bear most of the disease burden. There is a similar connection between education and tobacco consumption, as those with less education also tend to have considerably higher rates of smoking. Tobacco consumption also has a harmful effect on household income and economic development. Poor smokers spend their scarce household income on tobacco, thus increasing their vulnerability. According to PATH Canada & Work for a Better Bangladesh (2002), 'for the poor, daily spending on tobacco represents a daily drain on scant family resources. Yet in many countries it is precisely the poor who use tobacco the most. In Bangladesh, smoking rates are twice as high in the lowest income group as in the highest'.

Given the tobacco industry's efforts to capture more consumers in developing countries, States need to intervene to protect the human rights of their citizens against the negative effects that these strategies will have on their health, life, and standard of living. Moreover, as the tobacco epidemic disproportionately affects poor people, tobacco control should be a State priority. The United Nations (UN) Independent Expert on Human Rights and Extreme Poverty urged the UN Human Rights Council (UNHRC) to give priority 'to persons living in extreme poverty to ensure that they enjoy their civil and political rights and at the very least a minimum core content of all economic, social and cultural rights' (UNHRC, 2010).

The globalization of the tobacco epidemic has led to intensified tobacco control worldwide. In this context, the WHO used its constitutional power to negotiate a treaty to establish standards for tobacco control regulation. In 2005, the Framework Convention on Tobacco Control (FCTC) entered into force. The FCTC imposes obligations on State Parties in areas such as smoke-free environments, tobacco advertising, promotion and sponsorship, and health warnings. The FCTC plays a central role in linking tobacco control and human rights.

The United Nations has recently joined the global effort to build a stronger connection between tobacco control, non-communicable diseases (NCDs), and human rights. A UN high-level meeting on NCDs took place in September 2011, and the UN General Assembly President concluded that '[the] Public Health Pendulum has swung too far, focusing too much on too few illnesses', and pledged to 'examine options to bolster prevision efforts' (UN General Assembly, 2011). The only other high-level UN summit devoted to a health issue was on HIV/AIDS, which transformed the global response to the HIV pandemic. Advocates hope that the NCD summit meeting will have the same kind of impact. The plan of action seeks to 'achieve a suggested global goal by 2040 of a world essentially free from tobacco where less than 5% of the population uses tobacco' (Beaglehole et al., 2011). This strategy also calls for the immediate implementation of FCTC measures.

In reaction to these global responses to the tobacco pandemic, the tobacco industry has invoked the rhetoric of fundamental rights in resisting effective tobacco control laws and regulations (Jacobson & Soliman, 2002). In this chapter, we demonstrate the weakness and duplicity of the industry's arguments, and argue that tobacco control and human rights are mutually reinforcing. We analyse some of the archetypal arguments the industry raises worldwide to attack tobacco control regulation with an emphasis on smoke-free legislation, and using a human rights-based approach, we conclude that the tobacco control measures enshrined in the FCTC are fully in line with human rights law. By examining emerging trends in tobacco control litigation, we expand the connections between human rights and tobacco control. This chapter does not offer an exhaustive account of the relationship between tobacco control and human rights, but rather focuses on some of the relevant connections.

The first part of this chapter discusses the connection between tobacco control and human rights. It describes human rights obligations, vis-à-vis tobacco control, and examines in closer detail the connection between the FCTC and human rights. It also analyses ways to strengthen the connection between tobacco control and human rights, with a special emphasis on the role human rights can play to monitor and enforce the FCTC. The second part of the chapter critically examines industry arguments against tobacco regulation, while showing how they are flawed from a human rights perspective. We examine recent tobacco control cases that help exemplify this connection between tobacco control and human rights. Finally, in the concluding part of the chapter, we identify new areas of concern in tobacco control and human rights, such as industry arguments based on trade and investment law and connections with intellectual property rights.

The relationship between tobacco control and human rights

Human rights discourse, as applied to tobacco control, needs to move away from a negative/positive rights human rights dichotomy and embrace a classification based on the type of State obligation (respect, protect, or fulfil). This will better clarify the connections between these two fields and will help advance tobacco control through a human rights approach. Drawing connections between the right to health and the FCTC, we argue that the FCTC can inform the concrete content of the right to health. Finally, the human rights system can strengthen monitoring and enforcement of the FCTC.

Respect, protect, fulfil, and tobacco control

Human rights were traditionally classified into two broad categories, negative and positive rights (Alston et al., 2008; Ferrajoli, 2001). According to this classification, civil and political rights were considered negative rights, while economic, social, and cultural rights were seen as positive rights.

Negative rights were understood as imposing obligations on States to refrain from certain conduct (Alston et al., 2008). On the other hand, positive rights require States to affirmatively engage in certain activities, and develop positive measures to comply with human rights obligations, including the expenditure of resources (Alston et al., 2008).

This twofold characterization of human rights is being replaced with a threefold classification that focuses on the type of State obligation and not on the nature of the right; therefore, it applies to civil and political, and economic, social, and cultural rights (Koch, 2005). According to this threefold typology, adopted by the Committee on Economic, Social, and Cultural Rights (CESCR), States have obligations to *respect*, to *protect*, and to *fulfil* all human rights.

The *obligation to respect* requires States to refrain from directly (or indirectly) violating human rights or interfering with their realization. Specific to tobacco control, States must refrain from actively promoting the use of tobacco products (Cabrera & Madrazo, 2010).

Second, the *obligation to protect* requires States to take measures to prevent third parties' interference with human rights. This obligation is essential for developing and expanding a human rights-based approach to tobacco control. Governments have a legal obligation, enshrined in human rights law, to regulate the tobacco industry to prevent the industry from interfering with the right to health and other human rights. For example, governments must ban misleading advertisement of tobacco products (light, mild, etc.) in order to protect the right to health, right to information, and rights of consumers (Cabrera & Madrazo, 2010).

Finally, the *obligation to fulfil* requires governments to adopt all appropriate legislative, administrative, budgetary, and other measures needed for the realization of human rights (Cabrera & Madrazo, 2010). This obligation requires governments to enact comprehensive tobacco control legislation that guarantees the right to health.

The tobacco industry claims that the choice of whether to smoke is a human right and governments should not be allowed to dictate when and where people smoke (Jacobson & Soliman, 2002). The industry uses the mantle of individual choice to rally public opinion against tobacco control laws, often dictating the terms of the debate and putting tobacco control advocates on the defensive (Jacobson & Soliman, 2002).

One effective way to combat these deceitful claims is through socioeconomic rights, particularly the right to health, which are embedded in many younger constitutional democracies, particularly in Africa, Latin America, and Eastern Europe. Moreover, in some countries that do not enshrine socioeconomic rights explicitly in the constitution, courts have interpreted other rights, such as the right to life, to encompass affirmative entitlements, such as the right to health.

While the industry has succeeded in increasing scrutiny of tobacco control laws, the industry itself has largely escaped scrutiny over its own human rights violations (Crow, 2005). The tobacco industry has 'asserted [their] own rights with great success', but an examination of the industry's role in human rights violations exposes major abuses (Crow, 2005). The tobacco industry, although a non-State actor, violates many fundamental rights, such as the right to a healthy workplace, the rights of children, and the rights to health and life.

Recent developments on human rights obligations of non-State actors show that they bear responsibility. For instance, a 2011 UN report stated that the responsibility to respect human rights requires that business enterprises:

> (a) Avoid causing or contributing to adverse human rights impacts through their own activities, and address such impacts when they occur;
>
> (b) Seek to prevent or mitigate adverse human rights impacts that are directly linked to their operations, products or services by their business relationships, even if they have not contributed to those impacts. (UNOHCHR, 2011, Principle 13)

These emerging debates could influence the way in which tobacco control and human rights relate to each other.

In sum, two changes in human rights discourse advances tobacco control. First, human rights jurisprudence has increasingly moved away from the rigid division between negative and positive rights, towards an understanding based on the type and nature of State obligations. Second, the tobacco industry has been able to co-opt human rights language by emphasizing State interference with individual rights. Such strategies put tobacco control advocates on the defensive, requiring them to argue that other rights must be balanced against (and ultimately outweigh) individual rights. Modern tobacco control strategies would be better served by highlighting the responsibility of the State to respect, protect, and fulfil the right to health, right to life, and other related human rights, and by emphasizing the human rights violations perpetrated by the tobacco industry.

The FCTC and human rights

As of November 2012, 176 countries had ratified the FCTC (WHO, 2011b). This means that the FCTC covers approximately 90% of the world's population (Framework Convention Alliance, 2010). The FCTC and its accompanying guidelines, issued by the Conference of the Parties, set forth minimum standards of measures governments must implement to reduce the harmful effects of tobacco products. The FCTC has generated global momentum for increased regulation of tobacco. The process leading to FCTC implementation at the country level has pushed governments and public health groups to better understand the role that law can play in protecting the public's health (O'Neill Institute for National and Global Health, 2012).

The relationship between the FCTC and human rights can be examined from two different perspectives. First, looking at the concrete human rights references and provisions included in the FCTC, we can examine the influence that human rights discourse has on the FCTC. Second, we can examine how the FCTC impacts human rights. The FCTC, as an international treaty, can be used to inform human rights obligations, such as the right to health.

Notably, there are few concrete human rights references in the text of the treaty, besides those in the FCTC's preamble (to Article 12 of the International Covenant on Economic, Social, and Cultural Rights (ICESCR) as well as to the Convention on the Rights of the Child (CRC), and to the Convention on the Elimination of All Forms of Discrimination against Women (CEDAW) (Taylor, 2005). Beyond these non-binding references, the FCTC contains virtually no references to human rights (Taylor, 2005). Despite the lack of human rights language in the FCTC, the treaty can be used to promote human rights in tobacco control if argued creatively.

Human rights provisions in the FCTC

Preamble: 'priority to the right to protect public health'

The use of tobacco products is significantly detrimental to the public's health. In both developed and developing countries, millions of people die every year from tobacco-related diseases, such as lung and throat cancer and cardiovascular disease (Ezzati & Lopez, 2003). Despite this well-known fact, many governments have failed to enact adequate measures to prevent the spread of tobacco consumption. These governments' failures violate their citizens' rights to health and life (Crow, 2005).

Throughout the FCTC, there is an explicit priority to protect the public's health. From the very first line of the FCTC's preamble, the Parties to the Convention assert a determination 'to give priority to their right to protect public health' (WHO, 2003). A central priority of the FCTC is to protect the right to health from third parties that may be endangering that right. When tensions arise between the right to health and other rights or interests, the FCTC prioritizes the protection of public health. One clear example comes from Article 8's protection from exposure to tobacco smoke in public places. By restricting smoking in public locations, the State specifically protects smokers and non-smokers alike from the harm that second-hand smoke represents. Similarly, Article 9 promotes public health rights by requiring the regulation, testing, and monitoring of tobacco products. Such regulations are expected to protect consumers from the product manipulation that the tobacco industry has practised for decades in numerous countries (Cabrera & Madrazo, 2010).

Right to access information

The FCTC places a strong emphasis on the right to access information. Tobacco companies have forcefully advertised and promoted their products. These methods range from deceptive packaging and labelling practices, to sponsoring sports events and music concerts to deliberately targeting children and adolescents, to downplaying the risks of tobacco smoking (Crow, 2005). All of these methods focus on manipulating information about tobacco products, a practice that the FCTC seeks to eliminate.

Several sections of the FCTC protect the right to access information. Article 10 creates an obligation for States to 'adopt and implement effective measures for *public disclosure of information* about the toxic constituents of the tobacco products and the emissions that they may produce' (Emphasis added; WHO, 2003). Similarly, Articles 11 and 12 provide strong protections for the right to access information. Article 11 requires governments to adopt regulations ensuring that 'tobacco product packaging and labelling do not promote a tobacco product by any means that are false, misleading, deceptive or likely to create an erroneous impression about its characteristics, health effects, hazards or emissions' (WHO, 2003). Meanwhile, Article 12 calls for 'broad access to . . . education and public awareness programs on the health risks . . . to tobacco smoke' (WHO, 2003). These provisions promote several different aspects of the right to access to information, but they all protect this right, using strong and unambiguous language.

By protecting the right of access to information, the FCTC invokes a right that is widely recognized in the human rights sphere. This right has been articulated in the constitutions of many countries (Bishop, 2006). It was also recognised in the early history of the United Nations. In 1946, the UN General Assembly resolved: 'Freedom of information is a fundamental human right and the touchstone for all freedoms to which the United Nations is consecrated' (UN General Assembly, 1946). At a regional level, in a 2003 resolution, the General Assembly of the Organization of American States (OAS) recognized the importance of access to information. In this resolution, the OAS General Assembly reaffirmed the statement of Article 13 of the American Convention of Human Rights in that everyone has the freedom to seek, receive, and impart information. As discussed later in this chapter, this right, in combination with the right to health, should more than counteract the tobacco industry's arguments over its right to freedom of expression.

FCTC and human rights: a two-way relationship

The FCTC has important implications for international human rights law. By ratifying the FCTC, Member-States acknowledge that the tobacco pandemic is a major threat to public health and that the FCTC is the minimum standard to protect the public's health. The FCTC creates a floor, a set of minimum tobacco control measures State Parties must implement. This requires States to develop laws and policies at the domestic level that meet these minimum international standards, and in doing so States protect the right to health. By setting concrete standards against which State action can be measured, the FCTC informs the content of the right to health (Cabrera & Madrazo, 2010).

As an international treaty, the FCTC can be used as a standard to measure whether States are fulfilling their obligations derived from the right to health, as they exist under international human rights law. The FCTC establishes the specific content of the minimum obligations States have with regard to tobacco control. If a State fails to implement the minimum tobacco control measures outlined in the FCTC, it could be found in violation of its obligations under the right to health (Cabrera & Madrazo, 2010).

The ICESCR plays an essential role in building this connection. In its General Comment 14, the CESCR (the treaty monitoring body in charge of interpreting and monitoring the implementation of the ICESCR) analysed and developed the content of the right to health (ICESCR, Article 12). In this general comment, the CESCR defined concrete State obligations arising from the right to health.

The CESCR clearly articulated the connection between tobacco control and the obligation to protect the right to health when it stated that:

> Violations of the obligation to protect follow from the failure of a State to take all necessary measures to safeguard persons within their jurisdiction from infringements of the right to health by third parties. This category includes such omissions as . . . the failure to discourage production, marketing, and consumption of tobacco. (CESCR, 2000, paragraph 51)

The FCTC can also help inform the content of other human rights, for instance, 'the right of everyone to the enjoyment of just and favourable conditions of work which ensure, in particular . . . (b) Safe and healthy working conditions', as established in Article 7 of the ICESCR (ICESCR, 1966). Tobacco smoke contains thousands of known chemicals, of which at least 250 are highly toxic to human health and their well-being (WHO, 2007). In response to this, the WHO established a permissible limit of 'zero' on human exposure to second-hand smoke. The WHO's policy recommendations for protection from exposure to second-hand smoke state, there is *no safe level* of environmental tobacco smoke (ETS) exposure, and, therefore, the only effective way of protecting individuals from the harmful effects of second-hand smoke is an absolute ban on smoking in workplaces and other public areas (WHO, 2007). Pursuant to Article 8 of the FCTC, State Parties have a duty to protect their inhabitants from undue, involuntary exposure to second-hand tobacco smoke (WHO, 2003). The FCTC sets a legal minimum standard regarding what 'safe and healthy working conditions' mean in relation to exposure to second-hand smoke.

Human rights bodies have been expanding the connection between the FCTC and human rights obligations, and have stressed that tobacco control is an integral component in the protection of the right to health. In 2009, in the periodic review of Brazil, the CESCR expressly commented on the relationship between the right to health and tobacco control. The 'CESCR expressly welcomed the Brazilian government's ratification of the FCTC' (Cabrera & Madrazo, 2010). However, the CESCR expressed concern that it was 'still permissible to promote the use of tobacco through advertising in the State Party [Brazil] and that . . . smoking is permitted in areas specially designed for the purpose' (CESCR, 2009, paragraph 30). In this instance, the CESCR connects tobacco control measures, smoke-free places (FCTC, Article 8), and banning advertising, promotion and sponsorship of tobacco products (FCTC, Article 13). The CESCR used the FCTC as a standard to measure Brazil's compliance with its right to health obligations. Finally, the CESCR concludes by recommending that Brazil 'take measures to ban the promotion of tobacco products and enact legislation to ensure that all enclosed public environments are completely free of tobacco' (CESCR, 2009, paragraph 30).

Other UN bodies have also followed the CESCR in linking tobacco control and human rights. In the periodic review of Argentina, the committee in charge of monitoring the implementation of the CEDAW (CEDAW Committee) addressed the connection between tobacco control and gender. When reviewing Argentina's implementation and compliance with Article 12 of CEDAW (women and health), the CEDAW Committee required the government to provide concrete information on the connection between tobacco control and women, and inquired about government gender-sensitive tobacco control policies. In its concluding observations, the CEDAW Committee expressed concern 'about the widespread use of tobacco among women in Argentina and the serious health impact of tobacco on women. The CEDAW Committee is particularly concerned that women are often targets in tobacco advertising campaigns, which encourage and increase the usage of tobacco among women, resulting in tobacco-related diseases and deaths' (CEDAW, 2010, paragraph 39). The CEDAW Committee urged Argentina to ratify and implement the FCTC, and to 'put in place legislation aimed at banning smoking in public spaces and restricting tobacco advertising' (CEDAW, 2010, paragraph 40). More recently, in October 2012, the UN Human Rights Council, in its universal periodic review of Argentina, also recommended that Argentina '[c]onsider the possibility in ratifying the WHO Framework Convention on Tobacco Control', linking again human rights with the FCTC (UNHRC, 2012).

Using the UN system to promote tobacco control also provides an opportunity to monitor the implementation of the FCTC. The FCTC lacks formal monitoring mechanisms and does not have an avenue for civil society to formally participate and inform the status of the FCTC implementation at the domestic level. In contrast, UN treaty-based bodies have formal mechanisms to monitor the implementation of UN treaties, which allow civil society to inform the process. There are several ways in which civil society organizations can participate, and one of the most widely used is by submitting shadow (alternative) reports. Those reports highlight human rights violations of the State and provide an alternative account of governments' implementation of human rights treaties.

Brazil's review by the CESCR provides a good illustration to build this connection between tobacco control, the FCTC, and human rights. International organizations, academic and civil society organizations, in partnership with local non-governmental organizations (NGOs), filed a shadow report entitled 'Preventing and Reducing Tobacco Use in Brazil: Pending Tasks' (O'Neill Institute for National & Global Health et al., 2009). This report builds a connection between the right to health (ICESCR, Article 12), tobacco control, and the FCTC. The CESCR used the arguments developed in the report to evaluate the government tobacco control actions. Moreover, some of the recommendations issued by the CESCR are based on arguments developed on the shadow report, and connected with the FCTC (Articles 8 and 13). In sum, when evaluating Brazil's compliance with Article 12 of the FCTC, the CESCR was expressing a clear vision of tobacco control as necessary for the right to health. The UN human rights system (through its treaty monitoring bodies) can provide an avenue for finding states accountable for their failures to implement the FCTC.

Strengthening the relationship between human rights and tobacco control: case study on smoke-free places

The tobacco industry often uses fundamental rights arguments to challenge tobacco control policies (Katz, 2005). The regulation of tobacco products involves complex trade-offs in terms of various rights. Strict regulation of marketing and consumption, for instance, can conflict with property rights and freedom of expression; and stringent smoking laws could be seen to conflict with the right to autonomy and self-determination (what the tobacco industry has tried to label as 'freedom to smoke').

In combating the tobacco industry's claims over fundamental rights, it is important to examine which, if any, industry claims have merit. The 'freedom to smoke' or 'right to smoke', for instance, has no basis in law; all States reserve the right to ban or regulate substances that are addictive and harmful to their populations. Other claims, such as those related to commercial freedom, do have some basis in law, but are not strong claims. Using an analytical framework (proportionality) to measure how different rights interact with one another and to determine which right should prevail in cases of conflict is the key to determining how human rights should be used to advance tobacco control efforts. In any analysis balancing the rights of industry against the rights of individuals, it is necessary to remember that there is 'little or no redeeming value for tobacco consumption', meaning that 'any balancing or proportionality tests applied to tobacco regulation are likely to weigh heavily in favour of more far reaching restrictions, more regulation, and less misleading information' (O'Neill Institute for National and Global Health, 2012).

The following section provides examples of how the industry has characterized tensions between human rights and tobacco control measures, in the context of smoke-free areas. We provide a concrete account of industry arguments, which, for the most part, do not have solid grounding under human rights law.

In challenging tobacco control laws, one of the most frequently made fundamental rights arguments made by the tobacco industry is that 'smoke-free places' measures violate the right to private property (Cabrera & Madrazo, 2010). The tobacco industry has used a few variations of how the right to property is infringed by bans on indoor smoking, none of which withstand a thorough examination from a human rights law perspective. To begin with, the right to property is not absolute. Although recognized in international human rights law, the right to property can be limited or restricted by the State, in particular to protect other fundamental rights. Most States use some form of balancing test to determine whether a regulation is an acceptable limitation of property rights.

The Inter-American Commission on Human Rights recently identified the elements of the proportionality test. The Commission held that in order for a restriction to be lawful and not an arbitrary interference in the right, restrictions must comply with the following requirements: (1) have been 'imposed through a law'; (2) respond 'to a legitimate aim to raise a social interest or to preserve the general well-being in a democratic society'; and (3) be 'proportional in the sense of being reasonable to obtain this aim and, in any case, of not sacrificing the essence of the right' (Inter-American Commission on Human Rights, 2009).

Well-drafted tobacco control laws fully meet this proportionality test. The 'lawfulness' prong is the easiest hurdle; if the regulation is passed in compliance with a State's regular lawmaking process, this requirement is fulfilled. In tobacco control laws, 'legitimate aims' and 'proportionality' tests are not difficult to meet either. Tobacco control laws aim to further the right to life, to a safe and clean environment, and to the preservation of health, all of which advance 'legitimate' social purposes (O'Neill Institute for National and Global Health, 2012). Furthermore, many countries have ratified and incorporated the FCTC into their domestic legislation, adding a further legal *obligation* to enact strong tobacco control laws (O'Neill Institute for National and Global Health, 2012). The proportionality test is a factual one, but as long as the tobacco restrictions do not harm the 'essence of the right to property', the limitations on the right are lawful (Inter-American Commission on Human Rights, 2009).

In measuring these balancing tests as they relate to smoke-free areas, it is important to remember the real harm caused by second-hand tobacco smoke. Government agencies and scientists have warned that there is 'no safe level of exposure to second-hand smoke' (US Surgeon General, 2007) and, according to a recent Pan-American Health Organization (PAHO) report, 'there is no level of exposure at which [second-hand smoke] has been found to be harmless to humans' (Pan American Health Organization, 2006). There is no controversy in the medical and scientific communities over this issue. Organizations such as the WHO, PAHO, and the US Surgeon General have categorically stated that exposure to second-hand smoke creates a serious risk to long-term health. The WHO's most recent estimates put the global death toll from tobacco at 6 million annual deaths (WHO, 2011a).

Despite these data, second-hand smoke continues to be a problem in the developing world. A recent study in seven Latin American countries found second-hand smoke in 94% of the public locations surveyed, with second-hand smoke found not only in bars and restaurants, but also in schools, government buildings, and other places where smoking was prohibited by law (Navas-Acien et al., 2004).

In weighing the balancing test in the right to property, it is important to recall these figures. Smoking carries no social benefits, but it causes a plethora of social harms. It is difficult to think how a regulation might have a more clear-cut 'legitimate aim'. This legitimacy of purpose leads to a second fundamental point regarding smoke-free area laws: States are not merely permitted, but are required, to enact laws to protect their citizens from the harms of second-hand smoke.

As described earlier, governments' attempts to reduce second-hand smoke exposure through smoke-free area laws do not violate owners' right to property. Indeed, under a human rights framework, governments may violate numerous other human rights by *failing* to enact smoke-free area laws and allowing continued exposure to the harms of second-hand smoke. Exposure to second-hand smoke poses a violation of numerous fundamental rights enshrined in international law, including the right to health; rights of the child; right to equal protection; right to just, equitable, and satisfactory conditions of work; and the right to a healthy environment (PAHO, 2006).

In courts from Peru and India to Uganda, judges have found that second-hand smoke violates fundamental rights such as the right to health, the right to life, and the right to a safe and clean environment. These courts have ordered government to enact stricter tobacco control regulations (PAHO, 2006). For instance, and with regard to the right to just, equitable, and satisfactory conditions of work, in a 2002 Canadian case, the Ontario Workplace Safety and Insurance Board awarded a non-smoking waitress compensation as a result of her contracting terminal lung cancer due to daily exposure to second-hand smoke during her employment (Laghi, 2002). Similar cases in the United States have also found a causal connection between smoke-filled workplaces and lung cancer (Douglas, 2004).

Such cases support the argument that there are strong rights-based arguments in favour of smoke-free areas. Although the tobacco industry claims that smoke-free areas are a violation of property rights, a workers' rights argument powerfully counteracts that claim. This argument could be more persuasive to advance policy debate, as public opinion is sympathetic to arguments that support regulation whose purposes is to protect non-smoking citizens from the hazardous effects of second-hand smoke (Katz, 2005).

Related to claims that smoke-free areas violate property rights, the tobacco industry has also asserted that they violate the rights to commerce and economic freedom. Mexico's federal tobacco law, approved in February 2008, has been challenged by numerous restaurants, hotels, and other service providers with close ties to the tobacco industry on the grounds of undue restrictions on the right to commerce and other fundamental rights (Cabrera & Madrazo, 2010). Similarly, the Chamber of Commerce in Guatemala challenged the Guatemalan Smoke-Free Places Law on the grounds that it restricted economic freedom (Cabrera & Madrazo, 2010).

The right to economic freedom is wide-ranging and many constitutions afford a freedom for industry, commerce, and work (O'Neill Institute for National and Global Health, 2012). The tobacco industry has invoked these provisions to argue, for example, that restrictions on smoking in public places are harmful to competition and to the exercise of lawful economic activity. But similarly to the arguments developed earlier, these arguments fail any balancing test due to the overwhelming interest in protecting the public's health from tobacco use and exposure to second-hand smoke.

This line of argument does not look promising for the tobacco industry. In a 2010 decision, the Guatemalan Constitutional Court upheld a smoke-free law, basing its decision, in part, on the Guatemalan government's obligation to protect the right to health and the right to life. The Constitutional Court resort to these rights as enshrined in both Guatemala's Constitution and in the international human rights treaties that Guatemala had ratified, such as the ICESCR. In an inclusive and comprehensive definition of the right to health the Guatemalan Court stated:

> A safe household, a clean environment, proper nutrition and correct information on the prevention of diseases are the bases of a healthy life. The right to health also implies that the people have control over their body and health. The right to health compels the States to generate conditions in which all may live as healthily as possible. Such conditions include the guaranteed availability of health services, healthy and safe working conditions, adequate housing and nutritional foods. (Constitutional Court of Guatemala, 2010)

The Guatemalan Constitutional Court carried out a thorough analysis of the arguments raised by the chamber of commerce in challenging the smoke-free law. The Constitutional Court resorted to international human rights treaties, such as the ICESCR, but more importantly it expressly refers to the FCTC, and to Article 8 of the FCTC, to develop its reasoning. The Constitutional Court clearly understood the relationship between different rights, e.g. right to freedom of commerce and right to health, and correctly applies a proportionality test.

Along the same lines, the Peruvian Constitutional Tribunal confirmed the constitutionality and legality of a law establishing smoke-free places. The Court held that the law satisfied a proportionality test, according to which the right to health was placed above the rights allegedly violated. The Tribunal additionally stated that FCTC provisions clearly establish that 100% smoke-free environments are more protective of health than separate smoking areas, and that there is a 'duty of the State to protect the right to health at the maximum level possible' (Peruvian Constitutional Tribunal, 2011). Like the Guatemalan Court, the Peruvian Tribunal used international human rights standards to interpret the FCTC and concluded that the FCTC 'is a human rights treaty, since it seeks to clearly, expressly and directly protect the basic right to health protection recognized in Article 7 of the Constitution [of Peru]' (Peruvian Constitutional Tribunal, 2011).

The future of human rights and tobacco control

As we have argued throughout this chapter, human rights and tobacco control are mutually reinforcing frameworks, supported both by human rights law and the FCTC—two complementary regimes in international law. Using human rights can be effective not only in defending tobacco control laws, but also to affirmatively advance tobacco control at the national level. The FCTC shapes the content of the right to health, and health-related rights, such as the right to life and a clean environment, as well as the right to information. Finally, regional and international human rights systems can also provide an avenue for monitoring the implementation of the FCTC. While the FCTC Conference of the Parties develops a mechanism to monitor implementation of the FCTC, international and regional human rights systems can monitor the implementation of FCTC duties.

Constitutional court decisions ranging from Colombia and Guatemala to India that have upheld tobacco control laws and driven tobacco control reform show great promise. There seems to be a shift both in how the public perceives tobacco control, and also in how courts interpret tobacco control norms in line with human rights. Additionally, decisions such as the one emerging from the Constitutional Tribunal in Peru illustrate the interrelated connection between human rights and tobacco control. For instance, the Peruvian Constitutional Tribunal states that:

> According to Article 3 of the WHO Framework Convention on Tobacco Control the aim of reducing the use and exposure to tobacco smoke must be achieved 'continually', it is found constitutionally prohibited that, in the face of the tobacco epidemic, any steps, legislative or otherwise, be taken in the future that would provide a lesser degree of protection to the fundamental right to health than is presently provided by current legislation. (Peruvian Constitutional Tribunal, 2011)

This decision expressly references the principle of progressive realization/non-retrogression, which applies to rights enshrined in the ICESCR. This decision has consequences that go beyond tobacco control, as the Tribunal's interpretations of progressive realization and non-retrogression would also apply to the right to health more broadly and set a high standard of protection.

In response, the industry is moving vigorously towards defending their corporate interests, challenging State powers to protect the public. Tobacco industry claims are not simply based on the rights of commerce and speech, but now include trade, investment, and intellectual property treaty rights. In a particularly disturbing case, Phillip Morris International (PMI) filed an arbitration request against Uruguay in front of the International Centre for Settlement of Investment Disputes (ICSID), challenging Uruguay's health warnings regulations. Not only is it alarming that the tobacco industry would challenge a sovereign State's public health regulations (which are in fact mandated under international human rights law as well as the FCTC), but also that PMI would challenge a developing country such as Uruguay.

Australia implemented a 'plain packaging law' at the end of 2012. The law reduces branding on product packaging to the display of brand and variant names in standardized font styles and sizes, with the remainder of a pack's surface to be taken up by health warnings and a plain background. The tobacco industry challenged the law under the Australian Constitution, but the Supreme Court of Australia upheld the law. However, legal challenges are still pending both before an Investment Tribunal and before the World Trade Organization.

Courts all over the world are moving towards recognizing the link between human rights and tobacco control, and are deciding cases in favour of tobacco control laws, over industry interests. Importantly, there is also growing international support that would push States to make this connection. For example, in October 2010, the PAHO Directing Council issued a resolution on health and human rights urging States to 'strengthen the technical capacity of the health authority to provide support for the formulation of health policies and plans consistent with the applicable international human rights instruments related to health' (PAHO, 2010). The tobacco control movement needs to capitalize on this momentum and work actively to strengthen the connection between human rights and tobacco control, both in litigation and in policy development.

Acknowledgements

This chapter is an updated, abbreviated version of a previously published article Human rights and the Framework Convention on Tobacco Control: Mutually Reinforcing Systems, by Oscar A. Cabrera and Lawrence O. Gostin, *International Journal of Law in Context*, Volume 7, Special Issue 03 (September 2011), pp. 285–303, Copyright © 2011 Cambridge University Press. Adapted with permission.

For their support in updating the article's information for this chapter, the authors would like to thank Paula Avila and Ana Ayala from the O'Neill Institute for National and Global Health Law.

References

Alston, P., Goodman, R., and Steiner, H. (2008). *International Human Rights in Context: Law, Politics, Morals.* Oxford University Press: Oxford.

Beaglehole, R., Bonita, R., Horton, R., *et al.* (2011). Priority actions for the non-communicable disease crisis. *Lancet*, 377, 1438–1447.

Bishop, C. (2006). *Access to Information as a Human Right: Analysis of the United Nations Human Rights Committee.* Paper Presented at the Annual Meeting of the International Communication Association, Dresden International Congress Centre, Dresden, Germany. Available at: <http://www.allacademic.com/meta/p91640_index.html> (accessed 14 November 2012).

Bollyky, T.J. and Gostin, L.O. (2010). The United States engagement in global tobacco control: proposal for comprehensive funding and strategies. *Journal of the American Medical Association*, 301, 2637–2038.

Cabrera, O. and Madrazo, A. (2010). Human rights as a tool for tobacco control in Latin America. *Salud Publica de Mexico*, 52, 288–297.

CEDAW. (2010). *Concluding Observations for Argentina.* Committee on the Elimination of Discrimination against Women (CEDAW): New York, NY. Available at: <http://www2.ohchr.org/english/bodies/cedaw/cedaws46.htm> (accessed 15 November 2012).

CESCR. (2000). *General Comment 14: The Right to the Highest Attainable Standard of Health (Article 12 of the International Covenant on Economic, Social and Cultural Rights).* Committee on Economic, Social and Cultural Rights (CESCR): Geneva.

CESCR. (2009). *Concluding Observations: Brazil.* Committee on Economic, Social, and Cultural Rights (CESCR): Geneva. Available at: <http://www2.ohchr.org/english/bodies/cescr/cescrs42.htm> (accessed 15 November 2012).

Constitutional Court of Guatemala. (2010). *Guatemala Chamber of Commerce* v. *Government of Guatemala.* DOCKET 2158-2009.

Crow, M.E. (2005). The human rights responsibilities of multinational tobacco companies. *Tobacco Control*, 1, ii14–ii18.

Douglas, C. (2004). *The Americans with Disabilities Act: Effective Legal Protection Against Secondhand Smoke Exposure.* A Law Synopsis by the Tobacco Control Legal Consortium: San Francisco, CA. Available at: <http://www.wmitchell.edu/tobaccolaw/resources/douglas.pdf> (accessed 15 November 2012).

Ezzati, M. and Lopez, A. (2003). Estimates of global mortality attributable to smoking in 2000. *Lancet*, 362, 847–852.

Ferrajoli, L. (2001). *Derechos y Garantías. La Ley del más Débil* (2nd Ed.). Editorial Trotta: Madrid.

Framework Convention Alliance (2010). *Updated Status of the WHO FCTC Ratification and Accession by Country.* Available at: <http://www.fctc.org/index.php?option=com_content&view=article&id=401:updated-status-of-the-who-fctc-ratification-and-accession-by-country-afghanistan-and-cote-divoire&catid=173:general&Itemid=200> (accessed 15 November 2012).

General Assembly of the Organization of American States. (2003). *Resolution AG/Res. 1932 (XXXIII-O/03)'*, 10 June 2003.

Gostin, L.O. (2007). Global regulatory strategies for tobacco control. *Journal of the American Medical Association*, 298, 2057–2059.

ICESCR. (1966). *International Covenant on Economic, Social and Cultural Rights, Art. 11(2), 993 UNTS 3*, 16 December 1966.

Inter-American Commission on Human Rights. (2009). *Asociación Nacional de Ex Servidores del Instituto Peruano de Seguridad Social* v. *Perú.* Case 12.670. Report No. 38/09.

Jacobson, P. and Soliman, S. (2002). Co-opting the health and human rights movements. *Journal of Law, Medicine & Ethics*, 30, 605–715.

Katz, J.E. (2005). Individual rights advocacy in tobacco control policies: an assessment and recommendation. *Tobacco Control*, 1, ii31–ii37.

Koch, I.E. (2005). Dichotomies, trichotomies or waves of duties? *Human Rights Law Review*, 5, 81–103.

Laghi, B. (2002). Ailing ex-waitress wins secondhand smoke case. *The Globe and Mail, Ontario*. Available at: <http://www.theglobeandmail.com/news/national/ailing-ex-waitress-wins-second-hand-smoke-case/article489722/> (accessed 15 November 2012).

Navas-Acien, A., Peruga, A., Breysse, P., *et al.* (2004). Secondhand tobacco smoke in public places in Latin America, 2002–2003. *Journal of the American Medical Association*, 291, 2741–2745.

O'Neill Institute for National and Global Health Law. (2012). *Tobacco Industry Strategy in Latin American Courts: A Litigation Guide*. O'Neill Institute for National and Global Health Law: Washington, DC.

O'Neill Institute for National and Global Health Law, Campaign for Tobacco-Free Kids, Aliança de Controle de Tobagismo. (2009). *Shadow Report to the Periodic Report by the Government of Brazil: Preventing and Reducing Tobacco Use in Brazil: Pending Tasks*. Available at: <http://www2.ohchr.org/english/bodies/cescr/cescrs42.htm> and <http://www.law.georgetown.edu/oneillinstitute/global-health-law/global-tobacco_control.cfm>.

PAHO. (2006). *Exposure to Secondhand Tobacco Smoke in the Americas*. Pan American Health Organization (PAHO): Washington DC. Available at: <http://new.paho.org/hq/dmdocuments/2009/HR_SHS_eng_tool.pdf> (accessed 15 November 2012).

PAHO. (2010). *Resolution CD50.R8. Health and Human Rights*. Pan American Health Organization (PAHO): Washington, DC.

PATH Canada and Work for a Better Bangladesh. (2002). *Fact Sheet: Tobacco and Poverty*. PATH Canada and Work for a Better Bangladesh: Dhaka. Available at: <http://www.healthbridge.ca/poverty_factsheet> (accessed 15 November 2012).

Peruvian Constitutional Tribunal. (2011). *Jaime Barco Rodas Contra el Artículo 3° de la ley N. 28705*—Ley General para la Prevención y Control de los Riesgos del Consumo de Tabaco, unconstitutionality proceeding, July 2011, p. 148 (unofficial translation for this article).

Taylor, A. (2005). Trade, human rights and the WHO Framework Convention on Tobacco Control: just what the doctor ordered? In T. Cottier, J. Pauwelyn, and E. Bürgi (Eds.), *Human Rights and International Trade*, pp. 322–333. Oxford University Press: Oxford.

UN General Assembly. (1946). '*Resolution 59(1)*', 65th Plenary Meeting, 14 December 1946.

UN General Assembly. (2011). *Full Media Release*. United Nations: New York, NY. Available at: <http://www.un.org/News/Press/docs/2011/ga11146.doc.htm> (accessed 15 November 2012).

UN Human Rights Council. (2010). *Report of the Independent Expert on the Question of Human Rights and Extreme Poverty, Magdalena Sepúlveda Carmona, on the Draft Guiding Principles on Extreme Poverty and Human Rights*. 6 August 2010, A/HRC/15/41. UN Office of the High Commissioner for Human Rights (UNOHCHR): Geneva.

UN Human Rights Council. (2012). *Working Group on the Universal Periodic, Fourteenth Session*. Geneva, 22 October–5 November 2012, Draft Report. Available at: <http://www.upr-info.org/IMG/pdf/a_hrc_wg.6_14_l.2.pdf> (accessed 15 November 2012).

UNOHCHR. (2011). *Report of the Special Representative of the Secretary General on the Issue of Human Rights and Transnational Corporations and Other Business Enterprises, John Ruggie*. 21 March 2011, A/HRC/17/31. UN Office of the High Commissioner for Human Rights (UNOHCHR): Geneva.

US Surgeon General. (2007). *The Health Consequences of Involuntary Exposure to Tobacco Smoke: There is No Risk-Free Level of Exposure to Secondhand Smoke*. Factsheet. US Surgeon General: Washington, DC. Available at: <http://www.surgeongeneral.gov/library/secondhandsmoke/factsheets/factsheet7.html> (accessed 15 November 2012).

WHO. (2003). *WHO Framework Convention on Tobacco Control (FCTC)*. World Health Organization (WHO): Geneva. Available at: <http://www.who.int/fctc/text_download/en/index.html> (accessed 15 November 2012).

WHO. (2004). *Tobacco and Poverty: A Vicious Cycle*. World Health Organization (WHO): Geneva. Available at: <http://www.who.int/tobacco/resources/publications/wntd/2004/en/index.html> (accessed 15 November 2012).

WHO. (2007). *Protection from Exposure to Second-Hand Tobacco Smoke. Policy Recommendations.* World Health Organization (WHO): Geneva. Available at: <http://whqlibdoc.who.int/publications/2007/9789241563413_eng.pdf> (accessed 15 November 2012).

WHO. (2011a). *Global Status Report on Noncommunicable Diseases 2010.* World Health Organization (WHO): Geneva. Available at: <http://www.who.int/nmh/publications/ncd_report2010/en/> (accessed 15 November 2012).

WHO. (2011b). *Parties to the WHO Framework Convention on Tobacco Control.* World Health Organization (WHO): Geneva. Available at: <http://www.who.int/fctc/signatories_parties/en/index.html> (accessed 15 November 2012).

Chapter 20

Women's health and human rights: struggles to engender social transformation

Alicia Ely Yamin

Where, after all, do universal human rights begin? In small places, close to home—so close and so small that they cannot be seen on any map of the world. Yet they are the world of the individual person: the neighborhood he lives in; the school or college he attends; the factory, farm or office where he works. Such are the places where every man, woman and child seeks equal justice, equal opportunity, equal dignity without discrimination. Unless these rights have meaning there, they have little meaning anywhere. Without concerted citizen action to uphold them close to home, we shall look in vain for progress in the larger world.

Introduction

Women's health and rights are affected disproportionately by all of the issues discussed in this volume's other chapters—poverty, infectious diseases, international development agendas, and all the rest. Yet, as has been noted before, the advancement of women's human rights in particular must permeate those small and often 'private' spaces, from the bedroom and household to the workplace and classroom, which historically have been neglected in international human rights law (Charlesworth & Chinkin, 2000; Chavkin & Chesler, 2008; Cook et al., 2003). It is largely in those intimate spaces in which our relationships and identities are formed, where the power dynamics constructed in the larger society are revealed, and where women are too often treated as less than fully human.

Every year in Afghanistan and India, among other places, many young women are doused with kerosene and set ablaze to die when they come to their marriages with what are perceived to be insufficient dowries, while in South Africa, lesbians are frequently subjected to 'corrective' rape, often under the supervision of their own families or communities (Britton, 2006; Raj et al., 2008). In the 21st century, women across the global South are still consigned to back-breaking labour and accorded few or no choices over their lives from birth until death, and pregnant women are often treated with no more dignity than gestating farm animals. And, around the globe, in countries of varying levels of development, millions of girls' and women's voices are still not heard and their lives not fully valued because, in addition to whatever other social disadvantage they may face, they were born female.

As we approach the 65th anniversary of the Universal Declaration of Human Rights (UDHR), women continue to be defined in their local communities as well as in global development discourse by their sexuality rather than their humanity, with tremendous implications for how their health needs are addressed (Cook et al., 2003; Reichenbach, 2009). Women's sexuality, as well as their fertility, is understood as needing to be controlled and managed, whether to meet demographic targets set in international development conferences or to comply with local cultural and religious norms. Given how dramatically contested the idea of women controlling their own bodies—let alone their sexual desires and identities—has been historically, it is not surprising that the struggle for women's health and rights has generally focused on sexual and reproductive health and rights (SRHR). Thus, this chapter will also emphasize SRHR.

In telling the story of the evolution of international human rights and women's health, this chapter sets out to show how approaching women's health in terms of human rights changes the way we understand both women's health and human rights norms. Indeed, efforts to advance women's health and human rights have produced enormous changes in international human rights law, as well as in paradigms of development and health policy and programming. However, it is also painfully evident that formidable challenges remain not only in translating legal progress into reality for millions of women on the proverbial ground, but also in defending the conceptual advances and standard-setting that have already been achieved. In looking ahead to the future, the chapter concludes with a caution that any meaningful social transformation in this important area requires gendered approaches to international human rights law and development agendas, which recognize women's full humanity.

Origins and development of women's health rights in international treaties

Article 25 of the UDHR notably sets out the right to 'a standard of living for the health and well-being of himself and of his family' (UN, 1948, Article 25(1)). The choice of the male pronoun is not merely a reflection on the semantic usage of the day; the vision of humanity enshrined in the UDHR is largely one of heterosexual male heads of household who support women and children. Article 25 goes on to note that 'motherhood and childhood are entitled to special care and assistance' (UN, 1948, Article 25(2)) and mentions 'widowhood' as a condition requiring consideration from the State in regards to the adequacy of a standard of living.

Despite the quoted remarks cited at the beginning of this chapter from Eleanor Roosevelt, former US First Lady and prominent member of the United Nations (UN) Commission on Human Rights, the drafting process for these theoretically universal norms was almost entirely devoid of women's participation and input (Charlesworth & Chinkin, 2000; Normand & Zaidi, 2008). Further, as international human rights became yet another domain for Cold War battles over ideologies, a narrow liberal understanding of rights as shields from government interference in the public sphere—e.g. freedom from torture by State agents, freedom from interference with political expression—came to predominate in the construction of norms as well as in their institutional interpretation. Such an understanding was ill-suited to meet women's health needs, as women and girls most often face torture and cruel, inhuman, and degrading treatment (CIDT) at the hands of their domestic partners and fathers, and are silenced by cultural norms that also have enormous health consequences, such as early marriage and pregnancy and female genital cutting/mutilation.

During the Cold War, civil and political (CP) rights and economic, social, and cultural (ESC) rights were divided into twin covenants, in which the obligations had very different status under the law. Women's and girls' health is affected by a broad array of human rights, both CP and ESC rights. But health per se was treated as an ESC right, and was therefore subject to progressive realization in accordance with a State's 'maximum available resources' (CESCR, 2000) Article 12(1) of the ICESCR set out the right of everyone to the 'highest attainable standard of physical and mental health'. Rather than attempt to define 'health', as the Constitution of the World Health Organization (WHO) had done, Article 12(2) set out obligations State Parties undertake with respect to realizing the right, which importantly included both medical care for all in the event of sickness, and preconditions for health, such as nutrition and environmental hygiene.

The absence of any mention of reproductive health in Article 12 is notable. As discussed later, this omission and others relating to the gendered dimensions of the right to health, were later in large measure corrected by the Committee on Economic, Social and Cultural Rights (CESCR) in 2000 in its General Comment 14 elucidating the meaning of Article 12:

> The provision for the reduction of the stillbirth rate and of infant mortality and for the healthy development of the child (Art. 12.2 a) may be understood as requiring measures to improve child and maternal health, sexual and reproductive health services, including access to family planning, pre- and post-natal care, emergency obstetric services and access to information, as well as to resources necessary to act on that information. (CESCR, 2000)

By the 1970s, the advent of widely accessible family planning methods held the promise of allowing women to control their own fertility and, in turn, dramatic improvements for women's health and rights. At the same time, women's movements in many countries had made enormous strides in achieving legislative as well as social changes advancing women's equality, and at the United Nations the Commission of the Status of Women had begun its work. Although the UDHR and the twin covenants on CP and ESC rights had prohibited discrimination on a number of grounds including sex, the Convention on the Elimination of All Forms of Discrimination against Women (CEDAW), which entered into force in 1981 after a long period of debate and ratifications, was a landmark treaty for women's health in a number of respects.

First, the CEDAW was the first international treaty to include obligations relating to both categories of rights, which was critical to women's health. Discrimination that prevents women from enjoying full political participation or freedom of information and association, for example, is often the source of women's suffering, just as lack of access to services or education can be. The CEDAW did however retain the formulas distinguishing immediate effect with respect to CP rights and progressive realization within maximum available resources for ESC rights, such as health.

Second, the erosion of the public–private distinction was critical for women's health because the actors responsible for women's suffering are often private actors, including domestic partners and community members. Traditionally, States were the exclusive subjects of international law, but the CEDAW found obligations of States to eliminate discrimination by private, non-State actors as well. For example, the CEDAW explicitly construed certain cultural practices, such as female genital cutting/mutilation as structural forms of discrimination against women and called upon State Parties to eliminate them, along with all forms of trafficking of and exploitation of women (UN General Assembly, 1979, Articles 5(a) and 6).

Third, the CEDAW reflected an increasingly sophisticated understanding of the need for both formal and substantive equality for women. Article 12(1) of the CEDAW states: 'State Parties shall take all appropriate measures to eliminate discrimination against women in the field of health care in order to ensure, on a basis of equality of men and women, access to health care services, including those related to family planning' (UN General Assembly, 1979). Article 14 calls on State Parties to: 'take all appropriate measures to eliminate discrimination against women in rural areas', including 'access to adequate health care facilities, including information, counselling and services in family planning' (UN General Assembly, 1979).

Formal equality—the notion that similarly situated people should be treated equally independent of outcome—has historically been a central goal of women's rights struggles, as well as the struggles of other disadvantaged groups. It is not just that women in many countries are still not considered fully human under the law, and therefore do not possess all of the rights accorded to men; in a real sense, having rights makes women human as our understanding of humanness is legally and socially constructed. Formal equality further implies that the right to health, like all rights, is only meaningful if its content can be universally provided, i.e. 'on the basis of equality between men and women' and with an eye towards eliminating discrimination and disparities faced by rural women.

Although it is critical, formal equality is often radically inadequate to achieve equal enjoyment of women's health rights, because it does not necessarily address the underlying inequalities in power, access to resources, and socioeconomic and political circumstances women face. Prohibitions on substantive discrimination therefore call for adopting 'measures to prevent, diminish, and eliminate the conditions or attitudes which cause substantive or de facto discrimination'. Thus, the question in achieving substantive equality is not how to treat men and women in the same way, but what is required for them to equally enjoy their right to health. The CEDAW recognizes this dimension of equality, asserting in Article 12(2):

> [n]ot withstanding the [obligation of State Parties to take all appropriate measures to eliminate discrimination against women in the field of health care in order to ensure, on a basis of equality of men and women, access to health care services,] State Parties shall ensure to women appropriate services in connection with pregnancy, confinement and the post-natal period, granting free services where necessary, as well as adequate nutrition during pregnancy and lactation.

That is, the biological differences between men and women call for different sets of goods and services in order for women to be genuinely treated equally with respect to access to healthcare. To treat men and women in a uniform manner would itself constitute substantive discrimination.

International law in this respect has evolved considerably in recent decades with respect to substantive equality and goes beyond domestic law in many jurisdictions in recognizing that achieving substantive equality may require adopting temporary or permanent positive measures with respect to women—or other groups—to combat the constraining effects of socially constructed circumstances (CESCR, 2000).

In 1999, General Recommendation 12 from the Committee on the Elimination of Discrimination against Women (CEDAW Committee), the body in charge of monitoring the implementation of the CEDAW, further clarified the nature of State Parties' obligations with respect to eliminating discrimination against women in healthcare. It also set out core obligations of States Parties, as did General Comment 14 from the CESCR (CEDAW, 1999; CESCR, 2009).

Building on the work from CEDAW as well as major conferences regarding women's health and SRHR in the 1990s, the CESCR noted in General Comment 14 that:

> To eliminate discrimination against women, there is a need to develop and implement a comprehensive national strategy for promoting women's right to health throughout their life span. Such a strategy should include interventions aimed at the prevention and treatment of diseases affecting women, as well

as policies to provide access to a full range of high quality and affordable health care, including sexual and reproductive services. A major goal should be reducing women's health risks, particularly lowering rates of maternal mortality and protecting women from domestic violence. (CESCR, 2000)

In practice, the CEDAW Committee, together with the CESCR, has generally adopted a flexible approach to examining discrimination against women in health. For example, the CESCR has called for 'the disaggregation of health and socioeconomic data according to sex [as] essential for identifying and remedying inequalities in health', and *de facto* disparities between women and men have been sufficient for CESCR and CEDAW Committee to conclude that there is evidence of discrimination with respect to women's health.

Progressive clarification of norms and appropriation of human rights discourse

In the 1990s, three seminal international conferences went far in clarifying standards with respect to women's health and rights. The 1993 Vienna Conference on Human Rights established women's rights as human rights. A year later, the 1994 International Conference on Population and Development (ICPD) held in Cairo, Egypt, marked a notable paradigm shift from development based on demographic imperatives and control of women's fertility to one of reproductive health and rights in which women (and men) were placed at the centre as decision-makers over their own lives (Roseman & Reichenbach, 2009) The Fourth World Conference on Women held in Beijing, China, in 1995, reaffirmed the vision set out in Cairo, and extended it to other spheres of women's health and lives.

By the mid-1990s when the Cairo and Beijing conferences took place, the disastrous effects that the structural adjustment programmes (SAPs) imposed on much of the world had wreaked havoc on poor people's health, and on women's health in particular, had become painfully apparent. As Brooke Schoepf and colleagues write, 'although SAP policies appeared to be gender-blind, they were not gender-neutral' (Schoepf et al., 2002). In addition to a disproportionate effect on access to care from the introduction of user fees and privatization, 'women's work burdens increased as they were pressed to supply an increasing share of family incomes, their earnings crucial to support children's nutrition and health as well as their own. Thus poor women . . . bore the brunt of SAP austerity (Schoepf et al., 2002). By the mid-1990s the gendered impacts on the growing HIV pandemic were also becoming evident.

At the same time, by the mid-1990s, activism in reproductive health had shifted away from concerns solely with women's autonomy, and the more dramatic rejections of the 'medicalization' of reproduction, to asserting demands for rights of access and information to appropriate services. Indeed, the SHRH community led other parts of the burgeoning health and human rights field in moving beyond consideration of the impacts of CP rights violations on health and restrictive health policies on CP rights to develop conceptually and practically what Jonathan Mann and colleagues referred to as the 'inextricable linkage' between health and human rights (Mann et al., 1994).

Both the ICPD Programme of Action and the Beijing Platform for Action represented the culmination of years of advocacy and coalition-building among women's movements around the world, including at Vienna. They also represented a major appropriation of human rights language and processes by activists who had until the 1990s not fully embraced human rights. The results had tremendous implications not just for women's health, but also for international law.

The ICPD Programme of Action called for 'sustained economic growth in the context of sustainable development, education, especially for girls, gender equity and equality; infant, child and maternal mortality reduction; and the provision of universal access to reproductive health services, including family planning and sexual health' (UN, 1994). In so doing, it embedded approaches to population dynamics in the context of other economic and social issues, including women's empowerment.

Importantly, the ICPD Programme of Action also established a comprehensive definition of reproductive health, which drew together many programmatic elements, such as family planning, maternal health, and sexually transmitted infections, which had been treated in a fragmented manner previously: 'Reproductive health is a state of complete physical, mental and social well-being and not merely the absence of disease or infirmity, in all matters relating to the reproductive system and to its functions and processes' (UN, 1994, paragraph 7.2). In echoing the 'complete state of well-being' in the WHO Constitution, as applied to 'all matters relating to the reproductive system and to its functions and processes', the ICPD Programme of Action very deliberately reaffirmed the need to understand health, and reproductive health in particular, in a much broader manner than the narrow and de-contextualized biomedical paradigm permitted.

Sexual rights have been further elaborated subsequently, but the ICPD Programme of Action makes clear that reproductive health includes sexual health, 'the purpose of which is the enhancement of life and personal relations, and not merely counselling and care related to reproduction and sexually transmitted disease'; it addresses the reproductive processes, functions and system at all stages of life, in the context of 'complete physical, mental and social well-being' (UN, 1994) (see also Yogyakarta Principles on sexual rights for applications of rights in relation to sexual orientation and gender identity; International Commission of Jurists, 2007). Sexual and reproductive health (SRH) is predicated on the ability of men and women to have a:

> Responsible, satisfying and safe sex life and that they have the capability to reproduce and the freedom to decide if, when and how often to do so. Implicit in this are the rights of men and women to be informed of and to have access to safe, effective, affordable and acceptable methods of fertility regulation of their choice, and the right of access to appropriate health care services that will enable women to go safely through pregnancy and childbirth and provide couples with the best chance of having a healthy infant. (UN, 1994, paragraph 72; WHO, 2012)

Sexual and reproductive health also requires 'equal relationships between men and women in matters of sexual relations and reproduction, including full respect for the integrity of the person, [and] mutual respect, consent, and shared responsibility for sexual behaviour and its consequences'; it also requires that women 'have control over and decide freely and responsibly on matters related to their sexuality, including SRH, free of coercion, discrimination and violence' (UN, 1995, paragraph 96). Of note, there have been several efforts by intergovernmental agencies such as the WHO and Pan-American Health Organization (PAHO) to further refine the definition:

> Sexual health is the experience of the ongoing process of physical, psychological and, socio-cultural well being related to sexuality. Sexual health is evidenced in the free and responsible expressions of sexual capabilities that foster harmonious personal and social wellness, enriching individual and social life. It is not merely the absence of dysfunction, disease and/or infirmity. For sexual health to be attained and maintained it is necessary that the sexual rights of all people be recognized and upheld. (PAHO and WHO, 2000)

Given the controversial subject matter, the ICPD Programme of Action was careful to state that the substance of reproductive rights had already been 'recognized in national laws, international human rights documents and other consensus documents', and that it was not creating any new rights. In effect, it was merely clarifying their nature:

> These rights rest on the recognition of the basic right of all couples and individuals to decide freely and responsibly the number, spacing and timing of their children and to have the information and means to do so, and the right to attain the highest standard of sexual and reproductive health. It also includes their right to make decisions concerning reproduction free of discrimination, coercion and violence, as expressed in human rights documents. (UN, 1994, paragraph 7.3)

Crucially, the ICPD Programme of Action also explicitly recognized the interdependence and indivisibility of CP rights and ESC rights, noting that SRHR included the rights to bodily integrity and security of person, to non-discrimination and equality between women and men, as well as an array of economic and social rights.

The Beijing Platform for Action reaffirmed and built on what had been established at the ICPD in Cairo a year earlier: 'Women have the right to the enjoyment of the highest attainable standard of physical and mental health. The enjoyment of this right is vital to their life and well-being and their ability to participate in all areas of public and private life. Health is a state of complete physical, mental and social well-being and not merely the absence of disease or infirmity' (UN, 1995, paragraph 89). After again echoing the WHO's expansive definition of health, the Beijing Platform for Action went on to note:

> Women's health involves their emotional, social and physical well-being and is determined by the social, political, and economic context of their lives, as well as by biology. However, health and well-being elude the majority of women. A major barrier for women to the achievement of the highest attainable standard of health is inequality, both between men and women and among women in different geographical regions, social classes, and indigenous and ethnic groups. (UN, 1995, paragraph 89)

Thus, there was a clear recognition not only of health being multidimensional and embedded in the realities of women's lives, but also of women's health being particularly subject to social determinants. Together with Cairo, these definitions reflect an understanding of women's health as not merely a matter of 'natural' biological causes.

On the contrary, patterns of women's health and illness are the products of social relations and social choices—of laws, policies, programmes, institutional arrangements, and practices that on the one hand promote not only formal but also substantive equality, and on the other can exacerbate inequalities. From gender-based violence to lack of access to family planning, reproductive ill health was caused not by natural biological factors but by human decisions and actions that reflected women's lack of power over their lives and within their societies. For example, both the criminalization of services (including abortion) and the criminalization of activities (such as sex work and intravenous drug use) are determining factors in the distribution of morbidity and mortality in relation to SRH (UN General Assembly, 2010). Thus, law is more usefully seen as framing the possibilities for women's SRH than as a distal factor, as is sometimes portrayed in conventional public health models of causality.

The Beijing Platform for Action went beyond SRH, and set out areas of concern relating to women's health more broadly. These included: poor quality and lack of responsiveness of health services; gender-specific barriers; gender inequality in preconditions to health such as nutrition; sexual- and gender-based violence, including physical and psychological abuse; HIV and other sexually transmitted diseases; mental disorders related to marginalization, powerlessness, and poverty, along with overwork and stress and the growing incidence of domestic violence as well as substance abuse; health concerns of older women; environmental health hazards and differential susceptibility; need for statistical data disaggregated by gender; and the need for clinical trials and health research on women (UN, 1995).

In the wake of these landmark conferences, there were further efforts to embed their bold construction of women's health rights in binding international law. In 1999 and 2000, respectively, CEDAW Committee and the CESCR issued a general recommendation and a general comment—widely considered to be authoritative interpretations of the provisions of the relevant treaties—which reflected the language and concepts of Cairo and Beijing. For example, the CESCR's General Comment 14, which explicated Article 12 of the International Covenant on Economic, Social and Cultural Rights (ICESCR), set out the need for specific plans and programmes to address women's health as well as a gender perspective: 'A gender-based approach recognizes that biological and socio-cultural factors play a significant role in influencing the health of men and women' (CESCR, 2000).

The optional protocol to the CEDAW, which enables individual complaint procedures, has already shown dramatic consequences for women's health. In the 2011 *Alyne da Silva* v. *Brazil* case, CEDAW Committee held the Brazilian government responsible for a failure to provide adequate maternal health services, reflecting a pattern of discrimination based on intersecting inequalities related to race and gender, which resulted in the death of Alyne da Silva Pimentel, a 28-year-old Afro-Brazilian woman, from pregnancy complications after her local health centre misdiagnosed her symptoms and delayed providing her with emergency care (CEDAW, 2011a). The ruling in this case sets ground-breaking precedents for international law beyond women's health, with respect to the obligations of States to expend sufficient resources to enable people to realize the enjoyment of their rights to health, and by extension other social rights; to exercise due diligence in investigating, overseeing and when necessary prosecuting conduct by private actors, including service providers; and to address substantive discrimination based on patterns of intersecting inequalities. The optional protocol to the ICESCR, entered into force in 2013, has similar potential.

At the regional level, additional treaties have further addressed issues critical to women's health. The Inter-American Convention on the Eradication of Violence Against Women (*Convención Belém do Pará*) entered into force in 1994, while a campaign for a regional convention on SRHR has been used by the Latin American Committee for the Defense of Women's Rights (*CLADEM*, by its Spanish acronym) as a political organizing and educational tool since the late 1990s.

In Africa, the Optional Protocol on Women's Human Rights to the African Charter on Human and People's Rights entered into force in 2003. The Maputo Protocol, as it is known, was extremely bold in that it enshrined abortion as a human right (African Union, 2005). Article 14 of the Maputo Protocol, which has now been ratified by 23 countries in the region, asserts the obligation of States Parties to 'ensure the right to health of women, including sexual and reproductive health', and then goes on to call for all appropriate measures to inter alia, 'protect the reproductive rights of women by authorising medical abortion in cases of sexual assault, rape, incest, and where the continued pregnancy endangers the mental and physical health of the mother or the life of the mother or the foetus' (African Union, 2005). Laws in many countries in sub-Saharan Africa are ambiguous with respect to allowances for therapeutic abortion, with the notable exception of South Africa, thus the Maputo Protocol's call for decriminalizing therapeutic abortion could potentially be used to push the boundaries of domestic constitutions and national legislation.

In practice, however, abortion is routinely denied and medical professionals often feel under an obligation to inform the police about women reporting to health facilities with post-abortion complications. This is not only the case in sub-Saharan Africa. The CEDAW addressed this issue in a 2011 landmark decision in *L.C.* v. *Peru* in which it held that Peru must amend its law to allow women to obtain an abortion in cases of rape and sexual assault; establish a mechanism to ensure the availability of those services; and guarantee access to abortion services when a woman's life or health is in danger, which is legal in Peru (CEDAW, 2011b). *L.C.* v. *Peru* followed a

2005 decision by the UN Human Rights Committee on Peru's abortion laws, *K.L.* v. *Peru*. In that decision, the UN Human Rights Committee had found that Peru's failure to institute regulations regarding the provision of legal therapeutic abortion violated the right to life as well as process rights under the International Covenant on Civil and Political Rights. Unfortunately, *KL* v. *Peru* was largely unimplemented despite strong civil society activism around it (UN Human Rights Committee, 2005).

Not surprisingly, abortion has proven one of the most contentious issues in SRHR. However, translating women's health rights more broadly into practice has proven to be a Sisyphean struggle around the globe. Although 'bringing Cairo and Beijing home' resulted in sweeping legal and policy changes in many countries, including a far greater attention to certain issues such as violence against women, it did not produce the expected changes in programming or practices on the ground (Berer, 2012). Further, the conceptual paradigm shift achieved in Cairo, and reiterated in the language of the Beijing Platform for Action, largely did not permeate the mainstream public health and development communities. The precariousness of the achievements at Cairo and Beijing became painfully evident in the creation of the UN Millennium Development Goals (MDGs) in 2001.

The Millennium Development Goals and efforts to operationalize rights-based approaches to women's health

Just a few years after women's movements around the world were celebrating the comprehensive vision of SRH and women's health enshrined in Cairo and Beijing, the MDGs seemed to retract those global promises to advance women's SRHR by means of sweeping societal reforms. The MDGs were based upon the 2000 UN Millennium Declaration, which set out a global commitment to fight poverty, and although suffused with human rights and equality language, contained no explicit references to SRHR. In explaining how this was possible, Crossette writes, 'Government delegations, embattled UN agency officials, and influential actors within the [UN] Secretariat all played parts in the story' (Crossette, 2005). Berer has written of the 'Unholy Alliance' among conservative Islamic States, the Vatican, and the increasingly powerful evangelical Christians in the United States, who had 'lost' their battles at the ICPD in Cairo as well as in Beijing but reasserted themselves with a vengeance in both international and domestic fora (Berer, 2001).

After strong US endorsement of reproductive rights by then US First Lady Hillary Clinton at the Beijing conference in 1995, anxiety over further alienating the fundamentalist Right silenced political support for SRHR by the Democrats during the protracted 2000 US election campaign period. The leadership of the United Nations Population Fund (UNFPA), an institution that had played a critical role in Cairo and Beijing, had also shifted and become far more political. Among all the different reasons, Crosette argues that perhaps the 'most tragic' was strong opposition from the G-77, which had newly reconfigured power dynamics (Crossette, 2005).

The MDGs were formulated by technocrats who merely translated the UN Millennium Declaration into eight goals, with corresponding targets and indicators. Therefore it was not surprising that there was only one goal that specifically related to women's health: MDG 5, which called for improving maternal health. MDG 3 aimed to 'Promote gender equality and empower women', but selected the feeble targets of eliminating gender disparity in primary and secondary education, preferably by 2005, and in all levels of education no later than 2015 (UN, 2012). Arguably all of the MDGs, as they relate to poverty reduction, are of tremendous importance to women's health and could be understood to have a gendered dimension, from HIV/AIDS to water and sanitation. By and large, however, implementation of the MDGs was done through technocratic approaches, avoiding the changes in social structures and power relations called for in the ICPD Programme of Action and the Beijing Platform for Action.

Thus, the contested terrain of SRHR had been reduced to the relatively depoliticized realm of maternal health; women's health needs were once again largely reduced in the international development agenda to their capacity as vessels for children. MDG 5 called for a reduction in mortality ratios by 75% from 1990 levels by 2015. As maternal mortality ratios do not reflect fertility levels, and due to an outcry from the women's health movement and the UNFPA, a second target—'universal access to reproductive health'—was added in 2007. Target 5B included indicators on family planning as well as adolescent birth rates, but did not reiterate the ICPD's commitment to the inclusion of 'sexual health'.

The international women's movement justifiably perceived the MDGs to be a betrayal of Cairo and Beijing, and a reneging on the commitments that governments had made in the 1990s. Even the belated and grudging addition of family planning in Target 5B was a tremendous political struggle. It is however important to recognize, as Jeff Waage and colleagues state, that it was not the maternal health community that had sought to exclude other issues: 'The maternal health community always recognised that access to contraception and safe induced abortion services would reduce a subset of maternal deaths, but sought care for all women including those who wanted to give birth, particularly those needing emergency obstetric care' (Waage et al., 2010).

At the same time as many in the women's health movement were alienated from the MDGs process, a critical mass of interest in maternal health as a human rights issue began to develop. In the last decade, work on maternal mortality as a human rights issue has led to cutting edge human rights advocacy, ranging from path-breaking litigation to work on budgets and economic and fiscal policies. It also engaged actors within the health domain, including service delivery organizations, in adopting 'rights-based approaches' to their maternal health work (Yamin, 2010). Further, mainstream human rights organizations which had not traditionally focused on SHRH, such as Human Rights Watch and Amnesty International, dedicated substantial amounts of staff and time to the issue of maternal mortality; Amnesty International even launched a global campaign on maternal mortality (Amnesty International, 2009, 2010, 2011; Human Rights Watch, 2011).

The MDG Task Force Report on Children and Women's Health set out from the beginning the need to adopt human rights principles and frameworks in achieving MDG 5 (Freedman et al., 2005). The then-Special Rapporteur on the right to health, Paul Hunt, took up maternal mortality as one of the key issues in his mandate and played a pivotal role in the way it was conceptualized in terms of a focus on the right to health (UN General Assembly, 2006). Although uniformly recognizing the need to situate maternal health rights within a larger framework of SRHR, much of the scholarship as well as advocacy on maternal mortality and human rights, including by this author (Yamin, 2008, 2010), focused on clarifying obligations relating to the right to health (Amnesty International, 2010; Freedman et al., 2005; Physicians for Human Rights, 2007; Yamin & Maine, 1999). At least in part a reaction to the historic neglect of economic and social rights by the human rights community, this focus was an attempt to demonstrate the added value of a human rights framework in areas traditionally dominated by conventional public health and development (Human Rights Council, 2009; Yamin, 2005, 2010).

Work on maternal health—where health systems play an undeniable role—also shaped the development of rights-based approaches to health, coming to emphasize the centrality of health systems to the realization of the right to health. As Professor Hunt and Gunilla Backman assert:

> In any society, an effective health system is a core institution, no less than a fair justice system or democratic political system . . . It is only through building and strengthening health systems that it will be possible to secure sustainable development, poverty reduction, economic prosperity, improved health for individuals and populations, as well as the right to the highest attainable standard of health. (Hunt & Backman, 2008)

Lynn Freedman and colleagues emphasize that improving health systems cannot be seen as a technocratic exercise; by bringing human rights to bear, transforming health systems can and should be understood as a means of constructing social citizenship for women in a society—and most critically for poor, rural and marginalized women (Freedman et al., 2005).

Recent years have witnessed an extraordinary degree of high-level engagement in the issue of maternal mortality as a human rights issue by the UN Human Rights Council, which has issued two historic resolutions and as of this writing is poised to issue a third (Human Rights Council, 2009, 2010). In 2011, the Human Rights Council requested that the Office of the High Commissioner prepare a 'Concise Technical Guidance on the application of a human-rights based approach to the implementation of policies and programmes to reduce preventable maternal morbidity and mortality', to be presented at its 21st session in 2012 (Human Rights Council, 2012). This Technical Guidance is the first operational guidance of its kind on the implications of a human rights-based approach to any development issue and implementation is an important precedent to set, not only for SRH and women's health, but also for the operationalization of human rights-based approaches to other health and development issues through the Human Rights Council, and human rights bodies of the United Nations generally.

Although by mid-2010, new global estimates of maternal mortality seemed to indicate that more progress had been made than previously understood, inconsistencies between those studies, gaps in the underlying data, and the unevenness of progress continued to spur a sense of urgency with respect to maternal mortality (Hogan et al., 2010; WHO, 2010b). At the MDG Summit, the UN Secretary-General launched a Global Strategy on Women's and Children's Health (Global Strategy). Notably, both the outcome document of the 2010 MDG Summit and the Global Strategy acknowledged failures of accountability in the MDG process and included multiple references to human rights (WHO, 2011; UN, 2010). The Global Strategy called for the WHO to chair an 'accountability process' on women's and children's health to implement the Global Strategy (The Partnership for Maternal Newborn and Child Health, 2011). That process, in turn, became the WHO Information and Accountability Commission on Women's and Children's Health (WHO, 2011).

The WHO Commission, in turn, called for both national accountability mechanisms, and an international level Expert Review Group (ERG) starting in 2012 and ending in 2015, which is to report annually to the UN Secretary-General 'on the results and resources related to the Global Strategy and on the progress in implementing the Commission's recommendations' (WHO, 2011). The establishment of the ERG and national accountability mechanisms reflect important recognitions of the need to institutionalize and operationalize human rights in approaches to women's health, and are potentially significant steps towards doing so. As of this writing, however, we have yet to see whether these accountability mechanisms can play a meaningful role in addressing the fundamental causes of high levels of maternal mortality, which are social rather than medical, and whether they can broaden governmental approaches to maternal health to recapture some of the dimensions of SRHR lost in the MDG process, and the WHO Commission's work.

Indeed, as the world approaches the 20-year review of the ICPD Programme of Action and also plans for a post-MDG development agenda, women's health is very much at play in global and national debates but the horizon does not appear rosy. Despite some progress in embedding human rights in efforts to address maternal mortality, these have largely remained around the edges of mainstream development discourse. Indeed, the focus on measurement of maternal mortality rates (MMRs) has largely displaced the important political debates suggested by the ICPD Programme of Action and the Beijing Platform for Action about what societal reforms are necessary to achieve women's SRHR and health rights more broadly (Yamin & Falb, 2012). Funding and programming has in many cases shifted from SRHR to reproductive, maternal newborn, and child health. Further, although in 2012 there has been a tremendous resurgence of interest and funding for family planning, long neglected in the MDGs, it has largely been as a sustainable development issue (UK Aid & Bill & Melinda Gates Foundation, 2012). Population control is once again being seen as fundamental to sustained economic growth but is remarkably disconnected from consideration of the need to address the larger social and economic contexts, as the ICPD Programme of Action had established, including inequalities in access to income and basic services as well as women's lack of power over their lives.

Conclusions

Human rights are sites of struggle as well as tools of struggle and nowhere has this been more evident than in the tumultuous history of women's health rights, and in particular women's SRHR. From gender-based violence to lack of access to family planning or abortion services, women's suffering is caused by and large not by 'natural' biological factors but rather by human decisions and actions that reflect women's lack of power over their lives and within their societies. This is not only true with respect to SRH; from nutritional deficiencies in low-income countries to disparities in diabetes rates and lack of access to cancer and cardiovascular disease detection and treatment in middle- and high-income countries, patterns of societal discrimination are inscribed in women's bodies (Brinton et al., 2010; Krieger, 2002; Yeshou et al., 2010).

Looking forward there is no reason to believe that struggles over the control of women's bodies and lives will abate any time soon. Recent backlashes against SRHR have led to conservative legislative proposals in Spain as well as the United States, and some of Eastern Europe, as well as across Latin America and some of Africa. Social constructions of women as animals and objects—as less than deserving of having full agency in their lives—are in no way limited to the global South. Between 2011 and 2012, nearly a thousand legislative bills were proposed and sometimes passed in the US Congress and state legislatures eliminating contraception in health insurance regimes, requiring intrusive vaginal ultrasounds before abortion, and redefining rape and personhood (Johnson, 2012). In the US state of Georgia in 2011, Republican representative Terry England argued on the floor of the Georgia legislature in favour of making it illegal for women who are carrying a stillborn foetus or one that is likely to die before it reaches term to have the dead foetus removed. Analogizing women to cows and pigs, which he said he had delivered both dead and alive on his farm, he portrayed that type of situation as a natural misfortune to be borne by human women as it is by barnyard animals (Dunham, 2012).

Sixty-five years after the UDHR proclaimed that all human beings are born free and equal in dignity and rights, one of the lessons from the history of struggles to advance women's health and rights is that women's claim to full humanness is unstable, and indeed still precarious even in the 21st century. The construction of women's identity in terms of reproductive capacity, and the projections of sexual mores and fantasies, both at national and international levels, are so widespread—and so internalized by many women themselves—that they determine the very possibilities for women to enjoy their rights to health.

Taking seriously the need for both formal and substantive equality between men and women in health, as well as among classes and other populations of women, calls for tectonic shifts in economic and social policies and programmes, as well as laws in some cases; cultural norms; and politics—and fundamentally in the 'conditions under which we are born, grow, live, work and age' in the phrase of the WHO Commission on Social Determinants on Health (WHO, 2009). It would require 'tackling the inequitable distribution of power, money, and resources' that serve as 'the structural drivers of those conditions of daily life — globally, nationally, and locally'; as well as far more systematic efforts to measure the problem, evaluate actions, and expand the knowledge base in order to understand dynamics of gender inequality and health (WHO, 2009). Taking gender equality seriously would also carry implications for the organization of health systems, and specifically for current debates about universalization of care, i.e. for the processes whereby previously underserved groups are covered, new services and medications are added to healthcare regimes, and the reduction of cost sharing (WHO, 2010).

Even in a complex and daunting global political context, the shaping of a new global development agenda as a successor to the MDGs presents an historic opportunity to fight for a framework as well as goals, targets, and indicators on gender equality and women's health, which recognize how diverse women face intersecting inequalities and disadvantages within and across societies. It is also an opportunity to try to ensure alignment with international human rights standards, such as the ICPD Programme of Action as well as international treaty law, together with implementation mechanisms that afford meaningful accountability and participation. It is still unclear what the post-2015 development agenda will bring for women's health and rights. However, it is abundantly clear that 'a social and international order' in which *everyone* can realize the rights and freedoms set forth in the UDHR (UN, 1948, Article 28) requires dismantling private tyrannies as well as public ones. It requires transformation in legal and political institutions but also within bedrooms and households and communities—those small spaces close to home, to which Mrs Roosevelt referred.

Acknowledgements

I am grateful to Rebecca Cantor, Lauren Masterson, and Kathryn Falb for assistance in the preparation of this chapter for publication.

References

African Union. (2005). *Protocol to the African Charter on Human and Peoples' Rights on the Rights of Women in Africa*. Adopted by the African Union on 11 July 2003, Maputo, Mozambique.

Amnesty International. (2009). *Giving Life, Risking Death: Maternal Mortality in Burkino Faso*. Amnesty International: London.

Amnesty International. (2010). *Deadly Delivery: The Maternal Health Care Crisis in the USA*. Amnesty International: London.

Amnesty International. (2011). *At a Crossroads: Sierra Leone's Free Health Care Policy*. Amnesty International: London.

Berer, M. (2001). Images, reproductive health and the collateral damage to women of fundamentalism and war. *Reproductive Health Matters*, 9, 6–11.

Berer, M. (2012). Maternal mortality or women's health: time for action. *Reproductive Health Matters*, 20, 5–10.

Brinton, E.A., Hopkins, P.N., and Sankaran, G. (2010). Cardiovascular disease in women: risk factors and risk reduction. In P. Murthy and S.C. Lanford (Eds.), *Women's Global Health and Human Rights*, pp. 161–175. Jones and Barlett Publishers: Sudbury, MA.

Britton, H. (2006). Organising against gender violence in South Africa. *Journal of Southern African Studies*, 22, 145–163.

CESCR. (2000). *General Comment 14: The right to the highest attainable standard of health (article 12 of the International Covenant on Economic, Social and Cultural Rights)*. Committee on Economic, Social and Cultural Rights (CESCR): Geneva.

CESCR. (2009). *General Comment No. 20: Non-Discrimination in Economic, Social, and Cultural Rights*. Committee on Economic, Social and Cultural Rights (CESCR): Geneva.

Charlesworth, H. and Chinkin, C.M. (2000). *The Boundaries of International Law: A Feminist Analysis*. Manchester University Press: Manchester.

Chavkin, W. and Chesler, E. (2008). *Where Human Rights Begin: Health, Sexuality, and Women in The New Millennium*. Rutgers University Press: New Brunswick, NJ.

CEDAW. (1999). *General Recommendation 24, Article 12 (Women and Health)*. United Nations Committee on the Elimination of Discrimination Against Women (CEDAW): Geneva.

CEDAW. (2011a). *Alyne da Silva Pimentel* v. *Brazil*. United Nations Committee on the Elimination of Discrimination Against Women (CEDAW): Geneva.

CEDAW. (2011b). *L.C.* v. *Peru. CEDAW/C/50/D/22/2009*. United Nations Committee on the Elimination of Discrimination Against Women (CEDAW): Geneva.

Cook, R., Dickens, B., and Falthalla, M. (2003). *Reproductive Health and Human Rights: Integrating Medicine, Ethics, and Law*. Oxford University Press: Oxford.

Crossette, B. (2005). Reproductive health and the millennium development goals: the missing link. *Studies of Family Planning*, 36, 71–79.

Dunham, D. (2012). *Georgia rep wants to force women to carry stillborn fetuses . . . like cows do*. Available at: http://blisstree.com/live/georgia-rep-wants-to-force-women-to-carry-stillborn-fetuses-like-cows-do-693/ (accessed 11 August 2012).

Freedman, L.P., Waldman, R.J., De Pinho, H., *et al.* (2005). *UN Millennium Project 2005: Who's Got the Power? Transforming Health Systems for Women and Children*. United Nations Development Programme (UNDP): London.

Hogan, M.C., Foreman, K.J., Naghavi, M., *et al.* (2010). Maternal mortality for 181 countries: 1980–2008: a systematic analysis of progress towards millennium development goal 5. *Lancet*, 375, 1609.

Human Rights Council. (2009). *Resolution 11/8: Preventable Maternal Mortality and Morbidity and Human Rights*. United Nations: Geneva.

Human Rights Council. (2010). *Resolution on Maternal Mortality*. United Nations: Geneva.

Human Rights Council. (2012). *Technical Guidance on the Application of a Human Rights-Based approach to the implementation of policies and programmes to reduce preventable maternal morbidity and mortality*, A/HRC/21/22. United Nations: Geneva.

Human Rights Watch. (2011). *Stop Making Excuses: Accountability for Maternal Health Care in South Africa*. Human Rights Watch: New York, NY.

Hunt, P. and Backman, G. (2008). Health systems and the right to the highest attainable standard of health. *Health and Human Rights*, 10, 81–92.

International Commission of Jurists (2007). *Yogyakarta Principles: Principles on the application of international human rights law in relation to sexual orientation and gender identity*. Available at: <http://www.unhcr.org/refworld/docid/48244e602.html> (accessed 8 February 2013).

Johnson, D. (2012, 21 June). Mothers Beware! *New York Review of Books*, pp. 23–26.

Krieger, N. (2002). Genders, sexes, and health: what are the connections—and why does it matter? *International Journal of Epidemiology*, 32, 652–657.

Mann, J., Gostin, L., Gruskin, S., *et al.* (1994). Health and human rights. *Health and Human Rights*, 1, 6–23.

Normand, R. and Zaidi, S. (2008). *Human Rights at the UN: The Political History of the Universal Justice.* Indiana University Press: Bloomington, IN.

PAHO and WHO. (2000). *Promotion of Sexual Health: Recommendations for Action. Proceedings of a Regional Consultation Convened by PAHO and WHO in Collaboration with the World Association for Sexology.* Antigua Guatemala, Guatemala. Pan American Health Organization (PAHO): Washington, DC; and World Health Organization (WHO): Geneva.

The Partnership for Maternal Newborn and Child Health. (2011). *Analysing Commitments to Advance the Global Strategy for Women's and Children's Health.* The PMNCH 2011 Report: Geneva.

Physicians for Human Rights. (2007). *Deadly Delays: Maternal Mortality in Peru—A Rights-Based Approach to Safe Motherhood.* Physicians for Human Rights: Cambridge, MA.

Raj, A., Gomez, C., and Silverman, J.G. (2008). Driven to a fiery death—the tragedy of self-immolation in Afghanistan. *New England Journal of Medicine*, 358, 2201–2203.

Reichenbach, L. (2009). The global reproductive health agenda: opportunities and challenges for the future. In L. Reichenbach and M.J. Roseman (Eds.), *Reproductive Health and Human Rights: The Way Forward*, pp. 21–40. University of Pennsylvania Press: Philadelphia, PA.

Roseman, M.J. and Reichenbach, L. (2009). Global reproductive health and rights: reflections on ICPD. In L. Reichenbach and M.J. Roseman (Eds.), *Reproductive Health and Human Rights: The Way Forward*, pp. 3–20. University of Pennsylvania Press: Philadelphia, PA.

Schoepf, B., Schoepf, C., and Millen, J. (2002). Theoretical therapies, remote remedies: SAPs and the political ecology of poverty and health in Africa. In J.Y. Kim, J.V. Millen, A. Irwin, *et al.* (Eds.), *Dying for Growth: Global Inequality and the Health of the Poor*, pp. 99–121. Common Courage Press: Monroe, ME.

Tyler, P. (1995, 6 September). Hillary Clinton, in China, details abuse of women. *The New York Times.*

UK Aid, and Bill and Melinda Gates Foundation. (2012). *London Summit on Family Planning.* Available at: <http://www.londonfamilyplanningsummit.co.uk/> (accessed 12 August 2012).

UN General Assembly. (1979). *Convention on the Elimination of All Forms of Discrimination against Women.* UN General Assembly: New York, NY.

UN General Assembly. (2006). *The Right of Everyone to the Enjoyment of the Highest Attainable Standard of Physical and Mental Health.* A/61/338. United Nations General Assembly: New York, NY.

UN General Assembly. (2010). *Report of the Special Rapporteur on the Right of Everyone to the Enjoyment of the Highest Attainable Standard of Physical and Mental Health.* A/65/255. United Nations General Assembly: New York, NY.

UN Human Rights Committee. (2005). *K.L.* v. *Peru.* CCPR/C/85/d/1153/2003. United Nations Human Rights Committee: New York, NY.

UN. (1948). *Universal Declaration of Human Rights.* United Nations: New York, NY.

UN. (1958). *Remarks by Eleanor Roosevelt at presentation of booklet on human rights, In Your Hands, to the United Nations Commission on Human Rights.* United Nations: New York, NY.

UN. (1994). *Programme of Action Adopted by the International Conference on Population and Development (ICPD).* Cairo, Egypt. A/CONF.171/13. United Nations: New York, NY.

UN. (1995). *Beijing Declaration and Platform for Action.* Beijing, China. A/CONF.177/20. United Nations: New York, NY.

UN. (2010). *UN Global Strategy on Women's and Children's Health.* United Nations: New York, NY.

UN. (2012). *Millennium Development Goals. Goal 3: Promote Gender Equality and Empower Women.* Available at: <http://www.un.org/millenniumgoals/gender.shtml> (accessed 12 August 2012).

Waage, J., Banerji, R., Campbell, O., *et al.* (2010). *The Millennium Development Goals: A Cross-Sectoral Analysis and Principles for Goal Setting after 2015* (Supplementary Web Appendix). Available at: <http://download.thelancet.com/flatcontentassets/pdfs/S0140673610611968-mmc1.pdf> (accessed 8 November 2012).

WHO. (2009). *Closing the Gap in a Generation: Health Equity through Action on the Social Determinants of Health*. World Health Organization (WHO): Geneva.

WHO. (2010). *World Health Report: Trends in Maternal Mortality: 1990 to 2008*. World Health Organization (WHO): Geneva.

WHO. (2011). *Commission on Information and Accountability for Women's and Children's Health: Keeping Promises, Measuring Results*. World Health Organization (WHO): Geneva.

WHO. (2012). *Reproductive Health*. World Health Organization (WHO): Geneva. Available at: <http://www.who.int/topics/reproductive_health/en/> (accessed 11 August 2012).

Yamin, A.E. (2005). *Learning to Dance: Advancing Women's Reproductive Health and Well-Being From the Perspectives of Public Health and Human Rights*. FXB Center for Health and Human Rights: Cambridge, MA.

Yamin, A.E. (2008). Fulfilling women's right to health—addressing maternal mortality. *Journal of Ambulatory Care Management*, 31, 193–195.

Yamin, A.E. (2010). Toward transformative accountability: applying a rights-based approach to fulfill maternal health obligations. *SUR*, 7, 95–121.

Yamin, A.E. and Falb, K.L. (2012). Counting what we know, knowing what to count: sexual and reproductive rights, maternal health, and the Millennium Development Goals. *Nordic Journal of Human Rights*, 3, 350–371.

Yamin, A.E. and Maine, D.P. (1999). Maternal mortality as a human rights issue: measuring compliance with international treaty obligations. *Human Rights Quarterly*, 21, 563–607.

Yeshou, D., Detwiler, M.R., and Smith, D.A. (2010). The global scourge of the 21st century—diabetes—and worse for women. In P. Murthy and C. Lanford Smith (Eds.), *Women's Global Health and Human Rights*, pp. 177–196. Jones and Bartlett Publishers: Sudbury, MA.

Chapter 21

The right to health in prison

Joanne Mariner and Rebecca Schleifer

Introduction

The enjoyment of the right to health in prison is most often conspicuous by its absence. Those who doubt this claim should pick the country of their choice and scan random news articles on prison health conditions there. In the United States, for example, where prison overcrowding has reached record levels and financially strapped states are trying to reduce imprisonment costs, prison health conditions are often dire (O'Dell, 2012). Critically ill inmates at state prisons in Arizona 'have begged prison officials for medical treatment . . . only to be told to "be patient", that "it's all in your head", or that they should "pray" to be cured' (Shen, 2012); and prisoners with serious mental illnesses at St. Tammany jail in Louisiana have waited weeks or months before receiving treatment (Vargas, 2012).

The neglect that these news articles describe is all too typical. Many, if not most places of detention around the world are overcrowded, violent, and dirty, with poor sanitary conditions, meagre or unhealthy food, inadequate ventilation, scant medical facilities, a shortage of medicines, and few if any medically trained staff (Human Rights Watch, 2010, 2011, 2012a, 2012b; Human Rights Watch & ACLU, 2010). Because the health problems of prisoners tend to be considerable, rates of infectious disease—and mortality rates—tend to be much higher than those experienced by the rest of society. Yet, since prisoners and their families come overwhelmingly from low socioeconomic strata with little political influence, they are poorly situated to press for improvements. And because they are usually forgotten and sometimes demonized by the public, there is little public pressure to enforce prisoners' right to health.

The population affected by these problems is sizeable. Over 10 million people are currently incarcerated in penal institutions and detention centres around the world (Walmsley, 2011). This figure represents only the prisoner population at any given moment in time, and, therefore, significantly underestimates the total number of people who pass through jails, prisons, police lock-ups, and other facilities on an annual basis (UNODC, 2011). Notably, more than a third of those incarcerated in prisons or jails—an estimated 10 million people each year—are pre-trial detainees being held pending the outcome of legal proceedings, people who are, in theory, presumed innocent of criminal behaviour (Schönteich, 2008). Prisons in some jurisdictions also hold people detained for alcohol or drug addiction treatment, and hundreds of thousands of others are held in administrative detention centres for reasons such as drug treatment, threatening national security, immigration violations, or 're-education' (Walmsley, 2011; Human Rights Watch, 2012c; Open Society Institute, 2009; Todrys et al., 2011).

This chapter reviews the international standards that guarantee, in principle, prisoners' right to health. It delineates not only the requirements set out under these standards, but also describes strategies for ensuring that these standards are met. An interesting point to note at the outset is that the right to health in prison lies at the nexus of so-called 'positive' and 'negative' rights. Having taken the step of depriving prisoners of their liberty and their ability to provide for their own healthcare, the government is under an affirmative obligation to protect their right to health. In other words, in many instances the only way for the government to comply with its duty not to subject prisoners to ill-treatment is for it to provide adequate healthcare.

The prison environment

The conditions in prisons, jails, police lockups, and other places of detention are often highly conducive to poor health and the spread of disease. Severe overcrowding, a near-universal problem—combined with poor food, water, sanitation, and ventilation, and a lack of provision for healthcare—makes many prisons a petri dish for the propagation of bacterial and viral infections. Prison violence and sexual abuse create additional physical and mental health problems. The stress of imprisonment increases the risk of suicide and other forms of self-harm.

Exacerbating the deleterious impact of these conditions, the population that enters prison is heavily skewed towards people with serious health problems and chronic untreated diseases (Jürgens et al., 2011). A significant proportion of prisoners come from the poorest, most marginalized groups in society, which often lack reliable access to healthcare. They include sex workers, individuals addicted to drugs, and people with psychosocial or intellectual disabilities. Rates of infectious diseases—including extremely serious diseases such as tuberculosis (TB), HIV, and hepatitis C—are generally much higher in the prison population than in the rest of society. Indeed, HIV prevalence in prisons worldwide has been estimated at two to 50 times that of the non-prison population, depending on the country, and viral hepatitis rates are believed to be even higher (WHO et al., 2007). The risk of TB in prisons is on average more than 20 times higher among prisoners than non-prisoners—making TB one of the leading causes of death in many countries' prisons—and the disease often takes multi-drug resistant forms due to poor adherence (Baussano et al., 2010; O'Grady et al., 2011).

The lack of adequate, suitably qualified healthcare staff and medical equipment is a problem in many prison systems worldwide. The isolation of prison health services from the general health system, often in a separate ministry, frustrates delivery of care in prison and continuity of care on entry or release (Jürgens et al., 2011). The growth of the prison population, alongside epidemics of HIV and other complex, chronic health conditions, has created additional challenges to providing adequate healthcare. The privatization of prisons in some jurisdictions (notably the United States) has complicated efforts to address prisoners' health needs by introducing incentives to increase incarceration, while becoming less accountable to public oversight (Herivel & Wright, 2003).

Besides an overall lack of medical staff, facilities, and services in many places of detention, there are also many cases of stubborn resistance to instituting certain preventive health measures, even when such measures are available to the broader public. In particular, although expert organizations such as the World Health Organization (WHO), the United Nations (UN) Office on Drugs and Crime (UNODC), and the Joint United Nations Programme on HIV/AIDS (UNAIDS) recommend that prisoners be given access to drug dependence treatment (including opioid substitution therapy), needle and syringe exchange services, and condoms, such services are rarely provided in places of detention. This situation persists in the face of strong evidence that such measures are inexpensive and effective, and a lack of evidence that they pose a security risk.

Condoms are unavailable in most prisons, despite clear awareness that sexual activity takes place behind bars and an expert consensus that their availability does not lead to an increase in prison sex (Human Rights Watch, 2007; WHO, 2007). Laws criminalizing consensual sex between adult men ('sodomy laws'), which exist in more than 80 countries, policies barring sex between prisoners, and outright discrimination against men who have sex with men frustrate efforts to distribute condoms in prison (Human Rights Watch, 2004, 2007; Kyomya et al., 2012). Similarly, only about ten countries currently allow needle/syringe programmes in some of their prisons, and about 41 allow opioid substitution therapy. At the same time, at least 37 countries offer opioid substitution therapy in community settings but not in prisons (Larney & Dolan, 2009). Moreover, the vast majority of harm reduction measures in prison fall far short of a comprehensive standard. Even in countries where harm reduction measures are allowed, many of these programmes are incomplete, small in scale, and available only in selected penal facilities (Stoicescu, 2012).

Incarceration poses serious health risks to prisoners on release, including high risk of drug overdose (Merrall et al., 2010), reduced capacity to adhere to antiretroviral therapy (Baillargeon 2009), and increased homelessness, unemployment, and other social determinants of health associated with higher rates of HIV, TB, and hepatitis C (Awofeso, 2010; CDC, 2010). Incarceration also disrupts social networks that limit HIV and other infectious disease transmission, increasing risk to prisoners and to the community outside prison (Adimora & Schoenbach, 2005; Burris et al., 2004).

Relevant international human rights standards

Under international human rights law, prisoners retain their fundamental rights and freedoms, albeit with some limitations, particularly on their rights to liberty and freedom of movement. Although prisoners may be subject to the restrictions required by their closed environment, their conditions of confinement should not unnecessarily aggravate the suffering inherent in imprisonment (UNHRC, 1992a).

Prisoners' right to health is protected by provisions in an array of widely ratified international human rights treaties, including the International Covenant on Civil and Political Rights (ICCPR, 1966); the International Covenant on Economic, Social and Cultural Rights (ICESCR, 1966); the Convention against Torture and Other Cruel, Inhuman or Degrading Treatment or Punishment (CAT, 1984); the Convention on the Elimination of All Forms of Discrimination against Women (CEDAW, 1979); the Convention on the Rights of Persons with Disabilities (CRPD, 2006); and the Convention on the Rights of the Child (CRC, 1989). It is also protected by provisions in a number of regional treaties, including the European Convention for the Protection of Human Rights and Fundamental Freedoms (ECHR, 2010); the European Convention for the Prevention of Torture and Inhuman or Degrading Treatment or Punishment (ECPT, 1987); European Social Charter, 1961; the American Convention on Human Rights (ACHR, 1969); the African Charter on Human and Peoples' Rights (African Charter on Human and People's Rights, 1981); and the Additional Protocol to the American Convention on Human Rights in the Area of Economic, Social and Cultural Rights, also known as the 'Protocol of San Salvador' (Organization of American States, 1988). Some of these treaties specifically articulate the right to health, while others such as the ICCPR and the CAT provide for the right to humane treatment, right to life, and freedom from torture, which all implicate detaining authorities' obligations with respect to the health of prisoners.

Each treaty also establishes an independent body charged with monitoring State compliance with treaty obligations and providing guidance to States in fulfilling them. Some monitoring bodies are even authorized to carry out prison visits. For example, the European Committee for the Prevention of Torture and Inhuman or Degrading Treatment or Punishment (CPT), the expert body established to monitor prison conditions and the treatment of prisoners in Europe, is specifically empowered to visit 'any place within its jurisdiction where persons are deprived of their liberty by a public authority' (ECPT, 1987).

Several other international instruments provide further guidance on how governments may comply with their legal obligation to respect prisoners' right to health. The earliest, but perhaps most comprehensive and specific, are the Standard Minimum Rules for the Treatment of Prisoners, adopted in 1957 by the UN Economic and Social Council (United Nations Standard Minimum Rules for the Treatment of Prisoners, 1957). Other relevant instruments include the Body of Principles for the Protection of All Persons under Any Form of Detention or Imprisonment; the Basic Principles for the Treatment of Prisoners; and the Principles of Medical Ethics relevant to the Role of Health Personnel, particularly Physicians, in the Protection of Prisoners and Detainees against Torture and Other Cruel, Inhuman or Degrading Treatment or Punishment; (UN General Assembly, 1982, 1988, 1990b). The Rules for the Protection of Juveniles Deprived of their Liberty and the Standard Minimum Rules for the Administration of Juvenile Justice lay out additional specifications of the conditions under which children may be detained (UN General Assembly, 1985, 1990a).

Although these instruments are not treaties, and do not have direct binding effect under international law, they may provide authoritative guidance as to the practical content of binding treaty standards (UNHRC, 1992a, 1994). Prison rights experts, noting their influence on international human rights jurisprudence, have observed that in many cases they have been recognized as 'minimum legal requirements for governments to meet' (Lines, 2008).

The scope and content of international protections on prisoners' right to health

Like all other persons, prisoners enjoy the right to the highest attainable standard of physical and mental health (ICESCR, 1966). They are also guaranteed the right to life and the right to be free of torture and cruel, inhuman or degrading treatment or punishment, and they must be treated with humanity and with respect for their inherent dignity (CAT, 1984; ICCPR, 1966). Notably, the prohibition on torture and other ill-treatment is a matter of *jus cogens*, a peremptory norm of customary international binding on every State regardless of whether it has ratified any particular treaty prohibiting such treatment (Nowak & McArthur, 2008; UNCAT, 2007). The UN General Assembly has explicitly affirmed that this right extends to all individuals detained by the State (UN General Assembly, 1988).

Under international law, States have an obligation to ensure medical care to prisoners at least equivalent to that available to the population outside of prison (CAT, 1984; ICCPR, 1966; ICESCR, 1966; Lines, 2006, 2008). States that are party to the ICESCR have committed to take steps to the maximum of their available resources, with a view to achieving progressively the full realization of the right to health. However, all Parties to the ICESCR regardless of their economic situation must guarantee minimum core obligations with respect to the right to health, including to persons behind bars. These include providing essential primary care; granting non-discriminatory access to healthcare, especially for vulnerable or marginalized groups; providing essential drugs; ensuring the equitable distribution of health facilities, goods, and services; and ensuring access to basic shelter, housing, sanitation, and potable water. Obligations of comparable priority include ensuring reproductive, maternal, and child healthcare; taking measures to prevent, treat, and control epidemic and endemic diseases; providing education and access to information for important health problems; and providing appropriate training for health personnel, including education on health and human rights (CESCR, 2000). Core obligations are non-derogable. To justify a failure to meet other ICESCR obligations, a State must show that 'every effort has nevertheless been made to use all available resources at its disposal in order to satisfy, as a matter of priority, the obligations outlined above' (CESCR, 2000; Council of Europe, 2001). The Committee on Economic, Social, and Cultural Rights (CESCR) has made clear that 'available resources' includes international economic and technical assistance, emphasizing the duty of governments and other actors in a position to assist to provide funding and other assistance to enable developing countries to fulfil core and related obligations (CESCR, 2000).

The UN Human Rights Committee, the expert UN body that monitors compliance with the ICCPR, has acknowledged that while there is no specific right to health under the ICCPR, questions on health in detention may be raised under Article 6 (right to life), Article 7 (freedom from torture), and Article 10 (humane treatment) (UNHRC, 1990, 1992a, 1992b, 1994, 2003a). The Committee has explained that the right to life 'should not be interpreted narrowly', and that further, governments must adopt 'positive measures' to increase life expectancy and eliminate epidemics (UNHRC, 1982). The Committee has further stressed that 'the State Party by arresting and detaining individuals takes the responsibility to care for their life. It is up to the State party by organizing its detention facilities to know about the state of health of the detainees as far as may be reasonably expected. Lack of financial means cannot reduce this responsibility' (UNHRC, 2002b). Therefore, according to the Committee, it is 'incumbent on States to ensure the right of life of detainees, and not incumbent on the latter to request protection' (UNHRC, 2002b). The Committee Against Torture, which monitors compliance with the Convention against Torture, has also found that failure to provide adequate medical care can violate the CAT's prohibition of cruel, inhuman, or degrading treatment (UNCAT, 1998, 2012a).

International health and human rights instruments also make clear that incarcerated persons are entitled to the same level and quality of healthcare as is available in the surrounding community, without discrimination based on their status as prisoners (CESCR, 2000; UN General Assembly, 1990b; UNODC et al., 2006). The UN Principles of Medical Ethics relevant to the Protection of Prisoners against Torture specifically state that 'Health personnel . . . charged with the medical care of prisoners and detainees have a duty to provide them with protection of their physical and mental health and treatment of disease of the same quality and standard as is afforded to those who are not imprisoned or detained' (UN General Assembly, 1982, Principle 1).

In fact, in some circumstances, the State's obligation to safeguard the lives and health of people in custody, and to protect them from ill-treatment, may require the authorities to ensure a *higher* standard of care to incarcerated persons than to those outside prison, who are not wholly dependent upon the State for the protection of their health and welfare (CAT, 1984; ICCPR, 1966; ICESCR, 1966; Lines, 2006). This positive State obligation derives from the fact that prisoners are 'powerless and can no longer protect [their] rights through their own initiative' (UN General Assembly, 2009). The African Commission on Human and Peoples' Rights, among others, has accordingly emphasized that the State's obligation to protect the right to health 'is heightened in cases where an individual is in its custody' (African Commission on Human and Peoples' Rights, 1998).

Adequate healthcare

The prohibition on torture and other ill-treatment, and the rights to life and to humane treatment, impose positive obligations on States to take action to safeguard the health of prisoners, including by guaranteeing a certain minimum adequate standard of healthcare to those in custody.

In the most serious cases, the State's failure to provide access to healthcare may implicate prisoners' right to life (UNHRC, 2002a). As the UN Human Rights Committee has pointed out, when the State arrests and detains people, it 'takes the responsibility to care for their life' (UNHRC,

2002b). The Human Rights Committee, the European Court of Human Rights, and the African Commission have all adjudicated cases in which a violation of the right to life was found due to the State's failure to provide needed medical attention to incarcerated persons (African Commission on Human and Peoples' Rights, 2000; ECHR, 2002; UNHRC, 2002b). An important prison health issue for which the right to life is especially relevant is the State's obligation to provide prisoners with HIV equal access to life-saving antiretroviral treatment. Access to TB treatment is equally critical. While in theory prisoners should receive care that is at least equivalent to that available to the outside community, in practice prisoners in many places have little or no access to HIV- and TB-related prevention and care (Jürgens et al., 2011; Todrys & Amon, 2012).

Even where not life threatening, the State's failure to provide adequate healthcare to incarcerated persons may violate the prohibition on cruel, inhuman, or degrading treatment (CPT, 2002; ECHR, 2006). It may also violate the requirement that incarcerated persons be treated with respect for their inherent dignity (UNHRC, 1990). This is particularly likely when inadequate healthcare is one of a broader array of problems, whose impact can be assessed cumulatively, or when a prisoner is denied medical attention for injuries received during beatings or other physical abuse by State agents (Lines, 2008). The UN Human Rights Committee, Inter-American Court of Human Rights, and Inter-American Commission on Human Rights, for example, have all identified poor healthcare as one of the factors resulting in a finding of abusive treatment. The UN Committee against Torture (UNCAT), similarly, has called on countries to improve prisoners' access to healthcare during its periodic assessments of countries' compliance with the Convention against Torture (UNCAT, 2003, 2011, 2012a, 2012b, 2012c).

The right to healthcare in prison includes the right to timely care (UNHRC, 2003b; UN Standard Minimum Rules for the Treatment of Prisoners, 1957; UN General Assembly, 1988). An unwarranted delay in needed medical treatment, which extends the prisoner's suffering and can entail negative health consequences, has been held to violate the right to life and protections against torture and ill-treatment in the ICCPR and the ECHR (ECHR, 2005, 2011; UNHRC, 2002b, 2003b). The Standard Minimum Rules for the Treatment of Prisoners codifies this rule in its Article 25, which provides that the 'medical officer . . . should daily see all sick prisoners, all who complain of illness, and any prisoner to whom his attention is specially directed' (UN Standard Minimum Rules for the Treatment of Prisoners, 1957).

Importantly, the right to health in prison not only requires State authorities to provide prisoners who are sick or injured with access to care, it also requires them to give access to preventive care (Lines, 2008). Steps must be taken to prevent the spread of disease, particularly with serious diseases such as HIV and TB (CESCR, 2003, 2011). When the failure to provide preventive healthcare has extremely harmful consequences, the State's failure to take such preventive steps may violate the prohibition on cruel, inhuman, or degrading treatment (ECHR, 2003; UNHRC, 2002c, 2002d). A concern for preventing such prohibited ill-treatment should inform the debate over condom distribution and other harm reduction measures, which have been recommended by expert agencies such as the WHO, UNAIDS, and UNODC as a matter of policy (UNODC, 2011).

Healthy conditions of confinement

Some experts affirm that the right to health encompasses the right to healthy living conditions, given that such conditions provide the crucial 'underlying determinants of health' (CESCR, 2000). Key elements include 'food and nutrition, housing, access to safe and potable water and adequate sanitation . . . and a healthy environment' (CESCR, 2000). It is clear, moreover, that the prohibition on torture and ill-treatment extends to conditions of confinement, as does the requirement of respect for human dignity (UNHRC, 1992a, 1992b).

A range of human rights bodies, including the UNCAT, the UNHRC, the UN Special Rapporteur on torture, and the European Court of Human Rights, have specifically identified overcrowding as one of the poor conditions that negatively affect the health of prisoners (Lines, 2008). In its concluding observations on Georgia, for example, the Human Rights Committee pointed to overcrowding as one of the factors that had led to a 'high rate of infectious disease and a very alarming mortality rate' in the country's prisons (UNHRC, 1997a). The UN Special Rapporteur on the right to health has noted, similarly, that overcrowding and a lack of privacy in prison 'tend to exacerbate mental disabilities' (UNCHR, 2005). Other prison conditions that human rights bodies have condemned for their deleterious impact on health include poor sanitary conditions, a lack of clean water, insufficient food, the presence of insects and other vermin, and 'airless' and stuffy cells.

Informed consent

The right to health also includes the right to refuse medical treatment, a right that has traditionally been in great jeopardy in the prison context. Forced medical experimentation has long been a hazard of imprisonment, so much so that the ICCPR's prohibition on torture and cruel, inhuman, or degrading treatment includes a specific protection against such experimentation (ICCPR, 1966). To enforce prisoners' right to refuse treatment, prisoners have a right to informed consent: in particular, to be provided with information 'sufficient to enable them to make an informed choice about their treatment options, and that they are able to refuse treatment if they so choose' (UNODC et al., 2006). As a group of UN Special Rapporteurs have explained, '[f]rom the perspective of the right to health, informed consent to medical treatment is essential, as is its 'logical corollary' the right to refuse treatment' (UNCHR, 2006). This right extends not only to unwanted medical treatment, but also to medical testing (UNODC et al., 2006).

Confidentiality of medical information

Prisoners enjoy a right to confidential medical information, though it may be limited by the demands of incarceration. Article 12 of the ICESCR guarantees protection of the confidentiality of personal health information as part of the right to health (CESCR, 2000). Efforts to ensure confidentiality of medical information are critical to ensuring other rights, including access to healthcare, as well as protection against discrimination and violence based on health status. For example, prisoners living with HIV routinely face discrimination, and sometimes violence, when their HIV status is disclosed. The fear of disclosure keeps some from seeking testing or treatment.

While prisoners do not enjoy absolute protection for the confidentiality of their medical information, breaches must be strictly justified. In practice, confidentiality may be unjustifiably broken through deliberate acts and omissions by prison officials that lack a sound penological justification. For example, HIV-positive prisoners in some countries are housed in segregated units and dressed in uniforms that disclose their status (Human Rights Watch & ACLU, 2010). In many cases, misinformation about HIV test results in prison policies that promote the disclosure of confidential information, and in turn fuel discrimination against prisoners living with HIV, dissuading people from undergoing HIV testing.

Mental health

Prisoners' right to health extends equally to mental health, and prison authorities are under the obligation to provide prisoners with adequate and necessary mental healthcare. The Convention on the Rights of Persons with Disabilities, which applies to people with long-term mental health problems, reaffirms the rights of people with disabilities to 'the highest attainable standard of health without discrimination on the basis of disability' (CRPD, 2006). It also recognizes within this right an obligation of States to 'provide those health services needed by persons with disabilities specifically because of their disabilities', which would include mental health services (CRPD, 2006). The Standard Minimum Rules affirm that all prisons should have a psychiatric service 'for the diagnosis and, in proper cases, the treatment of States of mental abnormality'. (UN Standard Minimum Rules for the Treatment of Prisoners, 1957). In his February 2013 report to the UN Human Rights Council (UNHRC), the Special Rapporteur on torture wrote that the CRPD superseded the 1991 Principles for the Protection of Mental Illness and should be reviewed in this light. Disability rights experts agree, and caution against pointing to the principles as an example. The UNHRC has, accordingly, found a lack of mental health services in prison to be a violation of prisoners' rights (UNHRC, 2002d). In a UK case involving a mentally ill prisoner who mortally beat another mentally ill prisoner, the European Court of Human Rights found that poor mental health services—and, in particular, a failure to provide adequate mental health screening—violated the victim's right to life (ECHR, 2002). Other cases have found a lack of adequate mental health services to be part of a pattern of cruel, inhuman, or degrading treatment (UNCHR, 2006; UNHRC, 1997b).

Without proper care, mentally ill prisoners suffer painful and debilitating symptoms. They may be afflicted with delusions and hallucinations, terrible fears, or extreme mood swings. With this in mind, it should be recalled that the prohibition on torture and ill-treatment applies 'not only to acts that cause physical pain but also to acts that cause mental suffering to the victim' (UNHRC, 1992b).

A form of imprisonment that may have a particularly negative mental health impact is solitary confinement or, as it is often called, administrative segregation. In light of the 'severe mental pain or suffering solitary confinement may cause', the UN Special Rapporteur on torture has called for the practice to be abolished. As he emphasized, '[n]egative health effects can occur after only a few days in solitary confinement, and the health risks rise with each additional day spent in such conditions' (UN General Assembly, 2011).

Particular groups

Different types of prisoners—such as women, older prisoners, children, indigenous people, and prisoners with disabilities—may have particular health needs, and should be provided access to healthcare that is appropriate to those needs. Accordingly, additional legal frameworks exist to protect them. Women, for example, should be given access to adequate gynaecological or maternity care; children may need vaccinations. Older prisoners may have a range of special needs, given their higher propensity for impaired mobility, hearing, and vision loss, as well as cognitive limitations including dementia, and chronic, disabling, and terminal illnesses (Human Rights Watch, 2012a).

Equally important, State authorities must take the particular vulnerabilities of different types of prisoners into account when taking steps that impact prisoners' health. A case in point is solitary confinement, which should never be used for juveniles and persons with psychosocial disabilities (UN General Assembly, 2011). The UNCAT, generally critical of solitary confinement, has called for the abolition of solitary confinement for persons with serious or acute mental illness (UNCAT, 2012b). As one US judge explained, putting mentally ill prisoners in solitary confinement 'is the mental equivalent of putting an asthmatic in a place with little air' (*Madrid* v. *Gomez*, 1995).

Remedies and reform

As closed institutions populated by largely despised groups, prisons are rarely the subject of public attention or concern; their immense problems hardly ever break into public consciousness. To force State authorities to pay greater attention to problems that they would rather ignore, therefore, the work of international and regional monitoring bodies—such as the European Committee for the Prevention of Torture and the Subcommittee on Prevention of Torture and other Cruel, Inhuman or Degrading Treatment or Punishment—is crucial. Unfortunately, many States are not a party to the treaties that establish these prison monitoring mechanisms, and even States that do belong to them often ignore or fail fully to implement the recommendations made by the monitoring bodies.

Moreover, overwhelming structural problems mean that documenting and revealing human rights abuses in prison are not enough. In country after country around the world, penal facilities and places of detention are seriously overcrowded and woefully under-resourced. The abusive conditions that result routinely violate prisoners' right to health, as well as an array of other rights. Given the reality of prison overcrowding, and the lack of public willingness to spend money to allocate funds to improving the situation of prisoners, it may be that the most effective way to respond to poor prison health conditions is not to focus narrowly on improving access to healthcare, but to think more generally about ways to reduce the numbers of people sent to prison.

Some prisoners are incarcerated for unjust or illegitimate reasons; they should simply be released. In addition, States should rely more on non-custodial alternatives to incarceration such as bail, community service, supervised release, and parole. States also need to address the larger failures of the criminal justice system: problems that contribute to high rates of pre-trial detention and the over-representation of marginalized people in prison.

Conclusion

Nearly all prisoners eventually return to society, and when they go back to their home communities they bring with them the marks of their prison experience, including, in many cases, poor physical and mental health, untreated injuries, and infectious diseases. Therefore, it should be clear that the current disastrous state of prison health conditions and care not only harms prisoners and prison staff, but it has a negative impact on their larger communities. Because attending to the health of prisoners is a matter of public health, it is crucial for State authorities to provide prisoners with decent living conditions and with adequate, care when they become ill, and to integrate healthcare services in prison with such services outside of prison.

Done correctly, prison healthcare can help both prisoners and society, reaching members of high-risk communities who might otherwise go without care. While respecting the right to health in prison should be taken seriously as a matter of human rights law, it also merits attention as a matter of policy.

References

ACHR. (1969). *American Convention on Human Rights.* Adopted 22 November 1969.

Adimora, A.A. and Schoenbach, V. J. (2005). Social context, sexual networks, and racial disparities in rates of sexually transmitted infections. *Journal of Infectious Diseases*, 191, S115–122.

African Charter on Human and Peoples' Rights. (1981). *African Charter on Human and Peoples' Rights ('Banjul Charter').* OAU Doc. CAB/LEG/67/3 rev. 5, 21 I.L.M. 58 (1982), entry into force 21 October 1986.

African Commission on Human and Peoples' Rights. (1998). *International Pen and Others* v. *Nigeria.* Comm. Nos. 137/94, 139/94, 154/96 and 161/97.

African Commission on Human and Peoples' Rights. (2000). *Malawi African Association and others* v. *Mauritania.* Comm. Nos. 54/91, 61/91, 98/93, 164/97 and 210/98.

Awefoso, N. (2010). Prison as social determinants of hepatitis C virus and tuberculosis infections. *Public Health Reports*, 125, 25–34.

Baillargeon, J., Giordano, T.P., Rich, J.D., *et al.* (2009). Accessing antiretroviral therapy following release from prison. *Journal of the American Medical Association*, 301, 848–857.

Baussano, I., Williams, B.G., Nunn, P., *et al.* (2010). Tuberculosis in prisons: a systematic review. *PLoS Medicine*, 7, e1000381.

Burris, S., Blankenship, K.M., Donoghoe, M., *et al.* (2004). Addressing the 'risk environment' for injection drug users: the mysterious case of the missing cop. *Milbank Quarterly*, 82, 125–156.

CAT. (1984). *Convention against Torture and other Cruel, Inhuman or Degrading Treatment or Punishment.* G.A. res. 39/46, annex, 39 U.N. GAOR Supp. (no. 51) at 197, U.N. Doc. A/39/51, adopted 10 December 1984, entry into force 26 June 1987.

CEDAW. (1979). *Convention on the Elimination of All Forms of Discrimination against Women.* Adopted 18 December 1979, entry into force 23 September 1981.

Centers for Disease Control and Prevention. (CDC). (2010). *Establishing a Holistic Framework to Reduce Inequities in HIV, Viral Hepatitis, STDs, and TB in The United States: An NCHHSTP White Paper on Social Determinants Of Health, 2010.* Centers for Disease Control: Atlanta, GA. Available at: <http://www.cdc.gov/socialdeterminants/docs/SDH-White-Paper-2010.pdf> (accessed 7 November 2012).

CESCR. (2000). *General Comment 14: The right to the highest attainable standard of health (article 12 of the International Covenant on Economic, Social and Cultural Rights).* Doc. No. E/C. 12/2000/4. Committee on Economic, Social, and Cultural Rights (CESCR): Geneva.

CESCR. (2003). *Concluding Observations of the Committee on Economic, Social and Cultural Rights: Republic of Moldova.* Doc. No. E/C.12/Add.91. Committee on Economic, Social, and Cultural Rights (CESCR): Geneva.

CESCR. (2011). *Concluding Observations of the Committee on Economic, Social and Cultural Rights: Russian Federation.* Doc. No. E/C.12/Rus/CO/5. Committee on Economic, Social, and Cultural Rights (CESCR): Geneva.

Council of Europe. (2001). *11th General Report on the CPT's Activities Covering the Period 1 January 2000 to 31 December 2000.* Strasbourg, Council of Europe, 2001 (CPT/Inf (2001) 16.

CPT. (2002). *CPT standards.* Doc. No. CPT/Inf/E (2002) 1—Rev. 2011. European Committee for the Prevention of Torture and Inhuman or Degrading Treatment or Punishment (CPT), Council of Europe: Geneva.

CRC. (1989). *Convention on the Rights of the Child.* Adopted and opened for signature, ratification and accession by General Assembly resolution 44/25, 20 November 1989, entry into force 2 September 1990, in accordance with article 49.

CRPD. (2006). *Convention on the Rights of Persons with Disabilities.* A. Res. 61/106, annex I, U.N. GAOR, 61st Sess., Supp. (No. 49) at 65, UN Doc. A/61/49. Adopted 13 December 2006, entry into force 3 May 2008.

ECHR. (2002). *Edwards and another* v. *United Kingdom*, application no. 46477/99.

ECHR. (2003). *Pantea* v. *Romania*, application no. 33343/96.

ECHR. (2005). *Nevmerzhitsky* v. *Ukraine*, application no. 54825/00.

ECHR. (2006). *Melnik* v. *Ukraine*, application no. 72286/01.

ECHR. (2011). *Vasyukov* v. *Russia*, application no. 2974/05.

ECHR. (2010). *European Convention for the Protection of Human Rights and Fundamental Freedoms.* Rome, 4.XI.1950, as amended by Protocols No. 11 and No. 14, entry into force 1 June 2010.

ECPT. (1987). *European Convention for the Prevention of Torture and Inhuman or Degrading Treatment or Punishment.* Doc. No. CPT/Inf/C (2002) 1 [EN] (Part 1)—Strasbourg, 26.XI.1987. Text amended according to the provisions of Protocols No. 1 (ETS No. 151) and No. 2 (ETS No. 152) which entered into force on 1 March 2002.

European Social Charter. (1961). *ETS 35—Social Charter*. Turin, 18.X.1961. Council of Europe: Strasbourg.

Herivel, T. and Wright, P. (2003). *Prison Nation: the Warehousing of America's Poor*. Routledge: New York, NY.

Human Rights Watch. (2004). *Hated To Death: Homophobia, Violence and Jamaica's HIV/AIDS Epidemic*. Human Rights Watch: New York, NY. Available at: <http://www.hrw.org/sites/default/files/reports/jamaica1104.pdf> (accessed 7 November 2012).

Human Rights Watch. (2007). *Ensure Access to Condoms in US Prisons and Jails*. Human Rights Watch: New York, NY. Available at: <http://www.hrw.org/sites/default/files/reports/condoms0307web.pdf> (accessed 7 November 2012).

Human Rights Watch. (2010). *Unjust and Unhealthy: HIV, TB, and Abuse in Zambian Prisons*. Human Rights Watch: New York, NY. Available at: <http://www.hrw.org/sites/default/files/reports/zambia0410webwcover.pdf> (accessed 7 November 2012).

Human Rights Watch. (2011). *'Even Dead Bodies Must Work': Health, Hard Labor, and Abuse in Ugandan Prisons*. Human Rights Watch: New York, NY. Available at: <http://www.hrw.org/sites/default/files/reports/uganda0711webwcover.pdf> (accessed 7 November 2012).

Human Rights Watch. (2012a). *Old Behind Bars: The Aging Prison Population in the United States*. Human Rights Watch: New York, NY. Available at: <http://www.hrw.org/sites/default/files/reports/usprisons0112webwcover_0.pdf> (accessed 7 November 2012).

Human Rights Watch. (2012b). *'Prison Is Not For Me': Arbitrary Detention in South Sudan*. Human Rights Watch: New York, NY. Available at: <http://www.hrw.org/sites/default/files/reports/southsudan0612_forinsert4Upload.pdf> (accessed 7 November 2012).

Human Rights Watch. (2012c). *Torture in The Name Of Treatment: Human Rights Abuses in Vietnam, China, Cambodia, and Lao PDR*. Human Rights Watch: New York, NY. Available at: <http://www.hrw.org/sites/default/files/reports/HHR%20Drug%20Detention%20Brochure_LOWRES.pdf> (accessed 7 November 2012).

Human Rights Watch and ACLU. (2010). *Sentenced to Stigma: Segregation of HIV-Positive Prisoners in Alabama and South Carolina*. Human Rights Watch and American Civil Liberties Union (ACLU): New York, NY. Available at: <http://www.aclu.org/files/assets/health0410webwcover.pdf> (accessed 7 November 2012).

ICCPR. (1966). *International Covenant on Civil and Political Rights*. G.A. Res. 2200A (XXI), 21 U.N. GAOR Supp. (no. 16) at 52. Adopted 16 December 1966, UN Doc. A/6316 (1966), 999 U.N.T.S. 171, entry into force 23 March 1976.

ICESCR. (1966). *International Covenant on Economic, Social and Cultural Rights*. Res 2200A (XXI), 21 U.N. GAOR Supp. (No. 16) at 49. Adopted 16 December 1966, G.A, UN Doc. A/6316 993 U.N. T.S. 3, entry into force 3 January 1976.

Jürgens, R., Nowak, M., and Day, M. (2011). HIV and incarceration: Prisons and detention, *Journal of the International AIDS Society*, 14, 26. doi:10.1186/1758-2652-14-26.

Kyomya, M., Todrys, K. W., and Amon, J. J. (2012). Laws against sodomy and the HIV epidemic in African prisons. *Lancet*, 380, 310–312.

Larney, S. and Dolan, K. (2009). A literature review of international implementation of opioid substitution treatment in prisons: Equivalence of care? *European Addiction Research*, 15, 107–112.

Lines, R. (2006). From equivalence of standards to equivalence of objectives: The entitlement of prisoners to health care standards higher than those outside prisons. *International Journal of Prisoner Health*, 2, 269–280.

Lines, R. (2008). The right to health of prisoners in international human rights law. *International Journal of Prison Health*, 4, 3–53.

Madrid v. *Gomez*. (1995). 889 F Supp. 1146, 1265.

Merrall, L.C., Kariminia, A., Binswanger, I.A., *et al.* (2010). Meta-analysis of drug-related deaths soon after release from prison. *Addiction*, 105, 1545–1554.

Nowak, M. and McArthur, E. (2008). *The United Nations Convention Against Torture: A Commentary.* Oxford University Press: New York, NY.

O'Dell, L. (2012). *Inmates at VA women's prison allege shoddy health care amounts to cruel and unusual punishment.* Available at: <http://www.therepublic.com/view/story/bbca8f8f8f30427d867d911234cf2c81/VA—Prisoners-Health-Lawsuit> (accessed 7 November 2012).

O'Grady, J., Hoelscher, M., Atun, R., *et al.* (2011). Tuberculosis in prisons in sub-Saharan Africa—the need for improved health services, surveillance and control. *Tuberculosis*, 91, 173–178.

Organization of American States. (1988). *Additional Protocol to the American Convention on Human Rights in the Area of Economic, Social and Cultural Rights ('Protocol of San Salvador').* Adopted in San Salvador on November 17.

Schönteich, M. (2008). *The scale and consequences of pretrial detention around the world.* Open Society Justice Initiative. Open Society Institute: New York, NY. Available at: <http://www.opensocietyfoundations.org/publications/justice-initiatives-pretrial-detention> (accessed 9 November 2012).

Shen, A. (2012). *States' Efforts to Privatize Prison Health Care Create 'Inhumane' Conditions.* ThinkProgress: Washington, DC. Available at: <http://thinkprogress.org/health/2012/07/23/563131/states-privatized-prison-health-care> (accessed 7 November 2012).

Stoicescu, C. (2012). *The Global State Of Harm Reduction: Towards an Integrated Response.* Harm Reduction International: London. Available at: <http://www.ihra.net/files/2012/07/24/GlobalState2012_Web.pdf> (accessed 7 November 2012).

Todrys, K.W. and Amon, J.J. (2012). Criminal justice reform as HIV and TB prevention in African prisons. *PLoS Medicine*, 9, e1001215.

Todrys, K.W., Amon, J.J., Malembeka, G., *et al.* (2011). Imprisoned and imperiled: Access to HIV and TB prevention and treatment, and denial of human rights in Zambian prisons, *Journal of the International AIDS Society*, 14, 8. doi:10.1186/1758–2652–14–8.

UNCAT. (1998). *Concluding Observations: New Zealand.* UN Doc. A/53/44, paras. 167–178. United Nations Committee Against Torture (UNCAT): New York, NY.

UNCAT. (2003). *Concluding Observations: Belgium.* UN Doc. CAT/C/CR/30/6. United Nations Committee Against Torture (UNCAT): New York, NY.

UNCAT. (2007). *General Comment No. 2: Implementation of article 2 by States Parties.* UN Doc. CAT/C/GC/2/CRP.1/Rev.4, para. 1. United Nations Committee Against Torture (UNCAT): New York, NY.

UNCAT. (2011). *Concluding Observations: Ireland.* UN Doc. CAT/C/IRL/CO/1, para. 14. United Nations Committee Against Torture (UNCAT): New York.

UNCAT. (2012a). *Concluding Observations: Cuba.* UN Doc. CAT/C/CUB/CO/2, para. 10. United Nations Committee Against Torture (UNCAT): New York.

UNCAT. (2012b). *Concluding Observations: Canada.* UN Doc. CAT/C/CAN/CO/6. United Nations Committee Against Torture (UNCAT): New York.

UNCAT. (2012c). *Concluding Observations: Greece.* UN Doc. CAT/C/GRC/CO/5-6, paras. 14 and 20. United Nations Committee Against Torture (UNCAT): New York.

UNCHR. (2005). *Report of the United Nations Special Rapporteur on the Right of Everyone to the Enjoyment of the Highest Attainable Standard of Physical and Mental Health, Paul Hunt.* UN Doc. E/CN.4/2005/51. United Nations: New York, NY.

UNCHR. (2006). *Joint Report on the Situation of Detainees at Guantanamo Bay.* UN Doc. E/CN.4/2006/120. United Nations Commission on Human Rights (UNCHR): Geneva.

UN General Assembly. (1982). *Principles of Medical Ethics relevant to the Role of Health Personnel, particularly Physicians, in the Protection of Prisoners and Detainees against Torture and Other Cruel, Inhuman or Degrading Treatment or Punishment.* UN Doc. A/RES/37/194. United Nations: New York.

UN General Assembly. (1985). *United Nations Standard Minimum Rules for the Administration of Juvenile Justice ('The Beijing Rules').* UN Doc. A/RES/40/33. United Nations: New York, NY.

UN General Assembly. (1990a). *United Nations Rules for the Protection of Juveniles Deprived of their Liberty.* G.A. Res. 45/113, UN Doc. A/RES/45/113. United Nations: New York, NY.

UN General Assembly. (1990b). *Basic Principles for the Treatment of Prisoners.* Adopted 14 December 1990, G.A. Res. 45/111, annex, 45 U.N. GAOR Supp. (No. 49A), UN Doc. A/45/49. United Nations: New York, NY.

UN General Assembly. (1988). *Body of Principles for the Protection of All Persons under Any Form of Detention or Imprisonment.* G.A. Res. 43/173, annex, UN Doc. A/RES/43/173. United Nations: New York, NY.

UN General Assembly. (2009). *Interim Report of the Special Rapporteur on Torture and Other Cruel, Inhuman or Degrading Treatment or Punishment.* UN Doc. A/64/215. United Nations: New York, NY.

UN General Assembly. (2011). *Interim Report of the Special Rapporteur on Torture and Other Cruel, Inhuman or Degrading Treatment or Punishment.* UN Doc. A/66/268. United Nations: New York, NY.

UNHRC. (1982). *General Comment 6, Article 6, Sixteenth session, 1982.* Compilation of General Comments and General Recommendations Adopted by Human Rights Treaty Bodies, UN Doc. HRI/GEN/1/Rev. 1 at 6. United Nations Human Rights Committee (UNHRC): Geneva.

UNHRC. (1990). *Pinto v Trinidad and Tobago.* Communication No. 232/1987, UN Doc A/45/40. United Nations Human Rights Committee (UNHRC): Geneva.

UNHRC. (1992a). *General Comment 21, Article 10, Forty-fourth session, 1992.* Compilation of General Comments and General Recommendations Adopted by Human Rights Treaty Bodies, UN Doc. HRI/GEN/1/Rev. 1 at 33. United Nations Human Rights Committee (UNHRC): Geneva.

UNHRC. (1992b). *General Comment 20, Article 7, Forty-fourth session, 1992.* Compilation of General Comments and General Recommendations Adopted by Human Rights Treaty Bodies, UN Doc. HRI/GEN/1/Rev. 1 at 30. United Nations Human Rights Committee (UNHRC): Geneva.

UNHRC. (1994). *Womah Mukong v Cameroon.* Communication No. 458/1991, UN Doc. CCPR/C/51/D/458/1991. United Nations Human Rights Committee (UNHRC): Geneva.

UNHRC. (1997a). *Concluding Observations: Georgia.* UN Doc. CCPR/C/79/Add.75. United Nations Human Rights Committee (UNHRC): Geneva.

UNHRC. (1997b). *Williams v Jamaica.* Communication No. 609/1995, UN Doc. CCPR/C/61/D/609/1995. United Nations Human Rights Committee (UNHRC): Geneva.

UNHRC. (2002a). *Concluding Observations: Georgia.* UN Doc. CCPR/CO/74/GEO. United Nations Human Rights Committee (UNHRC): Geneva.

UNHRC. (2002b). *Lantsova v Russian Federation.* 763/1997, UNHCR 74th session, UN Doc. CCPR/C/74/763/1997. United Nations Human Rights Committee (UNHRC): Geneva.

UNHRC. (2002c). *Concluding Observations: Moldova.* UN Doc. A/57/40 vol. I 76. United Nations Human Rights Committee (UNHRC): Geneva.

UNHRC. (2002d). *Sahadath v Trinidad and Tobago.* Communication No. 684/1996, UN Doc. CCPR/C/684/1996. United Nations Human Rights Committee (UNHRC): Geneva.

UNHRC. (2003a). *Cabal and Pasini v Australia.* UN Doc. CCPR/C/78/D/1020/2002. United Nations Human Rights Committee (UNHRC): Geneva.

UNHRC. (2003b). *Concluding Observations: Portugal.* UN Doc. CCPR/CO/78/PRT. United Nations Human Rights Committee (UNHRC): Geneva.

United Nations Office on Drugs and Crime (UNODC). (2011). *HIV in prisons: Situation and needs assessment toolkit.* United Nations Office on Drugs and Crime (UNODC): Vienna. Available at: <http://www.unodc.org/documents/hiv-aids/publications/HIV_in_prisons_situation_and_needs_assessment_document.pdf> (accessed 7 November 2012).

United Nations Office on Drugs, World Health Organization, and Joint United Nations Program on HIV/AIDS (UNAIDS). (2006). *HIV/AIDS prevention, care, treatment and support in prison settings a framework for an effective national response.* United Nations Office on Drugs and Crime, Vienna, World

Health Organization (WHO), Geneva, UNAIDS, Geneva. Available at: <http://www.unodc.org/pdf/HIV-AIDS_prisons_July06.pdf> (accessed 7 November 2012).

United Nations Standard Minimum Rules for the Treatment of Prisoners (SMR). (1957). *Adopted by the First United Nations Congress on the Prevention of Crime and the Treatment of Offenders.* Held at Geneva in 1955, and approved by the Economic and Social Council by its resolution 663 C (XXIV) of 31 July 1957, and 2076 (LXII) of 13 May 1977.

Vargas, R.A. (2012, 17 July). St. Tammany jail provides inadequate mental health care, suicide prevention, federal investigation finds. *The Times-Picayune.* Available at: <http://www.nola.com/crime/index.ssf/2012/07/st_tammany_jail_provides_inade.html> (accessed 7 November 2012).

Walmsley, R. (2011). *World Prison Population List* (9th Ed.). International Centre for Prison Studies: London.

WHO. (2007). *Health in Prisons: A WHO Guide to the Essentials in Prison Health.* WHO Regional Office for Europe: Copenhagen.

WHO, UNODC, and UNAIDS. (2007). *Effectiveness of evidence to address HIV in prisons.* World Health Organization (WHO), United Nations Office on Drugs and Crime (UNODC), and Joint United Nations Programme on HIV/AIDS (UNAIDS): Geneva. Available at: <http://whqlibdoc.who.int/publications/2007/9789241596190_eng.pdf> (accessed 7 November 2012).

Chapter 22

Access to medical products, vaccines, and medical technologies

Stephen P. Marks and Adriana L. Benedict

Introduction

The human right to medical products, vaccines, and medical technologies—which is understood here as including access to medicines, to vaccines, and to devices and procedures—is a derivative right from the rights to health as well as the right to benefit from scientific progress. When the main human rights instruments were drafted, the idea that lack of access to these commodities compromised human rights was not considered, except to the extent that these were reasonable measures constituting healthcare. Subsequently, and particularly as a result of the HIV pandemic, the vital need for treatment of HIV-positive individuals contributed to the progressive acknowledgement that access to medicines, including antiretroviral therapy (ART), was an internationally recognized human right. This argument has been extended from medicines to other life-saving health goods and from HIV/AIDS to the full range of health conditions that account for the disproportionate levels of mortality and morbidity in developing countries.

Today, access to medical products, vaccines, and medical technologies can be affirmed as a human right insofar as it is a significant component of two rights contained in the International Covenant on Economic, Social and Cultural Rights (ICESCR), namely, the right to health (Article 12) and the right 'to share in scientific advancement and its benefits' (Article 15(1)(b)) (UN General Assembly, 1996). The same Article 15 affirms the right 'to the protection of the moral and material interests resulting from any scientific, literary or artistic production' (Article 15(1)(c)) (UN General Assembly, 1996), according to which creative ideas and expressions of the human mind that possess commercial value receive the legal protection of property rights called intellectual property (IP) rights. The major legal mechanisms for protecting IPRs are copyrights, patents, and trademarks, which grant owners the exclusive right to make, sell, or use their original work products. There is an apparent contradiction between these two rights when applied to access to medical commodities: Article 15(1)(c) seems to protect the 'right' of companies to earn a profit from the products they develop, including by setting prices that render them inaccessible to the destitute sick, while Article 15(1)(b) seems to protect the 'right' of those destitute sick to benefit from the development of new medical products. The way out of this dilemma is to distinguish IP rights from human rights and consider them a temporary monopoly established for the valid social purpose of encouraging scientific invention and artistic creation. In other words, an IPR is a legally protected interest of a lower order than a human right, which implies a superior moral and legal claim. This distinction should not be interpreted to imply that IP rights do not have social value for, indeed, they have a very high value, justifying reasonably limiting Article 15 rights to promote innovation and creativity. However, as this chapter will seek to demonstrate, where the right to health is seriously impinged by IP rights, the human rights of those affected—to benefit from scientific progress and to health—prevail.

In order to assess the role and significance of access to medical products, vaccines, and medical technologies (hereinafter referred to collectively as 'health goods') in the context of the right to health, this chapter will focus on how these health goods have been addressed in global health and in relation to the evolving definition of the right to the highest attainable standard of health, on the one hand, and in relation to protection of intellectual property and other means to promote advances in science and technology, on the other.

Access to health goods

While much attention has been devoted to the concept of access to medicines, and specifically to essential medicines, the broader concept used in this chapter is based on the World Health Organization (WHO) building blocks of health systems, which include 'medical products, vaccines and technologies of assured quality, safety, efficacy and cost-effectiveness'; along with service delivery; health workforce; information; financing; and leadership and governance (stewardship) (WHO, 2007). Inclusion of this broader spectrum of goods is most compatible with the progressive realization of the right to health.

Numerous factors contribute to making health goods available in developing countries, including affordable prices; government commitment through a well-conceived and implemented national medicines policy; adequate, sustainable, and equitable public sector financing; generic substitution; transparent and widely disseminated consumer information; efficient distribution; control of taxes, duties and other markups; and careful selection and monitoring (WHO, 2004). The UN Millennium Project (2005) has identified six categories of barriers to access: inadequate national commitment; inadequate human resources; failure of the international community to keep its promises to developing countries; lack of coordination of international aid; obstacles created by the World Trade Organization (WTO) Agreement on Trade-Related Aspects of Intellectual Property (TRIPS); and the failure of the current incentive structure for research and development (R&D) to address priority health needs of developing countries. While several large international foundations (such as the Bill & Melinda Gates Foundation and the William J. Clinton Foundation) have successfully negotiated increased access through reduced prices for medicines by guaranteeing purchases and continuous demand, such strategies only address a fraction of the access gap. Similarly, donation programmes, albeit commendable, fail to address the systemic challenges requiring sustainable commitments and strategies (Holt et al., 2012).

While the literature has historically focused primarily on access to medicines, many of the considerations for access to vaccines and medical technologies are similar. As just mentioned, this chapter will therefore assume a degree of commonality among these categories in extrapolating lessons from access to medicines to the broader category of health goods. Nevertheless, to provide adequate context, the subcategories are briefly defined and introduced next.

Medical products (medicines)

Pre-eminent among 'medical products' are drugs for prevention, care, or treatment which must be available to those who need them 'on time, reliably, in sufficient quantity, and at reasonable cost' (WHO, 2007). As stated the historical focus on 'essential medicines' is just one component of the right to health's inclusion of medical products. Because the right to the highest attainable standard of health is a progressive right, it should not be limited to those medicines formally designated as 'essential' (a category which does not formally encompass many life-saving medicines due to arguably surmountable and therefore largely irrelevant cost-effectiveness and other considerations). The United Nations (UN) Development Group defines 'access' in the context of medicines as 'continuously available and affordable at public or private health facilities or drug outlets that are within one hour's walk of the population' (UN Development Group, 2003).

In 1975, half of the world's population was without access to life-saving and other essential medicines (UN Millennium Project, 2005). While this proportion has decreased to about one-third of the world's population, the absolute number has remained constant at approximately two billion people (Hogerzeil & Mirza, 2011). According to the WHO, public sector availability of essential medicines in 27 developing countries averages 34.9% (WHO, 2009a). Even where they are available, medicines may be inaccessible because they are unaffordable. The regional public sector availability of generic medicines (which are more affordable than their brand-name counterparts) is estimated to range from 29.4% in Africa to 54.4% in the Americas (Cameron et al., 2009).

Vaccines

Vaccines are defined by the WHO as 'biological products with effects that can exceed the induction of immunological protection against specific diseases', and primarily involve preparations intended to produce immunity to a disease by stimulating the production of antibodies (WHO, 2009b). Immunization can save between two and three million lives annually in all age groups, and the principal strategy for achieving this aim is the Global Immunization Vision and Strategy (GIVS), launched in 2006 by the WHO and the United Nations Children's Fund (UNICEF) under the guiding principle that '[a]ll people—without distinction of race, religion, political belief, economic or social condition—have a right to equal access to the needed vaccines and interventions' (WHO & UNICEF, 2006). GIVS is a ten-year framework which aims to increase the quantity and quality of immunizations in an equitable manner, particularly in low- and middle-income countries, where, according to the World Health Assembly (WHA), 'access to safe and effective vaccines is a human right that is not currently enjoyed by all people' (WHA, 2011). In order to uphold its commitment to immunization as a human right by focusing on vulnerable populations, GIVS recently shifted its emphasis from 'Reaching All Districts' to 'Reaching All Communities' (WHA, 2011).

A mid-term review of GIVS's progress found that although three-quarters of countries had achieved or were on track to achieve 90% or more coverage by 2015 for two key vaccines, DTP3 and MCV, nearly one-third of developing and least-developed countries were not on track, and nearly one-quarter of 68 priority countries had not made any progress (Brown et al., 2011). Access to newer vaccines paints a similarly dismal picture: over 83% of cervical cancer cases and deaths (preventable by human papilloma virus (HPV) vaccines) occur in developing countries (Erdman, 2009).

Medical technologies

Medical technologies encompass a wide range of devices, diagnostics, and technological processes used to detect, monitor, or treat medical conditions. 'Medical devices' in particular, have been defined to cover numerous products ranging from simple tongue depressors and bedpans to complex programmable pacemakers with micro-chip technology and laser surgical devices' (US FDA, 2010). For purposes of regulatory control in the United States, for example, a medical device is:

> [A]n instrument, apparatus, implement, machine, contrivance, implant, in vitro reagent, or other similar or related article, including a component part, or accessory which is . . . intended for use in the

> diagnosis of disease or other conditions, or in the cure, mitigation, treatment, or prevention of disease, in man or other animals, or intended to affect the structure or any function of the body of man or other animals, and which does not achieve any of its primary intended purposes through chemical action within or on the body of man or other animals and which is not dependent upon being metabolized for the achievement of any of its primary intended purposes. (US Congress, 1936)

Because they often require advanced technological infrastructure, access to medical technologies is arguably even more difficult for developing countries than drugs and vaccines. For example, at least ten countries have no radiotherapy units; access to computed tomography (CT) scanners in developing countries is less than 2% of that in high-income countries; and shortages of sterilizing equipment, syringes, and needles in some countries make up to 40% of all injections unsafe (WHO, 2011). Strategic Objective 11 of the WHO's Medium-Term Strategic Plan 2008–2013 includes as its first aim: 'Access to essential medical products and technologies, as part of the fulfillment of the right to health, recognized in countries' constitutions or national legislation' (WHO, 2008).

Evolving international human rights standards

Core human rights instruments have been applied to the problem of access to health goods by UN bodies, particularly the Office of the High Commissioner for Human Rights, the Commission on Human Rights, the Special Rapporteurs on the right of everyone to the enjoyment of the highest attainable standard of physical and mental health (Special Rapporteur on the right to health), the Committee on Economic, Social and Cultural Rights (CESCR), and the UN Human Rights Council.

The UN Sub-Commission on the Promotion and Protection of Human Rights declared in 2000 that 'the implementation of the TRIPS Agreement does not adequately reflect the fundamental nature and indivisibility of all human rights, including the right of everyone to enjoy the benefits of scientific progress and its applications, the right to health,' and that 'there are apparent conflicts between the intellectual property rights regime embodied in the TRIPS Agreement, on the one hand, and international human rights law, on the other' (UN Sub-Commission on the Promotion and Protection of Human Rights, 2000). It also reminded 'all [g]overnments of the primacy of human rights obligations over economic policies and agreements' and requested that the UN High Commissioner for Human Rights prepare a report on the impact of the TRIPS Agreement on human rights, which she completed the following year (UN Commission on Human Rights, 2001).

The UN Commission on Human Rights, for its part, adopted a resolution that same year recognizing 'that access to medication in the context of pandemics such as HIV/AIDS is one fundamental element for achieving progressively the full realization of the right [to health]' (UN Commission on Human Rights, 2001). It called on States 'to refrain from taking measures which would deny or limit equal access for all persons to preventive, curative or palliative pharmaceuticals or medical technologies used to treat pandemics such as HIV/AIDS or the most common opportunistic infections that accompany them,' and, clearly with TRIPS in mind, 'to ensure that . . . the application of international agreements is supportive of public health policies which promote broad access to safe, effective and affordable preventive, curative or palliative pharmaceuticals and medical technologies' (UN Commission on Human Rights, 2001). The United States—which has historically pushed for 'TRIPS-plus' provisions (which restrict TRIPS flexibilities intended to preserve developing countries' promotion of access to medicines (Morin, 2009))—was the only government to abstain from this resolution.

Following numerous studies and resolutions, the UN Human Rights Council adopted resolution 12/24 in October 2009 concerning 'access to medicines in the context of the right of everyone to the enjoyment of the highest attainable standard of physical and mental health' (UN Human Rights Council, 2009). In the resolution, the Council not only recognized 'that access to medicine is one of the fundamental elements in achieving progressively the full realization of the right of everyone to the enjoyment of the highest attainable standard of physical and mental health', but also encouraged 'all States to apply measures and procedures for enforcing intellectual property rights in such a manner as to avoid creating barriers to the legitimate trade of medicines, and to provide for safeguards against the abuse of such measures and procedures' (UN Human Rights Council, 2009). There were no objections or abstentions to this resolution.

Similarly, the CESCR issued a Statement on Human Rights and Intellectual Property, in which it considered that 'intellectual property rights must be balanced with the right . . . to enjoy the benefits of scientific progress and its applications', and concluded by calling for 'a mechanism for a human rights review of intellectual property systems' (CESCR, 2001). Indeed, the CESCR, in its General Comment No. 14, had interpreted the obligation under ICESCR Article 12(2)(d) to include 'the provision of essential drugs' (CESCR, 2000). In clarifying the obligations of State Parties, the CESCR included 'essential drugs, as defined by the WHO Action Programme on Essential Drugs', among the essential facilities, goods and services, which must be available in sufficient quantity within the State (CESCR, 2000). As part of their obligation to protect, State Parties have a duty 'to control the marketing of medical equipment and medicines by third parties' (CESCR, 2000), which strongly suggests that States should intervene where anti-competitive marketing of medicines and medical technologies is detrimental to the right to health. In General Comment No. 17, the CESCR challenged head-on the assumption of the international trade regime that the rights of companies holding pharmaceutical patents were of the same order as the rights of those who need the medicines, by treating the former as a temporary, revocable monopoly, and the latter as universal human rights (CESCR, 2006).

Both Special Rapporteurs on the right to health have actively sought to promote and further define the meaning of access to medicines from a human rights perspective. The first Special Rapporteur on the right to health, Paul Hunt, submitted a report to the UN General Assembly summarizing the responsibilities of States and of pharmaceutical companies with respect to access to medicines (UN General Assembly, 2006). Following consultation with States, non-governmental organizations (NGOs), academics, pharmaceutical companies, UN agencies, national human rights institutions, and other stakeholders, Professor Hunt presented the Human Rights Guidelines for Pharmaceutical Companies in Relation to Access to Medicines (UN General Assembly, 2008), calling upon companies to: recognize the importance of human rights in their corporate mission, provide board-level responsibility and accountability for its access strategy, publicly commit to contribute to R&D for neglected diseases, and respect the right of countries to use TRIPS flexibilities. Regarding patents and licensing, the guidelines called on drug companies to 'respect the right of countries to use, to the full, the provisions in . . . TRIPS . . . which allow flexibility for the purpose of promoting access to medicines, including the provisions relating to compulsory licensing and parallel imports', and, more generally, to 'respect the letter and spirit of the Doha Declaration' (UN General Assembly, 2008).

The second Special Rapporteur on the right to health, Anand Grover, submitted a report to the UN Human Rights Council analysing the use of TRIPS flexibilities and the adverse effect on access to medicines of 'TRIPS-plus' provisions found in free trade agreements (FTAs) (UN Human Rights Council, 2009). The following year, pursuant to Council resolution 12/24, quoted earlier, the Office of the United Nations High Commissioner for Human Rights (OHCHR) convened an expert consultation on access to medicines as a fundamental component of the right to health for an exchange of views, and requested that the Special Rapporteur present a summary of the discussions (UN Human Rights Council, 2011). In his summary, Mr Grover concluded:

> While some countries lack sufficient awareness about the use of TRIPS flexibilities and have limited technical capacity to implement them, others have not streamlined their patent laws sufficiently to facilitate use of such flexibilities. Furthermore, pressure from developed countries and multinational pharmaceutical corporations have played a prominent role in shaping the implementation of TRIPS flexibilities in developing and least developed countries. For example, a number of developing countries, while attempting to implement TRIPS flexibilities to address public health concerns, have experienced pressures from developed countries and multinational pharmaceutical corporations. (UN Human Rights Council, 2011, paragraph 47)

Mr Grover's report enumerated 13 recommendations for governments to progressively realize access to medicines as a component of the right to health (UN Human Rights Council, 2011).

Civil society consensus statements, such as the Montréal Statement on the Human Right to Essential Medicines (Marks, 2009; Pogge, 2007) and the Washington Declaration on Intellectual Property and the Public Interest (Global Congress on Intellectual Property and the Public Interest, 2011), have complemented the evolution of the United Nations' position in this realm. Similarly, the Universities Allied for Essential Medicines (UAEM) has adopted the Philadelphia Consensus Statement, stating, 'We believe that access to medical care and treatment is a basic human right' (UAEM, 2006). In addition, several NGOs, such as Médecins Sans Frontières (MSF) and Oxfam, have launched campaigns on access to essential medicines (Marks, 2009).

Domestic implementation and litigation

While international commitments have laid the foundations and garnered strong political will for improving access to health goods as a component of the right to health, commitments at the domestic level vary in the extent to which they render this right enforceable. Though in some cases national constitutions or their associated directive principles include specific mention of access to health goods (Kinney & Clark, 2004), in others, and often in addition, access is governed by statutes translated into administrative and regulatory provisions. At this level, national health systems and essential medicines lists often define the scope of access to health goods in the public sector (e.g., through government procurement or health insurance schemes) (Laing et al., 2003; Quick et al., 2002). Medicines included on essential medicines lists are intended to be those that are required to address the population's priority health care needs, selected on the bases of disease prevalence, efficacy and safety, and cost-effectiveness (Hogerzeil et al., 2006). However, as noted earlier, access to medicines as a component of the right to health calls for progressive realization of universal access to the highest attainable standard of health, including some health goods that might otherwise be excluded from public sector guarantees due to high cost.

In recent years, developing countries have adopted innovative strategies for making health goods more accessible. For instance, Mexico's health system reform has made high-cost health technologies widely accessible through its rights-based approach to catastrophic health insurance (see Frenk & Gómez-Dantés, Chapter 14, 'Realizing the right to healthcare in Mexico'), Brazil has strategically used TRIPS flexibilities to support its National AIDS Program (Flynn, 2011), and India has developed a generic industry so prolific that it has been called the 'pharmacy of the developing world' (Waning et al., 2010). Indeed, the success of these national strategies relies heavily on their ability to adapt to global development and distribution frameworks (Shadlen, 2011).

In the past couple of decades, courts have increasingly played a role in expanding the scope of access to high-cost health goods as a component of the right to health in developing countries (Byrne, 2009; Hogerzeil et al., 2006; also see De Negri Filho, Chapter 12: 'Brazil: a long journey towards a universal healthcare system'). As a result of the outcry over unaffordable drug pricing in countries confronted by the HIV pandemic, AIDS activists began to affirm access to medicines as a right under international law (Ferreira, 2002; Shadlen, 2007; Torres, 2002; Yamin, 2003). While countless health rights cases have involved individual requests for medicines included or excluded in national essential medicines lists or public insurance schemes, patient advocacy groups have also been successful in achieving significant resource re-allocations for vulnerable populations. The first major successful group claim for antiretroviral (ARV) drugs was brought before the Constitutional Court of South Africa (2002) by the South African Treatment Action Campaign (TAC) (Berger, 2002; Forman, 2008; Patterson & London, 2002). TAC had become South Africa's largest organization for people living with HIV, and was one of the first patient advocacy groups to build international solidarity in articulating health as a human right. Having played a critical role in incorporating health into the South African government's National Action Plan for the Protection and Promotion of Human Rights in 1998, the TAC successfully challenged the Ministry of Health's decision not to provide comprehensive ARV drugs for the prevention of mother-to-child transmission of HIV as a violation of the constitutionally protected right to health.

Some countries in Latin America where health is a justiciable constitutional right have seen a recent explosion in the use of judicial remedies to achieve access to health goods (Lamprea & Andia, 2010). In Colombia—where litigation concerning access to medicines and medical technologies became so prolific that the Constitutional Court in 2008 ordered a rights-based health reform—the courts have had to wrestle with the sustainability and fairness of resource-intensive judicial activism (Yamin & Parra-Vera, 2009). When courts are asked to determine what will satisfy the right to health in the absence of complete objective criteria to determine the optimal fair distribution of finite resources, their decisions have the potential to undermine democratic deliberation in administrative and legislative priority-setting. This may be especially problematic when access to courts is affected by socioeconomic criteria that tend to exclude the most vulnerable populations (Ferraz & Vieira, 2008).

In some cases, when additional human rights concerns, such as non-discrimination, have been at stake, group petitions have been heard by regional jurisdictions. Preeminent among these are the cases of *D* v. *United Kingdom*, decided by the European Court of Human Rights (1997), and *Jorge Odir Miranda Cortez, et al.* v. *El Salvador*, decided by the Inter-American Commission on Human Rights (2001). These supra-national rulings have significant domestic implications: referencing these cases, a favourable decision was granted to a group of HIV patients by the Ecuador Constitutional Court (2004) in *Mendoza and Ors* v. *Ministry of Public Health*, which found that the constitutional right to health required that the Ministry of Health continue its HIV treatment programme. The unprecedented success of collective HIV medicines cases ultimately set the stage for rights-based arguments for other health technologies (Matthews, 2011).

With global implications, BRIC (Brazil, Russia, India, China) countries and emerging economies have seen a rise in litigation concerning the scope of TRIPS flexibilities (Matthews, 2011). India in particular has recently served as a battleground between 'Big Pharma' and health rights advocates, not only with the upholding of its first compulsory license for a cancer drug, but also with a recent Supreme Court of India decision. In *Novartis AG* v. *Union of India*, Novartis, a Swiss pharmaceutical company, successfully challenged the meaning of Section 3(d) of the Indian Patent Law, which uses the flexibility in TRIPS Article 27 to limit the scope of patentable subject matter to new chemical entities in order to curb the practice of patent 'evergreening' (the filing of patents for incremental improvements to keep cheaper generic alternatives off the market) (Mueller, 2007). Additionally, in the few countries where they exist, patent opposition mechanisms—which provide a forum for public input regarding the validity of patent claims—can be a useful platform for health rights advocates to counter the anti-competitive effects of frivolous patent applications. To address these challenges on a broader scale, Yu (2008), George (2011), and Reiter (in press) have called for South-South collaboration in promoting access to generics and re-framing intellectual property principles to promote access to health goods.

Access implications of intellectual property and international trade regimes

Access to health goods—especially in developing countries where the vast majority of populations are uninsured or woefully underinsured—is largely determined by affordability (Maskus, 2002). While market competition promotes lower prices, IP protections encourage high prices via patents that assign drug companies monopoly rights to prevent unauthorized use (Attaran & Gillespie-White, 2001; Barbosa, 2007). As noted earlier, from the human rights perspective, IP rights are considered to be of a lower order than human rights, which imply a superior moral and legal claim, whereas IP rights merely establish temporary monopolies for the purpose of encouraging useful innovation (CESCR, 2006). Within developing countries, these monopolies render many health products unaffordable—and therefore inaccessible—for most people, without necessarily serving to further incentivize innovation (Chaudhuri, 2007; Chien, 2003; Westerhaus & Castro, 2006).

IP protections are strengthened, to the detriment of access, when coupled with patent linkage and 'evergreening' (Baker, 2008; Kesselheim, 2008). 'Patent linkage' refers to the way in which patents are linked to domestic regulatory and marketing approval, which is often associated with data exclusivity for the patent holder. 'Data exclusivity' allows patent holders to delay generic market entry by preventing generic companies from using clinical trial and other key data for a set number of years from the date of regulatory approval, which can often exceed the life of the original patent. Other practices that are often referred to as patent 'evergreening'—because they extend the length of a technology's patent protections—include: staggering patent applications (e.g. for various steps of a process, new uses, or alternate delivery methods); filing new patent applications for new mixtures or 'incremental innovation' (e.g. for modifications and improvements to an existing product); infringement suits in response to generic companies' regulatory applications; and 'pay for delay', in which a patent holder pays a generic company to delay market entry (Amin, in press; Correa, 2004). In many instances, additional patent applications themselves can extend the life of a patent, as IP rights are often licensed so as to be circumscribed not by the term of the existing patent, but by the term during which any pending patent applications, or even appeals, remain unresolved (George, 2012).

Strong IP protections, patent linkage, and patent evergreening have become increasingly insurmountable barriers to access to health goods as the international trade regime has progressively universalized the protection of these practices as the status quo (Abbott, 2006; Sell, 2011; 't Hoen, 2003). At the international level, TRIPS governs the minimum IP protections a WTO Member Country must enforce, requiring protection of patents for 20 years. These rights are subject to both domestic and international enforcement, and countries that fail to protect patents may be brought before the WTO's dispute settlement body by another government. Generally, access to health goods is reduced when developing countries implement TRIPS provisions relating to IP protection (Oliveira et al., 2004; Orsi et al., 2003).

Critically, certain TRIPS flexibilities exist to ensure that patent protections do not become barriers to access in developing countries (Sell, 2002). These flexibilities provide developing countries with the legal basis for parallel importation (importing cheaper generics from countries where relevant patents have not been filed or have expired) and compulsory licensing (manufacturing generic versions without the patent holder's authorization under certain conditions of necessity).

In partial response to pressure brought by UN bodies and NGOs mentioned previously, the fourth ministerial conference of the WTO reaffirmed TRIPS flexibilities in the Doha Declaration on the TRIPS Agreement and Public Health in November 2001. Significantly, the ministers agreed in the Doha Declaration 'that the TRIPS agreement does not and should not prevent members from taking measures to . . . promote access to medicines for all' (WTO, 2001). To drive the point home, the Declaration added, 'In this connection, we reaffirm the right of WTO members to use, to the full, the provisions in the TRIPS Agreement, which provide flexibility for this purpose' (WTO, 2001), and that:

> Each Member has the right to grant compulsory licences and the freedom to determine the grounds upon which such licences are granted . . . [and] the right to determine what constitutes a national emergency or other circumstances of extreme urgency, it being understood that public health crises, including those relating to HIV/AIDS, tuberculosis, malaria and other epidemics, can represent a national emergency or other circumstances of extreme urgency. (WTO, 2001, paragraph 5(c))

The next paragraph instructed the Council for TRIPS to find an expeditious solution to the problem of compulsory licensing for countries 'with insufficient or no manufacturing capacities in the pharmaceutical sector' (WTO, 2001). This was done with the WTO General Council's authorization of 'third-party compulsory licensing', allowing a manufacturer in another State to produce and export a compulsorily licensed product specifically for the benefit of the State issuing the compulsory license (WTO, 2003). The Doha Declaration also extended the deadline to 2016 for the least-developed countries to implement provisions on pharmaceutical patents (WTO, 2001).

Despite the Doha Declaration, powerful corporate and political influences discourage developing countries from taking full advantage of TRIPS flexibilities in promoting access to health goods. As early as 1998, parallel importation was challenged by 40 pharmaceutical companies (initially backed by the United States) opposed to South Africa's Medicines Act (*The Pharmaceutical Manufacturer's Association and Others* v. *The President of the Republic of South Africa* (1998)). However, the case was dropped following global public criticism of the companies' weak assertions concerning non-compliance with TRIPS (Forman, 2008; Nagan, 2002).

Similarly, compulsory licensing has been avoided on many occasions despite a clearly defined need and civil society pressure (Musungu & Oh, 2006). Despite being TRIPS-compliant, the first instances of compulsory licensing of ARVs in Thailand and Brazil resulted in hostile political repercussions, such as inclusion in the US Trade Representative's 'Special 301' watch list (Ford et al., 2007) (even though the United States itself has issued a number of compulsory licenses (Love, 2007)). By 2011, 17 countries—mostly upper-middle-income countries—had issued a total of only 24 compulsory licenses, primarily for HIV medicines (Kuhn & Beall, 2012). When India issued its first compulsory licence in 2012 for a cancer drug, effectively lowering its price by 97% (Mukherjee, 2012), the decision was admonished by a US Patent and Trademark Office official claiming that her Office actively discouraged such practices (Rea, 2012). Nevertheless, India's first compulsory licence (the second-ever licence for a cancer drug) was well-received by many (Bhaumik & Biswas, 2012), and was soon followed by changes in Chinese patent law, and similar considerations in Brazil, to facilitate compulsory licensing (Unnikrishnan, 2012). In response, several pharmaceutical companies made commitments to slash some cancer drug prices (Whalen, 2012), and some generic manufacturers made concerted efforts to target drugs 'ripe' for compulsory licensing (Pilla, 2012). With compulsory licensing on the rise and increasing policy cohesion among the world's largest generic suppliers, it remains to be seen to what extent compulsory licensing can be used as a sustainable, effective legal tool safeguarded by TRIPS.

What is perfectly clear, however, is that the current global trade framework does not support access to health goods as a component of the right to health. Trade agreements and investment treaties over the past couple of decades have had clear adverse effects on affordability of health goods in developing countries as a result of broad patent protections and associated foreign investors' rights, which, taken together, effectively block affordable generic alternatives (Correa, 2004; Costanza, 2009; Dwyer, 2007). Hundreds of 'TRIPS-plus' provisions in FTAs, bilateral investment treaties/investment promotion and protection agreements (BITs/BIPAs), and other multilateral agreements (such as the proposed Trans-Pacific Partnership Agreement) seek to impose more stringent standards of intellectual property protection for health goods than those found in TRIPS (Castro, 2006; Fink & Reichenmiller, 2006; Flynn & et al., 2011; Matthews, 2005). These TRIPS-plus provisions include, *inter alia,* broader patentability standards (extending patent protection to, e.g. 'incremental innovation'), additional categories of patentable products (e.g. medical procedures, which most countries exclude from patentability), international patent linkage, extended data exclusivity periods, narrower permissions for compulsory licensing and parallel importation, and overly broad definitions of counterfeit medicines implicating generic products (Correa, 2006; Scherer & Watal, 2002; Sell, 2007; Shukla & Sangal, 2009). Additionally, bilateral and multilateral agreements that include IP rights in their definition of protected 'investments,' subject domestic access-related policies—such as pharmaceutical price controls and industry regulations—to direct challenge by foreign investors via international arbitration (Rutledge, 2012).

Even in the absence of prohibitive treaty provisions, powerful corporate and political pressure—especially that surrounding ongoing negotiations—can influence governments to implement TRIPS-plus policies instead of using TRIPS flexibilities. To this end, the United States has been primarily criticized for pushing TRIPS-plus provisions in FTAs (Pogge et al., 2010), while the European Union has been seen as overly eager to enforce the WTO trade framework (De Bievre, 2006; Mullard, 2010). The European Parliament has responded to civil society concerns regarding TRIPS-plus provisions with a resolution calling for avoidance of such provisions in EU FTAs (European Parliament, 2007) but it is yet to be seen how effective this will be in practice.

Research and development

At an even more fundamental level, access to health goods depends largely on the research and development (R&D) framework, which rewards innovations based on commercial incentives (Grabowski, 2002; Pécoul et al., 1999). These incentives, however, disproportionately represent the buying power of high-income nations, and fail to capture the medical needs of developing countries, which not only have fewer financial resources, but are also characterized by distinct disease profiles. The Commission on Macroeconomics and Health has usefully categorized diseases that are equally predominant in high-income and developing countries as Type I diseases, those that have a disproportionate burden in developing countries as Type II, and those that are almost exclusively found in developing countries as Type III (also referred to as 'neglected tropical diseases') (WHO, 2001). While access to health goods for Type I diseases may be restricted by broad IP rights intended to promote R&D, access to health goods for most Type II and all Type III diseases—sometimes referred to as 'diseases of the bottom billion'—suffers from the additional challenge of *insufficient* R&D (Røttingen et al., 2012). Because Type II and Type III diseases disproportionately affect poor populations and account for a greater proportion of morbidity in the developing world, they are not profitable pharmaceutical targets, and therefore require non-traditional approaches to incentivize their R&D (Oprea et al., 2009).

In an effort to address this innovation gap, the World Health Assembly (WHA) passed a resolution to establish the Commission on Intellectual Property Rights, Innovation and Public Health (CIPIH) to collect relevant data and proposals from governments, academia, product development partnerships, and industry, including funding and incentives for the creation of health goods for developing countries (WHA, 2003). Following consideration of CIPIH's report, the WHA established the Intergovernmental Working Group on Public Health, Innovation and Intellectual Property and adopted in 2008 the Global Strategy and Plan of Action on Public Health, Innovation, and Intellectual Property (WHA, 2006, 2008, 2009). This Global Strategy both acknowledges that IP rights are 'an important incentive for the development of new health-care products' and quotes the provisions of the Universal Declaration of Human Rights on sharing in scientific advances and its benefits and protection of moral and material interest resulting from scientific production (WHA, 2008). As a rare example of explicit balancing of IP rights and human rights outside of the UN human rights bodies, it is significant that among the 'principles' of the strategy, is this restatement from the preamble of the WHO Constitution: 'the enjoyment of the highest attainable standard of health is one of the fundamental rights of every human being without distinction of race relation, political belief, economic or social condition' (WHA, 2008).

While the Global Strategy and Plan of Action strategically prioritized goals and identified actions for governments, industry, and the WHO, lack of concrete targets and financing requirements has prevented its effective utilization or adoption of accountability measures. However, two consecutive working groups have fulfilled the Global Strategy's mandate to 'establish a results-oriented and time-limited expert working group under the auspices of WHO and linking up with other relevant groups to examine current financing and coordination of research and development...' (WHA, 2008).

In 2012, the second of these, Consultative Expert Working Group on Research and Development: Financing and Coordination (CEWG), garnered international support for a 'Global R&D Convention' that would establish an evidence-based process for medical R&D priority-setting. It would also finance a dedicated R&D fund for the developing world through minor contributions from WHO Member-States (approximately 0.01% of gross domestic product) and support innovative R&D funding mechanisms, as well as establish principles aimed at ensuring access to innovation (CEWG, 2012; MSF Access Campaign, 2012; Karunakaran, 2012). Importantly, the CEWG emphasizes the importance of de-linking R&D from product prices, and experts have noted that this complex challenge will require countries to work together in determining the best options for commitment, administrative, decision-making, financial, oversight, and compliance mechanisms (Røttingen et al., 2012).

A number of alternative 'push' (prior) and 'pull' (ad hoc and post hoc) incentive mechanisms have been proposed to address the R&D gaps inherent in the market-based innovation paradigm (Hecht et al., 2009). 'Pull' mechanisms—such as advance market commitments (e.g. donor commitments to provide incentives to vaccine makers to produce vaccines for developing countries), prize funds, and expedited regulatory review (e.g. the FDA's Priority Review Vouchers, Accelerated Approval, and Fast-Track regulatory review)—reward R&D outcomes by facilitating commercialization of valuable but less profitable health products (Love & Hubbard, 2007; Robertson et al., 2012; Towse & Kettler, 2005). Several 'pull' mechanism proposals have yet to be tested. For instance, 'pay-for-performance' patents, such as those contemplated by the proposed Health Impact Fund, would use government and donor financing to reimburse patent holders on the basis of health impact in lieu of normal profits gained from market exclusivity (Pogge, 2010; Banerjee et al., 2010). Other proposals include patent buy-outs (Outterson, 2006), transferable IP rights and market exclusivity (Spellburg et al., 2008), and reduction of patent length (Center for Global Health R&D Policy Assessment, 2012).

'Push' mechanisms, on the other hand, incentivize earlier stages of product development. Patent pools, for instance, bring patents into a collectively owned and managed pool that can issue voluntary licences to generic companies for product development (Choi, 2003). The UNITAID Medicines Patent Pool, which is funded by a tax on airline ticket sales, has pooled patents to facilitate voluntary licensing of four chemical entities which, when combined, are a powerful fixed-dose antiretroviral combination (UNITAID, 2012). More recently, the World Intellectual Property Organization (WIPO) Re:Search initiative, a royalty-free patent pool for neglected tropical disease R&D, has resulted in its first agreement between universities and pharmaceutical companies to research new treatments for Chagas disease, sleeping sickness, schistosomiasis, and tuberculosis (WIPO, 2012).

Other 'push' mechanisms that have seen some success include targeted disease-specific funding (Blume-Kohout, 2012), health innovation networks for developing countries (Morel et al., 2005), capacity-building and technology transfer initiatives (Friede et al., 2011), open-source and crowd-sourced R&D for neglected diseases (Årdal & Røttingen, 2012; Maurer et al., 2004; Munos, 2010) and private-public product development partnerships (Frost & Reich, 2008; Nwaka & Ridley, 2003). 'Push' mechanisms that have been proposed but not yet tested include taxes on patents (Beall & Kuhn, 2012); and making undisclosed clinical trial data an international public good (Reichman, 2006). Similarly, innovative financial models that de-link R&D incentives from profits include: cost sharing for clinical trials (Lewis et al., 2007); an International Finance Facility for Immunization (IFFIm, 2012); neglected disease and global health tax credits (Rao, 2011); additional fees on patent applications called 'Green IP' (Nitta, 2006); and selling expedited regulatory review vouchers to raise money for neglected disease R&D (Center for Global Health R&D Policy Assessment, 2012; Moran, 2005).

While it is of the utmost importance, de-linking R&D from prices is just the first step in promoting access to health goods. Regardless of the R&D mechanism, health innovations needs to be licensed responsibly to ensure that publicly funded research benefits global health in an equitable way. To this end, global access licensing incorporates into health technology licenses terms such as agreements not to enforce patents in developing countries, march-in rights for public institutions, and tiered royalties. Global access licensing has increasingly been used by academic institutions to ensure that health-related innovations—especially diagnostics and medical devices, which are commonly developed in academia—reach the global poor (Chokshi, 2006). The UAEM, mentioned earlier, has been a key player in promoting global access licensing alongside neglected disease research, including through efforts to monitor implementation of the multi-institution Statement of Principles and Strategies for the Equitable Dissemination of Medical Technologies (AUTM, 2009). Similarly, the Access to Medicines Index (ATMI) ranks pharmaceutical companies based on their efforts, including through responsible licensing, to increase access to medicines; a proposed Access to Medical Devices Index may enhance these efforts (ATMI, 2012).

Conclusion

This chapter has reviewed the evolving international human rights standards that relate to access to medicines, vaccines, and medical technologies, and identified the gap between the commitment in principle to enhancing this access as part of the right to health and the right to benefit from scientific progress, on the one hand, and the obstacles posed by the IP and international trade regimes, on the other. The sheer breadth and complexity of the legal, economic, political, ethical, and technical considerations surrounding universal access to health goods cannot be properly addressed in one chapter. We noted progress in domestic implementation and increased use of judicial remedies in achieving access to life-saving health goods. Other strategies that were not addressed in this chapter include increasing generic manufacturing capacities in developing countries, public health insurance schemes, and strengthening supply-chain infrastructure (Kaplan & Lang, 2005; Rovira, 2006).

The trend in access to health goods, particularly in developing countries, provides evidence for policies in global health to increase access at all stages of the process, from setting research priorities for the development of new drugs, to manufacturing, pricing, marketing, and distribution. Critical challenges remain. While the international trade regime has to some extent adjusted to the political imperative of promoting development and strategies defined by the international financial institutions in poverty reduction programmes and the UN system in the Millennium Development Goals, it has not, so far, been receptive to the claim that access to health goods is guaranteed by a human right to health and the right to benefit from scientific progress. Similarly, the medical R&D system has not yet adapted to the global imperatives of these human rights calling for both availability and affordability of medical products. The developments described in this chapter are signs that the human right to medical products, vaccines, and medical technologies has advanced in terms of its normative content and its legal recognition. Nevertheless, if the political will and adequate resources can effectively be mobilized, it is not beyond reach to ensure reliable and sustainable implementation and accountability frameworks, accommodation with the international trade regime, and incentives for innovation and affordable pricing of the health goods component of the human right to health.

Acknowledgement

Some part of this chapter draw from Marks, S.P. (2009). Access to essential medicines as a component of the right to health. In A. Clapham and M. Robinson (Eds.), Realizing the Right to Health, pp. 82–101. (The Swiss Human Rights Book Series.) Rüffer & Rub: Zurich.

References

Abbott, F.M. (2006). The cycle of action and reaction: developments and trends in intellectual property and health. In P. Roffe, G. Tansey, and D.V. Eugui (Eds.), *Negotiating Health: Intellectual Property and Access to Medicines*, pp. 27–41. Earthscan: London.

Access to Medicine Index. (2012). *Access to Medicine Index*. Available at: <http://www.accesstomedicineindex.org/> (accessed 10 October 2012).

Amin, T. (in press). Re-visiting the patents and access to medicines dichotomy: an evaluation of TRIPS implementation and public health safeguards in developing countries. In O. Aginam, J. Harrington, and P. Yu (Eds.), *Global Governance of HIV/AIDS: Intellectual Property and Access to Essential Medicines*. Northampton: Edward Elgar Publishing Ltd.

Årdal, C. and Røttingen, J.-A. (2012). Open source drug discovery in practice: a case study. *PLOS Neglected Tropical Diseases*, 6(9), 1827.

Attaran, A. and Gillespie-White, L. (2001). Do patents for antiretroviral drugs constrain access to AIDS treatment in Africa? *Journal of the American Medical Association*, 286(15), 1886–1892.

AUTM. (2009). *Statement of Principles and Strategies for the Equitable Dissemination of Medical Technologies*. Available at: <https://www.autm.net/Content/NavigationMenu/TechTransfer/GlobalHealth/statementofprincliples.pdf> (accessed 10 October 2012).

Baker, B.K. (2008). Ending drug registration apartheid: Taming data exclusivity and patent/registration linkage. *American Journal of Law and Medicine*, 34(2–3), 303–344.

Banerjee, A., Hollis, A., and Pogge, T. (2010). The Health Impact Fund: incentives for improving access to medicines. *Lancet*, 375(9709), 166–169.

Barbosa, D.B. (2007). *Why Intellectual Property May Create Competition Problems*. Available at: <http://papers.ssrn.com/sol3/papers.cfm?abstract_id=1006085> (accessed 20 September 2010).

Beall, R. and Kuhn, R. (2012). Trends in compulsory licensing of pharmaceuticals since the Doha Declaration: a database analysis. *PLOS Medicine*, 9(1), e1001154.

Berger, J.M. (2002). Litigation strategies to gain access to treatment for HIV/AIDS: the case of South Africa's Treatment Action Campaign. *Wisconsin International Law Journal*, 20, 597–609.

Bhaumik, S. and Biswas, T. (2012). From outlier to trendsetter. *Canadian Medical Association Journal*, 184(12), E635–E636.

Blume-Kohout, M.E. (2012). Does targeted, disease-specific public research funding influence pharmaceutical innovation? *Journal of Policy Analysis and Management*, 31(3), 641–660.

Brown, D.W., Burton, A., Gacic-Dobo, M., *et al.* (2011). A mid-term assessment of progress towards the immunization coverage goal of the Global Immunization Vision and Strategy (GIVS). *BMC Public Health*, 11, 806.

Byrne, I. (2009). Enforcing the right to health: innovative lessons from domestic courts. In A. Clapham and M. Robinson (Eds.), *Realizing the Right to Health*, pp. 525–557. (The Swiss Human Rights Book Series.) Rüffer & Rub: Zurich.

Cameron, A., Ewen, M., Ross-Degnan, D., *et al.* (2009). Medicine prices, availability, and affordability in 36 developing and middle-income countries: a secondary analysis. *Lancet*, 373(9659), 632.

Castro, R. (2006). Intellectual Property rights in bilateral investment treaties and access to medicines: the case of Latin America. *Journal of World Intellectual Property*, 9(5), 548–572.

Center for Global Health R&D Policy Assessment. (2012). *Policy Innovations. Results for Development Institute*. Available at: <http://healthresearchpolicy.org/innovation> (accessed 20 September 2012).

CESCR. (2000). *General Comment 14: The right to the highest attainable standard of health (article 12 of the International Covenant on Economic, Social and Cultural Rights)*. Committee on Economic, Social and Cultural Rights (CESCR): Geneva.

CESCR. (2001). *Human Rights and Intellectual Property: Statement by the Committee on Economic Social and Cultural Rights*. UN Doc. E/C.12/2001/15, 14 December 2001. Committee on Economic, Social and Cultural Rights (CESCR): Geneva.

CESCR. (2006). *General Comment No. 17 on the Right of Everyone to Benefit from the Protection of the Moral and Material Interests Resulting from any Scientific, Literary or Artistic Production of Which He or She is the Author*. UN doc. E/C. 12/GC/17. Committee on Economic, Social and Cultural Rights (CESCR): Geneva.

CEWG. (2012). *Research and development to meet the needs of developing countries: Strengthening global financing and coordination*. World Health Organization (WHO): Geneva.

Chaudhuri, S. (2007). *Is Product Patent Protection Necessary in Developing Countries for Innovation?: R&D by Indian Pharmaceutical Companies after TRIPS*. Working Paper Series, 614, Indian Institute of Management: Calcutta.

Chien, C. (2003). Cheap drugs at what price to innovation: Does the compulsory licensing of pharmaceuticals hurt innovation? *Berkeley Technology Law Journal*, 18(1), 1–57.

Choi, J.P. (2003). *Patent Pools and Cross-Licensing in the Shadow of Patent Litigation*. CESifo Working Paper, 1070. Available at: <http://papers.ssrn.com/sol3/papers.cfm?abstract_id=466062> (accessed 20 September 2012).

Chokshi, D.A. (2006). Improving access to medicines in poor countries: The role of universities. *PLOS Medicine*, 3(6), e136.

Constitutional Court of Colombia. (2008). *Sentencia T-760. Sala Segunda de Revisión*, 31 July 2008.

Constitutional Court of Ecuador. (2004). *Mendoza and Ors v. Ministry of Public Health and the Director of the National AIDS-HIV-STI Program*. Tribunal Constitucional, 3ra. Sala. Resolucion No. 0749-2003–RA.

Constitutional Court of South Africa. (2002). *Minister of Health* v. *Treatment Action Campaign*. 5 SA 721.

Correa, C.M. (2004). Bilateralism in intellectual property: defeating the WTO system for access to medicines. *Case Western Reserve Journal of International Law*, 36, 79.

Correa, C.M. (2006). Implications of bilateral free trade agreements on access to medicines, *Bulletin of the World Health Organization*, 84(5), 399–404.

Costanza, L. (2009). *The Security of International Investments: A Synthesis of Impacts on Public Policies and Domestic Law in Host States*. LLM Dissertation (Laws 592), Faculty of Law, Victoria University of Wellington, New Zealand. [Online.] Available at: <http://researcharchive.vuw.ac.nz/bitstream/handle/10063/1145/thesis.pdf?sequence=1> (accessed 20 September 2012).

De Bievre, D. (2006). The EU regulatory trade agenda and the quest for WTO enforcement. *Journal of European Public Policy*, 13(6), 851–866.

Dwyer, L. (2007). Patent protection and access to medicine: the Colombian and Peruvian Trade Promotion Agreements. *Law and Business Review*, 13, 825.

Erdman, J.N. (2009). Human rights in health equity: cervical cancer and HPV vaccines. *American Journal of Law and Medicine*, 35(2–3), 365–387.

European Court of Human Rights. (1997). *D* v. *United Kingdom*. Case No. 146/1996/767/964.

European Parliament. (2007). *Resolution of 12 July 2007 on the TRIPS agreement and access to medicines*. Text adopted: P.6_TA(2007)0353.

Ferraz, O.M. and Vieira, F. (2008). Direito à Saúde, Recursos Escassos e Equidade: Os Riscos da Interpretação Judicial Dominante. *Revista de Ciências Sociais*, 52(1), 223–251.

Ferreira, L. (2002). The human rights obligations of multinational pharmaceutical corporations. *Fordham Law Review*, 71(3), 1133–1179.

Fink, C. and Reichenmiller, P. (2006). Tightening TRIPS: intellectual property Provisions of U.S. free trade agreements. In R. Newfarmer (Ed.), *Trade, Doha, and Development: A Window into the Issues*, pp. 285–299. World Bank: Washington, DC.

Flynn, M. (2011). Corporate power and state resistance: Brazil's use of TRIPS flexibilities for its national AIDS program. In K. C. Shadlen (Ed.), *Intellectual Property, Pharmaceuticals and Public Health: Access to Drugs in Developing Countries*, pp. 149–177. Northampton: Edward Elgar Publishing, Inc.

Flynn, S.M., Kaminski, M.E., Baker, B.K., *et al.* (2011). *Public Interest Analysis of the US TPP Proposal for an IP Chapter*. PIJIP Research Paper Series, 21. Available at: <http://digitalcommons.wcl.american.edu/cgi/viewcontent.cgi?article=1023&context=research> (accessed 20 September 2012).

Ford, N., Wilson, D., Costa Chavez, G., *et al.* (2007). Sustaining access to antiretroviral therapies in the less-developed world: lessons from Brazil and Thailand. *AIDS*, 21(Supp. 4), S21–S29

Forman, L. (2008). 'Rights' and wrongs: what utility for the right to health in reforming trade rules on medicines? *Health and Human Rights: An International Journal*, 10(2), 37–52

Friede, M., Palkonyay, L., Alfonso, C., *et al.* (2011). WHO initiative to increase global and equitable access to influenza vaccine in the event of a pandemic: Supporting developing country production capacity through technology transfer. *Vaccine*, 29(Supp. 1), A2–A7.

Frost, L.J. and Reich, M. (2008). *Access: How do Good Health Technologies Get to Poor People in Poor Countries?* Harvard Center for Population and International Health: Cambridge, MA.

George, E. (2011). South Africa and South-South cooperation to reframe global intellectual property principles and promote access to essential medicines. *Indiana Journal of Global Legal Studies*, 18(1), 167–197.

George, J. (2012). Patent pool: Legitimising big pharma's practices? *Access*, 3(1). Available at: <http://www.lawyerscollective.org/files/Access%20-%20Vol%20III,%20No_%201.pdf> (accessed 20 September 2012).

Global Congress on Intellectual Property and the Public Interest. (2011). *Washington Declaration on Intellectual Property and the Public Interest*. Adopted 27 August 2011 at Washington College of Law, Washington, DC.

Grabowski, H. (2002). Patents, innovation and access to new pharmaceuticals. *Journal of International Economic Law*, 5(4), 849–860.

Hecht, R., Wilson, P., and Palriwala, A. (2009). Improving health R&D financing for developing countries: A menu of innovative policy options. *Health Affairs*, 28(4), 974–985.

Hogerzeil, H.V. and Mirza, Z. (2011). *The World Medicines Situation 2011: Access to Essential Medicines as Part of the Right to Health*. World Health Organization (WHO): Geneva.

Hogerzeil, H.V., Samson, M., Casanovas, J.V., *et al.* (2006). Is access to essential medicines as part of the fulfillment of the right to health enforceable through the courts? *Lancet*, 368(9532), 305–311.

Holt, F., Gillam, S.J., and Ngondi, J.M. (2012). Improving access to medicines for neglected tropical diseases in developing countries: lessons from three emerging economies. *PLOS Neglected Tropical Disease*, 6(2), e1390.

IFFIm. (2012). *IFFIm: Supporting GAVI*. Available at: <http://www.iffim.org/index.aspx> (accessed 10 October 2012).

Inter-American Commission on Human Rights. (2001). *Jorge Odir Miranda Cortez* et al. v. *El Salvador*. Case 12.249, Report No. 27/09.

Kaplan, W.A. and Laing, R. (2005). *Local Production: Industrial Policy and Access to Medicines. Health, Nutrition and Population Discussion Paper*. World Health Organization (WHO): Geneva.

Karunakaran, K. (2012, 5 July). Why India needs to back a new R&D treaty in health sector. *The Economic Times*. Available at: <http://articles.economictimes.indiatimes.com/2012-07-05/news/32551747_1_treaty-r-d-indian-firms> (accessed 10 October 2012).

Kesselheim, A.S. (2008). Think globally, prescribe locally: how rational pharmaceutical policy in the US can improve global access to essential medicines. *American Journal of Law and Medicine*, 34(2–3), 125–139.

Kinney, E.D. and Clark, B.A. (2004). Provisions for health and health care in the constitutions of the countries of the world. *Cornell International Law Journal*, 37, 285.

Kuhn, R. and Beall, R.F. (2012). The time for pharmaceutical compulsory licensing has expired. *Nature Medicine*, 18(8), 1168.

Laing, R., Waning, B., and Gray, A. (2003). 25 years of the WHO Essential Medicines Lists: progress and challenges. *Lancet*, 361(9370), 1723–1729.

Lamprea, E. and Andia, T. (2010). *Local Maladies, Global Remedies: Rethinking Right to Health Duties. Global Justice, Stanford University*. [Online.] Available at: <http://iis-db.stanford.edu/evnts/6170/Global_Justice_May_21_2010.pdf> (accessed 20 September 2012).

Lewis, T.R., Reichman, J.H., and So, A.D. (2007). The case for public funding and public oversight of clinical trials. *The Economists' Voice*, 4(1), Art. 3.

Love, J. (2007). *Recent Examples of the Use of Compulsory License on Patents*. Knowledge Ecology International: Washington, DC. Available at: <http://www.keionline.org/misc-docs/recent_cls_8mar07.pdf> (accessed 20 September 2012).

Love, J. and Hubbard, T. (2007). The big idea: prizes to stimulate R&D for new medicines. *Chicago-Kent Law Review*, 82(3), 1519–1554.

Marks, S.P. (2009). Access to essential medicines as a component of the right to health. In A. Clapham and M. Robinson (Eds.), *Realizing the Right to Health*, pp. 82–101. (The Swiss Human Rights Book Series.) Rüffer & Rub: Zurich.

Maskus, K.E. (2002). Ensuring access to essential medicines: some economic considerations. *Wisconsin International Law Journal*, 20(2), 563–579.

Matthews, D.N. (2005). TRIPS flexibilities and access to medicines in developing countries: the problem with technical assistance and free trade agreements. *European Intellectual Property Review*, 27, 420–427.

Matthews, D. (2011). When framing meets law: using human rights as a practical instrument to facilitate access to medicines in developing countries. *The WIPO Journal*, 3(1), 113–127.

Maurer, S.M., Rai, A., and Sali, A. (2004). Finding cures for tropical disease: is open source an answer? *PLOS Medicine*, 1(3), e56.

Moran, M. (2005). *Fast Track Options as a Fundraising Mechanism to Support R&D into Neglected Diseases*. Pharmaceutical R&D Policy Project, London School of Economics: London. Available at: <http://www.who.int/intellectualproperty/submissions/Mary.Moran2.pdf> (accessed 10 October 2012).

Morel, C.M., Acharya, T., Broun, D., *et al.* (2005). Health innovation networks to help developing countries address neglected diseases. *Science*, 309, 401–403.

Morin, J.-F. (2009). Multilateralizing TRIPs-plus agreements: is the US strategy a failure? *Journal of World Intellectual Property*, 12, 175–197.

MSF Access Campaign. (2012). *How a Global R&D Convention Could Fill the Gaps Left by Today's Medical Innovation System*. Médecins Sans Frontières (MSF): New York, NY. Available at: <http://www.msfaccess.org/sites/default/files/MSF_assets/Innovation/Docs/MedInno_Briefing_GlobalConventionRD_ENG_2012Update.pdf> (accessed 10 October 2012).

Mueller, J.M. (2007). Taking TRIPS to India—Novartis, patent law and access to medicines. *New England Journal of Medicine*, 356, 541–543.

Mukherjee, R. (2012, 16 August). Big pharma lobbies hard to curb generics. *Times of India*. Available at: (accessed 20 September 2012).

Mullard, A. (2010). EU implicated in controversial counterfeiting bill. *Lancet*, 375(9723), 1335.

Munos, B. (2010). Can open-source drug R&D repower pharmaceutical innovation? *Nature Reviews Drug Discovery*, 5, 723–729.

Musungu, S.F. and Oh, C. (2006). *The Use of Flexibilities in TRIPS by Developing Countries: Can They Promote Access to Medicines?* World Health Organization (WHO): Geneva.

Nagan, W.P. (2002). International intellectual property, access to health care, and human rights: South Africa v. United States. *Florida Journal of International Law*, 14, 155.

Nitta, I. (2006). *Patent Insurance (Green Intellectual Property) Scheme: A Financial Prescription for Neglected Diseases?* Available at: <http://www.who.int/phi/GreenIP.pdf> (accessed 10 October 2012).

Nwaka, S. and Ridley, R.G. (2003). Virtual drug discovery and development for neglected diseases through public-private partnerships. *Nature Reviews Drug Discovery*, 2, 919–928.

Oliveira, M.A., Zepeda Bermudez, J.A., Costa Chavez, G., *et al.* (2004). Has the implementation of the TRIPS agreement in Latin America and the Caribbean produced intellectual property legislation that favours public health? *Bulletin of the World Health Organization*, 82(11), 815–821.

Oprea, L., Braunack-Mayer, A., and Gericke, C.A., 2009. Ethical issues in funding research and development of drugs for neglected tropical diseases. *Journal of Medical Ethics*, 35, 310–314.

Orsi, F., Hasenclever, L., Fialho, B., *et al.* (2003). Intellectual property rights, anti-AIDS policy and generic drugs: lessons from the Brazilian public health program. In J.-P. Moatti, B. Coriat, Y. Souteyrand, *et al.* (Eds.), *Economics of AIDS and Access to HIV/AIDS Care in Developing Countries: Issues and Challenges*, pp. 109–134. Le Publier: Paris.

Outterson, K. (2006). Innovations for low- and middle-income countries. *American Journal of Law and Medicine*, 32, 159–173.

Patterson, D. and London, L. (2002). International law, human rights and HIV/AIDS. *Bulletin of the World Health Organization*, 80(12), 964–969.

Pécoul, B., Chirac, P., Trouiller, P., *et al.* (1999). Access to essential drugs in poor countries: a lost battle? *Journal of the American Medical Association*, 281(4), 361–367.

The Pharmaceutical Manufacturer's Association and Others v. *The President of the Republic of South Africa*. (1998). Case no. 4183/98, Trans. Prov. Div., South Africa.

Pilla, V. (2012, 19 July). Natco targets drugs ripe for compulsory licensing. *Livemint & The Wall Street Journal*. Available at: <http://www.livemint.com/Companies/ZR7YHsT0xTb6e9ppKDIAuN/Natco-targets-drugs-ripe-for-compulsory-licensing.html> (accessed 20 September 2012).

Pogge, T. (2007). Montréal statement on the human right to essential medicines. *Cambridge Quarterly of Healthcare Ethics*, 16(1), 104–108.

Pogge, T., Rimmer, M., and Rubenstein, K. (2010). *Incentives for Global Public Health: Patent Law and Access to Essential Medicines.* Cambridge: Cambridge University Press.

Quick, J.D., Hogerzeil, H.V., Velásquez, G., and Lembit, R. (2002). Twenty-five years of essential medicines. *Bulletin of the World Health Organization*, 80(11), 913–914.

Rao, A. (2011). *Can an R&D Tax Credit Expand Investment in Product Development for Global Health?* Results for Development Institute: Washington, DC. Available at: <http://healthresearchpolicy.org/sites/healthresearchpolicy.org/files/assessments/files/Tax%20Credit%20Draft%20Consultation%20Draft%202%2028.pdf> (accessed 10 October 2012).

Rea, T.S. (2012, 2 July). USPTO on the hill: supporting U.S. innovators in global markets. *Director's Forum: David Kappos' Public Blog, uspto.gov*. Available at: <http://www.uspto.gov/blog/director/entry/uspto_on_the_hill_supporting> (accessed 20 September 2012).

Reichman, J.H. (2006). The international legal status of undisclosed clinical trial data: from private to public goods? In P. Roffe, G. Tansey, and D.V. Eugui (Eds.), *Negotiating Health: Intellectual Property and Access to Medicines*, pp. 133–150. Earthscan: London.

Reiter, B. (in press). Overcoming coloniality: the potential of south-south dialogue about citizenship, participatory democracy, and development between Brazil and India. In A. Gangopadhyay (Ed.), *India Brazil Dialogue*. Cambridge: Cambridge University Press.

Robertson, A.S., Stefanakis, R., Joseph, D., *et al.* (2012). The impact of the US Priority Review Voucher on private-sector investment in global health research and development. *PLOS Neglected Tropical Diseases*, 6(8), e1750.

Røttingen, J.-A., Chamas, C., Goyal, L.C., *et al.* (2012). Securing the public good of health research and development for developing countries. *Bulletin of the World Health Organization*, 90(5), 398–400.

Rovira, J. (2006). Creating and promoting domestic drug manufacturing capacities: a solution for developing countries? In P. Roffe, G. Tansey, and D.V. Eugui (Eds.), *Negotiating Health: Intellectual Property and Access to Medicines*, pp. 227–240. London: Earthscan.

Rutledge, P.B. (2012). TRIPS and BITS: An essay on compulsory licenses, expropriation, and international arbitration. *North Carolina Journal of Law & Technology*, 13, 149.

Scherer, F.M. and Watal, J. (2002). Post-TRIPS options for access to patented medicines in developing nations. *Journal of International Economic Law*, 5(4), 913–939.

Sell, S.K. (2002). TRIPS and the Access to Medicines campaign. *Wisconsin International Law Journal*, 20, 481.

Sell, S.K. (2007). TRIPS-plus free trade agreements and access to medicines. *Liverpool Law Review*, 28(1), 41–75.

Sell, S.K. (2011). TRIPS was never enough: vertical forum shifting, FTAs, ACTA, and TPP. *Journal of Intellectual Property Law*, 18, 447.

Shadlen, K.C. (2007). The political economy of AIDS treatment: Intellectual property and the transformation of generic supply. *International Studies Quarterly*, 51(3), 559–581.

Shadlen, K.C. (2011). The politics of patents and drugs in Brazil and Mexico: the industrial bases of health policies. In K.C. Shadlen (Ed.), *Intellectual Property, Pharmaceuticals and Public Health: Access to Drugs in Developing Countries*, pp. 41–58. Northampton: Edward Elgar Publishing, Inc.

Shukla, N. and Sangal, T. (2009). Generic drug industry in India: the counterfeit spin. *Journal of Intellectual Property Rights*, 14(3), 236–240.

Spellburg, B., Guidos, R., Gilbert, D., *et al.* (2008). The epidemic of antibiotic-resistant infections: a call to action for the medical community from the Infectious Diseases Society of America. *Clinical Infectious Diseases*, 46(2), 155–164.

Supreme Court of India. (forthcoming). *Novartis AG* v. *Union of India* [4 Madras L.J. 1153, on appeal].

'T Hoen, E. (2003). TRIPS, pharmaceutical patents and access to essential medicines: Seattle, Doha and beyond. In J.-P.Moatti, T. Barnett, B. Coriat, *et al.* (Eds.), *Economics of AIDS and Access to HIV/AIDS Care in Developing Countries: Issues and Challenges*, pp. 39–67. Paris: Le Publier.

Torres, M.A. (2002). The human right to health, national courts, and access to HIV/AIDS treatment: a case study from Venezuela. *Chicago Journal of International Law*, 3, 105.

Towse, A. and Kettler, H. (2005). Advance price or purchase commitments to create markets for treatments for diseases of poverty: lessons from three policies. *Bulletin of the World Health Organization*, 83(4), 301–307.

UAEM. (2006). *Philadelphia Consensus Statement on University Policies for Health-Related Innovations.* Available at: <http://essentialmedicine.org/sites/default/files/archive/philadelphia-consensus-statement.pdf> (accessed 12 November 2012).

UN Commission on Human Rights, 57th Session, (2001). *Resolution 2001/33, Access to Medication in the Context of Pandemics such as HIV/AIDS.* UN Doc. E/CN.4/RES/2001/33.

UN Development Group. (2003). *Indicators for Monitoring the Millennium Development Goals.* United Nations (UN): New York, NY.

UN General Assembly. (1996). *International Covenant on Economic, Social and Cultural Rights.* UNTS 993/3. United Nations (UN): New York, NY.

UN General Assembly. (2006). *Report of the Special Rapporteur on the Right of Everyone to the Highest Attainable Standard of Physical and Mental Health, Paul Hunt.* UN Doc. A/61/338. United Nations (UN): New York, NY.

UN General Assembly. (2008). *Report of the Special Rapporteur on the Right of Everyone to the Highest Attainable Standard of Physical and Mental Health, Paul Hunt.* UN Doc. A/63/263. United Nations (UN): New York, NY.

UN Human Rights Council. (2009). *11th Session. Report of the Special Rapporteur on the Right of Everyone to the Highest Attainable Standard of Physical and Mental Health, Anand Grover.* UN Doc A/HRC/11/12. United Nations (UN): New York, NY.

UN Human Rights Council. (2011). *17th session. Report of the Special Rapporteur on the Right of Everyone to the Enjoyment of the Highest Attainable Standard of Physical and Mental Health: Expert Consultation on Access to Medicines as a Fundamental Component of the Right to Health.* UN Doc. A/HRC/17/43. United Nations (UN): New York, NY.

UN Millennium Project. (2005). *Task Force on HIV/AIDS, Malaria, TB and Access to Medicines, Working Group on Essential Medicines. Prescription for Healthy Development: Increasing Access to Medicines.* Earthscan: London.

UN Sub-Commission on the Promotion and Protection of Human Rights. (2000). *51st Session. Intellectual Property Rights and Human Rights.* UN Doc. E/CN.4/RES/2000/7. United Nations (UN): New York, NY.

UN Sub-Commission on the Promotion and Protection of Human Rights. (2001). *52nd Session. The Impact of the Agreement on Trade-Related Aspects of Intellectual Property Rights on Human Rights: Report of the High Commissioner.* UN Doc. E/CN.4/Sub.2/2001/13. United Nations (UN): New York, NY.

UNITAID. (2012). *Medicines Patent Pool.* [Website.] Available at: <http://www.medicinespatentpool.org/> (accessed 20 September 2012).

Unnikrishnan, C.H. (2012, 21 June). Big pharma firms may learn to live with compulsory licensing. *The Livemint & The Wall Street Journal.* Available at: http://www.livemint.com/2012/06/21214055/Big-pharma-firms-may-learn-to.html (accessed 20 September 2012).

US Congress. (1936). Federal Food, Drug and Cosmetic Act, 21 U.S.C. § 321(h).

US FDA. (2010). US Department of Health and Human Services, Food and Drug Administration, Medical Devices, 1 March 2010. Available at: <http://www.fda.gov/medicaldevices/deviceregulationandguidance/overview/classifyyourdevice/ucm051512.htm> (accessed 22 October 2012).

WHA. (2003). *56th Session. Resolution WHA56.27—Intellectual Property Rights, Innovation and Public Health.* WHA56/27. World Health Assembly (WHA): Geneva.

WHA. (2006). *59th Session. Resolution 59.24—Public Health, Innovation, Essential Health Research and Intellectual Property Rights: Towards a Global Strategy and Plan of Action.* WHA59/24. World Health Assembly (WHA): Geneva.

WHA. (2008). *61st Session. Resolution 61.21—Global Strategy and Plan of Action on Public Health, Innovation and Intellectual Property*. WHA61/21. World Health Assembly (WHA): Geneva.

WHA. (2009). *62nd Session. Resolution 62.16—Global Strategy and Plan of Action on Public Health, Innovation and Intellectual Property*. WHA62/16. World Health Assembly (WHA): Geneva.

WHA. (2011). *64th Session. Global Immunization Vision and Strategy: Progress Report and Strategic Direction for the Decade of Vaccines*. WHA64/14. World Health Assembly (WHA): Geneva.

WHO. (2001). *Commission on Macroeconomics and Health, 2001. Macroeconomics and Health: Investing in Health for Economic Development*. World Health Organization (WHO): Geneva.

WHO. (2004). *WHO Medicines Strategy 2004–2007: Countries at the Core*. World Health Organization (WHO): Geneva.

WHO. (2007). *Everybody's Business: Strengthening Health Systems to Improve Health Outcomes. WHO's Framework for Action*. World Health Organization (WHO): Geneva.

WHO. (2008). *Medium-Term Strategic Plan 2008-2013 and Programme Budget 2008–2009*. World Health Organization (WHO): Geneva.

WHO. (2009a). *Continuity and Change: Implementing the Third WHO Medicines Strategy 2008–2013*. World Health Organization (WHO): Geneva.

WHO. (2009b). *Immunization Safety*. World Health Organization (WHO): Geneva. Available at: <http://www.who.int/immunization_safety/en/>(accessed 20 September 2012).

WHO. (2011). *First WHO Global Forum on Medical Devices: Context, Outcomes and Future Actions*. World Health Organization (WHO): Geneva.

WHO and UNICEF. (2006). *GIVS: Global Immunization and Vaccine Strategy 2006-2015*. World Health Organization (WHO) and United Nations Children's Fund (UNICEF): Geneva.

WIPO. (2012). *WIPO Re:Search*. [Website.] World Intellectual Property Organization (WIPO): Geneva. Available at: <http://www.wipo.int/research/en/> (accessed 10 October 2012).

WTO. (2001). *Ministerial Conference, Fourth Session, Doha, 9–14 November 2001, Declaration on the Trips Agreement and Public Health*. WTO Doc. WT/MIN(01)/DEC/W/2. World Trade Organization (WTO): Geneva.

WTO. (2003). *General Council Implementation of paragraph 6 of the Doha Declaration on the TRIPS Agreement and Public Health. Decision of the General Council of 30 August 2003*. WT/L/540 and Corr. 1. World Trade Organization (WTO): Geneva.

Waning, B., Diedrichsen, E., and Moon, S. (2010). A lifeline to treatment: the role of Indian generic manufacturers in supplying antiretroviral medicines to developing countries. *Journal of the International AIDS Society*, 13, 35.

Westerhaus, M. and Castro, A. (2006). How do intellectual property law and international trade agreements affect access to antiretroviral therapy? *PLOS Medicine*, 3(8), 1230–1236.

Whalen, J. (2012, 23 March). Cancer drugs get cheaper in India. *Wall Street Journal*. Available at: <http://online.wsj.com/article/SB10001424052702303812904577297673910205972.html> (accessed 20 September 2012).

Yamin, A.E. (2003). Not just a tragedy: access to medications as a right under international law. *Boston University International Law Journal*, 21, 325–371.

Yamin, A.E. and Parra-Vera, O. (2009). How do courts set health policy? The case of the Colombian Constitutional Court. *PLOS Medicine*, 6(2), 147–150.

Yu, P.K. (2008). Access to medicines, BRICS alliance, and collective action. *American Journal of Law and Medicine*, 34, 345–394.

Chapter 23

Nutrition and human rights: why meeting nutrient needs should be a human right

Martin W. Bloem and Saskia de Pee

Introduction

Throughout the ages, extreme poverty has been among the world's most critical problems. At the 2000 United Nations (UN) Millennium Summit, world leaders from 189 countries committed themselves to a set of eight time-bound targets that, when achieved, would end extreme poverty worldwide by 2015 (Horton, 2002).

These UN Millennium Development Goals (MDGs) are to:

- End hunger and extreme poverty;
- Ensure universal education;
- Ensure gender equality;
- Increase child survival;
- Reduce maternal mortality;
- Reduce the prevalence and impact of HIV/AIDS;
- Ensure environmental sustainability; and
- Improve global partnerships (UN General Assembly, 2000).

The first goal had two components: an economic goal and a hunger goal. The hunger goal had two major indicators: the number of undernourished people, and the percentage of underweight children under five.

Hunger, defined by the UN Food and Agriculture Organization (FAO) as undernourishment, remains a critical issue and the most recent State of Food Insecurity report estimated that about 870 million people are undernourished (FAO et al., 2012). Undernourishment is estimated as the number of people that are likely not meeting their energy requirements. The estimate is based on data on available calories (food production + import – export); energy requirements of different members of the population; access to food among different groups of the population; and variability of intra-household distribution. As such, it is important to note that it is not an estimate that assesses the adequacy of energy intake at individual level or nutritional status (FAO et al., 2012).

The second indicator of the hunger element of MDG 1 is the prevalence of underweight among children less than five years of age. Underweight is defined as having a weight-for-age less than –2 Z-scores of the median of the World Health Organization (WHO) Child Growth Standards. The WHO Child Growth Standards is a reference based on a multicountry study that included children from selected healthy and privileged populations from Brazil, Ghana, India, Norway, Oman, and the United States (WHO Multicentre Growth Reference Study Group, 2006). The latest data from United Nations Children's Fund (UNICEF), WHO, and the World Bank showed that about 100 million under-fives are underweight (UNICEF et al., 2012). In contrast with undernourishment, underweight is measured at individual level through household surveys from representative samples and is an indicator of nutritional status of the body, rather than of just energy intake (de Onis, 2007).

Although child undernutrition has long been used as an indicator or proxy for poverty, the world has never united behind making prevention of undernutrition a goal in itself. This is partially due to the fact that nutrition is so core to human development and so important throughout the life cycle and 'owned' by many disciplines that the world never agreed upon one single roadmap.

This chapter will focus on stunting or chronic undernutrition because we will argue that this is the most relevant nutrition problem in the context of human rights. There are 165 million children under the age of five who are stunted, according to the latest report of UNICEF et al. (2012). After a 2008 series on nutrition in *The Lancet* (Horton, 2008), a global movement known as 'scaling up nutrition' (SUN) was initiated; it generated momentum around this issue and has been joined by hundreds of agencies from governments, non-governmental organizations (NGOs), international agencies, the UN, private sector, donors, and civil society (Black et al., 2008; SUN, 2012; UNICEF et al., 2012).

This chapter posits that being stunted at the age of two years is a reflection of inequity; has long-term negative health, economic, and social consequences for the individual, their offspring as well as the population they live in; and deprives them from the possibilities to have equal chances for the rest of their life. Therefore, there is a need to include the prevention of chronic undernutrition, or stunting, as a 'human right'.

Stunting—a definition

The term 'stunting' refers to short-for-age, where short is defined by comparing one's length with that of individuals of the same age and sex in a reference population. For young children aged 0–59 months, the WHO's child growth standards (WHO Multicentre Growth Reference Study Group, 2006) are used for comparison. In that multicountry reference population, 2.3% of the children have a height that is more than two standard deviations lower than the median value (also stated as <–2 SD or <–2 Z-scores) of children of the same age and sex, which is explained by normal biological variation (WHO Multicentre Growth Reference Study Group, 2006). Thus, for any other population that is compared to this reference, a prevalence of stunting higher than 2.3% indicates that children in that population are affected by stunting. From a public health point of view a prevalence <20% is considered low, 20% to <30% medium, 30% to <40% high, and ≥40% very high.

What 'stunting' indicates

Stunting reflects inadequate growth and is due to an inadequate nutrient intake in comparison to nutrient needs, also called 'undernutrition'. The inadequacy of nutrient intake does not exclusively affect growth in length, but also development of the brain and the immune system. And while not meeting requirements due to consumption of a diet that is not nutritious enough is the main cause, factors that increase needs, reduce intake, and/or reduce absorption of nutrients, such as illness, are also important.

Stunting is a relatively easy indicator to measure, and a much more specific consequence of undernutrition than, for example, morbidity (related to immune system) or intellectual capacity (related to brain development). Thus, because stunting is due to not meeting nutrient requirements, it does not only reflect suboptimal linear growth, it reflects undernutrition during a critical period of development, in particular from conception until two years of age. Inadequate nutrition during that period has severe consequences for life, because many developmental processes occur only during certain stages of life, and cannot be re-done later in life (Victora et al., 2008).

For example, during pregnancy, an infant's brain will develop more than 100 billion nerve cells, resulting in a weight of approximately 400 grams at birth (Dekaban & Sadowsky, 1978). At 12 months of age the brain weighs about 1,000 grams and by 24 months of age the brain has reached 80% of its adult size (Dekaban & Sadowsky, 1978). The next developmental process that greatly contributes to brain growth and maturation is myelination. Myelination begins early in the third trimester of pregnancy with the most rapid period of myelination occurring in the first two years of life, and also here nutrition plays a very important role (Gunston et al., 1992).

Lack of adequate nutrients in the first 1,000 days of life will lead to irreversible gaps in brain development (Victora et al., 2008). Furthermore, the brain of a young child that does not interact much with her environment because of being tired due to anaemia develops fewer neuron connections and is left with a different brain structure and lower brain weight compared to a child that has been able to develop to her full potential. Thus the outcome of brain development by the age of two years, in which nutrition plays a large role, determines to a large extent a person's mental capacity for the rest of his/her life, including success in schooling and income earning (Hoddinott et al., 2008; Victora et al., 2008).

It is important to realize that not only stunted children are affected by undernutrition, also non-stunted children of populations with a considerable prevalence of stunting are likely to be affected, just not to the extent that their height is lower than that of 97.7% of the reference population. For example, it could be that their height should have been at the 70th percentile of the reference population (70% is shorter than this height and 30% is taller), but is only at 30%, which is considerably lower than the child's potential. Thus, in populations affected by stunting, children who are not stunted enough to be classified as such are also unlikely to have reached their full potential for growth and development, including brain development.

Stunting develops during life *in utero* and the first two years after birth. It is a process of suboptimal growth and development that gradually accumulates to such an extent that body length is below that of 97.7% of children in the reference population (WHO Multicentre Growth Reference Study Group, 2006). Because of this gradual process, the prevalence of stunting increases with age, with most of the increase occurring between birth and 24 months. Beyond 24 months of age, stunting prevalence may still increase, but at a much smaller pace (WHO Multicentre Growth Reference Study Group, 2006). Also, children born with a low birth weight (<2,500 grams) due to restricted intrauterine growth have been exposed to undernutrition *in utero* and are at great risk of remaining stunted. Girls who grow up stunted are more likely to suffer complications during childbirth, because they have a smaller pelvis (Özaltin, 2010). This risk increases when they themselves are well nourished before and during their pregnancy and are expecting a normal weight baby. Breaking the intergenerational cycle of undernutrition thus also requires good obstetric care.

The development of stunting usually co-occurs with micronutrient deficiencies, because several micronutrients are important for growth, and because foods that are rich in nutrients essential for linear growth are also good sources of other micronutrients (Allen, 2006; de Pee and Bloem, 2009). However, contrary to stunting, micronutrient deficiencies can, and should, be treated and prevented at any time during life. Although this does not mean that one can catch up on missed developmental opportunities, current, and future damage due to existing micronutrient deficiencies can be prevented.

Consequences of stunting

Stunting, because it indicates undernutrition early in life, which affects many essential life processes, has been linked to increased morbidity and mortality, delayed mental development, poor school performance, and reduced intellectual capacity (Hoddinott et al., 2008; Victora et al., 2008). This in turn affects income in adult life as well as economic productivity at national level. Furthermore, stunting is also related to increased risk of non-communicable disease later in life, such as diabetes, overweight and obesity, and cardiovascular disease (Victora et al., 2008). And women of short stature are at greater risk of obstetric complications and of delivering an infant with low birth weight, which contributes to the intergenerational cycle of malnutrition (Özaltin et al., 2010). Due to these severe consequences of stunting developed during early life, and the fact that much of this damage cannot be undone later in life, its prevention is essential.

Prevention of stunting

The prevalence of stunting among children aged 24 to 59 months in a population is a rough indicator of the risk of an individual newborn child to become stunted over the next two years of life as well. Prevention of undernutrition should start early in life, with interventions among at-risk populations (areas with high prevalence, lower socioeconomic groups, etc.) that improve nutrition of pregnant and lactating mothers, ensure exclusive breastfeeding during the first six months of life, and enable provision of adequate complementary feeding in addition to breastfeeding for children aged six to 23 months.

The ultimate aim of interventions to prevent stunting should be that nutrient requirements of the individual child, and also during life *in utero*, are met and that illness is prevented. An individual needs approximately 40 different nutrients, in different amounts, in order to grow, develop, and remain healthy (Golden, 2009). Meeting these requirements requires consumption of an adequately diverse diet, including breast milk, plant source foods (vegetables, fruits, staples), animal source foods (dairy, eggs, fish, meat), and fortified foods, and from each of those categories a variety of foods should be consumed (de Pee, 2009).

Where such a variety of foods is not accessible, for example, due to financial constraints (Chastre et al., 2007), or not available, specially formulated foods may be required that fill the so-called 'nutrient gap'. Since such a nutrient gap is difficult to quantify precisely, is different for every individual, and different between regions and countries, some best estimates and assumptions have to be made for the development of specially formulated foods and complementary food supplements, and cost considerations are also important.

A home-fortification approach, where a small amount of a powder- or lipid-based spread (<20 grams, <100 kcal/day) is added to home-prepared foods, which adds vitamins, minerals, and some other essential nutrients that are likely to not be available from the prevailing diet in adequate amounts, is a promising strategy for preventing stunting, because it hardly changes the local diet and food practices. Another option is the introduction of specially formulated complementary foods, such as infant porridges that have a good content of essential nutrients.

Stunting leads to lifelong inequity

While understanding and addressing the entire spectrum of nutrition challenges is critical and should be done through multisector solutions, the issue of child stunting/chronic undernutrition is clearly distinct. Consumption of a diverse diet is the only way to ensure that nutrient needs are being met and being able to do so requires that such foods are accessible, but this is often not the case for households of lower socioeconomic status (Menon et al., 2000; Rah et al., 2010; Thorne-Lyman, 2010). Therefore, stunting/chronic undernutrition is an important problem of inequity.

Given evidence on the irreversible effects on physical and cognitive development, educational attainment, and future productivity of a child, stunting deprives a two-year-old child of his/her inherent right to reach in an equitable way their full biologic potential and ability to have a healthy and prosperous life.

Nutrition in 'human rights' documents

Nutrition is mentioned sparsely in the various 'human rights' documents, but it has been argued that this is because nutrition is not a right in itself but an element of health or an outcome of lack of access to food.

Article 25 of the Universal Declaration of Human Rights (UDHR) mentions both health and access to food as rights:

> Everyone has the right to a standard of living adequate for the health and well-being of himself and of his family, including food, clothing, housing and medical care and necessary social services, and the right to security in the event of unemployment, sickness, disability, widowhood, old age or other lack of livelihood in circumstances beyond his control. (UDHR, 1948)

The International Covenant on Economic, Social and Cultural Rights (ICESCR) provides the most comprehensive article on the right to health in international human rights law. Nutrition is mentioned as one of the determinants of health. Indeed, Article 12 of the ICESCR recognizes the right of everyone to 'the enjoyment of the highest attainable standard of physical and mental health' (ICESCR, 1966), with 'health' understood not just as a right to be healthy, but as a right to control one's own health and body (including reproduction), and be free from interference such as torture or medical experimentation. States must protect this right by ensuring that everyone within their jurisdiction has access to the underlying determinants of health, such as clean water, sanitation, food, nutrition, and housing, and through a comprehensive system of healthcare, which is available to everyone without discrimination, and economically accessible to all.

Article 12.2 of the ICESCR requires Parties to take specific steps to improve the health of their citizens, including reducing infant mortality and improving child health; improving environmental and workplace health; preventing, controlling, and treating epidemic diseases; and creating conditions to ensure equal and timely access to medical services for all. These are considered to be 'illustrative, non-exhaustive examples', rather than a complete statement of Parties' obligations (CESCR, 2000, paragraph 7).

The Committee on Economic, Social, and Cultural Rights (CESCR) defines the 'right to food' as follows:

> The right to adequate food is realized when every man, woman and child, alone or in community with others, has physical and economic access at all times to adequate food or means for its procurement. The right to adequate food shall therefore not be interpreted in a narrow or restrictive sense, which equates it with a minimum package of calories, proteins and other specific nutrients. The right to adequate food will have to be realized progressively. However, States have a core obligation to take the necessary action to mitigate and alleviate hunger as provided for in paragraph 2 of article 11, even in times of natural or other disasters. (CESCR, 1999, paragraph 6)

Nutrition is only considered as a determinant to health and the right to food only mentioned access to 'nutritious food' but none of the 'human rights' documents recognizes the importance of nutrients in the sense that all required nutrients should be provided in adequate amounts. The particular need of children aged six to 24 months for nutrient-dense foods is very specific and the fact that these needs are difficult to meet from local foods for large segments of the world population supports the need for a discussion on the right to nutrients to prevent chronic undernutrition.

Discussion

The nutrition field has never had one home and has been an orphan both in the health as well as the agriculture sector. In the late 19th and early 20th centuries, nutritional science was developed particularly by medically trained professionals in Europe and the United States. The research was particularly focused on vitamin and mineral deficiencies, and the quality of diets. At the same time, agriculturalists were fighting against recurrent famines, and the development of new grain varieties, fertilizers, and innovative agriculture practices led to the 'green revolution'.

Although the medical world recognized suboptimal nutritional status as a determinant of health, and clinical deficiencies of specific nutrients as syndromes/diseases, stunting was not, as yet, fully recognized and was definitely not regarded as a health issue in itself. Meanwhile, agriculturists had put all their efforts towards increasing the production of staple foods, mainly focusing on the prevention of hunger. In terms of nutrition, agriculturists translated hunger into lack of access to an adequate amount of food or energy.

Illustrative of the different points of view of the medical profession and of the agriculturists is the fact that the number of hungry people, also known as 'undernourished' people, reported by the FAO, World Food Program, and International Fund for Agricultural Development on an annual basis, has caloric insufficiency as the basis, whereas the magnitude of the problem of undernutrition reported by the WHO and UNICEF is expressed as the number of stunted, wasted, and underweight children under five years of age. The number of undernourished is estimated based on national availability of calories (production + import – export), caloric needs of the population, and a certain distribution of calories among and within households.

Due to similar names but a very distinct meaning of the terms 'undernourished' and 'undernutrition', the different populations that are examined for whether they are affected (the entire world's population versus children under five years of age), and the very different methods used to estimate the numbers, these numbers tell a very different part of the story and cannot be harmonized. This fact is often poorly understood by policymakers as they are presented with numbers such as 868 million hungry or undernourished people (FAO et al., 2012) and 165 million stunted children (UNICEF et al., 2012). Expressing these as percentages, i.e. 12% of the world population and 26% of all under-fives in the world, may be more appropriate. When we consider that the current prevalence of stunting is lower than it was in recent decades, we can deduct that approximately one-third of the world population today suffers the consequences of having been stunted in early childhood, which is considerably more than the 12% that has an inadequate caloric intake and attests to the different magnitude and causes of these two problems.

The biological consequences of poor nutrition are different among different age groups, by gender, and among subpopulations, which is partly due to different needs. The WHO and the FAO worked with a number of technical expert groups on energy requirements, vitamin and mineral requirements, and requirements for other nutrients. The 'right to food' documents have only recognized to a limited extent the different implications of a lack of nutritious food for the various age groups.

The role of the private sector, particularly the food industry, is critical for achieving adequate nutrition and preventing stunting. The increase of the average height of populations in Europe and the United States, as well as parts of East Asia and Latin America, in the second half of the 20th century, coincided with dramatic economic development. Because access to healthcare, water and sanitation, and primary education did not change much during this period in these parts of the world, the improvement of nutritional status was to a large extent due to better access among the lower economic strata of these populations to a more diverse diet, including improved, processed, complementary foods as well as animal source foods such as dairy products (Floud et al., 2011). A good example is the average height of the Dutch male population, which increased from 165 cm in 1935 to 185 cm at the end of the 20th century (Larnkjær et al., 2006). Increased height, which reflects better nutrition, is associated with higher intelligence quotient, lower risk of cardiovascular diseases, but a slight increase of some kind of cancers, however, overall with a more healthy population (Floud et al., 2011).

The increase in prevalence of cardiovascular diseases, obesity, type-2 diabetes, cancers, and other chronic diseases since the 1960s—which are related to overconsumption of foods that have a high content of fats and/or sugars but at the same time a low content of vitamins, minerals, and other essential nutrients, and are also related to undernutrition in early childhood—has made the nutrition field even more complicated. While the 'green revolution' had prevented major famines, more and more groups are criticizing the approach and call on countries, agencies, and the private sector to put less emphasis on monoculture agribusiness and fast-food production and more emphasis on food diversification and lowering intake of high-sugar and high-fat foods. Although the private sector has contributed to increasing the height of many populations, addressing the increase of nutrition-related chronic disease is critically important and requires close cooperation between the public and private sector.

As mentioned in the introduction, the 2008 series on nutrition in *The Lancet* (Horton, 2008) was the beginning of change. The series reported a slow progress in the global reduction of stunting despite the vast array of evidence of the consequences as well as of effective interventions to address it (Bhutta et al., 2008). This resulted in the SUN movement, which was launched by a group of politicians and nutritionists and is currently the most important and widely supported effort to support countries in addressing nutritional problems, particularly stunting. The SUN process adopted the set of nutrition goals endorsed by the World Health Assembly in 2012, including a 40% reduction of the global number of children under five who are stunted by 2025 (WHO, 2012). By September 2012, 33 countries had committed themselves to SUN, that is, to fighting the problem of stunting in a transparent manner.

Civil society recently produced a report on 'the right to food' in which Shuftan and Jonsson authored a specific chapter on the right to nutrition (Shuftan & Jonsson, 2011). However, they mainly emphasized strategies to make multilateral and bilateral donors accountable for ensuring access to adequate food and nutrition and criticized both the SUN process and the use of ready-to-use-foods as examples of technical top-down strategies (Right to Food and Nutrition Watch, 2011). While we recognize that the root causes of stunting are multifactorial and rooted in poverty and inequality, the strategies to prevent stunting by ensuring adequate nutrient intake by adding, where necessary, appropriately formulated complementary foods and complementary food supplements to young children's diets are straightforward, at least in the short term (de Pee and Bloem 2009).

Given evidence on the irreversible effects to physical and cognitive development, educational attainment, and future productivity of a child, stunting deprives a child from the age of two of his/her inherent right to reach in an equitable way his/her full biologic potential and ability to have a healthy and prosperous life.

There is an urgent need to give every child equal opportunities at the age of two by ensuring that his/her rights to required nutrients during the first 1,000 days of life are met. There is a parallel with the way in which HIV/AIDS is addressed. While the causes of HIV infection are multifactorial, and to a large extent related to inequality, the treatment of HIV is considered a primary right and central to HIV/AIDS strategies. In the HIV/AIDS community it is accepted that every HIV-infected person in the world has the right to treatment, while at the same time, policies and programs are implemented for preventing the spread of HIV infections (and it should be noted that treatment also contributes to prevention). We should do the same in the nutrition field, by recognizing the right to nutrients and the prevention of chronic undernutrition, or stunting, as a human right. In so doing, we must ensure that appropriate complementary foods and food supplements become available and affordable for consumption by children at risk of undernutrition, where and for whom that is required.

References

Allen, L.H. (2006). Causes of nutrition-related public health problems of preschool children: available diet. *Journal of Pediatric Gastroenterology and Nutrition*, 43, S8–S12.

Bhutta, Z.A., Ahmed, T., Black, R.E., *et al.* (2008). What works? Interventions for maternal and child undernutrition and survival. *Lancet*, 371, 417–440.

Black, R., Allen, L., Bhutta, Z., *et al.* (2008). Maternal and child undernutrition: global and regional exposures and health consequences. *Lancet*, 371, 243–260.

CESCR. (1999). *General Comment 12: The Right to Adequate Food. (Article 11 of the International Covenant on Economic, Social and Cultural Rights).* Committee on Economic, Social and Cultural Rights (CESCR): Geneva.

CESCR. (2000). *General Comment 14: The Right to the Highest Attainable Standard of Health (Article 12 of the International Covenant on Economic, Social and Cultural Rights).* Committee on Economic, Social and Cultural Rights (CESCR): Geneva.

Chastre, C., Duffield A., Kindness H., *et al.* (2007). *The Minimum Cost of a Healthy Diet: Findings from Piloting a New Methodology in Four Study Locations.* Save the Children: Westport, CT. Available at: <http://motherchildnutrition.org/malnutrition/pdf/mcn-stc-minimum-cost-of-a-healthy-diet.pdf> (accessed 9 November 2012).

Dekaban, A.S. and Sadowsky, D. (1978). Changes in brain weights during the span of human life: relation of brain weights to body heights and body weights. *Annals of Neurology*, 4, 345–356.

de Onis, M., Onyango, AW., Borghi, E., *et al.* (2007). Development of a WHO growth reference for school-aged children and adolescents. *Bulletin of the World Health Organization*, 85(9), 660–667.

de Pee, S. and Bloem, M.W. (2009). Current and potential role of specially formulated foods and food supplements for preventing malnutrition among 6- to 23-month-old children and for treating moderate malnutrition among 6- to 59-month-old children. *Food and Nutrition Bulletin*, 30, S434–S463.

FAO, WFP, and IFAD. (2012). *The State of Food Insecurity in the World 2012.* Food and Agriculture Organization (FAO), World Food Program (WFP), and International Fund for Agricultural Development (IFAD): Rome. Available at: <http://www.fao.org/publications/sofi/en/> (accessed 9 November 2012).

Floud, R., Fogel, R.W., Harris, B., *et al.* (2011). *The Changing Body, Health, Nutrition, and Human Development in the Western World since 1700.* Cambridge University Press: Cambridge.

Golden, M.H. (2009). Proposed recommended nutrient densities for moderately malnourished children. *Food and Nutrition Bulletin*, 30, S267–S342.

Gunston, G.D., Burkimsher, D., Malan, H., *et al.* (1992). Reversible cerebral shrinkage in kwashiorkor: an MRI study. *Archives of Disease in Childhood*, 67(8), 1030–1032.

Hoddinott, J., Maluccio, J.A., Behrman, J.R., *et al.* (2008). Effect of a nutrition intervention during early childhood on economic productivity in Guatemalan adults. *Lancet*, 371, 411–416.

Horton, R. (2002). The health (and wealth) of nations. *Lancet*, 359, 993–994.

Horton, R. (2008). Maternal and child undernutrition: an urgent opportunity. *Lancet*, 371, 179.

ICESCR. (1966). *International Covenant on Economic, Social and Cultural Rights*. Office of the UN High Commissioner for Human Rights: Geneva.

Larnkjær, A., Schrøder, S.A., Schmidt, I.N., *et al.* (2006). Secular change in adult stature has come to a halt in northern Europe and Italy. *Acta Paediatrica*, 95, 754–755.

Menon, P., Ruel, M.T., and Morris, S.S. (2000). Socio-economic differentials in child stunting are consistently larger in urban than in rural areas. *Food and Nutrition Bulletin*, 21, 282–289.

Özaltin, E., Hill, K., and Subramanian, S.V. (2010). Association of maternal stature with offspring mortality, underweight, and stunting in low- to middle-income countries. *Journal of the American Medical Association*, 303, 1507–1516.

Rah, J.H., Akhter, N., Semba, R.D., *et al.* (2010). Low dietary diversity is a predictor of child stunting in rural Bangladesh. *European Journal of Clinical Nutrition*, 64, 1393–1398.

Right to Food and Nutrition Watch. (2011). *Claiming Human Rights: The Accountability Challenge 2011*. Wilma Strothenke, FIAN International: Heidelberg.

Sari, M., de Pee, S., Bloem, M.W., *et al.* (2010). Higher household expenditure on animal-source and nongrain foods lowers the risk of stunting among children 0–59 months old in Indonesia: implications of rising food prices. *Journal of Nutrition*, 140, 196S–201S.

Shuftan, C. and Jonsson, U. (2011). *The Right to Nutritional Strategies to Hold Multilateral and Bilateral Donors Accountable in Right to Food and Nutrition Watch. Claiming Human Rights: The Accountability Challenge 2011*. FIAN International: Heidelberg.

SUN. (2012). *SUN Movement Progress Report, 2011–2012*. Scaling Up Nutrition (SUN): Geneva.

Thorne-Lyman, A.L., Valpiani, N., Sun, K., *et al.* (2010). Household dietary diversity and food expenditures are closely linked in rural Bangladesh, increasing the risk of malnutrition due to the financial crisis. *Journal of Nutrition*, 140, 183S–189S.

UDHR. (1948). *Universal Declaration of Human Rights*. UN General Assembly: New York, NY.

UN Commission on Human Rights. (2001). *The Right to Good. Report by the Special Rapporteur on the Right to Food*. E/CN.4/2001/53. UN Commission on Human Rights: Geneva.

UN General Assembly. (2000). *Millennium Development Goals*. UN General Assembly: New York, NY.

UNICEF, WHO, and World Bank. (2012). *UNICEF—WHO—World Bank Joint Child Malnutrition Estimates*. United Nations Children's Fund (UNICEF) and World Health Organization (WHO): Geneva; World Bank: Washington, DC. Available at: <http://www.who.int/nutgrowthdb/jme_unicef_who_wb.pdf> (accessed 9 November 2012).

Victora, C.G., Adair, L., Fall, C., *et al.*, for the Maternal and Child Undernutrition Study Group. (2008). Maternal and child undernutrition: consequences for adult health and human capital. *Lancet*, 371, 340–357.

WHO. (2012). *WHO Maternal, Infant, and Young Child Nutrition: Draft Comprehensive Implementation Plan*. 65th World Health Assembly 2012: A65/11. World Health Organization (WHO): Geneva.

WHO Multicentre Growth Reference Study Group. (2006). WHO child growth standards based on length/height, weight and age. *Acta Paediatrica Supplement*, 450, 76–85.

Chapter 24

Primum non nocere and the right to health

José M. Zuniga and Imane Sidibé

Introduction

Any chapter focused on the issue of health workers as advocates for the human right to health would be incomplete without reference to the late Jonathan Mann, a champion of the cause who over several decades helped to move our societal discourse by demanding health workers stand behind health as a right of all people. In so doing, he recognized the inherent conflicts in making a commitment to challenge the notion of health as a purchasable privilege. Nonetheless, Dr Mann believed that doing nothing demeans health workers even as it may give the illusion of benefiting the medical profession through the health marketplace. He thus charged health workers to challenge the status quo of health as a privilege for the 'haves' of the world, and to do so at every opportunity and across cultural, economic, political, social, and other domains.

A chapter on the health workforce and the right to health could thus take many directions, and it could span across a range of issues. After all, health workers are not only purveyors but also consumers of health services and, as important, victims of a variety of rights violations both in their personal and professional lives. Female health workers, for example, have been subjected to the 'glass ceiling' effect in their work environments or suffered mistreatment in conflict zones, but as consumers they may also have experienced women's health violations. This chapter is thus focused on: (1) framing health worker engagement on the right to health as defined by human rights instruments and the work of various right to health advocates; (2) addressing the human resources for health crises plaguing numerous countries and their impact on advancing the right to health; (3) protecting health workers in their work environments, including conflict zones, and empowering them to fulfil their life-saving and life-enhancing work; and (4) holding health workers accountable for human rights abuses and violations.

Health worker engagement in advancing the right to health

When articulating the role of health workers in advancing the right to health, its advocates point to various human rights instruments that form a legal entitlement, notably:

- Article 25 of the Universal Declaration of Human Rights (UDHR) states that 'everyone has the right to a standard of living *adequate for health and wellbeing* of himself and of his family, including food, clothing, housing, *and medical care*, and necessary social services' (Emphasis added; UN General Assembly, 1948).
- Article 12 of the International Covenant on Economic, Social and Cultural Rights (ICESCR) recognizes 'the right of everyone to the enjoyment of the *highest attainable standard of physical and mental health*' (Emphasis added; ICESCR, 1966).

- The right to health is recognized, inter alia, in Article 5 of the International Convention on the Elimination of All Forms of Racial Discrimination (ICERD, 1965); Articles 11.1 and 12 of the Convention on the Elimination of All Forms of Discrimination against Women (CEDAW, 1979); and Article 24 of the Convention on the Rights of the Child (CRC, 1989).
- The right to health was more fully elaborated this decade in General Comment 14, which states that 'every human being is entitled to the enjoyment of the *highest attainable standard of health conducive to living a life in dignity*' (Emphasis added; CESCR, 2000).

Importantly, in defining health 'as a state of complete physical, mental, and social well-being and not merely the absence of disease or infirmity' (1946), the World Health Organization (WHO) established a means by which to escape the trap of thinking about health from a purely biomedical perspective to a more robust sense of an individual's well-being. Introducing societal dimensions into both the WHO's definition and efforts to achieve the state of complete well-being, the Declaration of Alma-Ata of 1978 expressed its view of health 'as a social goal whose realization requires the action of many other social and economic sectors in addition to the health sector' (WHO, 1978). The Ottawa Charter for Health Promotion wove into this fabric critical language around the importance of health promotion, proposing a 'process of enabling people to increase control over, and to improve, their health' (Ottawa Charter for Health Promotion, 1986).

Rounding out these documents is the Declaration of Geneva, which was adopted by the General Assembly of the World Medical Association (WMA) in 1948. It declared the medical profession's dedication to humanitarianism, and was intended as an update (some argue a revision) of the Oath of Hippocrates. As currently worded in its sixth iteration, the Declaration requires medical professionals make the following pledges, among others:

- 'The health of my patient will be my first consideration.'
- 'I will not permit considerations of religion, nationality, race, party politics or social standing to intervene between my duty and my patient.'
- 'I will maintain the utmost respect for human life, from the time of its conception, even under threat, I will not use my medical knowledge contrary to the laws of humanity.'

(WMA, 1948)

Yet, beyond these documents and their goals of enshrining the right to health, decades of work to define, promote, and protect the right have taught us two practical and highly relevant lessons regarding its implementation. First, the actual content, meaning, and appropriate method(s) to secure the fulfilment of rights requires interpretation at community and national levels. Second, there is anaemic enforcement in the narrow sense of human rights standards. There is no police power to force a government which violates human rights to address the wrong it has committed. International law operates according to the concept of horizontal enforcement, or mutual consent among States, and the human rights movement itself is based ultimately on people's belief in rights as rights. Therefore, it is only when rights are accepted as such, as extraordinarily strong societal claims based on legitimate societal consensus that they have power. Of course, this is also true for what are thought of as regular laws. If lawmakers or the laws themselves lack legitimacy, they will be ignored and, in the case of laws, exist only on the books.

Ultimately, the central issues for promoting and protecting rights are education and leadership so that people know about their rights and want to hold their leaders accountable for carrying out the governments' responsibilities. To the extent that people believe in them, rights achieve the cultural and social legitimacy which alone confers real power behind the concept of a human right. Without a strong prior commitment to the right, there can be no progress.

With respect to healthcare, first and foremost, a clear affirmation is needed, based on modern human rights documents and instruments of international law, to affirm that a right to health exists. Practically, this means that we must first inform and educate the public, and the political classes, that this right exists even though it is not enumerated in many national constitutions. Second, since there is not and will not be a universal or ultimate authority which can describe precisely the content of a minimum basic standard of care, participatory involvement is necessary to create and to compromise on those aspects of health and healthcare that form the foundation of advancing the right to health. Finally, governments have an obligation to progressively realize this right to health. This means setting targets which establish the basis for accountability in determining whether the government is meetings its responsibilities, and it also means making health a right whose parameters must be defined as a political issue.

Dr Mann and other advocates have articulated and through their work defined what health workers might do to advance the concept of and achieve a commitment to the right to health (Mann et al., 1999):

- There is a need to state the right clearly: medical care for prevention and treatment of illness is a human right.
- The human rights movement calls upon health workers as healers and as citizens of the modern world to look within and do something practical, concrete, and immediate—as both individuals and groups of health workers (e.g. Médecins Sans Frontières (MSF), Partners in Health (PIH), Physicians for Human Rights (PHR)) have engaged in through medical humanitarianism. With respect to medical care, this also translates into close attention to two fundamental aspects of human rights: respect for dignity and non-discrimination (which are elaborated upon later in this chapter). The UDHR starts by declaring that 'all people are born equal in dignity and rights', with dignity placed first (UN General Assembly, 1948). There is an affirmative responsibility to strengthen, in specific, immediate, and concrete ways, respect for dignity within healthcare practices and systems. Indeed, the healthcare system itself is rife with practices which are inadvertently impure and deny dignity.
- Health workers can become activists for catalysing action around the right to health, especially since they wield enormous societal legitimacy and are therefore uniquely placed to advance a rights-based agenda (i.e. PHR). Despite the conservative reputation of the profession of medicine as stakeholders in the status quo from which they are deemed to derive financial power, status, and benefits, medicine also embodies an ethos of challenge to the status quo.
- Health workers must refrain from abetting, facilitating, or engaging in any action—discrimination and stigmatization; non-consensual experimentation, testing, or medical treatment; torture and cruel, inhumane, or degrading treatment—that thwarts the right to health and, by extension, the general well-being of their patients.

Beyond these appeals to professional and social responsibility, there is one other argument for health worker engagement in advocating the human right to health: the impact on the providers of medical care when such care (preventive and curative) is considered a privilege rather than a right. If medical care is a privilege, the provider is merely a seller of services. Much like all services sold, while there is an ethics to the matter, the seller of services is ultimately just a commercially oriented entity. The seller has no larger responsibility to ensure justice or to ensure that the world is well shod. Nor does society need have any further regard for the seller than it does for any other merchant. In contrast, to consider healthcare a right engages medicine as a larger calling. To serve the ill and those at risk for illness, to comfort, and to accompany—these are human acts which to many lie beyond the marketplace, even an ethically managed marketplace.

Yet, while there is a need for health worker engagement in advancing the right to health agenda, they are themselves facing significant challenges to their ability to deliver health services. These challenges, which by extension also affect the ability of the health systems within which these health workers operate, include burgeoning human resources for health crises that have a deleterious impact on the right to health.

The human resources for health crisis and its impact on the right to health

The World Health Report 2006—*Working Together for Health*—featured an expert assessment of the global human resources for health crisis. The report revealed an estimated shortage of almost 4.3 million physicians, midwives, nurses, and support workers worldwide, and noted the shortage was most acute in the poorest countries of the world, especially sub-Saharan Africa countries, where health workers are most needed (WHO, 2006a).

The deficit of adequate numbers of health workers has already had and portends to have many more detrimental effects in global health. The health workforce shortage has been noted as a significant factor in the failure to meet the health-related United Nations (UN) Millennium Development Goals (MDGs) (UN, 2011). The MDGs, it should be noted, contain no mention of and thus no goals related to non-communicable diseases (NCDs), despite statistics indicating that an estimated 36 million deaths, or 63% of the 57 million deaths which occurred globally in 2008, were due to NCDs, comprised of mainly cardiovascular diseases (48%), cancers (21%), chronic respiratory diseases, (12%), and diabetes (3.5%) (WHO, 2012a). These statistics encompass high-, middle-, and low-income countries, which are witnessing increased burdens on their health systems and by extension upon health workers. It is upon this sobering backdrop of increased morbidity and mortality due to communicable *and* non-communicable diseases, as well as the various other causes of ill health and death, that the human resources for health crisis is put into greatest relief.

The historical and structural factors that created, and work to perpetuate, the human resources for health crisis going forwards are manifold, and themselves would merit their own chapter(s). This section delves into one of the most pressing—the migration of health workers.

The decades-long human resources for health crisis

Concerns about the international movement of health workers first emerged in the 1940s when large numbers of European health professionals began migrating to the United Kingdom and the United States in the aftermath of World War II. As concerns mounted, the WHO conducted the first-ever study on the migration of health professionals and published its findings in 1979 (Mejia et al., 1979). Since that time, the situation has alternately improved and become more dire, but has consistently grown more complex (Khadria, 2010). While the principal factors prompting health workers to leave their home countries are generally agreed to be unchanging (i.e. escape from hardship and the pursuit of greater opportunity), the patterns of migration and efforts to manage this 'fatal flow' have varied among both recipient and source countries (Khadria, 2010).

In a world of unequal economic development and lack of political freedom, the possibility of a better life elsewhere (including both regional migration within country as well as international migration) will always be a threat to employee retention. When the additional factor of worldwide professional shortages comes into play, however, the picture quickly becomes more than just an issue of the right to the pursuit of a better life. If left entirely up to market forces, the relatively greater financial resources of rich countries means they can simply import/purchase their way out of their human resource crunches. But when health worker shortages also exist in the very nations from which rich countries are importing them (with many of these countries also facing higher burdens of disease than the importing ones), this leads to a vicious cycle of competitive recruiting, workforce instability, and recrimination. Numerous countries, including Ghana, Jamaica, Nigeria, South Africa, Uganda, and Zambia, have suffered significant 'brain drain' losses (Mackey & Liang, 2012). Over three-quarters of the countries of sub-Saharan Africa, for example, do not meet the minimum acceptable physician per capita ratio of the WHO's 'Health for All' standard: one physician per 5,000 persons (WHO, 2006a).

Morbidity and mortality from endemic infectious diseases in many sub-Saharan African countries, most notably the HIV pandemic, have only exacerbated these trends. With 11% of the world's population and 24% of the global burden of disease, sub-Saharan Africa has only 3% of the estimated 60 million medical professionals in the world (WHO, 2006a). A worker-disease index (WDI) has been developed to quantify this relationship. A WDI of 1.0 represents parity between global burden of disease and share of the world's health workforce. With 24% of the global burden of disease and 3% of the world's health workforce, sub-Saharan Africa's WDI is 0.125—compared to a WDI of 3.7 for Canada and the United States, with 37% of health workers and 10% of global disease burden (Mackey & Liang, 2012).

Deteriorating demographics in affluent countries

The primary factors cited as drivers of demand for foreign-trained medical professionals in the major importing countries (Australia, Canada, the Gulf States, New Zealand, and the United States) are these countries' ageing, increasingly obese populations, and the chronic diseases associated with these conditions; high-tech medicine requiring greater numbers of skilled technicians; poor health resource planning; rural to urban migration; and competition from neighbouring countries. Expansion of insurance coverage in Canada and the United Kingdom also added to pressure on healthcare systems, just as expansive new healthcare legislation in the United States is expected to do beginning in 2014. It is estimated that with full implementation of the Patient Accountability and Affordable Care Act in the United States, as many as 32 million previously uninsured patients will be added to healthcare rolls by 2019—an increase of more than 25% (CBO, 2012).

The US Bureau of Labor Statistics (BLS) has projected a need for approximately 25,000 new physicians per year by 2020 (BLS, 2011), and yet only between 16,000 and 17,000 students graduate annually from US medical schools (AAMC, 2011)—this as a result of too few institutions, instructor shortages, and caps placed on the number of students who can be matriculated annually. International medical graduates are typically counted on to make up the approximately 5,000-head shortfall between the number of US hospital residency positions and the annual stock of newly trained physicians (Mullan, 2000). Overall, the AAMC anticipates a shortage of 130,600 physicians in the United States by 2025 (AAMC, 2008). The United States, of course, is not the only country failing to train adequate numbers of medical professionals: in New Zealand and the United Kingdom, international medical graduates are relied upon for more than 30% of the health workforce, while in Australia, Canada, and the United States, that percentage is somewhat lower (OECD, 2010). In the Gulf States, such as Kuwait and the United Arab Emirates, more than 50% of the health workforce is comprised of immigrants (WHO, 2010). Considered as a whole, Organization for Economic Cooperation and Development (OECD) Member-Countries are reported to source approximately 20% of their physicians from abroad (WHO, 2006a).

Health worker crisis and the effect on right to health

Financial losses to exporting countries are often emphasized in health worker migration analyses, such as one indicating the estimated loss across nine sub-Saharan African countries with high HIV/AIDS prevalence at approximately US$2.17 billion (Mills et al., 2011). But, a more insidious destruction is sometimes overlooked. Competitive recruiting of the highly skilled, highly motivated health workers and the chronic workforce instability this creates often result in a disproportionate loss of health professionals most likely to participate in leadership, managerial, and training roles as well as a more systemic loss of institutional knowledge, further weakening a country's health system. From this regard, calls for the payment of monetary damages to make up for public education and training expenses of importing countries would seem simplistic and unlikely to address these institutional and long reverberating deficits.

The Joint Learning Initiative (JLI) spearheaded by Harvard University, Rockefeller University, and the WHO cautions against a damage analysis based on the simple number of health worker émigrés, noting that often the denominator, more than the numerator, needs to be considered (Chen et al., 2004). Even where the absolute number of health workers lost may not be large, this outflow can nonetheless be seriously damaging to domestic health systems where shortages, poor health system infrastructures, and high burdens of disease exist. As a result, many of these countries end up unable to provide basic health and disease prevention services. The shortage of health workers in many sub-Saharan African countries has not only slowed the scale-up of HIV treatment programmes but also the expansion of immunization, antituberculosis, and other health programmes (WHO, 2006a), and threatens the ability to implement biomedical prevention interventions such as treatment as prevention (IAPAC, 2012).

Patterns of health worker migration

While it is tempting to see these 'fatal flows' of skilled workers as solely unidirectional, the reality in most, and perhaps all countries, is of a more complicated dynamic. Developed and developing countries alike are often both the destination and the source of skilled workers. A popular example is the case of South Africa. Close to 40% of South Africa's physicians are reported to have left the country to destinations such as Australia, Canada, the United Kingdom, or the United States over the past 16 years (Naicker et al., 2009; WHO, 2006a). At the same time, largely as a result of this physician emigration, South Africa itself (as well as neighbouring Botswana and Namibia) has become a destination for health professionals. In 2008, for example, Uganda's Minister of Health Stephen Malinga reported that 350 of the country's 1,900 Ugandan-trained physicians had left his country—200 of them for South Africa (Wasswa, 2008). By 2006, of the 34,000 physicians registering every year in South Africa, 16% were foreign-trained physicians, many from other African countries such as Ghana, Kenya, Nigeria, and Zambia (de Vries et al., 2009; Naicker et al., 2009).

Migration in developing countries is reported to happen in a stepwise fashion. Skilled workers tend to move from the poorer regions to cities within a country or province, and then to higher-income countries. As the vacancies in urban areas left by migrating workers are filled by those leaving rural posts, rural health worker shortages grow still more severe. In South Africa, for example, 46% of the country's population is reported to live in rural areas (World Bank, 2012), yet a mere 12% of physicians and 19% of nurses live in these areas (Hamilton & Yau, 2004). Health professionals will also move to progressively more developed countries: from the Democratic Republic of the Congo to Kenya, for example, and then south to Botswana, Namibia, or South Africa. In most countries there is also movement from the public to the private sector (including international non-governmental organizations (NGOs) with operations in-country), particularly where there are considerable differences in working conditions and administrative organization. While many international health organizations and bilateral aid agencies with in-country presence are careful not to recruit from the local labour supply by offering above-market salaries, at least explicitly, higher pay scales are not always the prime motivating factor.

Among industrialized countries, too, there is an ever-changing pattern of movement. Canadian physicians and nurses, for example, are lured to the United States by higher salaries, lower taxes, and a more temperate climate. In response, Canada turns to South Africa (and to a lesser extent, to Nigeria and Uganda) as a rich source of clinicians. South Africa, due to its advanced economic position relative to many other countries in sub-Saharan Africa, then ends up importing health workers from other Commonwealth nations of the region, such as Kenya, Malawi, Uganda, and Zambia. It is thus no surprise that Malawi, with 0.02 physicians per 1,000 persons, faces one of the lowest ratios of physicians per capita (WHO, 2006a)—thus forcing its Ministry of Health to experiment with alternate ways of delivering quality healthcare services to its citizens, including through task-shifting to non-physicians clinicians (WHO, 2008).

Similarly, the United Kingdom replaces its health professionals who move to the United States and Canada with physicians and nurses from Germany. Germany, in turn, hosts a significant and growing number of clinicians from the Czech Republic. In anticipation of a mass exodus after European Union expansion in 2004, Czech health systems targeted recruitment of Slovakian physicians, nurses, and pharmacists. All through this cycle, health benefits of a more robust health workforce are enjoyed by the importing country, to the detriment of countries whose health workers leave—an unintended consequence that inarguably violates the right to health for all.

Yet, despite these unintended consequences, there is a cogent argument, backed by its own set of legal and other instruments, that places the right to health, in this instance, squarely in conflict with the right to migrate—that is, the right to move from one nation or society to another. Ultimately this right, along with the right to liberty and the right to own property wherever it is possible, are derived from an individual's right to life as enshrined in the UDHR's Article 3 and the clear articulation of Article 1 of the UDHR which states that 'all humans are born free and equal in dignity and rights' (UN General Assembly, 1948). For this reason, in attempting to curb practices which serve to perpetuate human resources for health crises (e.g. aggressive recruiting and resultant brain-drain) the WHO, through a Global Code of Practice on the International Recruitment of Health Personnel, clearly articulated that 'nothing in the Code should be interpreted as limiting the freedom of health personnel, in accordance with applicable laws, to migrate to countries that wish to admit them and employ them' (WHA, 2010).

Empowering and protecting health workers

Poor management, in addition to the inability to address the motivation of health workers, remains a primary barrier to ensuring their empowerment. At a time when the current health workforce remains critically low in numbers and unable to address the burden faced in many countries, finding sustainable solutions to increase retention rates as well as the quality of work delivered is indispensable (Anyangwe & Mtonga, 2007; JLI, 2004; Kinoti & Livelsley, 2009; Narasimhan et al., 2004).

In 1957, American psychologist Frederick Herzberg developed the hygiene–motivation theory, which described the various characteristics that should be provided in the workplace to ensure the continuous support and motivation of employees (Amabile, 1993). Motivational factors included recognition for achievements in the workplace or the possibility for advancement; hygiene factors included the potential for remuneration and benefits, as well as positive working conditions (Gawel, 1997). These factors were all found to be directly linked to the overall performance and satisfaction of the employee within the workplace (Miner, 2005; Syptak et al., 1999). While the examples given previously play a paramount role in the overall motivation of health workers and the quality of services that they deliver, salary remains one, if not the greatest predictor of both (Willis-Shattuck et al., 2008). In many low- and middle-income countries, the inadequate remuneration of health professionals has greatly affected their job performance and overall job satisfaction, not to mention their willingness to continue to work within a certain setting (Kotzee & Couper, 2006). In cases of little to no remuneration, health workers are entirely stripped of their basic human right to livelihood that makes possible an adequate standard of living (ICESCR, 1966; UN General Assembly, 1948). The expectation imposed upon health workers to deliver quality health services becomes unjustifiable in circumstances of no to little financial safety or stability, including where the concept of equal pay for equal work is not the standard to which all are held accountable. These types of violations have been experienced, for example, by community health workers (CHWs) (Lehmann & Sanders, 2007; Rahman et al., 2010). This group of lay providers, trained as paraprofessionals in some settings, strengthens and represents the only link—however tenuous—between health service coverage and community involvement. In many countries, however, this cadre has not been adequately integrated into health systems as a recognized cadre of health worker. Past practices as well as a lack of a regulatory framework have led to the expectation, in countries and by international NGOs, that CHWs should be 'volunteers', motivated solely by the improvement of the health status in their communities (Battacharyya et al., 2001; Lehmann & Sanders, 2007).

Low remuneration of health professionals, rampant in many developing world nations, also further affects both the availability of health workers and their job performance due to financial burdens that lead to coping mechanisms that can prove detrimental to the health system (Van Lerberghe et al., 2002). For example, there have been documented cases of public sector health workers conducting private practice hours, selling medicine outside of their health centres or clinics, and overcharging for services (Delcheva et al., 1997; Israr et al., 2000; Parker & Newbrander, 1994). In addition, studies have shown that health workers who do not earn a living wage will often take a second job to supplement their incomes, which then leads to over-work and burn out (Willis-Shattuck et al., 2008).

Multiple documents and instruments enshrine the human right to basic labour protections, including adequate and safe working conditions (ICESCR, 1966; OAU, 1981; UN General Assembly, 1948). Yet, health workers also face poor working conditions in many settings (including the lack of electricity, no running water, and the inability to dispose of hazardous waste). Shortages of equipment, the lack of a solid infrastructure, and medicine stock-outs make their work environment less reliable and sustainable, resulting in poor patient outcomes (Thorton, 2012). Furthermore, such working conditions mean that health workers remain consistently exposed to disease or infection. Each year, an estimated 16,000 hepatitis C virus infections and from 200 to 5,000 HIV infections occur among health workers due to injuries involving needle sticks and other sharps (Rapiti et al., 2005). Universal precautions are necessary in order to prevent health workers from acquiring communicable and potentially life-threatening diseases. In addition, health workers must be vaccinated as a preventative measure against vaccine-preventable diseases such as hepatitis B virus infection. If an injury occurs, health workers must have access to post-exposure prophylaxis, which, if used correctly after a sharps-related injury, can greatly reduce the likelihood of infection (in some cases of HIV exposure, when zidovudine was used, it reduced infection likelihood by 81%) (Rapiti et al., 2005). Guidelines issued by the WHO, International Labor Organization (ILO), and the Joint United Nations Programme on HIV/AIDS (UNAIDS) guide policymakers on how to incorporate universal protection of health workers in practice. The guidelines recommend increasing access to PEP, ensuring paid leave for all absences due to illness, and compensation packages (such as early retirement benefits for premature work stoppage due to infection) (WHO/ILO/UNAIDS, 2011). In addition to these policy guidelines, the WHO's Treat, Train, and Retain initiative laid out a plan to address workforce challenges. 'Treat' ensures HIV care services are made available to support health workers in need; 'Train' entails preparing health workers to deliver HIV services; and 'Retain' aims to ensure the satisfaction of health workers in the workplace through appropriate management of motivational and hygiene factors (WHO, 2006b).

Health worker rights in war and conflict

During regional and national conflicts, health workers are in particular danger. The four Geneva Conventions of 1949 established international law that made it a right for individuals to receive healthcare and obliged 'all parties to a conflict to search for and collect the wounded after battle, and to facilitate access to [healthcare] facilities' (ICRC, 2011a). A set of symbols—a red cross, a crystal, and a crescent—was adopted as a signal to combatants that individuals wearing one of those symbols on their attire (or driving with the symbol displayed on their vehicle) were healthcare providers and should be protected from violence under international law (ICRC, 2011a). Despite the passage of these laws, violations continue to be widespread. Direct and indirect threats to healthcare exist in conflict zones. Direct threats include physical violence against health workers or their clinics (e.g. bombing, physical assault, and looting), kidnappings (either for ransoms or to treat enemy combatants), and assassination attempts occur often. Some health workers choose to spend the night at their clinics rather than risk the journey home at the end of the day (ICRC, 2011a). Indirect threats are just as damaging to a health system located within a conflict zone. When fighting is present in a community, routes to and from a hospital, for example, are either obstructed or extremely dangerous, meaning that the ability to get to a hospital or dispatch emergency vehicles to where they are needed is made impossible (ICRC, 2011a). Fighting can also disrupt electricity, water, and prevent the delivery of crucial supplies (ICRC, 2011a). The mass exodus of health workers from dangerous regions leaves health centres understaffed and unable to meet the overwhelming demand that armed conflict can provoke. Finally, preventative health measures (such as vaccine campaigns or health promotion programmes) are halted until the security situation improves (ICRC, 2011a).

Evidence of these violations has been documented in multiple countries including Bahrain, Iraq, Kosovo, and Syria (Iacopino et al., 2001; ICRC, 2011b; Owley, 2011; PHR, 2011a). In Iraq, for instance, the ICRC states that between 2003 and 2006, the Ministry of Health reported a loss of more than half of its health workforce due to emigration—the primary factor cited was fear for personal safety (ICRC, 2011b). During the Arab Spring in February 2011, Bahrainis participated in the fervour that swept the region, staging protests in the capital. The government's response was a violent crack-down on protesters; the use of rubber bullets and physical beatings, tear gas, bird shot, and chemical agents (PHR, 2011b). Following the protests, healthcare professionals discovered treating the injuries of protesters were arrested and, in some cases, tortured and physically assaulted (Owley, 2011). According to UN Secretary-General Ban Ki-moon, the international community has remained incapable of adequately monitoring and ensuring the safety of the vulnerable populations facing these dire situations (Ki-moon, 2008). Health workers must be assured security in order for their duties to be carried out effectively. Pressure on rights-based agencies (in particular the WHO) to establish mechanisms for health workers to denounce crimes against humanity targeting them or their facilities, led to the drafting of a new resolution that was adopted by the World Health Assembly (WHA) in May 2012 (WHO, 2012b). This resolution decrees that the WHO will take a lead role, with support from other bodies, in 'provid[ing] leadership at the global level in developing methods for systematic collection and dissemination of data on attacks on health facilities, health workers, health transports, and patients in complex humanitarian emergencies' (WHO, 2012b). If implementation is successful, the WHO and its Member-States will push for State responsibility and accountability regarding the safety of health workers in conflict and war zones, therefore, alleviating further burden on the delivery of adequate health services to those in need.

Health worker accountability for human rights violations

Regrettably, health workers have themselves been perpetrators of human rights abuses and violations. These abuses and violations have ranged from health workers conducting medical or scientific experimentation without a subject's consent (informed or otherwise), to engaging in torture or cruel, inhumane, or degrading behaviours that promote disrespect towards and loss of dignity for vulnerable populations.

Engaging in torture

Article 5 of the UDHR states that 'no one shall be subjected to torture or to cruel, inhumane, or degrading treatment or punishment' (UN General Assembly, 1948); its aim is to preserve basic human dignity. Yet, despite the UDHR's efforts to criminalize perpetrators of torture or abuse, such atrocities continue to occur. Further undermining the basic rights and provision of healthcare for citizens are the documented instances in which health workers, who are meant to uphold a relationship with their patients and provide a safe environment, are the perpetrators of human rights abuses.

A major human rights challenge is identifying health workers who partake in the abuse of patients or detainees, and putting an end to their actions—including in the case of health workers identified as accomplices in the torture of detainees through the act of intentionally concealing the inhumane treatment of detainees (Iacopino & Xenakis, 2011). This violation of medical ethics has been identified and condemned by the international community since the Nuremberg Trials, which took place after World War II. In response to these trials, the Nuremberg Code, the first of its kind to enumerate a series of international human rights principles focused on the professional responsibilities of healthcare providers (Elnimeiri, 2008; Smith, 1999). The code was formulated by a panel of American judges who presided over the court cases of Nazi physicians who were accused of crimes against humanity (Shuster, 1997). The first of 12 proceedings—the Doctors' Trial—began with an opening statement, an excerpt of which follows:

> The defendants in this case are charged with murders, tortures, and other atrocities committed in the name of medical science. The victims of these crimes are numbered in the hundreds of thousands. [. . .] The 20 physicians in the dock range from leaders of German scientific medicine, with excellent international reputations, down to the dregs of the German medical profession. [. . .] All of them violated the Hippocratic commandments which they had solemnly sworn to uphold and abide by, including the fundamental principle never to do harm – *primum non nocere*. (*United States* v *Karl Brandt et al.*, 1946)

Since the Nuremberg Code, various other medical ethics codes have been adopted, including the 'Physician's Oath' contained in the WMA's Declaration of Geneva, as well as the Fourth Geneva Convention in 1949, all condemning the use of medical knowledge for harmful actions against humanity (Geneva Convention IV, 1949; WMA, 1948). The Fourth Geneva Convention went even further by specifically incorporating rights against the torture of prisoners of war and other 'noncombatants' (Geneva Convention IV, 1949). Yet, despite the medical principles by which health workers are expected to abide, examples of torture at the hands of these professionals continue to be documented. In a report issued by the International Committee of the Red Cross (ICRC), alleged terrorists held in a US Central Intelligence Agency detention programme ICRC observers visited in 2006 at Guántanamo Bay, Cuba, were physically abused and sexually assaulted, and appropriate medical care and services were withheld (ICRC, 2007). The ICRC reported that health professionals had a leading role in 'selecting and rationalizing' abusive techniques (such as suffocation by water) used to force detainees to provide intelligence, and that health workers supervised torture in a direct violation of medical ethics (Allen et al., 2009; ICRC, 2007). The ICRC, for example, reported on a case in which a psychologist adviser, who served as a member of the behavioural science consultation team at Guántanamo Bay in 2002 and 2003, '[was accused] of developing a plan of coercive interview techniques, including isolation and sleep and food deprivation' (ICRC, 2007). Health workers at Guántanamo Bay were also documented falsifying medical records to disguise acts of torture inflicted upon detainees (Iacopino & Xenakis, 2011).

As recent as early 2012, in a brazen government ploy, volunteer health workers working with MSF in Misrata, Libya, were manipulated into unwittingly participating in human rights abuses by treating hundreds of torture-related injuries among detainees of a centre in that conflict-embroiled city. They stopped treating these patients because 'torture was so rampant that some detainees were brought for care only to make them fit for further interrogation' (MSF, 2012). In reporting to the Libyan government both the victims' claims and the enlistment of health professionals to inadvertently aid or abet these crimes, MSF reminded the Libyan government that doing so violated enforceable prohibitions against medical professionals participating in torture (MSF, 2012)—international covenants and declarations meant to avoid the atrocities of World War II.

Multiple agencies and committees, such as the Office of the High Commissioner for Human Rights, the Committee against Torture, and the UN Human Rights Committee have attempted to document cases of abuse and torture to ensure that the principles dictating human rights are upheld (Slama et al., 2009; Triantaphyllis et al., 2012). But, even in the presence of medical codes of conduct prohibiting health professional engagement in torture, and international covenants and laws meant to prevent governments from utilizing health professionals as pawns in committing human rights violations, there remains a need for strategies that will reinforce existing codes, covenants, and laws that provide mechanisms for identifying perpetrators—both individuals and States—and holding them accountable for their actions.

Informed consent

Informed consent principles have been adopted by or included in numerous foundational international documents that almost all States have acknowledged in some way, including the Nuremburg Code, the International Covenant on Civil and Political Rights, the WMA's Declaration of Helsinki (1964), and the International Ethical Guidelines for Biomedical Research Involving Human Subjects developed by the Council for International Organizations of Medical Science.

In clinical practice, the doctrine of informed consent rose to dominance during the course of the 20th century, replacing the medical ethos founded on trust in physicians' decisions—often on the assumption that the 'doctor knows best'. With respect to medical research on human subjects, informed consent requirements gained prominence in reaction to abuses that led to such influential responses as the Nuremberg Code. The Code was meant to forever curb the type of cruelty on the part of Nazi physicians that made possible their experiments in concentration camps across Third Reich-occupied countries in World War II (Faden & Beauchamp, 1986). It did so by categorically stating that 'the voluntary consent of the human subject is absolutely essential' (Nuremberg Code, 1949).

Not surprisingly, since the 1940s, and bolstered by violations such as those committed in relation to the Cold War era radiation experiments conducted in the United States over three decades (Advisory Committee on Human Radiation Experiments, 1995), the medical and research communities took a hard line with respect to the issue of informed consent. Physician-researchers, however, gradually began to chafe at the overly restrictive language of the Nuremberg Code, arguing it was not applicable to their reality because it focused upon human rights through a strictly legal lens, and increasingly did not reflect modern research agendas. The WMA accommodated these concerns by promoting its Declaration of Helsinki, a more permissive document whose subtitle reads, *Recommendations Guiding Doctors in Clinical Research* (Annas, 1999). This and other attempts to dilute the necessary prerequisite of informed consent to medical testing and treatment is based upon a myopic view that imposing this requirement presents a barrier to the ability of researchers to advance the goals of science (Malloy, 1998). The public health community learned, from the HIV experience of the mid- to late-1980s and into the early 1990s, valuable lessons in relation to implementing HIV and other sexually transmitted infection (STI) testing interventions on a non-consensual basis—if the individual and, by extension in this instance, the population targeted for the intervention (e.g. men who have sex with men), are not willing participants, not only is this individual/population further socially stigmatized, but the short-term benefit of testing is outweighed by the long-term harm of driving HIV and STI epidemics underground (Eisenstat, 1991).

To be fair, there exists a need for dictum less restrictive than the Nuremberg Code in relation to informed consent. An emerging picture is that the need for informed consent depends upon many variables. The level of valid consent to an intervention may vary according to the type of intervention, as may the level of decision-making capacity necessary for valid consent (Beauchamp, 2010; Buchanan & Brock, 1989). Robust informed consent, which requires detailed information and the ability to make informed decisions, is relatively unwaivable, but it may also not always be necessary. The riskier the intervention, the more it represents a definitive 'critical life choice' (Archard, 2008). As some bioethicists argue, the more value-laden and controversial, the more private the area of the body the intervention targets, the more conflicted and unsupervised the clinician or clinician-researcher, the higher the need for robust informed consent (Joffe & Truog, 2010; Miller, 2010). On other occasions, the need for robust informed consent and, perhaps, for consent of any form, is lesser (Miller, 2010). On those occasions, high costs may easily override that need.

Does the need for informed consent depend, among other variables, on whether the consent is for research or for care? Current consent procedures for research tend to be more demanding and more regulated than consent procedures for equally intrusive care (Levine, 1988). Bioethicists increasingly want to explain why this is the case. A standard account is that the proper goal of research is to gather generalizable knowledge, and not to help the individual, and that this different goal enhances the need for protections such as informed consent (Fried, 1974). However, actual goals often differ from proper goals. The research community might say that most researchers are highly committed to promoting study participants' health, and claim that many clinicians seek primarily financial gain, sometimes at the patient's expense. In addition, some studies are so safe, when reviewed independently, that (with or without consent) they impose virtually no risk. Another rationale for fewer consent requirements in care is that the relationship between the clinician and the patient is typically a fiduciary and privileged one whereas the relationship between the investigator and the study participant is rarely fiduciary (Joffe & Truog, 2010). But this rationale could easily work the other way around: assuming that the fiduciary relationship is a ground for informed consent (Joffe & Truog, 2010), the more fiduciary clinical relationship should demand more, not less, by way of informed consent.

Regardless of who wins the bioethical argument, and which side prevails—rigid law or merely guidance—the fact remains that the right to health requires duty-bearers, including health workers, to respect certain individual freedoms, including the rights to informed consent and to refuse medical experimentation as well as non-consensual testing and treatment.

Stigma and discrimination

Beyond human rights violations in the form of torture, health workers have been documented engaging in discriminatory and stigmatizing actions—including of fellow health workers in the instance of those who are themselves living with HIV/AIDS or a mental health condition. Whether verbal, psychological or, in some cases, physical, these abusive actions can lead to the social isolation of individuals, or at times, entire communities of people. Such actions impede the attainment of positive health outcomes, and present a barrier for those seeking health promotion as well as prevention and medical services. In addition to Article 25 of the UDHR, these violations are condemned by Article 12 of the ICESCR, which states that all people have the basic human 'right to the enjoyment of the highest attainable standard of physical and mental health' (ICESCR, 1966). By refusing adequate healthcare to a patient, and especially if this refusal is based on discriminatory or stigmatizing behaviour on the part of the health worker, he/she is betraying the sworn duty under the Oath of Hippocrates to never cause intentional harm to a person in need of care.

There are documented instances of health workers intentionally creating hostile environments for patients, especially vulnerable populations. Before understanding why health workers engage in the abuse of patients through stigmatization or discrimination, it would be beneficial to define the terms 'stigma' and 'discrimination' in the context of healthcare. Both terms tend to be used interchangeably despite the distinct meaning that each embodies. Stigma in health is related to the degrading and intentional social ostracizing of an individual due to his/her health status (Gruskin & Ferguson, 2009). This type of ill-treatment is easily identified and has been referred to as the 'tip of the iceberg' (Castro & Farmer, 2005) due to the complex nature of the underlying determinants which are not as easily defined. The health-related definition of discrimination refers to the denial of health rights by laws or institutions, governmental and non-governmental, based on an individual's health status (Gruskin & Ferguson, 2009). Unlike stigma, which tends to be caused by social unacceptability, fear, or misperceptions, discrimination directly violates a person's ability to maintain equal status within a system, therefore, negating international human rights principles, including that of the right to health. However, the two definitions remain rather intertwined as discrimination tends to be preceded by stigma and is considered a form of 'enacted stigma' (Parker et al., 2002).

Evidence of stigma and discrimination at the hands of health workers demonstrates that it has occurred in various healthcare settings, particularly towards people living with HIV/AIDS or patients with mental conditions; people with low socioeconomic status; a different religion from that of the healthcare provider; differing sexual orientation or gender identity; and/or histories of substance use or engagement in commercial sex trade.

Sexually transmitted infections

In the case of STIs, health worker attitudes and the intentional exclusion of patients with STIs, particularly HIV and syphilis, are driving the epidemics underground, thus making it more challenging to attain better health outcomes. With respect to HIV/AIDS, it is not uncommon to find patients who have either felt devalued or fear that they will be mistreated by the health system and by care providers simply because of an HIV-positive diagnosis. A 2008 study on stigma and HIV/AIDS conducted in Belize found that physicians and nurses were disclosing patients' HIV status to each other without receiving the patient's consent to do so (Andrewin & Chien, 2008). In another study conducted in India, Vaishali Mahendra and colleagues identified that health workers had disclosed the HIV status of patients without permission to the patients' family members (Mahendra et al., 2007). In addition, the staff at the health centre openly displayed its knowledge of patients' HIV status by burning the sheets that HIV-positive patients had slept on, or charged additional fees to patients for supplies that were used to control an STI (Mahendra et al., 2007). A 2006 study conducted in Los Angeles showed that more than half of the nurses and obstetricians surveyed had cited their practice of refusing to provide care to HIV-positive patients, knowing that they had no legal basis to support their actions (Sears & Ho, 2006). Unfortunately, healthcare workers have caused long-lasting emotional, psychological, and physical damage to patients; whether it is driven by fear of infection, the association of HIV with immoral behaviour, or a lack of education and understanding surrounding the impact of stigma (Nyblade et al., 2009).

As recognized by the 2011 Political Declaration on HIV/AIDS adopted by the UN General Assembly, these unwelcoming environments negatively impact the ability of patients to access prevention, care, and treatment services, as well as further weaken the state of the health system and its availability to those who are most in need (UN General Assembly, 2011). That is why Section 80 of this latest Political Declaration specifically commits UN Member-States to 'commit to national HIV and AIDS strategies that promote and protect human rights, including programmes aimed at eliminating stigma and discrimination against people living with and affected by HIV, including their families' (UN General Assembly, 2011).

Mental health and substance use

Another vulnerable group of individuals who find themselves marginalized and poorly treated by health workers are mental health patients and substance users. A literature review of the attitudes of nurses towards their patients living with a mental condition revealed that many nurses feared the mentally unwell. The nurses believed the patients were not curable; they were simply draining hospital resources in a futile attempt to fix an unfixable situation (Ross & Goldner, 2009). In Nigeria, 73.5% of healthcare professionals, in a study conducted regarding patients with a mental health challenge, associated the patients' illness with witchcraft and believed that they had previously been 'evildoers' despite their extensive knowledge of mental illness; this made the health providers fearful of any contact with the patients and further alienated them from care (Ewhrudjakpor, 2009). Many healthcare providers also believe mental health conditions are a consequence of substance use, therefore, directly impacting the manner in which substance users are likely to be treated (Ewhrudjakpor, 2009; Kabir et al., 2004; Ross & Goldner, 2009). Substance users are sometimes considered dangerous and difficult to handle due to the routine complexity of their cases (Peckover & Chidlaw, 2007); health workers may view them as 'second class patients with little or no clinical or social value' (Hunt & Derricot, 2001). This type of stigma may arise from the fear that health providers have surrounding the often unpredictable nature of the patient or because the drugs the patient uses are illegal, which immediately carries a pre-existing social discrimination (Hunt & Derricot, 2001). Additionally, there is the belief that the patient is responsible for causing him or herself undue harm which makes them less deserving of care (McLaughlin & Long, 1996; Skinner et al., 2007).

Refusal of care based on religious beliefs

Religion, race, socioeconomic status, and sexual orientation can sometimes be predictors of the access and quality of the care obtained by patients. Health workers have been documented giving differential treatment to patients because of religious beliefs; for instance, treatment is particularly influenced in the domain of sexual reproductive health. The term 'conscientious objection' of services is employed for health workers refusing to provide specific services; a legal phenomenon under which they remain protected because providing a certain service goes against their belief system (Zampas & Andion-Ibañez, 2012). For example, in 2008, Italy's Ministry of Health documented that approximately 70% of gynaecologists refused to perform abortions on the grounds that doing so was against their morals (Zampas & Andion-Ibañez, 2012). Other healthcare providers, notably pharmacists, have been documented worldwide refusing to provide contraception (including emergency contraception to victims of rape) due to a 'conscientious objection' (Teliska, 2005).

Patients of lower socioeconomic status or of certain races are also at risk of being devalued and disregarded by health workers. A US survey of African Americans showed that more than 60% had felt discriminated against at some point due to their colour or race, and over half of those surveyed had felt they were discriminated against based on their socioeconomic status (Bird & Bogart, 2001). Discrimination has also arisen due to the sexual orientation of the patient; refusal of care is common as well as healthcare providers openly degrading the patient (James & Platzer, 1999). Lesbian, gay, bisexual, and transgender (LGBT) individuals 'have been attacked, arrested, tortured, killed, sentenced to death, committed to medical or psychiatric institutions, and treated with "aversion therapy" including electroshock therapy or forced rape' (Mahon, 2009). These individuals find that health service environments are often unwelcoming and judgemental, a feeling that impacts the patient's access to care and their willingness to disclose their orientation, resulting in a lack of tailored care and health promotion services (Hunt, 2004). Additionally, because being homosexual is against the law in many countries, safe sex practices and other health concerns that are linked to sexual orientation are not addressed, driving LGBT health outcomes significantly lower (Dean et al., 2000).

The deleterious impacts of negative healthcare provider attitudes on the delivery of care to marginalized populations must be addressed by providing effective programmes that aim to sensitize these professionals and ensure equality in access to high-quality care and treatment for all in need regardless of any factor that may contribute to the 'other-ization' of any given individual or group of individuals.

Conclusion

We can examine the instruments of modern human rights and international law and find clear evidence of a right to health. But any legal exegesis would be simply a diversion from the real issues that impede the progressive realization of this fundamental human right. The heart of the matter is a question of belief followed by concrete actions. We must believe in and act to advance the right to health. We must believe and ensure that those individuals who are tasked with delivering health services—preventive and curative—that lead to positive health outcomes and, thus, to health for all, are empowered within their work environments and health systems, as well as protected from injury (occupational and otherwise). And we must believe and exclaim that health workers bear a special responsibility under the Oath of Hippocrates to first do no harm (*primum non nocere*), which translates into avoiding discriminatory and stigmatizing actions, truly involving their patients (including those enrolled in clinical trials) in decision-making through informed consent mechanisms, and, as important, refusing to engage in torture and degrading acts that dehumanize both victims and perpetrators.

We cannot shy away from these beliefs, which embody the most precious values of the medical profession. The medical marketplace is indeed value-laden, and thus pretending to the status of neutral or value-free domains translates into failing to advocate the progressive realization of the right to health. The quest towards achieving health as a right will take time, yet it serves to remind us all, including those who make up the global health workforce, with whom we stand and why. As Dr Mann posited, 'We are in the vanguard of a movement. We have a deeper belief that the world can be changed, and in doing that, we give value to the world' (FXB Center for Health and Human Rights, 2012).

Acknowledgements

The authors wish to acknowledge the invaluable contributions of Joan Holloway and Alexandra Zimbelman towards this chapter.

References

AAMC. (2008). *The Complexities of Physician Supply and Demand: Projections Through 2025*. Association of American Medical Colleges (AAMC): Washington, DC.

AAMC. (2011). *AAMC Facts, Table 27, Total Graduates by US Medical School and Sex, 2007–2011*. Association of American Medical Colleges (AAMC): Washington, DC.

Advisory Committee on Human Radiation Experiments. (1995). *Final Report*. Department of Energy: Washington, DC.

Allen, S., Keller, A., Reisner, S., *et al.* (2009). *Aiding Torture: Health Professionals' Ethics and Human Rights Violations Revealed in the May 2004 CIA Inspector General's Report*. Physicians for Human Rights: Cambridge, MA.

Amabile, T.M. (1993). Motivational synergy: toward new conceptualizations of intrinsic and extrinsic motivation in the workplace. *Human Resource Management Review*, 3(3), 185–201.

Andrewin, A. and Chien, L.Y. (2008). Stigmatization of patients with HIV/AIDS among doctors and nurses in Belize. *AIDS Patient Care and STDs*, 22(11), 897–906.

Annas, G.J. (1999). Questing for grails: duplicity, betrayal, and self-deception in postmodern medical research. In J.M. Mann, S. Gruskin, M.A. Grodin, *et al.* (Eds.), *Health and Human Rights*, pp. 373–399. Routledge: New York, NY.

Anyangwe, S. and Mtonga, C. (2007). Inequities in the global health workforce: the greatest impediment to health in sub-Saharan Africa. *International Journal of Environmental Research and Public Health*, 4(2), 93–100.

Archard, D. (2008). Informed consent: autonomy and self-ownership. *Journal of Applied Philosophy*, 25(1), 19–34.

Beauchamp, T.L. (2010). Autonomy and consent. In F.G. Miller, and A. Wertheimer (Eds.), *The Ethics of Consent*, pp. 55–78. Oxford University Press: New York, NY.

Bhattacharyya, K., Leban, K., Winch, P., *et al.* (2001). *Community Health Worker Incentives and Disincentives: How They Affect Motivation, Retention and Sustainability*. BASICS II: Arlington, VA.

Bird, S.T. and Bogart, L.M. (2001). Perceived race-based and socioeconomic status (SES)-based discrimination in interactions with health care providers. *Ethnicity & Disease*, 11(3), 554–563.

BLS, US Bureau of Labor. (2011). *Occupational Outlook Handbook, 2012–2013 Edition*. Bureau of Labor Statistics (BLS): Washington, DC.

Buchanan, A.E. and Brock, D.W. (1989). *Deciding for Others: The Ethics of Surrogate Decision-Making*. Cambridge University Press: Cambridge.

Castro, A. and Farmer, P. (2005). Understanding and addressing AIDS-related stigma: from anthropological theory to clinical practice in Haiti. *American Journal of Public Health*, 95(1), 53–59.

CBO. (2012). *Updated Estimates for the Insurance Coverage Provisions of the Affordable Care Act*. Congressional Budget Office (CBO): Washington, DC.

CEDAW. (1979). *Convention on the Elimination of All Forms of Discrimination against Women*. UN General Assembly: New York, NY.

CESCR. (2000). *General Comment 14: The right to the highest attainable standard of health (article 12 of the International Covenant on Economic, Social and Cultural Rights)*. Committee on Economic, Social and Cultural Rights (CESCR): Geneva.

Chen, L., Evans, T., Anand, S., *et al.* (2004). Human resources for health: overcoming the crisis. *Lancet*, 364, 1984–1990.

CRC. (1989). *Convention on the Rights of the Child*. United Nations Office of the High Commissioner for Human Rights: Geneva.

Dean, L., Meyer, I.H., Robinson, K., *et al.* (2000). Lesbian, gay, bisexual, and transgender health: findings and concerns. *Journal of the Gay and Lesbian Medical Association*, 4(3), 101–151.

Delcheva, E., Balabanova, D., and Mckee, M. (1997). Under-the-counter payments for health care: evidence from Bulgaria. *Health Policy (Amsterdam, Netherlands)*, 42(2), 89–100.

De Vries, H., Sanderson, P., Janta, B., *et al.* (2009). *International Comparison of Ten Medical Regulatory Systems: Egypt, Germany, Greece, India, Italy, Nigeria, Pakistan, Poland, South Africa and Spain*. RAND Corporation: Santa Monica, CA.

Eisenstat, S. (1991). Analysis of the rationality of mandatory testing for the HIV antibody: balancing the governmental public health interests with the individual's privacy interest. *University of Pittsburgh Law Review*, 52, 327–387.

Elnimeiri, M.K.M. (2008). Nuremberg Code: a landmark document on medical research ethics. *Sudanese Journal of Public Health*, 3(2), 94–96.

Ewhrudjakpor, C. (2009). Knowledge, beliefs and attitudes of health care providers towards the mentally ill in Delta State, Nigeria. *EthnoMed*, 3(1), 19–25.

Faden, R.R. and Beauchamp, T.L. (1986). *A History and Theory of Informed Consent*. Oxford University Press: New York, NY.

Fried, C. (1974). *Medical Experimentation: Personal Integrity and Social Policy*. North-Holland Publishing Company: New York, NY.

FXB Center for Health and Human Rights. (2012). *From Vision to Action: The First 11 Years*. FXB Center for Health and Human Rights: Boston, MA. Available at: <http://blogs.sph.harvard.edu/fxb/files/2012/10/Vision_to_Action.pdf> (accessed 10 October 2012).

Gawel, J.E. (1997). Herzberg's theory of motivation and Maslow's hierarchy of needs. *Practical Assessment, Research & Evaluation*, 5(11).

Geneva Convention IV. (1949). *Geneva Convention Relative to the Protection of Civilian Persons in Time of War*. Diplomatic Conference of Geneva of 1949: Geneva.

Gruskin, S. and Ferguson, L. (2009). Using indicators to determine the contribution of human rights to public health efforts. *Bulletin of the World Health Organization*, 87(9), 714–719.

Hamilton, K. and Yau, J. (2004). *The Global Tug-of-War for Health Care Workers*. Migration Policy Institute: Washington, DC.

Hunt, N. and Derricott, J. (2001). Smackheads, crackheads and other junkies: dimensions of the stigma of drug use. In T. Mason (Ed.), *Stigma and Social Exclusion in Healthcare*, pp. 190–205. Routledge: London.

Hunt, P. (2004). *Report of the Special Rapporteur on the Right to Everyone to the Enjoyment of the Highest Attainable Standard of Physical and Mental Health*. UN Doc. E/CN.4/2004/49. United Nations (UN): Geneva.

IAPAC. (2012). *Consensus Statement on Controlling the HIV Epidemic with Antiretrovirals: Treatment as Prevention and Pre-Exposure Prophylaxis*. International Association of Physicians in AIDS Care (IAPAC): Washington, DC. Available at: <http://www.iapac.org/tasp_prep/assets/TPSlon12_consensus.pdf> (accessed 7 September 2012).

ICESCR. (1966). *International Covenant on Economic, Social and Cultural Rights*. Office of the UN High Commissioner for Human Rights: Geneva. Available at: <http://www2.ohchr.org/english/law/pdf/cescr.pdf> (accessed 20 September 2012).

ICRC. (2007). *ICRC Report on the Treatment of Fourteen 'High Value Detainees' in CIA Custody*. International Committee of the Red Cross (ICRC): Geneva.

ICRC. (2011a). *Health Care in Danger: Making the Case*. International Committee of the Red Cross (ICRC): Geneva.

ICRC. (2011b). *Health Care in Danger: A Sixteen-Country Study*. International Committee of the Red Cross (ICRC): Geneva.

ILO, UNAIDS, and WHO. (2011). *The Joint WHO-ILO-UNAIDS Policy Guidelines on Improving Health Workers' Access to HIV and TB Prevention, Treatment, Care and Support Services: A Guidance Note*. International Labor Organization (ILO), Joint United Nations Program on AIDS (UNAIDS), and World Health Organization (WHO): Geneva.

Iacopino, V., Frank, M.W., Bauer, H.M., *et al.* (2001). A population-based assessment of human rights abuses committed against ethnic Albanian refugees from Kosovo. *American Journal of Public Health*, 91(12), 2013–2018.

Iacopino, V. and Xenakis, S.N. (2011). Neglect of medical evidence of torture in Guantánamo Bay: a case series. *PLoS Medicine*, 8(4), e1001027. Available at: <http://dx.doi.org/10.1371%2Fjournal.pmed.1001027> (accessed 17 September 2012).

International Convention on the Elimination of All Forms of Racial Discrimination (ICERD) (1965). GA res 2106 (XX), Annex, 20 UN GAOR Supp (No 14) at 47, UN Doc A/6014, 660 UNTS 195.

Israr, S.M., Razum, O., Ndiforchu, V., *et al.* (2000). Coping strategies of health personnel during economic crisis: a case study from Cameroon. *Tropical Medicine & International Health*, 5(4), 288–292.

JLI. (2004). *Human Resources for Health: Overcoming the Crisis*. Joint Learning Initiative (JLI): Cambridge, MA.

James, T. and Platzer, H. (1999). Ethical considerations in qualitative research with vulnerable groups: exploring lesbians' and gay men's experiences of health care—a personal perspective. *Nursing Ethics*, 6(1), 73–81.

Joffe, S. and Truog, R.D. (2010). Consent to medical care: the importance of fiduciary context. In F.G. Miller and A. Wertheimer (Eds.), *The Ethics of Consent*, pp. 347–374. Oxford University Press: New York, NY.

Kabir, M., Iliyasu, Z., Abubakar, I., *et al.* (2004). Perception and beliefs about mental illness among adults in Karfi village, northern Nigeria. *BMC International Health and Human Rights*, 4(1), 3.

Kadhria, B. (2010). *The Future of Health Worker Migration*. International Organization for Migration (IOM): Geneva.

Ki-moon, B. (2008). *The Responsibility to Deliver*. Opening Remarks of the UN Secretary-General at Year-End Press Conference, 17 December 2008. Available at: <http://www.un.org/apps/news/infocus/sgspeeches/statments_full.asp?statID=387#.UQ_yCWf-CM4> (accessed 17 December 2012).

Kinoti, S.N. and Livesley, N. (2009). *Overcoming Human-Resources- for-Health Challenges at the Service Delivery Level*. Elizabeth Glaser Pediatric AIDS Foundation: Washington, DC.

Kotzee, T.J. and Couper, I.D. (2006). What interventions do South African qualified doctors think will retain them in rural hospitals of the Limpopo province of South Africa? *Rural Remote Health*, 6(3), 581.

Lehmann, U. and Sanders, D. (2007). *Community Health Workers: What Do We Know About Them? The State of the Evidence on Programmes, Activities, Costs an Impact on Health Outcomes of Using Community Health Workers*. World Health Organization: Geneva.

Levine, R.J. (1988). *Ethics and Regulation of Clinical Research* (2nd Ed.). Yale University Press: New Haven, CT.

Mackey, T.J. and Liang, B.A. (2012). Rebalancing brain drain: Exploring resource reallocation to address health worker migration and promote global health. *Health Policy*, 107(1), 66–73.

Mahendra, V.S., Gilborn, L., Bharat, S., *et al.* (2007). Understanding and measuring AIDS-related stigma in health care settings: a developing country perspective. *Journal of Social Aspects of HIV/AIDS*, 4(2), 616–625.

Mahon, C. (2009). Sexual orientation, gender identity, and the right to health. In A. Clapham, M. Robinson, C. Mahon, *et al.* (Eds.), *Realizing the Right to Health*, pp. 235–248. Rüffer and Rub: Zurich.

Malloy, S.E. (1998). Beyond misguided paternalism: resuscitating the right to refuse medical treatment. *Wake Forest Law* Review, 33, 1035–1091.

Mann, J.M., Gostin, L., Gruskin, S., *et al.* (1999). Health and human rights. In J.M. Mann, S. Gruskin, M.A. Grodin, *et al.* (Eds.), *Health and Human Rights*, pp. 8–20. Routledge: New York, NY.

Manongi, R., Marchant, T., and Bygbjerg, I.C. (2006). Improving motivation among primary health care workers in Tanzania: a health worker perspective. *Human Resources for Health*, 4(6), 6.

Mclaughlin, D. and Long, A. (1996). An extended literature review of health professionals' perceptions of illicit drugs and their clients who use them. *Journal of Psychiatric and Mental Health Nursing*, 3(5), 283–238.

Mejia, A., Pizurki, H., Royston, E., *et al.* (1979). *Physician and Nurse Migration: Analysis and Policy Implications.* World Health Organization (WHO): Geneva.

Miller, F.G. (2010). Consent to clinical research. In F.G. Miller and A. Wertheimer (Eds.), *The Ethics of Consent*, pp. 375–404. Oxford University Press: New York, NY.

Mills, E.J., Kanters, S., Hagopian, A., *et al.* (2011). The financial cost of doctors emigrating from sub-Saharan Africa: human capital analysis. *British Medical Journal*, 343, d7031.

Miner, J.B. (2005). *Organizational Behaviour 1: Essential Theories of Motivation and Leadership*. ME Sharp, Inc.: Armonk, NY.

MSF. (2012). *Libya: Detainees Tortured and Denied Medical Care.* Médecins Sans Frontières (MSF): Brussels. Available at: <http://www.msf.org/msf/articles/2012/01/libya-detainees-tortured-and-denied-medical-care.cfm> (accessed 17 September 2012).

Mullan, F. (2000). The case for more US medical students. *New England Journal of Medicine*, 343(3), 213–217.

Naicker, S., Plange-Rhule, J., Tutt, R.C., and Eastwood, J.B. (2009). Shortage of healthcare workers in developing countries—Africa. *Ethnicity & Disease*, 19(1), S1-60–64.

Narasimhan, V., Brown, H., Pablos-Mendez, A., *et al.* (2004). Responding to the global human resources crisis. *Lancet*, 363(9419), 1469–1472.

Nuremberg Code. (1949). *Trials of War Criminals before the Nuremberg Military Tribunals under Control Council Law No. 10*, Vol. 2, pp. 181–182. U.S. Government Printing Office: Washington, DC.

Nyblade, L., Stangl, A., Weiss, E., *et al.* (2009). Combating HIV stigma in health care settings: what works? *Journal of the International AIDS Society*, 12, 15. Available at: <http://www.ncbi.nlm.nih.gov/pmc/articles/PMC2731724/pdf/1758-2652-12-15.pdf> (accessed 10 October 2012).

OAU. (1981). *African Charter on Human and People's Rights* ('Banjul Charter'). Organization of African Unity (OAU): Addis Ababa (now the African Union).

OECD. (2010). *International Migration of Health Workers: Improving International Co-Operation to Address the Global Health Workforce Crisis.* Organization for Economic Cooperation and Development (OECD): Paris.

Ottawa Charter for Health Promotion. (1986). Ottawa Charter For Health Promotion. *Health Promotion International*, 1(4), 405.

Owley, C. (2011). *Bahraini Healthcare Leaders Jailed & Tortured for Treating Injured Protestors.* Available at: <http://wfnhp.aft.org/news/bahraini-healthcare-leaders-jailed-tortured-treating-injured-protestors> (accessed 24 September 2012).

Parker, D. and Newbrander, W. (1994). Tackling wastage and inefficiency in the health sector. *World Health Forum*, 15(2), 107–113.

Parker, R., Aggleton, P., Attawell, K., *et al.* (2002). *HIV/AIDS-related Stigma and Discrimination: A Conceptual Framework and an Agenda for Action.* Population Council: New York, NY.

Peckover, S. and Chidlaw, R.G. (2007). Too frightened to care? Accounts by district nurses working with clients who misuse substances. *Health & Social Care in the Community*, 15(3), 238–245.

PHR. (2011a). *PHR Releases Accounts of Violence in Syria: Violations of Medical Neutrality and Attacks on Civilians Described by Syrian Citizens*. Physicians for Human Rights (PHR): Washington, DC.

PHR. (2011b). *Persecution of Health Workers*. Physicians for Human Rights (PHR): Washington, DC.

Rahman, S., Ali, N., Jennings, L., *et al.* (2010). Factors affecting recruitment and retention of community health workers in a newborn care intervention in Bangladesh. *Human Resources for Health*, 8(1), 12.

Rapiti, E., Prüss-Üstün, A., and Hutin, Y. (2005). *Assessing the Burden of Disease from Sharps Injuries to Health-Care Workers at National and Local Levels*. World Health Organization (WHO): Geneva.

Ross, C.A. and Goldner, E.M. (2009). Stigma, negative attitudes and discrimination towards mental illness within the nursing profession: a review of the literature. *Journal of Psychiatric and Mental Health Nursing*, 16(6), 558–567.

Sears, B. and Ho, D. (2006). *HIV Discrimination in Health Care Services in Los Angeles County: The Results of Three Testing Studies*. The Williams Institute: University of California, Los Angeles, CA.

Shuster, E. (1997). Fifty years later: the significance of the Nuremberg Code. *New England Journal of Medicine*, 337(20), 1436–1440.

Skinner, N., Feather, N.T., Freeman, T., *et al.* (2007). Stigma and discrimination in health-care provision to drug users: the role of values, affect, and deservingness judgments. *Journal of Applied Social Psychology*, 37(1), 163–186.

Slama, S., Wolff, H., and Loutan, L. (2009). The right to health in prisons: implications in a borderless world. In A. Clapham, and M. Robinson (Eds.), *Realizing the Right to Health*, pp. 185–212. Rüffer & Rub: Zurich.

Smith, D. (1999). The legacy of Nuremberg: sustaining human rights. *Cornell Law Forum*, 25(3), 2–7.

Syptak, J.M., Marsland, D.W., and Ulmer, D. (1999). Job satisfaction: putting theory into practice. *Family Practice Management*, 6(9), 26–30.

Teliska, H. (2005) Obstacles to access: how pharmacist refusal clauses undermine the basic health care needs of rural and low-income women. *Berkeley Journal of Gender Law & Justice*, 20, 229–233.

Thorton, P. (2012). *Our Side of the Story: Ugandan Health Workers Speak Up*. VSO International: London.

Triantaphyllis, C., Ezer, T., and Cohen, J. (2012). *Twenty Mechanisms for Addressing Torture in Health Care*. Open Society Foundations (OSF): New York, NY.

UN. (2011). *The Millennium Development Goals Report 2011*. United Nations (UN): New York, NY.

UN General Assembly. (1948). *Universal Declaration of Human Rights*. UN General Assembly: Paris.

UN General Assembly. (2011). *Political Declaration on HIV/AIDS*. UN General Assembly: New York, NY.

United States v. Karl Brandt et al. (1946). *Trials of War Criminals Before the Nuremberg Military Tribunals Under Control Council Law 10*, Vol. 1 (Superintendent of Documents, US Government Printing Office, 1950: Washington, DC); Military Tribunal, Case 1.

Van Lerberghe, W., Conceicao, C., Van Damme, W., *et al.* (2002). When staff is underpaid: dealing with the individual coping strategies of health personnel. *Bulletin of the World Health Organization*, 80(7), 581–584.

WHA. (2010). *Global Code of Practice on the International Recruitment of Health Personnel*. World Health Assembly (WHA): Geneva.

WHO. (1946). *Preamble to the Constitution of the World Health Organization*. World Health Organization (WHO): Geneva.

WHO. (1978). *Declaration of Alma-Ata*. World Health Organization (WHO): Geneva.

WHO. (2006a). *Working Together for Health: The World Health Report 2006*. World Health Organization (WHO): Geneva.

WHO. (2006b). *Treat, Train, Retain: The AIDS and Health Workforce Plan*. World Health Organization (WHO): Geneva.

WHO. (2008). *Task-Shifting: Global Recommendations and Guidelines*. World Health Organization (WHO): Geneva.

WHO. (2010). *Migration of Health Workers*. World Health Organization (WHO): Geneva.

WHO. (2012a). *World Health Statistics: A Snapshot of Global Health*. World Health Organization (WHO): Geneva.

WHO. (2012b). *WHO's Response and Role as the Health Cluster Lead in Meeting the Growing Demands of Health in Humanitarian Emergencies*. World Health Organization (WHO): Geneva.

WMA. (1948). *Declaration of Geneva: Physician's Oath*. World Medical Association (WMA): Geneva.

WMA. (1964). *Declaration of Helsinki: Recommendations Guiding Doctors in Clinical Research*. World Medical Association (WMA): Geneva.

Wasswa, H. (2008). Rich states 'snatch' trained doctors from poor countries. *British Medical Journal*, 336, 579.

Willis-Shattuck, M., Bidwell, P., Thomas, S., *et al.* (2008). Motivation and retention of health workers in developing countries: a systematic review. *BMC Health Services Research*, 8(1), 247.

WorldBank. (2012). *World Development Indicators 2012*. World Bank: Washington, DC.

Zampas, C. and Andion-Ibañez, X. (2012). Conscientious objection to sexual and reproductive health services: international human rights standards and European law and practice. *European Journal of Health Law*, 19(3), 231–256.

Chapter 25

Combating torture and other ill-treatment

Michael Bochenek

Introduction

It is safe to say that torture and other forms of ill-treatment occur in most countries of the world. In 2011, for example, Amnesty International recorded acts of torture and other ill-treatment in at least 101 countries (Amnesty International, 2012a). The last time Amnesty International undertook a more comprehensive survey of its research files, examining all information received between 1997 and mid-2000 in preparation for its third global campaign against torture, it found that it had received reports of torture and ill-treatment by State agents in over 150 countries in all regions of the world, nearly every country it was actively working on (Amnesty International, 2000).

Reports prepared by Amnesty International, Human Rights Watch, and other groups make for rough reading, whatever the topic. It is particularly difficult to go through the pages of a report that details acts of torture—acts that are stunning in their brutality and inhumanity whether casually inflicted or meticulously planned.

Torturers are endlessly, maliciously inventive. In addition to blows and kicks, beatings with truncheons and machine guns, whipping, burning, rape, and the like, Amnesty International has documented innumerable other forms of torture: people forced into stress positions, exposure to excessive cold or heat for prolonged periods, suspension from the ceiling by the wrists, gouging out flesh with pinchers, the use of pliers to remove teeth during interrogations, bottles and other objects inserted into vaginas and anuses, electric shocks to the mouth and genitals, forcing people to perform abusive acts on each other, and forcing them to watch as their children, parents, or spouses are beaten, raped, or killed, among other practices. Even apparently benign activities such as playing music can be turned to the infliction of suffering.

Some instruments and methods of torture acquire chillingly imaginative nicknames. In one of Rio de Janeiro's juvenile detention centres, guards beat children with wooden clubs named for a pop star and a cartoon character (Human Rights Watch, 2005a). Types of torture include 'the parrot's perch', 'the telephone', and 'the flying carpet'. These terms are often employed menacingly by prison guards and police to warn their targets of the consequences of non-compliance.

Whatever its form, torture is profoundly invasive, robbing people of their sense of dignity and security. The aim of these acts is to break the spirit and coerce a confession, to punish people for crimes they are thought to have committed, or simply to punish them for who they are.

The mental impact of torture is frequently as significant, if not far more so, than the physical consequences. A man who was suspended by his bound wrists from the ceiling and given electric shocks through wires attached to his toes and penis during interrogations by Egypt's State Security Investigations Service (SSI) over the course of a week in 2004 told Amnesty International, 'The worst thing that happened to me was taking my clothes off because it affects my psychology' (Amnesty International, 2007a). Not only do the mental consequences of torture in many cases last far longer than the physical effects, they can also extend to family members or, some scholars have argued, entire communities.

It goes without saying that torture and other forms of cruel, inhuman, and degrading treatment are health issues. Ill-treatment is in some cases so severe that its victims die as a result. Even when such acts do not cause death, they have obvious health consequences. Torture and other ill-treatment can also be the result of denial of healthcare. And, in some cases, they are carried out by or with the complicity of health professionals.

International law flatly prohibits torture, always and everywhere. Other cruel, inhuman, and degrading treatment or punishment—other forms of ill-treatment that do not meet the definition of torture because, for instance, they are not committed for a purpose such as compelling a confession or obtaining information—are also prohibited (Convention against Torture and Other Cruel, Inhuman or Degrading Treatment or Punishment, 1987).

As one human rights lawyer has observed, the international prohibition on torture is, in fact, 'arguably the most absolute in all international human rights law. The State may not torture in times of war or other national emergency, for any purpose whatsoever, no matter how many lives may be at stake' (PoKempner, 2005). Torture is a crime in international law. Its use in armed conflict is a war crime, and its systematic or widespread use can amount to a crime against humanity (Rome Statute of the International Criminal Court, 2002).

Because torture is universally condemned, those who engage in acts of torture usually take care to conceal their acts, or at the very least commit those acts only when they are reasonably certain that they will not be called to account. Darius Rejali writes in his book *Torture and Democracy* of 'the case of an officer in Mobutu's Zaire who stopped his soldiers from beating a prisoner with sticks, saying, "It will leave scars and we will get complaints from Amnesty International"' (Rejali, 2009).

Even when acts of torture are brazen, as when armed groups film and occasionally post the abuses they commit, torturers tend to operate in the belief that they do so with impunity.

A discussion of this length on a subject as vast as torture and other forms of ill-treatment is necessarily limited. This chapter examines some of the common contexts in which Amnesty International and other human rights groups have documented torture and other cruel, inhuman, and degrading treatment or punishment. It does not attempt to address the health consequences that result from torture and other ill-treatment. Nor does it attempt to address and refute the 'ticking bomb' justification for torture; Waldron and others have capably done so (Waldron, 2005, 2010).

This chapter first reviews the international prohibition of torture and other forms of cruel, inhuman, and degrading treatment or punishment, examining the sources of the international prohibition, the definition set forth in the Convention against Torture and Other Cruel, Inhuman or Degrading Treatment or Punishment (CAT), the interpretations of the elements of torture by international and regional courts and other authorities, and the absolute nature of the prohibition.

The second section examines policing and detention practices, circumstances where Amnesty International frequently encounters evidence of torture. Torture and other ill-treatment by police, prison guards, and others in these settings can range from isolated, opportunistic acts of cruelty at one end of the spectrum to the routine implementation at the other, with most falling somewhere in between.

The chapter then turns to the acts of torture and ill-treatment systematically perpetrated by the United States and other governments after the attacks of 11 September 2001. These acts, and the policies that permitted them, are well documented, but they are significant because they combine so many of the worst practices: the use of spurious legal analysis to justify torture, the complicity of health professionals, the forthright use of tactics that individually have long been acknowledged to be acts of torture, and the cumulative use of these tactics to bring detainees to their breaking point.

Other forms of ill-treatment that do not necessarily meet the definition of torture are also common in places of detention; these are discussed in the fourth section of this chapter, which also notes some of the other circumstances in which ill-treatment occurs with regularity.

The fifth section of the chapter discusses legal prohibitions on particular forms of medical care, so that the physician who provides the care risks imprisonment, substantial fines, or the loss of his or her livelihood. For example, women in many countries cannot obtain abortions even if their health or lives are threatened by pregnancy. Nicaragua, with its total ban on abortion, is the starkest case, but many other countries place unacceptable restrictions on abortion in law and practice. Amnesty International has argued that such situations do indeed amount to torture.

Amnesty International has run three global campaigns against torture—in 1973, 1984, and 2000 (Amnesty International, 1973, 1984, 2000, 2003). Through these campaigns and its regular monitoring and reporting, it has developed a series of recommendations to combat torture. The chapter closes by summarizing the policy steps that States should take to prevent torture and other forms of ill-treatment and to address these human rights violations when they do occur.

The international prohibition of torture and other ill-treatment

The right to be free from torture and other forms of cruel, inhuman, and degrading treatment or punishment is proclaimed in the Universal Declaration of Human Rights (UDHR). In addition to the CAT, the International Covenant on Civil and Political Rights (ICCPR), the Convention on the Rights of the Child (CRC), the Convention on the Rights of Persons with Disabilities (CRPD), and regional treaties prohibit torture and other cruel, inhuman, and degrading treatment or punishment. The prohibition of torture and other ill-treatment is also reaffirmed in numerous international and regional standards.

The acknowledgement of the prohibition is such that it is part of customary international law, meaning that it is binding on all States (Committee against Torture, 2008). In fact, the prohibition of torture is a peremptory norm of international law, or *jus cogens*, a norm that prevails over conflicting treaty prohibitions or other sources of law (Commission on Human Rights, 1986; de Wet, 2004).

Human rights treaties explicitly provide that some human rights may be subject to certain limitations, for instance to protect the rights of others or for the protection of public order or public health. Under these principles, laws against defamation are generally permissible even though they limit the exercise of free expression because such laws protect the rights of others (Human Rights Committee, 2011). Restrictions on the time, place, and manner of a public assembly may be legitimate means of ensuring that the assembly remains peaceful (OSCE Guidelines on Freedom of Peaceful Assembly, 2007, paragraph 80). Some narrowly tailored limits on the right to movement might be allowable to counter a demonstrable threat posed by contagious disease (Boggio et al., 2008). In all such cases, the limitation must be necessary to achieve a legitimate interest and proportionate to that objective.

These treaties also allow States to derogate from a wider range of human rights during times of public emergency. Derogation effectively exempts a State from its obligation to respect particular human rights. To do so, the State must meet stringent standards, including the requirement that '[t]he circumstances invoked . . . constitute an exceptional and imminent public danger, threatening the existence of the nation' (Commission on Human Rights, 1982; Human Rights Committee, 2001; Siracusa Principles, 1984).

But there are no exceptions to prohibition of torture and other ill-treatment (Committee against Torture, 2008). It is among the rights that States may never derogate from, not 'even for the asserted purpose of preserving the life of the nation' (Human Rights Committee, 1992; Siracusa Principles, 1984). In fact, States must take special precautions during times of public emergency to ensure protection from torture and other forms of cruel, inhuman, or degrading treatment or punishment (Siracusa Principles, 1984).

The CAT defines torture as acts that consist of the intentional infliction of severe pain or suffering, physical or mental, involve a public official, and are committed for a specific purpose, such as extracting a confession, obtaining information, intimidating, coercing or punishing a person, 'or for any reason based on discrimination of any kind' (Convention against Torture, 1987). Pain and suffering 'arising only from, inherent in or incidental to lawful sanctions' are excluded from the definition of torture (Convention against Torture, 1987). The International Criminal Tribunal for the Former Yugoslavia (ICTY) observed in the *Celebici* case that the examples given in the purpose element of Article 1—securing a confession or information, intimidation, punishment, discrimination—'do not constitute an exhaustive list, and should be regarded as merely representative' (*Prosecutor* v. *Delalic et al.*, 1998).

The Convention does not define other forms of cruel, inhuman, and degrading treatment or punishment. The Body of Principles for the Protection of All Persons under Any Form of Detention or Imprisonment, adopted by the UN General Assembly in 1988, note, 'The term "cruel, inhuman, or degrading treatment or punishment" should be interpreted so as to extend the widest possible protection against abuses, whether physical or mental, including the holding of a detained or imprisoned person in conditions which deprive him, temporarily or permanently, of the use of any of his natural senses, such as sight or hearing, or of his awareness of place and the passing of time' (Body of Principles for the Protection of All Persons Under Any Form of Detention or Imprisonment, 1988, Principle 6).

In general, the Committee against Torture and the Human Rights Committee (HRC) have avoided drawing sharp distinctions between torture and other forms of prohibited ill-treatment. The Committee against Torture notes that '[i]n practice, the definitional threshold between ill-treatment and torture is often not clear' (Committee against Torture, 2008). These committees instead simply note violations of the prohibition of torture and other cruel, inhuman, and degrading treatment or punishment taken as a whole.

In contrast, the European Court of Human Rights has often relied on 'the intensity of the suffering inflicted' to distinguish between torture and other forms of inhuman and degrading treatment (*Atkas* v. *Turkey*, 2003; *Ireland* v. *United Kingdom*, 1980; Reidy, 2002). Some judgements of the ICTY have also described the element of severity as a 'distinguishing characteristic of torture that sets it apart from similar offences' (*Prosecutor* v. *Kvocka*, 2001).

Nevertheless, the European Court's approach has been widely criticized, including by several of the judges who took part in the hearing of *Ireland* v. *United Kingdom*, the 1978 case that announced that rule; Amnesty International; and legal scholars (Amnesty International, 1978; *Ireland* v. *UK*, 1978; O'Boyle, 1977; Rodley, 2011). The Inter-American Court of Human Rights does not follow the approach of *Ireland* v. *United Kingdom* and instead assesses on a case-by-case basis whether acts, individually or in combination, amount to torture (*Caesar* v. *Trinidad and Tobago*, 2005; *Loayza Tamayo* v. *Peru*, 1997). Recent decisions of the European Court of Human Rights have referred to the definition in the CAT, in an apparent adjustment to the way it assesses severity (*Selmouni* v. *France*, 1999).

One danger of the European Court of Human Rights's 'intensity of suffering' approach in *Ireland* v. *United Kingdom*, even as it has developed in more recent cases, is that it requires courts to make fine distinctions without clear standards or accurate means of measurement. Because 'intensity of suffering' is necessarily subjective and thus difficult, if not impossible, to gauge with any precision, psychological forms of torture would be at particular risk of being improperly viewed as not amounting to torture under this approach. It is not apparent, for example, how an 'intensity of suffering' analysis would assess purely psychological forms of torture, for instance in one case before the Inter-American Court of Human Rights in which Guatemalan authorities subjected a woman to eight days of captivity and interrogation, during which they repeatedly threatened to kill her, showed her photographs of mutilated corpses, and told her that they had abducted her son (*Caso Maritza Urrutia* v. *Guatemala*, 2003). Using the CAT's definition as a reference, the Inter-American Court found these acts to constitute forms of psychological torture.

At the extreme, the risk of the 'intensity of suffering' approach is illustrated by the United States' effort, discussed later in this chapter, to legitimize torture by minimizing, and frequently dismissing, the suffering those practices inflict. As Waldron writes, 'Insisting on exact definitions may sound very lawyerly, but there is something disturbing about it when the quest for precision is put to work in the service of a mentality that says, "Give us a definition so we have something to work around, something to game, a determinate envelope to push"' (Waldron, 2005). He continues, '*There are some scales one really should not be on*, and with respect to which one really does not have a legitimate interest in knowing precisely how far along the scale one is permitted to go' (Waldron, 2005).

To the extent that it is useful to distinguish between acts of torture and other forms of cruel, inhuman, and degrading treatment, an approach that is more consistent with the definition in the CAT is to examine whether the acts are inflicted for a purpose such as one listed in Article 1. Manfred Nowak, writing as the United Nations [UN] Special Rapporteur on torture, usefully noted that '[a]cts which fall short of this definition [of torture], particularly acts without the elements of intent or acts not carried out for the specific purposes outlined, may comprise [cruel, inhuman, and degrading treatment] under Article 16 of the Convention' (Commission on Human Rights, 2005).

Torture and other forms of cruel, inhuman, and degrading treatment or punishment are equally prohibited, so it is not immediately apparent why it is helpful to assess whether an act is torture or another form of prohibited ill-treatment. As the Committee against Torture observes, '[t]he obligations to prevent torture and other cruel, inhuman or degrading treatment or punishment . . . are indivisible, interdependent and interrelated' (Committee against Torture, 2008). But the State has some additional obligations to respond to torture, for example, to ensure that torture is a criminal offence and to refrain from deporting or extraditing a person to a country where he or she would be at risk of torture (Convention against Torture, 1987). And torture receives particular condemnation that other forms of ill-treatment do not: in the words of one US appellate court, 'the torturer has become like the pirate and slave trader before him *hostis humani generis*, an enemy of all mankind' (*Filartiga* v. *Pena-Irala*, 1980).

Torture during arrest, interrogation, detention, and other policing practices

The temptation to resort to acts of torture and other mistreatment during arrest and detention can be high, especially for those police forces and prison authorities who are poorly paid and receive little training on proper methods of criminal investigation, effective crowd control, and good detention practices. These and other human rights violations are a foreseeable consequence whenever States disregard the presumption of innocence, the prohibition on arbitrary arrest and detention, and other due process protections; guarantees of free expression, assembly, and association; and other core human rights protections.

Members of religious and ethnic minorities, migrants, individuals who are (or are thought to be) gay, lesbian, or transgender, and unpopular groups are often targeted—in many cases, simply to punish them for who they are.

Torture and ill-treatment are in large part the consequence of inadequate State policies: the failure to pay and train staff, to protect victims from abuse, to monitor and hold official wrongdoers accountable leads to situations that encourage torture and other forms of ill-treatment.

Often, as well, State policy approaches are not simply negligent but also affirmatively encourage officials to disregard procedures and principles that help prevent torture. For example, authorities may exploit legitimate public concerns over high crime rates, gang violence, and organized crime to cut corners on human rights, presumably on the theory that human rights hamper policing. In Mexico, there are widespread reports of torture, along with enforced disappearances, unlawful killings, and excessive use of force by the Mexican armed forces in their campaign against the drug cartels operating in that country (Human Rights Watch, 2011a). Torture is a regular feature of policing in Brazil (Amnesty International, 2005, 2007b; Human Rights Watch, 2009; IHRC & Justiça Global, 2011). *Mano dura* ('iron fist') approaches to fighting crime in Central America and the Dominican Republic are invitations to engage in police abuses, not only to torture but also to engage in extrajudicial executions under 'shoot to kill' orders and carry out enforced disappearances (Amnesty International, 2011a).

As these examples and others demonstrate, State authorities may be tempted to turn to torture and other human rights violations when they feel under threat. There is a high correlation, for example, between the use of states of emergency and torture: one illustration is Egypt, where a 31-year state of emergency in force until May 2012 was characterized by 'an endemic practice of incommunicado detention and torture, the use of military and exceptional courts that do not meet fair trial standards and the routine violation of the rights to freedom of expression, assembly and association' (Amnesty International, 2012b; International Federation for Human Rights, 2010).

States' responses to the Arab Spring provide particularly brutal examples of the use torture as a defensive strategy, in many cases outside of the context of arrest, lawful detention, and fair trial:

- In Egypt, for instance, thousands of peaceful protesters were beaten or tortured, and 840 killed, in the 18 days before President Hosni Mubarak announced his resignation in February 2011 (Amnesty International, 2011b).
- In Libya, after Col. Mu'ammar al-Gaddafi responded to street protests by declaring open season on anyone he and his son Saif al-Islam deemed unfaithful to his regime. The country spiralled into armed conflict, and his forces abducted and tortured thousands of captured opposition fighters and other detainees before he was captured and killed while in custody (Amnesty International, 2011c). And at the time of this writing, transitional authorities have been unable or unwilling to rein in the militias that formed in opposition to Gaddafi's rule and which now are engaging in extrajudicial killings, arbitrary arrests, torture, and forcible displacement in the name of revenge (Amnesty International, 2012c).
- In Syria, where at the time of this writing crimes against humanity and other human rights violations have been ongoing for more than a year, children as young as ten have been arrested, detained, and tortured; hundreds more children and thousands of adults have been killed in Homs, Houla, and elsewhere in the country, and even more people have been forced to flee their homes (Amnesty International, 2012d, 2012e, 2012f). Amnesty International has called for the UN Security Council to refer the situation in Syria to the International Criminal Court (Amnesty International, 2012l).

Authorities in Bahrain, Iraq, and Yemen have also responded to peaceful protests with excessive force and tortured or otherwise ill-treated those arrested for taking part in protests (Amnesty International, 2011d, 2011e, 2012g, 2012k).

Elsewhere in the world, political opposition leaders, reporters, and human rights defenders are subjected to torture and other ill-treatment. For instance, journalists and human rights defenders in Russia, Tajikistan, Turkmenistan, and Uzbekistan regularly report that they are harassed, intimidated, and beaten. In North Korea, hundreds of thousands endure arbitrary detention, forced labour, torture and other ill-treatment in the country's numerous political prison camps.

Once torture becomes an established State practice, it is hard to eradicate. Egypt's SSI under Mubarak was notorious for torture. It was disbanded in 2011 by the Supreme Council of the Armed Forces, which assumed control of the country after Mubarak's resignation. But torture did not end with the dissolution of the SSI; the armed forces continued to employ it (Amnesty International, 2012h). In Libya, detainees held by militias after Gaddafi's death told Amnesty International that they had been 'suspended in contorted positions; beaten for hours with whips, cables, plastic hoses, metal chains and bars, and wooden sticks; and given electric shocks with live wires and taser-like electro-shock weapons. The patterns of injury observed were consistent with their testimonies. Medical reports confirmed the use of torture on several detainees who had died' (Amnesty International, 2012i).

Argentina's *Proceso*, the campaign of repression waged by the military dictatorship between 1976 and 1983, and its analogues in Brazil, Uruguay, and other countries represent what may be as far as a State can go in inflicting terror on its own people without actually committing genocide. In the late 1970s and early 1980s, in the name of fighting subversion, each of these countries systematically subjected thousands of citizens deemed suspect to enforced disappearance, torture, and in many cases summary execution (Arquidiocese de São Paulo, 1985; CONADEP, 2003; Feitlowitz, 1998; Gaspari, 2002; Weschler, 1990). The term 'subversive' was broadly construed—in Argentina, a chart used at the Air Force Academy in Buenos Aires identified an astonishing number of subversive interests, including the influence of the post-Vatican II Catholic Church and various Protestant sects, drug addiction, homosexuality, divorce, 'hippie-ness', lay education, and art, newspapers, radio, television, cinema, theatre, magazines, and books (Simpson & Bennett, 1985). In Uruguay, as Steve Crawshaw and John Jackson mention in *Small Acts of Resistance*, 'A performance of Ravel's *Piano Concerto for Left Hand* was cancelled because the title sounded leftishly dangerous' (Crawshaw & Jackson, 2010).

Torture in the name of countering terror

Something of the logic of the *Proceso* echoes in the counterterrorism tactics employed by the United States after 11 September 2001. The analogy does not stretch very far, of course. But US authorities used the rhetoric of war (formally undeclared, worldwide, against persons largely unknown), bolstered by a quasi-legal concept of national self-defence, to justify a variety of human rights violations.

We now know that the United States systematically transferred suspects clandestinely between jurisdictions and arranged for their secret detention in 'black sites'. US authorities carried out these transfers to countries whose law enforcement agencies routinely use torture. As Human Rights Watch concluded, '[e]vidence suggests that torture in such cases was not a regrettable consequence of rendition; it may have been the purpose' (Human Rights Watch, 2011b).

In addition, there is ample reason to believe that US advisers took part in interrogations of detainees who they knew or should have known had just been tortured. Some number of these detainees—George W. Bush, former US President, puts it at three—were subjected to water-boarding (forcing water into the nose and mouth of a detainee so that he begins to drown); these and dozens more endured other coercive interrogation practices that were, plainly put, acts of torture. US officials developed an overall policy of detention as an 'enabler for interrogation', in the words of Maj. Gen. Geoffrey Miller, Guantánamo's detention and interrogation centre commander (Hersh, 2004a). And they relied heavily on the participation of psychiatrists and other health professionals. These policies were authorized by President Bush and other senior Bush Administration officials (Amnesty International, 2011f; Bush, 2010; *The Washington Times*, 2008) and were justified by a set of legal opinions that relied on 'a definition of torture so narrow that it would have exculpated Saddam Hussein', as Yale Law School Dean Harold Koh remarked in 2005 (Confirmation Hearing, 2005). This in spite of the fact that the United States had criticized other countries for engaging in these same acts, and in the case of water-boarding, despite legal precedent construing the technique as torture (Malinowski, 2005; Wallach, 2006).

US soldiers and contractors were told, 'The gloves are coming off, gentlemen, regarding these detainees, [name withheld by editors] has made it clear that we want these individuals broken' (Danner, 2004). It was utterly predictable that some of the soldiers and contractors who ultimately oversaw detainees would take the memos and the statements of their superiors as permission to cross all lines.

Thanks to Seymour Hersh's three-part *New Yorker* series and subsequent disclosures, we know that the infamous photographs from Abu Ghraib were not an isolated incident (Hersh, 2004a, 2004b, 2004c). The abusive practices at Abu Ghraib included using military working dogs to intimidate detainees, threatening detainees with rape, beating detainees with broom handles and chairs, and sodomizing a detainee with various objects, including a broomstick (Hersh, 2004a).

'In fact, the only exceptional aspect of the abuse at Abu Ghraib may have been that it was photographed', Reed Brody of Human Rights Watch wrote in a June 2004 report (Human Rights Watch, 2004a). Nor were abusive practices confined to Abu Ghraib. For example, a US Army special agent who investigated two homicides at Bagram testified at a military commission hearing that she had interviewed detainees who described 'being forced to stand, being sleep deprived, kicked, hit, beaten . . . Shackling was quite common at that facility, as was hooding' (Author's Notes, 2008).

At Guantánamo, some detainees were enrolled in the euphemistically named 'frequent flier' programme, meaning that they were moved from cell to cell every few hours in order to disrupt their sleep and daily routines in an effort to disorient them. One of these detainees, Mohammed Jawad (who had been captured when he was under age 18), was moved 112 times over a 14-day period, an average of once every three hours (Author's Notes, 2008; Frakt, 2009a, 2009b, 2011). Another detainee, Omar Khadr (captured at age 15), 'was moved every three hours for 21 days', *The Globe and Mail* reported after it reviewed documents held by Canada's Department of Foreign Affairs (El Akkad, 2008). In Jawad's case, the military judge found that 'the scheme was calculated to profoundly disrupt his mental sense' and ruled that 'under the circumstances, subjecting this Accused to the "frequent flier" program from 7–20 May 2004, constitutes abusive conduct and cruel and inhuman treatment' (*USA* v. *Mohammed Jawad*, 2008).

Other abusive practices in use at Guantánamo included 'Change of Scenery Down' (exposure to extreme temperatures as well as deprivation of light and sound) as well as 'sleep adjustment', the practice of reversing sleep cycles from night to day and back again. Some detainees were subjected to interrogations for periods up to 20 hours. In addition, as five UN mandate holders observed in a joint report to the UN Commission on Human Rights, 'Reports indicate that although 30 days of isolation was the maximum period permissible, detainees were put back in isolation after very short breaks, so that they were in quasi-isolation for up to 18 months' (Commission on Human Rights, 2006).

One of the most damning reports of US conduct in the years after 2001 comes from a leaked report by the International Committee of the Red Cross (ICRC), which generally does not make its findings public. When the ICRC interviewed 14 'high-value' detainees who had been transferred from CIA detention to Guantánamo Bay, it found that they had been subjected to 'a harsh regime employing a combination of physical and psychological ill-treatment with the aim of obtaining compliance and extracting information' (ICRC, 2007).

The men were held in 'continuous solitary confinement and incommunicado detention' throughout their time in the CIA programme—16 months for some, more than three years for 11 of the men, and four and a half years in one case. 'Even their guards were usually masked and, other than the absolute minimum, did not communicate in any way with the detainees' (ICRC, 2007).

During their time in the CIA programme, the men endured suffocation by water; 'prolonged stress standing position, naked, held with the arms extended and chained above the head'; 'beatings by use of a collar held around the detainee's neck and used to forcefully bang the head and body against the wall'; beating and kicking; confinement to a box; prolonged nudity for several weeks or months; sleep deprivation 'through use of forced stress positions (standing or sitting), cold water and use of repetitive or loud music'; exposure to cold temperature, including by immersion in cold water or having cold water poured over the body; prolonged shackling of hands and/or feet; forced shaving of head and beard; and deprivation or restrictions on solid food for periods of three days up to one month (ICRC, 2007). They were also subjected to a variety of threats, 'including of ill-treatment in the form of "water boarding," electric shocks, infection with HIV, sodomy of the detainee, and the arrest and rape of his family, torture, being brought close to death, and of an interrogation process to which "no rules applied"' (ICRC, 2007).

The 14 men had been arrested in Djibouti, Pakistan, Thailand, and the United Arab Emirates, and then transferred after a month to another country, likely Afghanistan (ICRC, 2007). They were moved throughout the time they were held, probably to places of detention in several countries. In fact, four of the men believed that they had been held in Guantánamo for periods between one week and one year in 2003 and 2004—they had been allowed outdoors during the earlier period of detention, and they recognized it when they were transferred out of CIA custody in 2006. If so, the ICRC had been denied notice of their presence and access to them during its regular detention visits (ICRC, 2007).

During these transfers, detainees were blindfolded, made to wear diapers, and shackled at the hands and feet. 'The journey times obviously varied considerably and ranged from one hour to over 24 to 36 hours. The detainee was not allowed to go to the toilet and if necessary was obliged to urinate or defecate into the diaper' (ICRC, 2007). Some were transported on their backs with their hands cuffed behind them. The effect was to subject them to mental strain, 'increasing their sense of orientation and isolation' (ICRC, 2007) and making them more vulnerable to interrogation.

Two days after the attacks in the United States, a front-page article in *Le Monde* declared, 'We are all Americans' (Colombani, 2001). But the outpouring of solidarity that followed the attacks of 11 September 2001 turned quickly to disbelief and condemnation. And the cases against several of those held in Guantánamo collapsed after confessions and other evidence was ruled the product of torture and thrown out. In the end, the United States' wholesale reliance on torture, enforced disappearance, and other abusive practices have done it significant damage with very little, if any, benefit.

Other forms of ill-treatment

International law also prohibits other forms of cruel, inhuman, and degrading treatment or punishment. Again, places of detention are one of the principal settings in which such ill-treatment occurs. Those in hospitals, group homes, foster homes, and similar settings, particularly persons with mental illness, mental disability, and physical disability, are also often subjected to ill-treatment. Ill-treatment in detention and other custodial settings can last for years, with immediate and long-term consequences for physical and mental health.

Overcrowding is common, increasing the risk of violence and making it more likely that facilities will fail to meet basic standards of health and hygiene. As the African Commission's Special Rapporteur on prisons and places of detention wrote in an April 2011 report:

> Unacceptable levels of overcrowding, disease, physical and psychological abuse by officials and inmates alike, violence, malnutrition, poor hygienic conditions, old dilapidated facilities, inadequate medical care for inmates and high mortality rates among inmates are still prevalent in most of our prisons. Overcrowding in particular not only leads to a myriad of abuses of the rights of inmates, but also further strains already overworked staff and further complicates the management of prisons. (African Commission on Human and Peoples' Rights, 2011)

To take just two examples, and by no means the worst in their respective regions, institutions in Ghana designed to hold 8,000 detainees were holding 13,500 in September 2011, meaning that they were operating at 170% of capacity (Amnesty International, 2012j). In Brazil, a study by the *Núcleo de Estudos da Violência* found that the prison population exceeded the capacity of the system by 58%, based on 2008 data (Salla et al., 2009). National statistics do not give a full picture of overcrowding, however, since many facilities are significantly overburdened than suggested by the national average. Ghana's Nsawam Central Prison, for example, built in 1960 to hold up to 717 men, housed approximately 3,280 inmates in September 2011, meaning that it was operating at nearly 460% of capacity (Amnesty International, 2012j). Moreover, it is difficult to estimate true prison capacity objectively, and capacity figures are easy to manipulate (Human Rights Watch, 2005a, 1998).

Detention centres in much of the world are overcrowded for two related reasons. First, pre-trial detention is often used reflexively—alternatives such as release on specified conditions, the posting of a bond, the surrender of travel documents, or regular reporting requirements are unavailable or extended only to a privileged few. Pre-trial detention is the norm even when there is little evidence to support the charge or where the charge is a minor one. Cases may be adjourned repeatedly rather than dismissed if witnesses do not appear, if prosecutors are otherwise unprepared to try the case, or if no defence counsel is available. Poor recordkeeping can result in indefinite detention: Some of the detainees Amnesty International interviewed in Nigerian prisons in 2007 had been in pre-trial detention for longer than the prison sentence they were likely to receive if eventually convicted (Amnesty International, 2008).

Second, alternatives to traditional prison sentences are comparatively rare. 'A lot of prisoners [do not] have to be in prison—they have committed petty theft. Community service could be an alternative. Some prisoners have committed traffic offences but have not paid a fine so they are in prison for six months to a year', a Ghanaian prison official commented to Amnesty International in September 2011 (Amnesty International, 2012j).

International standards and good detention practice call for detainees to be classified according to offence, vulnerability, and similar characteristics in order to maintain good order, minimize the risk of victimization, and encourage rehabilitation. But many detention facilities fail to separate according to even the most basic categories. Those awaiting trial or sentence are sometimes mixed with convicted prisoners (Amnesty International, 2012j). Persons with mental illnesses are often held in the general prison population, in some cases, not because they have been accused of committing a crime but instead because there is no other place for them to go (Amnesty International, 2008; Human Rights Watch, 2003). In Nigeria, for instance, Amnesty International found that an elderly woman in Enugu Prison who had been classified as a 'civil lunatic' was housed in a cell with no bed, mattress, or bedding; she sat naked on the dirt floor in the middle of her cell rocking back and forth, her arms wrapped around her breasts (Amnesty International, 2008). Children are mixed with adults, particular in police lockups or in immigration detention facilities (Amnesty International, 2008, 2010b, 2011g). Men and women may also be held together. An inspection of Venezuela's prisons in 1996 for Human Rights Watch revealed that inmates in the remote Ciudad Bolívar prison had torn down the wall that separated the men's and women's sections, meaning that the 40 women mingled with a male population of more than 1,000. The women reported finding male partners as quickly as possible (Human Rights Watch, 1997). More recently, the Committee against Torture has rebuked Honduras, Nicaragua, and other countries for failing to separate men and women in detention (Committee against Torture, 2009a, 2009b).

Incommunicado detention—where nobody except the authorities has contact with the detainee—is strictly prohibited. Other forms of solitary confinement may be permissible if they are of short duration, necessary to accomplish a legitimate objective, and proportionate to the circumstances. Too often, however, these limitations are not observed.

In addition, detainees are frequently subjected to arbitrary punishment, often for minor offences. Beatings are common. In fact, corporal punishment is permitted in some prison systems, in flagrant disregard of international standards. Other forms of punishment that are impermissible under international standards but often employed include shackling and isolation, sometimes for prolonged periods.

Verbal abuse is even more common. 'The officers insult you. They humiliate you. They make fun of you and why you are here', a woman detained in Ghana told Amnesty International (Amnesty International, 2012j).

Violence among detainees occurs on a daily basis, often unchecked by detention officials. In many cases, in fact, guards may encourage detainees to administer punishment among themselves on an informal basis. For example, in a 2007 case in Honduras, the non-governmental organization (NGO) *Arcoiris* reported that four other detainees beat, stripped, and raped a detainee after a police agent announced, once the detainee was locked in a cell with 57 other men, '*[M]iren, aquí les traigo a una princesita, ya saben lo que tienen que hacer*' ('Look, here I'm bringing you a little princess; you know what you have to do') (Human Rights Council, 2008).

Overcrowding puts intense pressures on already overburdened systems, combining with inadequate staffing, crumbling infrastructure, and inadequate supplies to produce conditions that are insalubrious in the extreme. The Rio de Janeiro public defender's office's description of one juvenile detention centre is typical:

> The infrastructure is precarious. The dormitories are dirty, fetid, and unhealthy, with leaks that have produced mold on the walls, making the place prone to respiratory illnesses and the dissemination of other infections, aggravated by the fact that the adolescents do not receive enough clothes to change them daily, as well as not having adequate facilities for their physiological needs and for daily bathing. (Human Rights Watch, 2005a)

The mother of one of the youths held in Rio de Janeiro's juvenile system reported, 'Their clothing takes on a revolting smell. They stay in those clothes. They sweat. They stay in dirty rooms, a lot of them in each room. They start to reek. So the guards call them, "You stinking bunch, you filth"' (Human Rights Watch, 2005).

The latrines are among the first things detainees usually show inspectors during prison inspections. Most of the time, there are one or two toilets for dozens or even hundreds of inmates. Some or all are broken; often there is no running water to flush the waste, so that maggots writhe in mounds of faeces. Or the only toilets are the buckets, bottles, and plastic bags that line the cell walls. Human rights researchers have repeatedly reported walking through standing waste water, saying the smell is indescribable. Sometimes access to toilets is limited to short periods during the day. Even then, guards may allow a day or two to go by before letting detainees use latrines, or they may give detainees just two or three minutes to use them.

It is not unusual for detainees to have to rely on family members to provide soap and other hygienic supplies. Detainees may also have to rely on family members to bring them food. In Guinea, after the government responded to a nationwide strike and protests in 2006 and 2007 by imposing curfews and restricting access to central Conakry, where the country's largest prison is located, the ICRC found that one-quarter of inmates were suffering from severe malnutrition, and the NGO *La Même Droits pour Tous* documented 13 deaths from malnutrition between December 2006 and February 2007 (Osborne, 2010).

Skin diseases such as scabies and fungal infections are common in many detention centres. Unprotected sex and exposure to blood through shared needles and razors increase the risk of viral infections, including HIV (Jürgens et al., 2011). Detainees are also at higher risk for tuberculosis (TB) (WHO, 2012).

Overcrowding can have additional health consequences. In Liberia's Monrovia Central Prison, where most detainees routinely sleep sitting up or in shifts because of the lack of space, some have created makeshift hammocks slung three or four metres above the floor. Detainees and prison staff told Amnesty International that people sometimes break their ribs or dislocate their shoulders from falling while they sleep (Amnesty International, 2011g).

Health services are often very limited or completely unavailable. Human Rights Watch found in 2010 that the Zambia Prisons Service employed just 14 healthcare workers to serve 15,300 inmates. Only 15 of the country's 86 prisons had clinics or sick bays (Human Rights Watch, 2010b). In Uganda, only 63 of the country's 223 prison units had some category of health worker in March 2011, Human Rights Watch reported (cited in Human Rights Watch, 2011c).

Measures that would help prevent against HIV transmission are often not fully implemented. Condom distribution, in particular, is limited or non-existent in many facilities, particularly in countries where same-sex sexual conduct is criminalized. 'If you give them condoms, you are encouraging them to sodomy', one nurse in Ghana told Amnesty International (Amnesty International, 2012j).

Other aspects of detention contribute to an experience that is both degrading and unhealthy. Time outside cells may be severely restricted—it is not uncommon for detainees to be locked up for two or three days or more at a time, sometimes in such close quarters that they cannot stretch out fully when they lie down.

Work opportunities, education, and other programming that would assist in rehabilitation may be unavailable or may be denied to particular categories of detainees. In many detention systems, for example, no such opportunities are available to pre-trial detainees because their time in detention is presumed to be brief, even if that is far from the case in practice. In Ghana, in contrast, as one inmate told Amnesty International, 'Condemned prisoners don't get a chance to work. Condemned prisoners are denied education because they say you don't get future so you don't get chance to learn' (Amnesty International, 2012j). The same logic—that it would be a waste of resources to provide rehabilitative services to those who will never return to society—often applies to death row inmates and, in some US states, to those who have been sentenced to life without parole (Human Rights Watch and Amnesty International, 2005).

Alternatively, detainees may be forced to engage in hard labour. In Uganda, thousands of detainees work for long hours to cultivate crops, clear fields, and gather firewood. Detainees who are considered to work too slowly are regularly beaten, and those who refuse to work have been handcuffed, stoned, or burned (Human Rights Watch, 2011c).

The absence of effective complaints mechanisms in many detention systems and general public apathy towards prison abuses mean that these abuses go unchecked.

Such conditions violate detainees' right to health (Lines, 2008). They also violate the prohibition on cruel, inhuman, and degrading treatment. As former UN Special Rapporteur on torture Nowak has concluded, 'Overcrowded and unhygienic prison conditions, together with lack of access to decent food, medicine, fresh air, daylight, and communication with the outside world soon amount to cruel, inhuman or degrading treatment, even in the absence of any physical violence' (Nowak, 2009).

Arrest and detention are not the only settings in which torture and other ill-treatment regularly occur. Elsewhere in the criminal justice setting, sentencing practices can violate the prohibition on torture and other cruel, inhuman, and degrading treatment. Courts in several Nigerian states, for example, can issue sentences of amputation (Amnesty International, 2008). In Malaysia, as many as 10,000 people each year are subjected to caning, a sentence that is available for more than 60 offences; caning is also used in Singapore, the Indonesian province of Aceh, and the Maldives (Amnesty International, 2010a, 2012h).

The United States stands out in the areas of criminal justice and detention practice. Approximately one-quarter of the world's jail and prison population is behind bars in the United States. The US justice system is remarkably punitive—not only does it imprison people in large numbers, but it does so for far longer than in other countries and for perhaps the widest range of crimes (Husak, 2008; Whitman, 2003). Children are tried as adults in large numbers. Racial and ethnic minorities are overrepresented at every stage of the process—they are more likely to be stopped and searched, more likely to be arrested, more likely to be detained pending trial, more likely to be convicted, less likely to receive alternatives to incarceration, and more likely to receive the harshest sentences, including the death penalty. Detention practices can be remarkably cruel: the needs of the increasing numbers of offenders with mental illness are not met, authorities often turn a blind eye to rape and other violence, tens of thousands of prisoners are held indefinitely in 'supermax' confinement with almost no sources of mental stimulation, and women may be shackled as they give birth, among other abusive practices.

In addition to the use of detention in criminal justice and immigration enforcement, involuntary confinement also occurs in psychiatric facilities and other institutions. Persons with mental disabilities can be deprived of their liberty in many countries with no due process, subjected to many of the same inhuman living conditions found in prisons and jails, and denied appropriate care and treatment (Gable et al., 2005; Gostin, 2008; Gostin & Gable, 2008).

Acts of torture and other cruel, inhuman, and degrading treatment or punishment are also frequently a component of labour exploitation. Ill-treatment is particularly common in domestic work, which is often excluded from the protection of labour laws (Amnesty International, 2010b; Human Rights Watch, 2004b; Sönmez et al., 2011). As the Committee on the Elimination of Discrimination against Women (CEDAW) has noted, 'Women migrant workers are more vulnerable to sexual abuse, sexual harassment and physical violence, especially in sectors where women predominate. Domestic workers are especially vulnerable to physical and sexual assault, food and sleep deprivation and cruelty by their employers' (CEDAW, 2008, paragraph 20).

Ill-treatment also commonly occurs in the context of land disputes, particularly during forced evictions. And it can occur in schools and in the home—acts of domestic violence and the corporal punishment of children, for example, are forms of cruel, inhuman, and degrading treatment.

These acts may be committed by State agents, such as a police officer who carries out an illegal eviction or a teacher who strikes his or her students. They may also be committed by private actors. In such cases, the State has an obligation to exercise due diligence to prevent ill-treatment and to investigate, prosecute, punish, and provide redress when ill-treatment does occur (*Velásquez-Rodríguez* v. *Honduras*, 1988).

Legislatively compelling complicity in torture

It is both a human rights abuse and a violation of professional ethics for health professionals to participate in torture and other acts of ill-treatment (Amnesty International, 2009c). For example, involuntary drug treatment and forced sterilization (including physical or chemical castration imposed punitively rather than as a medical procedure agreed by the patient and physician) do not comply with these standards (Barriga, 2012; Human Rights Watch, 2012; International Harm Reduction Development Program, 2010; Stinneford, 2006). Withholding needed treatment also breaches these standards. What if the law requires health professionals to refuse to provide essential medical care?

Abortion is a criminal offence in Nicaragua in all circumstances. The new Penal Code, introduced in 2008, provides for lengthy prison sentences for women and girls who seek an abortion and for health professionals who provide abortion services, even when an abortion is necessary to save the life or preserve the health of the woman. The revised law also provides for prison sentences for medical providers who cause unintentional harm to the foetus during the administration of medically indicated treatment to pregnant women and girls (Ley No. 164, 2008).

Nicaragua is not the only country that places unacceptable restrictions on abortion in law and practice. Chile and El Salvador, among other countries, also prohibit abortions even when a woman or girl's life or health is at risk (Center for Reproductive Rights, 2011; Shepard and Becerra, 2007). In countries that limit legal abortion only to cases of rape, incest, or health-threatening circumstances, women and girls often face considerable obstacles in actually obtaining one—they may experience long delays before they receive services, unnecessary referrals to other clinics, or demands for spousal permission. Some are denied abortions outright (Human Rights Watch, 2005b, 2006, 2010).

Foetal and/or maternal life and health can be put at risk by medical conditions experienced by the pregnant woman, whether these conditions are caused by the pregnancy (such as eclampsia or spontaneous abortion/miscarriage) or aggravated by it (such as malaria). Foetal and/or maternal life and health can also be put at risk by obstructed or premature labour.

In each situation of medical risk, physicians would aim to preserve or restore both foetal and maternal life and health. But if that is not possible, it is widely accepted medical practice to terminate a pregnancy where a woman or girl's life or health is at risk. In Nicaragua, in fact, the Ministry of Health's current protocols and best practice guidance recommend termination of the pregnancy in cases of severe pre-eclampsia, ectopic pregnancy, or other cases where the pregnancy poses a risk to the life or health of the patient (Ministry of Health, 2006).

Where there has been a stillbirth, a miscarriage or an unsafe abortion, medical care is necessary to repair damage and prevent the woman developing sepsis or some other condition that will cause her death. Decisions in these cases must often be taken very rapidly. Delay may cause permanent injury, such as infertility, or even death.

In addition, some medical interventions during pregnancy or delivery aimed at preserving maternal and/or foetal life and health can result in unintentional injury or death of the foetus. These include, for instance, malaria or cancer treatment and surgery or expedited delivery.

Nicaraguan physicians and other medical staff told Amnesty International they felt that, as a result of the new law, they had cause to be extremely concerned about treating pregnant women or assisting difficult births. Physicians said fear of criminal prosecution had caused otherwise preventable delays in the treatment of pregnant women with obstetric complications, even though physicians know that delays in treatment risk leading to permanent health damage to the patient, such as loss of fertility or permanent disability, or even the loss of her life.

Finally, it is generally accepted that Nicaragua's law will not reduce the number of abortions; instead, it will increase the number of unsafe abortions, a leading cause of maternal mortality.

Amnesty International concluded that Nicaragua had legislatively imposed torture. Withholding medically necessary abortions causes severe physical and mental pain and suffering—in fact, the severity is such that death may result. This pain and suffering was intentionally inflicted: the legislature intended to prohibit and criminalize abortion and was aware of the consequences when it did so. There is no legitimate State purpose for withholding essential medical services, and in fact the law requires health providers to act in a way that is contrary to accepted medical practice. The decision to withhold this care can really only have been taken for an improper purpose—punishment, coercion, discrimination or something akin to those motivations. Finally, the revision of the penal code was an 'act' by a 'public official': the changes were the result of legislative action. In short, all of the elements of torture, as set forth in the CAT, were present (Amnesty International, 2009a, 2009b).

To be sure, torture has particular legal implications that may be difficult to apply in this particular context. States must criminalise torture whenever it occurs, but it is not immediately clear how States would fulfil this obligation when torture is the consequence of a legislative act that requires somebody to refrain from particular action.

But in fact, this scenario is not so different from others in which an agent of the State is directed to perform an act of torture. In such cases, the individual who commits the act has no defence—as the Committee against Torture has observed, 'an order of a superior or public authority can never be invoked as a justification of torture' (Committee against Torture, 2008). The medical professional who faces the choice between either complying with the directive and committing an act of torture, on the one hand, or facing the consequences that result from non-compliance, on the other, is in a difficult position, but it is presumably precisely the position that was intended. Individual criminal responsibility for torture, with no defence of superior orders, serves as an additional check on torture.

The Committee against Torture, the UN body charged with providing authoritative guidance on States' obligations under the CAT, had previously concluded that restrictive abortion laws in Chile and Peru are cruel, inhuman, and degrading treatment (Committee against Torture, 2004, 2006). It had not gone as far as characterizing these restrictions as acts of torture. And in the end, it did not take that step in its consideration of Nicaragua, either. Its concluding observations contain a lengthy discussion of Nicaragua's general prohibition on abortion that calls for legal changes but avoids identifying the human rights violation with precision (Committee against Torture, 2009b).

Torture and other forms of cruel, inhuman, and degrading treatment or punishment are equally prohibited, so it is not crucial that the Committee did not clearly classify the consequences of Nicaragua's law as torture. From the perspective of achieving change, however, it would have been helpful. States are far more responsive to charges that they have engaged in torture than they are to other forms of ill-treatment. In addition, individual health professionals who would reluctantly comply with a law even if it resulted in ill-treatment might well balk at a course of action they knew to be torture.

Solutions

Amnesty International's three successive campaigns against torture identified a series of general recommendations to prevent torture. The UN Special Rapporteurs on torture have developed more comprehensive guidance. These recommendations make clear that combating torture and other forms of ill-treatment requires a multifaceted policy approach among other steps.

- States must eliminate practices that serve as 'preconditions' for torture.
- Opposition to torture must begin with unreserved condemnation of torture whenever it occurs. Public authorities must make clear to those under their command or supervision that torture will not be tolerated. Professional societies of health providers and lawyers should adopt and enforce clear ethical standards forbidding any complicity in acts of torture and other ill-treatment. And torture must be prohibited in the domestic legal framework.
- Secret and incommunicado detention, the practice of blindfolding and hooding detainees, and the use of military personnel to carry out law enforcement duties all make it more likely that torture and other ill-treatment will occur and will go unchallenged, thus these should be curtailed.
- Other prevention activities include effective training of public officials and education more generally about people's human rights and the obligations of States to ensure those rights.
- Regular visits to places of detention by independent monitoring bodies are crucial safeguards against torture. Independent monitors must have unrestricted access to all places of detention and all areas within each place of detention. They must be sufficiently resourced to allow it to conduct periodic unannounced visits. They should offer concrete recommendations for changes in detention practices, and they should refer appropriate cases for further investigation and prosecution.
- All allegations of torture and other ill-treatment must be promptly investigated. States must ensure that those who torture are held to account, including through criminal prosecution. They must provide full reparation to the victims of torture.
- And States must use international pressure to act as a check on each other. Measures such as human rights conditionality on non-humanitarian assistance are often criticized as blunt instruments—and are too often set aside for political expedience—but they can be effective if the States that insist on such terms are themselves complying with their international human rights obligations. Even more effective is robust participation in and support for UN and regional reporting processes, such as the Human Rights Council's Universal Periodic Review process, the reports of the Committee against Torture, the Human Rights Committee, other treaty bodies, and the work of the UN Special Rapporteur on torture.

Acknowledgments

Text extracts from Amnesty International, *Egypt: Systematic Abuses in the Name of Security*, Amnesty International, London, UK, Copyright 2007; Amnesty International, *Egypt Must Return to Rule of Law as State of Emergency Ends*, Amnesty International, Copyright 2012; available from <http://www.amnesty.org/en/news/egypt-must-return-rule-law-state-emergency-ends-2012-06-01>, and Amnesty International, *Militias Threaten Hopes for New Libya*, Amnesty International, London, UK, Copyright 2012 reproduced courtesy of Amnesty International. Copyright © Amnesty International Publications, 1 Easton Street, London WC1X 0DW, United Kingdom <http://www.amnesty.org>.

References

African Commission on Human and Peoples' Rights. (2011). *Activity Report of the Special Rapporteur on Prisons and Places of Detention in Africa, Honourable Commissioner Catherine Dupe Atoki*, 49th Ordinary Session, Banjul, The Gambia, 28 April–12 May 2011. African Commission on Human and Peoples' Rights: Banjul.

Amnesty International. (1973). *Report on Torture*. Amnesty International: London.

Amnesty International. (1978, 19 January). *Our organization must continue to combat torture anywhere in the world and that task makes it impossible for us to follow the restrictive standard set by the Court*. News Release, AI Index NWS 02/04/78.

Amnesty International. (1984). *Torture in the Eighties*. Amnesty International Publications: London.

Amnesty International. (2000). *Take a Step to Stamp Out Torture*. Amnesty International Publications: London.

Amnesty International. (2003). *Combating Torture: A Manual for Action*. Amnesty International Publications: London.

Amnesty International. (2005). *They Come in Shooting: Policing Socially Excluded Communities*. Amnesty International: London.

Amnesty International. (2007a). *Egypt: Systematic Abuses in the Name of Security*. Amnesty International: London.

Amnesty International. (2007b). *From Burning Buses to Caveirões: Searching for Human Security*. Amnesty International: London.

Amnesty International. (2008). *Nigeria: Prisoners' Rights Systematically Flouted*. Amnesty International: London.

Amnesty International. (2009a). *The Total Ban on Abortion in Nicaragua: Women's Lives and Health Endangered, Medical Professionals Criminalized*. Amnesty International: London.

Amnesty International. (2009b). *The Impact of the Complete Ban on Abortion in Nicaragua: Briefing to the United Nations Committee against Torture*. Amnesty International: London. Available at: <http://www.amnesty.org/en/library/asset/AMR43/005/2009/en/3394566e-4045-43f7-902c-b9f50181fcf5/amr430052009en.pdf> (accessed 4 June 2012).

Amnesty International. (2009c). *Codes of Ethics and Declarations Relevant to the Health Professions* (5th ed.). Amnesty International: London.

Amnesty International. (2010a). *A Blow to Humanity: Torture by Judicial Caning in Malaysia*. Amnesty International: London.

Amnesty International. (2010b). *Trapped: The Exploitation of Migrant Workers in Malaysia*. Amnesty International: London.

Amnesty International. (2011a). *Shut Up if You Don't Want to Be Killed: Human Rights Violations by Police in the Dominican Republic*. Amnesty International: London.

Amnesty International. (2011b). *Egypt Rises: Killings, Detention and Torture in the 25 January Revolution*. Amnesty International: London.

Amnesty International. (2011c). *The Battle for Libya: Killings, Disappearances and Torture*. Amnesty International: London.

Amnesty International. (2011d). *Days of Rage: Protests and Repression in Iraq*. Amnesty International: London.

Amnesty International. (2011e). *Moment of Truth for Yemen*. Amnesty International: London.

Amnesty International. (2011f). *Bringing George W. Bush to Justice: International Obligations of States to Which Former U.S. President George W. Bush May Travel*. Amnesty International: London.

Amnesty International. (2011g). *Good Intentions Are Not Enough: The Struggle to Reform Liberia's Prisons*. Amnesty International: London.

Amnesty International. (2012a). *Facts and Figures*. Available at: <http://files.amnesty.org/air12/fnf_air_2012_en.pdf> (accessed 23 May 2012).

Amnesty International. (2012b). *Egypt Must Return to Rule of Law as State of Emergency Ends*. Available at: <http://www.amnesty.org/en/news/egypt-must-return-rule-law-state-emergency-ends-2012-06-01> (accessed 1 June 2012).

Amnesty International. (2012c). *Libya: Rule of Law or Rule of Militias?* Amnesty International: London.

Amnesty International. (2012d). *I Wanted to Die: Syria's Torture Survivors Speak Out*. Amnesty International: London.

Amnesty International. (2012e). *Deadly Reprisals: Deliberate Killings and Other Abuses by Syria's Armed Forces*. Amnesty International: London.

Amnesty International. (2012f). *All-Out Repression: Purging Dissent in Aleppo, Syria*. Amnesty International: London.

Amnesty International. (2012g). *Flawed Reforms: Bahrain Fails to Achieve Justice for Protesters*. Amnesty International: London.

Amnesty International. (2012h). *Amnesty International Report 2012: The State of the World's Human Rights*. Amnesty International: London.

Amnesty International. (2012i). *Militias Threaten Hopes for New Libya*. Amnesty International: London.

Amnesty International. (2012j). *'Prisoners Are Bottom of the Pile': The Human Rights of Inmates in Ghana*. Amnesty International: London.

Amnesty International. (2012k). *Year of Rebellion: The State of Human Rights in the Middle East and North Africa*. Amnesty International: London.

Amnesty International. (2012l). Swift UN Action Needed on Syria after Houla Assault. Available at: <http://www.amnesty.org/en/news/swift-un-action-needed-syria-after-houla-assault-2012-05-28> (accessed 17 August 2012).

Arquidiocese de São Paulo. (1985). *Brasil: Nunca Mais*. Editora Vozes Ltd: Petrópolis.

Atkas v. *Turkey*. (2003). App. No. 24351/94, para. 313 (Eur. Ct. H.R. 24 April 2003). Available at: <http://hudoc.echr.coe.int/sites/eng/pages/search.aspx?i=001-61055> (accessed 12 August 2012).

Author's Notes. (2008). Military commission hearing of Mohammed Jawad, Guantánamo Bay, Cuba, 14 August 2008.

Barriga, S.R. (2012, 10 July). Ending forced sterilization of women and girls with disabilities. *The Huffington Post*.

Body of Principles for the Protection of All Persons under Any Form of Detention or Imprisonment. (1988). Adopted by UN General Assembly Resolution 43/173 of 9 December 1988.

Boggio, A., Zignol, M., Jaramillo, E., *et al.* (2008). Limitations on human rights: are they justifiable to reduce the burden of TB in the Era of MDR- and XDR-TB? *Health and Human Rights*, 10, 121–26.

Bush, G.W. (2010). *Decision Points*. Virgin Books: London.

Caesar v. *Trinidad and Tobago*. (2005). Ser. C, No. 123 (Inter-Am. Ct. H.R.).

Caso Maritza Urrutia v. *Guatemala*. (2003). Sentencia de 27 de noviembre de 2003 (fondo, reparaciones y costas) (Corte Inter-Am. D.H.), para. 51(a).

Center for Reproductive Rights. (2011). *Leyes sobre aborto en el mundo 2011*. Available at: <http://reproductiverights.org/sites/crr.civicactions.net/files/newsletter/crr_spanish_AbortionMap_2012.pdf> (accessed 4 June 2012).

Colombani, J.M. (2001, 13 September). Nous sommes tous Américans. *Le Monde*.

Commission on Human Rights. (1982). *Study of the Implications for Human Rights of Recent Developments Concerning Situations Known as States of Siege or Emergency*. Sub-Commission on Prevention of Discrimination and Protection of Minorities, 35th sess., provisional agenda item 10, UN Doc. E/CN.4/Sub.2/1982/15, para. 41 (1982) (by Nicole Questiaux).

Commission on Human Rights. (1986). *42d sess., agenda item 10(a), Torture and Other Cruel, Inhuman or Degrading Treatment or Punishment: Report by the Special Rapporteur, Mr. P. Kooijmans, Appointed Pursuant to Commission on Human Rights Resolution 1985/33.* U.N. Doc. E/CN.4/1986/15 (1986).

Commission on Human Rights. (2005). *62d sess., provisional agenda item 11(a).* U.N. Doc. E/CN.4/2006/6 (2005), para. 35.

Commission on Human Rights. (2006). *UN Economic and Social Council, Commission on Human Rights, 62d sess., provisional agenda items 10 and 11, Situation of Detainees at Guantánamo Bay: Report of the Chairperson-Rapporteur of the Working Group on Arbitrary Detention, Leila Zerrougui; the Special Rapporteur on Torture and Other Cruel, Inhuman or Degrading Treatment or Punishment, Manfred Nowak; the Special Rapporteur on Freedom of Religion or Belief, Asma Jahangir; and the Special Rapporteur on the Right of Everyone to the Enjoyment of the Highest Attainable Standard of Physical and Mental Health, Paul Hunt.* U.N. Doc. E/CN.4/2006/120 (2006).

Committee against Torture. (2004). *Conclusions and Recommendations of the Committee against Torture: Chile,* 32nd sess., 3–21 May 2004. UN Doc. CAT/C/CR/32/5 (2004), paras. 6(j), 7(m). Available at: <http://daccess-dds-ny.un.org/doc/UNDOC/GEN/G04/422/01/PDF/G0442201.pdf?OpenElement> (accessed 4 June 2012).

Committee against Torture. (2006). *Conclusions and Recommendations of the Committee against Torture: Peru,* 36th sess., 1–19 May 2006. UN Doc. CAT/C/PER/CO/4, para. 23.

Committee against Torture. (2008). *General Comment No. 2: Implementation of Article 2 by States Parties,* UN Doc. CAT/C/GC/2 (2008), para. 5.

Committee against Torture. (2009a). 42d sess., 27 April–15 May 2009. Concluding Observations of the Committee against Torture: Honduras. U.N. Doc. CAT/C/HND/CO/1 (2009).

Committee against Torture. (2009b). 42d sess., 27 April–15 May 2009. Concluding Observations of the Committee against Torture: Nicaragua. U.N. Doc. CAT/C/NIC/CO/1 (2009).

Committee on the Elimination of Discrimination against Women (CEDAW). (2008). *General Recommendation No. 26 on Women Migrant Workers,* UN Doc. CEDAW/C/2009/WP.1/R (2008), para. 20.

CONADEP. (2003). Nunca más: Informe de la Comisión Nacional sobre la Desparación de Personas (CONADEP) (6th ed.). Eudeba, Universidad de Buenos Aires: Buenos Aires.

Confirmation Hearing. (2005). On the Nomination of Alberto R. Gonzalez to be Attorney General of the United States: Hearing Before the S. Comm. on the Judiciary, 109th Cong. 534-37 (2005) (statement of Harold Hongju Koh, Dean, Yale Law School).

Convention against Torture and Other Cruel, Inhuman or Degrading Treatment or Punishment. (1987). Adopted 10 December 1984, 1465 U.N.T.S. 85 (entered into force 26 June 1987), art. (1).

Crawshaw, S. and Jackson, J. (2010). *Small Acts of Resistance: How Courage, Tenacity, and Ingenuity Can Change the World.* Union Square Press: New York, NY.

Danner, M. (2004, 7 September). Abu Ghraib: the hidden story. *The New York Review of Books.* Available at: <http://www.nybooks.com/articles/archives/2004/oct/07/abu-ghraib-the-hidden-story/?pagination=false>.

de Wet, E. (2004). The prohibition of torture as an international norm of *jus cogens* and its implications for national and customary law. *European Journal of International Law,* 15, 98–99.

El Akkad, O. (2008, 10 July). U.S. treatment of Khadr may have exceeded military's own guidelines. *The Globe and Mail.*

Feitlowitz, M. (1998). *A Lexicon of Terror: Argentina and the Legacies of Torture.* Oxford University Press: Oxford.

Filártiga v. *Peña-Irala.* (1980). 630 F.2d 876, 889 (2d Cir. 1980).

Frakt, D.J.R. (2009a). Closing argument at Guantanamo: the torture of Mohammed Jawad. *Harvard Human Rights Journal,* 22, 401–423.

Frakt, D.J.R. (2009b). The difficulty of defending detainees. *Washburn Law Journal*, 48, 381–406.

Frakt, D.J.R. (2011). Mohammed Jawad and the Military Commissions of Guantánamo. *Duke Law Journal*, 60, 1367–1411.

Gable, L., Vásquez, J., Gostin, L.O., *et al.* (2005). Mental health and due process in the Americas: protecting the human rights of persons involuntarily admitted to and detained in psychiatric institutions. *Pan American Journal of Public Health*, 18, 366–373.

Gaspari, E. (2002). *A ditadura escancarada*. Companhia das Letras: São Paulo.

Gostin, L.O. (2008). 'Old' and 'new' institutions for persons with mental illness: treatment, punishment or preventive confinement? *Public Health*, 122, 906–913.

Gostin, L.O. and Gable, L. (2008). Global mental health: changing norms, constant rights. *Georgetown Journal of International Affairs*, Winter/Spring, 83–92.

Hersh, S. (2004a, 10 May). Torture at Abu Ghraib. *The New Yorker*. Available at: <http://www.newyorker.com/archive/2004/05/10/040510fa_fact>.

Hersh, S. (2004b, 17 May). Chain of command. *The New Yorker*. Available at: <http://www.newyorker.com/archive/2004/05/17/040517fa_fact2>.

Hersh, S. (2004c, 24 May). The gray zone. *The New Yorker*. Available at: <http://www.newyorker.com/archive/2004/05/24/040524fa_fact>.

Human Rights Committee. (1992). *General Comment No. 20*, para. 3. UN Doc. HRI/GEN/1/Rev.1 at 30.

Human Rights Committee. (2001). *General Comment No. 29: States of Emergency*. UN Doc. CCPR/C/21/Rev.1/Add. 11 (2001).

Human Rights Committee. (2011). *General Comment No. 34: Article 19: Freedoms of Opinion and Expression*. UN Doc. CCPR/C/GC/34 (2011).

Human Rights Council. (2008). *Report of the Special Rapporteur on Torture and Other Cruel, Inhuman or Degrading Treatment or Punishment, Manfred Nowak, Addendum: Summary of Information, Including Individual Cases Transmitted to Governments and Replies Received*. 7th sess., agenda item 3, UN Doc. A/HRC/7/3/Add.1 (2008), para. 80.

Human Rights Watch. (1997). *Punishment Before Trial: Prison Conditions in Venezuela*. Human Rights Watch: New York, NY.

Human Rights Watch. (1998). *Behind Bars in Brazil*. Human Rights Watch: New York, NY.

Human Rights Watch. (2003). *Cruel Confinement: Abuses Against Detained Children in Northern Brazil*. Human Rights Watch: New York, NY.

Human Rights Watch. (2004a). *The Road to Abu Ghraib*. Human Rights Watch: New York, NY.

Human Rights Watch. (2004b). *Help Wanted: Abuses Against Female Migrant Domestic Workers in Indonesia and Malaysia*. Human Rights Watch: New York, NY.

Human Rights Watch. (2005a). *In the Dark: Hidden Abuses Against Detained Youth in Rio de Janeiro*. Human Rights Watch: New York, NY.

Human Rights Watch. (2005b). *Decisions Denied: Women's Access to Contraceptives and Abortion in Argentina*. Human Rights Watch: New York, NY.

Human Rights Watch. (2006). *The Second Assault: Obstructing Access to Legal Abortion after Rape in Mexico*. Human Rights Watch: New York, NY.

Human Rights Watch. (2009). *Lethal Force: Public Violence and Public Security in Rio de Janeiro and São Paulo*. Human Rights Watch: New York, NY.

Human Rights Watch. (2010a). *Illusions of Care: Lack of Accountability for Reproductive Rights in Argentina*. Human Rights Watch: New York, NY.

Human Rights Watch. (2010b). *Unjust and Unhealthy: HIV, TB, and Abuse in Zambian Prisons*. Human Rights Watch: New York, NY.

Human Rights Watch. (2011a). *Neither Rights Nor Security: Killings, Torture, and Disappearances in Mexico's 'War on Drugs'*. Human Rights Watch: New York, NY.

Human Rights Watch. (2011b). *Getting Away with Torture: The Bush Administration and the Mistreatment of Detainees*. Human Rights Watch: New York, NY.

Human Rights Watch. (2011c). *'Even Dead Bodies Must Work': Health, Hard Labour, and Abuse in Ugandan Prisons*. Human Rights Watch: New York, NY.

Human Rights Watch. (2012). *Torture in the Name of Treatment: Human Rights Abuses in Vietnam, China, Cambodia, and Lao PDR*. Human Rights Watch: New York, NY.

Human Rights Watch and Amnesty International. (2005). *The Rest of Their Lives: Life Without Parole for Child Offenders in the United States*. Human Rights Watch: New York, NY.

Husak, D. (2008). *Overcriminalization: The Limits of the Criminal Law*. Oxford University Press: Oxford.

ICRC. (2002). *ICRC Report on the Treatment of Fourteen 'High Value Detainees' in CIA Custody*. International Committee of the Red Cross (ICRC): Washington, DC.

IHRC and Justiça Global. (2011). *São Paulo sob achaque: Corrupção, crime organizado e violência institucional em maio de 2006*. IHRC and Justiça Global: Rio de Janeiro.

International Federation for Human Rights. (2010). *Egypt: Counter-Terrorism against the Background of an Endless State of Emergency*. FIDH: Paris.

International Harm Reduction Development Program. (2010). *Detention as Treatment: Detention of Methamphetamine Users in Cambodia, Laos, and Thailand*. Open Society Institute: New York, NY.

Ireland v. *United Kingdom*. (1978). App. No. 5310/71, 2 Eur. H.R. Rep. 25.

Jürgens, R., Nowak, M., and Day, M. (2011). HIV and incarceration: prisons and detention. *Journal of the International AIDS Society*, 14, 26.

Ley No. 164. (2008). *Código Penal* (Nicaragua), Arts. 143 and 145, as amended July 2008. Available at: <http://www.oas.org/juridico/mla/sp/nic/sp_nic_Nuevo_Codigo_Penal_%20Nicaragua_2007.pdf> (accessed 7 February 2013).

Lines, R. (2008). The right to health of prisoners in international human rights law. *International Journal of Prisoner Health*, 4, 3–53.

Loayza Tamayo v. *Peru*. (1997). Ser. C, No. 33 (Inter-Am. Ct. H.R.).

Malinowski, T. (2005). Banned State Department practices. In K. Roth and M. Worden (Eds.), *Torture: Does It Make Use Safer? Is It Ever Okay? A Human Rights Perspective*, pp. 142–144. The New Press: New York, NY.

McLemore, M. (2008). Access to condoms in U.S. prisons. *HIV/AIDS Policy and Law Review*, 13, 20–24.

Ministry of Health. (2006). *Rules and Protocols for the Management of Obstetric Complications*. December 2006 (on file with Amnesty International).

Nowak, M. (2009). Fact-finding on torture and ill-treatment and conditions of detention. *Journal of Human Rights Practice*, 1, 101–119.

O'Boyle, M. (1977). Torture and emergency powers under the European Convention on Human Rights: *Ireland* v. *United Kingdom*. *American Journal of International Law*, 71, 684–688.

Osborn, R.E. (2010). Correlates of violence in Guinea's Maison Centrale Prison: a statistical approach to documenting human rights abuses. *Health and Human Rights in Practice*, 12, 73–87.

OSCE Office for Democratic Institutions and Human Rights. (2007). *Guidelines on Freedom of Peaceful Assembly*. OSCE Office for Democratic Institutions and Human Rights: Warsaw.

PoKempner, D. (2005). Command responsibility for torture. In K. Roth and M. Worden (Eds.), *Torture: Does It Make Use Safer? Is It Ever Okay? A Human Rights Perspective*, pp. 158–72. The New Press: New York, NY.

Prosecutor v. *Delalic et al.* (1998). Case No. IT-96-21-T (ICTY Trial Chamber Judgement 1998), para. 470.

Prosecutor v. *Kvocka*. (2001). Case No. IT-98-30/1 (ITCY Trial Chamber Judgement 2001), para. 142.

Reidy, A. (2002). *The Prohibition of Torture: A Guide to the Implementation of Article 3 of the European Convention of Human Rights, Human Rights Handbooks, No. 6*. Directorate General of Human Rights, Council of Europe: Strasbourg.

Rejali, D. (2009). *Torture and Democracy*. Princeton University Press: Princeton, NJ.

Rodley, N. (2011). *The Treatment of Prisoners under International Law*. Oxford University Press: Oxford.

Rome Statue of the International Criminal Court. (2002). Art. 7(1), specifically arts. 7(1)(f) (torture), (g) (gender-based violence such as rape and sexual slavery), and (k) (other inhumane acts). UN General Assembly: Geneva.

Salla, F., Rodriguez Ballesteros, P., Espinoza, O., *et al.* (2009). *Democracy, Human Rights and Prison Conditions in South America*. Available at: <http://www.nevusp.org/downloads/down249.pdf> (accessed 1 June 2012).

Selmouni v. *France*. (1999). App. No. 25803/94 (Eur. Ct. H.R. 28 July 1999).

Shepard, B.L. and Becerra, L.C. (2007). Abortion policies and practices in Chile: ambiguities and dilemmas. *Reproductive Health Matters*, 15, 202–210.

Simpson, J. and Bennett, J. (1985). *The Disappeared and the Mothers of the Plaza: The Story of the 11,000 Argentines Who Vanished*. St. Martin's Press: New York, NY.

Siracusa Principles. (1984). *On the Limitation and Derogation Provisions in the International Covenant on Civil and Political Rights*. UN Doc. E/CN.4/1985/4, Annex (1984).

The Washington Times. (2008, 17 December). Interview of the Vice President by John Ward and John Solomon, *The Washington Times*, Vice President's West Wing Office. *The Washington Times*. Available at: <http://georgewbush-whitehouse.archives.gov/news/releases/2008/12/20081222.html> (accessed 4 June 2012).

Sönmez, S., Apostopoulos, Y., Tran, D., *et al.* (2011). Human rights and health disparities for workers in the UAE. *Health and Human Rights*, 13, 1–19.

Stinneford, J.F. (2006). Incapacitation through maiming: chemical castration, the eighth amendment, and the denial of human dignity. *University of St. Thomas Law Journal*, 3, 559 99.

USA v. *Mohammed Jawad*. (2008). D-008 Ruling, Ruling on Defense Motion to Dismiss: Torture of Detainee.

Velásquez-Rodríguez Case. (1988). Judgement of 29 July 1988, Inter-Am. Ct. H.R. (Ser. C) No 4.

Waldron, J. (1994). Vagueness in law and language: some philosophical issues. *California Law Review*, 82, 509–39.

Waldron, J. (2005). Torture and positive law: jurisprudence for the White House. *Columbia Law Review*, 105, 1715–1718, 1735.

Waldron, J. (2010). *Torture, Terror, and Trade-Offs: Philosophy for the White House*. Oxford University Press: Oxford.

Wallach, E. (2006). Drop by drop: forgetting the history of water torture in U.S. courts. *Columbia Journal of Transnational Law*, 45, 468–506.

Weschler, L. (1990). *A Miracle, a Universe: Settling Accounts with Torturers*. Pantheon Books: New York, NY.

Whitman, J.Q. (2003). *Harsh Justice: Criminal Punishment and the Widening Divide between America and Europe*. Oxford University Press: Oxford.

WHO. (2012). *Tuberculosis in Prisons*. World Health Organization (WHO): Geneva. Available at: <http://www.who.int/tb/challenges/prisons/story_1/en/index.html> (accessed 31 May 2012).

Chapter 26

Emergencies, disasters, conflicts, and human rights

Victoria Sutton

Introduction

The Universal Declaration of Human Rights (UDHR) has influenced individuals, foreign policy experts, and policymakers for decades in their efforts to improve the human condition throughout the world. As a testament to that influence, there are currently 'around two hundred assorted declarations, conventions, protocols, treaties, charters, and agreements, all dealing with the realization of human rights in the world [and] . . . no fewer than [65] mention . . . the [UDHR] as a source of authority and inspiration' (Morsink, 1999).

The UDHR was created on 10 December 1948, following World War II, when it was decided that the words that created the mission of the United Nations (UN) were not sufficiently well articulated. Eleanor Roosevelt, Chair of the committee that drafted the UDHR, said of the time leading up to its establishment: 'we must recognize that our mutual devotion to our own land must never blind us to the good of all lands and of all peoples . . . and that which injures any one of us, injures all of us. Only by remembering this will we finally have a chance to build a lasting peace' (Roosevelt, 1945). This statement has never been truer than in the face of an environmental disaster or conflicts that disrupt public health services when they are most needed.

In 2011, natural disasters alone killed 30,773 people, and injured 244.7 million worldwide (CRED et al., 2012). Economic damages from natural disasters were estimated to be US$366.1 billion and were the highest ever recorded (CRED et al., 2012). Between 300 and 400 environmental disasters occur each year in the world (CRED et al., 2012).

One of the most rapidly developing environmental disasters which challenged public health aid was the magnitude 7.0 earthquake that struck Haiti in 2010. The earthquake's characteristics produced devastating outcomes, but the aftermath of the shifting populations and influx of development workers to the island-nation set the stage for what proved to be a rapidly spreading and deadly cholera outbreak. This was the first cholera outbreak in more than a century (Walton & Ivers, 2011), and the public health infrastructure was inadequate to address the contagious nature of and rapid morbidity of the disease. On 8 November 2010, 48 hours after the flooding in Haiti, Médecins Sans Frontières (MSF) volunteers identified 200 cases and the next day more than 11,000 people were hospitalized of whom more than 700 died (Walton & Ivers, 2011). This disaster was felt acutely by those who shared the same hemisphere and raised awareness of the public health consequences that can increase the immediate suffering caused by the disaster itself.

This chapter will explore the influence of Article 25 of the UDHR on the response to international public health emergencies, including bioterrorism, international environmental disasters, and international conflicts. The combination of migration due to climate change or conflict presents new issues of law and policy; the need for public health services and the rapid growth of these refugee-type movements in the world will prove healthcare's importance and push this to the top of the political agenda in the coming years.

Article 25 as a source of law

The authority of Article 25 of the UDHR, as adopted by the UN General Assembly, could be considered either soft law or customary international law, so although it was originally created as a non-binding legal authority, its customary international law status suggests it is becoming binding as a matter of international law. Article 25(1) provides that '[e]veryone has the right to a standard of living adequate for the health of himself and his family, including food, clothing, housing and medical care, and necessary social services' (UDHR, 1948), laying the foundation for the international human rights actions and documents that followed.

The right to health set out in Article 25 has been the subject of work by the UN Human Rights Council (UNHRC), the former UN Commission on Human Rights, and the human rights special procedures. The UDHR is one of three foundational documents in international human rights law. The UDHR, the International Covenant on Civil and Political Rights (ICCPR), and the International Covenant on Economic, Social and Cultural Rights (ICESCR), all form the foundation of the UN system of human rights protections (Gable, 2007). The ICCPR and ICESCR were created in 1966 and were ratified and came into force in 1976 as binding law.

Article 12.2(d), 'The prevention, treatment and control of epidemic, endemic, occupational and other diseases', is explained in General Comment 14 with respect to disasters and emergencies as 'The right to treatment includes the creation of a system of urgent medical care in cases of accidents, epidemics and similar health hazards, and the provision of disaster relief and humanitarian assistance in emergency situations' (CESCR, 2000).

General comments have been developed to interpret the ICESCR, and General Comment 14 (CESCR, 2000) explains the right to health and the provision of health services, providing that health service 'extends to the underlying determinants of health, such as food and nutrition, housing, access to safe and potable water and adequate sanitation, safe and healthy working conditions, and a healthy environment' (CESCR, 2000).

The application of Article 25 to disasters and conflicts is a foundational instrument, although neither the word 'disasters' nor 'conflicts' is expressly included. The Covenants, however, take their authority and basis from the UDHR's Article 25.

The World Health Organization (WHO) Constitution defines health as 'a state of complete physical, mental, and social well-being and not merely the absence of disease or infirmity' (WHO, 1946). But the WHO goes further in defining health services as activities intended to restore and maintain health. This suggests that a clean environment as well as sanitary services and water would encompass the meaning of health services, 'a standard of living adequate for the health and well-being of himself and his family' (UDHR, 1948, Article 25).

The issue of State sovereignty

The development of international human rights law is a requirement that compromises a State's complete sovereignty over its citizens but in a way in which all the parties to the UDHR could agree. It is the Covenants where more of a compromise of sovereignty exists, so far as each party chooses to ratify them, because the Covenants are binding on the parties. Compromising sovereignty is often a stated reason that the United States declines signing treaties, as they have chosen not to ratify the UDHR. Some argue it is because doing so would impose actions on the State, such as providing access to universal healthcare (Heritage Foundation, 2012).

International relational ethics from foreign relations law and sovereignty

There are three essential ethical principles of international relational ethics which are important impositions on sovereignty: '(1) the inherent worth and dignity of individuals; (2) the community-defined public good; and (3) authentic relationships' (Fast et al., 2002). The focus on individuals maintains the aspect of human rights and the balance of public interests with the individual's interests in health. The community-defined public good, signals how the balancing of individual rights will be weighed against the public good which may change over time or with circumstances. Our weighing of individual rights against the public health interest and the community-defined public good still requires careful consideration of the inherent worth and dignity of individuals.

The third principle recognizes that it is the relationships between countries themselves which holds the most promise for ethical behaviour by governments and their adherence to the obligations they bear to their citizens. There is support in foreign relations law, which indicates four principles of international law apply in this case. First, there is State responsibility, defined in the Restatement of Foreign Relations Law (Comment D) that 'a State is responsible . . . for its own activities and those of individuals . . . under its jurisdiction. The State may be responsible, for instance, for not enacting necessary legislation, for not enforcing its laws against persons acting in its territories' (American Law Institute, 1986, §601). Second, the UN Charter includes as one of its purposes achieving 'international cooperation in solving international problems of an economic, social, cultural or, humanitarian character' (UN Charter, 1945, Article 1). An international legal principle, the duty to cooperate, is established by the 1970 UN Declaration of Principles on International Law, which stipulates that States have a duty to cooperate with each other (UN General Assembly, 1970).

Third, the duty to provide prior notification and to consult in good faith (UNEP, 1978) requires that nations provide prior notification to any State regarding potential damage that might occur, which could be translated to a duty to warn. Fourth, the international legal 'protective principle' recognizes the right of a sovereign State to prescribe law, and regulates conduct outside its territory for the purpose of protecting national security (American Law Institute, 1986, §402).

A laissez-faire form of international relations that has been the normative approach to international law will need to give way to the affirmative requirements of actions to ensure the 'health and well-being of everyone . . . his family, including food, clothing, housing and medical care and necessary social services' (UDHR, 1948, Article 25).

Pakistan flood in 2010 and discriminatory laws that are contradictory to the UDHR

Pakistan ratified the ICESCR on 17 April 2008 and the ICCPR on 23 June 2012 (UNTC, 2012), but in the case of the ICCPR, Pakistan registered a reservation, which observed the ICCPR unless it conflicted with Pakistani law. In this case, the pattern of discrimination against the Muslim sect known as the Ahmadis in particular (Khan, 2004) and specific prohibitions that infringe on the rights protected in the ICESCR in both the Pakistani Constitution and Pakistani law, create a situation of unenforceability against Pakistan. In essence, the State is complying with the terms of the ICESCR and ICCPR, but also the reservations it filed to ignore them when their own laws provided for officially sanctioned discrimination.

This conflict with the ICESCR and ICCPR and State sovereignty was evident during the 2010 flooding, which was one of the worst natural disasters in the history of Pakistan. The local clerics were the alleged source of the pressure to refuse aid to the Ahamdis as they struggled to survive the disaster conditions, which left them without food, water, or shelter (Malik, 2011). Without consent to enforce all aspects of the ICESCR and ICCPR, there were no available means to intrude into Pakistan's sovereign authority. Pakistan also did not sign the Optional Protocols for both the ICCPR and ICESR, which, although not yet enforceable because more signatures are needed for ratification before they enter into force, it signalled that Pakistan is not yet open to complaints filed from their jurisdiction.

Hurricane Katrina and the United States

The United States has ratified the ICCPR, with reservations, which specifically identify disaster situations with the understanding that discrimination only when 'solely' based on race will be considered a violation of the ICCPR. The US Constitution prohibits racial discrimination at both the state and federal levels, and disparate responses in a disaster can also violate the constitution if government actions are based solely on race. There has been no shortage of claims of international human rights violations by the United States, both during and after Hurricane Katrina struck New Orleans on 28 August 2005 (Edwards, 2006). A petition against the United States was filed with the Inter-American Commission for Human Rights (IACHR) for 'its exclusion of certain categories of immigrant survivors of Hurricane Katrina from federal disaster assistance', requesting injunctive measures to order the United States to take action to protect the right to life of these immigrants (International Human Rights Law Clinic (IHRLC), 2012). The IACHR responded by requesting information from the United States with regard to, among other things, access to healthcare in the disaster zone (IHRLC, 2012).

Humanitarian organizations and sovereignty

Non-governmental organizations (NGOs) engaged in humanitarian aid, though operating with neutrality and autonomously, may be faced with a choice when responding to an emergency, disaster, or conflict; either being prevented from entering a country or compromising their neutrality. For example, the Yemen government stopped the work of MSF when news media reported that the organization had condemned the acts of violence carried out by the Yemeni army against the Houthis in Saada. The reason for their expulsion was the Yemen government's claim that MSF had violated its neutrality by condemning the government. In order for the organization to resume work in the country, the government required that MSF offer public apologies for their criticism.

The WHO's International Health Regulations and public health emergencies

Disasters that involve diseases meeting the definition of a public health emergency of international concern trigger the application of binding regulations which require World Health Organization (WHO) Member-States to fashion responses that recognize human rights and human dignity. Member-States and Parties to International Health Regulations (IHRs) are bound by the regulations. These regulations require coordination of efforts across States to control the effect of any 'public health emergency of international concern' (PHEIC). In carrying out the requirements of the IHRs, Member-States must ensure 'full respect for the dignity, human rights, and fundamental freedoms of persons'. With regard to travellers, Member-States are required to 'treat travelers with respect for their dignity, human rights and fundamental freedoms, and minimize any discomfort or distress associated with such measures' (WHA, 2005).

The impetus to revise the existing IHRs in 2003, which had not been revised since they were first established in 1969 (WHO, 1969), came from the handling of the SARS outbreak which began in China. Based on an international norm, 'duty to warn', it was agreed among the 194 WHO Member-States that a binding regulation to warn other governments of PHEIC was necessary. In addition, the incorporation of the human rights references were in recognition of the actions of governments in the face of disease outbreaks or intentional bioterrorism, both of which would trigger the application of the regulations, if there was a determination that there was a PHEIC.

The future will likely dictate the kinds of actions for governments that will comport with human rights standards of 'human rights and fundamental freedoms and [that] minimize any discomfort or distress associated with such measures' (WHA, 2005). The likely source for determining what those measures might be would come from the actions taken during the 2003 severe acute respiratory syndrome (SARS) outbreak in Asia and North America, as well as the 2008 swine influenza outbreak in Mexico, which marked the first time that the IHRs were used and a pandemic was declared by the WHO under the regulations.

The lessons of SARS

In Hong Kong, where significant impacts were felt from the SARS outbreak, government actions included a quarantine of the building, the Amoy Gardens housing complex, where the first cases occurred (Rothstein et al., 2003). Officials used tape and restraint to prevent occupants from leaving the building, but afterwards they discovered that half of the residents had left the housing complex upon learning that it was to be quarantined. Uncertainty about the prospects of obtaining food and water during the quarantine may have exacerbated the non-quarantine compliance actions of the public.

During the SARS outbreak, Singapore had three index cases, all originating from people who had stayed at the Metropole Hotel in Hong Kong, where the first SARS case was traced to. Singapore had a number of laws and policies already in effect which provided for four-fifths of pay for employees on sick leave, as well as provisions for medical care during an emergency, although there is no publicly financed healthcare. Singapore's Environmental Public Health Act, Part IV, has strong measures for ordering a medical examination, ordering treatment in a hospital, and ordering quarantine if the person is suspected of having, or being a carrier of, an infectious disease. Using a Certificate of Urgency, the government was able to amend the Act through legislation in the Singapore Parliament, which provided very strict measures that 'were made within five categories: home quarantine orders, quarantine of premises, prevention of persons acting irresponsibly in a manner leading to the spread of infectious disease, compliance with disease control measures, and the handling of corpses when SARS is the suspected cause of death' (Rothstein et al., 2003).

The measures taken by the government to ensure that there were no human rights violations related to the SARS outbreak were exemplary. The potentially harsh economic effects of quarantine were mitigated by a Home Quarantine Order Allowance Scheme. According to the Singapore government's SARS website, the programme was administered by the Community Development Councils and was intended to defray the costs of home quarantine for self-employed persons and small businesses (those with 50 employees or less) that had to close as a result of SARS. The allowance of SGD$70 per day was paid to self-employed persons and employees of small businesses forced to close due to SARS. The government advised employers to treat the home quarantine period of its employees as paid hospital leave under the Employment Act, further relieving pressure on those forced to stay away from work (Rothstein et al., 2003).

For those who were quarantined at home, assistance with grocery shopping was offered, hotline numbers were provided, a daily update on television was presented regarding the status of the outbreak, free transportation for suspected cases of SARS was supplied, including for foreigners and visitors, and all care was subsidized at hospitals. Financial assistance was also provided to workers in hard-hit areas that required prolonged cessations of work due to SARS (SARS in Singapore, 2003).

In Canada, a number of SARS cases appeared in the Toronto and Ontario regions. Canada used both its federal Quarantine Act and provincial quarantine powers, but only issued seven quarantine orders during the course of the outbreak. Cooperation with isolation measures of staying home proved to be successful, and largely due to the affirmative steps taken by the federal and provincial governments to provide for basic human necessities during the isolation period. For example, the employment insurance regulations were amended (Employment Insurance Regulations, 1996) in order to remove the waiting period for sickness benefits to those who could not go to work either because they were in SARS quarantine or infected with SARS. Special employment insurance was also created for healthcare workers who were unable to work because of SARS and were not otherwise eligible for the government's Employment Insurance Act benefits. Another important action was to ensure that those quarantined did not face the financial danger of losing their homes, thus the government provided tax and mortgage relief to individuals having difficulty making their payments due to SARS-related quarantine. The Ontario provincial government provided qualified persons with unpaid leave in the event they were unable to work due to SARS, by enacting the SARS Assistance and Recovery Strategy Act (SARS Assistance and Recovery Strategy Act, 2003).

The actions that were taken in response to the SARS outbreak were not only consistent with rights-based provision of health services and food, as well as water and shelter, but they also alleviated the serious devastating effects of financial losses that could have led to a loss of health security.

The lessons of H1N1: the first official pandemic under international health regulations

In 2009, an outbreak of H1N1, called 'swine flu' (leading to the faulty conclusion that it was contracted from swine), had its epicentre in Mexico. This was the first event to utilize the IHRs' specific pandemic determination regulations (WHO, 2012) as well as their human rights guidance, which was particularly relevant to travellers. Air travel was not suspended, but checkpoints at airports in Europe and other regions used screening with questionnaires. No government-sanctioned blockades of trade or transportation were instituted, except in the case of Egypt and Russia. Egypt took the opportunity to order the destruction of swine in Cairo, which many believed was motivated by the dislike of swine by certain groups in Egypt. Six countries blocked the importation of swine, but Russia took the opportunity to block the importation of swine from North America, and all types of livestock and meat products from California, Kansas, New York, Ohio, and Texas (International Center for Trade and Sustainable Development, 2009), which allowed for a period of protectionism for their own livestock production industry.

Actions taken for political purposes, subordinating public health issues, resulted in second-order negative public health effects. These bans in Russia were without scientific basis and were violations of the General Agreement on Tariffs and Trade (GATT) phytosanitary rules, which require that trade blocks be based on scientifically defensible public health concerns as a result of the item being blocked from import. From a human rights perspective, these bans also unreasonably disrupted food availability for millions of Russians. In the case of Egypt, ironically, destruction of the swine which were used to consume garbage from Cairo, on the edge of the city, caused a crisis in garbage accumulating and vermin followed, creating conditions for more serious health threats due to the growing number of rats.

Conflicts and Article 25

War and conflicts have generated a great deal of international law specific to situations that conform to the Geneva Convention's norms on war and conflict. However, with new situations such as the redefinition of the term 'enemy combatant' to include unlawful combatants, as well as novel situations which lead to conflict and potentially war, the usefulness of the foundations in human rights law become essential. Reference to Article 25 of the UDHR is a starting point in the consideration of economic sanctions, for example, where food deprivation for civilians may be the logical outcome.

Right to access to medical care

Conflicts and war can create devastating results on the health of civilians where access to healthcare is impeded by the conflict. A study of conflict in the Congo region found that the mortality rate was higher in unstable provinces of the east and most of the deaths were from easily preventable and treatable illnesses rather than violence (WHO, 2002). Using regression analysis, the researchers concluded that mortality would have been at normal rates if the effects of impeding healthcare due to the conflict were removed (Coghlan et al., 2006).

Discrimination at the point of access to healthcare facilities is also another impediment to observing the right to health for civilians in a conflict zone. Any discrimination based on ethnic, religious, political, or other factors is a violation of the principle of medical neutrality. The principle of medical neutrality 'guarantees the provision of [healthcare] without discrimination to all injured and sick combatants and civilians in time of conflict' (WHO, 2002).

The protection of human health and access to medical services during armed conflict requires both human rights law and international humanitarian law to ensure that there are no gaps in protections (Perrin, 2009).

Food crises and conflict

As previously noted, Article 25(1) of the UDHR states that '[e]veryone has the right to a standard of living adequate for the health and well-being of himself and of his family, including food' (UDHR, 1948). Article 11(2) of the ICESCR states a recognition of 'the fundamental right of everyone to be free from hunger' (ICESCR, 1966). Building on that foundation, the Universal Declaration on the Eradication of Hunger and Malnutrition (UDEMH, 1974) has further articulated this right. But while the right to food is well established in international agreements, the duty to accept food is not as clear, and the duty to provide food and aid is even less so. However, the intentional use of food shortages to create a crisis and human deprivation in conflict and politically motivated strategies is well known but much more difficult to address in the international community (Marcus, 2003).

The former Soviet Union created the Ukrainian famine from 1928 to 1932, which killed between 5 million and 11 million people by starvation or related diseases (Björnson & Jonassohn, 1998) as part of a strategy to accelerate communism, which required the elimination of nationalism (which

Josef Stalin saw as a threat to his objective). The Ukraine was thought to be especially nationalistic, a political stance that was destroyed by breaking down the will of the population through starvation (Marcus, 2003). The famine was politically driven by excessive quotas for production set up by the former Soviet Union, which essentially left shortages of grain and food for the Ukraine. While food produced was either being exported or stored for 'emergencies', individuals were being prevented from buying or obtaining food in other ways, or from travelling abroad to obtain food and bringing it back into the country (Marcus, 2003).

The Ethiopian famine was induced by environmental conditions, but exacerbated by opportunistic political forces in 1983 to 1985 (Marcus, 2003). During the 1970s, drought conditions had created strains on food supplies, and the political opportunity arose to change economic and political policies to exacerbate the shortages causing starvation. The bombing of markets and air strikes as well as the restriction of travel further destroyed the ability for people to seek food to cope with the famine. More than 400,000 people died from starvation and related illnesses during the 1983 to 1985 period (Mayfield, 1995).

During the 1990s, the North Korean famine was also suspected of being politically motivated, although the North Korean government claimed that floods were responsible for the food shortages. More than one million people died due to the food shortages (Haggard & Noland, 2005). This crisis has continued until today (2012) and the international community has responded by providing aid and food, but there is ongoing suspicion that food is being diverted away from the starving population. For that reason, in early 2012, the United States declined to provide food to North Korea. Because the United States was negotiating with North Korea concerning its nuclear ambitions, and the launch of a missile was being planned, it was perceived that the United States was withholding food aid in exchange for policy concessions on the part of the North Koreans, which they would not accept. The United States has provided almost US$1 million in aid in the form of tents and tarps, but no food, given the proclivity to divert food from the people, according to the report (Reuters, 2011). In April 2012, the increasingly isolated country will mark the 100th birthday of the officially designated 'Eternal President' Kim Il-sung, and some believe that North Korea may have been hoarding food for the centennial event (Reuters, 2011). The famine is still ongoing, but with a closed society and drought factors, it is particularly difficult to identify the cause of the famine.

The intentional or reckless creation of a famine, which is intended to coerce or kill a population, is a form of genocide and, it has been argued, should be criminalized in international law, with stronger penalties than those provided by human rights law (Marcus, 2003). However, if economic sanctions are used against a country resulting in the starvation of its population is that a violation of international human rights law or is it consistent with conflict and war?

Economic sanctions and human rights law

The United States is credited with being the most frequent user of international economic sanctions in the world. These sanctions often involve restrictions on trade and financial transactions between persons subject to United States jurisdiction, which target the State and its citizens (Malloy, 1995). Because of the nature of these sanctions, their use must be balanced against the harm to innocent citizens, where shortages of food, water, and supplies can create a serious risk to life, and constitute an international human rights violation. Michael Malloy writes about the preference for sanctions over the use of military confrontation:

> The strategy of any effective sanctions program is to induce dysfunction in the trade and financial payments system of a target state with the goal of furthering a specific policy objective critical to the

> national interest. Given the concerns involved, it is probably counterproductive to limit the use of sanctions in an abstract or general way in order to protect human rights concerns. (Malloy, 1995)

The use of sanctions as a political strategy will almost always have unintended consequences for the citizens of the sanctioned nation, but is that preferable to war? In fact, the ICCPR authorizes derogation of some human rights in a time of public emergency (such as war). If that is the case, then war is devoid of the consideration of human rights, but only international humanitarian law is effective and should thus apply.

Global climate change, refugees, migration, and Article 25 Where they must flee the jurisdiction of their resident country, refugees that result from war and conflict are protected under auspices of the UN High Commission on Refugees (UNHCR). This is unclear when people become displaced but do not leave the jurisdiction of their country of residence. What is even less clear, though, and more daunting, is the lack of international law protecting refugees from devastating climate change or environmental disasters. While it is clear that the definition of a refugee under the UNHCR does not fit the climate change refugee (UNCSR, 1951), it seems possible that the internally displaced person status definition will fit an environmental refugee. But since international human rights law as it applies to refugee law, is uncertain, it does not appear advantageous to develop the law in this direction.

Because environmental disasters and the number of people being displaced by them are expected to increase, an examination of international human rights law and the progeny of Article 25 should be examined. This is especially necessary since estimates of the magnitude of displacements by the year 2050 due to climate change range from 25 million to 1 billion (IASC, 2008).

As an adaptation strategy, migration and resettlement have formally been incorporated into the range of strategies articulated in the Fourth Assessment Report of the Intergovernmental Panel on Climate Change, which identifies migration and displacement as being likely impacts of climate change due to extreme weather and climate events. But there is thus far no legal framework for addressing the need to protect climate- or environment-related migration or even statelessness that may result, for example, from the submerging of island nations.

Legal instruments that have been proposed to address climate change migration do not rely on human rights law, but, because the focus is on individuals, they have a basis in human rights law. Some of the proposals include: (1) a protocol to the UN Convention Relating to the Status of Refugees of 1951; (2) a protocol to the UN Framework Convention on Climate Change (UNFCCC); or (3) a new treaty altogether. In the negotiations leading up to the formal meeting of the parties (UN members which participate in the climate change treaty process), several meetings were held to craft language to address the growing problem of refugees due to environmental disasters thought to be triggered by climate change.

The parties addressed the climate change refugee issue with the following language during a November 2009 meeting: 'Activities related to national, regional and international migration, and displacement or planned relocation of persons affected by climate change while acknowledging the need to identify modalities of interstate cooperation to respond to the needs of affected populations who either cross an international frontier as a result of, or find themselves abroad and are unable to return owing to, the effects of climate change' (UNFCCC, 2008).

However, in December 2009, this language was removed from the documents prepared for the formal meeting, which consequently removed the climate change refugee concept from the much-needed debate. But in June 2010, at the Bonn meeting, another negotiations meeting leading up to the formal meeting, a weaker version was reintroduced, which led to the language accepted at the 2010 adaptation meeting in Cancún, Mexico, which 'invites' States to 'enhance action on adaptation . . . of 14(f) measures to enhance understanding, coordination, and cooperation with regard to climate change induced displacement, migration, and planned relocation, where appropriate, at the national, regional, and international levels' (UNFCC, 2008).

The Dhaka Declaration adopted at the Climate Vulnerability Forum in November 2011 also incorporated migration as an adaptation strategy for population displacement due to climate change or environmental disaster. Nonetheless, the language was the strongest yet to create a legal framework for addressing displacement. The Dhaka Declaration expressly called for the adoption of Article 14(f) of the Cancún language agreement noted earlier, and called for 'coordination and cooperation with regard to climate-induced displacements; migration and planned relocation; and in this respect called for the commencement of an international dialogue for an appropriate framework' (Climate Vulnerable Forum, 2011).

Conclusion

The UDHR has influenced individuals, foreign policy representatives, and policymakers for decades in their efforts to improve the human condition throughout the world. Currently 'around two hundred assorted declarations, conventions, protocols, treaties, charters, and agreements all dealing with the realization of human rights in the world [and] . . . no fewer than [65] mention . . . the [UDHR] as a source of authority and inspiration' (Morsink, 1999).

International public health emergencies, including bioterrorism, international environmental disasters, and international conflicts as well as the famine disasters that may be intentionally or recklessly created, can find their foundation in human rights in Article 25 of the UDHR. The strength of the framework built around Article 25 over the past 25 years is vitally important in a world where increasing populations, air travel, and threat of climate change will inevitably expose more people to environmental disasters, conflicts, and other public health emergencies.

Acknowledgements

Text extract from MY DAY © (1945) Eleanor Roosevelt/United Media Syndication. Dist. By UNIVERSAL UCLICK. Reprinted with permission. All rights reserved. Acknowledgements and thanks to Richard Rosen, Texas Tech University School of Law, Director, Center for Military Law for his guidance and advice on the conflict and humanitarian law and UDHR issues. This work was supported in part by a scholarship stipend from the Texas Tech University School of Law.

References

American Law Institute. (1986). *Restatement of the Law Third – The Foreign Relations Law of the United States. VI. The Law of the Environment.* American Law Institute: St. Paul, MN.

Björnson, K.S. and Jonassohn, K. (1998). *Genocide and Gross Human Rights Violations: In Comparative Perspective.* Transaction Publishers: Piscataway, NJ.

CESCR. (2000). *General Comment 14: The Right to the Highest Attainable Standard of Health (Article 12 of the International Covenant on Economic, Social and Cultural Rights).* Committee on Economic, Social and Cultural Rights (CESCR): Geneva. Available at: <http://www2.ohchr.org/english/bodies/cescr/comments.htm> (accessed 1 April 2012).

Climate Vulnerable Forum. (2011). *Dhaka Ministerial Declaration.* Adopted at Dhaka, Bangladesh on 14 November 2011.

Coghlan, B., Brennan, R.J., Ngoy, P., *et al.* (2006). Mortality in the Democratic Republic of the Congo: A nationwide survey. *Lancet*, 367, 44–51.

CRED, IRSS, and UCL. (2012). *Annual Disaster Statistical Review 2011*. Centre for Research on the Epidemiology of Disasters, Institute of Health and Society, Université catholique de Louvain: Brussels. Available at: <http://www.cred.be/publication/annual-disaster-statistical-review-2011> (accessed 1 April 2012).

Edwards, G. E. (2006). International human rights law violations before and after Hurricane Katrina: An international law framework for analysis. *Thurgood Marshall Law Review*, 31, 353–425.

Employment Insurance Regulations. (1996). *Employment Insurance Regulations: S.O.R./96-332*. Amended by S.O.R./2003-131 (P.C. 2003-474) (4 April 2003). Canada Employment Insurance Commission: Ottawa.

Fast, L., Neufeldt, R.C., and Schirch, L. (2002). Toward ethically grounded conflict interventions: Reevaluating challenges in the 21st century. *International Negotiation: A Journal of Theory and Practice*, 7, 185–207.

Gable, L. (2007). The proliferation of human rights in global health governance, *Journal of Law, Medicine and Ethics*, 35, 534–544.

Haggard, S. and Noland, M. (2005). *Human Rights: The Politics of Famine in North Korea*. US Committee for Human Rights in North Korea: Washington, DC.

Heritage Foundation. (2012). *Health Care*. The Heritage Foundation: Washington, DC. Available at: <http://www.heritage.org/issues/health-care> (accessed 1 April 2012).

IASC. (2008). *Climate Change, Migration and Displacement: Who will be affected?* Working paper submitted by the informal group on Migration/Displacement and Climate Change of the Inter-Agency Standing Committee (IASC): Geneva.

ICESCR. (1966). *International Covenant on Economic, Social and Cultural Rights, Art. 11(2), 993 UNTS 3*. International Covenant on Economic, Social and Cultural Rights (ICESCR): Geneva.

IHRLC. (2012). *Report*. International Human Rights Law Clinic (IHRLC), Berkeley Law: University of California, CA. Available at: <http://www.law.berkeley.edu/2974.htm> (accessed 1 April 2012).

International Center for Trade and Sustainable Development. (2009). String of pork bans follow swine flu outbreak. *Bridges Weekly Trade News Digest*, 13(15). Available at: <http://ictsd.org/i/news/bridgesweekly/45787/> (accessed 1 April 2012).

Khan, A.M. (2004). Persecution of the Ahmadiyya community in Pakistan: an analysis under international law and international relations. *Harvard Human Rights Journal*, 16, 217–245.

Malik, A. (2011). Denial of flood aid to members of the Ahmadiyya Muslim community in Pakistan. *Health and Human Rights: An International Journal*, 13(1). Available at: <http://www.hhrjournal.org/index.php/hhr/article/view/403/599> (accessed 1 April 2012).

Malloy, M.P. (1995). Economic sanctions and human rights: a delicate balance. *The Human Rights Brief*, 3(1), 12–14. (Publication of The Center for Human Rights and Humanitarian Law at Washington College of Law, American University: Washington, DC.) Available at: <http://www.wcl.american.edu/hrbrief/03/1malloy.pdf> (accessed 1 April 2012).

Marcus, D. (2003). Famine crimes in international law. *The American Journal of International Law*, 97, 245–281.

Mayfield, J.V. (1995). The prosecution of war crimes and respect for human rights: Ethiopia's balancing act. *Emory International Law Review*, 9, 553–593.

Morsink, J. (1999). *The Universal Declaration of Human Rights: Origins, Drafting, and Intent*. University of Pennsylvania Press: Philadelphia, PA.

Perrin, P. (2009). The right to health in armed conflict. In A. Clapham and M. Robinson (Eds.) *Swiss Human Rights Book, Vol. 3, Realizing the Right to Health*, pp. 157–172. Ruffer & Rub: Zurich.

Reuters. (2011). *Special Report: Famine Grips North Korea Rice Bowl*. Reuters: New York, NY. Available at: <http://www.reuters.com/article/2011/10/07/us-korea-north-food-idUSTRE7956DU20111007> (accessed 1 April 2012).

Roosevelt, E. (1945, 22 December). *My Day*. The Eleanor Roosevelt Papers Project: Washington DC. Available at: <http://www.gwu.edu/~erpapers/myday/displaydoc.cfm?_y=1945&_f=md000215> (accessed 1 April 2012).

Rothstein, M.A., Alcalde, G., Elster, N.R., *et al.* (2003). *Quarantine and Isolation: Lessons Learned from SARS, A Report to the Centers for Disease Control and Prevention.* Institute for Bioethics, Health Policy and Law, University of Louisville School of Medicine: Louisville, KY.

SARS Assistance and Recovery Strategy Act. (2003). *SARS Assistance and Recovery Strategy Act, Ch. 1.* Ontario, Canada.

SARS in Singapore. (2003, 17 April). SARS in Singapore: economic impact of SARS. *Channel News Asia.* Singapore. Available at: <http://www.channelnewsasia.com/sars/030417_mof.htm> (accessed 1 April 2012).

UDEMH. (1974). *Universal Declaration on the Eradication of Malnutrition and Hunger, GA Res. 3180 (XXVIII), Preamble.* UN General Assembly at the World Food Conference: New York, NY.

UN Charter. (1945). *United Nations Charter, Article 1.3.* Created 26 June 1945. United Nations (UN): San Francisco, CA.

UNEP. (1978). *UNEP Principles on Shared Natural Resources, Principle 6.* United Nations Environment Program (UNEP): Nairobi.

UNFCCC. (2008). *Protocol. Art. 14(f).* United Nations Framework Convention on Climate Change (UNFCCC): Geneva. Available at: <http://unfccc.int/essential_background/kyoto_protocol/items/1678.php> (accessed 1 April 2012).

UN General Assembly. (1948). *Universal Declaration of Human Rights.* UN General Assembly: Paris. Available at: <http://www.un.org/en/documents/udhr/index.shtml> (accessed 1 April 2012).

UN General Assembly. (1970). *UN Declaration of Principles on International Law Concerning Friendly Relations and Cooperation Among States in Accordance with the Charter of the United Nations.* Res. 2625 (24 October 1970). United Nations (UN): New York, NY.

United Nations Convention Relating to the Status of Refugees (1951). *United Nations Convention Relating to the Status of Refugees, Art. 1(a).* United Nations: New York, NY.

UNTC. (2012). *United Nations Treaty Collection: Chapter IV: Human rights.* United Nations: New York, NY. Available at: <http://treaties.un.org/Pages/Treaties.aspx?id=4&subid=A&lang=en> (accessed 1 April 2012).

Walton, D.A. and Ivers, L.C. (2011). Responding to cholera in post-earthquake Haiti. *New England Journal of Medicine*, 364, 3–5.

WHA. (2005). *International Health Regulations.* World Health Assembly (WHA): Geneva. Available at: <http://www.who.int/ihr/en/> accessed 1 April 2012).

WHO. (1946). *Preamble to the Constitution of the World Health Organization.* World Health Organization (WHO): New York, NY.

WHO. (1969). *The International Health Regulations.* World Health Organization (WHO): Geneva. Available at: <http://www.who.int/ihr/current/en/index.html> (accessed 1 April 2012).

WHO. (2002). *25 Questions on Health and Human Rights.* World Health Organization (WHO): Geneva. Available at: <http://www.who.int/entity/hhr/NEW37871OMSOK.pdf> (accessed 1 April 2012).

WHO. (2012). *Pandemic Alert System.* World Health Organization (WHO): Geneva. Available at: <http://www.who.int/csr/disease/swineflu/frequently_asked_questions/levels_pandemic_alert/en/index.html> (accessed 1 April 2012).

Chapter 27

Searching for a role for genomics in the right to health

Lisa Eckstein

Introduction

The optimism that underpinned the 1997 United Nations Educational, Scientific, and Cultural Organization (UNESCO) Universal Declaration on the Human Genome and Human Rights' call for the '[b]enefits from advances in biology, genetics and medicine, concerning the human genome, [to] be made available to all' is increasingly distant (UNESCO, 1997). A decade after the initial sequencing of the human genome, the hype surrounding the advances that would result has faded, replaced by a pervasive cynicism about the lack of tangible benefits associated with the 'omics' revolution. Instead, convincing arguments now abound that improved health outcomes are most likely to result from a focus on the social determinants of health rather than increased investments in genomic and related technologies. Particularly in the context of developing countries, genomic technologies might be considered a luxury that unjustifiably detracts from pressing public health needs. Is seeking a role for genomics in the right to health a futile or even detrimental quest?

This chapter takes a somewhat more optimistic view of the future role of genomic technology in the right to health:

- Genomics can contribute to meeting public health needs, including in developing countries, albeit in a measured way that must be balanced against the economic and social costs of implementation.
- Genomics can inform drug prescribing decisions—for example, by predicting likely adverse event outcomes—which can be applied to population-level decisions by national health authorities. Rapid molecular analyses of pathogens can facilitate responses to emerging and re-emerging infectious diseases.

Provided the requisite workforce and infrastructure is available, both of these areas provide opportunities for developing country innovation and commercialization.

Yet fostering a path to judicial, ethical, and contextual implementation of genomic technologies—in particular, in developing countries—is a daunting task. It requires surmounting practical hurdles that feature in many other chapters of this book, including but not limited to those of overstressed healthcare delivery systems, a paucity of trained healthcare professionals and ongoing workforce migration, and a lack of basic infrastructure. Moreover, implementation of genomic advances raises ethical, legal, and social issues (ELSI), encompassing concerns about individual privacy and discrimination, stigmatization of groups and communities, and the line between social and biological conceptions of race and ethnicity. Many of these ELSI concerns have been explored in the context of the United States and Europe, with little attention to their broader applicability.

The next section discusses the early expectations of genomic technologies for advancing health outcomes, and the limited extent to which these expectations have thus far been fulfilled. On most conceptions, genomic advances have shown lacklustre progress in preventing or treating the diseases responsible for the bulk of global morbidity and mortality. Nonetheless, genomic technologies are starting to play a valuable role in health and medical research and service delivery. Accordingly, the chapter features a discussion about general strategies for the responsible uptake of genomic technologies in developed countries—which are likely to comprise the bulk of genomic research and implementation in the near future—including grounding uptake in a 'public health genomics' ethos, which focuses on the evidence base for implementation and funding decisions, along with relevant ELSI.

The chapter next considers the multifaceted implications of genomic technologies for developing countries, recognizing the overwhelming challenges of implementation but also the potential value of genomics. On the one hand, ancestral genetic stratification may hinder the efficacy of certain genomic technologies developed in the United States and Europe for some other populations, exacerbating even further longstanding health disparities. On the other hand, the very potential for population-level genomic differences has fuelled steps by some developing countries to assert their own role in the genomics revolution, potentially stimulating social and economic benefits.

The chapter concludes with an analysis of two case studies: the use of genomics as a tool to improve HIV treatment, and ongoing efforts to apply pharmacogenomics to the global cardiovascular disease (CVD) epidemic. As a case study, HIV/AIDS is illustrative of the possibilities and challenges that beset the use of genomics to improve access to health and health outcomes in developing countries. In particular, genomics could ameliorate drug-related toxicities—currently responsible for approximately 25% of patients' failure to adhere to treatment (Ajay et al., 2008; d'Arminio Monforte et al., 2000). Genomic technologies also may be employed to minimize the development of HIV drug resistance. The application of genomics to CVD is further afield. While some drug therapies, such as warfarin, may benefit from genetic testing, significant genomic inroads for the majority of CVD treatment and prevention pathways remain elusive. Future progress depends on firmly grounding research in scientifically robust hypotheses and ethically responsible conduct.

Genomic medicine: from early hype to current expectations

The completion of the draft sequencing of the human genome in February 2001 was announced with huge fanfare. Unlocking the human genetic sequence was anticipated to lead to 'a new age in medicine' (Jeffords & Daschle, 2001). Indeed, one commentator went so far as to suggest that members of the public may greet the publication of the draft sequence 'with the same awestruck feeling that accompanied the landing of the first human on the moon and the detonation of the first atomic bomb' (Pääbo, 2001).

In the decade since the draft sequence was published, genomic information has generated some important health improvements—in particular, in the realm of pharmacogenomics, which seeks to understand the influence of genetic variation on drug response. Targeted clinical trials have managed to reduce drug development costs in certain circumstances—for example, the development of the breast cancer drug trastuzumab (Deverka et al., 2010). Pharmacogenomics is also playing an increasingly prominent role in drug prescribing, evidenced by the growing US Food and Drug Administration (FDA) *Table of Pharmacogenomic Biomarkers in Drug Labels*. Rapid molecular analyses have facilitated timely responses to emerging and re-emerging infectious diseases, including the development of diagnostics and potential therapeutics—seen, for example, in relation to the 2002/2003 severe acute respiratory syndrome (SARS) outbreak and the 2009 H1N1 influenza virus (Fricke et al., 2009).

Despite these laudable achievements, genomics has failed to translate into commonly applicable preventative health and medical interventions (Burke et al., 2010; Ioannidis, 2010; Knerr et al., 2010). The resultant disillusionment has been heightened all the more because of the 'artificially raised expectations' with which it was preceded (Burke et al., 2010). That said, dismissing genomics as peripheral to improving future health is premature. Scientific progress is, by nature, non-linear. In the coming decades, new research tools made possible by 'next-generation' gene sequencing techniques are likely to spawn far more nuanced biological understandings and resulting innovations. To get a sense of the increasing availability and decreasing cost of research tools, consider the two months and US$1 million dollars it took to sequence the first human genomes—those of genomics entrepreneur Craig Venter in 2007 and DNA pioneer James Watson in 2008. Yet in 2010, the whole genome of James Lupski, a prominent medical geneticist with Charcot–Marie–Tooth disease, was reportedly sequenced for as little as US$50,000 (Lupski et al., 2010).

In addition, far more interconnected understandings of genes and the environment are becoming possible: following the oft-quoted aphorism attributed to Judith Stern at the University of California Davis, 'genetics loads the gun but the environment pulls the trigger', (Kazaks & Stern, 2004). The manner in which genes are expressed is affected by such wide-ranging factors as maternal stress and nurturing, nutrition, exposure to toxins, and even social status (Dolinoy et al., 2007; Tung et al., 2012). As more holistic biological understandings become increasingly widespread, genomics' role in understanding and preventing the onset of common diseases may also expand. This raises the question of how genomics can best be harnessed as a component of the right to health. Various possible answers are explored in this chapter, which will be addressed within the context of developed countries, followed by a discussion about the far more complex question of how genomics might apply to the right to health in developing countries.

Genomics in developed countries

At least in the near future, the principal uptake of genomics will be in the context of developed countries. Already genomics and other emerging technologies are creeping into healthcare delivery systems, albeit at a slower pace than originally predicted. All developed countries have implemented newborn screening programmes to detect metabolic and other (mostly) genetic conditions (Burke et al., 2011). Reproductive genetic screening is also becoming increasingly prevalent, often targeted to a person's race or ethnicity: for example, Tay–Sachs and other disease screening for women of Ashkenazi Jewish descent. A limited number of drug-prescribing decisions take into account genomic information. As of March 2012, more than 70 FDA-approved drugs incorporate pharmacogenomics information in their drug labels, including information on drug exposure and variability in clinical response and risk for adverse events. Additional medical understanding is being generated by the greater than 1100 genetic sites that have now been associated with common traits and conditions (Lander, 2011).

These advances have, however, largely developed ad hoc, and evidence to support implementation of most genomic technologies remains patchy. In 2007, Khoury and colleagues estimated that less than 3% of published research focuses on the development of evidence-based guidelines on the value of a genomic application for health practice; the delivery and dissemination of such guidelines into health practice; and evaluation of the health outcomes of a genomic application in practice (Khoury et al., 2007). A more strategic approach to research and implementation, which shifts attention and funding from the initial stage of scientific discovery to the application, implementation, and evaluation of genome-based discoveries, could result in significant public health benefits (Burke et al., 2010). An important step towards achieving this goal will be the adoption of a 'public health genomics' ethos (Burke et al., 2006).

Economic barriers remain a key hurdle to the widespread uptake of genomic technologies, including pharmacogenomic markers and tests, in developed country healthcare systems. On the one hand, genomics has been touted as a means of reinvigorating pharmaceutical research and development, including concerns about the paucity of new molecular entities being brought to market. However, the potential for genomics to actually increase developmental productivity remains somewhat unclear (Cook et al., 2009). Perhaps more importantly, genomic technology uptake requires significant changes in the practices of the pharmaceutical industry, physicians, and healthcare payers. Many pharmaceutical companies have been reluctant to abandon the historically successful 'blockbuster' model, which seeks to develop and market drugs for the broadest possible patient group, in favour of developing drugs with more limited market potential (Aspinall & Hamermesh, 2007). Linking drugs to diagnostic genetic tests may complicate marketing to physicians and slow the diagnostic process, another barrier to industry uptake (Aspinall & Hamermesh, 2007). In the specific US context, further disincentives arise from the widespread pay-for-procedure approach, which encourages physicians to perform procedures rather than making early and accurate diagnoses (Aspinall & Hamermesh, 2007). Finally, payers, such as public and private health insurers, have been reluctant to cover genetic tests based on apprehension about overall costs should testing become widespread (Davis et al., 2009).

Uptake of genomic innovations in a manner conducive to public health also demands assessment of 'potential non-medical harms, such as stigmatization or the infringement of patient autonomy' (Rogowski et al., 2009). Early on, the importance of avoiding a '*GATTACA*-like' future caught the imagination of the public, scholars, and policymakers. The result was an explosion of journal articles, grey literature, and legislation seeking to address these issues. Article 11 of the 1997 Council of Europe Convention for the Protection of Human Rights and Dignity of the Human Being with regard to the Application of Biology and Medicine: Convention on Human Rights and Biomedicine prohibits in member countries any form of discrimination on the grounds of a person's genetic heritage (Council of Europe, 1997). Australia amended antidiscrimination laws to apply to discrimination based on real or perceived genetic status (Disability Discrimination and Other Human Rights Legislation Amendment Act, 2009). In the United States, the Genetic Information Nondiscrimination Act (GINA) of 2008 specifically prohibits insurers from using a person's genetic information in determining eligibility or premiums, and from requesting or requiring that a person undergo a genetic test (Genetic Information Nondiscrimination Act, 2008). The Act also prohibits employers from using a person's genetic information in making employment decisions (Genetic Information Nondiscrimination Act, 2008).

Ongoing ELSI concerns involve the availability of commercial direct-to-consumer genetic testing services, including varying levels of privacy protections, and doubtful test quality and validity. Further issues arise from the proliferation of genomic biobanks: of growing concern given the approximately 300 million biological samples stored in hospitals and research centres in the United States alone (Swede et al., 2007). While biobanks often ask donor permission for unrestricted data access for future research, there is no way for a donor to make a truly informed choice whether to accept the risks and benefits of as-yet unforeseen research—a central tenet of informed consent doctrines (Rothstein, 2005). More contentious still are commercial arrangements associated with repositories, including profits from drugs and research tools developed from donor materials, an issue that came to widespread public prominence with the 2010 bestselling book chronicling the development of hugely profitable cell lines harvested in the 1950s from an African American tobacco farmer without her knowledge or consent, and without a benefit-sharing mechanism

(Skloot, 2010). A promising regulatory model advocates biobank governance through a non-profit trusteeship guided by the public benefit (Winickoff & Winickoff, 2003); however, any cohesive uptake will require a daunting level of cooperation among diverse players including governments, research organizations, hospitals, and so forth.

Bioethics traditionally has focused on harm to individual patients and research participants: genomics raises the prospect of harm to racial, ethnic, and other socially identifiable groups. Most genomic research has proceeded on the basis that human races have retained significant amounts of genetic variation and, therefore, have collected samples based on a subject's race or ethnicity. Soo-Jin Lee describes the result as 'an infrastructure of racialization' (Lee, 2005): a situation that becomes all the more troubling when research touches on socially contentious traits and attracts a sensationalist media. Consider, for example, the New Zealand 'warrior gene' controversy. In 2006, scientists reported that a genetic variant in a region previously associated with behavioural disorders (quickly dubbed by the media 'the warrior gene') was 'strikingly overrepresented' in Māori males. Before his conference presentation, a lead researcher stated that 'obviously' the findings meant that Māori men were 'going to be more aggressive and violent and more likely to get involved in risk-taking behavior like gambling' (Australian Associated Press, 2006). Controversy immediately resulted. Other scientists critiqued the scientific rigor of the research (Crampton & Parkin, 2007; Merriman & Cameron, 2007), and a Māori politician pointed to social issues as the main contributors to Māori violence (Agençe France-Presse, 2006). Given what Juengst describes as population genetic research's capacity to 'drive scientific wedges into the social cracks that already divide people' (Juengst, 2007), instituting safeguards to the use of race and ethnicity in research—for example, through a 'race impact assessment' requirement—is an important issue for future policy attention.

Genomic advances may exacerbate national health disparities because of increased costs associated with technology uptake, or by overshadowing causes of disparities such as 'poverty, racism, unequal access to healthcare and cultural practices' (Rotimi & Jorde, 2010). For myriad interconnected reasons, disadvantaged persons are less likely to take up emerging technologies. In 2005, Armstrong and colleagues reported that, in the United States, white women were almost five times more likely to undergo counselling for the *BRCA1/2* gene variants, which predispose to breast and ovarian cancer, than African American women (Armstrong et al., 2005). This relationship remained even after adjusting for factors such as the probability of carrying the variant and socioeconomic status (Armstrong et al., 2005). A subsequent study reported that primary care physicians serving a high concentration of minority patients were significantly less likely to have ordered a genetic test or to have referred a patient to a genetic counsellor (Shields et al., 2008). Disparities in access to genetic tests may be exacerbated further by barriers such as lack of patient knowledge about genetic testing, lack of insurance coverage, and distrust in the medical system (Suther & Kiros, 2009).

In sum, genomic advances and other emerging technologies could contribute to health research and delivery in developed countries. However, realizing their potential requires close attention to the promotion of translational research, including studies on cost-effectiveness, along with ELSI at the individual and population level.

Genomics in developing countries

To what extent do genomic innovations have a future role in promoting the right to health in developing countries—countries which face seemingly more pressing health needs such as the alleviation of poverty and infectious diseases (Séguin et al., 2008a)? Benatar asks the prescient question: 'If drugs for malaria, tuberculosis, many tropical diseases, and HIV/AIDS have not been made available to billions in poor countries is it likely that the poor will benefit from advances in biotechnology?' (Benatar, 2002). Benatar describes, for example, the genetic engineering of insulin, which has created a product more expensive than animal insulin to suggest the likelihood that, 'as in the past [genomic] developments will be denied to the poor, or may only trickle down sporadically' (Benatar, 2002). Advocates of genomic uptake, on the other hand, stress its potential to 'offer innovative and potentially cost-effective solutions to major public health burdens', via both 'leapfrog' technologies and new ways of using existing genomic knowledge in a different environment (Kamal et al., 2011). Pharmacogenomic knowledge, for example, may allow developing countries to better decide the best interventions for their healthcare delivery systems (Pang, 2009)—in particular, by lessening the likelihood of adverse drug reactions and thereby improving patient compliance and reducing the subsequent emergence of drug-resistant pathogens (Warnich et al., 2011). More broadly, commentators suggest that genomics may strengthen developing countries' scientific capacities, enabling them 'to participate as equal partners in the global R&D enterprise' (Pang, 2009).

Challenges of transposing genomic technologies from developing countries

Health technologies developed in developed countries can prove suboptimal when applied in countries with different healthcare delivery systems, co-morbidities, and cultures. In the genomics context, this challenge is heightened further due to ancestral genetic stratification.

Broadly, ancestral genetic stratification refers to the 10% to 15% of total human genetic variation that is explained by differences between sub-Saharan Africans, Northern Europeans, and East Asians (Bamshad, 2005). Although this 'between-group' genetic variation is relatively small compared with 'within-group' variation, it is highly structured, meaning that a modest number of genotypes can accurately allocate anonymous individuals to ancestral population groups (Bamshad, 2005). Used uncritically, ancestral genetic stratification can be misleading. Importantly, there is no such thing as discrete genetic populations. The extent to which so-called populations differ in gene frequency depends on the number of populations that are sampled: the greater the number of populations genotyped, the more difficult it becomes to delineate population boundaries. Even references to genetic 'populations' warrant close scrutiny given their overlap with social categories of race and ethnicity (Knerr et al., 2010). Taking into account these caveats, recognizing potential differences in genetic variant frequencies is an important part of determining the relevance of technologies developed in Europe and the United States to other regions. Differences in gene frequencies are exacerbated further by widespread environmental differences that impact on gene expression patterns.

The vast majority of human genomics research (and consequent product development) has been undertaken in populations of European ancestry living in developed country conditions. Nearly 90% of genome-wide association studies, for example, have been carried out in populations of European ancestry. The MalariaGen Project is the only such study to have collected a large number of samples from African subjects (Rotimi & Jorde, 2010), an especially problematic situation given the overwhelming proportion of human genetic variation found solely within African populations (Rotimi & Jorde, 2010). Participants at a 2010 meeting in Ickworth, United Kingdom, which aimed to set an agenda for public health genomics (the Ickworth Group), noted the inapplicability of some genomic innovations in developing countries because of 'variations in social and environmental exposures, dietary intake, and a sustained limitation on daily calorie intake coupled with limited access to [healthcare]' (Burke et al., 2010; Warnich et al., 2011).

Factors contributing to developing country adoption of genomic technologies

Séguin and colleagues at the University of Toronto have studied extensively the economic and social factors that have contributed to genomic research and development in developing countries. At least theoretically, genotyping projects can provide local health benefits, including tools to better understand drug response, disease mechanisms, and disease susceptibility (Séguin et al., 2008a). Thailand, for example, has launched two genotyping initiatives: the Thai SNP Discovery Project, which is collecting and storing genetic samples from the Thai population, and the Thai Centre for Excellence in Life Sciences Pharmacogenomics Project, which is genotyping polymorphisms involved in drug response. Underpinning the establishment of these initiatives was the perceived lack of incentive for multinational corporations to ensure that therapeutic agents have a good response rate with few adverse effects within the Thai population (Séguin et al., 2008b). Unfortunately, despite the Thai project's public health-centred rationale, at present, genetic testing is not covered by the Thai public healthcare system. Accordingly, private Thai hospitals and the medical tourism industry will be the initial beneficiaries (Séguin et al., 2008b).

Guarding against 'safari' or 'helicopter' research (Boyer et al., 2011) is another reason for a developing country to enter into genomic research and development. For example, in Mexico, such concerns prompted an amendment to Mexico's General Health Law, which prohibits researchers from sampling genetic material or transporting such material outside Mexico without the Ministry of Health's prior approval (Séguin et al., 2008c). Mexico also established the National Institute of Genomic Medicine with the view that, 'if we do not carry out studies to understand our genomic patrimony that we possess, well, no one else will because they will be interested in their own populations;' moreover, should other countries seek to get this information, 'then it will cost us' (Séguin et al., 2008c).

Genomic research and development also may provide economic opportunities. The publicly funded Indian Genome Variation (IGV) consortium seeks to promote India's competitive edge in the lucrative global clinical trials market by improving selection specificity (Séguin et al., 2008c). The IGV also hopes to develop and commercialize new products, including in niche markets such as the application of genomics to traditional Indian medicines (Séguin et al., 2008c). Given the very early stage of development, any concrete benefits remain hypothetical. Yet Warnich and colleagues echo the views of many in developing countries when they state: 'It may be debated that [pharmacogenomics] research is "too late" for South Africa, or that it is too technologically advanced and not cost-effective. However . . . it seems more likely that not only are we 'just in time', but we could assume a place in the global genomic research community' (Warnich et al., 2011). The question is whether these hopes are realistic and worth pursuing, or reflect the premature hype that so often has surrounded genomics.

Barriers to implementing genomic advances

For most developing countries to implement genomic advances, capacity building is crucial. In sub-Saharan Africa, for example, 'limited facilities, financial support and human resources' have restricted the use of genomic research (Kamal et al., 2011). South African healthcare professionals have drawn particular attention to the need for bioinformatics skills to analyse genomic research (Warnich et al., 2011). These concerns feed into far broader issues surrounding the capacity of health systems in developing countries. Article 19 of the 1997 Universal Declaration on the Human Genome and Human Rights requires States to seek measures to develop and strengthen 'the capacity of developing countries to carry out research on human biology and genetics' and facilitate 'developing countries . . . benefit from the achievements of scientific and technological research' (UNESCO, 1997, Article 19). However, the extent to which these aspirations have been met is questionable. Wonkam and colleagues, in discussing the failure to build capacity in medical genetics services in Cameroon, calculated that of the 50 studies indexed in PubMed published since 1988 that used Cameroonian DNA samples, only seven included a Cameroonian collaborative centre and only 14 a Cameroonian author (Wonkam et al., 2010). There is little to suggest more proactive capacity-building practices are occurring elsewhere and calls continue for international collaboration and the promotion of global research infrastructure.

Capacity building must go beyond research and health services infrastructure to also encompass relevant ELSI: including enhancing the application of international principles of research ethics, and considering any necessary adjustment of, or addition to, these principles to accommodate local contexts. The Human Genetic Diversity Project (HGDP), which intended to sample, map, and archive human genetic variation from populations around the world, brought into focus the importance of close community involvement. The HGDP's targeting of indigenous peoples led to perceptions that indigenous peoples 'were being treated as examples of human fossils from whom samples had to be collected before they died out' (Dodson & Williamson, 1999). Worldwide controversy resulted, including charges of 'racism, commercialism, exploitation, and cultural imperialism' (Resnik, 1999). Ultimately, the HGDP was derailed due to lack of funding.

Informed consent—a principle often put forward as the cornerstone of research ethics—can require particular diligence in some developing country settings. Nyika Aceme of the African Malaria Network Trust has noted the need for researchers to explain studies to participants orally in much of the developing world, which is characterized by low literacy levels (Aceme, 2009). A number of concepts central to informing potential participants about the research project cannot easily be translated. Crucially, some African languages have no generally understood term for 'research' or 'science', leading community members to substitute therapeutic meanings (Molyneux et al., 2004). Vernacular issues are exacerbated in the context of research involving emerging technologies. Researchers have discussed the problems of translating terms such as 'candidate gene' or 'genotyping' to a Yoruba-speaking population in Nigeria, for example, because the lack of any Yoruba words for these concepts (Marshall & Rotimi, 2001).

In addition to being adequately understood and informed, consent must be voluntary: that is, participants must not come under undue pressure to participate in research. Empirical research suggests that participants in developing countries are less likely than those in developed countries to say that they can refuse to participate in or can withdraw from a trial (Mandava et al., 2012). Lack of voluntariness also could result from traditional respect for health professionals, with participants feeling that refusal would be 'impolite' (Chokshi et al., 2007). Previously in this chapter, concerns were raised about limits on the breadth of future genomic research to which subjects may consent, for example, through biobanks. Communicating the nature of 'future, often highly technical research projects' may be exacerbated further in a developing country context (Chokshi et al., 2007).

While informed consent typically is considered in the context of individual study participants, in developing country research the role of communities also demands consideration, including as gatekeepers to individual community members and as providers of culturally relevant information. The *International Ethical Guidelines for Biomedical Research Involving Human Subjects* issued by the Council for International Organizations of Medical Sciences (CIOMS) note the importance of respecting customs in some cultures that require an investigator, before approaching prospective subjects, to obtain permission from a community leader or some other authority (CIOMS & WHO, 2002). Investigators undertaking international collaborative research in rural Kenya have stressed the influence of prevailing community attitudes and beliefs in supporting 'free and informed' consent to research participation, advising that 'it may be very difficult, arguably impossible' to bridge 'important paradigmatic differences between researchers and participants in relation to the nature, goals, and activities in research' solely through interactions with individual prospective participants (Marsh et al., 2011). Carving out a role for communities in the informed consent process poses many challenges, including determining which persons represent a community, and potential conflicts between community and individual interests. Notably, the CIOMS guidelines make clear that in no case may permission from community leaders substitute for individual informed consent (CIOMS & WHO, 2002).

Risk–benefit analyses also raise specific issues in the context of developing country research. As a general principle of research ethics, the risks to which research participants are exposed must be reasonable in relation to expected benefits (Wendler & Miller, 2008). Many of the hazards that arise as regards genomic research in developing countries mirror those in developed countries, including privacy of research participants and their families, and potential discrimination and stigmatization of socially identifiable groups. Study benefits, however, are more circumspect given the likelihood that research benefits may accrue 'only to rich people within rich nations' (Knoppers et al., 2000). To ameliorate such global disparities, CIOMS and the Human Genome Organisation Ethics Committee advocate sharing benefits from human genetic research with international participant communities (CIOMS & WHO, 2002). While laudable, benefit-sharing arrangements should be balanced against the risk that so-called 'inclusion benefits' (benefits that result from trial participation) may unduly induce study participants and communities to enrol. The extent to which undue inducement applies in the context of genomic research is questionable: that is, the potential for research rewards to result in a sufficiently high chance that a subject will experience a harm that seriously contravenes his or her interests (Emanuel et al., 2005). Further research is warranted on the type and degree of harm that may result from genomic research, including in countries in which potential participants may have very different notions of harm than those in the United States and Europe. Given these varying harm conceptions, efforts to improve the internal capacity of developing countries to conduct ethical evaluations of research protocols are essential.

The promise and perils of genomic innovations are well illustrated in the context of two case studies that comprise the final part of this chapter: antiretroviral therapy (ART) for HIV, and CVD pharmacogenomics.

Case study 1: implications of pharmacogenomics for HIV treatment

The devastation that HIV/AIDS continues to reap, particularly in developing countries, is well outlined in other chapters of this book. Although we are far from achieving the lofty goal of universal access to ART, many developing countries have made considerable progress in providing their citizens with access to treatment (WHO et al., 2011). Two by-products of greater access are increasing concerns about drug-related toxicities and viral mutations leading to drug resistance (Gilks et al., 2006; Jordan et al., 2008). Genomics could play a valuable role in alleviating these concerns, but successful implementation requires navigating complex ELSI and scientific issues.

Using pharmacogenomics to minimize adverse drug reactions

Approximately 25% of patients fail to adhere completely to their ART as a consequence of adverse drug reactions (ADRs) (Ajay et al., 2008; d'Arminio Monforte et al., 2000). Genetic variation provides at least one reason for ADRs; accordingly, pharmacogenomics, at least theoretically, can help to better target HIV treatments. In developed countries, such drug targeting usually will occur at the individual patient level; and in developing countries, at the population and subpopulation level.

Abacavir, for example, has been prescribed as a component of combination antiretroviral regimens since 1999. Drug hypersensitivity—the major treatment-limiting toxicity—occurs in approximately 5% to 8% of patients within six weeks of commencing an abacavir-containing regimen (UNESCO, 1997). In 2002, scientists identified a strong association between a genetic variant—HLA-B*570—and hypersensitivity to the drug abacavir (Mallal et al., 2002). Current FDA labelling recommends screening patients for this allele before initiating ART containing abacavir (Food and Drug Administration, 2012). The US Department of Health and Human Services' Panel on Antiretroviral Guidelines for HIV-1-Infected Adults and Adolescents (which provides clinical guidance on the management of HIV followed by US clinicians and seen as a 'gold standard' internationally) also advocates testing for the HLA-B*570 variant to determine the optimum treatment regimen (Panel on Antiretroviral Guidelines for Adults and Adolescents, 2012). Cost-effectiveness studies conducted in the United States have reported cost savings resulting from prospective screening prior to initiating abacavir-containing treatment (Kauf et al., 2010).

Preventing abacavir-related ADRs has been held up as a paradigmatic example of a successful pharmacogenomics initiative. Its success stems, in particular, from the absence of an alternative drug with as favourable a cost and toxicity profile, the potential for genetic screening to avoid severe and prevalent toxicity, the potential for genetic screening to usefully discriminate between individual risk profiles, and the availability of a genetic screening test and high-quality laboratory services (Nolan, 2009). However, because of ancestral genetic stratification and applicable drug prescribing patterns, the public health benefits of genetic testing prior to commencement of abacavir treatment apply most clearly in developed country settings. Unfortunately, those persons for whom its success is most tenuous are those who already bear the brunt of the HIV/AIDS burden—namely, those in developing countries.

Potential for existing products to exacerbate health disparities

The use of pharmacogenomics to 'personalize' HIV treatment may have limited applicability to developing countries for three reasons: (1) differences in population-level frequencies of genetic variations, (2) different adverse event profiles for other reasons, and (3) different drug prescribing patterns, minimizing the pertinence of findings. As such, without close policy attention, genomics is likely to increase already dire global disparities in the burden of HIV/AIDS.

First, the HLA-B*5701 allele—the polymorphism on which the bulk of HIV/AIDS genomic attention has been focused—varies in frequency across population groups. To the extent that broad generalizations are possible (see earlier discussion on the limits of groupings based on ancestral genetic stratification), the allele is relatively common among Caucasians and some Indian populations (Nolan, 2009); but is considerably rarer in certain African populations (Warnich et al., 2011), and in some Asian populations, including the Japanese, Korean, and Taiwanese populations (Park et al., 2009). Considerable variation also occurs within countries. Notably, substantial differences in allele prevalence have been found in various African populations (Rotimi & Jorde, 2010). In Southern Thailand, the population had a frequency of 11%, whereas in Northeast Thailand the frequency was approximately 3% (Nolan et al., 2003; Phillips, 2006). The lower the frequency with which the genetic variant arises, the less the public health benefit of testing. Second, different adverse effects may arise in developing country populations because of the high prevalence of co-morbidities such as anaemia, malnutrition, and tuberculosis, along with possible differences in host genetics (Subbaraman et al., 2007). Finally, abacavir is not prescribed frequently in many developing countries. In South Africa, for example, abacavir is only included in the guidelines for treatment of infants and children (Warnich et al., 2011). Accordingly, far greater public health importance will attach to studies examining gene variants relevant to first- or second-line antiretroviral regimens—including efavirenz and nevirapine (Warnich et al., 2011). A variant of the multidrug resistance (*MDR1*) gene is associated with decreased risk of hepatotoxicity during treatment with nevirapine (Warnich et al., 2011). Persons of African descent tend to have a considerably lower prevalence of this allele than Caucasians and, therefore, are at higher risk for developing hepatotoxicity (Clarke & Mousa, 2009). Variations in drug metabolizing genes have a significant effect on the plasma concentration and half-life of efavirenz and nevirapine and, therefore, their toxicity (Clarke & Mousa, 2009).

In sum, although HLA-B*5701 screening is cost-effective in the United States and Europe, the allele's lower frequency in the populations prevalent in many developing countries—in addition to the significant resource constraints facing such countries—means that no such algorithm is likely to apply. Notably, neither of the commercially available genetic sequencing kits covers the *MDR1* gene, which likely has greater relevance in the developing country setting.

A space for developing country innovation

Market economics, among other reasons, explains why genomics, to date, primarily has been leveraged in a way that is best placed to assist developed countries. However, there may be a space for developing countries to fill the gap in ways that benefit their own economies and meet the needs of other developing countries. Thailand provides an interesting example of how developing countries could leverage market economics to their advantage.

By way of background, the Thai government began providing ART through its universal healthcare system in 2004, a scheme that costs upwards of 3.8 billion Baht (approximately US$117 million) each year. The Government Pharmaceutical Organization manufactures a generic fixed-dose combination of stavudine, lamivudine, and nevirapine. This provides 'an inexpensive and effective antiretroviral drug regimen for initiating treatment of naïve patients', but necessitates vigilance for adverse effects such as rash, Stevens–Johnson syndrome, and high nevirapine plasma concentration (Chantratita et al., 2011). In 2005, the Thailand Centre of Excellence for Life Sciences launched the HIV-1 Pharmacogenomics Project which identified several variants associated with nevirapine-induced skin rash, as well as a variant associated with lipodystrophy among Thai HIV-infected patients who had received a stavudine-containing antiretroviral regimen (Chantratita et al., 2011). Project participants now are developing a novel system to incorporate all genomic predictive markers associated with antiretroviral ADRs in the same LabChip, under the code name 'All-In-One PGX-HIV'. The system is estimated to cost purchasers 1500 Baht (approximately US$50). This pharmacogenetic screening system 'would be the first of its kind in the realization of personalized antiretroviral medicines, in which appropriate, inexpensive treatment is given to each individual patient in developing countries, according to genetic information' (Chantratita et al., 2011).

Using pharmacogenomics to limit viral mutations

Genomic innovations also have been used to minimize the resistance of HIV strains to antiviral drugs. In resource-rich countries, HIV drug resistance testing is adopted at the individual patient level to inform decision-making about the optimum drug regimen. Two FDA-approved kits—the

TRUGENE® HIV-1 Genotyping Kit and the ViroSeq® HIV-1 Genotyping System—are commercially available to detect HIV drug-resistant gene variants.

This level of personalized decision-making is unfeasible for developing countries, which rely on standardized treatment protocols for ART scale-up—usually one first-line regimen and one alternative, possibly along with one second-line regimen (Bennett, 2006). In addition, because of 'the prohibitive cost of the assay, the lack of adequately trained personnel, and laboratory infrastructures, access to resistance testing is still greatly limited' (Aghokeng et al., 2011). As a compromise, the World Health Organization (WHO) recommends that developing countries evaluate HIV drug resistance through laboratory-based surveillance (WHO, 2009). Perhaps of even greater concern are reports that commercially available kits (which are widely used and commercialized in African settings) are not optimized to report on non-β HIV subtypes (Jagodzinski et al., 2003): precisely the viral strands that predominate in sub-Saharan Africa (Aghokeng et al., 2011). As a part of ongoing clinical trials in Cameroon, researchers tested 145 samples for drug resistance using the ViroSeq® HIV-1 Genotyping System. The authors noted the system's high failure rate on the HIV-1 subtypes that predominate in Cameroon, which resulted in a more frequent need for repeated tests, affecting 'the overall assay cost and delay of result delivery' (Aghokeng et al., 2011). In other words, even when developing countries manage to purchase genetic assays, they fail to work as well as they would in developed country settings.

Some developing countries have developed in-house assays, which can be designed to better detect non-β HIV strains at a fraction of the cost of commercial test kits. Scientists from the US Centers for Disease Control and Prevention (CDC) and health departments in Malawi, Nigeria, Thailand, Vietnam, and Zambia, for example, reported developing and validating an in-house assay to survey and monitor HIV-1 drug resistance. The assay provided greater sensitivity to non-β subtypes at a cost per test of US$40.00, as compared with US$213.20 for TRUGENE® and US$172.86 for ViroSeq® (Praparattanapan et al., 2011; Zhou et al., 2011). However, their use is affected by issues such as a lack of trained technicians and requisite software and equipment (Praparattanapan et al., 2011).

Discussion

HIV/AIDS is a pressing public health problem consuming vast resources in many developing countries. The disease's burden is exacerbated by the poor applicability of many treatment tools in developing country contexts, including pharmacogenomics adverse event profiles and assays to monitor drug resistance. Pharmacogenomics could benefit healthcare planning by guiding the selection of drug regimens with minimal adverse effects for a country's population and subpopulations. Locally developed viral assays may better detect the most prevalent HIV strains. However, these advances come with social as well as economic costs.

Research to find which specific genetic variants give rise to which specific adverse events for which given population, and at what frequency, is an undoubtedly large undertaking. It requires representative genetic variation information for a given population, presumably through large-scale gene sequencing projects. A string of ELSI stem from such sequencing projects, including many discussed earlier in this chapter such as the difficulties of gaining informed consent, recognition of the role of community leaders, and the potential for demarcation between groups to lead to stigmatization or discrimination. Large-scale gene sequencing projects also are likely to be hindered by practical issues such as resourcing constraints, a limited trained workforce, and a lack of laboratory infrastructure. Similar practical barriers hinder the development of local assays to detect HIV mutations.

Case study 2: implications of pharmacogenomics for CVD

Cardiovascular disease is the leading cause of death in the world, and approximately 80% of the annual 35 million cardiovascular-related deaths in the world occur in low- and middle-income countries (Gersh et al., 2010). While public health and community-based prevention strategies will be paramount in stemming the tide of CVD, genomics could play an important role in improving and targeting treatment and prevention efforts. Pharmacogenomic testing may ensure that patients at risk for myopathy from statin therapy receive alternative treatments (Pereira & Weinshilboum, 2011). Similarly, it may identify, and preclude from clopidogrel treatment, those patients who have an impaired response due to a reduced ability to metabolize the drug (Pereira & Weinshilboum, 2011). The FDA *Table of Pharmacogenomic Biomarkers in Drug Labels* currently lists nine FDA-approved CVD drugs with pharmacogenomic information in their labels, in addition to two genetic variants associated with warfarin dosage (Food and Drug Administration, 2012). Yet, as evident from the preceding case study, genomic advances are rarely simple.

Warfarin, the most commonly prescribed oral anticoagulant globally (Myburgh et al., 2012; Ross et al., 2010), is a favourable example to consider more closely. Warfarin treatment is complicated by its narrow therapeutic index, and the marked variability of its effect and metabolism among persons. Accordingly, it is a frequent cause of emergency visits for ADRs (Budnitz et al., 2007), and a leading cause of ADR deaths (Ross et al., 2010). Traditional dosing approaches calculate an initial fixed dose based on clinical characteristics including race and ethnicity, followed by frequent physician monitoring. Several genes have been identified that may improve predictions of warfarin effect and metabolism: in particular, variants in the *CYP2C9* and *VKORC1* genes. In 2010, the FDA warfarin label was amended to recommend (but not require) physicians test a patient's genotype when selecting a starting dose (Food and Drug Administration, 2010). Despite scientific validation (International Warfarin Pharmacogenetics Consortium, 2009), US physicians and payers continue to question the cost effectiveness of genetic testing, and its ability to improve clinical outcomes (Carlquist & Anderson, 2011; Ray, 2010; Rosove & Grody, 2009).

Globally, pharmacogenomics' role in warfarin dosing is additionally challenging because of the variable relevance of particular genetic variants depending on a person's ancestry. In the United States, for example, much attention has focused on the CYP2C9*2 allele, which is rare in African populations and most populations from the Americas (Ross et al., 2010). No identified polymorphism of VKORC1—another stalwart of European-derived warfarin dosage guidelines—accounts for significant dose variance in African populations (Suarez-Kurtz & Botton, 2013). Moreover, specific warfarin dosage guidelines based on genotypes prevalent in African populations are lacking (Warnich et al., 2011). Some commentators also raise concerns that industry players could leverage global genomic variation for commercial advantage, further heightening health disparities (Roberts, 2011). AutoGenomics' development of an 'extended' assay provides an early example of this possibility, promoted in the competitive warfarin assay market as the only product that includes certain variants found in Japanese and African American persons (Ray, 2007).

Evidently, even seemingly promising spaces for pharmacogenomics require further work before any likely impact on global health outcomes. Genomic answers to more complex CVD questions appear further removed again. A common path that scientific researchers and others are pursuing to break through this seeming impasse is the use of racial and ethnic categories as a 'weak and imperfect proxy' (Collins, 2004) for genomic variation. Results have been scientifically and ethically dubious.

The slavery hypertension hypothesis, for example, seeks to explain excess hypertension in African Americans as compared with white Americans based on a genetic predisposition to conserve salt, exacerbated by selective pressure during the Atlantic passage due to salt and water depletion (Armelagos, 2005). The theory has been subject to scathing attack from historians and anthropologists, but continues to resonate in the popular media, including a 2007 endorsement by media magnate Oprah Winfrey (Obasogie, 2007). The hypertension community is more divided, with recent editorial comment in the journal *Hypertension* characterizing the hypothesis as 'hard to confirm or refute' (Fuchs, 2011). Yet in racially stratified countries such as the United States, environmental factors appear to provide far more explanatory force regarding CVD disparities. In a now famous study, physicians viewed interviews with hypothetical patients presenting symptoms of chest pain and made recommendations about the patient's care. The race and sex of a patient independently influenced physicians' perceptions of appropriate treatment, with black women significantly less likely to be referred for catheterization than white men (Schulman et al., 1999).

The FDA's 2005 registration of the first racially specific treatment—BiDil®, indicated for heart failure in self-identified African Americans—raises similar concerns. Once again, heart failure presents clear racial disparities, with the mortality rate in African Americans double or triple that in the white population (Yancy et al., 2011), in addition to differences in disease severity, outcomes, and response to therapy (Taylor et al., 2004). Notwithstanding the lack of an apparent genetic reason for such differences, researchers and the FDA accepted self-identified race as a 'useful proxy' for 'genomic and other physiologic characteristics that cause people to differ' (Temple & Stockbridge, 2007). BiDil® was a commercial failure, largely due to readily available generic versions of both of its constituent drugs. By January 2008, the sponsor company, NitroMed, announced that it was dramatically cutting employees and discontinuing marketing activities (Armstrong, 2008). The search for genomic causes of CVD in African Americans continues to receive widespread public funding. For such research to prove beneficial, far greater efforts are needed to transcend flawed racial and ethnic proxies and untangle the operative genomic and environmental causes of disease. This is true both as regards efforts to untangle domestic health disparities—as was the case with BiDil®—and as regards the application of genomics to global health disparities.

Conclusion

This chapter has sought to illustrate the potential role for genomics in future health research and healthcare delivery—in particular through better drug-prescribing decisions, streamlined clinical trials, and a more nuanced understanding of human biology. Undoubtedly, however, carving out a role for genomics in the right to health faces significant barriers. In developed countries—the region that is likely to comprise the bulk of genomic uptake in the near future, evidence of the efficacy of genomic advances, and their potential to add value to existing healthcare practices, must become a far greater component of the implementation pathway. The implications of uptake for health disparities should form a core component of any such analyses. Genomic research continues to generate new ELSI, many of which go beyond the individualistic focus of most research ethics guidelines. Stratification of genomic research based on participant race and ethnicity, for example, may result in racial or ethnic discrimination or stigmatization—a particular concern when the subject of research is socially contentious, as was the case with the New Zealand 'warrior gene' research.

Implementing genomic research and development in developing countries is more challenging still. Most countries face overwhelming health needs, pressing up against financial constraints. In the absence of dedicated external funding, the investments countries make towards genomic advances is money lost to other aspects of healthcare research and delivery. For now, the question raised is whether genomics is 'worth it', or, instead, whether the right to health demands looking to more firmly established social and environmental conditions. This question has no easy answer. Instead, each country or region must consider carefully their own reasons for looking towards genomic advances, and the potential sacrifices that genomic research activities might demand. Emerging economies such as those of Mexico and Thailand, for example, may seize on genomics as a means of building up broader research and development capacities and thereby becoming players in the global R&D enterprise. Tangible benefits are speculative, but by no means fanciful, as demonstrated by Thailand's early progress with developing HIV/AIDS pharmacogenomic testing kits. For countries with the greatest health and financial burdens, genomics—at least in the short term—is likely to play a far more contained role focused on the country's most immediate health problems. This may involve, for example, development of an in-house assay to test HIV drug resistance.

Importantly, however, the rapid rate of scientific progress suggests that in the not-too-distant future, genomics will be an ingrained component of best-practice healthcare. In order to 'future proof' this eventuality, regions and populations must be systematically included in underpinning research. This is of particular import for African populations, which are characterized by widespread genetic diversity and, accordingly, for who genomic advances developed in the context of the United States and Europe are least likely to succeed. Such inclusion demands continued progress on ELSI, including efforts to build up countries' capacity to independently undertake ethics review processes, thereby ensuring cultural sensitivity.

While the bulk of genomics' benefits are yet to be realized, there is a path to judicial, ethical, and contextual implementation of genomic sciences. Fostering a role for genomics in the right to health demands ongoing balancing of genomics' potential as against the immediate trade-offs that pursuing such potential demands, with an emphasis on using genomics to impact on the most immediate health needs. This provides our best chance of attaining a practical, yet forward-looking healthcare research and delivery system.

References

Aceme, N. (2009). Ethical and practical challenges surrounding genetic and genomic research in developing countries. *Acta Tropica*, 112, S21–S31.

Agençe France-Presse. (2006). *Maori slam 'warrior' gene study*. Available at: <http://www.abc.net.au/science/news/health/HealthRepublish_1710435.htm> (accessed 22 April 2012).

Aghokeng, A.F., Mpoudi-Ngole, E., Chia, J.E., *et al.* (2011). High failure rate of viroSeq^{TM} HIV-1 genotyping system for drug resistance testing in Cameroon, a context of broad HIV-1 genetic diversity. *Journal of Clinical Microbiology*, 49, 1635–1641.

Ajay, S., Roshni, V., Megha, M., *et al.* (2008). Adverse effects of antiretroviral treatment. *Indian Journal of Dermatology, Venereology and Leprology*, 74, 234–237.

Armelagos, G.J. (2005). The slavery hypertension hypothesis: natural selection and scientific investigation. *Transforming Anthropology*, 13, 119–124.

Armstrong, D. (2008). *NitroMed halts marketing of drug*. Available at: <http://online.wsj.com/article/SB120044147052292697.html> (accessed 11 July 2012).

Armstrong, K., Micco, E., Carney, A., *et al.* (2005). Racial differences in the use of BRCA1/2 testing among women with a family history of breast or ovarian cancer. *Journal of the American Medical Association*, 293, 1729–1736.

Aspinall, M. and Hamermesh, R. (2007). Realizing the promise of personalized medicine. *Harvard Business Review*, 85, 109–117.

Australian Associated Press. (2006). 'Warrior gene' blamed for Maori violence. *National Nine News*. Available at: <http://news.ninemsn.com.au/article.aspx?id=120718> (accessed 22 April 2012).

Bamshad, M. (2005). Genetic influences on health: does race matter? *Journal of the American Medical Association*, 294, 937–946.

Benatar, S. (2002). Human rights in the biotechnology era 1. *BMC International Health and Human Rights*, 2, 3–8.

Bennett, D.E. (2006). The requirement for surveillance of HIV drug resistance within antiretroviral rollout in the developing world. *Current Opinion in Infectious Diseases*, 19, 607–614.

Boyer, B.B., Dillard, D., Woodahl, E.L., *et al.* (2011). Ethical issues in developing pharmacogenetic research partnerships with American indigenous communities. *Clinical Pharmacology Therapy*, 89, 343–345.

Budnitz, D.S., Shehab, N., Kegler, S.R., *et al.* (2007). Medication use leading to emergency department visits for adverse drug events in older adults. *Annals of Internal Medicine*, 147, 755–765.

Burke, W., Burton, H., Hall, A., *et al.* (2010). Extending the reach of public health genomics: what should be the agenda for public health in an era of genome-based and 'personalized' medicine? *Genetics in Medicine*, 12, 785–791.

Burke, W., Khoury, M.J., Stewart, A., *et al.* (2006). The path from genome-based research to population health: development of an international public health genomics network. *Genetic Medicine*, 8, 451–458.

Burke, W., Tarini, B., Press, N.A., *et al.* (2011). Genetic screening. *Epidemiology Review*, 33, 148–164.

Carlquist, J.F. and Anderson, J.L. (2011). Using pharmacogenetics in real time to guide warfarin initiation—a clinician update. *Circulation*, 124, 2554–2559.

Chantratita, W., Chantarangsu, S., Kiertiburanakul, S., *et al.* (2011). Integrating HIV-1 pharmacogenomics into the universal coverage health- care system in Thailand: from scientific evidence to policy. *Pharmacogenomics & Pharmacoprotemics*, S6, 1–8.

Chokshi, D.A., Thera, M.A., Parker, M., *et al.* (2007). Valid consent for genomic epidemiology in developing countries. *PLoS Med*, 4, e95.

CIOMS and WHO. (2002). *International Ethical Guidelines for Biomedical Human Subjects*, Guideline 4. Council for International Organizations of Medical Sciences (CIOMS): Geneva.

Clarke, H. and Mousa, S.A. (2009). The implications of pharmacogenomics in the treatment of HIV-1-infected patients of African descent. *Pharmacogenomics and Personalized Medicine*, 2, 93–99.

Collins, F.S. (2004). What we do and don't know about 'race', 'ethnicity', genetics and health at the dawn of the genome era. *Nature Genetics*, 36, S13–S15.

Cook, J., Hunter, G., and Vernon, J.A. (2009). The future costs, risks and rewards of drug development: the economics of pharmacogenomics. *PharmacoEconomics*, 27, 355–363.

Council of Europe. (1997). *Convention for the Protection of Human Rights and Dignity of the Human Being with Regard to the Application of Biology and Medicine: Convention on Human Rights and Biomedicine.* Oviedo, 4 April, entered into force 1 December 1999. Available at: <http://conventions.coe.int/Treaty/en/Treaties/Html/164.htm> (accessed 23 October 2012).

Crampton, P. and Parkin, C. (2007). Warrior genes and risk-taking science. *New Zealand Medical Journal*, 120, U2439.

d'Arminio Monforte, A., Lepri, A.C., Rezza, G., *et al.* (2000). Insights into the reasons for discontinuation of the first highly active antiretroviral therapy (HAART) regimen in a cohort of antiretroviral naïve patients. *AIDS*, 14, 499–507.

Davis, J.C., Furstenthal, L., Desai, A.A., *et al.* (2009). The microeconomics of personalized medicine: today's challenge and tomorrow's promise. *Nature Reviews Drug Discovery*, 8, 279–286.

Deverka, P.A., Vernon, J., and McLeod, H.L. (2010). Economic opportunities and challenges for pharmacogenomics. *Annual Review of Pharmacology and Toxicology*, 50, 423–437.

Disability Discrimination Act (1992). (Cth) Amended by the *Disability Discrimination and Other Human Rights Legislation Amendment Act 2009* (Cth). Available at: <http://www.comlaw.gov.au/> (accessed 23 October 2012).

Dodson, M. and Williamson, R. (1999). Indigenous peoples and the morality of the human genome diversity project. *Journal of Medical Ethics*, 25, 204–208.

Dolinoy, D., Weidman, J.R., and Jirtle, R.L. (2007). Epigenetic gene regulation: linking early developmental environment to adult disease. *Reproductive Toxicology*, 23, 297–307.

Emanuel, E., Currie, X., and Herman, A. (2005). Undue inducement in clinical research in developing countries: is it a worry? *Lancet*, 366, 336–340.

Food and Drug Administration. (2010). *COUMADIN® TABLETS (warfarin sodium tablets, USP) crystalline; COUMADIN® FOR INJECTION (warfarin sodium for injection, USP)*. Available at: http://www.accessdata.fda.gov/drugsatfda_docs/label/2010/009218s108lbl.pdf (accessed 12 July 2012).

Food and Drug Administration. (2012). *Label for ziagen (abacavir sulfate)*. Available at: <http://www.accessdata.fda.gov/scripts/cder/drugsatfda/index.cfm?> (accessed 15 March 2012).

Fricke, W.F., Rasko, D.A., and Ravel, J. (2009). The role of genomics in the identification, prediction, and prevention of biological threats. *PLoS Biology*, 7, e1000217.

Fuchs, F.D. (2011). Why do black Americans have higher prevalence of hypertension? An enigma still unsolved. *Hypertension*, 57, 379–380.

Genetic Information Nondiscrimination Act. (2008). Public Law 110-233. 122 Stat. 881.

Gersh, B.J., Sliwa, K., Mayosi, B.M., *et al.* (2010). The epidemic of cardiovascular disease in the developing world: global implications. *European Heart Journal*, 31, 642–648.

Gilks, F., Crowley, S., Ekpini, R., *et al.* (2006). The WHO public-health approach to antiretroviral treatment against HIV in resource-limited settings. *Lancet*, 368, 505–510.

International Warfarin Pharmacogenetics Consortium. (2009). Estimation of the warfarin dose with clinical and pharmacogenetic data. *New England Journal of Medicine*, 360, 753–764.

Ioannidis, J.P. (2010). Expectations, validity, and reality in omics. *Journal of Clinical Epidemiology*, 63, 945–949.

Jagodzinski, L.L., Cooley, J.D., Weber, M., *et al.* (2003). Performance characteristics of human immunodeficiency virus type 1 (HIV-1) genotyping systems in sequence-based analysis of subtypes other than HIV-1 subtype B. *Journal of Clinical Microbiology*, 41, 998–1003.

Jeffords, J.M. and Daschle, T. (2001). Political issues in the genome era. *Science*, 291, 1249–1251.

Jordan, M.R., Bennett, D., Bertagnolio, S., *et al.* (2008). World Health Organization surveys to monitor HIV drug resistance prevention and associated factors in sentinel antiretroviral treatment sites. *Antiviral Therapy (London)*, 13, 15–23.

Juengst, E. (2007). FACE facts: Why human genetics will always provoke bioethics. *Journal of Law, Medicine & Ethics*, 32, 267–275.

Kamal, S.M., Warnich, L., Ferguson, L.R., *et al.* (2011). Forward look: tenth anniversary of the human genome sequence and 21st century post-genomics global health—a close up on Africa and women's health. *Current Pharmagenomics and Personalized Medicine*, 9, 148–155.

Kauf, T.L., Farkouh, R.A., Earnshaw, S.R., *et al.* (2010). Economic efficiency of genetic Screening to inform the use of abacavir sulfate in the treatment of HIV. *PharmacoEconomics*, 28, 1025–1039.

Kazaks, A. and Stern, J. (2004). Diet, physical activity, and behavior, pharmacotherapy of obesity: options and alternatives. In K.G. Hofbauer, U. Keller, and O. Boss (Eds.), *Pharmacology of Obesity*, pp. 387–405. CRC Press: Boca Raton, FL.

Khoury, M., Gwinn, M., Yoon, P.W., *et al.* (2007). The continuum of translation research in genomic medicine: how can we accelerate the appropriate integration of human genome discoveries into health care and disease prevention? *Genetics in Medicine*, 9, 665–674.

Knerr, S., Ramos, E., Nowinski, J., *et al.* (2010). Human difference in the genomic era: facilitating a socially responsible dialogue. *BMC Medical Genomics*, 3, 20.

Knoppers, B.M., Chadwick, R., Wakebe, H., *et al.* (2000). HUGO urges genetic benefit-sharing. *Community Genetics*, 3, 88–92.

Lander, E.S. (2011). Initial impact of the sequencing of the human genome. *Nature*, 470, 187–197.

Lee, S.S. (2005). Racializing drug design: implications of pharmacogenomics for health disparities. *American Journal of Public Health*, 95, 2133–2138.

Lupski, J., Reid, J., Gonzaga-Jaurequi, C., *et al.* (2010). Whole-genome sequencing in a patient with Charcot-Marie-Tooth neuropathy. *New England Journal of Medicine*, 362, 1181–1191.

Mallal, S., Nolan, D., Witt, C., *et al.* (2002). Association between presence of HLA-B*5701, HLA-DR7, and HLA-DQ3 and hypersensitivity to HIV-1 reverse-transcriptase inhibitor abacavir. *Lancet*, 359, 727–732.

Mandava, A., Pace, C., Campbell, B., *et al.* (2012). The quality of informed consent: mapping the landscape. A review of empirical data from developing and developed countries. *Journal of Medical Ethics*, 38, 356–365.

Marsh, V.M., Kamuya, D.K., Parker, M.J., *et al.* (2011). Working with concepts: the role of community in international collaborative biomedical research. *Public Health Ethics*, 4, 26–39.

Marshall, P.A., and Rotimi, C.N. (2001). Ethical challenges in community-based research. *American Journal of Medical Sciences*, 322, 241–245.

Merriman, T. and Cameron, W. (2007). Risk-taking: behind the warrior gene story. *New Zealand Medical Journal*, 120, U2440.

Molyneux, C.S., Peshu, N., and Marsh, K. (2004). Understanding of informed consent in a low-income setting: three case studies from the Kenyan coast. *Social Science and Medicine*, 59, 2547–2559.

Myburgh, R., Hochfeld, W.E., Dodgen, T.M., *et al.* (2012). Cardiovascular pharmacogenetics. *Pharmacology and Therapeutics*, 133, 280–290.

Nolan, D. (2009). HLA-B*5701 screening prior to abacavir prescription: clinical and laboratory aspects. *Critical Reviews in Clinical Laboratory Sciences*, 46, 153–165.

Nolan, D., Gaudieri, S., and Mallal, S. (2003). Pharmacogenetics: a practical role in predicting antiretroviral drug toxicity? *Journal of HIV Therapy*, 8, 36–41.

Obasogie, O.K. (2007, 17 May). Oprah's unhealthy mistake. *Los Angeles Times*. Available at: <http://articles.latimes.com/2007/may/17/opinion/oe-obasogie17> (accessed 10 July 2012).

Pääbo, S. (2001). The human genome and our view of ourselves. *Science*, 291, 1219–1220.

Panel on Antiretroviral Guidelines for Adults and Adolescents. (2012). *Guidelines for the Use of Antiretroviral Agents in HIV-1-Infected Adults and Adolescents*. Office of the AIDS Research Advisory Council: Bethesda, MD.

Pang, T. (2009). Pharmacogenomics and personalized medicine for the developing world—too soon or just-in-time? A personal view from the world health organization. *Current Pharmacogenomics and Personalized Medicine*, 7, 149–157.

Park, W.B., Choe, P.G., Song, K.H., *et al.* (2009). Should HLA-B*5701 screening be performed in every ethnic group before starting abacavir? *Clinical Infectious Diseases*, 48, 365–367.

Pereira, N.L. and Weinshilboum, R.M. (2011). The impact of pharmacogenomics on the management of cardiac disease. *Clinical Pharmacology and Therapeutics*, 90, 493–495.

Phillips, E.J. (2006). Genetic screening to prevent abacavir hypersensitivity reaction: are we there yet? *Clinical Infectious Diseases*, 43, 103–105.

Praparattanapan, J., Tragoolpua, Y., Wongtrakul, J., *et al.* (2011). *Comparisonof In-House HIV-1 Genotypic Drug Resistant Test with Commercial HIV-1 Genotypic Test Kit*. Available at: <http://imsear.hellis.org/handle/123456789/134993> (accessed 26 February 2012).

Ray, T. (2007). *Competition Heats Up in Warfarin Dx Market as New Tests Seek FDA OK*. Genomeweb. Available at: <http://www.genomeweb.com/dxpgx/competition-heats-warfarin-dx-market-new-tests-seek-fda-ok> (accessed 9 July 2012).

Ray, T. (2010). *FDA Updates Warfarin Labeling with PGx-Guided Dosing Ranges*. Genomeweb. Available at: <http://www.genomeweb.com/dxpgx/fda-updates-warfarin-labeling-pgx-guided-dosing-ranges> (accessed 11 July 2012).

Resnik, D.B. (1999). The human genome diversity project: ethical problems and solutions. *Politics and the Life Sciences*, 18, 15–23.

Roberts, D.E. (2011). *Fatal Invention: How Science, Politics, and Big Business Re-Create Race in the Twenty-First Century*. The New Press: New York, NY.

Rogowski, W.H., Grosse, S.D., and Khoury, M.J. (2009). Challenges of translating genetic tests into clinical and public health practice. *Nature Reviews Genetics*, 10, 489–495.

Rosove, M.H. and Grody, W.W. (2009). Should we be applying warfarin pharmacogenetics to clinical practice? No, not now. *Annals of Internal Medicine*, 151, 270–273.

Ross, K.A., Bigham, A.W., Edwards, M., *et al.* (2010). Worldwide allele frequency distribution of four polymorphisms associated with warfarin dose requirements. *Journal of Human Genetics*, 55, 582–589.

Rothstein, M.A. (2005). Expanding the ethical analysis of biobanks. *Journal of Law, Medicine, and Ethics*, 33, 89–101.

Rotimi, C. and Jorde, L. (2010). Ancestry and disease in the age of genomic medicine. *New England Journal of Medicine*, 363, 1551–1558.

Schulman, K.A., Berlin, J.A., Harless, W., *et al.* (1999). The effect of race and sex on physicians' recommendations for cardiac catheterization. *New England Journal of Medicine*, 340, 618–626.

Séguin, B., Hardy, B., Singer, P., *et al.* (2008a). Genomic medicine and developing countries: creating a room of their own. *Nature Reviews Genetics*, 9, 487–493.

Séguin, B., Hardy, B., Singer, P., *et al.* (2008b). Universal health care, genomic medicine and Thailand: investing in today and tomorrow. *Nature Reviews Genetics*, 9, S14–S19.

Séguin, B., Hardy, B., Singer, P., *et al.* (2008c). Genomics, public health and developing countries: the case of the Mexican national institute of genomic medicine (INMEGEN). *Nature Reviews Genetics*, 1, S5–S9.

Shields, A.E., Burke, W., and Levy, D.E. (2008). Differential use of available genetic tests among primary care physicians in the United States: results of a national survey. *Genetics in Medicine*, 10, 404–414.

Skloot, R. (2010). *The Immortal Life of Henrietta Lacks*. Broadway: New York, NY.

Suarez-Kurtz, G. and Botton, M.R. (2013). Pharmacogenomics of warfarin in populations of African descent. *British Journal of Clinical Pharmacology*, 75(2), 334–46.

Subbaraman, R., Chaquturu, S.K., Mayer, K.H., *et al.* (2007). Adverse effects of highly active antiretroviral therapy in developing countries. *Clinical Infectious Diseases*, 45, 1093–1101.

Suther, S. and Kiros, G.E. (2009). Barriers to the use of genetic testing: a study of racial and ethnic disparities. *Genetics in Medicine*, 11, 655–662.

Swede, H., Stone, C.L., and Norwood, A.R. (2007). National population-based biobanks for genetic research. *Genetics in Medicine*, 9, 141–129.

Taylor, A.L., Ziesche, S., Yancy, C., *et al.* (2004). Combination of isosorbide dinitrate and hydralazine in blacks with heart failure. *New England Journal of Medicine*, 351, 2049–2057.

Temple, R. and Stockbridge, N.L. (2007). BiDil for heart failure in black patients: the US Food and Drug Administration perspective. *Annals of Internal Medicine*, 146, 57–62.

Tung, J., Barreiro, L., Johnson, Z., *et al.* (2012). Social environment is associated with gene regulatory variation in the rhesus macaque immune system. *Proceedings of the National Academy of Sciences of the United States of America*, 109, 6490–6495.

UNESCO. (1997). *Universal Declaration of the Human Genome and Human Rights*. Available at: <http://portal.unesco.org/en/ev.php-URL_ID=13177&URL_DO=DO_TOPIC&URL_SECTION=201.html> (accessed 8 April 2011).

WHO. (2009). *Rapid Advice: Antiretroviral Therapy for HIV Infection in Adults and Adolescents*. World Health Organization (WHO): Geneva.

WHO, UNAIDS, and UNICEF. (2011). *Global HIV/AIDS Response: Epidemic Update and Health Sector Progress Towards Universal Access: Progress Report 2011*. World Health Organization (WHO): Geneva.

Warnich, L., Drogemoller, B.I., Pepper, M.S., *et al.* (2011). Pharmacogenomic research in South Africa: lessons learned and future opportunities in the rainbow nation. *Current Pharmacogenomics and Personalized Medicine*, 9, 191–207.

Wendler, D. and Miller, F.G. (2008). Risk-benefit analysis and the net risks test. In E. Emanuel, C. Grady, R. Crouch, *et al.* (Eds.), *The Oxford Textbook of Clinical Research Ethics*, pp. 503–11. Oxford University Press: New York, NY.

Winickoff, D.E. and Winickoff, R.N. (2003). The charitable trust as a model for genomic biobank. *New England Journal of Medicine*, 349, 1180–1184.

Wonkam, A., Muna, W., Ramesar, R., *et al.* (2010). Capacity-building in human genetics for developing countries: initiatives and perspectives in sub-Saharan Africa. *Public Health Genomics*, 13, 492–494.

Yancy, C.W., Wang, T.Y., Ventura, H.O., *et al.* (2011). The coalition to reduce racial and ethnic disparities in cardiovascular disease outcomes (credo). *Journal of the American College of Cardiology*, 57, 245–252.

Zhou, Z., Wagar, N., DeVos, J.R., *et al.* (2011). Optimization of a low cost and broadly sensitive genotyping assay for HIV-1 drug resistance surveillance and monitoring in resource-limited settings. *PLoS One*, 6, e28184.

Chapter 28

Financing governments: towards achieving the right to health

Joia S. Mukherjee

A universal notion

It is possible, and unfortunately common, to construe the right to health narrowly. The Constitution of the World Health Organization (WHO) states that every person is entitled to the 'highest *attainable* standard of health', (emphasis added; WHO, 1946). Yet, the determination of what is attainable, in which country, and for whom is embedded in the model in which the Sovereign state is the primary agent responsible for protecting, respecting, and fulfilling rights with the engagement of civil society in demanding their rights and holding their governments accountable.

Governments exist in an increasingly globalized world and the governments of poor countries cannot be judged as truly 'sovereign', enmeshed as they are in a geopolitical and historical context that has resulted in capital flows from the global South to the global North. This further results in unequal social determinants of health (Bell et al., 2010). Governments in resource-poor settings, without a sufficient tax base and stripped of the ability to profit from government-owned resources became, more than four decades ago, dependent upon loans to support their 'sovereign' States (Moss et al., 2006; Stone, 2004). These loans, most notably made by the World Bank and the International Monetary Fund (IMF), were designed with a strictly neoliberal economic view of development which holds that a healthy private sector with minimal government 'interference' is the best route to development (Marphatia, 2010). After decades of contraction, though, the public sector, while having the major responsibility for fulfilling the right to health, has limited resources to bring to bear towards the realization of the right to health (Gretchen et al., 2012; Pfeiffer, 2003; Pongou et al., 2006). If we view what is attainable against this backdrop, the provision of healthcare by the public sector of the 'sovereign' State alone becomes nearly impossible even if civil society is engaged in demanding their rights. As trade and profit are globalized, the accountability of duty bearers in enabling governments to respect, protect, and fulfil rights must be more explicitly defined.

Yet civil society engagement remains crucial–both with the sovereign State and non-State actors (particularly the international donor community) to deliver on the promise of the universal right to healthcare (Action for Global Health, 2012; Commonwealth Human Rights Initiative, 2011). Encouragingly, even among vulnerable people, these civil society movements have had success in advocating expanded access to health. Advocates of people living with disabilities demanded governmental change to make buildings accessible, and to end discrimination in hiring and education (Bagenstos, 2009). In many countries with newer constitutions, that right to health has been ratified in the form of constitutional embodiment. In countries such as Brazil and India, civil society movements have used cases of exclusion and suboptimal care to bring about legal action for fulfilling the right to health (Dasgupta, 2011; Fleury, 2011). In an increasingly globalized world, it is necessary for civil society to engage with the international community as well as government if the right to health is to be assured (Limwattananon et al., 2012).

The necessary interplay between civil society and government, with increased responsibility for all duty bearers, must work towards the realization of the right to health, which is judged not relative to the country in which one lives but rather is based on the accessibility of a standard package of the goods and services delivered with adequate quality to achieve health in the broadest sense. Over the past 15 years, scholars, activists, and governments have promoted internationally agreed upon goals that, when achieved, would mark progressive realization of the right to health. Work is being undertaken to quantitate the inputs needed to achieve these goals, including defining the role of nation-States themselves and other duty bearers in financing needed inputs, and how such a framework would be governed (Friedman & Gostin, 2012; Gostin, 2012). This chapter will examine the history of the right to health as it was framed within the International Covenant on Economic, Social and Cultural Rights (ICESCR) and the aspirations that followed the covenant, and how limiting public financing created a lack of a rights-based agenda for health. The chapter will also present the new paradigm of the 21st century for measuring the progressive realization of rights, and provide a powerful example of how civil society, governments, and other duty bearers have worked together to address one of the most pressing public health challenges of our time: HIV/AIDS.

The Alma-Ata Declaration versus the World Bank

The universality of human rights is a concept articulated in the Universal Declaration of Human Rights (UDHR), prompted in 1948 by the international moral outrage that followed the Holocaust—a State-orchestrated, systematic violation of the rights of specific ethnic and religious groups of people. Yet it took more than a decade for these concepts to be codified in the form of treaties—the ICESCR and the International Covenant on Civil and Political Rights (ICCPR). The Covenants and subsequent treaties have set up a two-pronged approach to human rights:

- Duty bearers (largely governments) are charged with respecting, protecting, and fulfiling rights.
- Civil society is responsible for participating in the process of the progressive realization of rights through demanding rights and holding governments accountable.

To establish the right to health it is critical to articulate the package of goods and services to be delivered. In 1978, the first International Conference on Primary Health Care was held in Alma-Ata, Kazakhstan, and was attended by health ministers and experts from 137 countries. They produced the Declaration of Alma-Ata (WHO & UNICEF, 1978), which advocated health as a right within a wider movement for social and economic rights including the right to food, potable water, and basic sanitation (Bryant & Richmond, 2008). The standards against which the attainment of rights would be measured included: 90% of children should have weight for age that corresponds to reference values; every family should be within a 15-minute walk of potable water; and women should have access to medically trained attendants for childbirth. There was unanimous agreement at Alma-Ata that these goals could not be achieved or sustained by the world's poorest governments without holding duty bearers outside of the sovereign State responsible for helping to finance these rights. Sadly, the proposed right to universal basic healthcare was attacked by international experts as naïve, too expensive, and not 'sustainable', and was rapidly replaced by the rubric of selective primary care, which was a much more limited package of preventive interventions, not rights based but rather driven by the cost constraints of individual country budgets (Walsh & Warren, 1979). However, the roots of the impoverished country budgets have historically been given little attention in formulating a movement for the right to health agenda.

First, we must address the historical underpinnings of the public sector in some of the world's impoverished countries. Countries such as Angola and Ghana, rich in natural resources, were plundered by northern empires. Any infrastructure that was developed sought to maximize the extraction of resources. Subjugates to this system had no right to the rich profits of their labour. In the 1960s and 1970s, many African nations were engaged in struggles against colonial powers for liberation. Not surprisingly, the cornerstone of many of these grassroots movements was the promise of social and economic rights—including to health and education (MacQueen, 1997). Subsequently, the end of colonialism worsened capital flight from African countries (Ndikumana & Boyce, 2008), leaving newly formed governments without the ability to collect tax, thus making the distribution of wealth towards social welfare impossible. Seeking other means to control their wealth, some post-colonial countries in Africa, Asia, and Latin America attempted to nationalize resources. Nationalization, however, was often met by military force from the global North. Most attempts to nationalize resources failed, leaving governments without revenue (De Witte, 2001; Doran, 2011).

The backdrop for these struggles was the Cold War and, in this setting, a dichotomous relationship between the free market and the public sector was imposed. The rhetoric, which promotes investments in the private sector as a more viable strategy for development as compared to investments in the public sector, continues today (Cutler & Gruber, 2012; Hill, 2010). While most developed countries have forms of social and economic rights or social protections—ranging from free education to healthcare to social security insurance—poor countries have not had sufficient capital to provide these basic rights to their citizens. By the mid-1970s, most developing nations, in the absence of a source of revenue to actualize the promise of a better life for their citizens, turned to the World Bank and the IMF for capital.

Loans from the World Bank were awarded under terms of 'structural adjustment', which tied loans to decreased public sector spending (sometimes called fiscal belt tightening), and to opening of markets through liberalization of trade barriers for Western goods (OECD, 2005). Structural adjustment programmes were justified under neoliberal, economic theory—also known as conservative macro-economic policy—which was promoted by international financial institutions starting in the 1970s, when demand from newly independent African countries was met by an increased supply of capital flows into international financial institutions from Organization of the Petroleum Exporting Countries (OPEC) profits. The predicted economic benefit that opening markets through trade liberalization and the privatization of State resources and services would have on economic development was bolstered by the fear of 'Dutch disease', a phenomenon of decline in manufacturing seen in Holland after a boom in revenues from gas reserves flowed into the public coffers (The Dutch Disease, 1977). Within a short time, many countries with little or no internal sources of revenue were set to default on their loans. The first crisis in loan repayment occurred in 1982, when Mexico informed the United States that it would not be able to service its debt, unilaterally announced a 90-day moratorium on making payments, and requested to renegotiate payment periods and new loans in order to fulfil its prior obligations (Burns et al., 2006). The 'rescue package' put forward by the United States ushered in structural adjustment programmes, which demanded significant reductions and spending caps in the public sector in favour of market solutions. Dependent upon loans tied to these principles, poor countries were able to spend very little on health owing to caps on spending. While developed nations spend 10% or more of their sizeable gross domestic product (GDP) on health, many of the poorest countries' health expenditures amount to as little as 2.5% of GDP (Pfeiffer, 2003). With little public sector spending on health, national expenditures are largely out of pocket and often catastrophic spending, resulting in poor outcomes and impoverishment for the most vulnerable (Smith-Spangler et al., 2012).

The health budgets of the poorest countries in the world suffered severely under these policies imposed on them by the World Bank and the IMF (Navarro, 2001). Without adequate public money to fund health, the Bamako Initiative of 1987 (Kanji, 1989) proposed supporting health programmes through user fees. The combination of constrained public budgets and the inability of the world's poor to afford user fees resulted in moribund health systems. By 2007, fully 35 years after Alma-Ata and decades of structural adjustments and failed cost recovery schemes having taken their toll, nearly 1.3 billion people worldwide lacked access to healthcare (ActionAid, 2007).

Fortunately, in the decade before the new millennium, there was an increasing realization in the development community that economic development was leaving many behind. In 2000, the United Nations (UN) hosted its 189 Member-States for the Millennium Summit, during which the various challenges facing the world were broadly addressed, including poverty, environmental threats, and human rights abuses and violations. From this Summit, the Millennium Development Goals (MDGs) were drafted and unanimously approved by UN Member-States (UN General Assembly, 2000). The eight MDGs address the major facets of development. Although the goals are not synonymous with the right to health (targets such as reducing maternal death by two-thirds mean many women are still excluded from access to health), their achievement could serve as a yardstick for the progressive realization of the right to health. The health-related MDGs include MDG 4 (regarding child health), MDG 5 (regarding women's reproductive health), and MDG 6 (regarding HIV, tuberculosis (TB), and malaria), are often referred to collectively as the health-related MDGs. Of the health-related MDGs, only MDG 6 has a clear stream of funding that helps both governments and civil society in meeting the goal of reducing morbidity and mortality from HIV, TB, and malaria. Moreover, the particular multilateral stream of funding created—the Global Fund to Fight AIDS, TB and Malaria (Global Fund), (which will be discussed later in this chapter)—made achieving MDG 6 possible for even some of the world's poorest countries (Barros et al., 2012). In contrast, the achievement of MDG 5—which seeks to reduce maternal mortality and increase access to reproductive health services for women—is lagging far behind MDG 6. This is largely because access to emergency obstetrical care (particularly blood, antibiotics, and Caesarean section) has been considered too expensive or complicated to include in government health plans in poor countries (UNICEF, 2010). To achieve the MDGs, which would surely decrease global inequality, it is estimated that health spending would need to reach US$60 per capita (World Bank, 2012). Yet, hampered by inadequate external and internal financing for health, as well as a lack of the coordination of health financing directed towards reducing disparities (Victora et al., 2003), as of 2010, only eight sub-Saharan African countries are on track to achieve the health-related MDGs. Most are achieving less than 50% of the gains that would be required to reach the goals by 2015, with progress on MDG 5 (maternal health) being particularly slow.

Financing the realization of the right to health

It is widely recognized that there are at least three critical pieces in the healthcare financing puzzle for resource-poor settings. First is that governments must increase the share of GDP that is spent on health. Beginning in 2000, increased calls for donor funding of HIV treatment and to achieve the MDGs resulted in a healthy dialogue about what countries themselves should commit to health, as well as reiterating calls for donor nations to commit 0.7% of overseas development assistance to health. In 2001, the same year as the UN General Assembly Special Session on AIDS, African heads of State met in Abuja, Nigeria, and pledged to spend at least 15% of their GDP to improve the health sector. At that time, African Union countries on average spent US$10 per capita on health, ranging from US$0.38 to US$380 per capita (WHO, 2012a; Zere et al., 2010).

Twenty-seven countries have increased the proportion of total government expenditures allocated to health since 2001. Only Rwanda and South Africa have achieved the Abuja Declaration target of 'at least 15%', and in the poorest countries the median level of real government spending on health from domestic resources has only increased from US$10 to US$14 per capita over the last decade. Seven countries actually reduced their relative government expenditures on health during the period (Kirigia et al., 2006).

To reach the Abuja Declaration targets is a complicated task. First, countries must commit to increasing the share of GDP that is allocated for health. Creating political will towards achieving universal health coverage is not a monolithic task. Civil society movements have been instrumental in some countries (e.g. Brazil, South Africa, Spain, Thailand) in demanding this increased government financing (People's Health Movement, 2012). In other countries, such as Rwanda, political will is less connected with civil society movements and more aligned with government agendas.

Reversing the tide: lessons from the AIDS movement

Discovered in 1981, AIDS spread rapidly around the globe (Mukherjee et al., 2003). The now 30-year epidemic has claimed tens of millions of lives, disproportionately among the poor on the African continent (Vella et al., 2012). In 1996, the advent of successful HIV treatment with antiretroviral therapy (ART) turned a universally fatal disease into one that was manageable but chronic and resulted in a 90% reduction of mortality among people on ART (Hammer et al., 1997; Palella et al., 1998). However, treatment was costly—initially US$10,000 per person per year. Thus, as recently as 2002, experts argued that HIV treatment in Africa and other resource-poor settings was not feasible. An honest assessment of the global situation at that time showed that access to life-saving treatment, even in the setting of epidemic disease, was not considered a right, but rather was decided by the market. The de facto criterion for receiving ART was the ability to pay. However, unlike any other disease in history, the HIV epidemic spurred an effective social movement marked by solidarity between the global North and South and grassroots engagement in the acceleration and distribution of scientific discoveries. Activists argued that to address the greatest health crisis in the past 500 years, a human rights-versus market-based approach was the only realistic strategy for an epidemic that is concentrated in poor and marginalized communities that have neither access to healthcare nor the ability to pay for treatment. The struggle for access to HIV treatment has achieved remarkable gains in realizing health as a right.

The roots of the AIDS movement sprang from activism against discrimination and evolved into the equitable distribution of ART. As the HIV epidemic reached unprecedented infection rates in the mid-1990s, ACT-UP and the Treatment Action Group (TAG) began advocating the US Food and Drug Administration (FDA) speed up development of new HIV therapies. Years of research and advocacy efforts paid off and new antiretroviral drugs were introduced in 1995, after which TAG members adjusted their efforts and began pushing pharmaceutical companies to conduct research on the effects of these new drugs. While ACT-UP and TAG allies were successfully pushing pharmaceutical companies to develop new and better HIV treatment, innovations in care remained inaccessible to HIV-infected individuals living in developing countries.

However, without access to the antiretroviral treatment that was becoming readily available in rich countries, the poor were continuing to suffer and die without access to medicines. In response, in the late 1990s, people living with AIDS and civil rights activists began pressuring pharmaceutical companies, scientists, clinicians, public health institutions, and government agencies to deliver treatment and care to the millions of HIV-positive people living in resource-poor countries. The principles that the disproportionate burden of AIDS on the poor merited special effort to achieve broader social equity and that such effort should be led by communities affected by the disease were unique factors in the call for treatment access. The essence of the movement depended upon life stories such as those of Ryan White, a young HIV-positive boy from the United States who highlighted profound discrimination towards people living with AIDS, and Zackie Achmat from South Africa who refused to take ART until his government committed to providing the therapy to all regardless of ability to pay. Enlisting more than 16,000 members, the South African-based Treatment Action Campaign (TAC) deployed strategies of 'treatment literacy' and 'community health advocacy', incorporating grassroots education into the science of HIV treatment. In addition, this group of civil society activists worked to hold the government accountable to the right to healthcare as it related to HIV treatment. In 2001, the TAC filed a lawsuit in South Africa's Constitutional Court on behalf of pregnant South African HIV-positive women who did not have access to ART to prevent transmission of the virus to their children. The TAC ultimately won the lawsuit when the court held that the government had in its responsibility to guarantee access to healthcare services. The Court ordered the government to take a series of steps aimed at ensuring access to comprehensive services to prevent mother-to-child transmission of HIV (Kapczynski & Berger, 2007).

Transnational momentum for treatment access continued to grow, and resulted in the formation of the Health Global Access Project (Health GAP). Today the successes achieved by TAG, ACT-UP, and Health GAP—just three of many civil society partners—are lauded within the global health community for their efforts, resulting in increased access to treatment for people living with HIV/AIDS by removing barriers to care. The success of this movement has been multifaceted, from engagement with the international community and duty bearers towards the creation a new global funding mechanism for HIV treatment, to rights-based arguments with the private sector over patents and sharing the fruits of scientific advancement. In addition, much of the money awarded for HIV treatment went to governments for programmes delivered free of charge within the public sector, in some cases far exceeding public sector spending caps imposed by international financial institutions. Although many struggles remain to maintain and expand funding for health as a right, the HIV treatment access movement has resulted in at least 6.6 million people in low- and middle-income countries receiving ART (WHO, 2012b).

The AIDS advocacy movement can serve as an example for the modern era as it stands as an important example of how deep and lasting transnational solidarity in civil society—applying strategic pressure on international duty bearers, governments, and the private sector—was successful in expanding a rights-based version of health in the face of a pandemic infectious disease. Civil society engagement and North–South solidarity produced remarkable achievements, including dramatic reductions in the price of ART, the development of large-scale funding, and the near universal provision of ART free of charge.

The movement successfully challenged neoliberal economic policy which historically restrained the amount of international aid poor countries could spend in the public sector. A major policy achievement of the AIDS movement was to argue that countries heavily affected by HIV must invest in treatment if they were ever to become 'self-sufficient'. Thus an international emergency response was created that exempted AIDS expenditure from fiscal space constraints. Breaking structural barriers on AIDS financing opened the door to develop a social strategy to deliver upon universal access. Activists lobbied rich governments to share responsibility for the health of all people living with HIV/AIDS. Under tremendous pressure, the donor governments pledged unprecedented support to the global AIDS fight, culminating in the creation of the Global Fund to Fight AIDS, Tuberculosis and Malaria (Global Fund)—the first large-scale, multilateral funding stream to assist governments in fulfilling the right to health. Before the Global Fund, a government's ability to respect, protect, and fulfil the right to healthcare was severely constrained by the domestic budget of the country. The international community's commitment to funding governments to deliver large-scale treatment access marks a new paradigm in a shared responsibility for realizing human rights.

The Global Fund, the world's largest financing institution for health, distributes its resources in such a way that deliberately harnesses the impact-potential of this powerful pairing of public and civil society sectors. As a result of the successful advocacy of the aforementioned organizations as well as several other non-governmental organizations (NGOs), plus deep political commitment from the United States and many other wealthy countries, the Global Fund was founded in 2002. It was the first funding entity to require that grants be submitted from a coalition of members from civil society, government entities, and the private sector, thus ensuring a rights-based approach to programmes approved by the Global Fund.

In 2007, the Global Fund's board voted to endorse 'dual-track financing' as its preferred composition for grant recipients. The approach calls for two equal 'principal recipients'—one a governmental implementer and the other an NGO—to submit a collaborative proposal for funding. The intentional pairing of public and civil society recipients offers a threefold advantage: faster use of grant funds for provision of care; increased sustainably through capacity-building of weaker sectors; and improved reach of service delivery to all populations, especially the most vulnerable (Global Fund, 2008). By setting dual-track financing as the standard approach to funding, the Global Fund recognizes the value of coordination between governments and NGOs to strengthen health systems by complementing each sector's advantages. Governments offer the unity of standardized national protocols and the capacity to bring programmes to scale; by contrast, local grassroots organizations ensure that target populations included marginalized patients and communities frequently neglected by public initiatives. Together, the principal recipients' combined efforts better assure health measures that are equitable, effective, and accountable to its citizens and patients.

Unfortunately, the Global Fund, for all its promise, has had significant financial and management challenges. In 2011, corruption and fraud involving more than US$34 million dollars by recipient countries led to the suspension of support by major European donors (Center for Strategic and International Studies, 2012). Round 11 of the Global Fund was cancelled, and no new monies were dispersed. Yet, millions of people depend on continued international financing for the treatment of HIV as well as for the expansion of services for tuberculosis and malaria. Efforts are currently underway to improve the management and leadership of the Global Fund. These changes are not only critical for survival of the Global Fund but also for what it represents: large-scale multilateral funding, committed by duty bearers, towards the progressive realization of the right health.

From AIDS to health system strengthening

The global AIDS movement catalysed 'global health' as a field distinct from 'international health' (and 'tropical medicine') and added delivery of curative care and longitudinal treatment to a public health agenda weighted in favour of health promotion and disease prevention. This was no zero-sum game. Anthony Fauci, Director of the US National Institute of Allergy and Infectious Diseases (NIAID), argues that global attention on AIDS reinvigorated support for fighting ancient killers such as malaria and TB (Fauci, 1999). New transnational funding mechanisms invested billions of US dollars in efforts to combat leading infectious killers and promote human health around the globe. Yet to address other major killers—non-communicable diseases such as cardiovascular disease and cancer—as well as the significant burdens placed on populations by chronic diseases such as mental illness and diabetes will take more funding and a robust infrastructure that can provide primary, secondary, and tertiary care.

The long-awaited availability of money for HIV prevention, care, and treatment in resource-poor settings laid bare the ravages of decades of wilful neglect of public infrastructure for health. Inadequate personnel, equipment, medicines, and physical infrastructure were never able to adequately address the basic primary healthcare needs of the population, let alone address HIV, a chronic infectious disease that fuelled the TB pandemic and an explosion in the number of orphaned children. Lack of infrastructure and materials with which to care for the sick and woefully inadequate compensation for their labour has led to trained health professionals fleeing areas with the greatest disease burden. Developing countries bear 90% of the global burden of disease armed with only 20% of the world's GDP and 12% of the world's health expenditures to combat this burden (Gottret & Schieber, 2006). Africa is particularly hard-hit, bearing fully one-quarter of the world's disease burden with 3% of the global health workforce, whose pay represents less than 1% of global health expenditures (WHO, 2006). With such paltry resources available in these settings, how do people get care? The short answer is that they do not. For this and many other reasons, life expectancy in Lesotho is 47 years (compared to 77 years in Cuba); in Haiti, 185 children per 1,000 die before their fifth birthday (compared to eight per 1,000 in the United States); and in Burundi 800 women die in childbirth for every 100,000 live births (as compared with four in Sweden) (WHO, 2012b). These rates are not unique across the continent.

While the success of the AIDS movement has catalysed innovative financing and increased investments in health, more must be done to assure the right to health for all. From the Paris Declaration on Aid Effectiveness (Paris Declaration on Aid Effectiveness, 2005) of 2005 to the recent Framework Convention on Global Health (Gostin, 2012), there is increasing momentum of a call for shared responsibility towards the right to health. However, real change must be radical in scope if it is to address health in its broadest construction and attend to the massively unequal social determinants. A fair accounting of the roots of inequality would necessitate a fair response. Many social commentators argue that the world's wealthiest nations and corporations have enriched themselves by impoverishing others through extraction of resources, labour, and the flight of untaxed capital to safe havens. Some systematic form of redistribution and governance (Ottersen et al., 2011) is therefore needed to achieve the right to health that is not dependent on politics or charity but rather on a globalized notion of justice and rights being the responsibility of all.

To this end, there are several novel solutions that have been proposed by those who seek to institutionalize a fair share of funding towards public goods of global importance such as healthcare and climate change remediation. In 2010, US Representative Peter Stark introduced the Investing in Our Future Act of 2010 (H.R.5783) to raise revenue for global health and climate change needs via a 0.005% levy on all foreign currency exchange transactions by large-scale traders (Redman, 2010). While the bill has yet to gain steam in the US Congress, there is an increasing global call for the so called 'Robin Hood' tax, which similarly advocates a tax on currency trading as a means to alleviating global poverty (Greenhouse & Bowley, 2011). Importantly, recent calls for the tax from advocates ranging from nurses in Chicago to Occupy Wall Street protesters link the economic plight of those in Europe and the United States with the poor in the global South (Suhr & Foley, 2012). This trend of transnational solidarity appears to be growing in strength and has included people from all parts of the economic spectrum (Stewart, 2011).

Conclusion

Revitalizing the public health infrastructure and improving the delivery of essentials such as vaccination, sanitation, and clean water, are critical aspects to addressing the social injustice that underlies disease, but treatment for endemic and epidemic diseases must also be made available.

Governments must take responsibility for the health of their people by setting rational, stable, and rights-based policies that guarantee healthcare for every citizen, but especially the most poor and vulnerable. Honouring their Abuja Declaration commitments (WHO, 2012a) would demonstrate bilateral responsibility. But, in an increasingly globalized world, the responsibility for realizing the right to health must not rest with the governments of the world's poorest countries alone, it is only with large-scale and ongoing international solidarity that poor governments will be able to address the right to health in a sustained way.

Civil society must have a continued and expanded voice. In this era of advanced technology, a broad-based international movement is growing. Advocacy to redress the violations of the basic right to health must recognize that more money is needed for health both now and for decades to come, and that calls for restrictions on government health spending, privatization, and market reforms serve to worsen inequality in healthcare and perpetuate social injustice. International financial institutions must grant further debt relief and reconsider the recommendations to use a market-driven framework for delivering healthcare to the world's poorest people. The AIDS movement and the movement for debt relief are among the first to try to reverse decades of progressive impoverishment of the public sector but more must be done.

References

Action for Global Health. (2012). *Civil society call to action on universal health coverage*. Available at: <http://www.actionforglobalhealth.eu/fileadmin/AfGH_Intranet/AFGH/Publications/UHC/UHC_Call_to_Action_eng2.pdf> (accessed 20 September 2012).

ActionAid. (2007). *Changing IMF Policies to Get More Doctors, Nurses and Teachers Hired in Developing Countries*. ActionAid: Washington, DC. Available at: <http://www.ifiwatchnet.org/sites/ifiwatchnet.org/files/4-pager%20—%20IMF%20and%20health.pdf> (accessed on 30 April 2009).

Bagenstos, S. (2009). *Law and the Contradictions of the Disability Rights Movement*. Yale University Press: New Haven, CT.

Barros, A.J.D., Ronsmans, C., Axelson, H., *et al.* (2012). Equity in maternal, newborn, and child health interventions in Countdown to 2015: a retrospective review of survey data from 54 countries. *Lancet*, 379, 1225–1233.

Bell, R., Taylor, S., and Marmot, M. (2010). Global health governance: commission on social determinants of health and the imperative for change. *Journal of Law, Medicine & Ethics*, 38(3), 470–485.

Bryant, J.H. and Richmond, J.B. (2008). Alma-Ata and primary health care: an evolving story. In H. Kris (Ed.), *International Encyclopedia of Public Health*, 152–174. Elsevier: Oxford.

Burns, K.D., Paluzzi, J.E., and Mukherjee, J.S. (2006). Poverty, health and human rights – time for action. *American Medical Student Association, Global Pulse*, 2(1), 40–45.

Center for Strategic and International Studies. (2012). *Righting the Global Fund*. <http://csis.org/files/publication/120227_Morrison_RightingGlobalFund_Web.pdf> (accessed 21 September 2012).

Commonwealth Human Rights Initiative. (2011). Civil society and national human rights institutions. *International Journal of Not-for-Profit Law*, 13(4).

Cutler, D.M. and Gruber, J. (2012). The affordable care act is constitutional. *Annals of Internal Medicine*, 156(9), 660–663.

Dasgupta, J. (2011). Ten years of negotiating rights around maternal health in Uttar Pradesh, India. *BMC International Health and Human Rights*, 11(3), S4.

De Witte, L. (2001). *The Assassination of Lumumba*. Verso: New York, NY.

Doran, M.S. (2011). The heirs of Nasser: who will benefit from the Second Arab revolution? *Foreign Affairs*, May/June.

The Dutch Disease (1977, 26 November). *The Economist*, pp. 82–83.

Fauci, A.S. (1999). The AIDS epidemic—considerations for the 21st century. *New England Journal of Medicine*, 341, 1046–1050.

Fleury, S. (2011). Brazil's health-care reform: social movements and civil society. *Lancet*, 21, 377(9779), 1724–1725.

Friedman, E.A. and Gostin, L.O. (2012). Pillars for progress on the right to health: harnessing the potential of human rights through a Framework Convention on Global Health. *Health and Human Rights*, 14(1), E4–E19.

Global Fund. (2008). *Civil Society Success on the Ground: Community Systems Strengthening and Dual Track Financing – Nine Illustrative Case Studies*. Report produced by The Global Fund to Fight AIDS, Tuberculosis, and Malaria & International HIV/AIDS Alliance. Global Fund: Washington, DC.

Gostin, L.O. (2012). A framework convention on global health: health for all, justice for all. *Journal of the American Medical Association*, 307(19), 2087–2092.

Gottret, P. and Schieber, G. (2006). *Health Financing Revisited: A Practitioner's Guide*. World Bank: Washington, DC. Available at: <http://siteresources.worldbank.org/INTHSD/Resources/topics/Health-Financing/HFRFull.pdf> (accessed 5 October 2012).

Greenhouse, S. and Bowley, G. (2011, 6 December). Tiny tax on financial trades gains advocates. *The New York Times*. Available at: <http://www.nytimes.com/2011/12/07/business/global/micro-tax-on-financial-trades-gains-advocates.html?pagewanted=all> (accessed 31 May 2012).

Gretchen, A., Stevens, G.A., Finucane, M.M., *et al.* (2012). Trends in mild, moderate, and severe stunting and underweight, and progress towards MDG 1 in 141 developing countries: a systematic analysis of population representative data. *Lancet*, 380(9844), 824–834.

Hammer, S.D., Squires, K.H., Hughes, M.D., *et al.* (1997). A controlled trial of two nucleoside analogues plus indinavir in persons with human immunodeficiency virus infection and cd4 cell counts of 200 per cubic millimeter or less. *New England Journal of Medicine*, 337, 725–733.

Hill, S. (2010). *Europe's Promise: Why the European Way Is the Best Hope in an Insecure Age*. University of California Press: Berkeley, CA.

Kanji, N. (1989). Charging for drugs in Africa: UNICEF's 'Bamako Initiative'. *Health Policy and Planning*, 4(2), 110–120.

Kapczynski, A. and Berger, J.M. (2007). *The Story of the TAC Case: The Potential and Limits of Socio-Economic Rights Litigation in South Africa*. Available at: <http://www.law.berkeley.edu/php-programs/faculty/facultyPubsPDF.php?facID=7238&pubID=2>.

Kirigia, J.M., Preker, A., Carrin, G., *et al.* (2006). An overview of health financing patterns and the way forward in the WHO African Region. *East African Medical Journal*, 83(9 Suppl), S1–S28.

Limwattananon, S., Tangcharoensathien, V., Tisayaticom, K., *et al.* (2012). Why has the Universal Coverage Scheme in Thailand achieved a pro-poor public subsidy for health care? *BMC Public Health*, 12 (suppl 1), S6.

MacQueen, N. (1997). *The Decolonization of Portuguese Africa: Metropolitan Revolution and the Dissolution of Empire*. Longman: London.

Marphatia, A.A. (2010). The adverse effects of International Monetary Fund programs on the health and education workforce. *International Journal of Health Services*, 40(1), 165–178.

Moss, T., Pettersson, G., and van de Walle, N. (2006). *An Aid-Institutions Paradox? A Review Essay on Aid Dependency and State Building in Sub-Saharan Africa*. Center for Global Development. Working Paper 74. Available at: <http://www.cgdev.org/content/publications/detail/5646/> (accessed 7 October 2012).

Mukherjee, J.S., Farmer, P.E., Niyizonkiza, D. (2003). Tackling HIV in resource poor countries. *British Medical Journal*, 327(7423), 1104–1106.

Navarro, V. (Ed.). (2001). *The Political Economy of Social Inequalities: Consequences for Health and the Quality of Life*. Baywood: Amityville, NY.

Ndikumana, L. and Boyce, J.K. (2008). *New Estimates of Capital Flight from Sub-Saharan African Countries: Linkages with External Borrowing and Policy Options*. Working Paper 166. Political Economy Research Institute, University of Massachusetts: Amherst, MA.

OECD. (2005). *Trade and Structural Adjustment, 2005*. Organization for Economic Cooperation and Development (OECD): Paris. Available at: <http://www.oecd.org/general/34753254.pdf> (accessed 17 September 2012).

Ottersen, O.P, Frenk, J., and Horton, R. (2011). University of Oslo Commission on Global Governance for Health, in collaboration with the Harvard Global Health Institute. *Lancet*, 378(9803), 1612–1613.

Palella, F.J., Delaney, K.M., Moorman, A.C., *et al.* (1998). Declining morbidity and mortality among patients with advanced human immunodeficiency virus infection. *New England Journal of Medicine*, 338(13), 853–860.

Paris Declaration on Aid Effectiveness. (2005). *Ownership, Harmonisation, Alignment, Results and Mutual Accountability*. Organization for Economic Cooperation and Development: Paris.

People's Health Movement. (2012). *The Cape Town Call to Action*. Available at: <http://www.phmovement.org/en/node/6537> (accessed 20 September 2012).

Pfeiffer, J. (2003). International NGOs and primary health care in Mozambique: the need for a new model of collaboration. *Social Science & Medicine*, 56(4), 725–738.

Pongou, R., Salomon, P.J., and Ezzati, M. (2006). Health impacts of macroeconomic crises and policies: determinants of variation in childhood malnutrition trends in Cameroon. *International Journal of Epidemiology*, 35(3), 648–656.

Redman, J. (2010). *Factsheet: Investing in Our Future Act of 2010 (H.R. 5783)—Using a Currency Transaction Levy to Raise Resources to Address Global Health and Climate Change in Developing Countries*. Available at: <http://www.ips-dc.org/articles/factsheet_investing_in_our_future_act_of_2010_hr_5783> (accessed 31 May 2012).

Smith-Spangler, C.M., Bhattacharya, J., and Goldhaber-Fiebert, J.D. (2012). Diabetes, its treatment, and catastrophic medical spending in 35 developing countries. *Diabetes Care*, 35(2), 319–326.

Stewart, H. (2011, 13 April). Robin Hood tax: 1000 economists urge G20 to accept Tobin tax: G20 finance ministers urged by experts from 53 countries to tax City speculators to help the world's poor. *The Guardian*. Available at: <http://www.guardian.co.uk/business/2011/apr/13/robin-hood-tax-economists-letter> (accessed 31 May 2012).

Stone, R.W. (2004). The political economy of IMF lending in Africa. *American Political Science Review*, 98(4), 577–591.

Suhr, J. and Foley, R.J. (2012, 18 May). Protesters in Chicago call for 'Robin Hood' tax. Nurses and thousands of other marchers demand a 'Robin Hood' tax on financial transactions. More protests are expected ahead of a NATO summit in Chicago. *Associated Press*.

UN General Assembly. (2000). *United Nations Millennium Declaration*. United Nations (UN) General Assembly: Geneva. Available at: <http://www.un.org/millennium/declaration/ares552e.pdf> (accessed 30 May 2012).

UNICEF. (2010). *Progress for Children: Advancing the MDGs with Equity*. United Nations Children's Fund (UNICEF): New York, NY. Available at: <http://www.unicef.org/publications/files/Progress_for_Children-No.9_EN_081710.pdf> (accessed 29 May 2012).

Vella, S., Schwartländer, B., Sow, S.P., *et al.* (2012). The history of antiretroviral therapy and of its implementation in resource-limited areas of the world. *AIDS*, 26(10), 1231–1241.

Victora, C.G., Wagstaff, A., Schellenberg, J.A., *et al.* (2003). Applying an equity lens to child health and mortality: more of the same is not enough. *Lancet*, 362, 233–241.

Walsh, J.A. and Warren, K.S. (1979). Selective primary health care: an interim strategy for disease control in developing countries. *New England Journal of Med*icine, 301(18), 967–974.

WHO. (1946). *Constitution of the World Health Association*. World Health Organization (WHO): Geneva. Available at: <http://www.who.int/governance/eb/constitution/en/> (accessed 29 May 2012).

WHO. (2006). *The World Health Report 2006: Working Together for Health*. World Health Organization (WHO): Geneva. Available at: <http://www.who.int/whr/2006/whr06_en.pdf> (accessed 5 October 2012).

WHO. (2012a). *The Abuja Declaration: 10 Years On*. World Health Organization (WHO): Geneva. Available at: <http://www.who.int/healthsystems/publications/Abuja10.pdf> (accessed 15 September 2012).

WHO. (2012b). *World Health Statistics Report, 2012*. Available at: <http://www.who.int/gho/publications/world_health_statistics/EN_WHS2012_Part1.pdf> (accessed, 7 October 2012).

WHO and UNICEF. (1978). *Primary Health Care. Report of the International Conference on Primary Health Care; 1978 September 6–12; Alma-Ata, USSR*. World Health Organization (WHO): Geneva.

World Bank. (2012). *The Costs of Attaining the Millennium Development Goals*. World Bank: Washington, DC. Available at: <http://www.worldbank.org/html/extdr/mdgassessment.pdf> (accessed 29 May 2012).

Zere, E., Walker, O., Kirigia, J., *et al*. (2010). Health financing in Malawi: evidence from National Health Accounts. *BMC International Health & Human Rights*, 10, 27. doi:10.1186/1472-698X-10-27.

Section 4

Conclusion

Chapter 29

The consequences of failure

Anand Grover, Brian Citro, and Mihir Mankad

Introduction

Countless hours, hundreds of billions of US dollars, and untold amounts of energy have been devoted to solving the world's myriad health problems. As can be seen from the varied perspectives that fill this book, the topic has generated great debate. There is, however, something of a universal baseline concerning the primary goals of the enterprise agreed upon by most involved: health systems should promote good health outcomes for all, they must be equitable and sustainable, and they should respect certain individual freedoms. Nevertheless, the development of such systems has been elusive, and there is a growing recognition that persistent failures to effectively address global health problems result in millions of preventable deaths annually. Communicable diseases such as HIV and tuberculosis (TB) continue to be leading causes of death in the world; commonly treatable illnesses, including diarrhoeal and lower respiratory infections, are leading causes of death in low-income countries; life-saving drugs are unavailable or unaffordable to millions who are in desperate need of them; and health systems across the world suffer from inadequate funding or inefficient allocation of resources.

As this book demonstrates, the health and human rights movement has developed substantially since its emergence in the late 20th century. Jonathan Mann, a pioneer in the global effort to combat HIV/AIDS, was among the first health leaders to recognize and note the interconnectedness of human rights and health. Prior to his contributions, health was discussed only at the margins of human rights. Dr Mann reoriented the discussion and articulated three fundamental ways in which health and human rights are related (Mann et al., 1999):

- First, and perhaps most importantly, he recognized that health is indeed a human rights issue—that health policies, programmes, and practices impact (negatively and positively) on human rights.
- Second, he recognized that many human rights issues are also health issues. That is, human rights violations and infringements on human dignity often result in poor health outcomes. According to Dr Mann, this causal relationship is essential to understanding the social factors that contribute to poor health and to successfully addressing global health concerns.
- Finally, he recognized that promotion and protection of human rights and promotion and protection of health are fundamentally linked. Dr Mann's work thus ushered in an era of global health governance wherein States, international organizations, and civil society recognize that health and human rights are inextricably linked.

The international right to health, established in Article 12 of the International Covenant on Economic, Social and Cultural Rights (ICESCR) and developed in General Comment 14 of the Committee on Economic, Social and Cultural Rights (CESCR), provides a framework through which to operationalize the linkages between health and human rights. The right to health framework includes a variety of conceptual and operational components that articulate and develop these linkages in greater detail. The right to health approach, in turn, operationalizes this framework and establishes a comprehensive approach grounded in law and founded upon normative human rights principles. The approach is well suited to address many of the current deficits and emerging problems in global health, compensating for shortcomings of traditional biomedical and public health approaches.

Most critically, the right to health approach: prioritizes the needs of vulnerable or marginalized groups; recognizes the role of underlying social, economic, and cultural determinants of health; protects personal freedoms and negative liberties; demands responsive, equitable, culturally appropriate, and sustainable health systems; and requires the active and informed participation of individuals and communities in all decisions affecting their health. Each of these aspects of the right establishes concomitant obligations on States undergirded by the normative imperative to respect human dignity and personal autonomy. Respect for dignity and autonomy requires States to: treat people as subjects rather than objects under the law; refrain from interfering in the intimate, emotional spheres wherein health-related decisions are made; and abstain from enacting laws or policies that increase physical or mental health risks for individuals or communities, instead taking positive steps to promote their health.

The right to health is articulated at the international and regional levels and is explicitly recognized in the constitutions of 115 countries (OHCHR, 2008). In several other countries, the right is recognized through legislation or judicial interpretation. The right to health, however, is far from being fully realized even in these jurisdictions. In each instance, only particular components are recognized and implemented and the right to health approach has not fully taken root. Even in countries where the right to health is explicitly recognized in the constitution, it often remains legally inoperable in practice and individuals and communities are unable to utilize the law to protect and fulfil the right. Moreover, in the absence of an operable right to health, people lack a comprehensive legal and normative framework with which to fully apprehend the varied and interrelated factors that affect their health, including underlying social, economic, and cultural determinants. In countries where the right to health is legally operable, however, individuals and communities have utilized the law to achieve significant advances in, among other things, access to health facilities, goods, and services. This has especially been the case in critical areas of health, including communicable diseases and access to medicines, where biomedical and public health approaches have failed to consistently secure desired outcomes.

The consequences of the failure to realize the right to health are, therefore, dire for the millions of people who lack access to basic health facilities, goods, and services. Vulnerable or marginalized groups across the world are most at risk in this regard and will be the most adversely affected by the failure to realize the right. Traditional biomedical and public health approaches have failed to prioritize their needs and to adequately address underlying social, economic, and cultural determinants of health. In developing countries, full realization of the right to health will ensure the development of responsive, effective, culturally appropriate, and sustainable health systems that prioritize the needs of vulnerable or marginalized groups and acknowledge the central role of the underlying social, economic, and cultural determinants of health. In wealthy countries, full realization of the right to health will ensure achievements in the promotion of positive health outcomes are protected and more equitably distributed across populations, as substantial inequalities exist between different groups within these countries.

This chapter will examine four essential aspects of the right to health: (1) the right as a legal entitlement in domestic law, (2) the prioritization of the needs of vulnerable or marginalized groups,

(3) the protection of personal freedoms and negative liberties, (4) and the participation of affected individuals and communities in all decisions affecting their health. Current deficits and emerging problems in global health will be considered in light of these four aspects of the right to health. The right to health approach, it will be demonstrated, provides not only the conceptual and legal tools, but also the flexibility and breadth required to address these multifaceted challenges. Specific attention will also be paid to the differences between the right to health approach and traditional biomedical and public health approaches in order to identify and clarify the consequences of the failure to realize the right to health.

Four central aspects of the right to health: addressing current deficits and emerging problems in global health

The consequences of the failure to realize the right to health are most evident in light of current deficits and emerging problems in global health analysed through the lens of the right to health. We will discuss four aspects of the right to health, and the right to health approach, that directly address current deficits and emerging global health problems. Among other things, the failure to realize the right to health amounts to a failure to adequately address these deficits and emerging problems as well as a failure to fulfil the normative imperative of the human rights regime more broadly.

Recognition of the right to health as a legal entitlement in domestic law

The right to health is a legal entitlement with positive and negative dimensions that establishes corresponding legal obligations for both State and non-State actors. At the international level, as mentioned earlier, the right is established by Article 12 of ICESCR and most fully elaborated in General Comment 14 (CESCR, 2000). In order for the right to health to be fully realized, however, it must be recognized in domestic law. Domestic recognition operationalizes the right and supports implementation of the right to health approach and is, therefore, a threshold concern. Inclusion of the right to health in the constitution in the form of a justiciable fundamental right is the highest form of domestic recognition.

Several reasons exist for the need to recognize the right to health in domestic law. First, there is a normative imperative to recognize the right to health as a legal entitlement in order to ensure respect for human dignity and personal autonomy in matters related to health. Second, domestic instantiation of the right to health is necessary to secure the legal mechanisms through which individuals and groups may directly affect changes in health laws and policies and to ensure governments formulate and implement appropriate policies at the outset. Third, domestic instantiation of the right to health in law is critical to guaranteeing sustainable resources and adequate financing for health at the national level.

In countries where the right to health is explicitly recognized in the constitution or has been judicially interpreted under constitutional principles such as the right to life, significant advances have been made towards realization of the right to health under the law, through legislation, and through administrative regulations and institutional arrangements. In these jurisdictions, a supportive constitutional environment allows individuals and groups to use the courts and legislature to obtain protections under the right to health and to realize positive dimensions of the right.

For example, the Indian government, driven to action by public interest litigation based on the right to health and through an ongoing dialogue with civil society and affected communities (*Sankalp Rehabilitation Trust & Anr.* v. *UOI & Ors*, 1999), scaled-up access to free, first-line antiretroviral treatment for HIV in India, which is now universal, and has begun to provide access to free second-line antiretroviral treatment under court order. In Kenya, the High Court ruled that sections of the country's Anti-Counterfeit Act must not be applied to generic medicines because these provisions would severely limit access to affordable and essential medicines in violation of the right to health in the Constitution of Kenya (High Court of Kenya, 2009).

The right to health in the Constitution of Brazil has been incorporated into the nation's Organic Law on Health, which is explicitly directed towards promoting, protecting, and ensuring the right to health (Brazil, 1990). Also in Brazil, in accordance with the constitutional right to health, the National Health Surveillance Agency has what is in effect a right of first review of patent applications and the power to supersede determinations of the patent authority in cases that are critical for public health purposes or otherwise implicate the right to health (Brazil, 1996). The Mental Health Act of Ghana, informed by explicit recognition of the right to health in the Constitution of Ghana, protects the right to non-discrimination, the right to information, and the right to participation of people living with mental illness (Government of Ghana, 2012). Argentina has enacted administrative guidelines for the examination of pharmaceutical patents from a public health perspective in order to ensure access to affordable medicines in the country in fulfilment of the right to health, which is protected through the right to life in the Constitution of Argentina (Ministry of Industry, Ministry of Health, National Industrial Property Institute, 2012).

The right to health, however, is either not recognized or is legally inoperable in a number of countries. This lacuna impedes the ability of individuals and groups to hold States accountable for the realization of their right to health. The needs of vulnerable or marginalized groups, who are often politically powerless, frequently go unmet when laws and policies affecting their health are unsupported by a constitutionally enshrined right to health. Without such explicit protection, legislation that aims to ensure basic protections for health, regulate the private health sector, or develop public health systems may lack a secure constitutional basis. The legal battle in the United States over the Patient Protection and Affordable Care Act of 2010 (Affordable Care Act) is one manifestation of this deficit.

Although the stated purpose of the Affordable Care Act is to 'provide affordable, quality [healthcare] for all Americans and reduce the growth in [healthcare] spending' (US Congress, 2009), the constitutional basis for the legislation is the commerce clause of the US Constitution, which grants the US Congress the power to regulate interstate commerce (United States Constitution, 1787). The stated purpose of the Affordable Care Act is thus not supported directly by the text of the US Constitution, as neither the right to health nor any other health-related rights are recognized therein. Though the legislation seeks to address critical deficits in the American health system—approximately 50 million people in the United States do not have health insurance (DeNavas-Walt, 2010)—this lack of recognition left the Affordable Care Act open to legal challenges on the grounds that it was an overextension of the US Congress's power to regulate. Although the US Supreme Court upheld the Affordable Care Act's constitutionality in June 2012, recognition of the right to health as a fundamental right in the US Constitution, provided the law a firm constitutional basis, shielding it from existential legal challenges on alternative constitutional grounds.

Funding for health systems and interventions that are not based on obligations under a constitutionally protected right to health are dependent upon political conditions, the market, international donor assistance, and the goodwill of private charitable organizations. Under the right to health, however, States have a duty to adequately finance health through budget prioritization, sustainable funding, and equitable resource allocation. The right to health also requires that special attention be paid to vulnerable or marginalized groups in this regard, including the poor and high-risk groups, such as people who use drugs, men who have sex with men, and prisoners and detainees. The challenge of ensuring adequate and sustainable funding for health has received greater attention as a result of the global financial crisis. Many low- and middle-income countries have become dependent upon international donor funding and now face an emerging crisis; these governments must account for acute shortfalls in funding for health as a result of a decrease in or withdrawal of bilateral and multilateral donor funding following the global financial crisis.

For instance, Burundi and Mozambique receive 100% and 68% of their TB resources from the Global Fund to Fight AIDS, Tuberculosis and Malaria (Global Fund), respectively (Slutsker, 2012). As a result of the cancellation of Round 11 of the Global Fund, approximately 63,000 TB patients in both countries are at risk of losing access to life-saving treatment (Slutsker, 2012). Vietnam faces similar challenges. The US government, through the US President's Emergency Plan for AIDS Relief (PEPFAR), provides funds for approximately 88% of Vietnam's HIV prevention and control efforts (PEPFAR, 2011). The United States, however, has proposed to cut PEPFAR funding for fiscal year 2013 by US$562.9 million, or 12.3% (amfAR, 2012). This is likely to result in a substantial decrease in funding for Vietnam. Moreover, Vietnam may soon experience additional cuts in funding from other donors, such as the Global Fund and the UK's Department for International Development, as a result of the country's transition from low- to a middle-income status (Martinez, 2008). These cuts will have a grave impact on the country's HIV prevention and control efforts unless the Vietnamese government prioritizes domestic funding for the HIV epidemic.

Ensuring adequate, sustainable, and equitable funding for health at the domestic level does not obviate the need for international assistance, as many countries simply lack sufficient funds in absolute terms to adequately finance a robust health sector. However, in countries where the right to health is a justiciable right recognized in law, the State has a duty to ensure adequate, sustainable, and equitable funding for health regardless of the financial constraints faced by the country. A fundamental right to health provides a firm basis in law with which to challenge low levels of public funding for health—including cuts in funding for publicly financed health facilities, goods, and services—and to ensure the needs of vulnerable or marginalized groups are prioritized in financing for health.

Prioritization of the needs of vulnerable or marginalized groups

The right to health requires that special attention be given to vulnerable or marginalized groups in national health systems through, among other things, targeted health interventions. Vulnerable or marginalized groups are those that may be socially, economically, or physically disadvantaged, such as the poor, children, older persons, women, persons with disabilities, ethnic minorities, sexual minorities, indigenous populations, assigned castes, and persons living with communicable diseases, including HIV and TB. The needs of these groups must be prioritized in order to ensure equitable access to quality health facilities, goods, and services for all. Vulnerable or marginalized groups must also be made a specific focus of health assessments at the national and global levels through the use of disaggregated epidemiological data and community-based research. In the absence of these data, the health concerns of these groups may go unobserved and thus unaddressed, particularly in countries where great social, economic, and cultural disparities exist. The failure to realize the right to health will result in the continued failure to prioritize the needs of vulnerable or marginalized groups throughout the world.

Many health systems are deficient in addressing the needs of vulnerable or marginalized groups. Primary healthcare—defined as essential and preventative healthcare universally accessible in the community at a cost the community can afford (WHO, 1978)—is critical to realizing the right to health for vulnerable or marginalized groups and ensuring more equitable distribution of positive health outcomes (Starfield et al., 2005). Lack of access to preventative and primary care services exacerbates and perpetuates the health problems faced by vulnerable or marginalized groups, including exposure to communicable diseases and high rates of maternal and infant mortality. Health sector development in many developing countries, however, has focused overwhelmingly on specialized secondary and tertiary care at the expense of preventative and primary care (De Maeseneer & Flinkenflögel, 2010). In these countries, public funding for secondary and tertiary care far outweighs spending on preventative and primary care, resulting in an inefficient allocation of public resources between primary, secondary, and tertiary care.

Privatization has also played a central role in shifting resources away from preventative and primary care and towards secondary and tertiary care sectors. Privatization facilitates the growth of highly specialized healthcare infrastructure because these sectors cater to and are supported by those who are able to pay for expensive diagnostic and treatment services. While quality secondary and tertiary care are essential components of a comprehensive health system, universally accessible, affordable primary healthcare is of principal importance to achieving positive health outcomes for all. This is particularly critical for vulnerable and marginalized groups who are often unable to afford specialized secondary and tertiary care. Moreover, when primary healthcare services are unavailable or inaccessible, secondary care, including emergency hospital care, becomes the first point of contact for many patients in the health system. This increases the total costs of the system and renders some otherwise preventable morbidities untreatable due to the late stage at which they are diagnosed.

In many developing countries, out-of-pocket expenditures on healthcare account for the large majority of health spending. Out-of-pocket expenditures, including informal, under-the-table payments or bribes made to health workers, disproportionately impact the poor who must pay considerably larger percentages of their income on healthcare than wealthy patients must pay for the same health services. For instance, in India it is estimated that more than 75% of all health spending is paid privately (Balarajan et al., 2011). As a result, it is unsurprising that expenditures on health are responsible for forcing more than half of the households in India into poverty each year (Balarajan et al., 2011). Under the right to health, health systems must account for the financial constraints of the poor and other vulnerable or marginalized groups in order to prioritize their needs through appropriate health financing arrangements. Pre-payment schemes, including progressively funded health insurance programmes and progressive taxation, may insulate the poor from catastrophic health expenditures and promote equitable access to health facilities, goods, and services (McIntyre, 2010). Moreover, under these schemes the poorest should be completely exempt from contributions in most cases. A failure to implement such programmes is likely to result in the continued lack of access to even basic health facilities, goods, and services for the poor and other vulnerable or marginalized groups.

In order to effectively address the needs of vulnerable or marginalized groups, the health risks and underlying social, economic, and cultural determinants of these groups must first be identified. The use of community-based research methods and disaggregated epidemiological data is critical in this regard. This is especially important in countries where positive health outcomes in the general population may conceal disparities between subgroups. Community-based research stresses a collaborative process and entails research with, rather than on, communities; it prioritizes the social, economic, and cultural context alongside health risk factors; it utilizes and affirms the value of communities' experiential knowledge; and it affords researchers access to closed or otherwise difficult to access communities (Leung et al., 2004). Community-based research thus holds great promise for the study of vulnerable and marginalized groups, by identifying their health risks and reaching these communities through targeted health interventions. Epidemiological data, disaggregated by indicators such as age, sex, ethnicity, race, income, education, sexual orientation, and religion, is essential to identifying, understanding, and addressing the health risks and underlying social, economic, and cultural determinants affecting vulnerable or marginalized groups (WHO, 2011). Community-based research and the collection and analysis of disaggregated epidemiological data are thus critical components of a health system that prioritizes the needs of vulnerable or marginalized groups.

Even in wealthy countries, many vulnerable or marginalized groups continue to experience consistently worse health outcomes than the rest of the population. The Roma, which comprise Europe's largest ethnic minority community, live shorter lives on average than non-Roma Europeans (Ringold et al., 2005) and experience significantly higher rates of infant mortality than the general population in some countries (UNICEF, 2011). They also experience reduced access to health facilities, goods, and services due to structural discrimination, exclusion from national health insurance schemes, and physical isolation (Council of Europe, 2012). In the United States, millions of migrant workers have considerably worse health than the general population (Holmes, 2006). Most migrant workers in the United States are agricultural workers, which is one of the most dangerous occupations in the country. As a result, migrant workers face serious occupational health risks due to unhygienic working conditions and occupational hazards, including exposure to pesticides and accidents. Moreover, only 5% to 10% of migrant agricultural workers have health insurance (Holmes, 2006), they experience much higher rates of TB (NCFH, 2009a), and their children experience higher rates of malnutrition (NCFH, 2009b) and are less likely to be immunized than other children in the United States (North Carolina Farmworker Institute, 2007). The right to health approach directly addresses this current deficit by calling on Europe and the United States to prioritize the needs of these groups in their health systems through, among other things, enacting targeted health interventions. Failure to realize the right to health is likely to result in the continued neglect of the Roma in Europe and migrant workers in the United States.

Transgendered and transsexual (trans) persons are a particularly vulnerable and marginalized community across the world. The increased recognition and developing social acceptance of trans persons, the recent acknowledgement of gender identity disorder by the mental health community, and technical advancements in the medical sciences have highlighted the emerging problems faced by this community. Among other challenges, trans persons face significant difficulties in accessing health goods and services, are at high risk for mental illness, and struggle to achieve recognition of their gender-reassignment under the law. These emerging problems are particularly acute in the developing world, where sexual minorities are highly stigmatized and face structural discrimination throughout society. In some developing countries, health services for trans persons, such as sex reassignment surgery and hormone replacement therapy, are completely unavailable or prohibitively expensive. In wealthy countries, these treatments are also very costly and may not be covered under private or public health insurance plans.

Trans persons face increased risks of mental illness as a result of stigmatization and discrimination. It is estimated that one in ten trans persons have difficulties with mental illness (Wylie et al., 2007). For trans persons suffering from gender identity disorder, withdrawing or withholding sex reassignment therapy often results in serious health complications, including anxiety, depression, suicidal ideation, and self-induced genital mutilation (APA, 2000). In many countries, including the United States, however, trans prisoners are routinely denied access to sex-reassignment therapy (Lee, 2008). Trans persons also suffer from a lack of recognition of their gender-reassignment under law, which negatively impacts on their dignity and results in significant administrative difficulties relating to marriage, employment, and other civic and social activities.

Under the right to health approach, trans persons are recognized as both vulnerable and marginalized as a group and their needs must therefore be prioritized. The impact of the underlying social, economic, and cultural determinants of their health, including stigmatization and discrimination, must also be further examined. The right to health approach provides a strong normative imperative against discrimination of any kind. The principle of non-discrimination is instrumental to increasing access to health goods and services for trans persons and to recognition of gender-reassignment under law. The failure to realize the right to health will contribute to the continuing stigmatization and discrimination of trans persons and their increased risk of poor physical and mental health.

Protection of freedoms and negative liberties

The right to health requires duty-bearers, including State and non-State actors, to respect certain individual freedoms and negative liberties. Negative liberties under the right to health include the following:

- The right to make health-related decisions free from State interference.
- The right to be free from medical experimentation and non-consensual testing and treatment.
- The right to privacy and confidentiality in health-related matters and information.
- The right to informed consent.

These freedoms are integral to human dignity and personal autonomy and there is thus a strong normative imperative not to infringe upon them. For instance, it has long been universally accepted that States are categorically prohibited from engaging in forced medical treatment of any kind, including forced sterilization and abortion. In fact, a central component of the foundation of the international human rights regime stems directly from the consensus that non-consensual treatment and medical experimentation transgress international norms (UN General Assembly, 1950).

Respect for freedoms under the right to health is also essential to the effectiveness and sustainability of health systems and interventions. Effectiveness and sustainability depends heavily upon the active and informed participation of affected individuals and communities, which is only possible if their participation is voluntary and based on principles of informed consent. Moreover, if we take a multidimensional view of what constitutes 'health' to include its emotional components and everyday functioning in social roles and activities, it is clear that respect for human dignity and personal autonomy is integral to the promotion of public health and achieving desired health outcomes (Ruger, 2006). Health systems and interventions that do not respect freedoms under the right to health infringe upon the dignity and autonomy of their participants and negatively impact on the social and emotional dimensions of their health. Systems and interventions that take a largely consequentialist approach and focus myopically on group health outcomes (understood narrowly) may thus actually lower the overall health of the group.

The protection of freedoms and negative liberties has been demonstrated to result in more sustainable public health interventions. For example, in the early days of the HIV epidemic, due to widespread fear and panic amongst policymakers and healthcare professionals, many public health interventions included non-consensual testing for HIV (Eisenstat, 1991). This approach was driven by a misunderstanding of the prevention and transmission of HIV and the fact that the communities primarily affected were otherwise vulnerable or marginalized populations, including men who have sex with men, sex workers, and injecting drug users. The social marginalization of these groups fuelled the practice of non-consensual testing. The history of successful HIV interventions, however, has confirmed the importance and centrality of informed consent in ensuring the willing participation of affected communities.

While top-down approaches to prevention of sexually transmitted infections (STIs) may work for short periods of time, more sustainable health interventions result from the active and informed participation of the community. For this, affected communities must play a central role in the formulation and implementation of health interventions, which is only possible through the informed consent of each individual. Community-based and -directed prevention programmes, such as the Sonagachi project in Kolkata, India, have resulted in substantially lower STI rates and have continued their success over longer periods of time (Dasgupta, 2011). In this project, as in other community-based and community-directed health interventions, wilful and informed community participation coupled with stakeholder buy-in and heightened awareness has generated self-sustaining health interventions as well as increased access to vulnerable groups whom public health workers might not otherwise reach (CASAM, 2008).

Informed consent is internationally recognized as a necessary prerequisite to medical testing and treatment in nearly all circumstances. Nevertheless, the right to informed consent has frequently been marginalized, diluted, or completely disregarded in health interventions based on the misguided notion that acquiring consent interferes with the expediency and efficacy of the intervention (Malloy, 1998). This is mistaken from both a public health and a human rights perspective and represents another current deficit in global health. Although most health interventions do respect the right to informed consent, the right to health approach prioritizes the right to informed consent and other freedoms, recognizing them as non-derogable rights central to human dignity and personal autonomy. Failing to adopt the right to health approach presents the risk of a descent into a predominantly consequentialist approach to public health that prioritizes narrow views of health and health outcomes of the group over the rights of individuals.

The threat posed by this current deficit in biomedical and public health approaches is most acute with respect to vulnerable or marginalized groups, and perhaps most conspicuous in the case of treatment for drug use. Around the world, people who use drugs are often compulsorily detained and subjected to non-consensual treatment in drug treatment facilities. This is particularly common in Asia (WHO, 2009). Treatment in these facilities is in most cases non-evidence-based or experimental, and those detained are often not drug dependent but rather have been detained only for drug use, which in and of itself is not a condition requiring treatment (WHO, 2009). Such programmes infringe upon the right to informed consent, the right to be free from medical experimentation and non-consensual testing and treatment, and in some cases may amount to cruel, inhuman, and degrading punishment. Moreover, in the large majority of cases, treatment in such facilities is ineffective in treating drug dependence and preventing drug use. For example, in Vietnam from 80% to 97% of people detained in compulsory drug treatment facilities returned to using drugs upon their release (Human Rights Watch, 2011).

In another example, it has been reported that during the last decade, the government of Uzbekistan has undertaken a covert campaign of non-consensual, compulsory sterilization of women (Open Society Foundation, 2011; World Organization Against Torture and Rapid Response Group, 2007). In some cases, women were not told that they were sterilized, and only discovered the fact after attempting pregnancy again or experiencing pain following childbirth. One of the purported rationales for this campaign underscores the core problem with consequentialist approaches to public health: the government is said to have implemented the programme in part to lower maternal and infant mortality rates in the country (BBC, 2012). The health intervention may ostensibly be successful on purely consequentialist grounds, based on the fact alone that fewer women would be physically capable of becoming pregnant. The right to health approach, in contrast, requires respect for women's right to make decisions concerning their sexual and reproductive health free from State interference. Forced sterilization is a gross violation of the right to be free from non-consensual treatment and it infringes upon the dignity and autonomy of women. In addition, forced sterilization and other non-consensual treatments result in poor health outcomes under a balanced, comprehensive understanding of women's health, which takes into account mental and emotional health and the ability to function in social roles and activities, including motherhood.

Non-consensual clinical trials for medicines and medical products by pharmaceutical companies represent one of a number of emerging global health problems that implicate negative liberties (Abadie, 2010). This problem is particularly critical in the developing world, which has increasingly become the site of clinical trials, as the costs of conducting trials in the developed world have increased tremendously over the past few decades (Glickman et al., 2009). Developing States often have weaker regulatory regimes, which may include less stringent medical testing regulations, such as those related to informed consent. Many States simply lack the technical and material capacity to monitor all necessary aspects of clinical trials and may suffer from weak governance in general and a lack of effective accountability mechanisms. In some cases, States may benefit financially from the operation of pharmaceutical companies within their borders which can discourage them from regulating clinical trials.

Some pharmaceutical companies have exploited these circumstances in order to lower costs associated with clinical trials and to avoid accountability for harm caused to participants, who often comprise poor or otherwise vulnerable communities. As a result, some of these trials have caused unnecessary and avoidable deaths and illnesses (Annas, 2009). Under the right to health approach, clinical trials must be conducted with the informed consent of each participant and States must ensure effective regulatory and accountability mechanisms are in place related to pharmaceuticals testing.

Active and informed participation

The right to health requires the active and informed participation of individuals and communities in all decisions affecting their health at all levels of governance. Participation is closely linked to fundamental principles of democratic governance and respect for personal autonomy and human dignity. Unlike under traditional biomedical and public health approaches, participation during all stages of health-related decision-making is a normative imperative under the right to health approach. Individuals and communities must therefore be allowed to participate fully in the formulation, implementation, monitoring, and evaluation of all policies and interventions that affect their health. Active and informed participation is further instrumental to ensuring health systems and interventions are responsive, effective, culturally appropriate, and sustainable.

Numerous international health-related instruments, including the World Health Organization (WHO) Constitution, the Declaration of Alma-Ata, the Ottawa Charter, and the Jakarta Declaration, recognize the centrality of individual participation in improving global health. However, many health systems and interventions continue to take a predominantly top-down approach, wherein health-related decisions are made with minimal input from affected individuals and communities. These health systems and interventions infringe upon the right of affected individuals and communities to participate in the formulation, implementation, monitoring, and evaluation of health policies and interventions and they neglect to incorporate the unique experiential knowledge of these communities. Moreover, individuals and communities are marginalized and disempowered when they are excluded from playing an active role in shaping health policies that impact their lives.

Health systems and interventions that do not incorporate the active and informed participation of affected individuals and communities are less likely to be effective and sustainable than community-based and -directed interventions. Community participation builds trust between decision-makers and affected communities and promotes culturally appropriate policies, which are key to formulating responsive and sustainable interventions. When communities participate fully in the formulation, implementation, monitoring, and evaluation of health policies and interventions, decision-makers are granted access to the community's unique experiential knowledge concerning its health and the underlying social, economic, and cultural determinants. In many cases, the bulk of this knowledge would otherwise be inaccessible to authorities and researchers if not for the cooperation of the community. Integration of this knowledge into the formulation and implementation of health policies and interventions improves health outcomes because it ensures policies and interventions respond to the specific needs of the community. As subjects of interventions, communities are also best situated to monitor and evaluate the effectiveness of health interventions and provide feedback needed to refine health policies.

As mentioned earlier, top-down interventions that fail to involve the active and informed participation of the affected communities represent another current deficit in global health. For example, interventions such as government-led condom distribution programmes have been effective in the short term, but have generally been unsustainable in the long term. This is due in part to the fact that the communities targeted by the interventions were not fully integrated into the formulation and implementation of the programmes. After the initial phases of these interventions, the community was unprepared or unwilling to take ownership of the programme due to the failure of decision-makers to incorporate their active and informed participation from the beginning.

In contrast, the Sonagachi project in Kolkata, India, described earlier, provides a model for community-directed health interventions. The project trained and educated sex workers in Kolkata's red light district on the prevention of STIs and condom use in an effort to prevent the transmission of STIs, including HIV (Dasgupta, 2011). Although the project began as a traditional public health intervention, it soon transformed into a community-directed project administered by sex workers themselves. It was further expanded to include literacy training for sex workers and child care for their children. As a result, not only were STI rates lowered significantly in the short term, low rates have been maintained and sex workers continue to administer the project (Dasgupta, 2011). Condom usage has also increased substantially, indicating the enhanced bargaining power of sex workers with their clients and the empowerment of the community generally.

In Nepal, a community-based health intervention aimed at strengthening the capacity of rural women's groups in matters related to maternal and antenatal healthcare successfully lowered maternal mortality rates, though it was not the primary objective of the intervention. The intervention succeeded by educating women on basic maternal and antenatal healthcare techniques so the women themselves were capable of administering certain aspects of maternal and antenatal care within their own communities. The intervention also resulted in heightened awareness of issues surrounding maternal health amongst participants, increased health-seeking behaviour amongst pregnant women, and improved hygiene in the case of home delivery (Manandhar et al., 2004).

Grassroots movements in the global effort to combat HIV/AIDS, including those led by the Treatment Action Campaign (TAC) in South Africa, have long advocated greater community participation in health-related decision-making and the development of community-based approaches to public health. The TAC has achieved substantial improvements in health outcomes for people living with HIV in South Africa through community-based activism and strategic litigation based on the right to health. For instance, pursuant to a legal challenge brought by the TAC, the Constitutional Court of South Africa held that the right to health in the Constitution of South Africa required the government to provide all public hospitals and clinics with nevirapine, an antiretroviral drug used to prevent mother-to-child transmission of HIV, and to develop a comprehensive policy to reduce perinatal transmission in the country (*Minister of Health* v. *Treatment Action Campaign*, 2002). Following the decision, the TAC continued to apply community-led pressure on the government of South Africa to ensure the Court's order was fully implemented (Heywood, 2009). The grassroots movement led by the TAC in South Africa exemplifies the achievements of community-directed health campaigns that have made use of the right to health approach.

While in some instances the active and informed participation of affected communities has been central to effective health interventions, many communities continue to be excluded from critical health-related decision-making processes. The lack of transparency and participation of affected communities in the negotiations surrounding free trade agreements and other bilateral and multilateral treaties is a significant emerging problem in this regard. To date, most governments have done very little to incorporate the participation of affected communities into these processes. Some governments have instead taken the position that the participation of groups outside the government-commissioned negotiation blocks would hinder rather than enhance negotiations. However, many of these agreements will greatly impact on the health of local communities through the introduction of domestic laws that, in effect, would restrict access to health goods and services. Therefore, it is essential that the active and informed participation of affected communities be integrated into treaty negotiation processes.

Several free trade agreements, including the Trans-Pacific Partnership Agreement (TPPA) and the European Union–India Free Trade Agreement (EU–India FTA), include provisions that, if implemented, could negatively impact on public health (UNAIDS/UNDP, 2012). For example, the TPPA and EU–India FTA require Member-States to strengthen intellectual property rights and lower standards for patenting medicines under domestic law. These laws would make it more difficult for generic drug producers to enter domestic pharmaceutical markets, which could severely restrict access to affordable medicines by limiting the availability of cheaper generic drugs. As a result, millions of people in India and other negotiating States, including Peru and Vietnam, would be unable to afford life-saving medicines. Civil society and community groups have repeatedly raised these concerns, but they have not been given a formal opportunity to provide input into the negotiating processes. Under these circumstances, agreements made at the international level, such as the TPPA and the EU–India FTA, that substantially impact on the health of millions of people may be completed without consultation with affected communities. The right to health approach provides a tool with which affected communities may demand a seat at the negotiation table when trade agreements threaten to impact on their health.

Conclusion

Current deficits in global health result in the poor health and unnecessary deaths of millions of people across the world. Emerging problems threaten to exacerbate this situation and pose significant challenges to traditional biomedical and public health approaches. Many of the world's health systems are currently in crisis. These systems are underfunded and they consistently fail to address the needs of vulnerable or marginalized groups, generating and perpetuating substantial disparities in health outcomes between countries and between groups within countries. Within these systems, the formulation and implementation of health policies and interventions do not adequately incorporate the active and informed participation of affected individuals and communities, infringing upon fundamental democratic principles and failing to utilize their experiential knowledge. Freedoms and negative liberties under the right to health, including the right to informed consent, are also inadequately protected in many instances. In order to address these persistent deficits and to tackle emerging health problems, current approaches to global health must be reformulated in line with the right to health.

The right to health approach is strongest where traditional approaches are weakest. The approach provides for a legal entitlement with both positive and negative dimensions, through which individuals and communities may demand access to health facilities, goods, and services, and according to which legislative and administrative health policies may be set. In contrast to traditional biomedical and public health approaches, the right to health approach protects freedoms and negative liberties as a matter of normative imperative, founded upon principles of human dignity and personal autonomy. The right to health approach prioritizes the needs of vulnerable or marginalized groups, whom existing approaches have consistently failed to serve. Finally, it requires the active and informed participation of individuals and communities in all decisions affecting their health at all levels of governance. Participation is essential to a responsive, effective, culturally appropriate, and sustainable health system.

The right to health approach moves us closer to the universal global health baseline: health systems that promote good health outcomes for all, that are equitable and sustainable, and that respect individual freedoms. It is therefore critical that all States, at all stages of health systems development, utilize the right to health approach in order to address current deficits and emerging problems in global health. The failure to realize and to incorporate the right to health approach into the existing global health paradigm will make it difficult, if not impossible, to achieve this universal baseline.

References

Abadie, R. (2010). *The Professional Guinea Pig: Big Pharma and the Risky World of Human Subjects*. Duke University Press Books: Durham, NC.

amfAR. (2012). *Averting Deaths, Lowering Costs and Beginning to End the HIV/AIDS Epidemic: The Investment Case for Maintaining PEPFAR Funding in FY13*. American Foundation for AIDS Research (amfAR): New York, NY. Available at: <http://www.amfar.org/uploadedFiles/_amfar.org/In_The_Community/Publications/Pepfar-Investment-April-2012.pdf> (accessed 19 June 2012).

Annas, G. (2009). Globalized clinical trials and informed consent. *New England Journal of Medicine*, 360, 2050–2053.

APA. (2000). *Diagnostic and Statistical Manual of Mental Disorders* (4th edition). American Psychiatric Association (APA): Washington, DC.

Balarajan, Y., Selvaraj, S., and Subramanian, S.V. (2011). India: towards universal health coverage 4: health care and equity in India. *Lancet*, 377(4), 505–555.

BBC World Service. (2012, 12 April). *Uzbekistan's Policy of Secretly Sterilising Women*. Available at: <http://www.bbc.co.uk/news/magazine-17612550> (accessed 12 April 2012).

Brazil. (1990). *Law No. 8.080*. [The Organic Law on Health.] Brasília: Governo Federal.

Brazil. (1996). *Law No. 9.279/1996, Article 229-C*. [Law of Industrial Property.] Brasília: Governo Federal.

Center for Advocacy on Stigma and Marginalization (CASAM). (2008). *Rights-Based Sex Workers Empowerment Guidelines: An Alternative HIV/AIDS Intervention Approach to the 100% Condom Use Programme*. India: Sampada Gramin Mahila Sanstha.

CESCR. (2000). *General Comment No. 14: The Right to the Highest Attainable Standard of Health (Article 12 of the International Covenant on Economic, Social and Cultural Rights)*. Committee on Economic, Social and Cultural Rights (CESCR): Geneva.

Council of Europe and Commissioner for Human Rights. (2012). *Human Rights of Roma and Travellers in Europe*. Available at: <http://www.coe.int/t/commissioner/source/prems/prems79611_GBR_CouvHumanRightsOfRoma_WEB.pdf> (accessed 26 June 2012).

Dasgupta, S. (2011). *Communication and Community Mobilization, Anti-Trafficking and Legitimization, Participation and Empowerment: HIV/AIDS Intervention and the Sonagachi Project*. Dissertation, Temple University, Philadelphia, PA.

De Maeseneer, J. and Flinkenflögel, M. (2010). Primary health care in Africa: do family physicians fit in? *British Journal of General Practice*, 60(573), 286–292.

DeNavas-Walt, C., Proctor, B., and Smith, J. (2010). *US Census Bureau, Current Population Reports, P. 60–238, Income, Poverty, and Health Insurance Coverage in the United States: 2009*. Washington, DC: US Government Printing Office.

Eisenstat, S. (1991). Analysis of the rationality of mandatory testing for the HIV antibody: balancing the governmental public health interests with the individual's privacy interest. *University of Pittsburgh Law Review*, 52(2), 327–382.

Glickman, S., McHutchison, J., Peterson, E., *et al.* (2009). Ethical and scientific implications of the globalization of clinical research. *New England Journal of Medicine*, 360, 816–823.

Government of Ghana. (2012). *Mental Health Act*. Government of Ghana: Accra.

Heywood, M. (2009). South Africa's Treatment Action Campaign: combining law and social mobilization to realize the right to health. *Journal of Human Rights Practice*, 1(1), 14–36.

High Court of Kenya at Nairobi. (2009). *P.A.O and 2 others* v. *the Attorney General of Kenya Petition No. 409 of 2009 Nairobi*. High Court of Kenya: Nairobi.

Holmes, S. (2006). An ethnographic study of the social context of migrant health in the United States. *PLOS Medicine*, 3(10), e448.

Human Rights Watch. (2011). *The Rehab Archipelago: Forced Labor and Other Abuses in Drug Detention Centers in Southern Vietnam*. Human Rights Watch: New York, NY.

Lee, A. (2008). Trans models in prison: the medicalization of gender identity and the eighth amendment right to sex reassignment therapy. *Harvard Journal of Law & Gender*, 31, 447–471.

Leung, M., Yen, I., and Minkler, M. (2004). Community-based participatory research: a promising approach for increasing epidemiology's relevance in the 21st century. *International Journal of Epidemiology*, 33(3), 499–506.

Malloy, S.E. (1998). Beyond misguided paternalism: resuscitating the right to refuse medical treatment. *Wake Forest Law Review*, 33, 1035–1091.

Manandhar, D., Osrin, D., Shrestha, B., *et al.* (2004). Effect of a participatory intervention with women's groups on birth outcomes in Nepal: cluster-randomised controlled trial. *Lancet*, 364, 970–979.

Mann, J.M., Gostin, L., Gruskin, S., *et al.* (1999). Health and human rights. In J.M. Mann, S. Gruskin, M.A. Grodin, *et al.* (Eds.), *Health and Human Rights*, pp. 8–20. Routledge: New York, NY.

Martinez, J. (2008). *How External Support for Health and HIV Will Evolve as Viet Nam Becomes a Middle-Income Country*. HLSP Institute: London.

McIntyre, D. (2010). WHR 2000 to WHR 2010: what progress in health care financing? *Health Policy and Planning*, 25(5), 349–351.

Minister of Health v. *Treatment Action Campaign*. (2002). 5 SA 721 (CC).

Ministry of Industry, Ministry of Health, and National Industrial Property Institute. (2012). *Joint Resolution 118/2012, 546/2012 and 107/2012. Adoption of Guidelines for Patentability Examination of Patent Applications for Chemical and Pharmaceutical Inventions*. Buenos Aires (2 May 2012).

NCFH. (2009a). *Tuberculosis*. National Center for Farmworker Health (NCFH). Buda, TX. Available at: <http://www.ncfh.org/docs/fs-What%20is%20TB.pdf> (accessed 24 June 2012).

NCFH. (2009b). *Maternal & Child Health Fact Sheet*. National Center for Farmworker Health (NCFH): Buda, TX. Available at: <http://www.ncfh.org/docs/fs-MATERNAL%20FACT%20SHEET.pdf> (accessed 24 June 2012).

North Carolina Farmworker Institute. (2007). *United States Farm Worker Factsheet*. Available at: <http://www.ncfarmworkers.org/2012/06/united-states-farmworker-factsheet/> (accessed 24 June 2012).

OHCHR. (2008). *Fact Sheet No. 31, The Right to Health*. Office of the High Commissioner for Human Rights (OHCHR): Geneva. Available at: <http://www.ohchr.org/Documents/Publications/Factsheet31.pdf> (accessed 24 June 2012).

Open Society Foundations. (2011). *Against Her Will: Forced Sterilization of Women Worldwide*. Available at: <http://www.soros.org/sites/default/files/against-her-will-20111003.pdf> (accessed 24 June 2012).

PEPFAR. (2011). *Vietnam Country Operational Plan 2011. Executive Summary*. United States President's Emergency Plan for AIDS Relief (PEPFAR): Hanoi. Available at: <http://www.pepfar.gov/documents/organization/199703.pdf> (accessed 24 June 2012).

Ringold, D., Orenstein, M.A., and Wilkens, E. (2005). *Roma in an Expanding Europe: Breaking the Poverty Cycle*. World Bank: Washington, DC. Available at: <http://siteresources.worldbank.org/EXTROMA/Resources/roma_in_expanding_europe.pdf> (accessed 20 June 2012).

Ruger, J. (2006). Toward a theory of a right to health: capability and incompletely theorized agreements. *Yale Journal of Law & the Humanities*, 18, 273–326.

Sankalp Rehabilitation Trust and Anr. v. *UOI and Ors.* (1999). WP 512.

Slutsker, M. (2012). *Human Impact of Global Fund Round 11 Cancellation*. [Blog entry.] Available at: <http://www.action.org/blog/post/human_impact_of_global_fund_round_11_cancellation> (accessed 26 March 2012).

Starfield, B., Shi, L., and Macinko, J. (2005) Contribution of primary care to health systems and health. *The Milbank Quarterly*, 83(3), 457–502.

UNAIDS/UNDP. (2012). *The Potential Impact of Free Trade Agreements on Public Health (Issue Brief)*. Joint United Nations Programme on HIV/AIDS (UNAIDS)/United Nations Development Programme (UNDP): Geneva.

UN General Assembly (1950). *Principles of International Law Recognized in the Charter of the Nuremberg Tribunal and in the Judgment of the Tribunal*, 5 UN GAOR Supp. (No. 12) at 11, U.N. Doc A/1316 (1950). United Nations (UN): Geneva.

UNICEF. (2011). *Women, Motherhood, and Early Childhood Development: Exploring the Question of How Poor Roma Women's Status and Situation Influences Children's Survival, Growth and Development*. United Nations Children's Fund (UNICEF) Regional Office Central and Eastern Europe and the Commonwealth of Independent States: Geneva. Available at: <http://www.unicef.org/ceecis/Women_Motherhood-07-21-2011-final-WEB%281%29.pdf> (accessed 25 June 2012).

United States Constitution. (1787). Article I, § 8, Clause 3.

US Congress. (2009). *111th Congress, 1st Session, H.R. 3962. A Bill to Provide Affordable, Quality Health Care for All Americans and Reduce the Growth in Health Care Spending, and for Other Purposes*. Available at: <http://housedocs.house.gov/rules/health/111_ahcaa.pdf> (accessed 18 June 2012).

WHO. (1978). *Declaration of Alma-Ata*. World Health Organization (WHO): Geneva.

WHO. (2009). *Assessment of Compulsory Treatment of People Who Use Drugs in Cambodia, China, Malaysia and Viet Nam: An Application of Selected Human Rights Principles*. World Health Organization (WHO): Geneva.

WHO. (2011). *Improving Equity in Health by Addressing Social Determinants* (The Commission on Social Determinants of Health Knowledge Networks, J. Lee, and R. Sadana, Eds.). Available at: <http://www.globalhealthequity.ca/webfm_send/154> (accessed 20 June 2012).

World Organisation Against Torture and Rapid Response Group. (2007). *Uzbekistan: Shadow Report UN Committee Against Torture, 39th Session*. Available at: <http://www.omct.org/files/2005/09/3070/uzb_report_un_cat_11_2007_eng.pdf> (accessed 24 June 2012).

Wylie, K., Hainsworth, K., and Ryles, S. (2007). The support needs of people awaiting a primary assessment at a UK gender reassignment programme. *International Journal of Transgenderism*, 10(2), 91–9.

Index

The index entries appear in letter-by-letter alphabetical order.

D

The manufacturer's authorised representative in the EU for product safety is Oxford University Press España S.A. of el Parque Empresarial San Fernando de Henares, Avenida de Castilla, 2 – 28830 Madrid (www.oup.es/en or product.safety@oup.com). OUP España S.A. also acts as importer into Spain of products made by the manufacturer.

www.ingramcontent.com/pod-product-compliance
Lightning Source LLC
LaVergne TN
LVHW062107200926
848484LV00007B/1613